Contents

Print and production

General reference

13

List of tables

List of figures

Introduction and context

1

This tenth edition of the *Print and Production Manual* is designed as a reference book for people who produce, specify and buy material. It contains a wealth of information that will help make them aware of issues involved in the successful completion of print projects.

This edition represents a significant update. The scope has been broadened to include more printed products and services, reflecting changes in an industry that is providing more services to its customers. Other changes have been made to coverage of e-commerce, new digital technological innovations and working practices. Digital prepress, workflows and administration are now the norm and have largely superseded traditional analogue methods. The printing section has been updated and includes a considerable amount of material on the digital technologies that are becoming increasingly common, including wide-format inkjet. The flexo section has been expanded, with greater emphasis on which is the best technology to use for a particular requirement, rather than a separate description of the potential methods that could be used. Finishing and distribution are also covered, along with mailing and export freight forwarding.

The context of printing

There is a bewildering array of ways for people and organisations to promote, teach, inform, entertain or do business with each other. Those are the basic functions of printed products, and now print faces stiff competition from alternative media as well as other print suppliers within a wider communication market. This manual aims to help produce the most effective products in the most efficient manner.

People have used technology to communicate from the days of cave painting. Before the invention of movable type in the late 15th century, a small army of scribes produced written proclamations and unique illustrated manuscripts for the clerics, professionals and aristocrats who controlled society. Then print became industrialised and created a manufacturing juggernaut that could publish multiple identical copies of books, newspapers, pamphlets and all sorts of promotional, educational, transactional and entertainment products.

The strength of print has been its ability to produce many copies of a document at a low unit cost. This mindset of trying to reduce costs has driven the industry for many years and is difficult to change. It is, however, important that a change is made. The final consumers of print products are people, and it is the changing needs and wishes of individuals that are driving the rapidly changing world of print. People are no longer content to be treated as part of a large group, and they demand to be treated as individuals. The strength of print is now a concern because a generic document may not be sufficient to engage individuals. Conventional print has undergone some changes, and there has been relentless decline in average run length of most print over the last 20 years. Prepress and make-ready developments have helped make short runs economic, and manufacturers have looked toward innovative new technologies to make the print run of just one copy, personalised for an individual consumer, an economic option. This is the wider context of the development of digital printing: making short run and customised print economically viable.

The printing industry is changing because people, the final consumers of print, are changing. Their requirements and needs are developing and changing for all products and services including print. The pressure is for cheaper print products that are produced in less time. There is also the demand for products to be better targeted at individuals resulting in drops in run length and increasing personalisation.

New printing technology has developed to take time and cost out of the process. Digital administration and e-commerce applications allow closer, faster communication between buyer and supplier to specify and track enquiries through to delivery. Digital workflows have smoothed the transition between the creative process, prepress production, printing and distribution. New printing presses have become increasingly efficient at reducing make-ready to cut the number of passes and to optimise the use of materials. The quality achievable, particularly from flexo and digital, has improved while litho has developed with more colours and special effects such as varnishing.

New technology has opened up the range of products that can economically be printed, and digital technology allows very short runs of the highest quality. Distributed engines allow simultaneous production in multiple locations while database technology, which can identify the requirements of individuals and print bespoke products, has enabled the growth of personalisation and helped to develop the customer relationship marketing programmes of many companies.

The arrival of the internet and worldwide web means that print now has real competition from an alternative media for the permanent publication of information. Parts of the printing industry are being absorbed into a wider communications industry taking in computers and telecommunications. Publishers can use multiple channels to get their message to consumers: print, internet, email, digital TV and SMS text messaging. For print to remain a leading channel, it is important to be able to use the most appropriate methods and suppliers.

How to use the manual

The content is arranged into three main sections:
► print buying issues
► production
► general reference section (including customs of the trade).

The print buying section aims to explain the issues other than price that people need to understand to make the best purchasing decision. Understanding the alternative processes will lead to the most appropriate production method being chosen, and considering the overall process might lead to re-engineering opportunities reducing time and cost. The need for clear specification and requests for quotation is explained along with the reasons why the capabilities of potential suppliers must be examined when deciding which quotes to accept.

The development of e-commerce to help all aspects of buying are discussed along with the growth in the use of the job definition format (JDF) and computer-integrated manufacturing (CIM). Quality control and assurance techniques for prepress, printing and materials are examined and electronic process control charts are provided. A range of industry-standard contract terms and conditions are provided with specifications for the supply of files and proofs.

The production section considers all aspects of modern reproduction and printing, and concentrates on the digital technologies that dominate the industry. There is a primer (or a reminder) covering the basics of digital graphics and colour theory. Origination and prepress are covered with emphasis on digital workflow based on PDF technology. The emerging use of media independent XML techniques is covered with the supply of certified print-ready files for direct conversion at the printers using computer-to-plate (CTP) technology.

The printing section has been significantly revised and gives details of the main technologies commonly used including litho, flexo, gravure, screen and digital printing, including wide-format inkjet. The section on choosing the most appropriate print process details the strengths and weaknesses of the different technologies for particular applications. Sections on inks and substrates (including digital colourant and inkjet) for both plastics and paper are included. A variety of binding and finishing processes are discussed, and despatch and distribution, including mailing and exporting, are covered. The impacts on the print supply chain provided by new digital technology, with several examples of how time, waste and cost can be reduced by changes in the overall approach, are discussed. The final part of the production section now includes examples of the use of e-commerce workflow systems, which are playing an increasingly important role in attempts to simplify the print supply chain. There are still examples of paper-based production control forms and check lists.

The general reference section contains a range of useful information. The appendix on typography includes a discussion on the use of typefaces for the internet. The final part is a detailed glossary covering the technical terms widely used in the printing and allied industries. This has been updated to include descriptions of many of the latest developments.

In considering the future it is useful to review the past. Table 1.1 provides a timeline of important advances in communication throughout human history. This clearly demonstrates several key factors:

▶ The pace of technological change and the adoption of new methods is increasing, while the lead time for new products is decreasing.

▶ The impact of technological change is incremental – once introduced it cannot be uninvented and the implications are often not what was intended.

▶ The history of new media does not involve replacement, although users of current technology tend to fear the worst as new media emerge. For example, film did not replace theatre; TV did not replace film and radio. Once established, the new media develops its characteristics and causes a change in the status quo.

▶ The history of communications contains many disruptive technologies that have caused significant industry changes and reorganisations.

TABLE 1.1 Timeline charting important developments in printing

BC 40,000	First known permanent human records – cave paintings in France
BC 8000	Use of representative symbology
BC 4000	Sumerians record commercial transactions on clay tablets
BC 3200	First Egyptian hieroglyphic records
BC 3000	Babylonians invent the abacus
BC 2700	Egyptians make papyrus from reeds and other Tapa materials
BC 1900	Babylonians develop the place–value number system where the value of a digit depends on the digit itself and its position within the number
BC 150	Chinese develop paper from bark and fibres
AD 105	Ts'ai Lun credited with the invention of paper in China
110	Woodblock printing begins in Korea
740	First printed newspaper in China
751	Arabs learn papermaking from the Chinese
820	Illuminated manuscripts produced by monks (continues until invention of the press)
1040	Chinese printers use movable type made from clay
1100	Multicolour printing used to create paper money in east Asia
1150	Papermaking introduced in Europe
1437	Johannes Gutenberg in Germany invents the printing press with movable metal type (parallel developments occurring in the Netherlands and Prague, the Czech Republic)
1455	42-line (Gutenberg) bible published in Mainz, Germany
1466	First advertising handbills
1476	William Caxton sets up Westminster Press
1594	*Mercurius Gallobelgicus*, the first magazine, is published in Cologne, Germany
1612	John Napier develops logarithms, uses the printed decimal point
1639	Stephen Day sets up first North American press
1642	Blaise Pascal builds geared adding machine, the Pascalene
1666	First European banknote printed by the Bank of Sweden
1725	William Ged invents stereotyping where a page of type is cast in a single mould
1737	Point system of font measurement developed by Parisian typecaster Pierre-Simon Fournier
1749	L'Abbé Nollet examines the effects of static electricity on the flow of drops from a capillary tube – origin of inkjet
1790	First cylindrical press invented
1796	Alois Senefelder invents lithography in Munich, Germany
1804	Fourdrinier brothers develop modern paper machine in France
1805	First typesetting machine invented by William Wing in the US
1806	Machine to print serial numbers on banknotes used in England
1814	First steam-driven printing press; Joseph Nicéphore Niépce takes the first photograph using a camera obscura with an eight-hour exposure
1826	First photographic negative
1820–34	Charles Babbage devises the Difference Engine, the forerunner of computers
1831	Development of the telegraph
1829	Typewriter patented by WA Burt; Louis Braille develops braille printing
1835	William Fox Talbot creates first photograph on sensitised paper
1837	Daguerreotype invented; Rowland Hill produces the first stamp
1838	Morse & Vail patent the telegraph
1841	Samuel Slocum patents the stapler; gravure printing invented by the Czech painter and graphic artist Karel Klic in Arnau/Ostböhmen
1842	Photograph first printed in newspaper
1848	Associated Press formed to use newly invented telegraph
1852	Photoengraving

TABLE 1.1 Timeline charting important developments in printing (continued)

1854	George Boole publishes his *Investigation of the Laws of Thought*, the system of symbolic and logical reasoning that will develop into the basis of computer software design
1867	Christopher Scholes invents the first practical, modern typewriter
1872	AM Ward issues the first mail order catalogue
1876	Alexander Graham Bell patents his 'electrical speech machine' (the telephone)
1877	Edison invents phonograph
1878	Illustrations appear in magazines
1882	Georg Meisenbach (1841–1912) patents the halftone screen (DRP 22244) used to print photographs in newspapers
1884	Ottmar Mergenthaler invents linotype
1895	First motion picture projectors; Marconi transmits first radio signal; cathode ray tube developed
1896	The Tabulating Machine Company established (merges to form CTR [Calculating, Tabulating & Recording Co. in 1911]; renamed International Business Machines, IBM, in 1924)
1897	Monotype typesetting developed; the first comic strip (Katzenjammer Kids) printed
1901	Marconi sends transatlantic radio signal
1903	Ira Washington Rubel invents the offset printing process accidentally when an impression is printed from a press cylinder direct onto the rubber blanket on the impression cylinder, then a sheet of paper is run and a sharp image is printed on the reverse
1904	John Fleming patents the diode vacuum tubes; Elsässische Maschinengesellschaft in Mülhausen builds the first rotogravure press
1906	First offset printing press developed by Rubel; photostats – photos of documents – developed
1907	Lumière brothers invent colour photography; Samuel Simon patents the use of silk as a printing screen – serigraphy, from the Latin word *seri* (silk) and the Greek word *graphein* (to write or draw)
1915	Property of germanium crystals to convert AC to direct current discovered by Manson Benedicts, foreshadowing semiconductors; first long-distance voice communication from Virginia to Paris
1929	FM radio transmission
1930	First large-scale analogue computer
1932	Herbert Land invents instant Polaroid photography
1937	Chester Carlson patents xerography – electrostatic imaging
1945	First computer bug found by Grace Murray Hopper (a trapped moth causes a relay failure)
1946	ENIAC, the first electronic digital computer goes online
1947	Transistor developed at Bell Labs by Shockley et al.
1950	Colour television tested; first commercial xerographic equipment
1951	UNIVAC (Universal Automatic Computer) is the first commercial computer; Siemens produces the first commercial inkjet printer, the Elema Oscilomink
1953	IBM introduces first computer model, the 701
1957	First dot-matrix printer; Monotype launches the mono-photo galley imagesetter
1958	Integrated circuit invented by Jack Kilby; Schawlow & Townes discover lasers
1959	Photoengraving – mass production of integrated circuits paves way for low-cost computers; Xerox introduces the first commercial copier
1962	Goss launches first web offset newspaper press
1963	Digital Equipment Corp. (DEC) introduces first minicomputer, the PDP-8; teletext invented
1964	Doug Engelbart invents the computer mouse
1965	DigiSet, the first computer photo-composition is introduced; CH Hertz and SE Simmonsson patent high-resolution continuous inkjet
1967	3M launches driography, later sold to Toray as waterless offset; Sweet and Cummings patent binary inkjet array
1968	Intel established; Alan Kay proposes the Dynabook, the beginnings of video editing display
1970	Floppy disk storage introduced; compact disk developed; Xerox establishes the Palo Alto Research Centre (PARC)
1972	ARPAnet launched, forerunner of the internet; first laser printers and page description languages developed
1973	Xerox PARC develops the Alto computer, the first machine with a graphical user interface (GUI); WYSIWYG editing, bitmapped display, overlapping windows and the first commercial use of the mouse; ethernet developed; first modem fax machines

TABLE 1.1 Timeline charting important developments in printing (continued)

1974	Charles Simonyi writes the first WYSIWYG application, Bravo
1975	IBM launches laser printer
1976	Monotype launches the Lasercomp, the first laser typesetter capable of imaging complete pages of text; IBM launches first inkjet printers
1977	Apple and Microsoft companies launched; Canon invents bubblejet thermal inkjet
1980	Scitex launches first electronic page make-up systems for images and tints
1982	John Warnock & Chuck Gescke found Adobe Systems and launch PostScript
1983	First laser imagesetters output one-piece film that include images as well as text
1984	Apple releases the Macintosh with graphical user interface
1985	Adobe launches PostScript, with the Laserwriter and Aldus PageMaker software forming the beginnings of desktop publishing
1986	Hope launches the first litho computer-to-plate system; *Today* is the first full-colour newspaper in UK
1990	Vutek grand-format inkjet printer, 1630, 4.8m wide for posters and graphics
1993	Indigo and Xeikon launch competitive high-quality digital colour presses
1997	4-back-4 sheet-fed perfectors operate commercially, boosting sheet-fed against small webs
1999	Print e-commerce systems launched
2000	CTP comes of age
2001	PDF workflows widely established
2002	64 and 72pp single-web heatset offset press formats introduced
2003	Digital plate usage overtakes film use in western Europe and North America
2004	High-quality colour digital presses are capable of 250ppm, lower quality inkjet 2000ppm. High-quality inkjet for packaging capable of 1200–2000m^2/hr. 4.3m wide gravure presses introduced
2005	Fastest inkjet system, Inca Digital Fastjet, in beta, capable of 300dpi at 6000m^2/hr

Source: Pira International Ltd

Acknowledgements

This publication has been updated and the editor and Pira International wish to formally thank many suppliers to the industry that provided information and images for use in this title. These suppliers include:

▶ Agfa Inc.
▶ Heidelberg
▶ MAN-Roland
▶ HP Indigo
▶ Xaar
▶ Spectra Inc. (a division of Dimatix)
▶ ROI Distribution
▶ Müller-Martini
▶ Fujifilm
▶ Canon
▶ Océ
▶ Kodak and Kodak VersaMark
▶ Creo Inc.
▶ Scitex Vision
▶ KBA
▶ Xerox.

Print buying and quality control

2

In a manual that covers such a broad range of production disciplines, advice on print buying or buying services from production companies is little more than a summary of principles. In practice there will be unique trading arrangements and pricing agreements that cannot be predicted here, where innovative methods of production are concerned and where new media services are involved.

This section should be read in conjunction with other appropriate sections of *The Print and Production Manual* and particularly with the quality control advice given in the printing section.

Print pricing and cost of production

Increasingly the specification and buying of print is part of the technical process of production, not merely a separate commercial activity. The basis for this is the fundamental print-buying maxim: the best deal will come from the supplier best qualified to produce the job. As print is bought to accomplish something, there is always pressure to achieve the lowest price. In many cases, however, the lowest price may not necessarily represent the best value to the buyer.

The corollary of this is that the best print buyer is the one who makes decisions based, at least in part, on a technical evaluation of the circumstances. The starting point, therefore, is to understand the techniques involved in production through a basic knowledge of the processes of origination and printing, and any other processes required for the job.

Many printers tend to be production led. Their concern is to obtain the best returns on their high levels of investment, so it is worth exploring the service and support of potential print suppliers.

The print industry has concentrated its efforts on minimising the unit cost of production through the reduction of make-ready and waste. In many cases, the supply of print is not a high enough priority for the customer to spend a great deal of time or money to provide benefits. The supplier can work with the customer to develop a strategy to re-engineer the chain on behalf of the client, offering a more efficient, reduced-cost solution. This approach is one of the major drivers for the growth of the specialist print management companies, able to apply their expertise across a range of suppliers. They tend to operate with larger print users where both parties can benefit from a strategic approach to print procurement.

The change will address the normally hidden costs of administration, wastage, warehousing and distribution. There are the client costs involved with print buying, salaries and overheads for staff dedicated to procurement, costs of receiving, storing and holding printed materials. Aspects to be examined will include all elements from raw materials to distribution:

- ► Paper and raw material sourcing
- ► Authoring, design and prepress
- ► Printing, finishing and binding
- ► Archiving (preparing and managing a digital asset management system)
- ► Warehousing and stock management

▶ Distribution

▶ Detailed customer service and helpdesk operation

▶ Fulfilment and support activities (database management, response handling).

There would be total activity reporting for all parties through improved administration systems, developed to provide maximum efficiency. The process re-engineering programme involves a three-stage approach: understanding current processes, designing appropriate alternatives and implementing the solution. It is a strategic review on the use of print and allied products.

Understand

The first stage involves a consultation exercise to understand the current situation and determine objectives to take out cost and time. It determines the total range of print and related communication products in use, with the scope of activities to be included (e.g. is mailing included, what about website design and e-commerce requirements?). The document audit aims to identify all current print products. It will include details of materials, processes, activities and stages involved, quantities and run lengths, delivery points, and waste and redundancy levels.

To provide the best business benefit, it is necessary to understand the business processes relevant to communication and documents. Client procurement systems and document use will be explored, covering administration procedure and detailing costs (if available). Key personnel and suppliers across the supply chain would be involved. Marketing objectives and CRM activities will be explored to determine any requirement for supporting technology.

Redesign

The process formally identifies costs and time in document usage. Process maps indicate opportunities to reduce cost and time. Printers will explore the application of appropriate technology to make improvements with the client exploring existing production processes and emerging new technologies.

The supplier will research the possibilities and typically run some from a workshop involving their staff, client personnel and any third-party stakeholders (design agencies, specialist finishing, distribution companies). An action plan for improvement should be generated from this.

Implement

Detailed plans setting out the business justification of the proposed differences should be formally documented, costed and justified for the client to consider. When approved, a contract between the parties will be drawn up and procedures changed.

The contract will incorporate a formal service level agreement (SLA) and regular ongoing project reviews. Like any project, the individual responsibilities on named personnel (at service provider and client) should be named, together with the proposed timescale. The costs would be negotiated as part of the agreement, normally initial costs would be borne by the supplier, amortised into a supply agreement, or a different agreement reached.

Detailed methodology

The initial product survey is a communication audit, determining the total range of printed and related communication products in use. These may typically include:

▶ Business cards

▶ General stationery (letterheads, compliments slips, envelopes)

▶ Business forms (pre-printed base forms, individual numbered/barcoded forms, multi-part sets, pads, A4 sheets)

▶ Labels

▶ Internal documentation

▶ Bills/statements (pre-printed base stock and personalisation)

▶ Marketing collateral material

▶ Brochures/catalogues

▶ Corporate brochure, report and accounts, corporate literature

▶ Security print

▶ Special/bespoke material

▶ Point-of-sale

▶ Packaging

▶ Distribution

▶ Mailing

▶ Fulfilment (if applicable).

Any communication audit should aim to identify all the currently used printed products for internal processes, communication with potential and existing customers, business to business, and to business to consumer. The use of any transactional documents and transactional mailing will be explored. Are any multi-version, multi-language editions required? Does the client need multi-media versions, repurposing for website?

To add value to the client, it is necessary to understand the business processes relevant to communication. This would involve detailed examination of the customer's business processes that are relevant to the use of print. An understanding of the structure of the client is vital, identifying key personnel and suppliers across the supply chain.

▶ Organisation structure

▶ Individual companies/business units

▶ Departmental structure

▶ Marketing requirements

▶ Identify key personnel and decision makers

▶ Explore purchasing systems and structures

▶ Explore administration systems

▶ Explore IT systems

▶ Identify key capabilities and strengths

▶ Requirements for EDI and existing systems

▶ E-commerce requirements

▶ Cooperation with other sources to fulfil complete service needs.

In most cases for significant users of print, supporting information is required. Is there any formal brand manual providing a corporate specification to promote the branding consistency? If so, a copy is required to detail all spot colours, typefaces and layouts. For each of the products identified, the following is ideally needed:

► Quantities required annually
► Number of individual orders, quantity per order
► Number of deliveries and points of delivery (addresses of individual departments within the same site/building)
► Average stock holdings (centrally and at users)
► Re-order trigger process, level and monitoring mechanism
► Procedure for replacement/update
► Waste levels (spoilage and document redundancy)
► Out of stock situations
► Cost and financial information (prices if available, cost of handling communication at the client)
► Order generation and invoice handling procedure, use of consolidated invoicing
► Material specification
► Paper – grade and grammage
► Inks/toners (any special colours/effects/security features)
► Varnish/sealer/spot varnish
► Lamination
► Production methods
► Number of suppliers
► Processes involved (web/sheet, litho/digital, finishing, mailing)
► Personalisation (PDF, PostScript, Mainframe Linecode, XML)
► Design/prepress
► Design agency contact
► Map workflow (PostScript/PDF)
► Supply of files/films
► Wastage levels (process and redundancy)
► Mailing procedures and consolidation.

This may yield a great deal of data and, to make it meaningful, it is translated into a series of business process maps and flowcharts. This process quantifies the processes, costs and time in document usage in a graphical manner. The diagrams are useful tools to identify activities where there are inefficiencies and opportunities for improvement.

► Design approval cycle
► Prepress workflow
► Material specification and purchase procedure
► Specification requirement (e.g. APACS regulations, mailpack weights)
► Specific end use (personalisation requirements, type of inserter)
► Paper supplier(s)

- ► Is the paper branded? Does it need to be?
- ► Grade and basis weight
- ► Ink/toner/varnish
- ► Production methodology.

Process maps will identify times involved and generation of waste for production:

- ► Design process
- ► File approval and transfer
- ► Prepress
- ► Proofing and proof approval cycle
- ► Platemaking
- ► Print make-ready
- ► Printing
- ► Finish/bind
- ► Store and hold stock
- ► Distribute
- ► Mailing.

For administration of standard products:

- ► Order entry at customer
- ► Initial trigger for reorder
- ► Stock monitoring and consolidation
- ► Raise order
- ► Receive order/check validity/provide confirmation
- ► Determine optimal reorder quantities
- ► Receipt of film/file
- ► Proofing needs
- ► Delivery notes
- ► Raise and send invoice
- ► Payment
- ► Reporting and trends.

For administration of new or updated bespoke products:

- ► Decision for new document
- ► Estimate
- ► Design and prepress
- ► Order entry at customer
- ► Raise order
- ► Receive order/check validity/provide confirmation
- ► Determine optimal reorder quantities
- ► Receipt of file
- ► Proofing needs
- ► Delivery notes
- ► Raise and send invoice

►   Payment

►   Reporting and trends.

When the current situation has been determined, the opportunities for process re-engineering will be examined. These will depend on the range of products involved and the objectives of the project. The business process maps indicate opportunities to reduce cost and time. At this stage the potential of new technology and IT developments will be considered to explore:

►   Consolidation of existing document product range

►   Supplier rationalisation

►   Improvement in usage of materials/processes

►   Paper choice

►   Prepress

►   Provide multi-version optimised media and format independent data

►   Colour management

►   JDF capability and link with administration systems

►   Optimise workflow

►   Remote proofing

►   Administration

►   Economic order quantities

►   Use of MIS/IT

►   Invoice consolidation

►   E-commerce opportunities

►   E-procurement, catalogue and shopping basket

►   Workflow management

►   Production – which print process is appropriate

►   Batching

►   Personalisation/DP capability

►   Stock and warehousing

►   Pick and pack

►   Distribution

►   Mailing.

These are the normal areas that can be changed to lead to improvements in the supply of printed products. The process should then explore areas where new technology can improve the business process of client, removing time and cost from the document cycle. Keeping in touch with the market developments will be repaid by being able to offer increased efficiencies to clients.

►   Consolidation of documents, optimal order quantities

►   Develop improved marketing communications

►   Direct mail

►   Direct marketing

►   Digital printing

▶ Database management – client profiles
▶ Fulfilment
▶ E-commerce offering.

The potential changes will be evaluated and new methods proposed as a presentation to the client management. This document should outline the potential benefits and detail how the process will be managed. The supplier will work with the client and its agents to achieve the best service levels for the communications solution. When required, a printer manages the service (taking a facilities management approach) where it acts as outsourcer or partner wherever appropriate.

▶ Provide expertise
▶ Design improvements and solutions
▶ Agree objectives, budget and time-scale
▶ Prepare and agree detailed contract
▶ Agree guarantees of service and quality
▶ Negotiate supply of equipment and services
▶ Implement
▶ Manage.

The supplier should aim to provide the widest range of products to minimise transaction costs for the client. This will involve working with approved design agencies, outside printers for services not available in-house and client-appointed service providers (mailing, distribution, warehousing) to provide a total service package. The additional activities often outside the remit of suppliers may include:

▶ Design
▶ Production
▶ Database management
▶ Website design and operation (updates and handling enquiries)
▶ Mailing and distribution
▶ Help-desk
▶ Call centre
▶ Warehousing
▶ Pick, pack and deliver
▶ Provide invisible back-office functionality.

This approach demonstrates the much wider scope of print procurement rather than being only a simple choice based on lowering the print prices from suppliers. The opportunity for lowest cost is to become a partner with the supplier(s), developing improved systems to provide a better and wider service. This will inevitably involve use of all types of printing technology and continual reviews should be carried out to check that the most effective process is being used.

Some printers are implementing Six Sigma statistical process control (SPC) programmes to determine their quality objectively and bring about a culture of continual improvement so customers can rank their suppliers (see page 58). The client can then prepare a list of important criteria such as colour fidelity, pack appearance, lack of common print faults, on-time delivery and score the performance objectively.

Production control

Any printer's qualifications do not reside simply in the machinery owned. They include all the practical considerations that will affect the ability to produce the product required to the schedule set by the buyer, and will enable him to produce the necessary balance of price, quality and service. Increasingly the methods of communication and provision of information to customers are seen as key factors.

The following factors will go towards building up the equation:

► skilled management
► production control
► appropriate machinery
► appropriate management systems and quality procedures
► MIS and e-commerce systems
► environmental policy
► skilled labour force
► capacity
► experience of similar work
► geographical location
► suitable communications
► appropriate transport
► availability of materials
► sound financial performance.

Good management in a printing organisation encompasses sales, production and administration. On the shop floor, it shows up as tight production control. With the customer, it results in good service.

Service from a print supplier is not simply a question of keeping to an agreed production schedule. The communication of information at every stage and quick and effective response to queries and requests is equally important. The increasing use of e-enabled systems allows clients to interrogate job status, request estimates and examine capacity directly, providing real-time information and reducing the overhead on the printer. Additional functionality may include help in the preparation of print-ready files without the need for expensive and time-consuming design and prepress operators at or outsourced by the customer. It is the improvement in administration that is the real benefit of e-commerce systems for printing.

It is usually possible to get some idea of a printer's service from the first contact, although a website may often be incomplete and misleading. If it is simple to establish communications, if estimates are quickly obtained, sensible questions are asked and good explanations are given about the resources and facilities of the supplier, then that augurs well for the future. If it is difficult to get an initial response from the printer, if it takes too long to estimate a job and the quotation is then confusing or does not match the specification, proceed no further. Such problems are symptomatic of deficiencies between the sales and marketing side of the organisation and the production side, not just between the salesperson and client.

Naturally, this assumes that there is a tight and exact specification for the job to be placed. Use forms wherever possible to achieve this since they give authority to the request and act as a checklist to ensure all aspects of the job are specified. Chapter 12 provides sample forms suitable for obtaining estimates; many printers offer interactive forms on their websites.

If large quantities of work are to be placed with the supplier, it may be worth arranging a site visit to inspect the printer's resources and meet the staff who would be involved. Most print companies are proud of their work and would be happy to accommodate this request. When visiting a factory, take the following steps:

► Look over the production control area to see how the company plans and schedules – manual or computerised, will it be easy for them to advise a delivery date?

► Meet line management, talk to them and form your own view about their competence and enthusiasm;

► Ask about quality control and check who is responsible. Is work examined by the production office on the shop floor and, if so, by whom? Does the company use densitometers or spectrophotometers? Do the presses have on-press monitoring? Maybe there are no formal checks at all (that may be acceptable if you have implicit faith in an experienced workforce). Does the company operate a documented, accredited quality management system?

► Check how the company handles incoming work: checking, proofing, making files print ready. Is it able to make (chargeable) late changes?

► Look over the machinery. Is it new or old? Does it appear well maintained? Is the housekeeping efficient? How is the factory laid out? Many experienced buyers have noted that an untidy factory almost invariably produces untidy work;

► Inspect the materials being used, the warehouse, how work-in-progress is stored and the level of waste produced;

► Try to assess the attitude of the workforce. Are they keen and enthusiastic or bored and indifferent? Do they want to impress you? If they don't, their work won't either;

► Above all, discuss work with staff and management as freely as possible. Ask about their development plans. Consider how they may be able to improve their service.

You will quickly form an impression of the type of company you are dealing with, how keen they are to work with you and how they perceive their working relationship with you. This is not necessary for you or them if you are placing one small job but, if you are to establish a longer-term relationship dealing with any quantity of work, the supplier should be pleased to show you his facilities and discuss his working methods.

Appropriate machinery

The print industry has a bewildering array of equipment that can be used to produce ostensibly the same product. Machines have different productivity rates and associated economics. Jobs should be placed on the most appropriate print machinery to achieve the required quality at the most economic level. Printers choose their machinery for a variety of reasons and the cost of producing a particular print product may vary widely according to the equipment used. In sheet-fed printing, for example, there is significant debate about the relative benefits of B1 (8 × A4pp to view) and B2 (4 × A4pp to view) presses. Make-ready costs are lower on the smaller press as plates are smaller and the capital cost of the machine is lower. For higher pagination publications, fewer sections and make-readies are necessary on the larger format press, resulting in fewer sections to handle in finishing. Running a four-page product two-up halves the print time but adds finishing operations. In web offset the choice of press pagination, cut-off and grain direction will alter the material requirements and cost of production. In practice the impact of different methods of production can be complex and costs can vary significantly.

Buyers who place their jobs with suppliers operating the most efficient and well-matched equipment will achieve the lowest prices. However, the downside to this is that it takes time to research the market and individual printers' capabilities to find out the best solutions. This is normally the domain of the professional print buyer or print management company rather than personnel who have to procure print as a small part of their job function.

A convention of printing companies is to produce a plant list. This lists all the machines in the factory and gives an indication of their purpose (e.g. maximum sheet size taken by the machine and number of stations on a binding line). It is important to appreciate that however competitive the quotation, the printer is at best a short-term solution to your problem if he does not have what you know to be the correct machinery for the purpose. It may suit him to do your work on an inefficient basis at that moment, but in due course he will either find more suitable work or go bust.

When placing a job, request information on the machines to be used in its production and satisfy yourself that they are appropriate. Appropriate does not necessarily mean the latest, state-of-the-art, gleaming piece of equipment. It simply means that the machine is a sensible choice for the type of work planned, and is not so old and decrepit that it is incapable of achieving either decent quality or productive speeds.

Quality procedures and MIS

Many printers, particularly large ones, have successfully implemented formal quality systems with external auditing such as ISO9001:2000, which is used to establish a management system that provides confidence in the conformance of a product to established or specified requirements. Management system refers to the structure for managing activities that transform inputs into a product or service that satisfy the customer's quality requirements, comply with regulations or meet environmental objectives. It is now the only standard against which a quality system can be certified by an external agency. The standard recognises that 'product' applies to services, processed material, and hardware and software intended for, or required by, customers.

Quality management is what a printer does to achieve:

▶ the customer's quality requirements

▶ applicable regulatory requirements

▶ customer satisfaction

▶ continual improvement of its performance in pursuit of these objectives.

These demonstrate the commitment of management to examine and understand all aspects of the company activities, and to undertake a systematic process improvement programme. Even if the organisation does not hold a formal certificate of quality, it should be able to demonstrate sensible procedures to prove their staff know the systems well enough to fulfil orders efficiently.

The role of the management information system at printers is increasingly important. The system will provide access to costing, estimating, scheduling, production control, work in progress, stock and distribution functions. Customers will have access to parts of the system.

Capacity

Both buyer and supplier can be opportunistic where a small, one-off job is concerned. The supplier may be able to quote a competitive price because there is a low point in production. The buyer may be able to take advantage of that price because his job will not be repeated and, if circumstances change later, there is no problem. However, if serious amounts of work are involved, both parties should satisfy themselves that the capacity really exists to produce this work to the schedules required by the buyer. This is obviously and undeniably the responsibility of both parties where regular productions such as periodicals are concerned, but it is also necessary if a continuing stream of work is envisaged.

Talk of priorities of jobs in printing companies should not be necessary other than in the context of balancing tightly scheduled production with work on longer schedules. In this context, it is the responsibility of the buyer to give a fair estimate of the volumes of work and the timings of that work likely to materialise. It is the responsibility of the printer to ensure he has the capacity to handle the work. He must allow for the inevitable machine downtime caused by breakdowns and servicing requirements, and hiatuses in labour supply caused by holidays and so forth.

It is the responsibility of both parties to ensure that they have understood the agreed production schedules and the implications of these schedules on the printer's loadings. Production schedules and capacity are one and the same thing. The purpose of a schedule is to ensure that the capacity is available to produce the work as and when agreed. Both parties should be clear whether the schedule they have agreed is stated in terms of working days or calendar days, and should remember to take into account national holidays and other unavoidable interruptions.

Refer to Chapter 12 for forms that can be used to work out project schedules. A supplier producing a steady stream of work similar to the jobs to be placed is the most reassuring guarantee.

It is in any event sensible to check samples of the supplier's work. Don't expect him to give you the last leather-bound multi-volume encyclopedia printed as a sample, but you should be able to keep and examine at your leisure spare copies of printed sheets, prepress samples and printed examples of repro work.

Printers can use e-auctions to bid for work at short notice to fill spare capacity that would otherwise remain unsold.

Similar work

If a supplier is already producing your sort of work for several customers, it is likely it is doing a reasonable job. In any event, never hesitate to check a supplier's reputation with other customers.

No one has an unblemished record, but any reputable organisation will have at least a few delighted customers who will be happy to endorse their claims. This is perfectly normal practice in the trade and will not be considered unreasonable.

If the supplier has not produced your type of work before, you must make a decision based on the importance of the job you are placing. If it is a large and significant project, you might be advised to place it with someone who has experience of similar work. If it is relatively low value and on a loose production schedule, you may be prepared to take a risk, especially if the supplier has the appropriate resources.

Location

There are some 13,000 printers in the UK, just under 100,000 across the EU. Suppliers from the emerging markets of eastern Europe and Asia are now competing for some products. A good starting point in the process of defining your needs is to decide whether there is a geographical limitation involved. Usually this depends on the type of work being placed, the amount of communication involved in its production and the delivery requirements. To many buyers there is a tyranny of distance, whether real or imagined.

Clients who want to now and again visit the printer's office to chat with him can suffer bad attacks of nerves if long distances are involved. In practice, the limitation tends to be self-defining. If the work being placed is substantial, the savings that may be possible by choosing one supplier in preference to another, wherever he is located, may be more significant than the inconvenience of distance or the expense of communication.

If the work is more limited, it will either be so straightforward that little communication is required (in which case it can be printed anywhere with the minimum of fuss) or so little cost will be involved that it is hardly worth casting too wide a net in the hope of saving a few pence on the quotation.

The situation changes if the customer is in a large city. Most of the major printing companies have representatives based in, or frequently visiting, the main towns and cities.

If the job is large enough to justify it, it may be worth buying print in another country. Two conditions must be satisfied if a buyer is to trade successfully with overseas suppliers:

▶ there should be enough work to justify the additional overhead that may result from communications taking place over a long distance;

▶ the supplier must have the administrative resources (and compatible languages) to deal with the extended lines of communication.

The work might need additional administration and the degree of this depends on the way in which the print buyer is trading with his overseas supplier. The common scenarios are:

▶ direct with the printer with no intermediaries

▶ through a sales office in one's own country run by the printer

▶ through a specialist print management intermediary

▶ through the customer's buying office in the country of supply.

The type of arrangement most appropriate will depend on the resources of the buyer and the supplier he is using. Clearly, much of the administrative work will be taken off the buyer's shoulders if his supplier has a local office prepared to handle all communication and transport of materials.

Sometimes, as relationships evolve, a buying organisation may begin trading through a local office but may, in due course, strike up such reliable contact with the factory that direct overseas trading becomes quicker and more effective. Other more adventurous systems may follow on from this. Many objections to using overseas suppliers have been overcome through the use of e-commerce, but some local knowledge can be useful. Remember to plan for contingencies, including potential physical delivery problems.

Currency is an issue when dealing with overseas suppliers. Depending on the volume of work you are buying and the agreement you have with your printers, you will either be quoted in the currency of the printer or in your local currency. If it is necessary to trade in the overseas currency, you must decide if you will need to cover yourself for this risk. If so, specialist financial advice will be needed.

Materials   Disappointment over paper, board or other materials is a common source of problems in the relationships between buyers and suppliers. Although it is possible to prepare rigorous technical specifications for paper and board that should ensure predictability, this is a risky business.

In almost every case, it is better to see a sample of the material to be used – and preferably a printed sample – than to rely on a specification. Indeed, it is inadvisable even to make a decision on the basis of a similar sheet of paper or sample of card since small variations in shade, substance or bulk can lead to bitter disappointment. This is a particular problem where overseas production is involved because the characteristics of materials considered significant in different parts of the world vary considerably.

Volatility of supply is also more acute in some areas of the world than in, for example, the UK or the US, and it may be more difficult to ensure consistency of supply in some overseas locations. The print buyer should, therefore, consider security of a consistent supply to be as important as the initial decision.

Environmental policy

A supplier's environmental performance may be a major consideration for print buyers from organisations that are keen to promote their environmental credentials. This manual is not the place for a detailed discussion of print's role in promoting environmental sustainability, but paper, and trees, are highly symbolic for many environmental organisations. It is important to promote the use of paper from sustainable forests, while increasing volume use of recycled material and reducing the use of volatile organic compounds (VOCs) helps mitigate many of the potential harmful impacts of the printing industry.

The ISO14000 family of standards on environmental management was developed to provide a practical toolbox to assist in the implementation of actions supportive of sustainable development. Increasing numbers of printers are becoming ISO14000 compliant; most others should be able to provide an environmental statement that demonstrates their commitment to good practice. A typical statement might read:

Printer Ltd: environmental statement

It is Printer's policy to continually seek to minimise any negative environmental impact from the pursuit of its various business interests, while continuing to produce high-quality products to its customers needs, specifications and satisfaction.

In this regard, Printer recognises that all activity will have some impact, and that this needs to be measured in a comprehensive and systematic manner.

To this end, the benefit of our products must be weighed against any ecological detriment, as a result of their manufacture, sale and ultimate disposal.

Environmental impact is therefore considered throughout our organisation in relation to:

1. The design and development of new products and processes.

2. Internal production methods, with particular emphasis on

  ► *reducing wastage*

  ► *reducing energy usage*

  ► *recycling of waste*

  ► *minimising and controlling hazardous substances (COSHH)*

  ► *controlling emissions whether to air, drainage or landfill, etc.*

  ► *optimising packaging of raw material and finished products*

  ► *eliminating the use of solvents and chemicals wherever possible*

  ► *using the most effective transport.*

It is Printer's policy to comply with, and aim to improve upon, all statutory environmental requirements, and to foster an informed and open approach to environmental concern.

The involvement of our employees, customers, suppliers, local communities and local authorities will be encouraged to assist us in the achievement of this policy.

Chief executive, Date

Customers should check how the supplier plans to comply with the statement and not just accept it as a given.

Envirowise (www.envirowise.gov.uk) is a useful resource for UK printers looking to improve their environmental performance; it offers practical support and advice to help companies improve their environmental credentials.

Estimates and charges

Printers will normally respond to a request for a quotation with an estimate containing a clearly defined outline specification that details quantities and delivery dates. For a regular relationship, the printer will often present a fixed-price menu allowing the client to do a ready-reckoner for costs. While convenient, it is good practice to obtain benchmark prices from several suppliers to ensure costs are under control.

Prepress

With the changes in technology being rapidly adopted, there is no standard way of estimating commercial prepress work except in cases where similar jobs such as books and periodicals are run. There will typically be a menu of prices for activities not directly provided by the client. Be particularly careful when examining a quote for the cost of additional proofs (if required) and for corrections. These are a popular way for printers and prepress houses to generate revenue.

A minimum charge is often invoked for small jobs, then bespoke activity charged at a set hourly rate. It is important that jobs are produced correctly according to industry standard for delivery to a printer. The production of contract and imposition proofs is a significant cost and it is often best to get the final printer to produce these to match their printing conditions.

Printing and binding

When final files are passed to the printer, it is the accepted ethic in the trade that the price quoted for printing is fixed according to the specification. Any technical complications leading to extra costs met along the way are the printer's problem. Issues rising from incorrect files are the responsibility of the customer, and significant additional costs will be passed to the customer. Printers normally:

▶ quote for prepress activities, including final proofing from suitable files. They will also highlight additional charges that may result from problems and delays due to prepress faults;

▶ quote a price for printing and binding a number of copies of the finished job, maybe with a run-on and run-back price for fewer or more copies, or;

▶ provide a quotation that identifies the consistent elements in the job and how they will be printed and bound, and specifies individual prices for each process.

The fixed method is suitable for simple, straightforward work where the specification is unlikely to change. The menu approach is preferred in the case of work where the buyer then needs a ready-reckoner to estimate the cost of change.

In essence, it is necessary to know the cost of printing each sheet that comprises the section of the job in permutations of colour required and the cost of binding those sheets.

A minimum quantity likely to be needed is used as the basis for the calculation, and a price per hundred or per thousand copies of the sheet is given as the run on. Since the printed sheet will comprise a number of pages of the final job, this is often quoted as, for example: €500 per 16 pages black on one side of the sheet, four colours on the reverse.

Folding

In the case of web-fed printing, where the folding is in line with the printing process, the cost of the folding will be included in the printing price. With sheetfed work, there will usually be an additional and identifiable cost for sheet handling and folding.

Binding

If a complicated binding method is involved, it is sensible for this also to be broken down into the constituent operations so that the cost of improving or reducing the specification can be estimated. If you are interested in the costs of alternative binding methods, this must be made known at the outset since in some instances it will affect the printing process.

Comparative estimating

It is desirable to persuade suppliers to present their quotations in a way that allows them to be easily be compared, hence requiring adequate detail within your printer's quotation. Additionally, a detailed response reveals the processes at which the supplier is most and least competitive. This helps to refine the choice of supplier, depending on the type of work you are placing and the processes involved in creating it.

Agreed price scales for repetitive work are a useful idea. They are a suitable basis for negotiation because the absence of continuous re-quotation can result in lower overheads.

Chapter 12 includes a range of typical forms for specifications. Various suppliers now provide expert help in their e-commerce systems to aid building up a specification from scratch, or have details of previous and standard jobs that can be modified to provide the specification. There is no industry standard for this type of function so there is a tendency for buyers to write short letters. Forms and e-commerce are a better idea because they remind the specifier of the points to be covered.

There are three major advantages to a supplier in dealing with a few customers placing large volumes of work rather than a proliferation of smaller projects:
► it becomes easier to plan good utilisation of labour and machine capacity
► sales overhead is reduced
► provided the customer is financially sound, less financial control is required.
These savings, which essentially amount to a better utilisation of overhead, are real enough provided the major customer is professional and efficient. But however large and influential the customer, if his working methods resemble a chimps' tea party, it will cost the printer more, rather than less, to run his account.

If a client is efficient and prepared to place a large and predictable volume of work with a supplier, then good prices should follow. In this context, remember that the good buyer is also a good salesman: he needs to sell the supplier the concept of the deal he is proposing.

This sort of discussion needs to be conducted at the appropriate level within the supplier's organisation. Do not attempt to bypass your usual rep with whom you place the one-off jobs but if you are proposing something on a grander scale, ask him if he will involve his sales director or managing director in such discussions. If he is sensible, he will be happy with this proposal. It will:

► avoid the complications of selling on your scheme at second-hand

► help to cement the supplier-buyer relationship

► lead to further suggestions about how the supplier's capacity can be taken up by the buyer.

Volume agreements

In areas of print buying where large volumes are the order of the day, it is not unusual for deals that represent millions of pounds' worth of work to be agreed and for this agreement to be used by the supplier as the basis for significant future investment plans.

Both parties must, of course, ensure that they can fulfil their contract whether it is legally binding or not. The supplier must have available the capacity he is selling with the flexibility he and his customers have agreed is necessary. The customer must be sure that the volumes of work he is predicting will come through according to the schedules agreed. The period over which such agreements can run and prices can be fixed is subject to a variety of influences outside the printing trade and must, therefore, be a matter for debate.

Caution is needed. Apart from external economic factors that the buyer and the supplier have no control of (e.g. inflation, price of raw materials, cost of power), the development of printing technology goes on apace and changes the economics of many of the processes year by year. You may, therefore, be reluctant to enter into agreements that extend beyond a year unless there are clearly understood clauses that are equitable but provide a means of escape for both parties in changing circumstances.

Contracts

Complicated legal contracts tend to be self-defeating. The subject matter is too volatile and legal restraints are unnecessary because it is a matter of fact that few trading relationships in the printing industry ever become the subject of litigation. By industrial standards, the financial sums involved are not huge, and the cost of establishing a legal basis for agreement, let alone activating it, is normally out of ratio to the business value.

In addition, the reputation of buyers and suppliers is widely known in the industry and the trader who misbehaves seriously is ill-advised. Not all professional buyers agree on this subject and, in some government departments in particular, there are quite complicated contractual arrangements for print buying.

One may make an exception in the case of magazine printing where both sides are entering into a substantial commitment over a potentially lengthy period and where levels of service may need to be specified with corresponding penalties for failure.

Paper

Methods of charging for paper are dealt with in Chapter 9; weight is still the governing factor in any given quality. The paper trade realises that the man in the street finds the mathematics of paper calculation and charging systems somewhat daunting, and the helpful merchant or printer expects to need to provide his estimates and costs in an intelligible form.

Getting quotes

The first step in getting quotes is to contact suppliers. When seeking quotations for a standard type of work that you are familiar with, and for which you know the range of responses likely, there is really no point in putting more than a handful of suppliers through the hoop of providing competitive quotes. With unusual work, or work that you do not normally handle, it may be worth talking to several potential suppliers in general terms before drawing up a shortlist of those with whom you wish to proceed further.

Three quotes

Three quotations on a job that requires competitive tendering is a comfortable number to work with, provided you believe each supplier is seriously capable of handling the work and is enthusiastic to get it. The type of work also determines the method by which you proceed to select the supplier.

In the case of straightforward printed matter, especially when only one type of supplier is involved, the whole business can probably be conducted by correspondence. With more complex jobs, you will need to see a representative and go through the work in some detail to ensure both parties understand everything.

It is worth noting a few basic tenets of communication at this preliminary stage. The first, and most important, rule is to ensure that each supplier is quoting on the same specification and, as far as you can control it, presenting his quote in the same way.

Your responsibility is to provide a concise, complete specification for the work along with any notes that may affect its production and, depending on circumstances, to dictate or agree a schedule.

Specifications

Specifications come in as many shapes, sizes and colours as butterflies and, given the volatile nature of printed matter, are almost as transient. However, it is essential that an initial firm specification is the subject of the comparative quotation analysis, and the printer's estimates are presented a way so that deviations from the specification can be calculated.

It is fruitless to attempt to dictate a format for the preparation of specs. They can be narrative or tabular, general or technical, depending on the style and technical skills of the buyer, and all this does not really matter provided the job has been properly described.

A set of sample specification forms can be found in Chapter 12. These present the bare minimum of information necessary about each job but are as basic as possible to avoid confusion and technical jargon. In a covering letter (on simple work) or face to face (on more complex material), make sure the supplier understands the specification and the schedules.

Schedules

Schedules, like specifications, can be presented in a variety of ways. The only vital qualification is that they must be unambiguous. A sample schedule is provided in Chapter 12.

Analysing quotes

If you have required conformity in the presentation of quotes, the task of comparing them will be relatively straightforward. Check that the service being offered by each supplier is comparable (and is at the level you require) and check that various incidentals are covered or quoted. In particular, watch out for:

► delivery charges

► packing charges

► additional sets of proofs beyond an agreed minimum

► charges for author's corrections on typesetting

► machine standing time due to late delivery of artwork

► a line that says subject to sight of copy.

All these are perfectly reasonable items in some circumstances. What the buyer and supplier must agree on is the nature of those circumstances. There is no advantage to either partner in having an agreement to see how it goes. There must be explicit understanding on what is and what isn't to be charged, or there could be problems when the invoice arrives.

If an analysis of three quotations shows widely varying bottom lines, and if you believe you have sensibly chosen suppliers who specialise in the type of work you are placing, something is probably wrong. Something has been misunderstood, or something has been omitted. Geographical location can result in significant variations in cost due to varying overheads (sometimes mitigated by lower delivery costs) but, as a general rule, variations in quotations of more than 10–12% for run-of-the-mill work need further investigation.

Terms of payment

Print suppliers should not be expected to be bankers. However, nearly all business is conducted on credit and to achieve a reasonable, commercial balance the cost of this facility needs to be estimated.

In the printing industry, terms of payment range from pro-forma invoicing (money up front) for the small and unknown customer, to 90 days or more to large and influential buyers. Whatever the arrangement, it is important to quantify its value. Supplier A quoting the same price as supplier B but on different credit terms is not quoting the same price at all.

The supplier might say that the variation in price is the cost to him of borrowing the money to finance the credit. In fact, although this is true enough, the way the price looks to the customer will be determined by what it costs the *buyer* to borrow money or, if he is a cash-rich operator, what he is getting in the way of interest on his cash. The relative advantages of credit will, therefore, depend on the cash flow position of the organisation that is buying.

Take into consideration whether paper is involved in the arrangement. Some of the printer's cash flow is current, as he works on your project. However, if you are obtaining your paper supplies through him, then this element will probably have been paid for either well in advance, in the case of paper held in stock, or at relatively high prices in the case of rapid delivery. It is not uncommon, therefore, to negotiate different payment terms for materials and print work.

Buying print

Communications between print buyer and printer are cost sensitive, time sensitive, ambiguous and, all too often, prone to error. Most large printers operate sophisticated management information systems to handle their administration, but these can be difficult to integrate with customers and partners in the manufacturing process.

Preferred suppliers

One method is to select one or two printers who can reliably offer a service that caters for most of the buyer's needs. For example, the part-time buyer who needs to order a range of small jobs – A4 leaflets, business cards, stationery, and occasionally needs a brochure, four-colour leaflet, or display card – may decide that his first range of material can be quickly and cheaply produced by the instant print shop in the high street. However, a local jobbing printer with a more extensive range of equipment can handle his more sophisticated needs.

Alternatively, he may feel that using two similar suppliers and splitting his work between them will ensure that he keeps them on their toes when it comes to price and service.

There are various scenarios that can work. The instant print shop has an apparent deficiency in that its range of products may be restricted. However, some instant print shops will act as a print broker and put those jobs that are too big for them to handle out to external suppliers.

For many organisations, there are multiple ordering points for small printed items. Instead of an ad hoc buying process, many use a print management company to streamline their purchases, obtaining a high degree of control and often significant cost savings.

Such savings are improved when the internal costs at the client – staff time, value of stock and duplication of production – are considered. Instead of employing specific print buyers, the function is outsourced to specialist service providers. With many organisations realising that a consistent branding approach is required, it makes sense to have a single point of control providing visibility of the purchases. The growth in print management is testament to these benefits.

There are several print market sectors, particularly business forms, where there is a high proportion of trade printing. These companies do not have the overhead of expensive direct sales and marketing teams, instead they sell to print managers or brokers. The lower overhead at suppliers is passed on to the broker, the client generally obtaining better prices than an open market approach where suppliers have the sales overhead. This allows the supplier to concentrate on manufacturing excellence and not involve so much management resource in promoting the sales of the company. The print management company might also take responsibility for warehousing and distribution, making the manufacturing simpler.

Successful print managers employ dedicated buyers and print supply chain logistics personnel to understand the suppliers and ensure an enquiry is sent to the most efficient supplier. Even the largest printers do not have the necessary equipment and capabilities to handle all types of job efficiently. Print managers do not have the burden of having to fill their printing capacity and can take a more objective view of the overall process.

Using a print management company

Many non-professional print buyers but buy relatively small amounts of printed material for promotions, marketing purposes or internal office use. Often buying will be distributed throughout an organisation, with individual branches and offices sourcing their own requirements. The principles involved in this type of activity are much the same as for the full-time, professional print buyer, but the style is different.

The office print buyer will typically adopt one of two methods of working. He will use a print broker or settle on one or two suppliers capable of handling 90% of the work required. What is certainly a bad option is to shop around for every small job to get the best price on each item. The administration and complication of working this way would almost certainly be out of proportion to the benefits achieved and, as a part-time enterprise, would be unrealistic.

Print brokers, also known as print farmers, get a mixed press in the print-buying trade. They can appear as unnecessary middlemen skimming margin off an already tight profit, or they are informed experts who save time and avoid mistakes by using specialist knowledge and buying power to achieve good prices and efficient relationships. Many will offer online systems to improve the specification and supply of printed items, controlling the branding and offering real-time information to the client. For a contract, the management company will prepare service level agreements (SLAs) for stock and bespoke items according to their complexity.

For the part-time print buyer who is required to operate in an unfamiliar market with limited knowledge of suppliers and prices, a print broker can be useful. The responsibilities of the print manager should include:
▶ representing the buyer to develop appropriate quality and schedule requirements through defined SLAs;
▶ handling the administration and all financial transactions, including the invoicing and credit control;
▶ providing transparency for comparative quotes if required;
▶ making the specification and ordering of stock and bespoke items straightforward;
▶ controlling the design and prepress work;
▶ providing real-time information on the status of jobs.
Provided the buyer understands the basis of the relationship, this can be an effective way of buying print, particularly for large, distributed organisations.

Print management is described differently by various participants in the market, from the print farmer to the document process outsourcer. It covers the practice of sourcing and buying print and services on behalf of a client. The print management sector comprises a range of different operations. First there are the large specialist outsourcing companies that concentrate on print and document management for large companies. They operate across many country markets and provide a high-tech, sophisticated service. The 'forms broking' sector specialises in providing complex business forms; this sector is extending its operations into commercial print, packaging and other sectors. The third sector is made up of print companies that buy print; they do not produce internally because they do not have the specialist manufacturing capability or the capacity. There is a growing trend for manufacturers to move into this sector to provide additional products and services for their customers, with some setting up dedicated print management operations.

The print management market in Europe was worth some €14.6 billion in 2004, 12.2% of the total print market. It is forecast to grow 26% to just over €18.4 billion by 2009, taking 14% of all print. While Germany boasts the largest print market, the UK has a larger print management market. The UK leads the print management sector in Europe with 14.5% of all print, which Pira forecasts will grow to 16.6% over the next five years as suppliers become more sophisticated and professional.

E-procurement

Examples of e-procurement screens and process capabilities are provided in Chapter 12.

A major trend that is changing the nature of print buying is the e-enablement of the process through the application of distributed communications based on standards to integrate administration into production. Methods are likely to be based on the job definition format (JDF), using XML..

The huge increase in e-commerce means that many disparate computer systems are having to communicate with one another. XML is used to enable business-to-business communication. Computers send and receive XML-tagged data across the web to exchange information.

XML facilitates the publishing production process and incorporates much of the administrative and process information to smooth out printing/publishing operations. In the case of print publishing, several proprietary systems on offer eventually coalesced into JDF – designed to enable the easy, comprehensive information interchange between customer and supplier.

JDF in process control of prepress

JDF is a data exchange standard that acts as a universal electronic job ticket for printing. It contains the process data needed from print specification and buying, print estimating, customer service, prepress, printing, finishing and despatch. JDF contains production and administration information, not content data. The key feature of JDF is the ability to carry a print job from creation to completion. JDF is able to link the production function and admin management information systems (MIS) at printers under nearly any precondition. as it is designed to be extremely versatile and comprehensive for businesses of all sizes.

JDF offers the promise of controlling and managing each job with less effort. It is comprehensive across the range of processes that make up print production and makes automated production control easier. Most importantly, the customer benefits because systems will work accurately and consistently together to produce the product the customer wants. Production will be better controlled so that printers can accurately estimate and fairly assess the costs involved. JDF is an open standard with most significant equipment and system vendors signed up to provide compatible components. Its objectives are:

▶ To provide consistent definition of the process, involving the whole workflow from commission to delivery;

▶ To create a flexible and extensible way of interfacing between processes defined by different suppliers, and the equipment involved to streamline production processes;

▶ To exchange data with MIS and e-commerce systems.

Digital administration of print

Print production is now largely digital. Designers prepare artwork to a standard suitable for printing, while some printers offer tools for non-expert customers to do the same. Page make-up systems, digital artwork applications, digital proofing, digital file transfer, computer to plate (CTP) and digital printing have all dramatically improved the overall productivity of print production. To complement this new efficiency in graphics workflows, there is a revolution taking place in the way the print supply chain is administered. Now administration systems, the IT applications that support the management of the process, are posing new questions on how the industry will respond to the development of e-procurement. Now, for the first time, the successful integration of front and back office with the digital production workflow will allow organisations to truly manage their print expenditure across their enterprise. Quotes can be requested online, suppliers selected by benchmarking cost, quality and delivery criteria, progress monitored and reports generated highlighting actual performance against key performance indices.

The challenge for the print industry is who will be best placed to offer the service. The product specifications for print vary greatly, from business cards to letterheads, complex business forms, transactional documents, promotional literature, direct mail and point of sale. No single printer has either the capital investment or the knowledge to produce all of a single client's requirements. There is an increasing trend for the appointment of a print-managed service provider who, while not printing the product directly, is responsible for implementation of the workflow and administration systems, buying print separately and managing the supply chain.

This move is challenging the traditional dynamics of the print industry. The managed service provider is becoming more powerful in the competitive matrix. Their value proposition is one of lower cost, an improvement in operational efficiency and the provision of the necessary management information.

Whatever the eventual impact of the increasing digitisation of print and administration processes on the competitive dynamics of the industry, the ultimate consequence, as with all industries, will be lower prices and shorter lead-times. Failure by companies to recognise this unavoidable consequence will mean a loss of competitiveness and, ultimately, jeopardy of their commercial livelihood.

Many organisations pay too much for printed material. There is a great deal of unnecessary duplication with one department re-creating work that others have done: the re-drawing of logos, the re-shooting and scanning of imagery and the production of graphic material when an acceptable alternative already exists as an asset of the organisation.

Purchases of paper or styles of printing are not consolidated and used to negotiate lower prices. Lack of knowledge of the print process among buyers results in printers being retained to do work that can be more economically and better produced elsewhere. The disjointed characteristics of the print value chain (marketing departments, agencies, prepress studios and printers) means that errors are common. Without an efficient system to administer the process, errors can occur at every handover: between client and designer, designer and artwork studio, studio and printer.

Organisations can start to both reduce their costs and improve efficiency by treating print as a line item in the P&L, developing strategies for the business as a whole and managing component parts on an ongoing basis. The key to achieving this new level of control is the increasing digitisation of both the workflow for print (the business process) and the administration systems (the management process).

Print workflows go digital

All commercial printing is digital. At some stage it is edited and created on a computer, only becoming analogue as a proof or a plate or even as a print. With Moore's Law still holding true and even accelerating (computer processing power doubles every 18 months at the same cost), and with the increasing availability of broad bandwidth, the print process will continue to become less artisan and more of a series of controlled IT applications. Today there are automatic page make-up systems, colour management systems, digital cameras, on-screen and digital proofing systems, CTP and digital printing. It is feasible to conduct the entire process in the electronic world, from the point of design through to the point of distribution.

For most, this move from manual to electronic activities has meant a lowering of unit cost, but not necessarily an attack on overall process costs. While prices have reduced, print is often still bought on limited criteria. Quality is a given. Buyers do not choose printers who cannot do the job – delivery times need to be met and unit costs need to be competitive. Often, though, inertia rules and print is placed with those who have delivered the product last. The key criterion appears to be trust. Service is so variable and errors so common, clients value the ability to delegate responsibility and be confident that the end product will meet their specification.

Today, however, assured quality within the print production process need not be left to the black art of printing. Using on-screen and digital proofing and electronic file transfer, imaging hubs can be created that are single entities controlling a client's entire artwork requirements. A single imaging entity can ensure effective management to the style-guide, and colour management is in the hands of people who understand both the brand attributes and the fingerprint of the press the work is going to. With on-screen and digital proofing, clients can be in any corner of the world. With digital file transfer and computer to plate, printers too can be close to their markets.

The essential element of this single managing entity is the asset management system linked to workflow. The management of content is key – to provide, prepare and manage artwork, resulting in greater visibility and control over the print process. The numbers of suppliers can be reduced, with benchmarks for quality being set and managed. Digitisation of production processes now enables a more coordinated supply chain; the key to delivering control is the extent to which administration systems can provide visibility of the component activities. The emergence of internet-based e-procurement helps solve many of the issues associated with promoting visibility and maintaining control for buyers. Where expenditure was never called out as a line item, strategies are now being developed to bring down costs and develop genuine competitive advantage.

Integrated administration systems

New systems are designed to integrate the business process with graphic arts production, linking printers' MIS with their production systems and giving customers and suppliers access to the system. Systems will allow many new functions to smooth the print production supply chain, from the initial customer idea to the reconciliation of the final invoice. Clients will have access to the system to initiate enquiries. A new job will have the specification built up from scratch or by changing an existing product. Simple expert systems advise print novices on areas that can create difficulties or ambiguity further down the chain. When completed, the detailed specification can be sent to a range of qualified suppliers to provide quotes and delivery dates. The system will have the capability of integrating directly into the suppliers' JDF-compliant MIS, so avoiding the need for printers' staff to input the job details (and possibly keying in an error). The response can be electronically sent to the system, where competitive quotes can be examined on a like-for-like basis and the purchase decision made. When an order is placed, it will be a simple execute file sending purchase details directly into the printer's system as well as preparing and providing the necessary files.

If required, customers can have access to the competitive tendering process ensuring that work is placed according to their key criteria (price, quality, delivery, turnaround of quotes). The system will log the print specification of the production equipment, and the job files will be prepared and optimised for the chosen production route. Colour management and pre-flight checking will be carried out and application or print-ready PDF files submitted ready for output according to the printer's needs. Hard-copy proofs or previously printed samples will be sent separately. The progress of jobs can be monitored when suppliers implement JDF- and CIP4-compliant production equipment, and the customer is aware of the progress. Invoices are easy to reconcile, the whole experience is smoothed and there are fewer places to introduce errors.

The following detail shows the extent of integration that is required for a system to deliver significant improvements. The activities to be covered by the system include:

- ▶ Finance
  - ▷ General ledgers
  - ▷ Sales order processing
  - ▷ Purchase order processing
  - ▷ Management and statutory reports
- ▶ Estimating
  - ▷ Costing of internal prepress and design, printing and finishing, warehousing, logistics and despatch
  - ▷ Fixed price matrices
  - ▷ RFQs to third-party suppliers
- ▶ Stock control
  - ▷ Raw materials
  - ▷ Part and finished goods
  - ▷ Multiple locations – multi-bin, consignment and at third parties
- ▶ Purchasing
  - ▷ Specification of goods
  - ▷ Supplier categorisation
  - ▷ Supplier ratings
- ▶ Invoicing
  - ▷ Consolidation, part invoices, to specific customer requirements
- ▶ Production and project planning
  - ▷ Scheduling
  - ▷ Control
  - ▷ Project management
- ▶ E-commerce
  - ▷ Customer interface – purchasing, catalogue of products, stock
  - ▷ Administrator interface – estimating, planning, production control, delivery
  - ▷ Supplier interface – material supply and purchase
- ▶ Specific graphics functionality
  - ▷ Digital asset management
  - ▷ Workflow management tools to allow improvements in the productivity of prepress and collaborative working with customers (e.g. remote proofing, colour management, web to print)
  - ▷ Automated page assembly, pagination, brand consistency
  - ▷ Project management and administration
  - ▷ Sophisticated dynamic document creation from templates for branded items.

The key is to provide graphics functionality to the business process for the range of clients involved, to simplify the print/communications supply chain and provide easier use for customers through controlled access. Specific examples are provided in Chapter 12.

Print buyers and print management companies will use these tools to find ways to improve the supply chain of any printed items, and reduce the costs and lead-time to improve the client performance. Additionally, the system will be used to provide a managed imaging service, encompassing prepress and design. The prepress function will involve a digital asset management system holding all content for clients. This will support re-use of material for different media, ensuring speedy response and guaranteeing the correct version to maintain brand integrity.

One of the key areas for all print users and suppliers is the way that orders can be developed and subsequently processed. The system will be used to manage the process in the following manner:

Estimating/RFQ The system will handle estimates for work produced internally and by third-party suppliers (either as a bespoke request for quotation or from an agreed price matrix). The greatest complexity will be for items bought externally where multiple estimates will be requested and analysed as part of the vendor management programme.

Specific jobs might consist of multiple separate elements and components (of prepress and print), from multiple suppliers that must be consolidated into a single estimate and then throughout manufacturing and despatch to multiple locations. The system should allow estimates to be produced from scratch, to allow revisions to an existing product or to enable standard products or processes to be combined.

Estimating performance, in terms of time taken to generate a response, must be included. This should provide prompts to estimator/customer service personnel of due dates to ensure service level agreements (SLAs) are exceeded.

Order processing Each order is provided with a unique reference (cross-referenced to customer order number) and the system generates works instruction and job bags or purchase orders to approved suppliers. The MIS provides internal production planning and capacity loading system for the prepress, printing and finishing operations and will be able to link to external suppliers, in time through standard JDF. The system will thus provide real-time job tracking with updates manually entered or linked to real-time data collection, according to the manufacturer's capabilities. Potential delivery problems will be highlighted well in advance. Contracted service level agreements for different customers and products will be monitored against actual performance.

Purchasing Effective print product sourcing and purchasing will become critical success factors for users of print. The system will provide transparency of the reverse tendering/estimating process with suppliers as shown in Figure 2.1 (overleaf).

FIGURE 2.1 Outline of procurement process

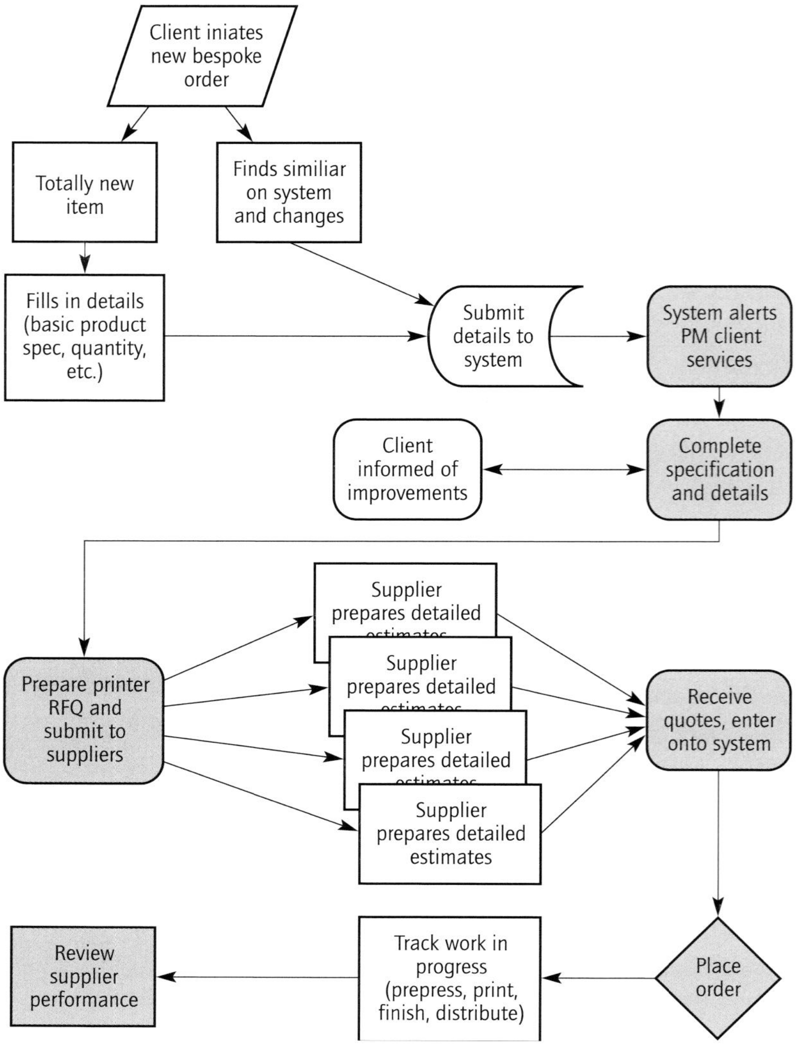

Source: Pira International Ltd

Approved supplier capabilities and product specifications will be maintained on the system with performance ratings (on price, quality, on-time delivery and specific criteria). The use of standard JDF-compatible MIS systems at printers will greatly ease integration, but there are few printers with such capability in general print markets. The system will support a vendor management system to monitor and rank suppliers on criteria of response to RFQ, technical capabilities, price, delivery performance, quality and other attributes to be agreed.

Warehouse and stock control Stock lifecycle management and warehouse management are important for managing print supply contracts. The MIS must be able to manage complex warehouse structures and a range of warehouse facilities such as box storage, pick and pack storage, fixed bin storage and high rack storage. Stock control is important, particularly the capability of linking to the e-commerce function at customers so allowing them to view a thumbnail of the document during ordering. Other important functions include:

► expected delivery date for items ordered not yet delivered

► acceptance of part-deliveries

► identify significant receipt of overs/unders

► multiple stock locations (some at suppliers, some at customers), in some cases for same items

► batch control and tracking, ability to identify supplier and order for stock items that may have more than one supplier

► stock consumption, reordering at agreed levels for stock items

► pick, pack and deliver notes, capability for part order fulfilment and fulfilment from multiple locations.

e-commerce for print There are two main types of e-commerce used in print procurement: workflow sites and e-auction sites. Basic system functionality should be accessible remotely via a web browser by approved personnel, clients and suppliers. For print service customers there will be full stock item catalogues and an ordering facility, linked to graphic displays of the documents and content involved. The authority to spend, order levels and specific views of available items will be configured according to clients' requirements. One key feature that will take cost out of the chain is the ability to link more closely with preferred print suppliers, enabling more efficient manufacturing. This might involve the system interrogating the technical specification of a stock item to be re-ordered then suggesting adding similar items to the order that could be manufactured at the same time (e.g. using spot colours on similar sheet size and substrate).

These topics are covered in greater detail in Chapter 12.

Controlling print quality

Print production comprises a combination of creative and technical processes. There are many factors that influence the perceived quality of the product. The approach taken to control these factors must recognise this within three distinct areas of influence:

► graphic design and original materials

► prepress processes

► production printing.

Graphic design and the original materials

Graphic design and the generation of original materials is essentially the creative part of the print production process, and judgements of quality are subjective. But they should also be influenced by technical considerations: how a design will be affected by the limitations of the printing process (see under quality and technical process specifications in Chapter 7, page 420. The selection of original materials that include consumable materials, such as paper, as well as artist's or photographic originals, requires as much technical as creative consideration.

Prepress processes

Judging quality in the prepress area is related primarily to the standards applied when processing an original design into the final films and plates that will be used for production printing. Judgement cannot be made in isolation since the output must be suitable for, and take account of, the characteristics of the printing process. Although quality control in the prepress area is defined by technical processes, there is inevitably some degree of subjective interpretation.

Printing

Quality in the production printing area is judged primarily on the ability to transfer ink from plate to substrate consistently, without defects, while complying with certain technical specifications. This area is least influenced by subjective judgements and is more capable of being controlled and specified by measurable parameters.

The final printed job can be judged to be of poor quality if acceptable standards are not simultaneously met in all these areas. Poor print quality can be due simply to poor design, prepress or printing, but it is just as likely to arise from work that, though excellent in all areas in its own right, has been carried out without consideration of the process as a whole. For example, the graphic designer may produce fabulous work but, ignoring limitations of the printing process, might provide material that will not reproduce well. Equally, separations and proofs may be produced that, although good, do not match the characteristics of the printing process. Both situations might result in poor final quality and dissatisfaction with the end product.

The three areas are often the responsibility of different departments or companies. This makes it is easy for one to blame another for a quality failure, but achieving acceptable results (the best quality that the process and materials allow) is possible only if print production, from design through to printing, is considered as a total system. It must be recognised that all processing stages are related to one another. Each stage needs to be controlled in its own right, but overall quality relies on communicating relevant information to all other operation stages.

Print production as a system

A controlled digital workflow for print is an integrated system. At each stage (from client, designer, prepress, platemaking, printing, binding and finishing) information can be passed ahead to help the set-up of equipment. It can also be passed back to ensure optimum quality from the process. For colour reproduction, the required information is conveyed in the form of the print characteristic specification, or colour profile of the press to be used. If a specific profile is not available, the buyer will use a widely accepted generic profile, such as the Eurostandard, and the printer will operate within such tolerances.

Standardised printing conditions allow an overall improvement in the quality of printed items while allowing maximum flexibility in placing a job with the buyer. The buyer can enhance the product by using suppliers with additional print units offering a wider colour gamut or incorporating metallics and fluorescents to achieve specialist effects.

The print characteristic and potential printing problems

The print characteristic is a quantitative definition of the transfer between the digital image and production print. It is affected by substrate, inks, tone transfer characteristics (dot gain) of the press and process. Colour management allows a suitable original, containing the maximum amount of information, to be rendered for any particular printing condition that has been profiled. Having provided a profile, the printer's main task is to maintain it within defined tolerances. To be able to do this, indeed to control any colour printing, requires an understanding of the important parameters and the influences that they have on the printed result. If a proof is to match job printing, it must duplicate the print characteristic attributes appropriate to the particular printing condition. The influencing attributes are:

► substrate
► solid ink colour
► secondary colour (trapping)
► tone transfer (dot gain)
► grey balance.

Although these are listed as individual attributes, they are not totally isolated from the influence of the others. This is particularly true for grey balance that is not a variable in its own right, but reflects the changes of any or all of the others.

Substrate

The substrate has a significant influence on the print characteristic with respect to both measured properties and the appearance of the printed result. Most people connected with print production will have experienced the difficulties associated with trying to match a print on uncoated paper with a proof printed on gloss-coated paper. The paper's surface, absorbency, and optical properties all contribute to affect the printed result. It is therefore important to have different specifications for different substrate categories.

Solid ink colour

The solid colour is mainly affected by the amount of ink or colorant transferred to the substrate. It is the main way the printer can adjust the overall result during a production run. As the process inks are manufactured to comply with recognised colour standards, the ink film thickness is the main thing to control, and the measurement of solid density provides an effective means of monitoring this. Note there may be significant colour differences between process colours in different countries. In the UK, for example, BS4666 has a warmer cyan and colder magenta than the German DIN 16538/9.

Secondary colour (trapping)

The secondary and tertiary colours are all affected by the primary ink's hue and ink film thickness and influenced by the trapping characteristics. It is possible to have little or no difference between two prints with respect to the primary colours but to see significant differences in secondary colours, particularly in saturated colours. Multicolour printing involves the overlapping of several ink films. It is important that an overprinting ink is accepted as well on printed areas of the sheet as it is on unprinted areas. Poor trapping means that less overprinting ink is laid down on the previously printed area so that there is a colour bias towards that of the underlying ink. This effect is demonstrated in Figure 2.2.

FIGURE 2.2 Poor trapping results in a colour bias towards that of the underlying ink

Good trapping – magenta on cyan

Poor trapping – magenta on cyan

Poor trapping – cyan on magenta

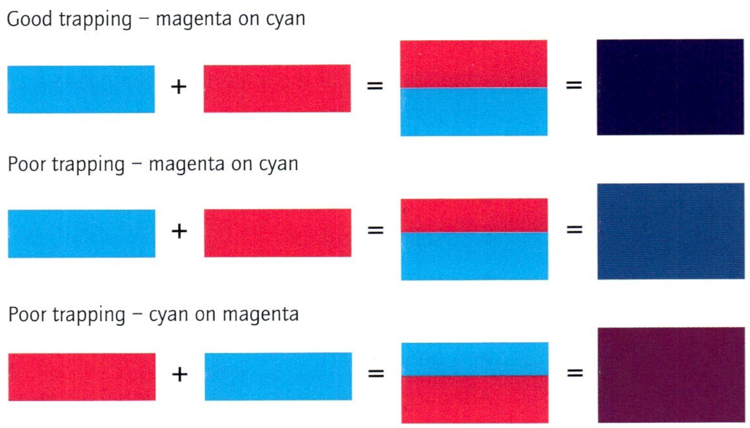

Source: Pira International Ltd

Tone transfer

The control of tone transfer (dot gain) is a major concern for all printed products that use halftone, irrespective of the printing process, but the problems experienced are not always recognised. All the printing processes, with the exception of gravure, have to create the visual impression of differences in tone or colour intensity by varying the area that is printed. Normally this is achieved with a regular pattern of dots, referred to as the halftone process, but it is possible to convey a comparable effect with lines or irregular patterns. This is used in the FM (frequency modulated) screening methods.

Irrespective of the method used, the discrete changes in intensity seen are dependent on the ratio of clean paper to the area of paper covered with ink. Variation in the overall intensity can be achieved by adjustment of inking level in an analogy with television where the contrast control is equivalent to relative changes in dot area, and the brightness control is equivalent to adjusting the level of inking. It means there are two ways to achieve the same intensity on the print. That is helpful because it allows leeway for adjustment but it can also cause problems. For example, a printed area with a density of 0.29 can be achieved with small dots at a high inking level or larger dots with lower inking. It does not mean that both conditions are correct because the larger dots result in lower contrast relative to the solid.

What is dot gain?

Dot gain is one of the most misunderstood properties of lithographic printing. It is an integral phenomenon of the offset process and is not an unwanted side effect. Dot gain reflects the change in the relative dot area between the original dot in a make-up application or PDF, exposed to plate should be identical with accurate calibration and the final dried ink dot on paper. The dot area may change through light scattering if film is used and there are mechanical forces exerted on the fluid ink during transfer from inking roller, to plate, to blanket and to paper. Optical effects of light becoming trapped around the edge of the dot further increase the apparent size of dots on paper. Problems arise when there is excessive dot gain that has not been taken into account in the reproduction process.

Printing from films gave rise to significant quality problems associated with changes in the relative sizes of printing dots across the tonal range. Platemaking and printing both affect the final printed dot size. The imagesetter produces dots on the film to a determined percentage coverage. When these dots are transferred to the printing plate, there will be a size change and further changes will also take place during the transfer of the image to the substrate. Although dots may reduce in size at some stages of the transfer, the cumulative overall effect is normally an increase. A simple illustration of the stages of dot gain, applicable in lithography when using positive film, is shown in Figure 2.3.

FIGURE 2.3 The cumulative effect of dot gain

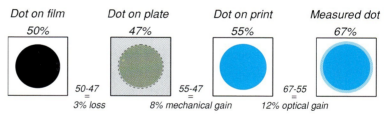

Source: Pira International Ltd

FIGURE 2.4 High dot gain requires lower inking to match the density of the halftone

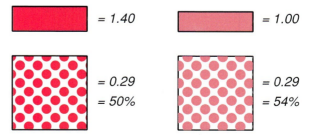

High dot gain requires lower inking to match the
density of the halftone

Source: Pira International Ltd

Although the term 'dot gain' is not used, this change in tone value during transfer is equally appropriate if the tone image is made up with lines or the patterns applicable in FM screening. The change to CTP technology has removed the changes in dot size associated with generating film and platemaking, but still requires calibration to produce optimal results.

How is dot area measured?

It is not easy to measure the geometric size of printed dots. For control, a densitometer is used to calculate the area from the integrated density on film and print, and a CCD plate reader measures the size of dots on plate. The calculation is referred to as the Murray-Davis equation and is built in as a function in most modern densitometers. This measurement incorporates all factors affecting the dot size, mechanical influences related to the press and optical properties associated with the paper. This calculated value is referred to as the apparent or effective dot area. Typical values for offset lithography using positive working plates from film would be 16–20% growth of a 40% dot on film and 10–15% at 80% for coated stock. With the development of CTP, the major variable of film exposure is eliminated and much lower dot gain (5–10%) results. With correct calibration this paves the way to an improvement in quality.

Dot gain problems

Inconsistent results from conventional platemaking from films can be due to dot gain variations. A typical example would be variation in the density of tint blocks from page to page, or from one publication to the next. This can be influenced by several factors: poor control when film contacting or platemaking, incorrect press adjustment or materials. Under normal printing conditions, dot gain occurs evenly all around the printed dot so the choice of dot shape – elliptical, round or square – will affect the result. If dot gain is not even it indicates a problem on-press such as doubling or slur. This must be cured by adjustment of the printing conditions.

An unacceptable colour match may occur when colours are specified in the form of percentage values for CMYK. Such a specification can produce only an acceptable colour match if the dot gain characteristics applicable when printing are nearly identical to those that applied when the colour was specified.

Achieving a colour match between proof and production printing requires all the important print characteristic attributes – substrate, ink colour, solid density and colour sequence – to be comparable for proof and production, but dot growth is the most significant of all the parameters. If the proof is produced with dot growth less than can be attained in the production printing, it is impossible to achieve the required intensity in all tones simultaneously.

The production result will typically appear desaturated and lacking in contrast when inking is adjusted to match midtone colours and densities. Alternatively, if ink levels are adjusted so that saturated colours are matched, the midtones are too dark and gradation is lost. In situations where the discrepancy in dot growth applies only to one colour, the disagreement may be apparent as a colour bias or cast. Such problems commonly become obvious in flesh tones and in neutral areas of the reproduction. If the dot gain of any one chromatic colour shifts significantly from that of the others, the neutral balance of the reproduction is noticeably upset. It is important to ensure that the spread of dot gain in the midtones does not become excessive. Users with CTP report significant reduction in the occurrence of such problems.

Grey balance

Grey balance is not a variable in its own right, but is affected by all the previously mentioned attributes. Grey balance is affected by the relationship of these attributes, one colour relative to another. It is possible to achieve a neutral result using the process colours, if the proportions of the three colours are correct one to another. Variation in the relative inking levels, dot gain characteristics or trapping, will cause a shift in the printed grey balance. People are particularly sensitive to these shifts, therefore, and reproductions of subject-matter with a large neutral content will be noticeably more affected than subjects that are more colourful.

Many printers issue technical specifications indicating the form in which they require films to be supplied, and the print characteristics required for proofs, based on their knowledge of their presses and materials. Generic standard specifications are also produced for specific sectors of the industry. These are aimed principally at satisfying the needs of advertisers who want to supply all magazines with separation films or data files to a common specification.

The International Federation of the Periodical Press (FIPP) has established a standard specification for colour separations in European web offset magazines. In North America, the *Specification for Web Offset Publications* (SWOP) has been agreed by a consensus of advertising agencies, magazine publishers, graphic arts associations and printers. For coldset newspapers, there is UK Offset Newspaper Specification (UKONS) in the UK; and *Specifications for Non-heat Advertising Print* (SNAP) in North America. See Chapter 3 for further details.

During the past few years an ISO technical committee for graphic technology has been working to develop a common set of technical specifications that formalises those previously referred to, but also extends the approach to processes other than offset lithography. These are specified under the following standard *ISO 12647 – Process control for the manufacture of halftone colour separations, proof and production prints. Part 1 Parameters and measurement methods, Part 2 Offset lithographic processes, Part 3 Coldset offset lithography and letterpress on newsprint, Part 4 Gravure, Part 5 Screen printing.*

Mechanical problems

Precision engineered printing presses may give rise to problems if they are not well maintained or set up correctly. Ink transfer may be inconsistent through incorrect pressure settings or uneven wear characteristics; loose and stretched blankets may lead to doubling and slur, as will worn and non-lubricated bearings of plate, blanket or impression cylinders.

Such problems lead to poor reproduction characteristics, which can be identified by use of colour bars and print control strips to monitor the process.

Print control images

To achieve predictable and consistent results, it is important to have process controls that enable the print characteristic to be monitored and controlled within acceptable limits. To make this control easier, the industry uses sensitive reference images. These are typically found on a control strip. They should be used at all the critical stages: proofing, platemaking and printing. With digital prepress, the strip is still needed. It will generally be incorporated by the imposition programme along with trim, fold and cut marks and so forth. Many suppliers offer digital control strips.

Whether digital or analogue film, the printed strips are invaluable in determining the state of a printed item. They will often assist print minders with on-press measurement in make-ready and consistent running. In the event of queries or quality problems, printed control strips allow systematic quantitative analysis of the printing conditions that are useful for printers to determine the nature of any problems.

2

FIGURE 2.5 'Typical' print control strip

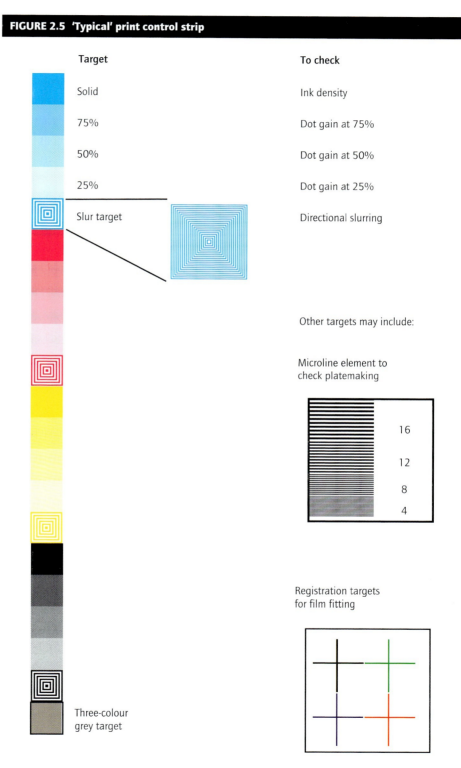

Target	To check
Solid	Ink density
75%	Dot gain at 75%
50%	Dot gain at 50%
25%	Dot gain at 25%
Slur target	Directional slurring

Other targets may include:

Microline element to
check platemaking

16
12
8
4

Registration targets
for film fitting

Three-colour
grey target

Print control targets. The elements are usually arranged in a line,
so as to occupy little space. Only first-generation films
or high-resolution image files should be used

Source: Pira International Ltd

Technical specifications of control strips

A wide range of control images is available for visual assessment and measurement. Some are available as individual elements but they will normally be used as part of a comprehensive continuous control strip. In the case of film, it is important that the control strips should be used in their original form and not duplicated. Not only does duplication infringe copyright, it also changes the tone value of halftone patches and the reproduction of fine lines or dots. This makes it impossible to use the control strip, for example, to provide a reliable measurement of dot gain without first verifying the tone value by measuring the control strip itself.

TABLE 2.1 Test images for monitoring attributes of the print characteristic

Attribute	Image element	Method of assessment
Ink colour and ink film thickness	Solid patch	Visual, colorimeter, spectrophotometer or densitometer
Tone transfer (platemaking)	Continuous tone step wedge	Visual
	Microlines	Magnifier
	Highlight and shadow dots	Magnifier
	Star target	Visual
Tone transfer (printing)	Star target	Visual
	Variable size elements	Magnifier
	Coarse and fine halftone area	Visual or densitometer
	Halftone patch	Densitometer
Tone transfer (slur and doubling)	Star target	Visual
	Concentric circle	Visual
	Line tints	Visual or densitometer
Trapping	Solid overprints	Visual or densitometer
Grey balance	Three-colour neutral halftone patch	Visual, densitometer or spectrophotometer

Source: Pira International Ltd

Which control strip? There is no simple answer to this question, as most are adequate. The choice really depends on the user. Is the preference for a frequent repeat of solids at the expense of, say, grey balance? Are visual dot gain assessment elements required? Are plate control elements to be incorporated into the colour bar, or are there separate elements? The answers to these questions must depend on the importance attached to each parameter. This is determined by the quality of work produced, the consistency of the raw materials used, and the press itself. Each element will be considered in detail within the context of the variables that need to be controlled, and an examination of the options and problems of measurement.

Position of control strips One important consideration when using control strips is their position on the printed sheet. It must be positioned where it will best experience conditions representative of the whole of the sheet, yet still be trimmed off easily during finishing operations. On sheet-fed presses it is normally found most convenient to locate control strips at the extreme back edge. However, it is best to avoid this position, if possible, as it suffers more significantly from the effects of sheet distortion and stretch; the centre or front half of the sheet is preferable. On web presses, inking is more consistent around the cylinder because there is no significant non-printing gap.

Solid colour fields

All the commercial colour strips contain several solid patches of each colour, repeated at intervals along the length of the strip. If the control strip is for a particular type of press, the spacing may correspond with the ink zone widths. From the point of view of ink feed control, the more frequently the solids are repeated the better. However, the more solid the patches, the less space for elements that provided for control of the other attributes. These solid fields can be evaluated visually, but it would be normal to use a densitometer to measure and ensure solid inking is even and within the specified tolerance.

FIGURE 2.6 Control strip of the primary printing colours

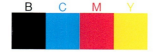

Source: Pira International Ltd

Secondary colour (trapping) fields

The capability to assess trapping is provided by a solid area of each of the overprints. The requirement for the control strip is quite straightforward: the two-colour overprint patch should be close to the solid areas of the individual colours to enable accurate measurement of trapping. Trapping does not vary greatly across the width of the sheet, assuming reasonably controlled inking, so it is not necessary to include frequent repeats of these patches across the width of the press. These fields may be assessed visually or with a densitometer or spectrophotometer.

FIGURE 2.7 The control strip showing secondary, as well as primary colour fields

Source: Pira International Ltd

Grey balance elements

Most control strips contain one or more steps, which include overprints of halftone areas of the three primary colours as a grey patch. Ideally these should appear as a neutral when printed at normal levels of ink density, dot gain and trapping. If printing to a reference standard condition, such as that defined in ISO 12647-2, the patches should be as defined in the standard. However, even if the pass sheet has a colour bias in these areas, it provides a very sensitive target for visual assessment or measurement. The human visual system is particularly adept at discriminating between tertiary colours and greys.

Ideally, the control strip should contain several grey steps of, say, 25%, 50% and 75%. This mini grey-scale would then be subject to both the platemaking and printing variables, and would indicate whether the grey balance of the printed image was being maintained. But for a print control strip it is normally necessary to settle for a single tone value, in which case a 70–75% neutral is suitable as it provides the best compromise between control of solid density and dot gain.

FIGURE 2.8 Grey balance fields

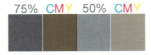

Source: Pira International Ltd

Tone transfer fields – platemaking and proofing

Most platemaking and analogue prepress proofing systems use the photomechanical transfer of the image from the film. In this process, fine lines and dots are particularly sensitive to small changes in the conditions of exposure and processing and are widely used to monitor and control this aspect of the overall control of tone transfer.

Microlines Microlines are used in film production but less so for direct plate imaging. There are specific control targets such as the Ugra Plate Control Wedge (PCW), and microlines may also be incorporated into a print control strip. The PCW consists of fine positive and negative lines, the finest of which is 4μm and the thickest 70μm. Under normal conditions, a positive working offset litho plate, with correct exposure, would show the positive 10–12μm line just reproduced. Similar target values are normally appropriate when used with positive working prepress proofing systems. The greater the thickness of the last reproduced line, the greater the loss of image in transfer.

FIGURE 2.9 Microlines, such as the Ugra Plate Control Wedge (PCW) may be incorporated into a print control strip

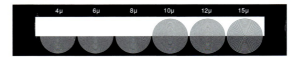

Source: Pira International Ltd

Shadow and highlight dots Shadow and highlight dots perform a similar function to the microlines. They typically consist of small areas of halftone dots with percentage values of 1–5% and 95–99%, in 1% increments. The normal exposure condition for offset plates will result in the 2% dot just being reproduced. The examples shown in Figure 2.10 are combined with microline targets.

FIGURE 2.10 Fogra control strip (left) and a System Brunner control strip (right), here combined with microline targets

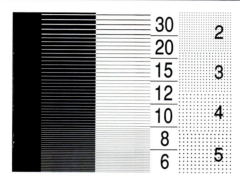

Source: Pira International Ltd

Tone transfer fields – printing

The tone transfer targets are a combination of visual and measurable elements. The visual ones are useful to indicate a problem but it is not normally possible to quantify the effect.

GATF Star Target The Graphic Arts Technical Foundation (GATF) Star Target was one of the first elements designed for the control of tone transfer to be widely used in the graphic arts industry. The target comprises lines that radiate out to form the spokes of a wheel, with the line thickness progressively reducing as they converge in the centre. In certain respects, it behaves like the microlines referred to previously but, because the line thickness is continuously variable and is not so fine, it offers rather more information for print control.

Its response to variations in platemaking and film contacting is similar to that of the microline target. The lines in the centre of the target are at their finest and they disappear to form a white centre. The size of the white centre is determined by the amount of image loss at platemaking. Conversely, image growth causes the lines to join together at the centre producing a solid circular area, the size of which determines the extent of image growth.

FIGURE 2.11 The GATF Star Target used for control of tone transfer

Source: Pira International Ltd

Variable dot size elements

With this type of element, an attempt is made to quantify the extent of image growth by evaluating the change in variable sized dots. The main example of this is the GATF Mid-tone Dot Gain Scale that is shown in Figure 2.12. When printed, the dots increase in size to bridge the gap between the edge of the dots and the crosses. It can be seen that as the numbered steps increase, the dot diameters reduce. Therefore, the extent of dot growth can be quantified by determining at what point the bridging takes place. If Step 10 is bridged and Step 15 is open, the dot growth is defined as 10%.

FIGURE 2.12 The GATF Mid-tone Dot Gain Scale

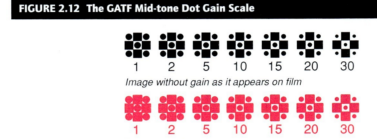

Source: Pira International Ltd

Halftone for measurement

This is a relatively straightforward field providing a precise tone value on the film that can be measured to determine dot gain on the print. The main consideration is the number of tone patches and their tonal values. The whole tone scale is important, but space makes it impractical to include more than two or three tone values in a control strip. These should normally be a midtone (40% or 50%) and a shadow tone (75% or 80%). The halftone patches on most commercially available control strips are produced at a screen ruling of 60 lines per centimetre, and for this reason technical specifications are normally defined at this screen ruling.

FIGURE 2.13 Tone patches on a control strip are normally limited to a midtone and a shadow tone

40%   80%

Source: Pira International Ltd

Tone transfer fields – slur and doubling

A certain degree of dot growth is unavoidable, but the increase in dot size may comprise two importantly different components. The increase may be predominantly symmetrical around the area of the dot or it may be more pronounced in one direction. The latter effect occurs when either slurring or doubling is present. Pronounced directional dot growth should be regarded as a fault, since it is neither consistent nor predictable. The control elements previously referred to for the monitoring of tone transfer will indicate the consequence of slur, but will not be able to isolate slur from normal dot growth. Slur and doubling targets aim to make this distinction, using line patterns as opposed to dots. Lines, unlike dots, have a direction and since both slur and doubling are directional effects they are able to show that it is occurring.

Star target The star target can indicate changes in growth through the size of the central solid area but, being a line target, it is able to indicate if this increase is directional. If there is slur, the central solid area will be formed as an ellipse, the short axis being the direction of slur. If doubling occurs, a figure of eight is formed in the centre, with the short axis indicating the direction of the double image.

FIGURE 2.14 Three examples of slur and doubling targets

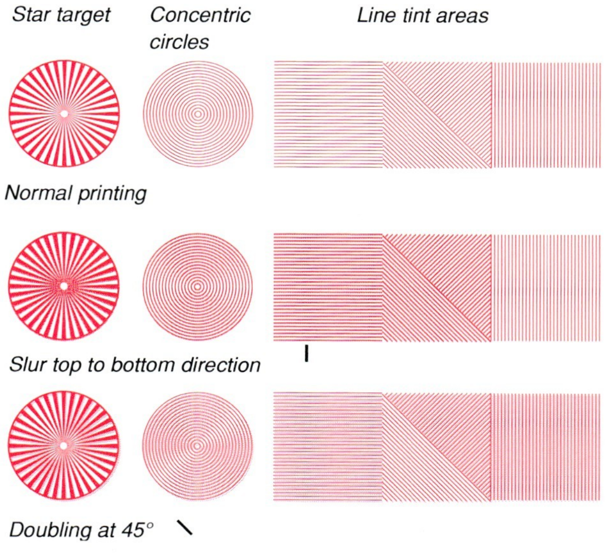

Source: Pira International Ltd

Concentric circles A concentric circle target, like the star target, is visually sensitive to both doubling and slur and can also distinguish between the two. The element consists of concentric circles having different diameters; the line thickness and gaps are equal so that the overall coverage of the target is 50%. The presence of slur is indicated by darker 90° segments in the circle while doubling produces smaller dark segments. The more segments, the greater the displacement of the double image.

Line tint areas Small line tint areas are the most common form of slur and doubling targets. The principle is simple: lines at right angles to the direction of slur increase in thickness, while lines normal to the direction of slur are unaffected. This creates different comparative densities. However, the targets are not able to distinguish between slur and doubling without being closely examined using magnification. Area measurements made on each patch with a densitometer can be used to determine the extent of slur and doubling by subtraction of one from the other.

Imaging control with CTP

The method of controlling image transfer when using CTP is different to that described for analogue plates. In analogue platemaking the objective is to achieve consistent transfer of the film image to the plate, and this is adequately achieved with the control strips described earlier. Consistent imaging is also of prime importance for CTP and there are digital control strips that enable this to be achieved with simple visual assessment. There are also occasions when actual tone values on plate must be determined, and this requires measurement.

With analogue plates, the tone values are fixed on the film and the scope for change during the transfer to plate is quite limited. With CTP, the data transfer can easily be adapted to achieve the required values on plate, and by implication the required values on the print. This provides the opportunity to match reference printing conditions and, where plates are made for specific presses, to modify the imaging to achieve the same tone transfer across a number of presses.

Digital control strips

The combination of digital data from different application programs, PDFs produced differently, with various different RIP and output device parameters, different types of plate and development conditions for plates as well as printing requirements for the transfer of tonal values place high demands on the control of the work as it progresses. System and equipment manufacturers supply a number of proprietary digital control strips for plate control, but the principal independent control strips are probably the Ugra/Fogra Digital Plate Control Wedge and the GATF Digital Plate Control Target.

FIGURE 2.15 Ugra/Fogra Digital Plate Control Wedge

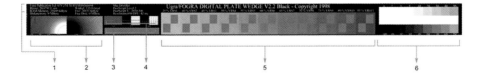

1 Information panel, 2 Resolution panel. 3 Geometrical diagnostic panels, 4 Checkered panels, 5 Visual reference steps (VRS), 6 Progress wedge

Source: Fogra

The visual reference steps (VRS) and the halftone wedge are the principal elements concerned with image transfer control. The VRS consist of pairs of coarse screen reference patches surrounded by fine screen areas (note these are not reproduced accurately in Figure 2.15). There are 11 VRS; they step up in 5% increments from 35% to 85% dot areas. Under ideal conditions and linear tone reproduction, the two fields in VRS 4 should appear to have the same tone value. When the two panels have a dot percentage of 50% they should blend with each other, i.e. the impression of brightness and the measurable tonal value should give a dot percentage of 50% in both areas. Due to the plate type, exposure calibration, developer and transfer characteristics, this is hardly ever actually achieved under operational conditions and shifts upwards or downwards occur. The VRS panels that are important for day-to-day production are those that enable the optimum setting to be chosen and output results to be achieved.

Deviations from the appearance of the VRS panels can be identified by a visual check. Other panels provide information about resolution as well as the progress wedge, with which the tonal value transfer can be checked. In order to eliminate production-dependent differences in plate materials, zero points are located between the rows of halftone panels. Consequently the position for the densitometry measurement of zero (substrate only) and the dot percentage are beside each other.

The resolution panel contains two semicircular panels. In the first panel positive lines radiate out from a point; in the second the lines are negative. The thickness of the lines corresponds to the theoretical resolution of the output device.

The geometrical diagnostics panels also contain lines that are oriented to the resolution setting of the output device. The checkered panels are below the geometrical diagnostics panel. Labels are positioned over each of the panels and the sides of the squares are one, two and four units long.

The line panels and checkerboard panels orient themselves to the respective resolution attitudes of the plate exposure.

The most important functions of the wedge are:

► Basic adjustment exposure/development over sensitive symmetry functions in the resolution panel, line panel and checkerboard panels;
► To control the tone values on the plate in the raster wedge with neighbouring zero-field for densitometry measurement;
► To control the stability of printing plate production concerning exposure and tone value correction with 11 visual reference stages;
► A procedure for the adaptation of digital printing plate production to the standardised edition print.

Process control tools

To control the printing process and optimise quality it is necessary to measure and calibrate reproduction characteristics throughout the process. Most modern digital equipment performs regular automatic measurement and calibration. Where hard copy proofs and print without on-line measurement take place there are several tools available to make the measurements.

The densitometer

The densitometer is the principal measurement tool to quantify and control the attributes that have been previously defined. The transmission densitometer is normally used to measure photographic images on film, and the reflection instrument to measure prints or proofs on paper. The reflection instrument measures the proportion of light that is absorbed by the printed ink film, but this is converted and displayed in the logarithmic optical density scale. The basic measurement principle of the densitometer is shown in Figure 2.16. When measuring the process colours, the measurement is made through the complementary filter. For example, to control the cyan ink film thickness, the amount of red light absorbed is needed and a red filter is applied.

FIGURE 2.16 The measurement principle of the densitometer

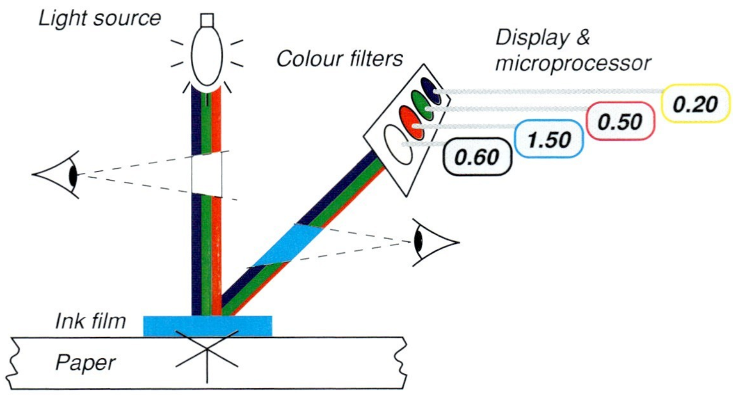

Source: Pira International Ltd

In modern instruments, measurements are simultaneously made through all filters but only the highest value is normally displayed. Most reflection densitometers contain a microprocessor and this enables additional information to be provided that is calculated from the density measurements. These may include the following:

▶ apparent dot area and dotgain
▶ relative print contrast
▶ percentage trap hue error
▶ greyness.

The densitometer filters are optimised for the purpose of measuring process colours. While this does not prevent the density measurement of special colours, the sensitivity to change may be reduced and it is possible that the same single filter density can be achieved when measuring two different colours. To accurately measure colour, a spectrophotometer or colorimeter is required.

The spectrophotometer

The spectrophotometer measures the proportion of light that is absorbed in narrow bands throughout the visible spectrum. When a sample colour is measured, it provides spectral reflectance data that is unique for each colour.

FIGURE 2.17 The measurement principle of a spectrophotometer

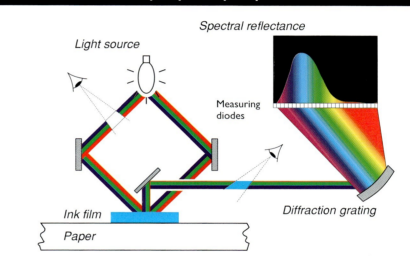

Source: Pira International Ltd

This is converted for normal use into a three-figure (CIELab) description. This takes account of the spectral composition of the light source and the spectral sensitivity of human vision. It also defines the colour's location within a three-dimensional colour space.

    The three-dimensional colour space is required because humans perceive colours to have three distinctly different attributes: hue, chroma and lightness. Hue is simply how humans perceive its colour to be – red, green, blue. Chroma, or saturation, describes a colour's colourfulness. Lightness describes the luminous intensity of a colour. When the colour has a location within this space, it is possible to indicate with a single value how different it is to a specified colour. This is referred to as the ΔE, colour difference, and a value of 2 is just perceivable. See Chapter 4 for more detail.

The colorimeter

The colorimeter is a less expensive instrument for measuring colour. It uses filters that are designed to mimic the response of the human visual system. It is suited to the measurement of colour differences rather than the absolute measurement of colour.

Tone value measurement on plate

There are basically two approaches to measuring the tone values reproduced on plate:
▶ reflection density and calculation of area
▶ planimetric measurement with dot area meter.

Densitometers

Most densitometer manufacturers now include an option for measuring plate dot area with their densitometers, or market a version specifically for plate measurement. While it is certainly possible to measure dot area on plates with a densitometer, there are a number of factors that must be considered with respect to the consistency and accuracy of measurement. These include:

▶ *Image contrast.* If the contrast between plate coating and base substrate is low the calculated dot area will be unreliable. For example, if the contrast is 1.0, a measured area of 50% will show a 1% change if the density of the tone value changes by 0.01. If the same change occurs with a plate having a contrast of 0.4 the calculated area will show a 3% change.

▶ *Plate grain.* All modern plates are grained. Light reflecting from the surface is scattered, the extent to which this happens depending on the nature of the grain. This will affect the readings between different manufacturers' plates. There are some indications to suggest that even within a single manufacturer's product small variations in graining can affect the measured dot area. Direction effects in the graining are also considered important, and consistent orientation of the instrument to the grip edge of the plate is recommended.

▶ *Plate processing.* The level of desensitising gum left on the plate after processing has been shown to affect the light scattering and therefore the measured value. It is recommended when making measurements that the desensitising solution be removed with warm water and buffed dry, leaving no water marks or streaks in the areas to be measured.

▶ *Measuring aperture.* To minimise the impact of these issues, the densitometer should obtain its measurement from the integration of as many dots as possible. This means using an instrument with as large a measuring aperture as possible.

▶ *The n factor.* Even if consideration is given to all these factors, the area measured is unlikely to be accurate. To improve the accuracy, the calculation will normally use the Yule-Nielsen formula with a suitable value for *n*. However, a different value is likely to be required for different manufacturers' plates, and to be completely accurate, the *n* value would need to change with the tone value.

From these comments it can be appreciated that it is not possible to be confident that the tone values measured with a densitometer will be an accurate indication of what is on the plate. If used with care, and bearing in mind the factors previously mentioned, the densitometer can be used to monitor consistency, but in this respect it offers little more than the digital control wedge.

Dot area planimeter

The measurement principle of the planimeter is quite different to that of the densitometer and significantly more accurate. The sampled tone value is captured on a CCD array, just like a digital camera but with optics that magnify the image. The threshold point between dot and background is determined automatically, and the dot area is then calculated by the ratio of image pixels to non-image pixels. More sophisticated instruments may refine the basic equation to improve accuracy. This principle of measurement means there is no need to measure 100% and zero coverage to calibrate the system, as is the case with the densitometer.

The accuracy of measurement is mainly dependent on the resolution of the captured image (particularly for fine screen rulings and FM screening) and on the device's ability to set thresholds accurately for the full tonal range. Although the planimeter is more accurate than the densitometer, it also has difficulty if the contrast of the image on the plate is low.

Linearisation and calibration

CTP systems provide a level of flexibility in imaging that is not possible with analogue platemaking, because the image data can be modified during screening in the RIP to achieve the required tone value on the plate. This is a practical application of colour management to achieve consistent reproduction across a range of presses.

Different RIP software may adopt slightly different approaches to linearisation and calibration. It is desirable to linearise the image transfer to plate independently to provide a base reference for monitoring stability. Having linearised the device, a characteristic curve is applied to achieve the requisite tone values on the plate. For example, to maintain the same print characteristic achieved when working with film, a linear transfer of data tone values to plate is not required. The tone values must be reduced to be equivalent to the reduction that happens when printing down with positive films.

This approach can be extended to modify the tone transfer characteristic achieved in printing, so as to comply with a reference condition or other presses. To do this, it is necessary to image plates with a linear transfer and print them at normal conditions and densities. From the resulting prints, the actual tone transfer characteristic (when using linear-imaged plates) is determined by measuring the apparent dot area for each tone on the control target. It is then possible to establish the correction curve necessary for printing to achieve the tone transfer of the reference condition. The procedure for doing this is shown in Figure 2.18.

First, plot the data to define the required curve for the reference condition, followed by the actual data derived from the print test, with linear-imaged plates. To define the plate calibration curve, start at a point where the required curve crosses a vertical grid line. From this point, move parallel with the horizontal axis until you meet the actual curve, and then move vertically until you meet the unity line. From this point move parallel with the horizontal axis until you meet the vertical grid line on which you started.

FIGURE 2.18 Determining the required plate correction curve necessary to modify actual printing curve to required printing curve

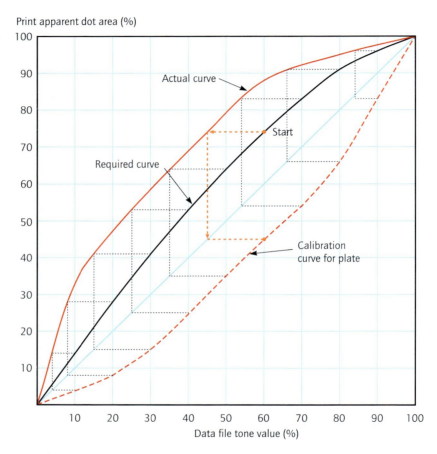

Source: Pira International Ltd

This defines one point on the calibration curve – repeat for other tone values and join the points with a curve. The data from this curve is used by the RIP in plate imaging to provide a plate that, when printed from, will achieve the required characteristic curve.

Closed-loop on-press colour control systems

During the 1990s several sheet-fed press manufacturers offered a scanning spectrophotometer quality system to check print quality. These were generally quite expensive and time consuming to operate. They relied on the press minder to adjust the press if the system detected a variation, but would provide a report detailing the consistency throughout the print run. The next generation of control systems hard-wired colorimeters and spectrophotometers after printing to monitor sheets and webs as they were printed. They scan and measure a colour bar on the moving web or sheet, and continually feed back data to the press ink-control console for ink-film thickness compensation. In addition to maintaining consistent colour quality, these systems are an efficient means of collecting real-time data for statistical process control and customer quality assurance.

After initial testing these systems have almost become a standard feature on new web presses and it's possible to retrofit them to existing presses. Micro control strips that take up little space are printed, while some manufacturers are developing pattern recognition systems that will measure the printed subject instead of needing a separate strip. Variables such as ink-fountain levels, fountain solution pH, ink-train temperature, roller stripes and durometer, blanket height and tension can be controlled, but aren't always, as a result of poor maintenance or inadequate systems or training.

Suppliers increasingly include colour control as part of their overall colour workflow tools. Printers achieve greater consistency and can provide documentation as part of a quality assurance programme for their customers. Komori offers a closed-loop scanning SpectroDensitometer that provides automatic measurement using densitometric and spectral evaluation functions, data collection and analysis. The system provides closed-loop press control as well as statistical process data reporting. MAN Roland has developed its sophisticated Pecom ClosedLoop systems for controlling both colour and cut-off registers and the ink density, as well as for scanning the webs. These automatically and reliably ensure constant quality and reduced waste on MAN Roland's LithoMan presses.

Heidelberg introduced the Prinect Web Centre, which includes Omnicon press controls and modules for automated presetting, machine control and data reporting. The Omni Makeready module automatically converts data from closed-loop colour controls for faster and more precise adjustment of ink settings during start-ups. Modules for data reporting and for integrating press performance data into a company's MIS are available. When Goss took over Heidelberg's web division it offered the capability to upgrade older machines with its Colour Control Interface Enhancement.

In sheet-fed Heidelberg developed a system for monitoring the colour process within an end-to-end workflow using small measuring elements, or mini spots. These are placed randomly on the print sheet and measured automatically by Prinect Image Control using a spectrophotometric procedure. Measurements can also be performed with manual measuring devices. In both cases, the data is recorded and tested by the Prinect Quality Monitor. Corrections during production can be effected in order to make adjustments to the plate calibration or the colour profiles of follow-up jobs. This data can also be used to record the print quality for customers – an important aspect in securing long-term customer loyalty. Colour management technology is built into the press and can be linked back to prepress to control both the proofing and the platesetter.

Quality assurance for printers and statistical process control

Besides satisfying client requirements, the printer may improve the performance of the business, obtaining better quality and greater productivity, by measuring and controlling all aspects of production. A systematic programme will generate much information including detailed, quantifiable performance statistics on the materials, equipment and processes in operation. Over time, the results may provide the basis for performance specification of materials allowing the printer to determine the costs of running different materials and so improving the process. Methods used internally are based on statistical process control (SPC) techniques, the modern version of which is Six Sigma.

Six Sigma is a quality management program to achieve high levels of consistency; it was pioneered at Motorola and GE and is now widely adopted. It is a highly disciplined process focusing on developing and delivering near-perfect products and services. Sigma is a statistical term that measures how far a given process deviates from perfection. The central idea behind Six Sigma is to measure how many defects there are in a process then act to eliminate them systematically, getting as close to zero defects as possible. There are two versions for existing and new processes:

► DMAIC is the basic methodology to improve existing processes
   ► Define out-of-tolerance range
   ► Measure key internal processes critical to quality
   ► Analyse why defects occur
   ► Improve the process to stay within tolerance
   ► Control the process to stay within goals.
► DMADV is the basic methodology of introducing new processes
   ► Define the process and where it would fail to meet customer needs
   ► Measure and determine if process meets customer needs
   ► Analyse the options to meet customer needs
   ► Design in changes to the process to meet customer needs
   ► Verify the changes have met customer needs.

Both use SPC as a management technique designed to improve quality and productivity through continuous measurement and corrective action to improve a process. There is inherent variability in all manufacturing processes. SPC critically examines all the stages to determine the limits of consistency due to the equipment in use. Variation outside these limits may result in defective product. Taking action to control the process will lower such occurrences. Systematic improvement will increase the uniformity of the output as it reduces mistakes and waste of material, personnel and machine time. Reducing waste transfers the man and machine time previously spent producing defective product into the manufacture of good product, and increasing the capacity of a plant.

Statistical process control is an integral part of a total quality management system. When SPC is used correctly, the printer will see significant improvements in both productivity and quality. The literature has many examples of SPC programmes applied to printing. These objectively define print quality and improve consistency while generating productivity improvements, reducing waste and eliminating spoilage.

Customers make a contract with the printer to deliver a number of copies at a particular time. Trade terms and conditions have developed over time, incorporating acceptable limits for variation in quantity and quality of a print run. The competitive nature of print and higher demands of clients is changing these terms. In many market sectors, clients demand delivery of a precise quantity of perfect product. Printers must change to develop systems to deliver exactly what the customer requires.

Printing is complex and brings together many materials under a range of conditions on fast-moving, precision machinery. The press conditions and materials used will affect the printed result, and in heatset web offset these variables include:

▶ Ink formulation and duct settings
▶ Drier and chill roll temperature
▶ Plate wear
▶ Blanket surface release properties and tension
▶ Cylinder and roller pressures
▶ Roller surface hardness
▶ Fount solution formulation, pH and conductivity, alcohol content (if used)
▶ Ink/fount emulsification
▶ Temperature of oven, rollers, plates, blankets, fount solution
▶ Press speed
▶ Web tension
▶ Prepress and platemaking
▶ Paper
▶ Relative humidity
▶ Ambient conditions.

These variables must be controlled or, at least, taken into account for the press to reach an equilibrium state and perform to an acceptable quality and productivity. Variation in colour or folding results in wasted time and raw materials. It is necessary to employ a specialist resource to sort the sub-standard product. Lithographic printing processes contain many variables across both product and the production. The printed appearance is governed by:

▶ Ink film thickness and density
▶ Highlight, mid-tone and shadow dot gain (sharpness)
▶ Process colour grey balance
▶ Ink trap
▶ Paper opacity, colour and brightness
▶ Absence of printing defects
▶ Gloss
▶ Ink contrast.

These are measurable print characteristics. They must be measured and then controlled by the pressman to match the proofs throughout a run.

The ethos of printing quality management is changing. It used to be reactive quality control after each production stage by checking film, plates and print. This method identified the poor quality after production and later replaced it with good quality. This changed towards integrated proactive quality assurance, and providing good quality product is now taken as given by customers. Quality tends to be a disqualifier rather than a qualifier as similar printing companies in a particular market compete with similar capital equipment. Applying an SPC system will prove and demonstrate their quality and acts as the means for them to differentiate themselves from competitors.

It is a fairly straightforward exercise to apply SPC to print if management provides leadership and commitment. The routine to follow is:

► Sample
► Analyse
► Control and improve.

The improvements will be in better quality and productivity.

For a quality improvement, the printer will measure and record a quantifiable printability characteristic (perhaps a densitometer reading of density, dot gain and trapping, or colorimetric measures of mid-tone grey) during the run of any job. Then plot the results as detailed make-ready to define printing characteristics and then a sub-set throughout the run to monitor consistency. To improve productivity, define a consistent runnability measure and record performance over time. The results must then be analysed and the management should initiate action (involving press crews) to eliminate the poor performers and reduce variability.

The traditional manual visual comparison to a pass sheet is not sufficient. With higher speed presses producing larger sheets, there is too much information to process quickly and accurately by eye. Printing is a dynamic process. One potential problem is overcorrection by the pressman. Studies have indicated that when a web press reached equilibrium it operated more consistently in terms of density and dot gain when left alone than when adjusted by operators.

Quality assurance of printing

Many companies adopted systematic quality management programmes gaining accreditation to ISO9001:2000 standards. In many sectors of print, and in supplying to printers, such qualification is a necessary marketing tool. This activity has resulted in the industry rigorously defining quality as conformance to a specification rather than using various difficult-to-define nebulous attributes of the product.

The successful application of process control to any manufacturing process will reduce the need for quality inspection by cutting the production of defective products. An initial inspection is made by sampling the run during production. This is later followed by detailed examination, normally off-line. The process is expensive involving specialist staff who may delay the completion of the job. Reactive quality control is not totally effective in identifying and removing poor-quality product. There is no totally reliable automatic image analysis fault-finding system for fast-moving presses, and this is often the role of the press minder.

If problems are discovered later, the printer has the choice of delivering fewer copies than ordered or starting re-work. Both are expensive and time consuming. Controlling the process is a proactive approach to production. Quality procedures change to examining the process itself rather than the resulting products. When the process is under control and operating within known, defined and accepted limits of variation the product is predictable and will fall within manufacturing specification.

Some customers buy print as a secondary product outside their main business activities, such as in packaging, some catalogues, technical documentation and instruction manuals rather than commercial print. They have led the demand for systematic proof that a quality standard is being achieved and maintained. These clients routinely use many sophisticated production and quality systems. They are now applying the same disciplines to buying printed products. The days of a printing company satisfying a customer by providing a few specials, or advance copies, chosen by the printer are numbered. It is difficult to define quality in commercial printing quantitatively. The definition must encompass all aspects of design, production and materials that go into the product and not just concentrate on the final manufacturing process of putting ink onto paper. If different contract proofs made to different specifications are supplied, it will be impossible to match the results accurately under the standard press conditions. The skill of the printer is in making an acceptable visual match across the whole sheet. Problems may surface later when an advertiser examines a single page in isolation from the 16 printed together when the result is a compromise with the other pages in the track.

There is no single measure that will adequately define printability to satisfy customers in the real world of commercial printing. In that world, printability is the subjective perception of a printed article by an individual. The individual who matters most is the paying customer and acceptable printability is a result that satisfies the customer for every copy. Such subjectivity in defining printability and passing the job is a major stumbling block to applying an objective print by numbers system. The printer can progress toward a quantitative printability by ensuring that each job is printed in the same manner on press using control strips to ensure consistency. Printers have used control strips for many years, often as a reactive diagnostic aid in the event of problems rather than proactively in quality assurance. Closed-loop systems will monitor the following print characteristics across the sheet:

► Density
► Dot gain
► Trapping
► Grey balance
► Colour (for spot colour applications).

Minders should check measurements manually if the machine is not equipped with automatic measuring. When the minder is satisfied that the press is performing correctly, then ink density is the most important measure to get even across the sheet. The readings demonstrate any necessary adjustments and prove that the press is performing correctly to achieve quick acceptance of the pass sheet. These characteristics will form the basis of a colour profile for use in colour management to optimise reproduction quality and provide good matching of proofs.

It is straightforward to measure subsequent sheets to ensure they are identical to the pass. During the run, the time taken means it is impractical to take all measurements manually across the sheet. Normally density and mid-tone dot gain measurements at fixed points across the sheet will prove consistency through the run. The production statistics can be exported for off-line analysis, as part of the JDF link with production equipment.

Simple manual systems can yield much valuable control information. Press minders will manually examine sample copies through the run, checking for colour, print to fold registration and for print faults. At regular intervals, the minder will remove and retain a copy, taking and recording density and dot gain across the sheet. The results could be directly entered into a database from densitometer, colorimeter or spectrophotometer. Most modern measuring instruments have data ports to link into a computer.

Examples of process control charts to define colour printing conditions

Measuring density characteristics forms the basis of a quantitative quality assurance programme. It is vital that the instruments are correctly calibrated. Figure 2.19 is a record of densitometer calibration. Examples of quality assurance record sheets for pass sheet and printed results are shown in Figure 2.20 and Figure 2.21. These charts can contain much data, including a description of the job and materials involved on a particular press as well as the print measurements.

Figure 2.22 is an example of a process control chart that is designed to monitor colour density from a particular measure. The characteristic could be end density of cyan, magenta, yellow and black from different pass sheets or throughout a run. It could be a measure from a proofing system recorded during a weekly calibration. The chart allows a range of values to be plotted together to give a simple visual representation of consistency over time.

All four of the charts on the pages that follow can be found in the Excel file SPC sheets contained on the accompanying CD. The spreadsheet is fully formatted for use.

FIGURE 2.19 Densitometer/spectrophotometer calibration assurance record

DENSITOMETER/SPECTROPHOTOMETER CALIBRATION ASSURANCE RECORD

Procedure

Check the calibration readings of the instrument on a weekly basis against the supplied calibration forme. Readings should be within ±0.02 units from the chart. If the instrument is not within ±0.02 units the instrument **MUST** be recalibrated.

Record the check and calibrations performed on the chart below

DATE	Cyan	Magenta	Yellow	Black	Within Spec.	Recalibrated OK	Signed
STANDARD							

Note: an electronic version of this form is supplied on the accompanying CD-rom.
Source: Pira International Ltd

FIGURE 2.20 Pass sheet quality assurance record

PASS SHEET QUALITY ASSURANCE RECORD

Date _____

Job _____

Section _____

Press _____

Job Stock _____ grammage _____ gsm

PRINTED RESULT

Sheet is free from print faults (misregister/slur/doubling) _____

		End Density	**Dot Gain** At 40%	At 80%
Black	A side	_____	_____ %	_____ %
	B side	_____	_____ %	_____ %
Cyan	A side	_____	_____ %	_____ %
	B side	_____	_____ %	_____ %
Magenta	A side	_____	_____ %	_____ %
	B side	_____	_____ %	_____ %
Yellow	A side	_____	_____ %	_____ %
	B side	_____	_____ %	_____ %
Spot 1	A side	_____	_____ %	_____ %
	B side	_____	_____ %	_____ %
Spot 2	A side	_____	_____ %	_____ %
	B side	_____	_____ %	_____ %

Trapping	Magenta on Cyan	Yellow on Cyan	Yellow on Magenta
A side	_____ %	_____ %	_____ %
B side	_____ %	_____ %	_____ %

Note: an electronic version of this form is supplied on the accompanying CD-rom.
Source: Pira International Ltd

FIGURE 2.21 On-press printed sheet quality assurance record

ON PRESS PRINTED SHEET QUALITY ASSURANCE RECORD

Date _____

Job _____

Press _____

Section _____

Job Stock _____ grammage _____ gsm

Please fill in density readings for A&B sides measuring at intervals of _____ 12345 impressions

Clock Reading	Time	Black (A)	Cyan (A)	Magenta (A)	Yellow (A)	Spot (A)	Black (B)	Cyan (B)	Magenta (B)	Yellow (B)	Spot (B)
Pass Sheet											
12345		1.7									
24690		1.75									
37035		1.8									
49380											
61725											
74070											
86415											
98760											
111105											
123450											
135795											
148140											
160485											
172830											
185175											
197520											
209865											
222210											
234555											
246900											
271590											

Note: an electronic version of this form is supplied on the accompanying CD-rom.

Source: Pira International Ltd

FIGURE 2.22 Process control chart for monitoring colour

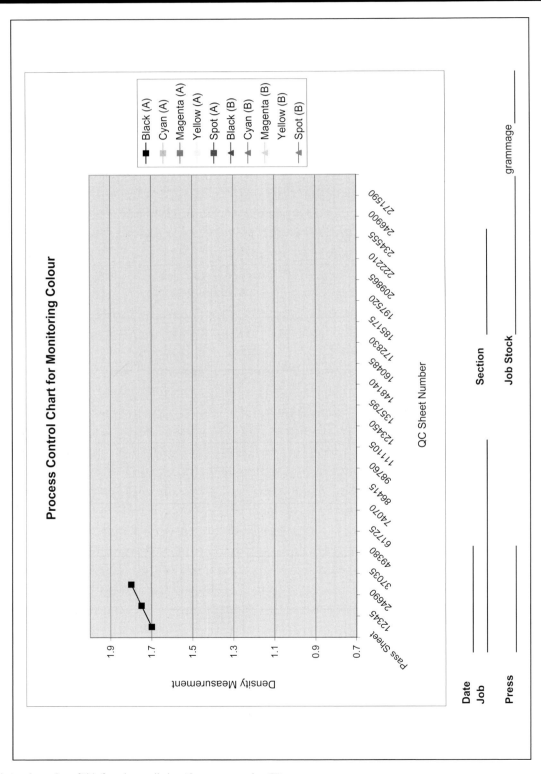

Note: an electronic version of this form is supplied on the accompanying CD-rom.

Source: Pira International Ltd

Such systematic measurement allows printers to demonstrate consistency to customers and ensure the optimum submission of files and proofs. It is necessary for publication printers to conform to the general market conditions, so allowing more consistency for publishers and advertisers. In practice, preparing the samples and recording the measurements is extremely time-consuming. There must be a real commitment from management to use and act on the results, otherwise the technical and production personnel will quickly find reasons to stop taking the measurements.

When such a system is in operation, the printer can develop acceptable limits of variation with the client. Printing is a dynamic process. Press vibration and the rotation of rollers and cylinders and transfer mechanisms of ink will result in cyclical variation between copies. Most of the time this is not noticeable and only stringent examination and measurement can show these differences. Most often they fall within practical error limits of measurement. Over a longer period, there may be slow drifts in condition resulting in a change. The minder will correct the drift as it occurs. At the end of a job, it is useful to discuss the results with the client to find how they regard the performance. Sharing the results, showing how the measured differences affect the visual result and deciding what is unacceptable allows an agreed quality standard to develop. After a few runs the client confidence should be increased as jobs are produced within acceptable variance. The press crews will learn the actions to reduce variation and improve quality, saving the expense of waste and rework.

There are useful marketing benefits of proving quality for some customers. Internally, the goal is to define a standard set of printing conditions for a particular press and stock. This definition should fall within the market requirements and ensure that the standard is met every time as a matter of routine. When this is achieved, the printer can maximise output from the expensive press time by checking films, proofs and plates before they get to press. When press crews can rely totally that all materials they use are correct they can develop standard make-ready procedures, using automation advances such as plate loading and plate scanning to pre-set the ink ducts. The make-ready will be much faster and involve less waste when the printer just concentrates on printing the test strip correctly by running the press at standard conditions. The printed work will match the contract proofs provided the proofs are made to match the press and the press is running normally.

The crew will spend time setting the press to its standard conditions during make-ready, rather than adjusting to compensate for incorrectly made proofs or an absorbent paper that has abnormal dot gain characteristics. With the commercial pressures on a plant to maximise throughput, press crews spend their time trying to change to the next job quickly rather than stepping back and involving all the plant to design a system to smooth the high price of printing.

With the development of reduced plate gap and gapless presses, there will be no room on the web to position traditional control strips. Sheetfed printers may be reluctant to pay for areas of print that are destined to be waste. Micro test forms positioned in circumferential folds across the web or analysing printed image area may evolve as control methods. Some form of measurement will be required to control the process.

Productivity improvement through SPC

The key paper and ink performance property for printers is runnability through their presses. There are no laboratory tests that correlate to press performance. The only informed way is to measure the performance of materials on press, then specify the best-performing material. Runnability should be defined as a unit measure of saleable print produced over a given time. The measure should be interpreted for factors that are not paper-related but might affect performance on press.

A quick check of condition on delivery may reveal damage but not all may become apparent until the reel is unwrapped. It is important that reel paper is kept in a clean area to avoid damage when a reel is stored. Any loose stones or solid litter may cause holes that need to be slabbed off as excessive waste. During the splice preparation, a minimum of paper should be slabbed off the reel. Good housekeeping in the printer's warehouse and liaison with the supplier to ensure good handling practice is useful. There should be no need to remove more than a few unwinds when the wrapper is removed. Training personnel involved in reel preparation to remove the least slab possible is a quick and effective way of reducing waste. A scale should be available to weigh any excess slab waste with an explanation for any reels with significant quantities over 1kg to 2kg. It is good practice to have a Polaroid camera available to take quick pictures of damaged reels to back up any discussions and claims against a supplier. A record detailing the slab and core waste, together with press count when the reel started and finished, provides evidence of paper performance before printing, and is useful to calculate the true basis weight and amount of paper used.

Systematic measurement and recording paper performance on press will generate much data. This will involve taking a measure from each press daily, sometimes more often when the stock changes between jobs. A relational database is vital to process this into useful information and relevant intelligence. It does not have to be particularly sophisticated, and any of the readily available PC or Macintosh products should be more than capable. Individual plants should construct their own database. The records must include three classes of fields:

Paper identification criteria
► Paper name (and hence mill and supplier)
► Paper grade
► Paper grammage
► Batch number (optional)

Plant records and job statistics
► Date
► Press (and folder configuration)
► Total copies produced in the period

Paper runnability data

► Metreage/N⁰ sheets of paper run
► Good copies produced
► Total copies produced
► Running time
► Total running and paper downtime
► N⁰ blanket washes
► N⁰ web breaks

This information may be entered automatically as shop floor data collection as part of the company-wide management information system, or manually from dockets filled out by the press crew. It is time-consuming to enter the data manually. Using a relational database increases the speed of data input when a series of paper identification codes is in use across the plant. From the runnability data calculations described above can be used to work out the press running waste, net and gross running speed, metreage per break and wash. This data is typically available in a pressroom, either from manual dockets or from shop floor data collection systems. Practically this means routinely recording these data on a daily basis, and then processing it into information. A new data record must be created every 24 hours and each time the paper changes on a press. When processing the data, the individual plant will exclude records if the run length is below a certain level, or if the performance is greatly affected by factors outside the normal operation. The runnability will be affected if the press has serious mechanical problems, and these abnormal records should be ignored. It is important that any machine downtime that is not connected with the paper performance is ignored. This means that press stops for new plates or for mechanical problems must be ignored when compiling the data. Make-ready will lower the performance as the press is being set up so make-ready time should be ignored. The data that should be recorded is:

► Total copies (sheets) produced = N_t
  The total quantity that the press produces in the unit time. Accurate counting seems difficult in many print operations. Good communication with the finishing department to compare recorded quantities is often useful to determine and remove any source of errors.
► Metreage of paper used $M = N_t \times N \times$ press cut off (m)
  Where N is the number of webs on a multi-web press. The number of webs must be taken into account when metreages per break or wash are compared. The actual metreage of a reel or number of sheets on a pallet put through the press are important measures. They should be compared with the metreage or quantity of sheets recorded on the paper label to see how accurate the supplier's measure is. If the length (or number of sheets) and weight of the paper are known, a precise measure of basis weight can be obtained. If this is higher than the nominal weight, the difference reflects a hidden source of paper waste that cannot be recovered.

► Good copies produced = N$_g$

Saleable copies passed through to the next production stage. If there is a subsequent problem unrelated to paper, e.g. an editorial mistake that requires reprinting, the copies should be regarded as good for the exercise of determining runnability.

► Waste copies produced = (N$_t$ − N$_g$)

The number of sub-standard copies produced including both necessary waste and accidental spoilage. The largest single cause of waste is setting up a job during make-ready. Most web press running waste comes from necessary reel splices together with blanket washes and web breaks that cause spoilage. Washes should be taken at the same time as a splice to minimise waste. There will be additional waste as minders take out samples and spoilage when they make press and folder adjustments.

► Printing time = T$_r$ (hr)

All press time while paper is being converted that does not include initial make-ready. The cut-off point for make-ready is necessarily arbitrary on the part of the press minder who is recording the time. This does not matter provided that the same cut-off point is used throughout the recording and it does not vary for a particular press or paper.

► Non-productive time due to paper problems = T$_p$ (hr)

The minder should account for all press downtime. There may be some discretion in assigning some downtime to a paper problem, particularly as a minder may occasionally look for a scapegoat to blame for a machine stop with no obvious cause. As long as the minders are consistent, the results should not be biased for or against any grades of paper. The largest components of press downtime due to paper are from web breaks, blanket washes and machine or folder jams.

With modern automatic blanket washing equipment the press may not always stop while a wash cycle occurs, taking perhaps less than a minute. Waste is incurred and the frequency of washes is an important contributor to productivity.

► Number of web breaks = Br

The major cause of press downtime in web offset printing is the web break. The continuous web breaks somewhere and the press instantly stops. It takes between 20 minutes and an hour to get back into production, wasting up to 2000m of paper. Web breaks may be due to definite paper faults, or to particular actions by press or printer or there may be no direct evidence one way or the other.

It is sometimes possible to determine the cause of the break. On occasions it is due to actions of the printer. Improper preparation of the reelstand splices, a mechanical fault in the folder, or tar dropping onto the moving web from the oven and sticking on the chill stacks can cause breaks. Most breaks fall into the no evidence bracket where there is no clear evidence of a paper fault or a press problem, but the break occurs and press time and paper are wasted as a result. The sleuth-like minder pieces together the two ends and finds a slime hole, a crease in the web, or a cut edge, or a poorly prepared mill splice. Whatever the cause of a break the result is lost press time and waste paper.

► Number of blanket washes = Wa

Material from paper surface and components of ink will gradually build up on the blanket, and sometimes the plate, during a press run. The build-up may not be solely attributable to the paper type, but the paper will certainly influence the degree and speed of any piling. The number of washes is only a useful indicator of build-up as press crews will normally wash blankets whenever the press stops.

From these data, the following runnability characteristics can be determined:

Gross running speed

The key runnability measurement for either a sheetfed or web printing press should be the gross running speed of paper through the press. This measures press performance over the preferred maximum unit of time, with non-paper down time ignored. Gross speed is calculated as:

$$\text{Gross running speed} = N_g / (T_r + T_p) \text{ (Copies hr}^{-1})$$

This measure is the most important for the printer as it measures the rate of production of good copies over a period of time.

Net running speed

While the press is running, the net paper run speed is obtained from:

$$\text{Net running speed} = N_t / T_r \text{ (Copies hr}^{-1})$$

In web printing, a measure of running speed expressed as copies an hour must be qualified because the cut off of the press and pagination of the product will vary. The paper speed through the press is the important measure to take account of different press format and cut off.

There may be single or twin webs. There are many press cut-off sizes, and in the UK the popular sizes are 587mm, 600mm, 625mm or 630mm for a 16-page press. Double circumference presses may be 1,200mm or 1,260mm. Shortgrain presses have cut offs of 897mm or 930mm. The new generation of gapless presses reduce the paper consumption to achieve the same format of final product. So an A4 product can come from a press with 612mm cut off instead of the conventional 630mm.

Press running waste

This measures the production of waste copies, and is more important on the inherently more wasteful web process than on sheetfed where waste sheets can be re-used. The figure does not include the slab and core waste in web printing that should be recorded separately, or any wrapper when the paper is bought by weight.

As an internal measurement, percentage of waste should be expressed as proportion of the good copies produced as a higher figure results. Then successful waste reduction provides a larger fall giving good motivation to the staff. For external discussion with customers, waste should be expressed as a percentage of the total copies giving a lower number.

$$\text{Press running waste} = (N_t - N_g)/N_g \times 100\% \text{ (Internal)}$$
$$\text{Press running waste} = (N_t - N_g) N_t \times 100\% \text{ (External)}$$

Metreage per web break

Measures the amount of paper run per web break from any cause.

$$\text{Meterage per web break} = (M \times N)/Br \text{ (m)}$$

N is the number of webs running on the press. Normally only one of the webs suffers a break before the press alarm system automatically severs all webs. The metreage per break is therefore the length of paper from all reelstands.

Metreage (or number of copies) per blanket wash

This measures the amount of paper run between blanket washes, expressed as impressions per wash for sheetfed applications.

$$\text{Metre per blanket wash} = M/(Wa \times N) \text{ (m)}$$

N is the number of webs running on the press. Build-up is seen on individual press units so the total metreage of paper recorded should be from just a single reelstand. This measure may not accurately reflect the tendency for the paper to suffer from build up as often not all the washes are recorded.

Interpretation of runnability results

The SPC programme is used to improve productivity by identifying the best performing materials and defining acceptable performance. Put simply, the higher the gross running speed the better the paper is for the printer because the higher speed means more saleable product in a given time. This is a compelling economic performance indicator for the printers' production staff to monitor. Reasons for a poor performer may be interesting, certainly for the supplier, but they must be a secondary consideration for the printer and publisher.

Runnability information is used to make a quantitative comparison of raw materials or machinery. These properties allow management to conduct useful sorts to be carried out to determine the effects of different presses and variables inside the plant as well as just the paper. It can help troubleshooting. When poor performance occurs, it is easy to compare with the performance of the same materials on different presses at different times. This information can help identify the root cause of the problem, and if it is the material or the process.

Care is needed when interpreting the data into meaningful information. A significant number of results are needed before the information becomes useful. The results should reflect paper properties, and not background noise and factors unrelated to paper. Runnability is influenced by the run length of the particular job and the numbers of copies run in the particular period. A modern press should outperform an older model, and an experienced crew will normally produce more than inexperienced minders.

The different presses with different crews will even out over a period of time if jobs are mixed across all machines. One method to allow for the different capabilities of presses is to express the gross running speed as a percentage of the manufacturer's maximum output rating for the press. When this figure is calculated on a daily basis over a period most printers will find they have significant room for improving production.

These factors should apply equally to all papers when examining paper performance. When these factors skew the results a value judgement is necessary to obtain worthwhile information. If a particular grade of paper is used on an older press with complicated in-line finishing equipment, it is not valid to compare the gross running speed with a new press producing sections from a high speed folder and automatic palletiser.

The data can be sorted by machine to provide relative performance statistics together with trends over time. It may be that patterns emerge showing that particular combinations of press and paper result in unacceptably poor performance. The supplier may argue with justification that the cause is within the press. If some corrective action improves the situation then printer and supplier benefit from constructive dialogue. If not, the printer should use an alternative material on that particular machinery to provide better productivity.

Large amounts of data will be generated, and press performance statistics for each day, or part of a day when a paper type changes, quickly build up. The results will show a wide range of performance for individual papers. It is important to understand the information and ensure that statistics are valid before discussing results publicly with suppliers. When a programme has been established the statistics can be used with the supplier to create a base level of performance. Significant variation from the base level should trigger an alarm for production staff and supplier to try to find a solution while the job is in progress rather than conducting a post-mortem after the event.

Quantitative runnability information allows a company to place a monetary value on the runnability. Actual productivity (good copies per hour) is compared to estimators' standards. Any variance from the standard can be expressed in monetary terms, as a cost per amount of paper. This measure can be used to give the paper purchaser the means to determine which paper should be used for any job. Two examples are presented below.

Examples

▶ For a sheet-fed press with a rate of €100 an hour, and an estimated gross production speed of 8000 copies per hour, a job runs four colours on both sides with two grades of 90gsm paper, A and B. Each sheet is 700 × 1000mm, so 1 tonne = 15,873 sheets. A has a gross running speed of 8500cph and sells for €600 per tonne. B has a gross running speed of 7500cph and sells for €550 per tonne.

Paper cost of production = price per sheet + [(hourly rate/gross run speed) × N°
of passes]

For A = €600/15,873 + [(€100/8,500) × 2]

       =3.78¢ + 2.35¢

       = 6.13¢

For B = €550/15,873 + [(€100/7,500) × 2]

       = 3.46¢ + 2.67¢

       = 6.13¢

So, in this example, a saving of €50 per tonne on the purchase price is eliminated by
a variance of just 6% from estimated running speed.

▶ A twin web offset press costed at €550 per hour runs 90gsm paper reels of width
900mm with press cut off of 630mm. Paper A sells for €550 per tonne and runs at
42,000cph while paper B sells for €500 per tonne and runs at 40,000cph.

Paper cost of production

= Kilo price × (cut off × web width × KgM^{-2}) + [(hourly rate/gross run speed)
× N° of webs]

For A = 0.55€Kg^{-1} × (0.63m × 0.90m × 0.09KgM^{-2}) + [(€550/42,000) × 2]

       = 2.80¢ + 2.62¢

       = 5.42¢

For B = 0.50€Kg^{-1} × (0.63m × 0.90m × 0.09KgM^{-2}) + [(€550/4,000) × 2]

       = 2.55¢ + 2.75¢

       = 5.40¢

In this case the cost saving of €50 per tonne for paper is eliminated by a variance
of as little as 2.5% from the estimated running speed.

It is a simple exercise to construct a spreadsheet to accurately factor the press running
performance of any paper into its overall cost. This provides the purchaser with useful
ammunition when trying to negotiate the best deal from a range of potential suppliers.
When a publisher supplies paper the printer can provide a valid preference for a particular
grade backed up by statistics rather than just a feeling for the relative performance.

**Printer–supplier
relationship**

Successful trading should allow both buyer and seller to profit from the transaction. Most
companies spend much time and effort building relationships with customers yet overlook
the potential benefits in forming similar bonds with suppliers. Printers generally do not like
to put all their eggs in one basket and become tied in to one supplier. Instead, they get
tied into many suppliers. It may profit printers to develop their suppliers to provide more
than just the goods and services at an acceptable cost. Suppliers are a potential source of
expertise and information for the client.

The printer's purchasing function

Commercial printing is a conversion process. It needs paper or board, ink, chemicals, plates, film, adhesives and other minor components. These raw materials will account for more than half the cost of a typical job. The purchasing function in a company can make a major contribution to the financial performance if it is performed well. It needs professional people supported by computerised databases and online systems to obtain the best value. Purchasing must be close to the operational areas ensuring that materials are performing to the maximum potential and looking for continual improvements.

There are two broadly opposite approaches to purchasing. The first is to treat raw materials as commodities and negotiate the lowest price from a wide group of suppliers. Much practical printing concentrates on buying the lowest-price paper or inks and contacting the supplier's technical and support operation only if there are problems in use. Many printers operate on a reactive, exception basis across their business. They concentrate on solving problems after the event rather than trying to eliminate problems before they occur.

Some organisations separate buying from operations and treat it as a profit centre. This approach can avoid costly duplication in a large multi-site company, but the performance must be examined closely. A buyer may obtain quotes on a particular grade of paper and demonstrate price savings by buying brand X rather than brand Y, but the true cost of producing using brand Y may not become apparent until the job is complete. Saving €15 per tonne can be swallowed up by the supplier delivering 2% over the ordered quantity of a heavier weight paper that has multiple breaks, blanket washes and jams on press. The purchasing manager has gained an apparent profit while the rest of the organisation suffers increased costs.

Alternatively, a company may choose to develop good relationships with a smaller number of key suppliers in a mutually beneficial win-win situation. The printer aims to rationalise suppliers and reduce the range of materials used to minimise variables in production. This allows the press crews a chance to learn the characteristics of materials and then improve the process. Buying from fewer suppliers increases the value of the account and hence market share to the supplier. The participants find it worthwhile to share results openly, and to develop superior products and processes.

Strategies for purchasing by printers

The economic objective of buying should be to obtain the best value for the company. This is to ensure the right material is in the right place at the right time, minimise waste and keep working capital tied up in stock at the lowest level possible. This goal should not be hidden away, but well publicised as a company objective and certainly discussed with suppliers and potential suppliers.

Obtaining value is best achieved through knowledge and understanding. Clearly define the purchasing requirement and act to negotiate from strength whenever possible. A strong position will come from knowing your internal processes and suppliers; what they are capable of and how materials perform through running an SPC programme to get quantitative runnability statistics.

Act to reduce the number of suppliers for key materials to the ones that provide the best-value material. Rationalise the materials used to a minimum to allow production personnel to get the benefit of a learning curve. Work with the internal production and planning functions to define requirements for special materials in advance to give suppliers reasonable lead times whenever possible. Giving time to suppliers allows them to manufacture and deliver efficiently at the right time for the printer.

Printer and paper maker

The relation between printer and papermaker can be strained with both parties seemingly at cross-purposes. Paper mills manufacture huge quantities of paper, and a single modern machine may produce 200,000 tonnes of consistent paper each year. The mill then markets it throughout the world through specialist distribution channels. Individual printers take only a tiny portion of the output and will use the paper in their particular manner. Often the local selling organisation will represent many different mills and their marketing and technical personnel do not fully understand all facets of the paper use. They deal second-hand and have to work according to the customs of the supplying mill, and often not directly influencing developments. This makes it difficult for the mill to monitor the press performance of all its products. Inevitably, the performance properties appear to be a compromise to printers.

Printer and paper maker do not have the same perception of paper. Printers sometimes get the feeling that their problems are not taken seriously enough by the paper maker, and the mill almost objects to printers spoiling paper by putting messy ink on it. Paper makers may feel that printers' machinery is often poorly maintained and not set up well enough to avoid problems that are passed straight to the mill as a paper problem. This puts a gulf between them that is bad for both parties.

A suitable strategy to overcome problems can occur only when a professional structured approach to gain mutual benefit is followed. Clear communication between printer and supplier is necessary. The printer must describe simply and clearly what they require from any material, and apply conditions of supply as part of a purchase contract. The paper maker should clearly explain what the expected performance characteristics should be together with actions if problems occur. Keeping accurate records of performance and sharing them with the supplier will lead to improvements and form the basis of acceptable runnability.

When agreement is reached, and an order placed, the printer should offer a normal contract with the order specifying the terms and conditions of supply for paper. An example could be:

XXXX company is actively working to refine and improve all operations. This involves minimising paper wastage and eliminating spoilage by providing the best-performing materials backed up by a supportive technical and administrative supplier organisation. XXXX company expects the supplier to deliver the ordered quantity of paper at the time agreed and in perfect condition. The gross running speed is the key determinant of runnability. It will be measured with the incidence of web breaks and blanket washes.

The printer will inform the paper maker when paper falls significantly below its normal standard and invite them to examine the run together. This may determine the reasons in printing or the service properties of the paper. If there is no direct evidence of poor paper then, unless conditions have significantly changed on press, the printer should expect some compensation for a poorly performing batch of paper. The press performance is part of the conditions for the supply of paper.

Reel-fed paper will be ordered by length not weight, and invoiced by the measured metreage delivered. Sheet-fed paper will be ordered by number of sheets required and not by weight. The company aims to receive the exact (to the next full reel) quantity ordered, no longer following the 'No less than' terms operated in the past. XXXX company will not accept over or under quantities. It will be the responsibility of the paper supplier to ensure that the correct amount of paper, in perfect condition, is delivered at the agreed time.

XXXX company wants to encourage constructive dialogue with preferred suppliers to determine the best way of meeting mutually beneficial objectives.

Beneficial relationships

The best commercial relationships are cases where both parties profit. The most obvious case is where one supplier takes a large share of the available orders in return for a discounted price based on bulk. This can normally be agreed with ink, plate and consumable suppliers, but rarely with paper makers or merchants. In many cases an increase in turnover may be accomplished by buying a range of materials from one source. Suppliers often act as agents for principals to supply all the needs of a printer from one source.

The two parties should explore the supply chain and look to remove areas of cost wherever possible. All transactions, from the initial promotion and sales contact through to the successful use of the product in a job and administration, should be analysed. Wherever wasteful practices are seen they should be changed. One method of improving the relationship is for a consignment stock holding agreement. This is a widespread practice in the supply of ink, press consumables, plates, film and chemistry, and blankets. Here, the supplier holds fast-moving stock at the customer. The printer draws materials as required and is invoiced at the end of a week or month for the materials consumed rather than delivered to the plant. This reduces working capital tied up in stock for the printer, and will smooth distribution for the supplier. He can replenish the stock on a regular planned weekly or monthly basis instead of ad-hoc. Consignment stocking could be useful for the supply of standard paper sizes for sheetfed printing. The supplier's representative visits the plant to check on stock, and to generate a top-up order with the customer's warehouse and store personnel.

With the development of e-procurement there is the opportunity to share information between management information systems of supplier and customer to smooth the administration and control stocks resulting in lower costs. There is a trend of increasing use of computers to handle routine data processing tasks. Modern logistics practices involve designing systems to smooth order processing and stock control.

Suppliers are a potentially valuable source of expertise that a printer can use. Ink manufacturers have experience of chemical industry legislation on hazardous materials and waste management and will be able to advise printers on best practice. Paper makers should provide insight on wider environmental issues facing the whole publishing industry. In some cases formal joint projects may yield developments that printer and supplier can use to gain a technical lead over the competition. In most cases building a good relationship with any supplier ensures a source of information about new developments and competitive industry activity. Any information, of course, must be validated. During a long-term relationship the company will learn the reliability and accuracy of any information and then how much attention to pay to it.

TABLE 2.2 Potential benefits of forming a supplier–printer relationship

For the supplier	For the printer
Guaranteed increase in sales volume and performance and bulk manufacture	Financial benefits from price, stockholding
	Less variation in materials
Lower sales cost	Less management time spent evaluating alternative suppliers and testing
Better feedback on performance of materials	Optimal performing materials
Steady planning of volume and capacity	Prices guaranteed for a specified period for planning
Efficient product distribution	Security of supply and simpler logistics of supply
Simpler administration	Just in time delivery
Simple invoicing	Simple payment
ß-testing of new products	Early information on new developments
Call on user expertise	Call on supplier expertise

Source: Pira International Ltd

Actions if there are problems

Problems occur during printing, and probably always will. They are bad news for both printer and supplier. Most problems with supplied materials tend to be interesting one-off examples. When problems recur a solution is usually found in changing the paper or ink and thoroughly washing the press. The material is then labelled as suspect and is not used again. Printers tend to have long unforgiving memories for materials that have not worked well at one time. In fact the problem may not necessarily be due to the material, but it is in the printer's perception.

The first course of action when a problem occurs is to get back into production quickly; then to identify the cause, take appropriate action and apportion blame. Most paper suppliers have a clause in their terms and conditions indemnifying against consequential loss if there is faulty material. When justified claims are raised the supplier will agree to reimburse the direct loss of wasted material and press time. They will not enter discussion about costs incurred in alternative printing and failing to finish a job on schedule. This situation often leads printers to exaggerate effects and causes, and the paper supplier to resist justifiable claims as it rightly wants to avoid spurious claims.

The major cause of web offset press downtime, by far, is the web break. The continuous web breaks somewhere and the press instantly stops. It takes between 20 minutes and an hour to get back into production wasting up to 2000m of paper. There are three categories of break: due to the printer, the paper or those with no definite evidence. It is sometimes possible to determine the cause of the break. On occasions the break is due to actions of the printer. An improper preparation of the reelstand splices, a mechanical fault in the folder, or tar dropping onto the moving web from the oven and sticking on the chill stacks can cause breaks. The largest category of breaks falls into the no evidence bracket. Here there is no clear evidence of a paper fault or a press problem, but the break occurs and press time and paper are both wasted as a result. A pressman will slow the machine in trying to avoid breaks so the possibility of a break may contribute to poor production. The sleuth-like minder pieces together the two ends and finds a slime hole, a crease or slit in the web, a cut edge, or a poorly prepared mill splice. These are presented to the supplier as evidence of poor paper, together with details of waste and lost press time, and a claim for compensation is negotiated.

Laboratory personnel perform tests on discrete paper samples while presses run continual reels or pallets of sheets. Paper is an organic material with an enormous array of fibres, coating and various bonding elements making up the sheet. There will be stresses and strains imparted to the paper as it passes through the press. These will vary in the infeed, printing units, oven, chills, slitters and in the folder. The paper itself will have an inherent strength, and areas where there is a weakness. This may be an obvious fault such as a slime hole or a nick in the edge, or it may be an area containing slightly less fibre but more coating, an imperfect edge from an unsharpened knife, or an uneven tension from the winder. Statistics show that a sheet containing more imperfections will be more likely to break. Modern web offset printing machinery puts ink onto paper at speeds of up to 3000ft per minute through the press. Any slight imperfections in paper may result in a no evidence break, which is bad news for the printer.

The idea should be to work to avoid claims. When they do occur a disciplined, controlled approach will lead to improved performance. Identify the cause of the problem and do not jump to conclusions that may overlook the real cause. When a printer implements a statistical process control programme there will be quantitative production and quality statistics relating to individual presses and grades of paper. Part of the specification may include an acceptable range of press runnability. When acceptable levels are not met the printer should sound the alarm and involve the support staff of the supplier.

Paper or ink testing will cover two stages. First the mill or merchant will supply paper samples to the printer, together with an approximate price. If this is of interest the supplier will deliver test reels or pallets for on-machine testing. The printer should use a standard procedure to test the material and provide that information back to the supplier. It is useful to provide an on-machine test form to ensure that the machine condition is recorded along with the results of the test. An example that could be used for ink and paper is given in Figure 2.23. The testing procedure should follow initial laboratory testing (or

FIGURE 2.23 On-press paper test form

ON PRESS PAPER TEST REPORT FORM

Date ... / ... / .0...

Customer.. Job..

Paper.. Grade .... GSM ....

Supplier.. Mill..

Sheet/web... Batch no...

Size/width ....

Amount of paper tested   ....

Customer services approval   ....

Instructions for printed copies

_____

_____

Press....................................

Ink grade... Supplier ....

Plates... Blanket..................................

Fount Solution... Concentration . . . . . %   Alcohol . . . . .%

pH................................ Conductivity................................. S-1................................... Temperature................................ ˚C

Print order .... Press speed ....

Machine minders report / comments:

_____

_____

                                                         Signed ....

Customer services report / comments:

_____

_____

_____

                                                         Signed ....

Source: Pira International Ltd

discussion of the supplier's test results), an on-machine trial, then an extended machine and commercial trial. Once approved, the routine use of the material should be subject to continual monitoring of performance in an SPC programme.

Purchasing decision making

There are many factors that influence the choice of a particular grade of material: availability, cost and quality. It is easy to determine the price of a material paid to a supplier. However, detailed measurement is necessary to determine the cost of downtime and sub-optimal running due to a material. The measured performance of paper and ink on press provides the basis for informed choice of the cheapest materials.

Sharing the requirements and performance with the supplier allows both parties to work together to achieve process improvements and lower costs, which are benefits for both sides. Mutually commercially beneficial agreements, such as JIT to reduce stock holding costs and over-delivery, can be made to work with good relationships. The printer might use an MRP II (manufacturing resources planning) system to get the right material to the right place at the right time and have the confidence to be able to rely on the performance. Linking to the planning and scheduling functions needs good information to be successful. The performance of the materials used must be predictable for closed-loop control of the process to be successful.

Just-in-time purchasing for printers

All sectors of print are seeing a trend toward lower print runs and more reprints as customers act to reduce their working capital tied up in slow-moving or redundant stock. This is particularly prevalent in packaging, labels and book production. The clients often apply just-in-time (JIT) ordering procedures with their suppliers. Such approaches can be usefully applied by printers to target five areas:

▶ No waste
▶ Firm schedules
▶ Quality
▶ Minimum set-up
▶ Positive relationships.

Printers cannot just impose JIT on a supplier to reduce stockholdings. Having the minimum amount of paper delivered from a new supplier for a one-off job with a fixed delivery date is an unnecessarily high-risk strategy. The quantity may not be met if any paper is damaged, and if there is a press or binder problem the delivery date may not be met. Successfully using a JIT process means understanding the material properties to build in a fall-back position if there are problems. They should work with suppliers to develop mutually beneficial relationships to lower the costs associated with using a product.

The correct use of specifications can provide dramatic improvements in performance on press by ensuring that all factors are suited to their purposes. Materials should be specified to use the highest grade in the budget range. As a supplier, building in unnecessary characteristics into a product is costly and acts to reduce profitability. If the customer is willing to pay then his finances are affected. For example, it is an unnecessary cost for newspapers to print heatset on coated paper when the market is coldset on newsprint. So over-specification is financially damaging. The characteristics that the manufacturer measures and controls may not be the important factors for the next step in the supply chain. It is not until the performances of materials are measured that the complete cost picture for the customer can be calculated. So it must be the customer who decides if a material is over-specified. Where a good relationship exists between client and supplier they can work together to develop a lower-cost, high-quality solution to the benefit of both.

Industry practices

3

Over many years the industry has developed a series of norms governing the agreements between buyer and seller. These are by no means definitive and may be superseded by specific supply agreements between trading partners. The relentless advance of new technology, with the emergence of digital workflows and administration, has meant that these documents are continually being updated. The latest versions are available from the authors' websites.

Particular contract details agreed between customer and supplier will take precedence over generic industry terms and conditions published by industry bodies in various locations. It is worth the buyer checking the small print (or conditions of acceptance in an e-commerce situation) when accepting an estimate or placing an order to ensure there are no terms that are contentious.

Most printers will provide their own standard terms and conditions, typically based on the BPIF example that follows.

Standard conditions of contract for printers

The British Printing Industries Federation (BPIF) issues a set of standard conditions for use by member firms that were produced after discussions with the Office of Fair Trading and which are printed below with permission of the BPIF.

For the standard conditions to have full legal force in any individual case, it is essential that they should be drawn to the customer's attention. It is not sufficient merely to print the conditions on the back of the estimate form. There must also be wording on the face of the form making reference to the printing on the back. This wording must be sufficiently prominent to prevent a customer alleging that he did not see it, and it is suggested that it should be printed as part of the estimate letter (i.e. above the signature) in preference to printing it at the foot of the form.

The wording could be on the following lines: 'This estimate is given subject to the standard conditions of contract issued by the British Printing Industries Federation and printed overleaf which conditions shall be deemed to be embodied in any contract based on or arising out of this estimate except as may be otherwise indicated herein or subsequently agreed in writing.'

Where a firm wishes to use its own conditions in addition to the standard conditions, these may be printed on the face of the estimate, preferably above the signature. They could also be printed on the reverse of the estimate, below the standard conditions, provided it is made clear that the additional clauses are not part of the standard conditions.

The unconditional acceptance by a customer of a printer's estimate constitutes a contract on the printer's conditions. Some customers, however, specify in their orders certain conditions of their own. A conditional acceptance of a printer's estimate is not binding on the printer until he confirms or accepts it in writing or by conduct. If the printer accepts such a counter-offer, the conditions it contains become added to or (where in conflict) substituted for those in the printer's original estimate. Where appropriate for 'printer' read 'binder'.

1. Price variation

Estimates are based on the printer's current costs of production and, unless otherwise agreed, are subject to amendment on, or at any time after acceptance, to meet any rise or fall in such costs.

2. Tax

Except in the case of a customer who is not contracting in the course of a business nor holding himself out as doing so, the printer reserves the right to charge the amount of any value added tax payable whether or not included on the estimate or invoice.

3. Preliminary work

All work carried out, whether experimentally or otherwise, at customer's request shall be charged.

4. Copy

A charge may be made to cover any additional work involved where copy supplied is not clear and legible.

5. Proofs

Proofs of all work may be submitted for the customer's approval, and the printer shall incur no liability for any errors not corrected by the customer in proofs submitted. Customer's alterations and additional proofs necessitated thereby shall be charged extra. When style, type or layout is left to the printer's judgement, changes made by the customer shall be charged extra.

6. Delivery and payment

► Delivery of work shall be accepted when tendered and the ownership shall pass, and payment becomes due, on notification that the work has been completed.

► Unless otherwise specified, the price quoted is for delivery of the work to the customer's address as set out in the estimate. A charge may be made to cover any extra costs involved for delivery to a different address.

► Should expedited delivery be agreed, an extra might be charged to cover overtime or other additional costs involved.

► Should work be suspended at the request of or delayed through any default of the customer for a period of 30 days, the printer shall then be entitled to payment for work carried out, materials specially ordered and other additional costs including storage.

7. Variations in quantity

In the case of continuous stationery production, every endeavour will be made to deliver the correct quantity ordered. However, quotations are conditional on the following margins being allowed for overs and shortages (measured in fold depths), the same to be charged or deducted:

▶ For quantities below 10,000, or where special papers or special features are required: 10% margin.

▶ Single-part or one-process work 10,000 to 50,000: 5% margin; over 50,000: 4% margin.

▶ Multi-part or multi-process work 10,000 to 50,000: 10% margin; over 50,000: 3% margin.

8. Claims

Advice of damage, delay or partial loss of goods in transit or of non-delivery must be given in writing to the printer and the carrier within three clear days of delivery (or, in the case of non-delivery, within 28 days of despatch of the goods). Any claim in respect thereof must be made in writing to the printer and the carrier within seven clear days of delivery (or, in the case of non-delivery, within 42 days of despatch). All other claims must be made in writing to the printer within 28 days of delivery. The printer shall not be liable in respect of any claim unless the aforementioned requirements have been complied with except in any particular case where the customer proves that:

(a) it was not possible to comply with the requirements and

(b) advice (where required) was given and the claim made as soon as reasonably possible.

9. Liability

The printer shall not be liable for any loss to the customer arising from delay in transit not caused by the printer.

10. Standing material

▶ Metal, film, glass and other materials owned by the printer and used by him in the production of type, plates, moulds, stereotypes, electrotypes, film-setting, negatives, positives and the like shall remain his exclusive property. When supplied by the customer, such items shall remain the customer's property.

▶ Type may be distributed and lithographic, photogravure or other work effaced immediately after the order is executed unless written arrangements are made to the contrary. In the latter event, rent may be charged.

11. Customer's property

▶ Except in the case of a customer who is not contracting in the course of a business nor holding himself out as doing so, customer's property and all property supplied to the printer by or on behalf of the customer shall while it is in the possession of the printer or in transit to or from the customer be deemed to be at customer's risk unless otherwise agreed and the customer should insure accordingly.

▶ The printer shall be entitled to make a reasonable charge for the storage of any customer's property left with the printer before receipt of the order or after notification to the customer of completion of the work.

12. Materials supplied by the customer

► The printer may reject any paper, plates or other materials supplied or specified by the customer, which appear to him to be unsuitable. Additional cost incurred if materials are found to be unsuitable during production may be charged except that if the whole or any part of such additional cost could have been avoided but for unreasonable delay by the printer in ascertaining the unsuitability of the materials then that amount shall not be charged to the customer.

► Where materials are so supplied or specified, the printer will take every care to secure the best results, but responsibility will not be accepted for imperfect work caused by defects in or unsuitability of materials so supplied or specified.

► Quantities of materials supplied shall be adequate to cover normal spoilage.

13. Insolvency

If the customer ceases to pay his debts in the ordinary course of business, cannot pay his debts as they become due or, being a company, is deemed to be unable to pay its debts, has a winding-up petition issued against it or being a person commits an act of bankruptcy or has a bankruptcy petition issued against him, the printer without prejudice to other remedies shall:

► have the right not to proceed further with the contract or any other work for the customer and be entitled to charge for work already carried out (whether completed or not) and materials purchased for the customer, such charge to be an immediate debt due to him, and

► in respect of all unpaid debts due from the customer have a general lien on all goods and property in his possession (whether worked on or not) and shall be entitled on the expiration of 14 days' notice to dispose of such goods or property in such manner and at such price as he thinks fit and to apply the proceeds towards such debts.

14. Illegal matter

► The printer shall not be required to print any matter that, in his opinion, is or may be of an illegal or libellous nature or an infringement of the proprietary or other rights of any third party.

► The printer shall be indemnified by the customer in respect of any claims, costs and expenses arising out of any libellous matter or any infringement of copyright, patent, design or any other proprietary or personal rights contained in any material printed for the customer. The indemnity shall extend to any amounts paid on a lawyer's advice in settlement of any claim.

15. Periodical publications

A contract for the printing of a periodical publication may not be terminated by either party unless 13 weeks' notice in writing is given in the case of periodicals produced monthly or more frequently or 26 weeks' notice in writing is given in the case of other periodicals. Notice may be given at any time but, wherever possible, should be given after completion of work on any one issue. Nevertheless the printer may terminate any such contract should any sum due remain unpaid.

16. Machine-readable codes

(a) In the case of machine-readable codes or symbols, the printer shall print the same as specified or approved by the customer in accordance with generally accepted standards and procedures.

(b) The customer shall be responsible for satisfying himself that the code or symbol will read correctly on the equipment likely to be used by those for whom the code or symbol is intended.

(c) The customer shall indemnify the printer against any claim by any party resulting from the code or symbol not reading or not reading correctly for any reason, except to the extent that such claim rises from any failure of the printer to comply with paragraph (a) above which is not attributable to error falling within the tolerances generally accepted in the trade in relation to printing of this sort.

17. Force majeure

The printer shall be under no liability if he shall be unable to carry out any provision of the contract for any reason beyond his control including (without limiting the foregoing) act of God, legislation, war, fire, flood, drought, failure of power supply, lock-out, strike or other action taken by employees in contemplation or furtherance of a dispute or owing to any inability to procure materials required for the performance of the contract. During the continuance of such a contingency, the customer may by written notice to the printer elect to terminate the contract and pay for work done and materials used, but subject thereto shall otherwise accept delivery when available.

18. Law

These conditions and all other express terms of the contract shall be governed and construed in accordance with the laws of England (Scotland in the case of Scottish printers).

British paper and board trade customs, 1988

Five Federations or Associations endorse this document. Representatives formally recorded their acceptance of its content by signing on behalf of their respective organisations. Terms marked * are described in Appendix C at the end of this document.

The British Paper and Board Industry Federation, The National Association of Paper Merchants, The Packaging Distributors Association, The British Box and Packaging Association, The British Printing Industries Federation.

This publication is a compilation of the customs and practices that have been found by individual British mills to be valuable and practical in handling their sales of paper and board. It has been developed in consultation with the signatory boards listed above. It is as complete as it has been possible to make it, and will constitute a ready method to ensure that both buyer and seller have the same understanding of a quotation or the terms of a sale.

These customs shall apply to all transactions except as otherwise specifically agreed in writing* by the parties. Nothing in these customs shall affect buyers' statutory rights under the Sale of Goods Act 1979. These customs are to be interpreted in accordance with the law of England.

This edition (1988) of *British Paper and Board Trade Customs* supersedes *British Paper and Board Trade Customs* (1974) including the amendments of February 1985, *The Code of Practice for Lined Cartonboard* (May 1982) and *The Code of Practice for Rigid Box Board* (March 1983).

It does not contain *The Code of Practice for Container Middles* (January 1985), *Recommended Quality Requirements for Continuous Stationery Paper*, and *Recommended Quality Requirements for Carbonless Papers for Continuous Stationery* and the *Memorandum on Pallet Specifications* all of which are available as separate publications.

Terms marked * are described in Appendix C (see page 105).

Part 1: **General – applying** **to all paper and board**	**Force majeure**

1. In the event of the delivery by the seller or acceptance by the buyer being wholly or partly prevented or interfered with by act of God, hostilities, threat of war, riot, industrial dispute, civil commotion, fire, drought, flood, restriction by Government or other competent authority, shortfall in anticipated supplies of raw material or by any of the following contingencies beyond the control of the party affected: interruption of transport, destruction or damage of premises, plant or machinery, or any other causes whether of similar character or not, beyond the control of the party affected including, in the case of the buyer, causes affecting the buyer's customer, the following provisions shall have effect:

    a. The party affected shall give to the other party immediate notice of cause preventing or interfering with delivery or acceptance and the extent to which delivery or acceptance is prevented or interfered with, and (if possible) the probable duration of the cause of prevention or interference.

    b. During the continuance of the cause of prevention or interference, delivery of the unfulfilled portion of the contract shall be suspended or, in the case of a partial prevention or interference, reduced until the cause shall have ceased to operate.

    c. Immediately the cause of the prevention or interference has ceased to operate, the party concerned shall give notice thereof to the other party, and as soon as practicable thereafter delivery shall be resumed in accordance with the terms of the contract.

    d. If a cause of prevention or interference shall continue for more than one calendar month after the stipulated date of delivery either party may by notice in writing to the other cancel that portion affected by the delay.

Price variation

2. In the event of a variation of costs necessarily and properly incurred by the seller after the acceptance of an order but before the date on which it is necessary to proceed with manufacture in order to meet the delivery requirements of the order, the price may be increased or decreased within the limits of such variation. This is subject to reasonable notice being given by either the seller or the buyer in respect of orders or balances of orders outstanding.

   The buyer shall have the option to cancel orders or balances of orders outstanding by notice in writing* to the seller within seven days of receiving the seller's notification of an increase in price. Any quotation should also be subject to variation in like manner unless specifically stated otherwise.

Details of order

3. a. Making specifications: Full particulars of the quality, quantity, grammage or thickness and format* of the material ordered, together with any other pertinent information, shall be provided by the buyer to the seller, in sufficient time to enable the manufacturer to comply with the making and/or delivery requirements.
   b. Technical specification: If any special technical or end-use properties are required they must be stated, and agreed in writing* by both parties, before the order is placed.
   c. Delivery specification: The buyer shall provide to the seller all necessary information for delivery of the goods to be effected.

Invoicing

4. a. The goods, having been despatched to meet the buyer's delivery requirements, they shall be invoiced, and such invoice shall become due and payable in accordance with the section headed 'Terms'. (paras 32–33)
   b. If the goods contracted for be ready for delivery on the specified date and the buyer does not then take delivery, they shall be invoiced forthwith and such invoice shall become due and payable in accordance with the section headed 'Terms'. (paras 32–33)

Storage

5. Goods stored by the seller after the date of invoice shall be subject to an economic and appropriate rent charge.

Insurance

6. Insurance of the goods shall remain the responsibility of the seller until delivery has been accepted at the specified destination.

Cancellation

7. Once accepted, an order may not be cancelled either wholly or in part except as permitted under the Force Majeure or Price Variation provisions of these customs or by agreement between the parties. Unless specifically agreed otherwise, neither party shall be liable to make any payment to the other on cancellation, whether by agreement or by such provisions, save that where the seller agrees to a cancellation at the request of the buyer or where the cancellation is due to *force majeure* affecting the buyer or the buyer's customer and not the seller then the following provisions shall (unless otherwise agreed) apply:

    a. No payment shall be made in respect of the seller's regular stock products except that when transit has commenced before cancellation the buyer shall reimburse the seller's reasonable costs involved including cost of re-delivery to the seller and the cost of any damage in transit.

    b. Where the buyer has ordered goods which are to be manufactured for the specific order and the buyer had been advised by the seller of the making date and any of the goods are in course of manufacture or have been completed in accordance with the contract at the time of the cancellation the buyer shall pay the contract price for those goods. Where cancellation is due to an event in respect of which a claim is available under the seller's insurance or would be available if the seller had insured as required by paragraph 6, the liability of the buyer under this paragraph shall be reduced accordingly.

Settlement of disputes

8. In the event of a dispute arising between buyer and seller that cannot be settled by agreement, the parties concerned (in preference to having recourse to the courts) may refer the matter *either* to the standing committee of the Paper Trade Customs *or* to Arbitration under the relevant acts.

STANDING COMMITTEE

9. A standing committee shall be appointed consisting of three persons appointed by and from each signatory body. The standing committee shall appoint a chairman who may be either independent from or one of their number. The chairman shall hold office during the pleasure of the standing committee and shall have a casting vote, which (if he is otherwise a member of the standing committee) shall be in addition to his vote as such a member. The standing committee shall also appoint a secretary through whom any request for its services should be made. A quorum for a meeting of the standing committee shall be six, among whom at least three signatory bodies are represented and none of whom is in the employ of or acting as agent for a party to any dispute or reference being considered.

    Where any business concerns a dispute or reference affecting members of one or more signatory bodies each relevant signatory body must be represented within the quorum. Decisions of the standing committee shall be by majority votes of those attending a meeting at which a quorum is present.

10. The standing committee has discretion in all cases whether to accept or refuse a reference and this provision may not be varied by any purported agreement between parties. Subject to this provision the standing committee may provide either of the following services:

    a. Interpretation of these customs in relation to any given set of facts referred to the standing committee either by the parties to a dispute or by any tribunal considering any matter involving such interpretation.

    b. Conciliation at the request of parties in dispute which will involve investigation and discussions in such manner as the standing committee thinks fit in each case with a view to making recommendations for settlement.

11. The secretary of the standing committee may give informal guidance to any interested person or body (whether or not a member of a signatory body) as to interpretation of these customs but has no authority to bind the standing committee.

12. In any case where the standing committee agrees to provide such service the standing committee may either perform the relevant function itself or may delegate the performance of the function to a sub-committee appointed by the standing committee. The sub-committee shall consist of two representatives of each signatory body involved and an independent chairman who shall have a casting vote only. Decisions of the sub-committee shall be by majority vote. The members of the sub-committee may, but need not, be members of the standing committee and shall not be in the employ of or acting as an agent for a party to any dispute or reference being considered.

13. The standing committee and any sub-committee shall each have the power to co-opt specialist advisers if thought fit who may participate in their meetings but not vote or count towards a quorum.

14. The standing committee shall not be bound to follow their earlier decision as to interpretation.

OTHER THAN BY STANDING COMMITTEE

15. If it is decided to settle by arbitration, otherwise than through the services of the standing committee, a dispute arising under any contract or order, including liability for any loss or damage as above, such disputes shall be settled in England and Wales under the Arbitration Acts, 1952–1979, or any statutory modifications or additions thereto or re-enactments thereof, or in Scotland and Northern Ireland under the appropriate law relating thereto.

16. Each party shall appoint an arbiter, but if either party fails to appoint an arbiter within ten days of notice in writing from the other party requiring them to do so, the arbiter appointed by the other party shall act for both parties and his award shall bind both parties as if he had been appointed sole arbiter by consent.

17. If the arbiters do not agree upon determination of liability and how the cost of the dispute shall be borne, they are to appoint an umpire to whom their findings are to be submitted. In such cases the final decision shall be that of the umpire.

18. No person in the employ of, or acting as an agent for either shall be eligible to act as arbiter or umpire.

Complaints and claims

PROCEDURE – HOME*

19. In respect of damage in transit complaints must be notified in writing* (other than upon the consignment note) to the carrier and supplier within three clear working days of delivery of the goods and any claim must be made in writing within seven clear days of the end of the transit of the consignment or the part of the consignment in respect of which the claim arises.

20. For non-delivery of the whole of the consignment or any separate package forming part of the consignment, notification in writing should be made within 28 days and the claim should be made in writing within 42 days after transit began.

21. Complaints arising on other grounds which can be revealed by immediate external and visual examination of the bulk delivery can only be accepted if made in writing to the supplier within 14 days after delivery and before the goods are used. If a defect is subsequently discovered during processing, a claim may be admissible provided the supplier is notified by the quickest possible means.

22. No acceptance of responsibility can be guaranteed for any claims lodged after three months from the date of delivery.

PROCEDURE – EXPORT*

23. Complaints on any grounds which can be revealed by immediate external and visual examination of the bulk delivery must be notified to the supplier by the quickest possible means within 14 days after the goods have reached their ultimate destination as stated on the order and before the goods are used.

24. If a defect is subsequently discovered during processing, a claim may be admissible provided the supplier is notified by the quickest possible means. No acceptance of responsibility can be guaranteed for any claims lodged after three months from the date of delivery at the ultimate destination.

SUCCESSIVE DELIVERIES

25. If any home or export order is to be executed in successive consignments, each such consignment shall rank and be treated as a separate entity. Any difference or dispute about one consignment shall not affect any other portion of the contract or order.

MEASUREMENT OF REEL LENGTH

26. In the event of any complaint being made for inaccurate measurement of the length of the material supplied on the reel, such complaint must be based solely upon the actual measurements. It shall not be based upon yield from the consignment concerned.

Materials of manufacture

27. Unless it is otherwise expressly stipulated in the order and agreed, the manufacturer shall be free to use his discretion in the selection of materials. It is expected however that the manufacturer would advise his customers of any significant changes that might affect performance, providing the end use is known.

Outturn sheets

28. Outturn sheets* may be supplied with the invoice on request and duplicate sheets shall be retained by the manufacturer for a period of 12 months after manufacture.

Conditions and methods of sampling and testing

29. The conditions and methods of sampling and testing in respect of any paper and boards in the scope of these Customs, unless agreed otherwise by buyer and seller, shall be the agreed standard tests prepared by the British Standards Institution. (Listed in Appendix A on page 88.)

Part II: Customs specific to paper

Scope of customs for paper

30. The scope of this section of the customs shall include all papers and boards, coated or uncoated, excluding:
    ► hand and mould made papers
    ► soft tissue paper
    ► newsprint
    ► boards as defined in the appropriate section of the customs.

Bases of sale

31. Paper shall be sold and invoiced:
    a. by 100 or 1000 sheets or any part thereof OR
    b. by ream* of 500 sheets OR
    c. by area OR
    d. by weight, in reels or sheets however packed OR
    e. by arrangement between buyer and seller.

Terms

QUOTATIONS

32. Unless otherwise stated, quotations are understood to be net and carriage paid to the address stated on the order. The choice of route and mode of delivery shall be at the discretion of the seller, unless otherwise agreed between buyer and seller.

TERMS OF PAYMENT

33. Goods invoiced and dispatched up to and including the last day of the calendar month shall be paid for before the end of the following month.

DELIVERY

34. Delivery in the United Kingdom of Great Britain and Northern Ireland shall include delivery at the buyer's warehouse or that of this consignee.

CHARGEABLE WEIGHT*

35. a. *Sheets*: For paper sold by weight in sheet form, the chargeable weight of a consignment shall be the product of the nominal net weight* of a unit of a stated number of sheets of the ordered size and grammage* and the number of such units, provided that the actual net weight of the consignment does not fall short of the chargeable weight as defined above by more than 2.5%, in which case the actual net weight shall be charged.

    b. Reels: For paper sold by weight in reel form, the chargeable weight of a consignment shall be either:

       i)   The actual weight of the reels excluding wooden and/or metal centres or

       ii) The nominal net weight calculated from the grammage and area supplied.

    [For details of sale of paper and board by area, please refer to 'Guidelines for Buying and Selling Printing and Writing Papers on the Reel by Area' (Appendix B, page 89).]

Manufacturing variations, cutting tolerances for graphic* papers only

REELS – MEASUREMENTS

36. Reels shall not vary from the ordered width by more than the following amounts:

    a.   plus or minus 2mm for reels up to and including 1000mm width

    b.   plus or minus 3mm for reels over 1000mm width.

REEL JOINS

37. At the time of placing an order the buyer and seller should agree the maximum number of joins or splices, the method of joining, their position in the reel and identification.

SHEETS – MEASUREMENTS

38. For paper guillotine trimmed or precision cut*, the permissible tolerance shall not be more than plus or minus 2mm.

39. In special circumstances, members of AMPW* will supply precision cut papers against making orders to the following tolerances when specifically requested to do so:

    ▶   cross direction* of the paper plus or minus 1mm;

    ▶   machine direction* of the paper plus or minus 2mm.

40. Mills reserve the right to make price adjustments when called upon to observe these tighter tolerances which are intended to satisfy printers' requirements when using convertible presses* for perfecting*.

41. Sheets not guillotine trimmed or precision cut shall not vary from the ordered measurement by more than the following:

a.   plus or minus 3mm for measurements up to and including 610mm;

b.   plus or minus 5mm for measurements over 610mm and up to and including 1245mm;

c.   plus or minus 6mm or measurements over 1245mm.

**Cutting tolerances
for all other papers**

REELS – MEASUREMENTS

42.   Reels shall not vary from the ordered width by more than the following amounts:

a.   plus or minus 3mm for reels up to and including 610mm in width

b.   plus or minus 5mm for reels over 610mm and up to and including 1245mm in width

c.   plus or minus 6mm for reels over 1245mm in width.

REEL JOINS

43.   At the time of placing an order the buyer and seller should agree the maximum number of joins or splices, the method of joining, their position in the reel and identification.

SHEETS – MEASUREMENTS

44.   For paper guillotine trimmed or precision cut, the permissible tolerance shall not be more than plus or minus 2mm.

45.   Sheets not guillotine trimmed or precision cut shall not vary from the ordered measurement by more than the following:

a.   plus or minus 3mm for measurements up to and including 610mm;

b.   plus or minus 5mm for measurements over 610mm and up to and including 1245mm;

c.   plus or minus 6mm for measurements over 1245mm.

**Other manufacturing
tolerances and
variations for all types
of paper (including
graphic papers)**

GRAMMAGE*

46.   Grammage readings obtained by using the methods of sampling, conditioning and testing detailed in Appendix A shall not vary from the ordered grammage by more than plus or minus 7.5% under 40 grammes per square metre or more than plus or minus 5% for 40 grammes per square metre and over.

THICKNESS

47.   Thickness readings obtained by using the methods of sampling conditioning and testing detailed in Appendix A shall not vary from the ordered thickness by more than:

a.   plus or minus 10% for thicknesses up to and including 100 micrometres*;

b.   plus or minus 7.5% for thicknesses over 100 micrometres.

QUANTITY VARIATION

48. Making orders are any orders for paper which are outside the normal stock range of the manufacturer and shall be deemed to be properly executed if the quantity supplied in each size and weight is within the following limits either way of the quantity ordered in each size and weight:

	Standard stock* quality and grammage in special sizes	Non-standard papers e.g. by reason of quality and/or grammage
Up to and including 1 tonne	10.0%	15.0%
Over 1 tonne and not exceeding 5 tonnes	5.0%	10.0%
Over 5 tonnes and not exceeding 10 tonnes	5.0%	7.5%
Over 10 tonnes and not exceeding 20 tonnes	3.75%	5.0%
Over 20 tonnes	2.5%	2.5%

DOUBLE TOLERANCE

49. In all cases covered by the above manufacturing variation clauses, where purchasers specify any tolerance exclusively in one direction, double tolerance shall apply in the other direction.

50. For example, if a customer orders 'not less than 6 tonnes' of a non-standard paper the tolerance on quantity supplied would be minus 0% plus 2 × 7.5% = 15% = 0.9 tonne. If a customer specifies for a non-graphic paper a reel width as 'not less than 590mm', the tolerance on this width would be minus 0mm plus 2 × 3mm = 6mm.

SQUARENESS

51. Adjacent edges of paper supplied as rectangular should form a right angle within a tolerance of plus or minus 0.003 radians (10'192). This may be checked by placing one side of the sheet in contact with a straight reference edge; a straight line is then constructed at right angles to the reference edge, passing through the corner under test: at a distance of one metre from the reference edge, the distance between the constructed line and the adjacent edge of the sheet should not exceed 3mm. For sheets less than one metre in length on the edge under test, the variation may be interpreted proportionally.

GENERAL

52. When tolerance measurements are to be determined, samples shall first be selected and conditioned in accordance with BS3430 and BS3431 (listed in Appendix A on page 102).

Packing

53. Returnable boards, frames, cases, stillages, pallets and special centres shall be clearly marked and shall be charged at appropriate rates. These charges shall be refunded in full when such packing material has been returned to the point of origin in good condition within an agreed period.

Dandy rolls* and supported sleeves*

54. Any buyer requiring a special watermark shall pay the papermaker in full for the provision of the roll or sleeve. The buyer, by agreement with the papermaker, may be allowed a credit of 2.5% on the value of each invoice for the paper made in the mill from the roll or sleeve until the total cost has been refunded, when the roll or sleeve *but not the design or its copyright* shall automatically become the property of the mill. The roll or sleeve shall be redeemable by the buyer within five years from the date of the last making of paper from the roll or sleeve concerned, upon repayment to the mill of the total amount of any such allowances. If no such allowances are made, the roll or sleeve shall remain the property of the buyer who may at any time require delivery thereof. No roll or sleeve shall be destroyed until the buyer has been given in writing* the opportunity of redemption.

    Any alterations to the roll or sleeve required by the buyer, or maintenance due to fair wear and tear, are the responsibility of the buyer, and the charge may be credited on the same basis as the original dandy roll or supported sleeve. The ownership of the watermark, dandy roll and supported sleeve shall be the subject of a written agreement between the buyer and the mill.

Breakage

55. Customary mill packages will not be broken.

Part III: Scope of customs for boards

56. Heavier grades of paper, described commercially as 'boards' primarily intended for the packaging and converting industries, but excluding fibre building board, matrix board, container middles and grey paper felt.

Bases of sale

57. Board shall be sold and invoiced:

   a   by weight, whether in sheets or reels OR

   b   by area OR

   c.   by number of sheets of a required size OR

   d.   by arrangement between buyer and seller.

Terms   **QUOTATIONS**

58. Unless otherwise stated, quotations are understood to be net and carriage paid to the address stated on the order. The choice of route and mode of delivery shall be at the discretion of the seller unless otherwise agreed between buyer and seller.

TERMS OF PAYMENT

59. Goods invoiced and dispatched up to and including the last day of the calendar month shall be paid for before the end of the following month.

DELIVERY

60. Delivery in the United Kingdom of Great Britain and Northern Ireland shall include delivery at the buyer's warehouse or that of his consignee.

CHARGEABLE WEIGHT*

61. The chargeable weight for sheets shall exclude the weight of the necessary wrapping materials. Board in reels shall be charged at gross weight inclusive of wrappers, centres and plugs (excluding wood or metal centres) which are not returnable.

62. The following manufacturing variations and general requirements replace the *Code of Practice for Lined Cartonboard* (May 1982) and the *Code of Practice for Rigid Boxboard* (March 1983) and cover the following classes of board.

   Class I   White-lined boards down to No2 white-lined chipboard;

   Class II   All other non-white boards lined with virgin pulp liners;

   Class III   Unlined chipboard and similar grades including 'greyboard'.

General requirements

63. Agreement on the following conditions and tolerances shall be taken as an expression of intention, and any deviation from these guidelines shall be the subject of negotiation between buyer and seller.

   a.   The supplier must not deliver material which the supplier could reasonably be expected to know would not be satisfactory for the described conversion process in the converter's plant and the end use if indicated.

b. Board manufacturers must ensure that, to the best of their knowledge, materials used or supplied by them are suitable for the purposes specified. The responsibility for ensuring the suitability of the finished product rests with the converter, though it may be necessary to agree specifications for particular individual outlets and purposes, e.g. the direct packaging of food as covered in the Statutory Instrument 1987 Nº 1523 or such other legislation as may, in future, apply.

c. The board shall be delivered in good condition in units of specified size and weight. For lined cartonboard, sheets shall be wrapped in suitable moisture-proof wrappers to protect them during transport. Reels will be similarly wrapped when requested.

d. All units of board, whether pallets, bundles or reels shall be clearly marked to customers' requirements with the order details for identification purposes. Machine direction* should be shown when requested by a uniform symbol (<—>) on every bundle and on two adjacent sides of a pallet.

(For lined carton board only, pallet loads or reels may be identified in relation to the manufacturing sequence and deckle position when required.)

Manufacturing variations and tolerances

SHEET DIMENSION TOLERANCES

64. The size of a sheet of board shall be defined by width and length, the second dimension being the way of the machine direction. When cutting sheets, dimensions shall be within the following tolerances:

Class of board	I	II	III
Machine direction	±2.5mm	±3mm	±3mm
Cross direction*	±1.5mm	±2mm	±2mm

The cross direction tolerances also refer to reels.

SQUARENESS

65. Adjacent edges of a board supplied as rectangular should form a right angle within a tolerance of plus or minus 0.003 radians (10'19") unless tighter specifications are agreed between buyer and seller. (This may be checked by placing one side of the sheet in contact with a straight reference edge; a straight line is then constructed at right angles to the reference edge, passing through the corner under test; at a distance of 1m from the reference edge, the distance between the constructed line and the adjacent edge of the sheet should not exceed 3mm. For sheets less than 1m in length on the edge under test, the variation may be interpreted proportionally.)

GRAMMAGE*

66. a. Permitted deviation of the individual specimen value from ordered grammage within a consignment (95% of the specimen measurements must be within the agreed tolerance).

	I	II	III
Unpasted	±5%	±5%	±5%
Pasted	±7%	±7%	±7%

b. From ordered grammages, the following sliding scale will apply for variation of the average grammage for a given order.

	I	II	III
Unpasted			
(up to & inc 10 tonnes)	±5%	±5%	±5%
(10 tonnes or over)	±3%	±5%	±5%
Pasted			
(up to & inc 10 tonnes)	±7%	±7%	±7%
(10 tonnes or over)	±5%	±7%	±7%

Thickness

67. These tolerances refer to the deviation of the individual specimen value from the ordered value within a consignment.

	I	II	III
Unpasted, the greater of	±4%	±5%	±7%
or	25μ	25μ	25μ
Pasted	±7%	±9%	

MOISTURE CONTENT

68. The moisture content of the board at the time of delivery or customer collection shall be uniformly distributed and as specified within the following tolerances.

	I	II	III
Unpasted	±1.5%	±2%	±2%
Pasted	±2%	±3%	

Note:

69. Tolerances for thickness and moisture content refer to the deviation of the individual specimen value from the ordered value within a consignment. 95% of the individual measurements must be within the agreed tolerances.

70. Achievement against tolerance is assessed for each parameter (i.e. grammage, thickness and moisture content) independently of the other two. The 95% achievement is therefore not cumulative.

QUANTITY

71. Orders shall be deemed to be properly executed if the quantity supplied in each size and weight is within the following limits either way of the quantity ordered in each size and weight:

	I	II	III
Up to 10 tonnes	±10%	±10%	±10%
Over 10 and up to 20 tonnes	±7.5%	±7.5%	±7.5%
Over 20 and up to 50 tonnes	±4%	±4%	±4%
Over 50 tonnes	±2.5%	±2.5%	±2.5%

COLOURED BOARDS

72. A higher differential for quantity shall be allowed for coloured board, of all classes as follows:

> up to 20 tonnes – plus or minus 15%
>
> over 20 tonnes – plus or minus 6.5%.

DOUBLE TOLERANCE

73. If a minimum or maximum quantity or dimension is specified, there shall be a double tolerance in the other direction.

BOARD SUPPLIED ON REELS

74. Cores or centres shall be of suitable strength to prevent collapse or distortion of the reel in normal handling.

EDGE ALIGNMENT

75. Reels and coils shall be tightly and evenly wound; the sides of the reel shall be visibly perpendicular to the axis of the core. The sides of the reel or coil shall not be dished by more than 25mm per metre of diameter.

    The maximum lateral displacement between the edges of successive laps shall not exceed the following:

	I	II	III
Coils or reels with a butt join	3mm	3mm	3mm
All other coils or reels	2mm	3mm	3mm

JOINS OR SPLICES

76. For orders up to five tonnes the total number of joins should not be more than the number of reels in the delivery. For orders of five tonnes and above, the number of joints shall not exceed the following percentages of the total number of reels in the consignment.

Quantity ordered	No joins per reel	Not>2 joins per reel	Not>3 joins per reel
5 tonnes and not exceeding 20 tonnes	50%	40%	10%
20 tonnes and over	60%	40%	Nil

STRAIGHT EDGE

77. The edge of a sheet or reel shall not deviate from a straight line by more than the following:

	I	II	III
Over a length of 1.5m	±1.5mm	±3mm	±3mm

SHAPE

78. The board as delivered shall be free from such wave or curl as can be anticipated to cause difficulties on modern converting*, printing and packaging machinery.

EDGES

79. Slit, chopped and guillotined edges of the board shall be sufficiently clean, firm and free from loose fibres and dust for the printing process where applicable.

TORN SHEETS, TABS

80. With the exception of count tabs, which are only acceptable where requested, and pallet binders, there should be no torn or folded sheets, no packing pieces (except at the start of the reel) nor loose pieces of board between sheets or in a reel which might impede the automatic feed of the converting/printing machine where applicable.

SURFACES

81. The board shall be sufficiently clean and free from fluff, loose fibres and non-fibrous contraries for the printing process specified. There shall be a minimum possible variation in shade of face, not only within a making but also between makings.

ACIDITY OF PRINTING SURFACES (pH VALUE)

82. The surface pH value measured by the appropriate method shall be not less than 5.0 on any surface specified to be printed.

Appendix A: British Standards referred to in British paper and board customs

BS 2924: Part 1: Method for determination of pH

BS 3430: Method for sampling to determine the average quality of paper and board

BS 3431: Method for the conditioning of paper and board for testing

BS 3432: Method for the determination of grammage* of paper and board

BS 3433: Method for determination of moisture content of paper and board by the oven-drying method

BS 3983: Part 2: Method for determining the single sheet thickness of paper and board and apparent density of board

Note: The most recent issue of the above standards is applicable in all cases.

Appendix B:
Guidelines for buying
and selling printing
and writing papers
on the reel by area

1. Introduction

The following are guidelines for the purchase and supply by area of printing and writing papers on reels. This is one of the conditions of sale included in the British Paper and Board Trade Customs 1988. The method reduces the amount of variation between the ordered and delivered surface area of the paper, compared with ordering and charging by weight. Where printing and writing papers on reels are bought and sold on an area basis, the preferred area is one thousand square metres (1000m²) or one thousand linear metres of a stated width (1000m × width).

2. Operation

Modern linear measuring devices available for fitting to slitter/rewinders, converting equipment, web-fed printing machines are accurate to +0.5% and may be equipped with visual digital display in metres or with a chart recorder providing a printout of the meterage of each set of reels.

Papermills so equipped will be able to give meterage figures for the reels they supply but will also continue to show the weight of reels for transport purposes.

3. Ordering by area

The customer will order the required number of square metres, or linear metres at specified reel widths, of the grade of paper required. The papermill converts the order to 'x' number of reels, each reel to be 'y' metres in length, at a nominal weight of 'z' kilogrammes per reel. (The same length and width can, if required, be designated as a quantity of sheets.)

Some mills may prefer to wind reels to the same length, which would be advantageous to supplier and customer in both practical and clerical terms. Prices that are quoted will include the cost of cores, packaging etc.

4. Tolerances

In calculating the total quantity to be ordered there is no longer any need to take account of core and wrappers or to allow for grammage variation (+5% above 40g/m²) as is necessary when ordering by weight. Variables to take into account are +1.0% to cover the tolerance of the linear measuring device, in addition to the making order tolerance. Making orders are any orders for paper which are outside the normal stock range of the manufacturer and shall be deemed to be properly executed if the quantity supplied in each size and grammage is within the following limits either way:

Quantity ordered	Standard stock* quality and grammage in special sizes	Non-standard papers e.g. by reason of quality and/or grammage
Up to 25 000 m²	10.0%	15.0%
25 to 50 000 m²	5.0%	10.0%
50 to 100 000 m²	5.0%	7.5%
100 to 200 000 m²	3.75%	5.0%
Over 200 000 m²	2.5%	2.5%

If a tolerance is excluded in one direction, double tolerance shall apply in the other direction.

5. Claims for short measure

For a claim for short measure to be successful the printer will need to account for all of the paper used. Such a claim must include the following information:

► length of paper issued from the store

► length of paper used, equivalent to quantity and size of both saleable and unsaleable products printed/converted

► length equivalent to unused paper waste, e.g. left on reel core or removed before printing/converting.

NB. This clause, if agreed between the parties, shall override para 26 of *British Paper and Board Trade Customs 1988*.

6. Prices

Basic list prices will be quoted in £s per 1000 m² or £'s per 1000 linear metres.

7. Costs

Costs of paper will be calculated as follows:

a. Cost per 1000 linear metres in width ordered:

$$\frac{\text{Reel width (mm)} \times \text{price in £s per 1000m}^2}{1000}$$

b. total cost of quantity ordered or invoiced:

$$\frac{\text{Reel width (mm)} \times \text{total linear metres} \times \text{price in £s per 1000 m}^2}{1\ 000\ 000}$$

or

$$\frac{\text{total linear metres} \times \text{price in £s per 1000 linear m of given width}}{1000}$$

8. Grammage

Grammage is no longer of prime consideration in respect of the cost of a given area of paper but will revert to the role of a quality control property together with other characteristics such as thickness, opacity etc.

9. Reel specification

It is desirable that a reel specification should accompany each consignment and contain the following information:

Main heading	Supplier	Customer
	Supplier ref no.	Customer order no.
	Grade	Reel width
	Quantity ordered	
For each reel	Reel no.	Length in metres
	Scale weight in kg	

10. Stock records, issue and receipt notes

Records will need to be maintained in reels and metres, which will be similar to methods used for sheets on pallets. The much greater accuracy and certainty of information will improve the correlation between stock records and physical stock and also permit a greater control of paper spoilage. When changing from a weight to an area basis for ordering and charging, it is necessary to ensure that all operatives concerned are fully trained in the procedure and in the terminology and units employed. The organisations associated with these guidelines are:

The British Paper and Board Industry Federation

The British Printing Industries Federation

The National Association of Paper Merchants

The Publishers Association.

Appendix C: Glossary for British paper and board customs

Definitions

Actual weight The weight of a unit or consignment of paper as recorded by accurate and properly maintained weighing equipment.

AMPW The Association of Makers of Printings and Writings.

Chargeable weight The weight of paper that a supplier is permitted to invoice to a buyer under the terms of these customs.

Convertible press A type of multi-unit, sheetfed printing press in which reversing equipment is provided between two adjacent units so that the sheet may be turned over and the following unit(s) print on the reverse side of the sheet in the same pass. Thus the press is capable of printing on one side or perfecting.

Converting Any process carried out on paper that alters its appearance or format or changes it into another product, e.g. printing, cutting, impregnating, laminating.

Cross direction That direction in the plane of a sheet of paper at right angles to the machine direction.

Cut sizes Term used to denote paper in small rectangular sheets. There is no agreed line of demarcation between 'large' and cut sizes but the latter would generally be applied to sheets of A3 format (297 × 420mm) and below.

Dandy roll A wire-covered roll of light construction used on the upper side of the forming fabric and rotating in contact with the wet web. If required, a design may be incorporated on the face of the roll to impart a watermark to the paper, e.g. laid lines, brand name or other symbols.

Export Refers to the relevant market area in the procedure for complaints and claims for goods sold outside of the United Kingdom and Northern Ireland.

Format The manner in which paper or board is presented for sale, e.g. in sheets or on reels. For sheets, format is taken to include dimensions and machine direction and, for reels, the width, internal diameter of cores and information on the amount of paper or board to be wound by specifying the overall diameter, length or weight.

Grammage The mass of a unit area of paper or board determined by the specified method of test and expressed in grammes per square metre (gsm).

Graphic papers Papers intended to be suitable for printing by conventional processes and/or inscribing with writing inks or similar applications.

Home Refers to the relevant market area in the procedure for complaints and claims for goods sold within the whole of the United Kingdom including Northern Ireland, Channel Islands, Isle of Man etc.

In writing Any method of communication that will provide a hard copy of the message, e.g. letter, telex, fax etc.

Machine direction That direction in a paper and board corresponding to the direction of travel of the web on the paper or board machine.

Micrometre A unit, used to express the thickness of paper and board, equivalent to one thousandth of a millimetre. Frequently abbreviated in trade parlance to micron (μm).

Net weight The weight of a unit or consignment of paper excluding tare (i.e. packaging material, cores etc.).

Nominal weight The weight of a unit or consignment of paper or board calculated from its nominal grammage, nominal dimensions and the number of sheets or total area supplied.

Outturn sheets Samples provided by a seller to a buyer, representative of a making, to illustrate its characteristics.

Perfecting The placing of an image on both sides of a sheet of paper in the same pass through a printing machine, or in a subsequent working.

Precision cut Term used for paper or board that has been cut from the reel to rectangular sheets in a precision cutter. Although no different from a rotary cutter in basic principle, the precision cutter is distinguished by its greater accuracy.

Ream A pack of 500 sheets of paper of the same quality, colour, grammage and format.

Stock papers Those qualities, colours, grammages and formats of paper that are advertised by the seller as being held in stock on a regular and continuing basis for prompt delivery.

Supported sleeve A device, for use in conjunction with an uncovered dandy roll, in the form of a cylindrical, wire-covered sleeve that may be fitted over the body of the dandy roll and removed when no longer required. In cases where a sleeve can be used, it is unnecessary to manufacture the more expensive complete dandy roll for a given watermark.

Working days Monday to Friday, excluding public holidays.

Trade customs of the printing industry of North America

1. Quotation

A quotation not accepted within 30 days may be changed.

2. Orders

Acceptance of orders is subject to credit approval and contingencies such as fire, water, strikes, theft, vandalism, acts of God, and other causes beyond the provider's control. Cancelled orders require compensation for incurred costs and related obligations.

3. Experimental work

Experimental or preliminary work performed at customer's request will be charged to the customer at the provider's current rates. This work cannot be used without the provider's written consent.

4. Creative work

Sketches, copy, dummies and all other creative work developed or furnished by the provider are the provider's exclusive property. The provider must give written approval for all use of this work and for any derivation of ideas from it.

5. Accuracy of specifications

Quotations are based on the accuracy of the specifications provided. The provider can re-quote a job at time of submission if copy, film, tapes, disks, or other input materials don't conform to the information on which the original quotation was based.

6. Preparatory materials

Art work, type, plates, negatives, positives, tapes, disks, and all other items supplied by the provider remain the provider's exclusive property.

7. Electronic manuscript or image

It is the customer's responsibility to maintain a copy of the original file. The provider is not responsible for accidental damage to media supplied by the customer or for the accuracy of furnished input or final output. Until digital input can be evaluated by the provider, no claims or promises are made about the provider's ability to work with jobs submitted in digital format, and no liability is assumed for problems that may arise. Any additional translating, editing, or programming needed to utilise customer-supplied files will be charged at prevailing rates.

8. Alterations/corrections

Customer alterations include all work performed in addition to the original specifications. All such work will be charged at the provider's current rates.

9. Prepress proofs

The provider will submit prepress proofs along with original copy for the customer's review and approval. Corrections will be returned to the provider on a master set marked 'OK', 'OK with corrections', or 'Revised proof required' and signed by the customer. Until the master set is received, no additional work will be performed. The provider will not be responsible for undetected production errors if:

▶ proofs are not required by the customer

▶ the work is printed per the customer's OK

▶ requests for changes are communicated orally.

10. Press proofs

Press proofs will not be furnished unless they have been required in writing in the provider's quotation. A press sheet can be submitted for the customer's approval as long as the customer is present at the press during makeready. Any press time lost or alterations/corrections made because of the customer's delay or change of mind will be charged at the provider's current rates.

11. Colour proofing

Because of differences in equipment, paper, inks, and other conditions between colour proofing and production pressroom operations, a reasonable variation in colour between colour proofs and the completed job is to be expected. When variation of this kind occurs, it will be considered acceptable performance.

12. Overruns or underruns

Overruns or underruns will not exceed 10% of the quantity ordered. The provider will bill for actual quantity delivered within this tolerance. If the customer requires a guaranteed quantity, the percentage of tolerance must be stated at the time of quotation.

13. Customer's property

The provider will only maintain fire and extended coverage on property belonging to the customer while the property is in the provider's possession. The provider's liability for this property will not exceed the amount recoverable from the insurance. Additional insurance coverage may be obtained if it is requested in writing, and if the premium is paid to the provider.

14. Delivery

Unless otherwise specified, the price quoted is for a single shipment, without storage, FOB provider's platform. Proposals are based on continuous and uninterrupted delivery of the complete order. If the specifications state otherwise, the provider will charge accordingly at current rates. Charges for delivery of materials and supplies from the customer to the provider, or from the customer's supplier to the provider, are not included in quotations unless specified. Title for finished work passes to the customer upon delivery to the carrier at shipping point; or upon mailing of invoices for the finished work or its segments, whichever occurs first.

15. Production schedules

Production schedules will be established and followed by both the customer and the provider. In the event that production schedules are not adhered to by the customer, delivery dates will be subject to renegotiation. There will be no liability or penalty for delays due to state of war, riot, civil disorder, fire, strikes, accidents, action of government or civil authority, acts of God, or other causes beyond the control of the provider. In such cases, schedules will be extended by an amount of time equal to delay incurred.

16. Customer-furnished materials

Materials furnished by customers or their suppliers are verified by delivery tickets. The provider bears no responsibility for discrepancies between delivery tickets and actual counts. Customer-supplied paper must be delivered according to specifications furnished by the provider. These specifications will include correct weight, thickness, pick resistance, and other technical requirements. Artwork, film, colour separations, special dies, tapes, disks, or other materials furnished by the customer must be usable by the provider without alterations or repair. Items not meeting this requirement will be repaired by the customer, or by the provider at the provider's current rates.

17. Outside purchases

Unless otherwise agreed in writing, all outside purchases as requested or authorised by the customer, are chargeable.

18. Terms/claims/liens

Payment is net cash 30 calendar days from date of invoice. Claims for defects, damages or shortages must be made by the customer in writing no later than ten calendar days after delivery. If no such claim is made, the provider and the customer will understand that the job has been accepted. By accepting the job, the customer acknowledges that the provider's performance has fully satisfied all terms, conditions and specifications.

The provider's liability will be limited to the quoted selling price of defective goods, without additional liability for special or consequential damages. As security for payment of any sum due under the terms of an agreement, the provider has the right to hold and place a lien on all customer property in the provider's possession. This right applies even if credit has been extended, notes have been accepted, trade acceptances have been made, or payment has been guaranteed. If payment is not made, the customer is liable for all collection costs incurred.

19. Liability

1. Disclaimer of Express Warranties: the provider warrants that the work is as described in the purchase order. The customer understands that all sketches, copy, dummies and preparatory work shown to the customer are intended only to illustrate the general type and quality of the work. They are not intended to represent the actual work performed.

2. Disclaimer of Implied Warranties: the provider warrants only that the work will conform to the description contained in the purchase order. The provider's maximum liability, whether by negligence, contract, or otherwise, will not exceed the return of the amount invoiced for the work in dispute. Under no circumstances will the provider be liable for specific, individual, or consequential damages.

20. Indemnification

The customer agrees to protect the provider from economic loss and any other harmful consequences that could arise in connection with the work. This means that the customer will:

hold the provider harmless and save, indemnify, and otherwise defend him/her against claims, demands, actions, and proceedings on any and all grounds. This will apply regardless of responsibility for negligence.

1. Copyrights. The customer also warrants that the subject matter to be printed is not copyrighted by a third party. The customer also recognises that because subject matter does not have to bear a copyright notice in order to be protected by copyright law, absence of such notice does not necessarily assure a right to reproduce. The customer further warrants that no copyright notice has been removed from any material used in preparing the subject matter for reproduction.

    To support these warranties, the customer agrees to indemnify and hold the provider harmless for all liability, damages, and attorney fees that may be incurred in any legal action connected with copyright infringement involving the work produced or provided.

2. Personal or economic rights. The customer also warrants that the work does not contain anything that is libelous or scandalous, or anything that threatens anyone's right to privacy or other personal or economic rights. The customer will, at the customer's sole expense, promptly and thoroughly defend the provider in all legal actions on these grounds as long as the provider:
    ▶ promptly notifies the customer of the legal action;
    ▶ gives the customer reasonable time to undertake and conduct a defense.
    The provider reserves the right to use his or her sole discretion in refusing to print anything he or she deems illegal, libelous, scandalous, improper or infringing upon copyright law.

21. Storage

The provider will retain intermediate materials until the related end product has been accepted by the customer. If requested by the customer, intermediate materials will be stored for an additional period at additional charge. The provider is not liable for any loss or damage to stored material beyond what is recoverable by the provider's fire and extended insurance coverage.

22. Taxes

All amounts due for taxes and assessments will be added to the customer's invoice and are the responsibility of the customer. No tax exemption will be granted unless the customer's 'Exemption Certificate' (or other official proof of exemption) accompanies the purchase order. If, after the customer has paid the invoice, it is determined that more tax is due, then the customer must promptly remit the required taxes to the taxing authority, or immediately reimburse the provider for any additional taxes paid.

23. Telecommunications

Unless otherwise agreed, the customer will pay for all transmission charges. The provider is not responsible for any errors, omissions, or extra costs resulting from faults in the transmission.

Customs of the trade for the manufacture of books

The conditions on which typesetters, printers and binders execute work for publishers are usually based on the standard conditions of contract issued by the British Printing Industries Federation (BPIF). However, such conditions do not fully cover all aspects of book production, and the purpose of [the following] is to clarify the current practices of the book trade on all relevant points.

[The following] is only intended to affect the position of printers and binders engaged in book manufacture. It should be noted that the customs recommended [here] can be varied by mutual agreement between the parties to a contract and will be without legal effect except insofar as they coincide with the existing legal position, or where they are specifically incorporated into a particular contract. Even where the customs do not have legal effect, however, publishers and book manufacturers may feel, in the event of dispute, that they provide a suitable basis for settlement.

The process of manufacturing books is complex, encompassing a multitude of stages, and calls for a high degree of cooperation and understanding between customers and manufacturers. This is reflected [here] and also in *Book Production Practice* published jointly by The British Printing Industries Federation and The Publishers Association (PA). These publications provide a comprehensive framework on which to base trouble-free working relationships.

Customs of the Trade for the Manufacture of Books was first produced in 1972 by a joint BPIF/PA working party and has been formally accepted by the BPIF and the PA.

This latest edition was prepared by another joint BPIF/PA working party, and it is hoped that all publishers and book manufacturers will find the guidelines it provides of value.

1. Data capture and typesetting

A Estimating

(a) Typesetters estimate and charge for setting copy as received, and may charge as extra any editing work for which they are made responsible, and any extra costs that may arise from illegible or unclear copy not previously seen.

(b) If a cast-off is required to ensure that the final extent of the book is a number of pages which can be economically manufactured, the typesetter is expected to cast-off the probable number of pages of good regular typescript to an accuracy of 5%. Cast-offs can only be guaranteed to be within an accuracy of 5% if a complete edited manuscript together with a full design, artwork and typographical specification is submitted to the typesetter. A charge may be made for casting-off where agreed. If the typesetter's cast-off is in error beyond this limit of 5%, no charge should be made for the extra setting involved and the typesetter may be asked to contribute to any additional expenses caused by the error provided that it can be shown that the discrepancy is the responsibility of the typesetter.

(c) The typesetter has no editorial responsibility. His task is to follow the publisher's instructions on style of setting, to set accurately from the manuscript and to correct his own errors without charge when these are marked on the proof. Where a revised proof is required, the publisher will only be responsible for checking the alterations made together with consequent changes. Care, however, needs to be taken where repagination as a consequent change is involved. As corrections can be ambiguous, it is highly recommended that publishers do request a revised proof, for the benefit of both parties. After proofs have been passed by the publisher, the typesetter is in no case liable for any error except errors introduced after the return of such passed proofs, in which case he may be required to correct the printed image in any sheets and bound books at no cost to the publisher. The typesetter/printer should return the press proofs to the publisher when the job is complete, unless otherwise instructed.

(d) The costs of any illustrations are normally charged as extra where these are not specifically estimated.

(e) All extra work asked for by the publishers, such as additional proofs, alterations to proofs, specimen pages, and press delays awaiting approval, and any experimental work carried out at the publisher's request (on disk, magnetic tape, sketches, artwork, positives, plates, presswork or binding, etc.) is charged for at supplier's current rate for such work. A charge for specimen pages may be credited by agreement against an order for setting the book.

(f) All charges arising from work extra to that covered by an estimate or scale of prices should be advised to the publisher before work commences, or, where this is impracticable, as soon as possible thereafter.

(g) Where style or layout is left to the typesetter's judgement, changes therefrom made by the publisher may be charged extra.

B Storage of electronic data

If the publisher wishes to update or re-use basic data in another form at a later date, he should clearly state on his original order his anticipated requirements. He also has the right at this stage to instruct the typesetter to store the data and to specify in what form (and whether fully corrected) it is to be stored; agreement on all matters, including costs, to be reached before work commences.

The final output (disks/tapes/CRC/film or any similar medium as specified by the publisher on his original order, or at the stage when contracts are agreed) becomes the property of the publisher when payment has been made in full.

If the typesetter agrees to store tapes/disks for the publisher he is responsible for regularly checking the condition of tapes and disks and re-running, as agreed between the two parties, to avoid corruption. The charge for re-running should normally be included in the storage charge being paid by the publisher, unless agreed otherwise, in which case the typesetter will charge the publisher the cost of re-running at a price to be agreed before work commences.

C Compatibility

Publishers should not assume compatibility between one typesetting system and another, even if the same equipment is being used. The publisher should enquire from the typesetter before placing the original order if the typesetter can supply data in a form that can be used elsewhere. The publisher might instruct the typesetter on his original order to store material in an agreed form for forward transmission.

In addition to the cost of the work, the publisher will be responsible for the material cost of the tape, disk, etc. together with insurance and storage costs, to be incorporated within the original estimate or as a separate charge – the method of charging to be agreed between parties concerned.

When transferring a tape or disk, the typesetter should provide information on the codes used where appropriate. Where a typesetter receives electronic data from a publisher he may charge for conversion programs and the manual addition of typographical codes, editorial alterations, etc. where these are required. It is open to the typesetter to negotiate with the publisher for the recovery of extra costs incurred through the supply of inadequately prepared disks.

If having agreed with the publisher to store data, the typesetter changes his system to a non-compatible system, the onus is on him to translate at his own cost any tapes/disks into an equally usable form for use on that changed system or, if the publisher wishes, hand over the original stored tapes/disks to the publishers. A change of system should not impose a cost penalty on publisher's work stored before the change.

2. Prepress platemaking, printing and binding

(a) Litho plates made by the printer are the property of the printer and may be destroyed after completion of printing (unless otherwise agreed with the publisher).

(b) Both film and photoset material used for litho platemaking become the property of the publisher when payment has been made in full. Film is usually held without storage charge for two years after invoice. Before making a storage charge for film, the printer should offer the publisher an opportunity to make his own storage arrangement. A charge to recover removal costs may be made for any film transferred, but it will be the printer's responsibility to check that the film is complete before despatch. All charges should be agreed with the publisher before implementation.

(c) Some film is produced by plate projection systems and cannot be processed without separate coded instructions, either on disk or in the form of magnetic cards. Where such instructions are individual to the work in question, rather than forming part of a more general database, these are also considered to be the publisher's property.

(d) Where offset printing is ordered separately from composition, the printer's responsibility is limited to reproducing the image supplied to him. However, any technical or other defect noticed by the printer in the material thus supplied should be brought to the publisher's attention as soon as possible.

(e) Estimates usually provide that materials, when supplied by the customer, including artwork, reproduction copy, tapes, film, plates, paper and binding materials shall be suitable for their purpose. Provided the publisher has been given adequate forewarning of costs, the printer or binder may charge for any additional work (such as retouching, film spotting, excess blanket-washing, paper conditioning, handling preprinted covers) incurred when materials are found during production to be inconsistent with the standards on which the estimates were based. Where it is not practical for such warning to be given, the publisher should be informed without delay and remedial costs passed on.

(f) Final intermediates used in the production of work for a publisher should not be destroyed or erased without the written agreement of the publisher, but the publisher should not expect the printer to store items indefinitely. The publisher is entitled to remove any such material on payment of appropriate handling charges.

(g) It is normally assumed that publisher's property (e.g. artwork, photographs, the property of third parties supplied by the publisher, etc.) is held and worked on by the printer/binder at the publisher's risk. The printer/binder should, however, exercise great care in handling and storing such property and if it is damaged before the production process is completed, the question of restitution should be the subject of negotiation between the parties. Camera-ready copy, artwork, photographs, etc. are normally returned to the publisher upon completion of manufacture unless otherwise agreed and should not be destroyed without the written agreement of the publisher.

(h) To avoid the possibility of subsequent disagreement, printing and binding orders should always be comprehensive, specifying precisely the materials the printer/binder is to use, and include the delivery date required and agreed price where appropriate.

(i) If a manufacturer folds more sheets than are covered by the publisher's initial instructions, he does so at his own risk. However, it is open to him to negotiate with the publisher to recover his folding costs if the sheets are then sold or bound.

(j) In the case of multi-volume sets, where individual volumes are not available separately, the manufacturer should charge for the production of complete sets only. Any surplus copies of individual volumes should be referred to the publisher for mutual agreement as to disposal.

(k) A storage charge may be proposed by the binder for any sheets, covers, bound stock and other material belonging to the publisher and kept on his behalf. A schedule of such items should be made to the publisher before any storage charge is made, and an opportunity given to the publisher to give disposal instructions.

(l) *Incidental imperfections* It is the responsibility of the printer or binder to make good incidental imperfections or, should this be impractical or unduly costly, he may opt to offer the publisher financial compensation as an alternative, on the basis of a fully annotated title page. This is intended to reflect the full printing and binding cost of the book and is customarily set at 25% of the published price; it is, however, accepted that it is open to the manufacturer to negotiate alternative arrangements with publishers of mass market paperbacks or specialised academic works with an extended stockholding life or where it is felt exceptional considerations apply.

(m) *Edition imperfections* It is recognised that when substantial numbers of an edition are delivered in a faulty condition, and the fault lies with the supplier, the precise remedy must be a matter for individual negotiation between publisher and printer or binder.

(n) It is the responsibility of the supplier despatching goods to ensure that accurate documentation is sent with them with a copy to the publisher.

(o) *Covers.* If the printer/binder has a specific manner in which he wants covers printed on a sheet, he should make it clear at the outset. Where covers are supplied to the binder it is the publisher's responsibility to ensure that imposition is correct. This might include the number of copies on a sheet, margins between covers for two-up binding, etc.

Trade binding

(a) When sheets, covers, or similar materials are to pass from a printer to a binder for further processing, the publisher is responsible for agreeing the necessary imposition between printer and binder.

(b) Unless specifically instructed, the binder will not count the sheets sent to him on receipt. The printer is responsible for supplying the correct number of usable sheets, including the agreed binder's spoilage allowance, and advising the binder and publisher in writing. This advice should be verified by the binder's count, which is normally carried out during the folding operation or, in the case of web-fed work or pre-folded sections, at the gathering stage.

(c) A binder cannot be held responsible for checking any defect relating to content, print quality or paper. He also relies on the printed folios to represent the correct page sequence. Any technical or other defects noticed by the binder in the material supplied for binding should be brought to the publisher's attention.

(d) The printer or binder cannot be held responsible for the transportation of components to his factory.

3. Ownership, insurance and liability

(a) Ownership of the work will normally pass to the publisher at the moment of payment in full, but a different arrangement may be mutually agreed between publisher and manufacturer.

(b) The publisher and the typesetter/printer/binder is each normally responsible for the insurance of his own property, including property in transit. The publisher's responsibility for the insurance of work done is from the earlier of:

(i) work delivered to the publisher, or to his nominated delivery address

(ii) payment in full by the publisher.

In this way the publisher insures the work from the moment when he has an insurable interest in it. The publisher is responsible for the insurance of material stored at his request in whatever form.

The typesetter is responsible in the case of a failure or loss of work in progress and should insure against such a likelihood. The value for insurance purposes should cover the cost of replacement of tapes and disks to the same stage as when they were lost or damaged. The publisher should insure for any consequential loss as a result of loss or damage.

The typesetter will not be responsible for any consequential loss.

(c) For insurance purposes the publisher's property on the supplier's premises includes all materials supplied by the publisher such as manuscripts, tapes and disks, artwork, photographs, transparencies, camera ready copy, film, paper and, where a trade binder is used, printed sheets and printed covers that have been paid for by the publisher.

(d) The typesetter/printer/binder is entitled not to proceed with any work which, in his opinion, is or may be of an illegal or libellous nature, or an infringement of third party rights.

4. Materials

(a) *Storage* As part of his service the printer holds publisher's white paper free of charge for 60 days pending instructions to print. If he is required to hold it for a longer period he may implement a storage charge, unless it is agreed that special circumstances exist, such as stock papers which are delivered and used in regular quantities.

(b) *Advice procedure* Paper supplied by the publisher should be advised to the printer before delivery and the advice note should specify the publisher and the title for which it is intended. On receipt of the paper, the printer should send the publisher an out-turn sheet quoting full details of the delivery and, if necessary, a report. Sheets and other goods provided by, or on behalf of, the publisher are not normally counted or checked when received, but the supplier should advise the publisher of any apparent shortages or damage as soon as discovered.

(c) *Paper supplied on reel* Before ordering, the publisher should ask the printer to specify the type of reel centre required, maximum diameter of reel and type of splice, and any other special requirements.

The publisher should instruct the paper supplier to ensure that the end wrapping is flat, any joins are clearly marked, that a specification giving full details of each consignment, including the actual metre length per reel, is sent when the reels are delivered, and that delivery dates are arranged with the printer.

The printer's spoilage is calculated on a length basis not on a weight basis. Reels are not checked when supplied, but the printer should advise the publisher of any shortage or damage as soon as possible.

(d) *Spoilage allowances* Where the publisher supplies the paper, the printer must specify in his estimate the quantity and sheet or reel size of paper required, including an allowance for printing and binding spoilage. It must be emphasised that this allowance should always be mutually agreed beforehand, particularly in the case of recycled or thin papers where higher than normal allowances may be required. Any use of material in excess of the specified quantity should be notified to the publisher and the cost borne by the printer, unless it is an agreed paper fault or change to the specification.

(e) *Binding* If the binding is to be done in quantities smaller than the print run, it is the publisher's responsibility to allow for the extra binder's spoilage required, if necessary by increasing the print order. Each individual binding order will necessitate a spoilage allowance. For the first and last sections the publisher may need to allow the binder more spoilage than for the rest of the book.

5. General

A Outwork

Certain elements of the work may have to be subcontracted because the supplier is not equipped to execute them. Where a supplier needs to subcontract work which he would normally do, he should consult his customer, where practical, before doing so. During the period of outwork the supplier retains sole responsibility for any costs incurred, the quality of the work, the production of the quantity of copies, and completion of the work by the date previously agreed; and for insurance in accordance with Section 3. A separate invoice must not be submitted, unless agreed in advance with the Publisher.

B Schedules and delays

(a) A production schedule, where timing is critical, should be submitted and agreed in writing, based on a realistic assessment of the circumstances at the time. Any delay on either side should be notified to the other parties concerned as soon as it is foreseen, and the remainder of the schedule re-negotiated.

If the manufacturer has reserved machinery time for a particular order at the customer's request and the order is postponed, then the customer and manufacturer should make every effort to find other suitable work to fill the reserved time. If neither party can find such suitable work, it is open to the manufacturer to seek to negotiate appropriate compensation.

(b) A broken promise of delivery by an agreed date does not constitute a breach of contract if it is caused by *force majeure* (as generally recognised in the printing industry) nor, if caused in any other way, does it involve a penalty unless:

1. a penalty for any delay in completion has been agreed; and

2. the customer has not himself defaulted on any dates in the agreed schedule for the work.

C Cancellation

Orders can only be cancelled on terms that compensate the supplier for any costs incurred for any material purchased or services performed, unless the publisher can demonstrate that the supplier is responsible for the grounds of cancellation.

D Terms of payment

Terms of payment, including any special arrangements such as stage payments and the charging of interest on overdue amounts, etc., should be agreed between supplier and customer before the order is placed. In the absence of such prior agreement, payment will be in 30 days.

The following are examples of current practice:

(a) Typesetting is customarily invoiced on completion of the contracted process. However, where a single supplier is responsible for composition and machining, the invoice may be rendered for the two processes if agreed in advance.

(b) Interim payments may, in certain circumstances, be negotiated for composition, machining or binding.

(c) It is normal practice to allow a plus or minus tolerance of 5% on the ordered quantity of books. If all books are bound in the first instance the invoiced quantity printed should be the same as the invoiced quantity bound when produced by the same supplier. If shortages occur, the publisher reserves the right to invoice the printer or binder for the excess use of materials (if supplied by the publisher) relative to that shortfall. It is a matter for negotiation between manufacturer and publisher as to how variations from these tolerances are dealt with.

If it is important that the publisher receives the exact number of copies ordered or not less than the exact number, this should be made clear when the quotation is sought and clearly stated on the order. This usually occurs with short-run printing.

(d) Except where covered by prior agreement, an invoice for composition may be rendered 60 days after completion of any proofing stage, where the proofs have not been returned to the supplier for further work to be done.

(e) Where materials are supplied by the printer, the charge for such materials shall be invoiced as part of the printing or binding as appropriate. Paper may only be invoiced in advance by the printer by prior agreement.

(f) The existence of an unresolved query on the invoice does not release the publisher from his obligation to pay the parts of the invoice not under query.

(g) VAT will be charged where appropriate whether or not it has been included in the estimate.

Customs of the trade for the production of periodicals

Although many origination houses and suppliers have detailed contracts with periodical publishers, their work is often also based on the standard conditions of contract issued by the British Printing Industries Federation. However, such conditions do not fully cover all aspects of periodical production and the purpose of this [section] is to clarify the customs of the periodical trade on all relevant points.

[This section] does not affect, and is not intended to affect, the position of the origination house and printer not engaged in magazine and journal production. It should also be noted that the customs recommended can be varied by mutual agreement between parties to a contract and that they are without legal effect unless they are specifically incorporated into a particular contract. Even where the customs do not have a legal effect, however, publishers and suppliers may feel that they provide a suitable basis for settlement in the event of a dispute.

Customs of the Trade for the Production of Periodicals was provided by a joint PPA/BPIF Working Party and has been formally accepted by the two associations, and registered at the Office of Fair Trading.

1. Terms of payment

Terms of payment, including such special arrangements as stage payments, are normally agreed between supplier and customer before the order is placed. In the absence of such prior agreement, payment is due 30 days from the date the printed work is delivered. It is in the interest of both parties that invoices are rendered as promptly as possible following delivery. The following are examples of current practice:

▶ Where prepress material is ordered separately, an invoice may be rendered on completion of this part of the contract;

▶ Where a single supplier is responsible for composition and machining, the invoice may be rendered on completion of machining;

▶ Where a single supplier is responsible for machining and binding, the invoice may be rendered on delivery of bound copies;

▶ Interim payments may be negotiated for unusually large, slow or complex orders for prepress work, machining or binding;

▶ Except where covered by a prior agreement, an invoice for prepress work may be rendered 60 days after completion of a proofing stage if the proofs have not been returned to the supplier for further work to be done.

2. Origination material

Regardless of ownership, origination material supplied by a publisher for the production of periodicals should not be destroyed without the written agreement of the publisher, but the publisher should not expect the supplier to store items indefinitely. A storage period, usually 13 months, should be agreed in advance.

Publisher's property (and artwork, photograph, the property of third parties supplied by the publisher) is normally held and worked on by the supplier at the publisher's risk. The supplier should, however, exercise reasonable care in handling and storing such property. Film, digital and origination materials produced by the supplier or origination house remain the property of the printer or origination house unless otherwise agreed. It is recommended that arrangements are made for such materials to become the property of the publisher when payment has been made in full.

There should be some specific arrangement regarding the loss or damage liability of transparencies from picture libraries because replacement value can be high. The supplier may need to break the seal, using all reasonable care, on photo library pictures in order to scan them, in which case the publisher would be liable for any damage to the material involved in so doing.

Paying for the faulty output of corrupted modems or disks is the publisher's liability. Also, if charges for modems or the use of fax are to be incurred as an extra, prior agreement is needed in respect of the basis of these charges, including a clear understanding of who is responsible for the maintenance and support of hardware and software. The same principle applies to messenger services (without prejudice to clause 7).

Lithographic plates made by the supplier are normally the property of the supplier and may be destroyed when printing is completed, unless the publisher has made a specific request to the contrary in writing.

3. Insurance

Publisher and supplier are each normally responsible for the insurance of their own property, including property in transit, but see clause 8 on paper. The publisher's responsibility for the insurance of work done is either from the time the work is:

▶ delivered to his nominated supplier;

▶ payment is made by the publisher, whichever is the earlier.

In this way the publishing company insures the work from the moment it has an insurable interest in it. The publisher is responsible for the insurance of material stored by the supplier at the publisher's request in whatever form, unless agreed specifically otherwise in writing. Value for insurance purposes should cover the cost of replacement to the same stage as when lost. Suppliers do not normally cover any liability for the publisher's consequential loss.

The agreement should clarify what materials or data are covered by the respective insurance arrangements of publisher and supplier, including the position with regard to materials supplied by other parties (inserts etc). Examples of publisher's property on the supplier's premises which should be insured are all material supplied by the publisher such as disks, manuscripts, artwork, photographs, transparencies, programming tapes, camera-ready copy, film, paper and printed sheets owned by the publisher or supplied from other suppliers (inserts etc.).

Where modem equipment is dedicated to a publisher or specific periodical, agreement is need on insurance against total failure and disaster recovery and third party misconduct.

4. Variations from quotation

The following are examples of current practice (the expression 'supplier' here includes the origination house).

▶ Suppliers quote and charge for handling copy as received. Charges for additional work, and any additional charge that may arise from illegible or unclear copy not previously seen, should be agreed. It is the responsibility of the supplier to ensure that the final output matches the final approved proof, subject to normal tolerances.

▶ Where style or layout is left to the supplier's judgement, changes made by the publisher may incur an extra charge.

▶ The charges for authors' corrections should be agreed between the publisher and the supplier.

▶ The publisher should agree with the supplier the number of proofs required and be charged accordingly. Publisher and supplier should be clear as to what type of proof is acceptable: dry colour (e.g. Cromalin or Matchprint), inkjet, dye sublimation or any other form.

▶ All extra work undertaken for the publisher may be charged at the rate agreed subject to prior authorisation, where practical. Causes of extra work include requests for additional proofs, alterations to proofs, extra planning, specimen pages, press delays and extra planning incurred by the late arrival of editorial material and delay in gaining approval. Additional experimental work carried out at the publisher's request (on sketches, artwork, positives, plates, press-work or binding, and so on) may also be charged at an agreed rate.

▶ Costs arising from work which the publisher and the supplier agree is additional to that covered by the quotation or scale of prices may be charged for at a reasonable rate.

▶ Overmatter produced but not used will be charged at the current rates.

5. Liability for error

Origination from manuscript or digital file

The supplier has no editorial responsibility other than to follow the publisher's instructions on style, to set accurately from the manuscript and to correct his own errors without charge when these are marked on the proof. After proofs have been passed by the publisher, the supplier is not liable for any error in origination, although errors introduced after the return of such passed proofs are the responsibility of the supplier. It should be established at the outset whether the supplier is responsible for reading and marking first proofs or whether first proofs will be corrected before dispatch to the publisher.

Offset printing ordered separately from origination

In the case of offset printing ordered separately from origination, the supplier's responsibility is limited to reproducing the image supplied by the publisher. Any technical or other defect noticed by the supplier in the material supplied by the publisher for reproduction should be brought to the publisher's attention.

Claims

In the event of a claim from the publisher for defective work, the supplier's liability is normally limited to the production value of the work and materials used in respect of the defective areas. However, in certain circumstances, it may be necessary for negotiations to take place between the publisher and the supplier.

6. Illegal matter

The supplier shall not be required to print any matter that, in his opinion is or may be, of an obscene, illegal or libellous nature or is an infringement of the proprietary or other rights of any third party. The supplier must immediately inform the publisher if these circumstances arise. The supplier is entitled to seek indemnification in writing by the publisher in respect of any claims, costs and expenses arising out of any libellous matter, or any infringement of copyright, patent, design or any proprietary or personal rights contained in any material originated or printed for the publisher.

The indemnity may extend to any amounts paid on a lawyer's advice in settlement of any claim.

7. Materials supplied by or on behalf of the publisher

▶ Estimates usually provide that materials when supplied by the customer, including disks, artwork, copy for reproduction, takes, film, plates and paper, are suitable for their purpose. Provided the publisher has adequate forewarning, where practical, of the cost, the supplier may charge for additional work (disk intervention, retouching, film spotting, extra planning, paper conditioning, excess blanket washing, reduced machine running speeds, handling pre-printed covers etc.) incurred when materials are found during production to be inconsistent with the standard on which the estimate was based.

► Standards for colour origination: The Periodical Publishers Association and the Periodical Printers Section of the BPIF both endorse the specification for offset printing produced by the International Federation of the Periodical Press. Copies of the latest version (published in January 1995) of this publication are available from PPA and the BPIF.

► Sheets, reels and other goods provided by, or on behalf of, the publisher are not normally counted or checked when received, but a routine should be agreed (as part of the BS5750 or ISO9000 standard for example) for handling documentary evidence of delivery. The supplier should advise the publisher of any apparent shortages or damage.

► It is the responsibility of the supplier that despatches the goods to ensure that accurate documentation is sent with them.

► Inserts as supplied to any agreed specification by a third party and delivered to the supplier should be clearly marked with the quantity, the title and issue for which they are intended and details of overs, and should be accompanied by written notification from the publisher for reference purposes. Adequate notification from the publisher on all inserts should be sent to the supplier.

8. Paper supplied by the publisher

Storage

The supplier and publisher should agree on a minimum quantity of the publisher's paper, defined by tonnage or by number of issues, to be stored free on the supplier's premises. The supplier will be responsible for storing this under suitable conditions. The supplier and publisher should agree which of them has the responsibility for insuring the publisher's paper while it is on the supplier's premises.

Advice procedure

Details of the paper supplied by the publisher should be given to the supplier before delivery. The advice note should specify the quantity, the title and the publisher for which it is intended and the paper should be clearly identified as being the property of the publisher. When the supplier receives the paper he should, in addition to reporting any discrepancies or damage, confirm the storage address.

Consumption

Paper should be used in the sequence in which it is delivered: oldest stock used first, unless otherwise agreed in writing. The supplier should send the publisher regular usage and stock returns, normally five days after the completion of printing of an issue. If requested by the publisher, the supplier should retain for inspection slab waste and wrappings from an issue.

Paper supplied on reel

Before ordering the paper, the publisher should confirm with the supplier the full specification of the type and size of reel core required, including width and maximum diameter.

Each reel should be clearly identified and the information provided on each reel label should be discussed with the supplier. Minimum requirements include: mill name, batch number, publisher, title, direction of unwind, metreage, date of making, weight, substance and reel width.

The publisher should instruct the paper supplier to ensure that the end wrapping is flat, so that the reels can be stored correctly on end, that documentation giving full details of each consignment is sent when the reels are delivered and that delivery dates are arranged with the supplier. It is the supplier's responsibility to ensure that reels are handled and stored efficiently.

The publisher should agree with the supplier the basis on which spoilage will be calculated (for example length, numbers of cut-offs, weight and the amount of waste slabbed off reels). There should be agreement that the amount of waste which is slabbed off reels should be kept to a maximum number of millimetres/kilos.

Defective material

When running paper, the supplier should advise the publisher of any defective material as soon as he is aware of it and should keep evidence.

Spoilage allowances

The supplier should specify in his quotation the quantity of paper to be supplied. A spoilage allowance for printing should be included in his calculations.

Guidelines for paper spoilage

It is impossible to give guidelines that will be applicable in all circumstances. Different types of press will result in significant variations. There are also, inevitably, specific problems which arise from week to week.

The points which should be taken into consideration include:

▶ length of run
▶ number of colours per section, number of webs
▶ type of binding
▶ weight and standard of paper (i.e. coated or uncoated)
▶ additional processes such as lamination, varnishing and so on
▶ quality of the final product
▶ age of equipment in use.

Waste agreements normally specify a number of cut-offs/sheets for make-ready and a percentage for running. The total number of sheets/cut-offs is then specified as a percentage waste and is used to make-ready in the bindery.

The spoilage allowance must be agreed between the two parties prior to the start of the contract. It is essential that suppliers and publishers are constantly vigilant to ensure that paper is not wasted by carelessness. This is an increasingly expensive commodity and both parties have a vested interest in keeping wastage to a minimum. Publishers sometimes agree with suppliers that when wastage levels are lower than the agreed norm the value of any savings should be shared.

The figures that follow are based on the printing of a magazine-format periodical of medium quality using the same coated paper throughout the run and include binding spoilage. They should not be used as a criterion for complex production, for high-quality magazines (where the spoilage may necessarily be higher), for tabloid newspaper-format publications where less critical quality may be acceptable or for production involving complicated binding requirements.

Start-up waste represents the number of sheets or cut-offs spoilt up to the first good copy. Running waste represents a percentage of copies normally spoilt in the printing, folding and binding process. Running waste normally reduces as print runs increase.

Example of web offset spoilage calculations:

	mono only	mono and spot	four colour
Running	8%	9%	10%
Start-up copies	2500	3500	4000
30,000 copies			
Start-up for a four-colour publication			4000
Running waste of 10.0% on a 30,000 print order			3000
Total waste			7000 copies

In order to get 30,000 good copies, a total of 37,000 copies will need to be produced, a spoilage allowance of 23.3% being required on the print order of 30,000.

Example of sheetfed spoilage calculations:

	mono only	mono and spot	four colour
Running	6%	7%	9%
Start-up	500	650	800
8000 copies			
Start-up for a four-colour publication			800
Running waste of 9% on a 8000 print order			720
Total waste			1520 copies

In order to get 8000 good copies, a total of 9520 copies will need to be produced, a spoilage allowance of 19% being required on the print order of 8000.

Any problems arising from the quality of paper stocks should be notified to the publisher immediately and discussions held to negotiate revised paper spoilage rates.

9. Schedule and delays

A production schedule for all work should be submitted and agreed in advance in writing, and should be based on a realistic assessment of the circumstances at the time. Any delay on either side should be notified to other parties concerned as soon as it is foreseen, and the remainder of the schedule re-negotiated. Any additional costs incurred by supplier or publisher must be agreed in advance on the basis of 'normal trading practice' of both parties.

10. Outwork

It is not acceptable for the supplier to sub-contract the publisher's work unless this has been agreed in advance. If there is outwork, the supplier retains sole responsibility for quality and quantity, for the completion of the work according to schedule and for insurance (see clause 3).

11. Liability

The supplier is not liable for any loss to the publisher arising from delay in transit not caused by the supplier or the supplier's sub-contractor.

12. Notice period and insolvency

A contract for the printing of a periodical may not be terminated by either party unless 13 weeks' notice in writing is given in the case of periodicals which are produced monthly or more frequently, and with 26 weeks' notice in writing in the case of bi-monthlies, quarterlies and annuals, unless the title is closed, where other arrangements may need to be made between publisher and supplier. Notice may be given at any time but wherever possible should be given after work on any one issue is completed.

Nevertheless, either party may terminate any such contract forthwith should the other be in breach of the agreement; both parties should note that this includes non-payment of sums due.

Both parties should ensure that there is provision in the terms and conditions for loss caused by the default of either party through default for reasons of insolvency or change of ownership. Legal advice should be sought in these circumstances.

13. Force majeure

Either party should be excused from performance of its obligations if and to the extent that such performance is hindered or prevented (directly or indirectly) by reason of any strike, lockout, labour disturbance, government action, riot, armed conflict, fire, flood, drought, failure of power supply, unavailability or breakdown of normal means of transport, inability to procure materials required for the performance of the contract, act of God or any other matter whatsoever beyond the party's reasonable control ('*force majeure* event') provided always that the party uses its best endeavours to limit the effect of the force majeure event. In the event that performance by either publisher or the supplier is prevented by any force majeure event, then either party may give the other written notice to terminate the contract and pay for work done and materials used, as mutually agreed, but subject to that should accept performance of the contract when reasonably practicable.

14. Disputes

Independent arbitration services are available to both parties if necessary. The BPIF will assist if its members are involved, offering a service that will appoint an independent arbitrator. Pira International is an alternative and the Institute of Printing maintains a list of accredited consultants. Some contracts include agreed procedures to be followed in the case of disputes.

15. Confidentiality

Each party to a contract is entitled to expect the other to respect the confidentiality of the details of the agreement, and the business of information supplied by the other party.

16. Law

An agreement should specify the law under which it is governed and in the UK this is usually English law.

FIPP specification for European gravure printing of periodicals

The specification for European gravure printing was set up to ensure a more uniform and standardised approach so that the same page appearing in several different magazines across Europe will, in each case, match the original (and each other) as closely as possible.

Introduction

The publication of specifications is an evolutionary process because it does, in fact, provide only a snapshot of technology available at that moment. As part of this evolutionary trend the FIPP Production Committee sought to publish a summary of the current practices of European gravure magazine printers for the benefit of publishers and advertisers.

The purpose of this specification is to ensure a more uniform and standardised approach so that the same page appearing in several different magazines across Europe will, in each case, match the original (and each other) as closely as possible. At present, this can be best achieved by supplying each printer with a set of final colour separation films and photo-mechanical proofs made in accordance with this specification. It is now becoming possible to supply digital data in place of final colour separation films. There are benefits to be derived from this but there are also some problems to be solved before it can become universally acceptable. FIPP is developing a specification addressing these issues.

Film separations
and proofing

This specification was produced by the International Federation of the Periodical Press (FIPP) and the European Rotogravure Association (ERA). Any questions concerning its use should be directed to: International Federation of the Periodical Press, Queens House, 55/56 Lincoln's Inn Fields, London WC2A 3LJ, UK. Telephone: (+44) (0)207 404 4169. Fax: (+44) (0)207 404 4170. Email: info@fipp.com. Web: www.fipp.com

1. Scope

This specification is for the supply of final films with proofs to publication gravure printers, for the printing of periodicals. Most European gravure printers are able to produce acceptable results from film separations made for the web offset litho printing process. Some problems may arise, however, with screen angles, screen rulings and highlight dots. These problems can be avoided by following this specification. There are other minor variations between individual gravure printers due to slight differences in the inks and these cannot be avoided when using a common set of separation films. These differences are not normally great enough to cause unacceptable results.

The forme cylinders may be engraved from digital data by scanning final films or opalines made from them. A few printers continue to use the etching process. This specification applies to all three methods of forme cylinder production.

2. Page design and colour specification

2.1 Fine lettering

Thin lines, box rules, medium and small size typematter and detail should ideally be reproduced in one colour only. Perfect registration of such images in more than one colour cannot be guaranteed and the slightest movement during the printing run will result in colour fringing.

2.2 Reverse lettering

Reversals should be made using a minimum of colour. Typematter or detail smaller than 8-point size should ideally be reversed out of one process colour only. When reversals out of more than one colour are necessary, it is best to use the dominant colour, e.g. black or cyan, for the shape of the letters and undercut the letter shapes, i.e. apply grip, in the subordinate colours. This will reduce register problems. Small letters or letters with fine serifs should not be used for reversals since the slightest mis-register will create colour fringing, showing colour in the white type areas. Care should also be taken to ensure the background for reverse lettering is dark enough to give good legibility.

2.3 Undercolour removal (UCR)/Grey component replacement (GCR)

Colour separations can be produced using either normal undercolour removal (UCR) or grey component replacement (GCR) techniques. Irrespective of the technique used, the maximum sum percentage of the four process colours in the dark shadow areas should not be greater than 280% when printing on uncoated paper. This figure may be exceeded for prestige work or when running on coated paper, but this may be at the expense of reduced press speeds and higher ink consumption and therefore must be discussed with the individual printer.

Levels of UCR or GCR will depend on subject matter and individual publisher and printer preference, and therefore must be discussed with the individual printer.

Where a large solid black background is to be reproduced it is recommended to run 40% cyan under the solid black to give extra density.

2.4 Overprinting

Care should be taken to ensure that lettering or detail to overprint will have sufficient contrast against the background tone to be legible.

2.5 Tint or special colour backgrounds

When a common colour background is required on more than one page or part of a feature, careful consideration should be given to the use of not more than two process colours to enable the printer to provide a consistent result across all areas.

A minimum of 8% in each process colour used in a tint block is recommended to ensure uniform reproduction. For single-colour tint areas, particularly yellow, to be clearly visible against unprinted paper, a minimum of 15% is suggested.

2.6 Grey balance

On proofs made with colourants to match the gravure process, typical neutral grey balance at 50% is yellow 38% , magenta 38% and cyan 50%. At 20%, yellow is 14%, magenta 14% and cyan 20%. The printed grey balance may vary slightly according to the ink formulations used by the printer.

2.7 Highlight dots

The minimum dot that can be held on the run with certainty is 5%. Colour separation films should, however, contain dots below this value to ensure smooth gradations and vignettes. In those cases where it is necessary to hold the edge of a picture it is preferable to use a dot of at least 8% in the dominant colour. Good firm film dot quality is essential.

3. Halftone screening

3.1 Screen ruling

Most gravure printers prefer to use 70 lines per centimetre (175 lines per inch) screen ruling, but films of 60 lines per centimetre (150 lines per inch) are acceptable. This applies for magazine printing on both coated and uncoated paper. If necessary, it is possible to engrave cylinders using a mixture of final films in the range of 60–70 lines per centimetre screen ruling. Films outside this range can be used but only in agreement with the printer.

3.2 Screen angles

Any normal combinations of angles can be used, but it is best to avoid 45° especially in the case of black. The use of 90°, 45° and 0° angle films can give rise to problems in the conversion process. Angles of 7.5° and 82.5° should be avoided except in the case of yellow. The reason is to ensure that no visible moiré patterning occurs as a result of the conversion process.

3.3 Dot shape

Dot shape has no significant effect in the engraving process since the shape of the ink cells is not determined by the shape of the dot on the film. Dot shape does, however, have an effect on the visual appearance of the proof, where elliptical dots appear to give smoother results and square dots slightly sharper results. It is important to keep to the same dot family within a set of colour separations.

4. Final film separations

4.1 Image orientation and presentation

Final film should be positives right reading emulsion down. They must be clearly marked for colour and contain register marks outside the trim area. Only minimal correction is permissible and must be on the non-emulsion side of the film.

4.2 Film quality

All films must be one piece, hard dot, free from kinks, spots and scratches, on 0.1mm thick (0.00in) polyester base. The clear film density should not exceed 0.05 and the solid tone density should be at least 3.5. Note: New film technologies may not achieve this specification, but may be acceptable to some printers. Note: Some printers engrave directly from the separation films. In this case the films should be 0.18mm thick polyester-based material.

5. Colour proofing

The customer proof should provide a consistent result that can be matched in production. Both the substrate and the colourants play an important part in achieving this objective. Photomechanical proofs such as Cromalin, Matchprint and Signature are suitable and are capable of giving a close, if not perfect, match to the production run. Direct Digital Colour Proofs such as Iris inkjet, Stork inkjet, Kodak Approval and 3M Digital Matchprint may be acceptable to the printer. The use of sheetfed offset litho ink-on-paper proofs is not recommended. In the absence of a specification for proofs from the individual printer, the following guidelines should be acceptable.

5.1 Substrate

Where possible, the substrate should be the same as with the production run. Under certain circumstances Cromalin proofs can be produced using the substrate from the production run.

For proofing systems where a proprietary substrate is required, a shade matching the production stock should be used. These are readily available. A CIELab colorimetric specification for the substrate for a typical magazine paper could be:

L* 92.0 ± 2.0
a* 1.0 ± 1.0
b* 4.0 ± 3.0

These values refer to CIE Daylight Illuminant D50, CIE Standard Observer 2°, a geometry of 45/0 and measurement on a stack of several sheets of the substrate (the so-called 'white backing').

5.2 Colour gamut

Colourants are available from the proofing system suppliers to conform to the ISO 2846 (CEI 13–67) standard litho inks. Other colourants are available to give closer conformity to gravure inks and these should be used wherever possible. Application data sheets are available from the different proofing systems' manufacturers providing their recommendations.

5.3 Control strips

Appropriate control strips must be evident on all proofs. They must be exposed emulsion side down, be in register, and only original films must be used. Standard 60 lines per centimetre (150 lines per inch) control strips will enable all the necessary control measurements to be made.

These are solid tone density and dot gain.

5.4 Solid tone density

When colourants which conform to typical gravure inks are used, the proof should give the following solid tone densities, as measured using densitometers with the filter characteristic indicated below:

Type of filter	yellow	magenta	cyan	black
Narrow band polarised	1.40	1.60	1.50	1.80
Narrow band non-polarised	1.25	1.40	1.30	1.50
Broad band polarised	1.00	1.50	1.40	1.80
Broad band non-polarised	0.90	1.30	1.25	1.50
Tolerance	±0.10	±0.10	±0.10	±0.10

To identify the type of densitometer filter, please consult the supplier or the instruction manual, or see Annex A (overleaf).

5.5 Dot gain

Dot gain is of far less importance in gravure printing than in litho printing. The reason is that the gravure process varies the ink film thickness as well as the dot size from highlight to shadow. It is important, however, that the proof is made in accordance with the same dot gains that would be used for web offset lithography on coated paper. The dot gain values at 40% dot should be in the range 17–21%.

5.6 Proofing sequence

If there is a choice of proofing sequence, it is recommended to proof in the same colour sequence as on the production run, i.e. yellow, magenta, cyan, black.

6. Viewing of originals and proofs

Correct viewing conditions are essential for effective appraisal of originals and proofs. The same applies for checking proofs with running copies. These viewing conditions must conform to ISO 3664 that corresponds with BS 950 part II. In brief, the illuminant should match CIE Daylight Illuminant D50, the illumination level should be 2000 lux, and the surround should be a neutral, medium-grey colour.

Annex A Information

Densitometer categorisation

The following information, in combination with 5.2, may be used to determine the appropriate density targets for a number of commonly used densitometers.

Narrow band polarised
APS 3
Gretag Series D 140/160/180/190
Macbeth Series 1240 PO
Techkon R412
Vipdens 800P/900P
X-Rite Series ELP 404/408/414/418/428

Narrow band non-polarised
Macbeth RD
914/918/920/1056/1118
Macbeth Series 1240/1250
Vipdens 800/900
X-Rite Series E 404/408/414/418/428

Broad band polarised
Gretag D1/122
Macbeth Series 1230 PO
X-Rite Series GLP 404/408/414/418/428

Broad band non-polarised

Cosar SOS 40/61

Macbeth Series 1230

Macbeth RD 917/923/926/514

X-Rite Series G 404/408/414/418/428

FIPP specification for European offset litho printed periodicals

The specification for European offset printing, published for all personnel involved in publishing, advertising, design, print and origination of film separations and proofs to be printed in offset litho periodicals. The purpose of the specification is to ensure not only a uniform input of material to the printer, but also to build into the proofs as many of the characteristics of the production run as possible.

Introduction

Since it was first published in July 1984, the *FIPP Specification for Offset Litho Printed Periodicals* has been accepted widely across Europe by all sides of the Graphic Arts Industry.

This (fourth) edition incorporates recent changes that have taken place in the constantly evolving technology in the industry.

This specification is published for the benefit of all personnel involved in publishing, advertising, design, printing and prepress activities.

The purpose of the specification is to ensure not only a uniform input of final films to the printer, but also to ensure the proofs match the production run as closely as possible. A standardised approach will provide more consistent reproduction across a spectrum of printers, papers and publications.

The FIPP Specification of European Offset Litho Printed Periodicals is the responsibility of the FIPP Production Committee which, chaired by David Richards of Readers' Digest, is composed of representatives from all sides of the Graphic Arts Industry.

Any questions concerning its use should be directed to: FIPP, Imperial House, 15–19 Kingsway, London WC2B 6UN. Tel: (+44) (0)171 379 3822.
Fax: (+44) (0)171 379 3866. E-mail: FIPP.NEMO@NEMO.GEIS.COM

Film separations and poofing

1. Scope

FIPP specification for the production of final films to be printed in periodicals and magazines by the offset litho process.

2. Page design and colour separation

2.1 Fine lettering

Fine lines, box rules, medium and small size typematter and detail should ideally be reproduced in one colour only. Perfect registration of such images in more than one colour cannot be guaranteed and the slightest movement during printing will result in colour fringing.

2.2 Reverse lettering

Reversals should be made using a minimum of colour. Typematter or detail smaller than 8pt size should, ideally, be reversed out of one process colour only. When reversals out of more than one colour are necessary it is best to use the dominant colour, e.g. black or cyan, for the shape of the letters and undercut the letter shapes, i.e. apply grip in the subordinate colours. This will reduce any effects of slight misregister.

Small letters with fine serifs should not be used for reversals since the slightest mis-register even with grip applied will create colour fringing showing colour in the white type areas. Care should also be taken to ensure the background for reverse lettering is dark enough to give good legibility.

2.3 Undercolour removal (UCR)/Grey component replacement (GCR)

Colour separations can be produced using either normal undercolour remover (UCR) or grey component replacement (GCR) techniques. Irrespective of the technique used, the maximum sum percentage of the four process colours in the shadow areas should not be greater than 300% when printing on coated paper. The use of uncoated paper or light weight coated paper may demand a lower ink coverage and this should be discussed between the individual printer and the publisher.

Levels of UCR or GCR will depend on subject matter as well as individual publisher and printer preference and should be discussed between the printer and the publisher concerned.

Where a large solid black background is to be reproduced, it is recommended to add 40% cyan under the solid black to give extra density.

2.4 Overprinting

Particular care should be taken to ensure that lettering or detail to overprint will have sufficient contrast against the background to be legible.

2.5 Tint or special colour background

When a common colour background is required on more than one page or parts of a feature, careful consideration should be given to the use of not more than two process colours to enable the printer to provide a consistent result across all areas.

2.6 Grey balance

On proofs made with colorants to match the offset litho process, typical neutral grey balance is produced by cyan at 50%, magenta 40% and yellow at 40%. With a 20% dot area of cyan, magenta is 14% and yellow is 14%.

3. Halftone screening

3.1 Screen ruling

Conventional screen rulings of 60 or 70 lines per centimetre (150 or 175 lines per inch) are preferable when used for printing on coated papers. Screen rulings of 48 or 54 lines per centimetre (120 or 133 lines per inch) are suitable for printing on uncoated papers.

3.2 Screen angles

Any standard combination of angles can be used in order to avoid moiré patterns. Good results are obtained with the yellow at 0° or 90° and the dominant chromatic colour at 45°.

3.3 Dot shape

Elliptical dot formations are recommended to assist smooth tonal changes where the first corner link-up is between 40% and 45% and the second corner link-up is between 55% and 65%.

3.4 FM (stochastic) screens

This screen process has become widely available in rips and in software packages for use in conjunction with film recorders. In the case of normal screening, the dots are equidistant but vary in size. In the case of FM screening the dots are all the same size, but the spacing between them varies. There is minimal risk of moiré patterns and the printed result appears more like continuous tone than halftone. On the other hand, because the tone transfer characteristics (dot gain/dot loss) are different, the printer and the publisher must be consulted before FM screen films are supplied.

4. Final film separations

4.1 Image orientation and presentation

The final film should be right reading emulsion side down. Each colour should be clearly marked and contain register marks outside the trim area. Only minimal correction is permissible and must be carried out on the non-emulsion side of the film. Some publishers may require more than one set of positives or negatives, please refer to individual rate cards.

4.2 Film quality

All films must be one piece 'hard dot' free from kinks spots or scratches on 0.1 mm (0.004 inch) thick polyester base. The clear film density should not exceed 0.05 and the solid tone density should be at least 3.5. The fringe on any dot should not be wider than 5 microns. Note: New film technologies may not achieve the above density specification but may be acceptable to some printers. In any case a mixture of film types is not recommended.

5. Colour proofing – technical detail

The colour proof should provide a result that can be matched in production printing. The parameters in this part of the specification have therefore been derived from production data and should be applied to both on-press and off-press proofing.

5.1 Proofing stock paper

Wherever possible the paper being used for production printing should be used for proofing. Otherwise one of the following categories will be acceptable, and should be selected to correspond with the journal's printing stock:

1) Coated super calendered woodfree pulp paper

2) Coated super calendered mechanical pulp paper

3) Web-sized super calendered mechanical pulp paper.

The typical physical properties for each of these categories are shown in the Table 3.1 (page 138).

Consult specific publishers as to which category of paper applies.

5.2 Colourants

The colourants should conform to European Standard CEI 30-89 Part 2 or equivalent national standards.

Annex A Information

Densitometer categorisation

The following information, in combination with 5.2, may be used to determine the appropriate density targets for a number of commonly used densitometers.

Narrow band polarised

APS 3

Gretag Series D 140/160/180/190

Macbeth Series 1240 PO

Techkon R412

Vipdens 800P/900P

X-Rite Series ELP 404/408/414/418/428

Narrow band non-polarised

Macbeth RD

914/918/920/1056/1118

Macbeth Series 1240/1250

Vipdens 800/900

X-Rite Series E 404/408/414/418/428

Broad band polarised

Gretag D1/122

Macbeth Series 1230 PO

X-Rite Series GLP 404/408/414/418/428

Broad band non-polarised
Cosar SOS 40/61

Macbeth Series 1230

Macbeth RD 917/923/926/514

X-Rite Series G 404/408/414/418/428

5.3 Dot gain
It is now universally understood that an increase in apparent tone value occurs between film and printed dot (dot gain). The level of increase depends on several factors, including ink flow properties, blankets and cylinder pressures, paper type, machine and dampening conditions, platemaking and others. It is vital that a similar level of dot gain, which is recognised to be representative of most production presses, is incorporated in the proofs. The lists of dot gains shown in Tables 3.2 and 3.3 (overleaf) is currently deemed representative for paper grades covered by these specifications when printing from either positive or negative working plates. Dot area is calculated using the Murray–Davies formula, with measurements made on 60 lines per centimetre (150 lines per inch) control strips.

Note: In order to maintain grey balance, the dot gain in cyan, magenta and yellow should be uniformly high or low. A tolerance window of ±2% is permitted. Dot gain in the black tends to be slightly higher and the tolerance window may be +4%–0%. In situations where it is possible to monitor only a single tone value, it should be a midtone (40–50%) rather than a shadow tone.

5.4 Proof densities
Proofs should have solid-tone densities, as shown in Table 3.4 for coated woodfree mechanical pulp super calendered papers and Table 3.5 for web-sized mechanical pulp super calendered paper (page 139), when measured on the categories of paper defined above in 5.1.

In the case of coated mechanical pulp super calendered paper, a tolerance of ±0.1 is allowable, but for coated woodfree super calendered paper −0.0 to +0.2 is acceptable, providing that, as with the former grade, deviations are uniformly high or low across the subjects on the sheet.

In the case of web-sized mechanical pulp super calendered papers a tolerance of ±0.1 is permitted but must be uniformly high or low. To identify the type of filter please consult the supplier of the densitometer and refer also to Annex A.

TABLE 3.1 Physical properties of different papers

	Coat woodfree	Coated mechanical	Uncoated mechanical
Toughness (using Bendtsen [ml/min])			
Based on BS 4420	10–20	20–40	40–60
Toughness (micrometers)			
Based on Parker Print-Surf	1.2–1.4	1.4–1.8	1.7–2.1
Brightness			
Based on ISO 2470 at 57 mm (%)	75-85	65–75	65–75
Oil absorbency			
Based on Pira SOAT test (seconds)	60–260	50–250	10–30
Colour (based on CIELab; D50 2° observer 0/45 or 45/0)			
L	93.00	87.00	88.00
a*	0.00	−1.00	0.00
b*	−3.00	3.00	8.00

TABLE 3.2 Coated woodfree/mechanical pulp super calendered papers

Dot gain values	Plate tint	Positive	Negative
	40%	18.00	25.00
	50%	19.00	26.00
	70%	16.00	21.00
	75%	14.00	19.00
	80%	12.00	16.00

TABLE 3.3 Web-sized mechanical pulp super calendered paper

Dot gain values	Plate tint	Positive	Negative
	40%	24.00	31.00
	50%	25.00	32.00
	70%	21.00	26.00
	75%	19.00	24.00
	80%	16.00	20.00

6. Color proofing – on-press

This section applies to both proofing and production press work, sometimes referred to as wet-proofing or on-press.

6.1 Control strips

Control strips must be evident on all proofs. They must be positioned across the line of inking to the full width of the subject concerned. They must be exposed with the photographic emulsion in contact with the surface of the plate. They must be proofed in register and original control strip films, not duplicates, must be used. The control strip, which should be obtained from a recognised source, must be 60 lines per centimetre (150 lines per inch), and provide the facility for the monitoring/measurement of plate exposure, solid ink densities, dot gain, ink trapping, slurring, doubling and grey balance. Duplicate or self-designed strips are not acceptable as they provide doubtful readings.

6.2 Proof platemaking

A microline target should be featured on all proofs. Positive plates should be exposed so that the rendering of positive lines begins no lower than 8 microns and not higher than 15 microns. The corresponding negative line range on negative plates is 6 microns to 12 microns.

6.3 Proof direction

Proofs should be inked in the same direction as will be applicable on the production press.

TABLE 3.4 Coated woodfree/mechanical pulp s/c papers				
Type of filter	**Cyan**	**Magenta**	**Yellow**	**Black**
Narrow-band polarised	1.40	1.50	1.40	1.80
Narrow-band non-polarised	1.20	1.30	1.20	1.40
Broad-band polarised	1.30	1.40	1.10	1.80
Broad-band non-polarised	1.20	1.30	1.00	1.40

TABLE 3.5 Web sized mechanical pulp s/c papers				
Type of filter	**Cyan**	**Magenta**	**Yellow**	**Black**
Narrow-band polarised	1.10	1.20	1.10	1.50
Narrow-band non-polarised	1.00	1.10	1.00	1.20
Broad-band polarised	1.10	1.20	0.90	1.50
Broad-band non-polarised	1.00	1.10	0.80	1.20

6.4 Proofing sequence

It is considered essential that the chromatic colours be proofed in the same sequence as production printing, which is normally as follows:

(1) cyan

(2) magenta

(3) yellow

The black printer may occupy any position in the sequence.

6.5 Proof presentation

a) *Type of proof*: in general four-colour composite proofs are sufficient, but for GCR a three-colour mix is also required. See also individual publication rate cards to check whether progressives are required by a publisher.

b) *Measurements*: the dot gain and solid density readings taken at the time of proofing in a number of positions across the sheet must be recorded on the four-colour copy of the progressives. The manufacturer and model of the densitometer used to take the measurements should be indicated.

c) *Corrections:* proofs should be free from corrections of a vital or major nature. For minor corrections where time does not allow for reproofing, indicate clearly both on the composite proofs and, if relevant, single colour proofs the exact nature of the corrections. It is very important that new proofs are supplied when changes have been made which affect the colour appearance.

7. Colour proofing – off-press

This section applies to all non-press proof production.

7.1 Control strips

The appropriate control strip for the particular proofing system should be evident on all proofs. If this strip does not provide facilities to measure/monitor solid density, exposure, dot gain, grey balance and trapping at 60 lines per centimetre (150 lines per inch), then an additional industry recognised control strip should appear on the proof. In all cases original and not duplicate control strip films must be used.

7.2 Proofing stock

Where possible the proof should be produced on the production stock, or on the applicable grade as specified in Part 6.1. If this is not possible, a proprietary substrate of a shade matching the production stock should be used.

7.3 General consideration

Production experience has shown that poor correlation can exist between production prints on coated paper and some off-press proofs, where the subject has critical quarter tones, e.g. magenta in flesh tones. The proof appears to have higher dot gain than the production print. The mismatch is most apparent where the production presses print with dot gain at the low end of the tolerance, and can be made worse if positive plates are over-exposed, or dampening levels result in over-emulsification of the ink. This fact should be borne in mind when passing proofs containing this type of subject matter.

8. Viewing of originals and proofs

Correct viewing conditions are essential for effective appraisal of originals and proofs. Lighting which corresponds to ISO Standard 3664 (BS950 Part 2) must be used at all prepress stages of colour evaluation and reproduction.

In brief the illuminant should match CIE Daylight Illuminant D50. The illumination level should be 2000 lux and the surround should be a neutral medium grey colour.

SWOP – specifications for web offset publications in North America

Specifications concerning practice in the US are available from: The Specifications for Web Offset Publications (SWOP), SWOP Incorporated Administration Office, 60 East 42nd Street, Suite 1416, New York, NY 10165-0015, US. Tel: (+1) 212 983 6042. Fax: (+1) 212 983 6043.

In North America, the *Specifications for Web Offset Publications* (SWOP) was agreed by a consensus of advertising agencies, magazine publishers, graphic arts associations and printers.

Printer's responsibilities

The printer is responsible for visually matching the supplied SWOP proof. This implies that the supplied film or file and proof are made to SWOP specifications, whether it is a press proof or off-press proof. Off-press proofs, which are currently the most common form of proof supplied to the printer, are to be made using SWOP Certified Systems. Since most production press forms will include pages from several different sources, the printer may not be able to match non-compliant proofs in running the press form.

Production presses should be analysed to determine their compatibility with SWOP proofing characteristics, and their ability to match a SWOP certified press proof. Production presses should be optimised to conditions as close to the target values as possible. Then the press can be adjusted, within tolerance, if a change is needed, to obtain the best overall visual match to the submitted proofs. The following guidelines list the controls and initial aim values that the printer can use to bring presses into SWOP compliance and to assure the faithful replication of supplied proofs. These guidelines are based on the use of N^o5 grade publication web offset paper and heatset process colour inks matched to SWOP aim values. It is the responsibility of the printer to check received digital files against the supplied proofs for content and colour breaks.

Viewing of proofs and printed signatures

Proofs and final printed product must be viewed and/or compared using 5000 Kelvin (D_{50}) illumination complying with ISO 3664:2000, Viewing conditions for graphic technology and photography. This standard and practice is now more important than ever due to increased usage of different dyes and pigments in the industry for proofing. Viewing booth manufacturers can provide compliance information.

Printer's colour control bar

A control bar running perpendicular to the direction of printing and suitable for measurement should be included on press forms. This bar should be 133-line screen and contain solid patches of each colour; 25%, 50% and 75% patches; two-colour and three-colour solid overprints; and target areas visually sensitive to slur and dot gain. The relationship between the trim size of a publication and the web press cut-off should allow for the inclusion of this control bar.

Control bars as described above may be obtained from GATF. Specify: 'GATF/SWOP Production Control Bar'. Other sources of similar bars are available.

Computer-to-plate (CTP)

CTP platesetters are usually calibrated by the manufacturer to reproduce exactly the per cent dot values on the plate that are specified in the electronic file. However, CTP systems have extended capabilities for changing the size of the dots from that which is stated in the digital file and output curves should be adjusted as necessary to result in final printing which best matches supplied SWOP proofs in colour and tone value. The entire reproduction scale is important in matching the proof, but particular attention should be paid to the mid-tone and minimum dot areas.

Control procedures are as important in CTP as they are in film-based platemaking. Digital control scales are available from RIT, GATF, Ugra and Fogra to evaluate and control CTP systems.

New classes of instruments are now available for measurement of tone value on plates.

Tone value increase (total dot gain)

Tone value increase (dot gain) reflects the difference between the dot on the film or in the digital file and the final printed dot. Output from digital files should be controlled by the printer to match SWOP proofing.

In order to maintain visual gray balance, the TVI value of the three colours should not differ by more than 4% from the target values. For example, if either cyan or magenta is +2% (22%) in TVI, yellow deviation should not be greater than −2% (16%).

Another way to explain this specification is: after adding 2 percentage points to the measured yellow TVI, process colours (Y, M, C) should not differ by more than 4 percentage points.

The table for total tone value increase (dot gain, physical and optical), as measured in the 50% 133-line screen target, is shown below.

	Target value	Tolerance
Yellow	18%	15–24%
Magenta	20%	17–26%
Cyan	20%	17–26%
Black	22%	19–28%

Production press tone value guidelines

Over the past several years many things, including newer and more stable presses running at faster speeds, a shift to positive printing, and more and better measurement techniques have improved the quality of production printing. Tone value increase (dot gain), with some production systems has been reported to be lower by many publications and has been confirmed in specific press tests conducted by SWOP, to be 18% and lower. This is especially evident when printing with positive plates. Other tests, however, also verify an abundance of publication printing with TVIs remaining in excess of 20%. Now, with the advent of computer-to-plate technology, printers have the opportunity to match the tone value of the supplied file or film with greater accuracy.

The printer's responsibility is to visually match the supplied SWOP proof. Since SWOP specifies proofing tone value increase levels at an average of approximately 20%, the guidelines have always allowed for slightly fuller production printing in order to at least approximate press proofs and the many off-press proofs presently in use.

These guidelines have worked well (i.e. facilitated highly acceptable printing) because of the insistence on grey balance and process control as the overriding factors in the matching process. The danger appears to be that, with CTP and the false notion that 'less gain is better', the printer could go too far by making plates with not enough tone value in mid-tones. This could create an inability to match the supplied proof by printing too light and an inability to run film supplied and digitally supplied pages in the same press form. Weight is also important in matching proofs along with grey balance and hue shifts, therefore, this new ability to control the process more closely should bring a higher level of quality to publication printing. Additionally, it should be re-emphasised that TVI or dot gain is neither good nor bad, whether it be high or low, but rather only detrimental if it is out of control, not consistent with the supplied SWOP proof or not in balance from colour to colour.

Screen angles

SWOP specifies that unscreened digital files be sent to the printer. The printer should assume responsibility to ensure that moiré patterns are not introduced into the printing when plates are produced digitally. In many cases, the prepress provider will notify the printer of the angles used to eliminate this problem if it was encountered in the prepress process. It is also possible, and probable in the future, that proofs will be supplied to the printer that are unscreened, and so will not have the ability to show a moiré problem. In any case, it is the printer's responsibility to notify the advertising agency or advertiser of the problem and work with them to resolve the problem. See the SWOP specification section, page 141 for recommended screen angles.

In the case of copy-dot files that have been converted to digital format by scanning from film supplied, the printer still has the responsibility to notify if a problem develops.

Printing inks

Process printing inks for web offset presses should match the colours of the SWOP/NAPIM standard reference proofing inks (ISO 2846-1) and have physical properties that enable the web printer to meet the SWOP print quality control parameters while maintaining web press performance requirements. Ink manufacturers should not be asked to deviate from these shades to match a particular off-press proof, nor should this be necessary, since only off-press proofing systems certified by SWOP for compliance to these ink colours may be used.

Solid ink density

Target values for printed ink density on production presses should be the densities determined as the centre point for each colour by use of the SWOP Hi-Lo Color Reference. The acceptable deviation in either direction from the centre point was previously equal to the total difference between the Hi and the Lo patches, or approximately ±.14 but is now ±.10 in density.

FIGURE 3.1 SWOP Hi-Lo Color Reference

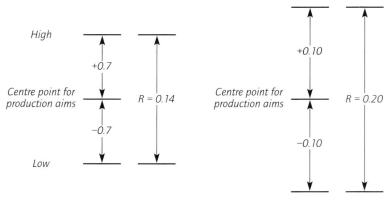

Source: Pira International Ltd

Acceptable density ranges for the proofs and production from SWOP Hi-Lo Color References. Note: actual density ranges will vary depending on the densitometer used to read the SWOP Hi-Lo colour references.

Note: printers often run higher black densities. Printers are cautioned, however, to make sure this does not increase dot gain to levels outside of SWOP specifications.

Print contrast

A general guideline for publication printing is that print contrast at the 75% tone value should fall within the following ranges (absolute, includes paper):

Yellow   20–30%
Magenta   30–40%
Black   35–45%

Other publication papers

Super calendered paper

Certain offset publications now print on super calendered (SC) paper. As with all other production stocks, the goal is to achieve as close a visual match to the submitted SWOP proofs as possible. The customer must determine the acceptability of the match, but there are certain techniques that will improve the potential to match the SC printed image to the SWOP proof. If possible, films and electronic files supplied for printing on SC paper should:

▶ Have screen rulings at 120 or 133 lines per inch at output;

▶ Have a maximum TAC between 260% and 280%. This is because less ink and water will require less oven heat, resulting in better print and paper gloss and minimal linting. TAC above the recommended specification will most probably cause dry back and after a few days, a chemical reaction will take place and the printing will appear flat compared with the original press side result;

▶ Incorporate appropriate output curves that are 3% to 5% less in mid-tones than normal SWOP curves, to compensate for the additional TVI (dot gain) experienced when running super calendered papers on production presses.

Press recommendations for running SC paper are as follows:

▶ Ink tacks – use lower than normal tack inks where tack progressively decreases (9, 9, 8 and 7). Normal sequence of inks is: black, cyan, magenta, yellow;

▶ Run the least amount of water possible without scumming. Ink and water balance are critical and this allows for lower oven temperatures, improved ink mileage, higher print gloss and fewer linting problems;

▶ Fountain solutions should have a pH of 3.8 to 4.5 and alcohol substitutes should be utilised;

▶ Plates should be fine grain. This minimises water pick-up;

▶ Quick release blankets should be used.

Nº 3 grade coated publication paper

It is widely known that many publications routinely use papers brighter than a Nº 5 grade coated paper for both covers and, sometimes, entire magazines. However, SWOP specifies the use of a Nº 5 grade coated as a common proofing paper. SWOP does not want to introduce a new or second proofing stock at this time since we believe that the present stock provides a good common denominator.

However, it would be for the benefit of the publication industry if production printing on a brighter (i.e. Nº 3 grade) stock could be colorimetrically characterised using the same methodology as the Nº 5 grade stock that has been characterised in the CGATS Technical Report 001, *Graphic technology – Color characterisation data for Type 1 printing*.

To this end, SWOP has recently endorsed a test printing, run on a representative sample of a Nº 3 grade coated paper and run to specific guidelines, which are in line with normal industry guidelines (such as tone value increase and density). The inks used were SWOP and ISO 2846-1 compliant. A statistical sampling of this press run has been sent to the CGATS SC4 committee with a request that they investigate the appropriateness of drafting a technical report, similar to CGATS TR 001.

Supply of digital files

The practice of supplying complete digital files for printing has largely been accepted in most developed print markets and works well on a daily basis. It is important to provide files optimised wherever possible, and the Periodical Publishers Association (PPA) provides a very useful resource in its pass4press initiative. The latest version, V5.0, released in 2005, is presented overleaf. The PPA website (www.pass4press.com) contains the latest versions of the specification together with useful downloads, including complete Distiller Job Option Settings to produced optimised PDFs for printing.

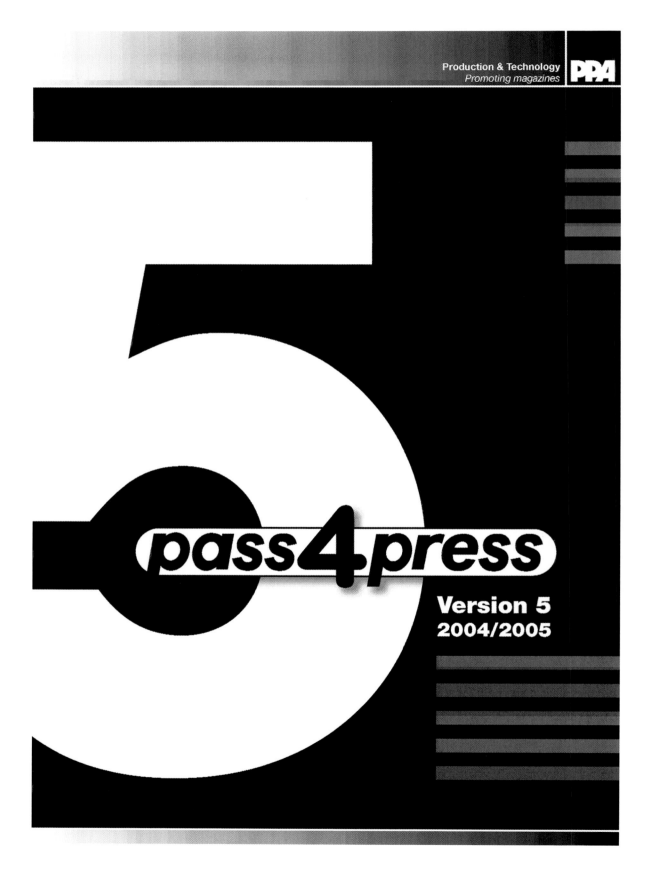

Production & Technology committee

Alice Beattie (Co-Chairman)	The National Magazine Company
Jasper Scott (Co-Chairman)	IPC Media
Rose Benjamin	PPA Executive
Sharon Bird	IDG Communications
Michele Cohen	Profile Media Group
Sarah Davidson	The Condé Nast Publications
Meurig Evans	Haymarket Business Publications
Andy Franks	Emap
Paul Gillott	Reed Business Information
Emma Goode	PSP Communications
Joanne Hurst	VNU Business Publications
Doreen Loughrey	CMP Information
Michael Mann	The Economist Group
Michael Murphy	Redwood
Debbie Read	IPC Media
Christopher Reed	William Reed Publishing
Vanessa Salter	Cedar Communications
Mal Skelton	BBC Magazines

Accreditation committee

Debbie Read (Chairman)	IPC Media
Tony Austin	Wyndeham Argent
Sarah Davidson	The Condé Nast Publications
Bob Marchant	Colour Therapy
Les Pipe	Colour Systems

Proof4press sub-group

Jack Bisset	Polestar
Brent Martin	DuPont
Andy Psarianos	FE Burman Limited
Marcus Kirby	Vertis prs
Pamela Raftery	St Ives

Pass4press committee

Debbie Read (Chairman)	IPC Media
Robert Banbury	The Economist Group
Jack Bisset	Polestar
Chris Burn	Agfa
Leonard Burns	Time-Life International
Michele Cohen	Profile Media Group
Raidel Chao-Batlle	The National Magazine Company
Steve Collins	Agfa
David Croaker	The National Magazine Company
Tim Daly	Interoute
Dominic Duffy	Applecart Solutions
Meurig Evans	Haymarket Business Publications
Barry Fitzpatrick	Wyndeham Graphics
Andy Franks	Emap
Paul Gillott	Reed Business Information
Chris Glynne	IPC Media
Nick Grote	DuPont
Catherine Harding-Wiltshire	BMJ Publishing Group
Joanne Izatt	The Condé Nast Publications
Glenn Joyce	The National Magazine Company
Marcus Kirby	Vertis prs
Bob Linford	Wyndeham Argent
Savio Luis	Vio Worldwide
Marcus Lynch	Adobe
Maria Machera	Creo
Frank Maeder	Southernprint
Bob Marchant	Colour Therapy
Brent Martin	DuPont
Richard Mason	Emap
Jonathan Moore	The Condé Nast Publications
Andy Psarianos	FE Burman Limited
Pamela Raftery	St Ives
Christopher Reed	William Reed Publishing

pass4press version 5 Introduction

pass4press

Dear Colleagues,

It has been five years since **pass4press** was originally launched, during which time we have seen an enormous amount of change in the industry in pursuit of a complete digital workflow. This brochure has been produced to incorporate revisions to the **pass4press** specification and to provide updates on developments with the preflighting and **proof4press** initiatives.

We cannot have a complete digital workflow if pictures are still submitted in an analogue form, therefore the committee has worked extremely hard this year to produce a set of best practice guidelines for the supply and processing of digital imagery. Details of these guidelines can be found within the separate **pic4press** brochure, which I hope you will find extremely useful.

The **pass4press** website (**www.pass4press.com**) will be updated throughout the year with any further developments and I am pleased to inform you that some videos have been produced giving step-by-step instructions of how to create **pass4press** files using the latest specifications. These have kindly been produced for us by **Darrin Stevens** at **Polestar** and they can be accessed via the **pass4press** website. If you would like to make any comments about **pass4press** or the website please contact **Rose Benjamin** at the **PPA** on **020 7404 4166**.

I would like to thank all the committee members who have given up their time, knowledge and expertise to help develop the **pass4press** specifications. Finally, I would like to offer a special thank you to **Jonathan Moore, The Condé Nast Publications**, for all his time and effort spent in producing this brochure.

Debbie

Debbie Read, IPC Media
pass4press committee chair

pass4press
The 5th element what you need for v5

Version 5 **pass4press** recommendations for creating the right file first time – best practice guidelines for preparing your documents and their elements

What version of pass4press should you use?
Last year's Version 4 guidelines introduced the more secure PDF/X specification, which is becoming the international standard for supplying high resolution print-quality files. Version 5 further refines the guidelines, and is now based solely on the PDF/X format. However, if you do not currently possess the software to make a **pass4press** Version 5 file you should use last year's Version 4 instructions until you upgrade your software. The diagram below illustrates which version PDF you should create based on what software you have available.

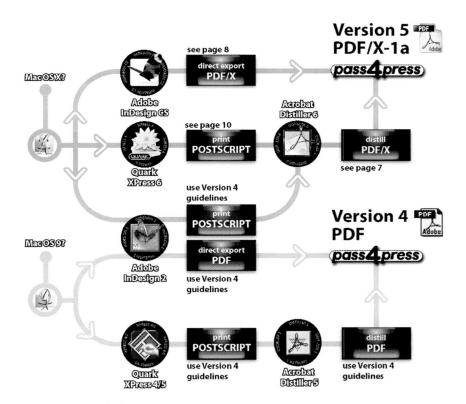

Proofing and file delivery
To streamline the process of receiving PDF files, it is suggested that a file naming convention is set up with your suppliers. It is recommended that all PDFs sent are given a relevant name that includes basic information, such as title, publication name and issue date, ie: **title_pubname_jan05.pdf**. The file name should be no more than 27 characters and should not include any non-standard characters, eg: **\:/*<>**. Please note that your file naming convention cannot be implemented without agreement from your pre-press and print suppliers. An email confirming the transmission of any digital file should be sent to the relevant production contact at the destination. Recordable media must be write-protected and contain only the files relevant to the job. Disks must be clearly labelled with a booking reference supplied by the publisher.

All proofs must conform to the **proof4press** guidelines (see page 12). It is important to flightcheck PDFs before transmission, either using standalone flightchecking software or a server solution such as the PPA's own **pass4press online flightchecking service, www.pass4press.com**.

 **V5:2004/5**

Preparation getting your files in shape

Recommended digital image specifications

Resolution and size: Colour or greyscale continuous-tone images should be saved at **300dpi**, bitmaps at **2400dpi**. Where known, the image's dimensions should be set to the final printed size. Images too small or too low resolution for their final use will have to be resupplied to prevent quality loss.

Format Ideally files should be saved as **TIFFs**, but **JPEG** compression can be used as a transmission format to speed up delivery times – see note below.

Compression Compression is split between lossy and loss-less formats. Lossy formats, such as JPEG, throw pixel information away to reduce file sizes, and rely on algorithms to rebuild the discarded data when decompressing (ie, opening) the file (see **Glossary** entry, p15). Loss-less formats such as **Stuffit** or **Zip** archives look for repeating code in a file, remove it and then tag that area so it can replace that part when the file is decompressed. The file therefore contains all the information from the original and is decompressed in its original format.

Colour Spaces Files should be in **DeviceGrey**, **DeviceCMYK**, **DeviceN** or **Separation** colour spaces, but must only include cyan, magenta, yellow and black separations. Any objects in **Device RGB**, **CalibratedRGB** or **LAB** must be converted before being imported into a layout application. **DeviceCMYK** should be in an appropriate CMYK colour space such as the **ECI's ISOWebcoated.icc** profile (**http://www.eci.org**). For more information see the **pic4press** documentation on submission and handling of images (**www.pass4press.com**).

Total Area Coverage Combined colour values should not exceed **310 per cent**. Note that some publishers may require a lower maximum depending on the substrate used.

Proofs Where necessary a CMYK, ripped proof of a supplied digital image should be provided according to the **proof4press** and **RIP standardisation guidelines**.

Vector software: Adobe Illustrator CS and Macromedia Freehand MX

Files originated in Illustrator or Freehand should have all fonts embedded or outlined. Their colour space should be set to CMYK and all transparent elements should be flattened. In **Illustrator**: use **Edit>Transparency Flattener Presets** set as per the example. **Freehand** 'fakes' its vector transparency effects by calculating overlapping colours, so does not need to have its files flattened. Any bitmaps contained within a vector file must be embedded. In Illustrator the rasterisation must be set in **Effects>Document Raster Effect Settings** set to CMYK and 300dpi. Freehand uses the native resolution of placed images and relies on their resolution being of sufficient quality, so does not need to be configured.

Page layout applications: Adobe InDesign CS and QuarkXPress 6

Colours: Delete any instance of non-CMYK colours. In **QuarkXPress**, select **Edit>Colours** to display all colours used: the icon to the left denotes whether it is RGB, CMYK or a Spot colour. Convert any non-CMYK colours using the **Model** tab. In **Adobe InDesign**, select **Window>Swatches**. Colour spaces are shown as a small icon on the right. You can also use the **Ink Manager** in the **Print** dialogue to convert Spots to CMYK. Note that if **colour management** is turned on in InDesign, all elements imported in the document which are of a different colour space than the output destination space will be transformed into the final document's working colour space when printed or exported directly to PDF.

Fonts: Delete any instances of fonts that are present in the document but not being used. In **QuarkXPress**, select **Utilities>Usage** and select the **Fonts** tab. Make sure no fonts are using psuedo bolds or italics. In **Adobe InDesign**, select **Type>Find Font**. This palette also displays a warning triangle next to any problem fonts.

Placed images: Go through your placed image files. Check resolutions and colour spaces, try to carry out any resising in **Adobe Photoshop**, rather than in your page layout application, as this adds to potential problems. Ideally every image should be placed at 100 per cent of its original size. This does not apply to pure vector artwork. Verify your images in **QuarkXPress** in **Utilities>Usage** in the **Pictures** tab. Click the **More Information** for additional details. In **InDesign** choose **Window>Links**. Problems will be displayed by warning icons next to the relevant image.

Page size: Finally, double-check your page document size is correct. In your page setup, create a custom paper size which is **the size of your document plus 20mm** in both width and depth to allow for registration marks to be added at the PDF creation stage. In this brochure a standard A4 page size is used as an example: make sure you enter dimensions which are relevant to your publication.

PDF/X-1a Overview

An outline of the **PDF/X** format in comparison to any other PDF, **PDF/X**'s future development and why the **PPA pass4press** committee is recommending its usage

What is new in pass4press Version 5?

With the release of **Version 5** of the **pass4press** specification comes a mandate that PDF files conform to **PDF/X-1a** as per the **Ghent PDF Workgroup 2004 Magazine Ads** specification.

Why PDF/X-1a?

PDF/X-1a:2001, to give the specification its full name, is a global agreement on how files for the whole of the print industry should be constructed. It goes further towards strengthening the reliability of digital workflows by giving clear and concise instructions on how to properly interpret these files. The PDF/X standards give application developers tangible guidelines to adhere to, allowing them to create better products. It is now simple to create and process files that conform to **PDF/X-1a**: **Adobe InDesign CS** can natively export the format, **QuarkXpress 6** can create **PostScript** files that can be converted to PDF/X using **Adobe Distiller 6**. Last year's Version 4 recommendations were to use PDF/X-1a where possible, reflecting the fact that software was only just becoming available that made it possible to use the format. **Version 5** of **pass4press** now uses **PDF/X-1a** as the foundation on which further market specific restrictions have been applied. This method has been coined as **PDF/X+** and is the intended way of using PDF/X.

What can I do in PDF/X-1a that I can't do with any other PDF?

Nothing. PDF/X is not an alternative to PDF – it is a focused subset limiting settings which are either not relevant or which commonly cause problems in a high-resolution printing environment. It is designed specifically for reliable pre-press data interchange. It is also an application standard, as well as a file format standard. In other words, it defines how applications creating and reading PDF/X files should behave.

How do I create a pass4press Version 5 file?

Follow the guidelines on the following pages to create a file that conforms to the **Version 5 pass4press** specification. You can also download a preset version of these settings for use in **Distiller 6** from the website, **www. pass4press.com**. It is very important that you flightcheck the file before transmission, either using standalone flightchecking software or a server solution such as the PPA's own **pass4press Online Flightchecking service, www.pass4press.com**.

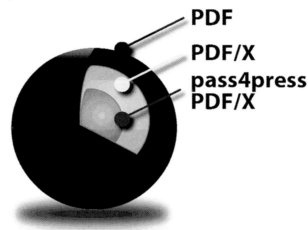

PDF

PDF/X

pass4press
PDF/X

What is the Ghent PDF Workgroup?

The **Ghent PDF Workgroup** is an international assembly of industry associations whose goal is to establish and disseminate process specifications for best practices in graphic arts workflows worldwide.

The following objectives are defined:

1: Streamline and coordinate the decision process between industry associations (worldwide) interested in best practices for graphic arts workflows.

2: Develop and maintain process specifications and associated documentation for best practices in graphic arts workflows.

3: Develop and maintain reference implementations for those process specifications to ensure the practical applicability of such specifications.

4: Actively promote adoption of the established specifications by the worldwide user and vendor community.

The **Ghent PDF Workgroup** consists of two membership classes: Association and Vendors.

Association members are graphic arts industry associations representing printers, publishers, design agencies, pre-press houses and/or similar companies.

Association members include:

Cebuco	Holland	**DAL TC**	Holland	**DDAP**	USA
DDPFF	Denmark	**DRRB**	Denmark	**ERA**	Europe
Febelgra	Belgium	**FICG**	France	**IDP Groep**	Holland
IPA	USA	**Medibel+**	Belgium	**PPA**	UK
Sicogif	France	**Taga Italia**	Italy	**VFG**	Austria
VIGC	Belgium	**VSD**	Switzerland		

Vendor members are software and/or hardware companies with an active interest in supporting the process specifications developed by the Workgroup.

Vendor Members include:

Adobe	**Agfa**	**Artwork Systems**	**Creo**	**Enfocus Software**
Esko Graphics	**Global Graphics**	**pub-specs**	**Quark Inc**	**Screen**

For more information visit: **www.ghentpdfworkgroup.org**

What are the specifications for a pass4press Version 5 file?

The following are **required** in order for a PDF file to be considered a valid **pass4press Version 5** file:
- *A PDF file shall be compliant to the ISO PDF/X-1a:2001 standard as defined by ISO 15930-1.*
- *A PDF file shall not be created with the Adobe PDFWriter product.*
- *A PDF file must either have no crop box defined or have a crop box set to the same size as the Media Box.*
- *No object in a PDF file shall be transparent.*
- *A PDF file shall not use Multiple Master fonts or Multiple Master instances.*
- *Embedded composite fonts which are not sub-set shall not be used in a PDF file.*
- *A PDF file shall not contain white text set to overprint.*
- *Images using 16 bits per sample shall not be used in PDF files.*
- *PDF files shall not use layers.*
- *A PDF file shall not contain annotations that are set to print.*
- *The number of pages in a PDF file shall be exactly one.*
- *Total area of coverage (TAC) of elements on a page should not exceed 310 per cent.*
- *Resolution of colour and greyscale images shall not be below 150 dpi.*
- *Resolution of 1-bit images (either regular images or image masks) shall not be below 550 dpi.*
- *1-bit images shall not use JBIG compression.*
- *Images shall not use JPEG2000 compression.*

The following are **not recommended** in PDF files and should generate a warning in preflight:
- *A PDF file should not contain objects that are completely off the page (as defined by the MediaBox).*
- *A PDF file should not contain custom UCR functions for objects in any colour space.*
- *A PDF file should not contain custom BG functions for objects in any colour space.*
- *A PDF file should not use black text smaller than 12 points that is set to knockout.*
- *A PDF file should not contain text that is smaller than 5 points or text that is smaller than 9 points and coloured with more then 2 colour separations.*
- *Resolution of colour and greyscale images should not be above 450 dpi.*
- *Resolution of 1-bit images (either regular images or image masks) should not be above 3600 dpi.*

Settings for preflight applications will be available on the website, **www.pass4press.com**

pass4press

Adobe InDesign CS export to PDF

Guidelines for exporting a **PDF/X** directly from **Adobe InDesign CS**. This example was created on an **Apple Macintosh** running **OS X 10.3.5**

1 In **Edit>Transparency Flattener Preset** click **New**, name the preset relevantly and enter the details as below. Click **OK** to store the settings.

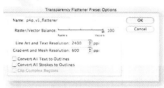

2 From the **File** menu select **Export**, in the **Format** pop-up select **Adobe PDF**. Name the file and select the folder that you want to save the PDF into, then click **Save**.

3 In the **General** tab select the page to print: typically a single page at a time. Set the **Compatibility** to **Acrobat 4 (PDF 1.3)** and deselect all of the listed **Options**.

4 In **Compression** set the options for how the PDF will handle placed images. Set **Bicubic Downsampling** to 450dpi for **Colour** images and 2400dpi for **Bitmaps**.

5 The **Marks And Bleeds** tab should be set as below: the indicated **Printer's Marks** should be enabled, the **Offset** set at 3mm and the **Bleed** set to 3mm all round.

6 The **Output Intent** should reflect the colour space of the document (see Output Intent on p15 and InDesign notes on p5). Use **Transparency Flattener Preset** from step 1.

7 The **Ink Manager** shows all the colour plates in the document, and will display any non-process colours in the document. Make sure only **CMYK** inks are present.

8 The **Security** tab allows you to assign access privileges to the resulting PDF file: enabling any security settings will fail **pass4press** compliance.

9 Before you click **Export** to save the PDF, select **Save Preset...**: this means these settings can be quickly accessed in future using the **Preset** pop-up menu.

8 **pass4press** V5:2004/5

Adobe InDesign CS print to PostScript

Printing a **PostScript** file from **Adobe InDesign CS**, to be converted to a **PDF/X** using **Acrobat Distiller 6.0**. This example was created on an **Apple Macintosh** running **Mac OS X 10.3.5**

① Open the **File>Print** menu and from the **Printer** pop-up menu choose **PostScript® File**. Select **Adobe PDF** in the **PPD** menu and enter the number of the page to print.

② In Setup, enter the size of your page plus 20mm in the **Paper Size** width and height boxes. Check the **Orientation** is portrait, the **Scale** 100% and **Page Position Centred**.

③ The **Marks And Bleeds** tab should be set as below: **All Printers' Marks** must be enabled, **Offset** set to 3mm and **Bleed** set to 3mm all round.

④ In the **Output** tab set the **Colour** option to **Composite CMYK** and **Flip** to **None**. Ensure the **Simulate Overprint** box is not checked. Click the **Ink Manager** button.

⑤ In the **Ink Manager**, make sure there are only the four CMYK colour plates shown in the order below and that no spot or RGB colours are present.

⑥ In **Graphics**, check that **Send Data** is set to **All**, that **Fonts Download** is set to **Subset**, that **PostScript®** is set to **Level 3** and that the **Data Format** is **Binary**.

⑦ The **Output Intent** should reflect the colour space of the document (see Output Intent on p15 and InDesign notes on p5).

If **InDesign's Colour Settings** are not configured all the options will be greyed out:

⑧ Make sure **OPI Image Replacement** is disabled. In **Transparency Flattener** set the **Preset** to the settings entered in Step One on page 8 to achieve the highest quality results.

⑨ Before you click **Save** to begin printing the **PostScript** file select **Save Preset**, in future you can then access these settings via the **Print Preset** menu.

pass4press V5:2004/5 **9**

pass4press

QuarkXpress 6 print to PostScript

Printing a **PostScript** file from **QuarkXpress 6.0**, to be converted to a **PDF/X** file using **Acrobat Distiller 6.0**. This example was created on an **Apple Macintosh** running **Mac OS X 10.3.5**

1 Select **Edit>Print** and **Printer**. Choose **Adobe PDF** in **Printer**, and in **Output Options** check **Save As File** and **PostScript**: click **Save** to choose the location.

2 Back at the main **Print Layout** window, set the **Layout** options as shown. The **Offset** box is in points: either enter **9pt** or **3mm** – which will be converted to **8.504pt**.

3 Change to the **Setup** tab. Make sure the **Paper Size** is **Custom**, and that the **Height** and **Width** is your page size plus 20mm. Ensure the page is 100% and centred.

4 Select **Output**: this lists the colours in the document and will display any rogue RGB or Spot colours. Make sure **Halftoning** is **Printer** and **Resolution** to **2400dpi**.

5 In the **Options** window set the **Output** to **Normal**, the **Data** format to **Binary** and check the **Full Resolution TIFF Output** box. **OPI** will be greyed out if not active.

6 **Layers** displays all the layers present in the document and shows the specific colours plates used on each individual layer – ensure all the required layers are active.

7 Set the **Bleed Type** to **Symmetric** and the amount to **3mm** to give the correct all-round bleed around the document's trim size. Check the **Clip At Bleed Edge** option.

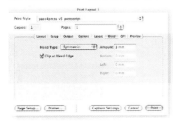

8 The **Preview** tab is a way to visually check the trim, bleed and media boxes are correct. Click **Print** to create the **PostScript** file.

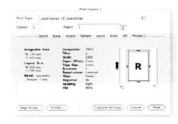

9 You can save most of the settings as a **Print Style** for easy re-use. Open **Edit>Print Styles** and select **New**. Enter a name and the settings as per the guidelines.

10 pass4press V5:2004/5

PDF/X-1a distilling in Adobe Acrobat 6

Creating a **PDF/X** file by printing a **PostScript** file from **Adobe InDesign 2.0.2** or **QuarkXpress 4.1.1** or higher. This example was created on an **Apple Macintosh** running **Mac OS X 10.3.5**

1 In **Distiller's** Settings menu, select **Edit Adobe PDF Settings....** In the **General** tab make sure the **Default Page Size** is set to the dimensions relevant to your publication.

2 In the **Images** tab set the **Compression** and **Sampling** options. The settings reduce very high resolution images down, but will not prevent the placement of low-res images.

3 The **Fonts** tab allows you to embed fonts into the PDF to ensure the correct fonts are rendered. **Subsetting** fonts means only characters used in the document are saved.

4 The **Color** tab is set to **Leave Colour Unchanged**; all placed images should already be **CMYK**. This tab also sets how the PDF will treat **Transfer Functions** (see FAQ).

5 The **pass4press Version 5 Advanced** settings are based on the **Ghent Workgroup's** European recommendations: tick the boxes as per the example.

6 This tab defines **PDF/X**-specific settings. The **Output Intent Profile Name** names a registered characterisation at **www.color.org** (see FAQ). Note **Trapping** option below.

7 To save the settings, click **Save As...** at the bottom of the window and fill in a relevant name. These settings are available pre-configured from **www.pass4press.com**

8 Drag-and-drop a **PostScript** file over the main **Distiller** window so it highlights – the file will be automatically distilled and saved to the same folder as the original postscript file.

9 In future you can simply open **Distiller**, select the **pass4press Version 5 PDF/X Job Options** and drop your **PostScript** file onto the **Distiller** window.

6a The **Trapped** flag must be set to **Insert False** if the job is not trapped or **Insert True** if it is trapped. Do not set this to **Leave Undefined**.

pass4press V5:2004/5 **11**

pass4press

proof4press proofing initiative update

The **proof4press** sub-committee is developing a 'standard' proofing method acceptable and relevant across the UK magazine industry

Introduction

proof4press is a standard for proofing to ensure that editorial and advertising material can be produced to a consistent and appropriate standard for the printing condition to be used, to give the printer the best chance of meeting the expectations created by the proof. **proof4press** will enable publishers, advertisers and printers to accept proofs from a variety of different accredited proofing devices and be confident that they will all fall within a tight tolerance. The **proof4press** standard is completely non-proprietary and is thus open for any vendor's RIP, ink, paper or proof engine combination to gain accreditation. In 2003 the first **proof4press** standard was announced and major proofing vendors such as **DuPont**, **Agfa** and **Creo** now have accredited solutions, with many other companies currently going through the process to gain accreditation.

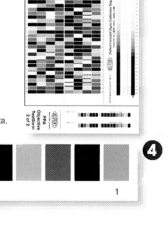

Proof4press accreditation

Any proofing manufacturing company can apply for **PPA proof4press accreditation**. The process of accreditation falls into four parts, detailed below:

1 Rip standardisation

The RIP for the proofing engine must pass the **pass4Press RIP Standardisation Test Form**. PDF files need to be interpreted in order to be displayed or printed. The results can vary from device to device. It is possible that the devices you are using have been configured incorrectly or were not intended to be used for the proofing of printing material. This test is designed to identify any discrepancies by means of a quick visual check. It is simple to understand and only takes minutes to run and analyse. Whilst this **Test Form** does not guarantee 100 per cent integrity it does conform to the RIP standards set by the PPA and adopted by suppliers to the UK magazine printing industry. More elaborate testing of complete workflows can be carried out with **ECI's Altona Suite** or the **Kensington Suite**. The **proof4press** sub-committee will require evidence to demonstrate that the verification test has been passed for a device to achieve accreditation. You can get test files, as well as the white papers, from the website at **www.pass4press.com**.

2 Visual assessments of proofs compared to target

A set of eight A4 images have been selected that are representative of typical magazine pages and are challenging to reproduce – the images cover a wide range of colours and gradations. The images, along with an **Objective Test Form** (see stage 3 below), are made available to the applicant, together with proofs of the images proofed to the **proof4press DP 10** target standard. If necessary, a proof can be output of the vendor's own test forms to assist with their colour management. Vendors seeking accreditation can arrange to submit their proofs for visual assessment by the **proof4press** sub-committee. If approved at the visual assessment stage, step 3 can commence. If the proofs do not pass visual assessment the vendor will be given guidelines and the opportunity to re-supply their proofs at the next scheduled meeting. A copy of the visual assessment form used by the **proof4press** sub-committee can be found on the **pass4press** website for reference.

3 Assessment of objective test form

The **Objective Test Form** (proofed using the same profile as the one used for the images passed in phase 2) will be measured with a spectrophotometer to check that the proof conforms to the expected standards and that all colours are within a **delta E tolerance** of **2** compared to the **proof4press DP 10** original target.

4 Input of data into proof4press verifier software

Once a pass has been given at the third phase, the data from the PPA control strip is input into the **proof4press** verifier software. The applicant will be encouraged to supervise the inputting of the data.

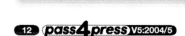

18   *proof4press*   1

The verifier software will then enable any supplier or receiver of proofs to check that the proof conforms to the standard. A proof will fail if any patch has a tolerance of greater than a **delta E** of **2** compared to the data that has been input into the software.

Proof4press verification

The **proof4press** standard is maintained by a verification process. Once a pass has been given at the accreditation stage, data from the **pass4press** control strip is input into the **proof4press** verifier software. The verifier software will then enable any supplier or receiver of proofs to check that the proof conforms to the standard. A proof will fail if any patch has a tolerance of greater than a **delta E** of **2** compared to the data that has been input into the software. The verifier software is available for purchase from **Laurie Mullaney Associates Ltd (www.lmal.co.uk)** or for further information see **www.pass4press.com**.

Accredited proofing devices

To get an up to date list of accredited proofing solutions, visit **www.pass4press.com**.

Using proof4press

Everyone can benefit from using **proof4press**. Publishers and advertisers should be looking to specify **proof4press** verified proofs as part of their specifications; repro houses and other suppliers of reproduction for print should be using **pass4press**-certified proofing devices; printers should be supporting **proof4press** as a proof that they are confident of matching on press.

Producers of **pass4press** proofs should have purchased the **pass4press** verifier software and have the required spectrophotometer to enable them to check from the **proof4press control strip** that the output falls within tolerance. Proofs that match the required standards will have a 'Pass' label embedded -- enabled from within the **pass4press** verifier software – and a copy of the **proof4press control strip** will be incorporated on all proofs. Receivers of **pass4press** proofs, whether advertisers, publishers or printers, should be looking for the **proof4press control strip** and the accreditation label, but should also consider using the verifier software themselves as a quality check on the incoming proofs and as a method of ensuring standards are maintained.

Proof4press developments

The initial **proof4press** standard created in 2003 reflected the widely-used **DP 10** target and is aimed at magazines produced on coated paper. Extensive work has been going on all year with a view to enlarging the range of proofing standards by covering a broader range of substrates. In common with other related initiatives, **pass4press** is seeking to align to internationally-recognised standards. To this end, the **ECI (European Colour Initiative)** profiles for **offset** are presently under consideration. The specific profiles under test are:

ISOcoated.icc Paper type 1 and 2, gloss and matte coated, 150 lpi (60/cm), FOGRA27L
ISOwebcoated.icc Paper type 3, gloss coated web (LWC), 150 lpi (60/cm), FOGRA28L
ISOuncoated.icc Paper type 4, uncoated white, 150 lpi (60/cm), FOGRA29L
ISOuncoatedyellowish.icc Paper type 5, uncoated slightly yellowish, 150 lpi (60/cm), FOGRA30L

Testing has already taken place using the internationally recognised **Altona Suite** and selected magazine images with a number of vendors and devices, but the committee feels that more extensive testing on a wider range of devices needs to be undertaken to establish the full gamut of the **ECI** tolerance range, before firm recommendations can be made. The intention is to be in a position to offer recommendations in advance of the 2005 PPA Conference.

pass4press
FAQ Questions you need answered

What is a PDF?
Portable Document Format. A digital file format developed by Adobe to be compact, cross-platform and capable of containing graphics. This makes it ideal for the distribution of files within the print publishing market.

How do I create a pass4press file?
Either by following the guidelines in this brochure or by using an accredited workflow system that is capable of producing **PDF** files which conform to the **pass4press** standard.

Why can't I supply a native Quark XPress or Adobe InDesign file?
Fonts are not embedded in these files, which means that as well as there being font legality issues, unpredictable results may occur. However, using the methods described in this brochure, you can export a **PDF** directly from Adobe InDesign that will adhere to the **pass4press Version 5** standard.

Why can't I use multiple master fonts?
Multiple Master fonts are incompatible with the majority of RIP devices currently in use, so should be avoided.

Do I need to supply a proof with my PDF?
Yes. Proofs must be 100 per cent of the final output size and created from the actual PDF being submitted. Proofs must not be produced from the original application files as the result will not accurately reflect the final print file.

Can I supply any type of proof?
No, the proof should be an approved colour contract proof that builds in dot gain and represents the printing colour space. RIP Standardisation Guidelines (p12) should be adhered to.

Will the PDF print as it views on screen?
No, not always. This is why it is essential that a proof is produced from the PDF file and that the proof is ripped according to the RIP Standardisation Guidelines.

What is a PDF/X file?
PDF/X is a focused subset of PDF designed for reliable pre-press interchange. PDF/X is also an application standard that defines how applications creating and reading PDF/X files should behave. PDF/X is now the recommended format, providing that all the **pass4press** parameters such as resolution and maximum ink density have been conformed to. The Output Intent should be set to the colour space your document has been created.

Why do problems arise with overprints?
Problems sometimes occur with different RIPs interpreting PDF files in different ways. RIP settings need to be standardised, which is why the pass4press committee has carried out RIP

standardisation – see page 12. Further details are available on the website: **www.pass4press.com**.

Can I create a pass4press version 5 file using Microsoft Windows?
Yes, settings for applications on a PC are virtually identical and guidelines and will be posted in PDF format on the website, **www.pass4press.com**, in the near future.

Why you need to set the trapping flag within your PDF
When creating a **pass4press Version 5 PDF** in **Acrobat Distiller** one of the options is to set the values for **Trapping**. The pass4press Version 5 specification recommends that this must be set to **True** if you have either already applied trapping or if you do not wish to have any trapping applied. This flag must otherwise be set to **False**. Bear in mind that when creating a composite (rather than a separated) **PostScript** file from **QuarkXpress** it will not include any trapping information, but all overprint and knockout informations set with the the trapping dialogue box will be retained. We recommend in this case that the flag is set to **False**. However, some PDF workflow systems may generate files which incorporate trapping information and should therefore set the flag to **True**. Note that if the flag is set to **False** it does not necessarily mean that any other party, such as the pre-press house or printer, will apply trapping at a later stage.

How do I fix trim or page boxes?
PDF files contain invisible boxes which define the geometry of the page. Applications like QuarkXpress, Acrobat Distiller 5.05 and above, as well as Adobe InDesign CS all create and handle page boxes correctly as long as the guidelines outlined in this document are followed. These boxes need to be present and defined correctly in order for processes such as automatic page positioning and automatic size checking to work. If the files have been created incorrectly these pages may need to be handled manually which could incur additional costs.
Adobe InDesign CS see page 8, Step 5 for exporting PDFs.
See page 9, Step 3 for printing a PostScript file.
QuarkXPress 6 See page 10, Step 2.

How do I avoid problems with transfer functions?
When saving to a Photoshop EPS or DCS file, you are presented with buttons that give options including halftone screens and transfer functions. All of these buttons should be left off unless they are specifically required for your job – check with your printer or pre-press supplier. When using the **pass4press** Acrobat Distiller 6.0 settings, any halftone, screening, orientation, or background information will be removed in the distilling process, but transfer curves will be applied. It is strongly recommended not to use transfer functions as a means of applying colour corrections or special effects within images as there are better methods available.

Glossary of terms what it all means

CMYK An abbreviation for cyan, magenta, yellow and black (or 'key').

Colour management A process used to ensure colour consistency across different input and output devices so that printed results match originals.

Compression The reduction in size of a digital file, which can be lossy or loss-less. Lossy formats (such as JPEG) permanently discard data – when the file is expanded the remaining data is used to rebuild the missing data, which can lead to a noticeable quality drop.

Downsampling The reduction in resolution of an image, whilst retaining sizing and positioning information.

DPI/PPI Dots per inch/pixels per inch. Measurements used to determine the resolution of printing images and text.

EPS Encapsulated PostScript. The EPS file format can contain both vector and bitmap graphics and is widely supported by most graphic applications. EPS files are often used as an intermediate way of transferring graphic elements from one application to another.

Halftone Screen A pattern of dots of different sizes used to simulate a continuous-tone image.

JPEG Joint Photographic Experts Group – the body that has defined compression standards. A JPEG trades image quality for file size. Compression can be set from 1 (lowest quality) to 12 (highest quality). Ideally the maximum setting should be used for print-quality images. Every time a JPEG is saved there is a potential quality drop, normally visible in the form of pixel 'blocks' appearing on the image. JPEGs are typically supplied at 72dpi in RGB. It is advisable to convert JPEGs to a loss-less format (ie, TIFF) if any work such as retouching is to be carried out. When images are embedded into **pass4press** PDFs they are compressed as maximum quality JPEGs.

LPI Lines per inch. A measurement for the number of lines per inch in the halftone grid.

OPI Open Pre-press Interface. A system in which low-resolution images are automatically replaced with high-resolution images on output. OPI comments are not acceptable within **pass4press** compliant PDF files.

Output Intent The PDF/X standard requires that all CYMK data be identified for a target printing condition using an Output Intent. For printing conditions included in the ICC registry, this may be conveyed by a pointer to the printing characterisation data (Output Condition Identifier). For other conditions a full output profile is required as the value of the DestOutputProfile key. If you are not sure which colour space you should use, talk to your printer or publisher, otherwise **pass4press** suggest the ECI's ISO web coated profile. See the ECI website for more information (http://www.eci.org).

Overprint The printing of one colour over another without knocking out the colour beneath, meaning colours merge.

Press dot gain The amount by which a halftone dot increases between the printing plate and printed sheets. This occurs when ink is absorbed by paper and is an inevitable part of the printing process – therefore it must be compensated for when scanning and be represented on the proof.

RGB The red, green and blue colour space used on scanning devices and computer displays. This colour space is not suitable for the printing process, so any element using it must be converted into CMYK before producing a PDF.

RIP Raster Image Processor. A software program or computer that interprets digital data (for instance, PostScript) and determines what value each individual pixel of a final output page bitmap should have. In short, the interpretation of vector data into rasterised information.

Spot Colour Colour printed with customised ink outside the four process colours of cyan, magenta, yellow and black, such as metallics or fluorescents. Spot colours are not currently acceptable within a **pass4press** PDF.

Total Area Coverage Total area coverage refers to the maximum amount of ink – expressed in the cumulative sum of dot percentages – of all the colours being printed in one area. For example, CMYK has a maximum of 400% ink – 100% of each colour. In Offset printing it is not desirable to print 400% of ink in one area as this can cause problems ranging from inconsistent results to ink drying problems. The recommended amount of TAC is dependant on many variables including paper type and printing process; **pass4press** recommends 310% maximum for the printing of magazines on heatset web offset printing on good quality coated paper, but stresses that in all cases one should verify with the printer or publisher for the recommended TAC.

TIFF Tagged Image File Format. The traditional rasterised bitmap file format for high-quality, print-usage image files, photographic in nature, which can theoretically be any resolution or colour space. TIFFs are typically used in print at 300dpi at 100% of their placed size. TIFFs can lose quality if enlarged.

Transfer Functions These are instructions to change the colour gradation of an image. They have traditionally been used to compensate for dot gain in output devices or for the creation of special effects. Transfer functions are rarely used today. The **pass4press** specification forbids the use of transfer functions within PDF files. It recommends that these effects are applied during the creation of a PDF file.

Trapping A pre-press operation that allows for variations in registration during printing. The effect is created mainly by allowing an overlap between adjacent areas of colour. The requirement for trapping is greatly reduced with digital workflows.

UCR/GCR Under-Colour Removal/ Grey Component Replacement. UCR replaces the grey component of neutral colours with black ink, whereas GCR replaces the grey component of all colours with black ink, to minimise the amount of ink used during printing.

pass4press
Version 5 2004/2005

produced by
Jonathan Moore
The Condé Nast Publications
printed by
FE Burman Limited

Background to imaging theory and colour

4

Birth of computer graphics

Samuel Finley Breese Morse (1791–1872) invented the first digital communication. He studied painting in London, where he heard about the newly discovered research into electromagnetism and he gained the inspiration for his telegraph system. Morse code is a character code that is used to electronically transmit messages over telegraph lines. It started the movement toward today's electronically networked world.

Bits and bytes

Digital files make up all commercially printed items today. Digital files are composed of bits of information. A bit, or **bi**nary digi**t**, is a partial electromagnetic charge held on a memory device in a computer. As technology has improved and developed, the necessary size of the charge has dropped to a relatively small number of electrons. This allows smaller, more powerful computers to store, transmit and manipulate digital information more quickly and easily.

This bit is a binary function and considered as two possible digits – 1 or 0, on or off – and every representation of digital information is comprised of a collection of bits. It is cumbersome to have to count in binary mode and one of the key developments in boosting the digital capabilities was to handle collections of bits rather than individual bits. If eight bits are combined together there are 256 permutations from 00000000 to 11111111. This is a byte and 1012 bytes is a kilobyte (k or kb), 1024kb is a megabyte (Mb), 1024Mb is a gigabyte (Gb) and 1024Gb is a terabyte (Tb). Terabyte databases of content are now common in digital memory archives. Tb hard disks will be in workstations relatively soon and the standard hard disk size in personal computers within five years. A terabyte contains 8,390,967,461,888 (8.4 trillion) discrete bits of information, which is a large amount of information by any definition.

The representation of information owes a great deal to the decision to group eight bits together to make a byte that makes up all web and printed images, text and pictures. When passed between computers there are two basic forms of file; often they will be combined to make up a complete page or document. These two fundamentally different types of computer graphic files are:

► raster
► vector.

Raster (bitmap) files

Raster files are made up of collections of lines made up of pixels that describe every addressable position of any image as an array of discrete addresses. Images are built by varying the attributes of the pixels. The total image is stored as a reference grid, or map, of each pixel's value. In a mono image, each pixel may be either 'on' (black) or 'off' (white). Each pixel needs only a single bit to record its state, hence the term 'bitmapped image'.

In a high-resolution, continuous tone colour, each pixel requires more than a single bit, they have 'depth'. There are three channels – red, blue and green – in RGB colour for the web, and four – cyan, magenta, yellow and black – for most printing applications. Each separation has its own collection of pixels. The size of raster files corresponds to the number of addressable positions and colours in the image. Bit depth is the number of bits used to store information about each pixel. The higher the depth, the more colours are stored in an image. For example, the lowest bit-depth one-bit graphics are capable only of showing two colours, black and white. This is because there are only two combinations of numbers in one bit, 0 and 1. Four-bit colour is capable of displaying 16 colours because there are 16 combinations of four bits; with eight-bit colour, there are 256 colours available. With 16-bit colour, a total of 65,536 are available, and in the case of 24-bit colour, 16,777,216 colours are available. Bit depth can refer to the bit depth of an image or monitor. The number of pixels in a raster file is determined when the file is created; if they are not to be seen in the final reproduction, they must not be enlarged too much as shown in the following images.

FIGURE 4.1   Mono halftone TIFF image, 134kb uncompressed

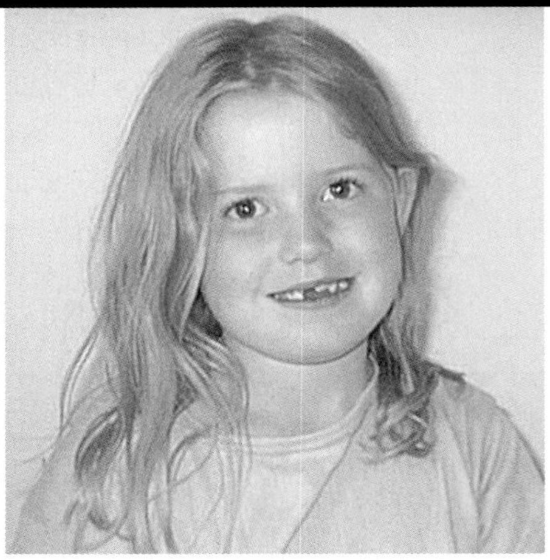

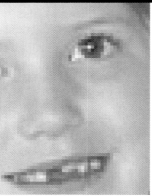

Source: Pira International Ltd

This image is satisfactory for mono reproduction at 3×4cm. When blown up too much, the individual pixels become too apparent, as shown in Figure 4.2 where a portion has been enlarged 15 times.

FIGURE 4.2   Portion of Figure 4.1 enlarged 15x, showing pixelation effects

Source: Pira International Ltd

For printing without such unsightly attributes, there is a limit to the degree of enlargement of a raster image and both the size and the number of the pixels it contains. The rule of thumb is to use a screen ruling of half the resolution of the image file at whatever the printed size is.

Continuous tone pictures are created by digital photography and scanning, along with creative artists and illustrators working directly in software, and generating images with no analogue original. The market-leading software for raster files image manipulation is Adobe PhotoShop.

Vector files

Vector files contain no pixel information. They comprise a list of mathematical descriptions of the boundaries of graphic objects used to create an image. They are the building components of the image rather than a representation of the finished graphic. Its simplest form is a straight line and the vector file contains the necessary data to describe the line's start position, length, direction of travel, thickness and colour. To become an image, the vector is drawn in software. The image is drawn from fundamental instructions within the file and the resolution of the final result depends on the output or viewing device. Vector images are not linked to any particular piece of hardware, and it is up to the application software to interpret the instructions correctly. It is the resolution-independence of vector graphics that allows the same font to be written to a 300dpi office printer and 3400dpi platesetter, and be reproduced at the optimum quality from both.

Another name for vector graphics is object or object-oriented graphics. This is because pictures formed this way remain as groups of simple objects and each element of that is stored as the instructions for its own reconstruction. The leading applications for the construction of vector graphics are Illustrator, Freehand and Corel Draw.

Figure 4.3 (overleaf) shows the comparison between a raster and a vector graphic of the same subject – a lower case g. If the raster version were to appear as smooth as the vector at the same size, the resolution of the raster would have to be so high that you could not see the individual pixels.

This shows a lower-case g character from the Antiqua font family. The outline of the character is positioned over a regular raster grid for a 10pt character at 150-line screen, the typical frequency of a halftone picture. At this resolution, the pixels in the grid are not capable of precisely rendering the shape of the character through the low resolution. To get a smooth, clear outline, significantly higher resolution is necessary, normally eight to ten times higher than for continuous tone pictures.

Vector graphics are inherently much smaller files than their raster equivalents. While it is possible to convert a photographic picture into a vector graphic, it is only likely to be used to create a special effect because it will lose its photo-realism in the process. Conversion is frequently done from printed or flat artwork of logos and simple designs so that they may be converted into a vector graphic by outlining the design for linework and particularly font characters.

FIGURE 4.3 Comparison between raster (bitmap) and vector font characters

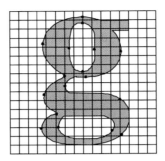

Raster grid overlaid with lower case
Antiqua 'g' outlined, bezier points in position

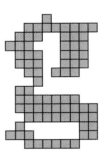

Vector font character   Pixels making up character

Source: Pira International Ltd

Fonts (founts)

A font is a collection of characters – upper- and lower-case letters, punctuation marks and numerals – in one size of one typeface. A typeface is the set of all sizes of one weight and style from a related set called a family. Two of the best known of all the thousands of type families available are probably Helvetica and Times. Within the type family there will be all the derivations of the basic design: bold, italic, extra bold, demi-bold, light, book, condensed and so on. The term font is increasingly being used as synonymous with typeface, but purists find the inaccuracy objectionable.

Depending on the software technology, the font will contain both a map of the character and the mathematical instructions for building the character outline, or just the instructions.

Font technology

Font technology issues do not give rise to the same degree of problems they once did. This does not mean that all problems have been solved by incorporating font outlines into PDF files but, with a bit of care and judicious use of preflighting software, most print-related issues can be solved.

In a computer system, the individual font characters are encoded in the form of binary numerical codes just as the numerals used in calculation programs are. A range of the codes is shown in Table 4.1. This is because the circuitry of a microprocessor can do only two things: calculate binary arithmetic operations and perform Boolean (true or false) logic operations.

Character	Binary Value
TABLE 4.1 Binary values of alphanumeric characters in 7-bit ASCII code	
1	00110001
2	00110010
3	00110011
4	00110100
5	00110101
6	00110111
A	1000001
B	1000010
C	1000011
D	1000100
E	1000101
F	1000111

Source: Pira International Ltd

Each character in a font has a particular shape and there are various ways of describing that shape on a computer. So when a personal computer saves the letter A to memory, it does not create an image of the letter A with tiny magnetic dots, but records a binary number that represents the letter A in a character code table. When the key for the letter A on the keyboard is pushed, the first thing that is generated is the character code for A. The computer uses that to load the character A from a font file listing with the same binary number and then displays it on screen.

A bitmapped font describes each character by drawing a picture of that character on a rectangular grid of pixels as a fixed bitmap array. The number of pixels in the letter does not change, so its rendered size on screen or print depends on the resolution of the device. To change size, a separate bitmap set is needed for every font size so raster fonts are less efficient in the use of computer resources than vector fonts. Many typographic purists maintain that the quality of the hand-crafted glyphs is much better than that produced by scaling algorithms, especially at small point sizes. They are always preferred in situations where text clarity is critical and screen space is at a premium. This technology is useful for representing small characters on web displays to make them as clear as possible.

Vector fonts (PostScript, TrueType and OpenType) describe the outline of the shape and then fill in the interior of that outline. Pierre Bézier was a French engineer who developed a routine to aid the body design of a car for Renault in the early 1970s. Bézier Curves are mathematical descriptions of smooth curves. His formula allowed a computer to use four points to create any curved segment, or spline. When these points are combined any shape can be created smoothly in digital form requiring a minimal amount of code. This type of mathematical description is used in PostScript and many computer programs.

An outline is composed of a set of paths. In Figure 4.3, the outline of letter g is described by three paths. The main one is on the outside and the two smaller ones are internal. Each of these paths is composed of a series of Bézier and line segments. Each spline is defined by control points and represented in the diagram by dots. Moving a control point will change the shape of the curve but does not alter where the spline begins or ends. A series of splines and lines are joined together to make a path. All paths in an outline font must be closed when it comes back and joins its start. A closed path has a direction that is essentially clockwise or anti-clockwise. When the outline character is drawn, everything in the interior of the outline should be filled. In the case of the g, there are two paths inside the main outline path and the interior of those two paths should be white rather than dark. The direction of the paths makes the distinction. Consider any point in the character and draw a line from that point out to infinity and count the number of times a path is crossed. Each time a clockwise path is crossed, add one to the count and subtract one for each anti-clockwise path. If the result of the count is non-zero then we fill the point dark, otherwise we leave it white. So to make the g above work, the outer path is clockwise and the two inner ones anti-clockwise and the loops are around a white interior.

As well as the outline scalable shape information, the font program contains additional information and hints to help the output device render the character outlines at different sizes. At small pixel sizes, the process of drawing the interior of an outline font is difficult to do well. Hinting mechanisms are statements to specify the location of key features of a character; then the RIP interprets these hints and makes the type more uniform on many output devices while reducing the overall size of font files. At its most basic level, hinting a font is a method of defining exactly which pixels are turned on in order to create the best possible character bitmap shape at small sizes and low resolutions. Since it is the outline that determines which pixels will constitute a character bitmap at a given size, it is often necessary to modify the outline to create a good bitmap image, effectively changing the outline until the desired combination of pixels is turned on. A hint is a mathematical instruction added to the font to distort a character's outline at particular sizes. Technically, hints result in operations that modify a contour's scaled control point co-ordinates before the outline is scan converted. In TrueType, a combination of these hints, and the resulting distortions, affords a fine degree of control over the bitmap shape produced.

English-language computers employ a basic seven-bit character code, the American Standard Code for Information Interchange (ASCII). This allows for a character set of 128 items of upper and lower case Latin letters, Arabic numerals, signs, and control characters to be used (2^7 = 128 code points). When an eight bit is used as a parity bit, that is a value used for checking whether or not data have been transmitted properly, then ASCII becomes an eight-bit, or one-byte (eight bits = one byte) character code. A true eight-bit character code allows up to 256 items to be encoded (2^8 = 256 code points).

In the case of languages such as Kanji, for example, which has a huge character set with tens of thousands of characters, a 16-bit, or two-byte, character code is used. A two-byte character code allows for up to 65,536 items to be encoded (2^{16} = 65,536 code points), but the standard character code used in Japanese personal computers at present, i.e. Japan Industrial Standard (JIS) X 0208–1990, lists only 6,879 characters.

TABLE 4.2 Character sets from several TrueType font sets on a PC

Character	Arial	Times New Roman	Wingdings
1			
2			
3			
4			
5			
6			
7			
8			
9			
10			
11			
12			
13			
14			
15	€	€	⊙
16			
17			
18			
19			
20	¶	¶	☆
21	§	§	▪
22			
23			
24			
25			
26			
27			
28			
29			
30			
31			
32			
33	!	!	(pen)
34	"	"	✂
35	#	#	(scissors)
36	$	$	(symbol)
37	%	%	(bell)
38	&	&	(open book)
39	'	'	(symbol)
40	(	(	☎
41	)	)	(symbol)
42	*	*	✉
43	+	+	(symbol)
44	,	,	(symbol)
45	-	-	(symbol)
46	.	.	(symbol)
47			
48	0	0	(folder)
49	1	1	(folder open)
50	2	2	(document)
51	3	3	(document)
52	4	4	(symbol)
53	5	5	(symbol)
54	6	6	(symbol)
55	7	7	(symbol)
56	8	8	(symbol)
57	9	9	(symbol)
58	:	:	(computer)
59	;	;	(symbol)
60	<	<	(symbol)
61	=	=	(symbol)
62	>	>	(symbol)
63	?	?	(pencil)
64	@	@	(symbol)
65	A	A	(symbol)
66	B	B	(symbol)
67	C	C	(symbol)
68	D	D	(symbol)
69	E	E	(symbol)
70	F	F	☞
71	G	G	(symbol)
72	H	H	(symbol)
73	I	I	✋
74	J	J	☺
75	K	K	☺
76	L	L	☹
77	M	M	(symbol)
78	N	N	(symbol)
79	O	O	(symbol)
80	P	P	(symbol)
81	Q	Q	✈
82	R	R	☼
83	S	S	●
84	T	T	✼
85	U	U	✞
86	V	V	✠
87	W	W	✡
88	X	X	✺
89	Y	Y	✶
90	Z	Z	☾
91	[	[	(symbol)
92	\	\	ॐ
93	]	]	✴
94	^	^	♈
95	_	_	♉
96	`	`	♊
97	a	a	♋
98	b	b	♌
99	c	c	♍
100	d	d	♎
101	e	e	♏
102	f	f	♐
103	g	G	♑
104	h	H	♒
105	i	I	♓
106	j	J	er
107	k	K	&
108	l	L	●
109	m	M	○
110	n	N	■
111	o	O	□
112	p	P	□
113	q	Q	□
114	r	R	□
115	s	S	•
116	t	T	◆
117	u	U	◆
118	v	V	❖
119	w	W	◆
120	x	X	⊠
121	y	Y	◹
122	z	Z	⌘
123	{	{	(symbol)
124	|	|	❀
125	}	}	"
126	~	~	"
127			
128	Ç	Ç	(symbol)
129	ü	Ü	✓
130	é	É	↑
131	â	Â	↓
132	ä	Ä	↗
133	à	À	→
134	å	Å	↙
135	ç	Ç	←
136	ê	Ê	↓
137	ë	Ë	↖
138	è	È	→
139	ï	Ï	⇦
140	î	Î	↘
141	ì	Ì	↗
142	Ä	Ä	(symbol)
143	Å	Å	(symbol)
144	É	É	(symbol)
145	æ	Æ	↘
146	Æ	Æ	(symbol)
147	ô	Ô	⇕
148	ö	Ö	(symbol)
149	ò	Ò	⇩
150	û	Û	✗
151	ù	Ù	□
152	ÿ	Ÿ	▦
153	Ö	Ö	⊠
154	Ü	Ü	➲
155	ø	ø	(symbol)
156	£	£	●
157	Ø	Ø	➢
158			◄
159	ƒ	ƒ	③
160	á	á	↑
161	í	í	↙
162	ó	ó	⇔
163	ú	ú	□
164	ñ	ñ	⇧
165	Ñ	Ñ	(symbol)
166	ª	ª	✚
167	º	º	(clock)
168	¿	¿	(clock)
169	®	®	✹
170	¬	¬	✷
171			(clock)
172			(clock)
173	¡	¡	○
174	«	«	★
175	»	»	(clock)
176			♉
177			♉
178			♉
179			○
180			○
181	Á	Á	(clock)
182			(clock)
183	À	À	(clock)
184	©	©	⤴
185			○
186			○
187	+	+	(symbol)
188	+	+	(symbol)
189	¢	¢	●
190	¥	¥	◎
191	+	+	(symbol)
192	+	+	(symbol)
193	-	-	(symbol)
194	-	-	(symbol)
195	+	+	(symbol)
196	-	-	(symbol)
197	+	+	(symbol)
198	ã	ã	↖
199	Ã	Ã	✍
200	+	+	(symbol)
201	+	+	(symbol)
202	-	-	(symbol)
203	-	-	(symbol)
204			○
205	-	-	(symbol)
206	+	+	(symbol)
207	€	€	⊙
208			⇨
209			(symbol)
210	Ê	Ê	↘
211	Ë	Ë	✄
212	È	È	(symbol)
213	I	I	✋
214	Í	Í	(symbol)
215	Î	Î	(symbol)
216	Ï	Ï	(symbol)
217	+	+	✚
218	+	+	(clock)
219			♉
220			♉
221			○
222	Ì	Ì	✠
223			♉
224	Ó	Ó	(symbol)
225	ß	ß	←
226	Ô	Ô	(symbol)
227	Ò	Ò	(symbol)
228	õ	õ	(symbol)
229	Õ	Õ	⊠
230	µ	µ	✿
231			☑
232			(symbol)
233	Ú	Ú	✈
234	Û	Û	(symbol)
235	Ù	Ù	(symbol)
236			⊠
237			(headphone)
238	-	-	✳
239	'	'	◈
240	-	-	(symbol)
241	±	±	(symbol)
242			♉
243			(clock)
244	¶	¶	☆
245	§	§	▪
246	÷	÷	(symbol)
247	¸	¸	(clock)
248	º	º	⊞
249	¨	¨	□
250	·	·	(clock)
251			(clock)
252			¤
253			◆
254			♉
255			

Source: Pira International Ltd

Table 4.2 shows the character sets for three common TrueType fonts on a PC with a standard UK keyboard. Arial and Times New Roman share the same characters while Wingdings provides a different array of symbols, each taking just one byte of computer memory to store. The main characters will always fall in the same position by convention making it easy for data exchange between different fonts and different operating systems. Difficulties may still arise with special characters (foreign, scientific or mathematical) and decorative marks such as bullets. Mapping of some characters is different on a Macintosh platform than on a Windows workstation. Even some mundane ones sometimes do not translate across when transferring between a Macintosh application using PostScript fonts and a PC with TrueType fonts, so care is needed to check. The ASCII code, having fixed the first 128 out of the full byte 256 possible characters, left the balance to be defined either by the operating system or the application.

PostScript fonts come in two parts: the screen font and the printer font. Screen fonts are low-resolution bitmaps which are used to display the character on the computer screen. The maps are made to correspond to a certain point size (typically at 72 ppi resolution) and contain information about the character width and spacing. If screen fonts are scaled to appear larger, their block nature quickly becomes visible with the character curves clearly showing jagged edges (the jaggies). Adobe's Type Manager (ATM) overcomes some of these problems. ATM improves the look of type on the computer screen by creating appropriately sized screen fonts (from the instructions in the printer fonts), as they are required. The ATM software has no influence on type sent to a PostScript printer, but it can be used to aid the appearance of PostScript fonts on non-PostScript printers.

Due to their low resolution, screen fonts are not suitable for sending to a printer or imagesetter. Printer fonts are vector descriptions of the character boundaries. When a document is sent to a PostScript imager, the application determines the screen fonts used and requests the equivalent printer fonts from the output device. If the fonts are not present on the printer and cannot be downloaded by the application, then the raster image processor (RIP) will either make a font substitution (choose a font that it thinks is near to the one requested) or use the screen font. In either case the result is likely to be unsatisfactory, and more likely a disaster. The RIP is the computer in the printer that translates the vector information describing the document layout and character constructions into the raster map needed to draw or write the final page image onto paper. PostScript fonts on different platforms, even though they may have identical names, may not contain the same character dimensions and spacings.

The graphics industry uses both TrueType and PostScript fonts that are based on slightly different technologies, and the new OpenType technology. PostScript uses cubic Bézier splines where each control point determines the slope of the spline at the corresponding end point. TrueType uses quadratic Bézier splines, and in these there is only one control point between two end points. That point determines the slope of the spline at both end points. Cubic splines are generally easier to edit (more shapes are possible with them). Any quadratic spline can be converted to a cubic spline with essentially no loss. A cubic spline can be converted to a quadratic with arbitrary precision, but there will be a slight loss of accuracy in most cases. This means it is easy to convert TrueType outlines to PostScript outlines, but harder to convert PostScript to TrueType.

OpenType is a PostScript font rendered into a TrueType format. It looks like a TrueType font except that the outline descriptions are PostScript Type2 font descriptions rather than TrueType. An OpenType font is essentially a double-byte TrueType font (meaning that it can contain some 65,000 glyphs, or representations of characters), augmented by a series of resources (called tables) that allow OpenType fonts to provide certain auxiliary features. This feature is hugely useful for non-Latin character sets.

So, in a font all of the points are described mathematically and it easy for a computer to calculate the required shape at output (or for display) using little memory. This means that for text each character can be stored as a single byte, and a 3,000-word article takes up only 3k of memory. At output, the vector file is translated into a bitmap according to the resolution of the output device. Most type looks satisfactory when imaged on a 600dpi laser printer while conventional printing type needs 2400dpi (maybe 1200 dpi for newsprint).

Font legality

When a font is bought, the user does not receive ownership of it. There are usage rules with all fonts and it is important to read the licence and be aware of the manufacturer's requirements for its use and distribution. Not all font owners have the same rules but here are some of the more common approaches to font use. A buyer of a font package is licensing the right to use it. Apart from as a security back-up, it is usually illegal to copy fonts and give copies to others, which includes printing companies. It is possible to legally send copies of fonts along with a job to a printer as long as the printer already has a licence to use it. There are two alternatives to sending a copy of the font with the job. One is to convert the fonts to outlines, but this is feasible only for layouts with small quantities of text such as display advertisements. The other is to embed the fonts within the document format. In this way they become an integral part of the file and cannot be saved separately by the recipient. This is probably the most important early driver for the success of PDF as a transfer mechanism.

Image printing

Conventional printing technology does not have the controllable capability of printing variable shades of an ink, and variations in colour density are produced by varying the physical area of the dot in a halftone screening process.

Screening

There are two ways of varying the area. In conventional screening, the image is split into a series of cells at a fixed position that contain a dot. The dot can vary in size from nothing to filling the complete cell. Newer, frequency modulated screening (FM, sometimes referred to as stochastic screening) uses the same sized dots and just adds more with no fixed position for each.

A platesetter (or imagesetter) is a recorder that shines laser light onto a photo-receptive media and selectively exposes an image. Text, linework and images are all produced from a vast array of tiny dots making up the final image. Text and linework are generally produced from vector files with a mathematical transformation performed by the RIP. High resolution is necessary to avoid noticeable jagged edges and other unsightly artefacts. A minimum of 1200 lines per inch is required for newspaper and about 2400lpi (or 2,540lpi) for commercial printing. This high resolution is fine for text where it is only at output that the outline is painted, but most continuous tone pictures are stored at much lower resolutions, typically 300 dots per inch for commercial colour printing onto a good surface.

The images are built up at the higher resolution with individual printing screened dots being output at 150dpi (much lower for newspaper and some flexo reproduction, higher for top-quality litho where 200dpi is not uncommon). The screen frequency can be represented by a grid as in Figure 4.4. Each square in this grid is a halftone cell and capable of holding one halftone dot. Think of each halftone screen as a grid that is superimposed on the image recorder resolution grid.

The recorder makes an extremely fine grid (named the resolution grid). The imagesetter spots composing the grid are called printer dots, and, in fact, image recorder resolution is measured in dots per inch (dpi). When the halftone grid is laid over the resolution grid, each halftone supercell is filled with imagesetter spots. Combinations of these spots make halftone dots.

FIGURE 4.4 Halftone dots and the imagesetter grid

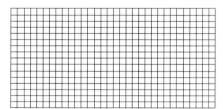

Platesetter (imagesetter) grid

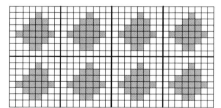

Pixels activated in grid to create a printable tint

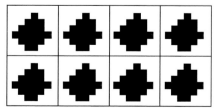

Screened dots for printing in 'Supercells'

Source: Pira International Ltd

To convert an image into a halftone, the halftone grid is superimposed and the colour value at that point is converted into a percentage dot. The percentage is then output as a dot using the particular screening algorithms to control frequency, angle and shape of the individual dots at the output device. The size of halftone cells is determined by the interaction of the screen frequency with the image recorder resolution. Each of the halftone cells in the figure comprises many spots created by the image recorder laser beam when it is focused on a point of media. Each spot in a halftone cell can be turned on (producing a colour dot) or left blank to give white. The combination of imagesetter spots produces a halftone dot of a specific size and shape. If a dot has to be larger, the image recorder turns on more spots; if smaller then fewer spots are exposed. PostScript uses at least 256 levels of grey to properly reproduce an image and platesetter manufacturers have adopted 256 grey levels as a minimum standard; each level expresses as a single byte of information.

There is a trade-off between screen frequencies and grey levels. Higher screen frequencies are finer and can reproduce more detail from the original file in more halftone cells. The platesetter resolution remains constant so the more halftone cells there are will contain fewer addressable spots. As the number of output spots decreases, so does the number of grey levels each halftone cell can reproduce. To create different shapes, spots are exposed in different sequences. These spot functions are determined by a RIP algorithm.

In FM (frequency modulated or stochastic) screening, the platesetter takes the image bitmap data and generates smaller dots that are not restricted to a fixed grid pattern. By varying the number of dots in a given area, any desired grey level can be generated. As the dots are significantly smaller than conventional halftone cells, FM screening can represent more detail. FM screening methods employ randomness, or noise generation, in determining where to place pixels. This produces smoother tone transitions and eliminates patterns that could lead to a moiré effect. Many digital printing devices use FM techniques to print small dots at high resolution, producing an apparently continuous tone image.

Colour reproduction – basic principles

This section provides an understanding of the basic principles of colour reproduction. It will help readers to appreciate some of the problems and limitations in printed colour reproductions, and understand some of the terminology.

Human vision

People use their eyes to receive light from the surroundings. Signals from light-receptive cells on the retina transmit a signal to the brain, which interprets the signal as vision. The retina of a person with normal colour vision provides a visual sensation when stimulated by electromagnetic radiation in the wavelength range 380–760 nm. The brain interprets this stimulation as light and colour. The sensation of colour will be different depending upon the precise balance, or combination, of wavelengths received. The sensation of white requires elements of all three thirds of the visible spectrum to be present. Millions of photoreceptor cells (about 126,500,000 in each eye) lie within the retina and these photoreceptors are divided into two groups: rods and cones.

FIGURE 4.5 Horizontal cross-section of the eye

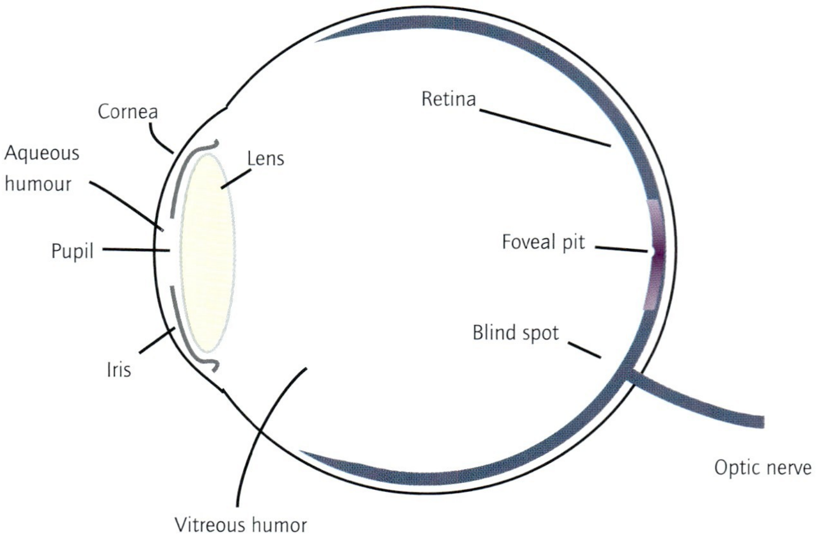

Source: Pira International Ltd

The rods – there are about 120,000,000 of these cells – are brightness sensors. The cones determine hue. They are concentrated in a small area of the retina opposite the optical axis of the lens and are divided into three groups:

▶   those that are broadly sensitive to the short wavelength third of the visible spectrum – blue;

▶   those that are broadly sensitive to the medium wavelength third of the spectrum – green;

▶   those that are broadly sensitive to the long wavelength third of the visible spectrum – red.

The eye takes in the light onto the receptor cells but it is the brain that interprets the result humans see. With the vast amount of information to process human beings have evolved mechanisms for the brain to make short cuts; these may not reflect reality. It is fairly easy to fool the eye (in fact all continuous tone printing of images uses this principle); in print production it is important to take steps to avoid being fooled.

Figure 4.6 shows one such effect. The yellow, cyan, magenta, green, blue and red circles are all identical in hue and strength yet humans see significant variation, particularly in density. This chromatic induction effect is due to the different surrounds, the brain perceives the relative rather than absolute colour.

FIGURE 4.6 Effect of chromatic induction

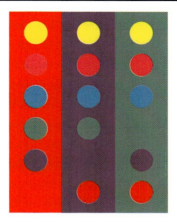

Source: Pira International Ltd

Colour definition and measurement

Defining and ordering colours

In printing there is often a need to communicate the colour of an object. A subjective description is insufficient. Scarlet, warm red, yellow shade red or bright red convey the general nature of the colour but they are not precise enough to convey the exact colour for most printed products. To describe the colour accurately, an objective system that defines the colour is needed. Three terms can be used to define a colour: hue, lightness and chroma (saturation).

Hue, lightness and chroma

Initially hue is used to describe a colour. Hue is how most humans perceive colour to be – red, green, blue, etc. Lightness then describes the luminous intensity of a colour. While it is easier to understand this attribute with respect to grey, it applies equally to colours. For a neutral grey, white has high lightness while black has low lightness. Similarly, yellow has high lightness and blue has lower lightness; sometimes the term 'value' is used to describe this attribute. The chroma, or saturation, describes the degree of intensity or colourfulness.

Colour definition using a physical sample

For many printed products, colour is specified through the provision of a physical sample. This may be a previously printed job or a sample of another product, perhaps a fabric or plastic. It is normal to specify many special solid colours using a reference sample from a colour specification and matching system.

The Pantone system is probably the most widely used and recognised. It provides a range of colours produced from 13 base colours, plus black and white, with a unique number to define each colour. There are additional metallic and fluorescent colours. Pantone notation is commonly found within computer-based graphic design software, which further widens its use in specifying the required colour.

Colour guides are also available to indicate the range of colours achieved with halftone combinations of the process colours – cyan, magenta, yellow and black. Again Pantone is the most common system to allow process colour combinations to be compared to colours defined in the solid colour guide. While the range of colours in such systems is smaller, they are valuable where special colours cannot be used and it is necessary to define a colour within the gamut of the process inks and the halftone process. There are also colour guides available that are produced with extended process colour sets, such as Pantone Hexachrome (CMYK + orange and green) and Opaltone (CMYK + red, green and blue).

While these physical systems have been widely adopted and provide both an acceptable method for defining a colour and, in the case of Pantone, a colour mixing system, they are not without their limitations or problems, particularly when defining colour standards. Limitations of physical colour specification systems include:

▶ manufacturing variation in the printing of sample books
▶ shelf life and fading of books
▶ limited range of colours and substrates (normally coated and uncoated stock)
▶ there is no definition of tolerances.

An objective system is needed for specifying colour and defining tolerances that involves measurement that correlates with the human perception of colour.

Defining colour by measurement

Human colour vision is complex. It involves physical, physiological and psychological influences, and an individual's experience can change over time as eyes age. A system for colour measurement must consider these influences. In practice there are three basic factors, vital to the appearance of colour, which form the basis for systems of colour measurement:

▶ a source of light;
▶ an object that will absorb some wavelengths of light and reflect others;
▶ a visual system that can provide the required sensation in the brain when appropriate wavelengths of light are received.

A useful colour measurement system must consider:

▶ a definition of the spectral output of the illuminates
▶ the measurement of the spectral reflectance of the sample
▶ a definition of 'normal' human colour vision (a standard observer).

The methods used today for colour measurement are based on systems and standards that have been developed through the Commission Internationale de l'Eclairage (CIE), the international body responsible for recommendations for photometry and colorimetry. Standards have been defined for a range of illuminates and the standard observer, the basis of a mathematical description of colour that converts a spectral reflectance measurement into a colour description that can be represented by a colour space model.

Spectral reflectance

The colour of an object or a print depends on the absorption of certain wavelengths of light and the reflection or transmission of others. A measurement of the amount of light reflected by the sample at different wavelengths provides an indication of its colour. This measurement may be used to provide a graphical representation of the colour, in the form of a curve on a graph.

FIGURE 4.7 Spectral reflectance curves of three process colours and a cyan/magenta overprint

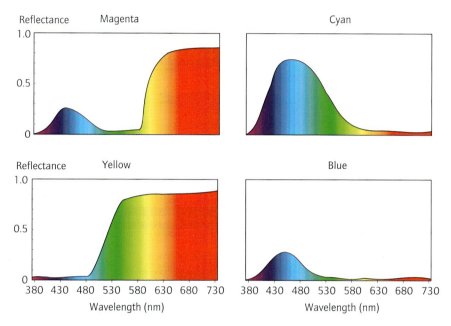

Source: Pira International Ltd

Examples for process colours and the magenta + cyan overprint are shown in Figure 4.7. These curves are spectral reflectance curves and they represent the fundamental physical measurement of a colour. The horizontal axis shows the wavelengths of light in the visible part of the spectrum; measurements are normally taken at 5–20nm intervals, depending on the instrument. The vertical axis shows the percentage of light reflected from the sample at each of the measured wavelengths. With experience, an individual can view the curve and obtain a good indication of the colour without seeing a printed sample.

Two printed samples with identical spectral reflectance curves will be perceived to be the same colour when viewed, but it is also possible for two samples with different spectral curves to be perceived to be a colour match. This is known as a metameric match – identical under one light source but different under another. When spectral reflectance is related to the colour of the light source and the colour sensitivity of the human visual system, it provides a meaningful way of measuring and defining colour.

CIE colour standards

In 1931 the CIE made an important step in standardising systems for colour measurement and order by specifying the spectral characteristics of standard illuminants and providing data relating to the standard observer. It also established methods for describing colour.

Standard Illuminants

A number of standard illuminants have now been defined. Those most relevant to printing are shown in Table 4.3. The spectral power distribution curves for two of the most important standard light illuminants are shown in Figure 4.8, overleaf.

TABLE 4.3 CIE standard illuminants

Standard		Nature of light
	Colour temperature	
A	Typical of tungsten light	2856 K
C	Representating bluish daylight	6800 K
D_{65}	Representing average indoor daylight	6504 K
D_{50}	Representing warm indoor daylight (widely used in colour vision and colorimetry)	5083 K

Source: Pira International Ltd

FIGURE 4.8 Spectral power distribution of CIE standard Illuminants A and D_{65}

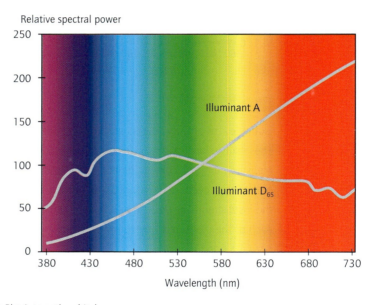

Source: Pira International Ltd

While these standards exist in terms of a specification of their spectral power distribution, and can be used in colorimetry calculations, it is not possible to obtain actual light sources that have an identical spectral power distribution. The widely available 'daylight' tubes that are used to represent D_{65} and D_{50} in colour viewing are the nearest that the lamp manufacturers are able to achieve. A comparison between the D_{65} standard and a typical fluorescent light source is shown in Figure 4.9.

FIGURE 4.9 Spectral energy distribution curves of daylight fluorescent light and Illuminant standard D$_{65}$

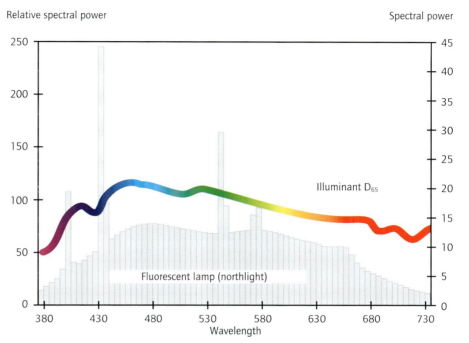

Source: Pira International Ltd

The CIE standard observer

The basis for the current understanding of human colour vision is experimental work carried out in the UK in the mid-1920s to determine the average or standard observer. A range of volunteers with normal colour vision were required to match monochromatic light of individual wavelengths by additively mixing proportions of red, green and blue light. From these experiments it was possible to define, for all colours of the spectrum, the amount of red, green and blue light required to be received by the eye in order to match that colour. The CIE used the results of this work to define the standard observer. More specifically, the data that defines this is referred to as the CIE colour-matching functions. It is provided as a data table, giving values for x (red), y (green) and z (blue), at wavelength increments of 5nm throughout the visible spectrum.

The original experimental work used apparatus that provided a viewing field with a cone angle of 2° (CIE 2° Standard Observer). Later experiments used a 10° angular field, and these results are used in the CIE 1964 10° Standard Observer. The 10° standard is more appropriate where the samples being measured are larger areas of colour. A graphical representation of the data for the colour-matching functions for the two standard observers – 2° and 10° – is shown in Figure 4.10.

FIGURE 4.10 CIE colour matching functions

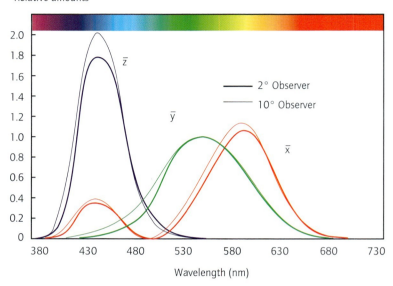

Source: Pira International Ltd

Tristimulus values

The colour-matching functions provide the means for converting any spectral curves into three numbers, the X, Y and Z tristimulus values that provide a unique definition of that colour. The tristimulus values represent the amount of red, green and blue cone response required by the standard observer to match the colour when viewed under a particular light source. A simple appreciation of how the tristimulus values are calculated can be obtained from Figure 4.11.

FIGURE 4.11 Diagrammatic representation of the calculation of the tristimulus values (X, Y, Z)

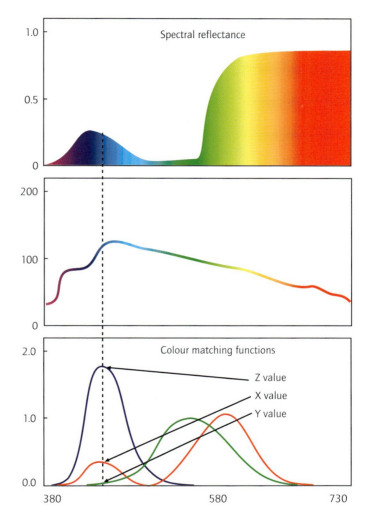

Source: Pira International Ltd

The diagram shows that for each incremental wavelength on the reflectance curve there is an associated power output from the illuminate and corresponding values for the required amount of red, green and blue response. These values are determined throughout the spectrum, at 10nm or 5nm intervals, and the resulting products are then summed. The three resulting values are multiplied by a constant factor, determined for the particular illuminate, to provide the X, Y and Z tristimulus values. The tristimulus values are the foundation for all subsequent colorimetric calculations. By understanding how the tristimulus values are calculated, it is possible to appreciate how a colour match can be observed between two colours whose spectral reflectance is different. Identical spectral reflectance curves will always provide the same tristimulus values, but it is also possible for this to be achieved with different spectral reflectance, as with a metameric pair.

Chromaticity values

The tristimulus values provide three numbers that can be used to identify any colour but they do not correlate directly with the lightness, hue and chroma that define the visual attributes of colour (except Y, which correlates with lightness). To improve the correlation, the CIE recommends using the x, y, z chromaticity coordinates. These are calculated from tristimulus values such that:

$$x = \frac{X}{(X+Y+Z)}$$

$$y = \frac{Y}{(X+Y+Z)}$$

$$z = \frac{Z}{(X+Y+Z)}$$

$$x + y + z = 1$$

The x, y coordinates of a colour can be plotted on a chromaticity diagram (Figure 4.12). The triangular-shaped locus shown on this diagram defines the visible colour gamut and is the result of plotting the chromaticity values from the colour-matching functions (2° Observer) at each wavelength. The straight line joining 380 to 730nm represents colours of red–purple, such as magenta, that do not exist in the spectrum but are obtained by mixing red and blue light.

FIGURE 4.12 CIE 1931 *x, y* chromaticity diagram (2° Observer data) showing the location of a CMY ink set printed on coated paper and illuminates D$_{65}$ and A

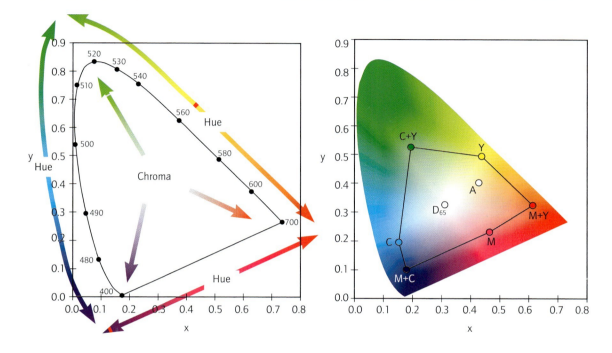

Source: Pira International Ltd

The notation *Yxy* specifies colours with *Y* being the lightness and *xy* being represented on the two axes of the chromaticity diagram, providing a means of plotting colours with respect to hue and chroma. As it is a two-dimensional diagram, white through to grey to black will all plot at the same point. The position of white and other colours on the diagram depends on the light source. The location of a perfect white diffuser is shown on the diagram when illuminated with standard illuminant D$_{65}$ and illuminant A. Increased chroma or saturation is represented by movement away from the neutral areas out towards the perimeter of the triangle, with hue represented at all points around the perimeter. Figure 4.12 shows the location of the three process colours and their overprints plotted on *x, y* chromaticity diagrams.

When viewing these two-dimensional diagrams, users should appreciate that some apparently different colours plot in the same position. The most obvious examples are greys through to white, but the same is true for other colours which are of the same hue but differ only in lightness. An example would be an orange and brown colour; brown can be considered to be a dark orange colour. To illustrate this point more clearly, sample Pantone colours have been selected and plotted on the chromaticity diagram in Figure 4.13. Access to a Pantone book will assist in an understanding of the diagram, by referring to the specific colours that are plotted. The sample colours can all be found on the same page. They represent a base colour orange and two colours produced by adding black to the base, together with a further two achieved with the addition of transparent white to the colour.

FIGURE 4.13 CIE x, y chromaticity diagram showing sample Pantone colours

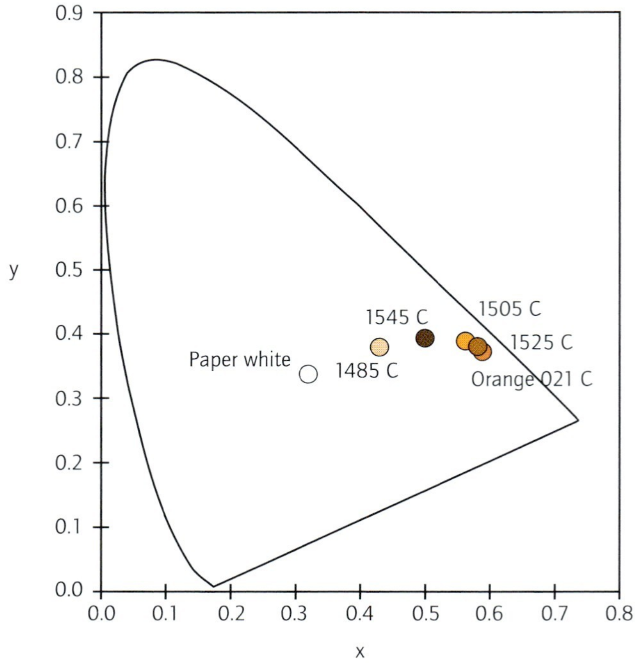

Source: Pira International Ltd

The diagram shows that the base orange, being a saturated colour, plots near to the perimeter of the triangular locus. The other colours have lower saturation, as a result of mixing black or white to the base orange, and these plot closer to the paper white. The samples also clearly indicate the limitations of plotting on a two-dimensional diagram.

CIELab ($L*a*b*$) colour space

The x, y chromaticity diagrams are limited in only being able to represent two dimensions. In 1976, the CIE recommended the CIELab ($L*a*b*$) uniform colour space for applications dealing with subtractive colorant mixtures such as those in the printing industry. The colour space is obtained by plotting the three values along the axis at right angles to one another. The $L*$ value represents lightness and the $a*$ and $b*$ are the chromatic axes that adopt the opponent response theory of colour vision, where $a* = $ red–green and $b* = $ yellow–blue. A three-dimensional diagrammatic representation of the CIELab colour space is shown in Figure 4.14. The aim is for equal visual colour difference to be proportional to distance within the colour space.

FIGURE 4.14   The CIELab (L*a*b*) colour space

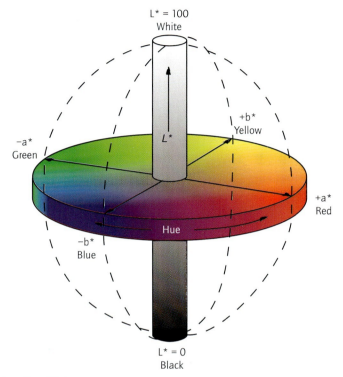

L* = 100
White

+b*
Yellow

−a*
Green

L*

+a*
Red

Hue

−b*
Blue

L* = 0
Black

Source: Pira International Ltd

The location of colours in the CIELab diagram cannot be easily represented on paper because it describes colour in a three-dimensional space. The normal solution is to display a two-dimensional graph of $a*$ and $b*$ axis, with the relevant lightness values represented by a separate single bar scale, or as a numeric value.

In order to understand more clearly how colours plot on the CIELab diagram, it is sensible once again to consider the sample Pantone colours. In Figure 4.15 the sample colours are plotted on the $a*$ $b*$ axis, which produces a characteristic plot of colour patches that have the same hue but differ in chroma. When plotted with an $L*$ $a*$ axis, the difference in lightness of these same colours is emphasised. Those samples with transparent white added move towards the paper in terms of lightness, and those to which black has been added plot towards the complete black. The relative position of colours in this diagram basically correlates with the perception of colour difference, as will be seen by examination of these samples in the Pantone book.

FIGURE 4.15 CIELab diagram showing Pantone colours – hue to chroma (left) lightness to chroma (right)

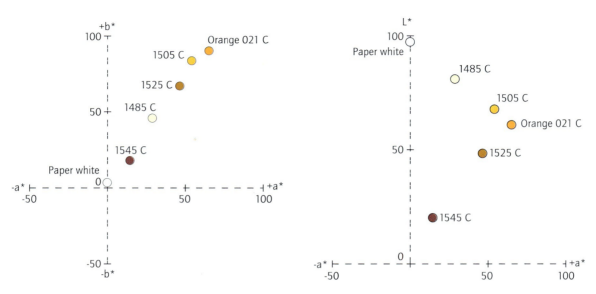

Source: Pira International Ltd

An alternative to CIELab is CIELCh (L*C*h°), where polar coordinates are used to define the location of a colour within the colour space. The lightness (L*) remains the same as with CIELab, but C* specifies chroma (distance along X or Y axis) and h° defines the hue angle (with X axis 0°). CIELCh is not an alternative colour space to CIELab, and the location and relationship of colours to each other remain the same; it is only the coordinate system that changes. Figure 4.16 illustrates the location of red (M+Y) and blue (C+M) plotted on the L*C*h° diagram.

FIGURE 4.16 Example colours plotted using CIELCh (L*C*h°)

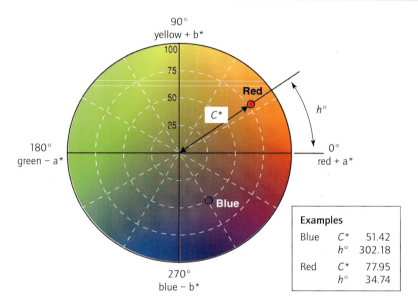

Examples		
Blue	*C**	51.42
	h°	302.18
Red	*C**	77.95
	h°	34.74

Source: Pira International Ltd

Colour differences and tolerances

An important application for CIELab is to define colour and differences between samples. Ideally, a single value would define the colour difference that correlates exactly with human visual perception irrespective of its position in the colour space. Equally perceived differences between pairs of light colours and pairs of dark colours or low chroma and high chroma would have identical colour difference values. The single value that is used to express the colour difference is the ∆E (the ∆ is Delta, representing difference). To determine the ΔE *ab the differences in ΔL^*, Δa^* and Δb^* between the reference and sample are measured, then the equation:

$$\Delta E^*ab = [(\Delta L^*)^2 + (\Delta a^*)^2 + (\Delta b^*)^2]^{0.5}$$

is used. This appears rather complicated but it is simply calculating the distance within the colour space between the reference and sample. This is represented diagrammatically in Figure 4.17.

FIGURE 4.17 Diagrammatic representation of ΔE*ab colour difference and tolerances

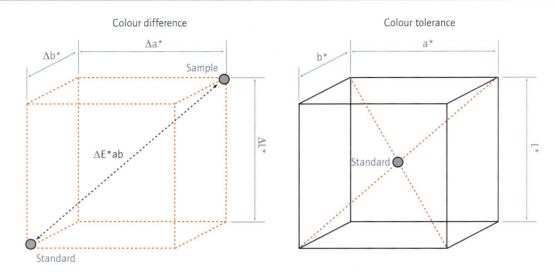

Source: Pira International Ltd

For example, Table 4.4 shows the calculation of the colour difference between the Pantone base orange and sample 1505. With reference to a Pantone colour guide book, it is possible gain an impression of what a ΔE10 represents in actual colour difference.

TABLE 4.4 Example calculation of colour difference (ΔE)

Pantone colour	L*	a*	b*
Orange base	62	61	72
1505 c	65	51	74
Δ_(difference)	3	10	2
ΔE*ab	$[(32) + (102) + (22)]^{1/2} = 10.63$		

Source: Pira International Ltd

The ΔE value defines the overall colour difference, which takes account of both lightness and chromatic differences, and is therefore, ideally suited to defining the permitted variation when colour printing. Table 4.5 indicates the ΔE values that can typically be applied to different situations.

TABLE 4.5 Colour difference description

ΔE*ab	0.5 to 2	Critical colour match, difference just perceptible to trained observer
ΔE*ab	2 to 4	Acceptable for most printing where side by side comparison is possible
ΔE*ab	4 to 8	Acceptable colour match where side by side comparison is not possible
ΔE*ab	above 8	Significant visual difference

Source: Pira International Ltd

Although the ΔE^*ab value is commonly used as a single number to define the total colour differences, there are occasions when it is desirable to consider the attributes of the colour difference separately. In this case, ΔL^* is used independently to define lightness differences, ΔC^* chroma differences and ΔH^* the difference in hue. Knowing the individual differences is helpful when establishing the required corrective action to improve a colour match, and in certain instances it is beneficial to define tolerances for each individual attribute.

Total colour difference, as provided by ΔE^*ab, is widely used for defining tolerances in printing but it does have some weaknesses. Partly due to the rectangular tolerance box that is defined around the standard (see Figure 4.17), and the equal weighting applied to all three attributes of the colour. In practice, humans do not detect differences in hue, chroma or lightness equally. The average observer will see hue differences first, then chroma differences and lightness differences last. Therefore the preferred tolerance would be a three-dimensional ellipsoid, as illustrated in Figure 4.18. Humans observe differences in low chroma colours more acutely than high chroma colours, therefore the size of the ellipsoid in different areas of the colour space should reflect this. The shape of the ellipsoid is determined by the weighting of lightness to chroma, chroma to hue, etc., and provision for this is made in some alternative colour difference equations.

FIGURE 4.18 Ellipsoid for colour tolerance as in CMC and CIE2000 colour difference calculations, also showing the reducing size of the tolerance ellipsoid with decreasing chroma (left)

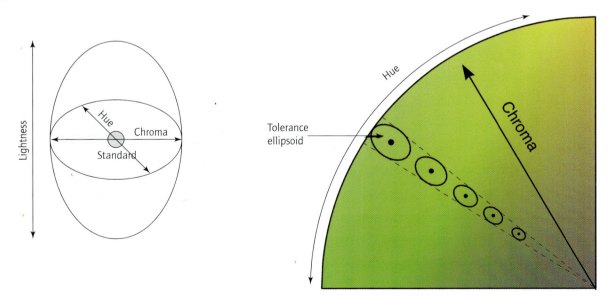

Source: Pira International Ltd

Colour measurement

To make a colour measurement requires a means of evaluating the reflected light from the sample. It must measure and determine the tristimulus values (X, Y and Z). This is accomplished using a spectrophotometer or a tristimulus colorimeter. A spectrophotometer determines the proportion of light reflected from the sample in discrete wavelengths throughout the visible spectrum, at 5, 10 or 20nm intervals, depending on the instrument. This enables the spectrophotometer to provide a complete spectral reflection curve from which the X, Y and Z tristimulus values are calculated. The colorimeter is in many respects similar to a densitometer. It measures the reflected light from the sample using filtered photocells. The filters are selected so that the resulting spectral sensitivities are a close match to the CIE colour-matching functions. Because it is difficult to find filtration that exactly matches the CIE colour-matching functions, this method provides limited accuracy. However, it offers a convenient method of providing simple, relatively low-cost colour difference measuring instruments. Because it does not provide a full spectral reflectance curve, the colorimeter is not able to provide an indication of the degree of metamerism in a colour match. A schematic representation of the two types of instrument is shown in Figures 4.19 and 4.20.

FIGURE 4.19 Schematic representation of a reflection spectrophotometer

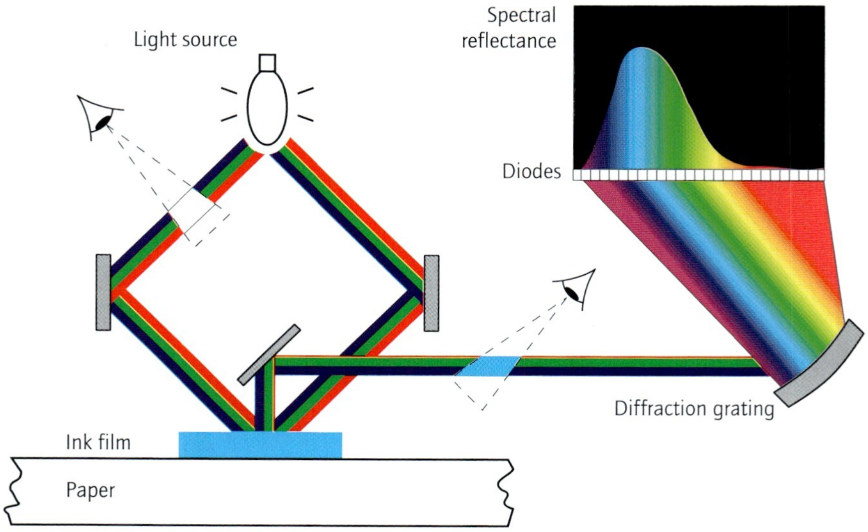

Source: Pira International Ltd

FIGURE 4.20 Schematic representation of a tristimulus colorimeter

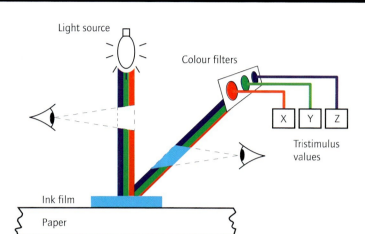

Source: Pira International Ltd

Additive colour

When the process of creating colour uses sources of light – such as the tiny points of phosphor on the surface of a domestic television tube, a computer screen or the projected light from a video projector – this is additive colour. The colour is created by adding together different amounts of the additive light primaries: red, green and blue (RGB). If all three of these are present, their combined effect will be white. If none of the light sources are available, the result will be black (the absence of light). All the other tones and hues that the device is able to present will be created by the precise control of the individual (and relative) brightness of the RGB sources, because mixing two primary colours creates a secondary colour; red plus blue makes magenta, red plus green makes yellow, and blue plus green makes cyan.

A colour monitor reproduces colours by presenting red, green and blue light from individual points that are so small that the eye cannot distinguish them as separate. The blending of these points by the eye creates the illusion of continuous colour (a similar idea to the principle of halftone described earlier). The individual points of colour are phosphor spots on the surface of the glass tube that are bombarded with a stream of electrons from three guns in the neck of the tube. The electrons excite the phosphor, which then glows. The more energy that is transferred from the electron guns, the more light the phosphors will emit; causing the phosphors to emit more or less light, depending on the signals received and creating the various colours seen on the screen. Thus, as the relative amounts of RGB are altered, so the whole range of colours may be produced.

The fact that the eye has three sets of cones or receptors is fundamental to most modern methods of colour reproduction, whether it is printing, photography or television. Additive colour reproduction is based on the understanding that, by selectively mixing three different lights, it is possible to stimulate the human vision to see different colours. If the receptors are all stimulated to a similar level, we perceive the colour as neutral (grey to white). The brain, in effect, mixes the stimuli in an additive manner.

FIGURE 4.21 Additive colour

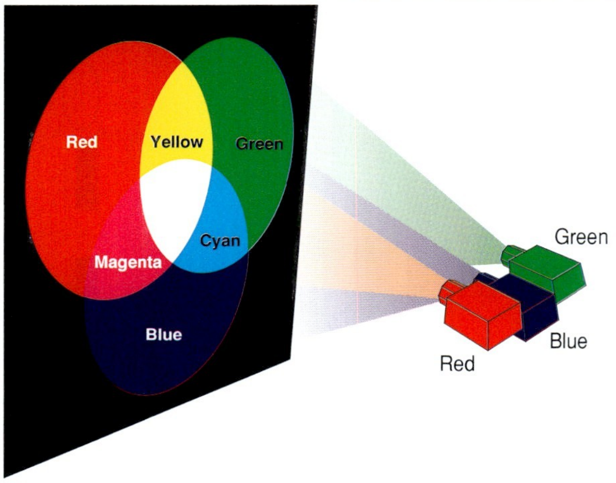

Source: Pira International Ltd

Additive colour works only for self-illuminating devices; it does not work for print because a printed page does not generate light. Print is viewed by the light that falls on its surface, which is then reflected back off the ink and paper. All process colour printed reproductions, and most colour photographs, are based on the subtractive principle.

Subtractive colour

Paper is normally white, as can be seen in the centre of Figure 4.21, and is a mixture of the three additive colours. Nothing has to be *added* to white to make colours because they are all already there. The means of creating the appearance of particular colours in photography and process-colour printing is subtractive colour, because it starts with white and *subtracts* from that white the colours that are not wanted. Additive colour starts with no light (black) and mixes light to build the colour wanted. In subtractive colour (printing), the unwanted wavelengths are carefully filtered out of white to leave behind those that are required.

The primary colours of subtractive reproduction are the secondary colours of the additive method, and in the realisation of that is the explanation of why they do what they do. The secondary colours of the additive system can be seen in the overlaps in Figure 4.21. The subtractive primaries are cyan (C), magenta (M) and yellow (Y).

Cyan is two-thirds of white light, created by mixing blue and green light, while white is created by blue, green and red. Another way to describe cyan is what is left when red light is removed from white. Magenta is blue plus red, or what is left when green is removed from white. Yellow is green plus red, or what is left when blue is removed from white.

If a single, transparent subtractive primary is printed on white paper, it will remove its complementary colour. So, cyan removes red, magenta removes green, and yellow removes blue. Controlling the overprinting of the three inks results in the required combination of wavelengths being subtracted. Where all three inks overprint, all three thirds of white are removed, leaving black. However, with ink on paper, the combination of the three inks alone cannot achieve a high enough density, so a fourth ink, black (K is used to describe the key colour), is needed to enhance shadow detail and dark colours. A bonus is that black ink is cheaper than the primary colours and will print clear, sharp text.

FIGURE 4.22 The subtractive process: yellow, magenta and cyan are the primary colours and red, green and blue become the secondary colours

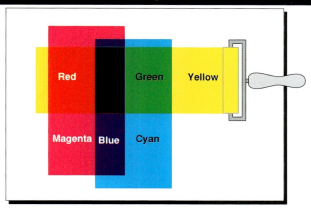

Source: Pira International Ltd

Figure 4.22 demonstrates the primary, secondary and tertiary combinations of yellow, magenta and cyan transparent inks. At first glance, subtractive colour mixture appears quite different from additive methods, but there is a clear relationship between the two. In practice, the printer considers subtractive mixture without reference to additive methods, but it is helpful, in understanding the process and its limitations, to be aware of the relationship.

The eye has receptors responsive to red, green and blue light, so it is these colours that have to be subtracted. Therefore the primary colours for a subtractive system are simply those that absorb (subtract) red, green and blue light. These are cyan, magenta and yellow, the three primary colours used in printing. Cyan absorbs red, magenta absorbs green and yellow absorbs blue. Thus if the three are overprinted, red, green and blue are absorbed, resulting in black. Cyan plus magenta absorbs red and green, leaving blue; magenta plus yellow absorbs green and blue, leaving red; and cyan plus yellow absorbs red and blue, leaving green (see Figure 4.23).

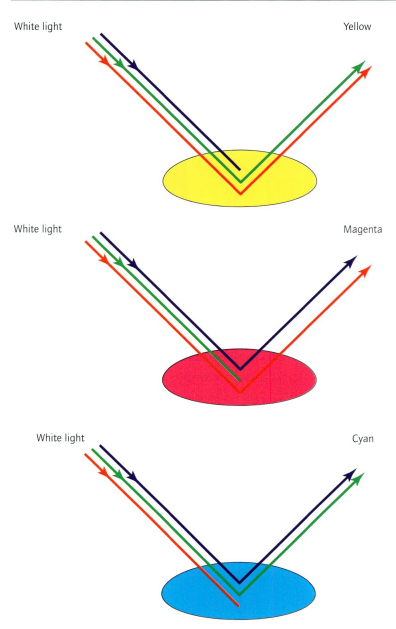

FIGURE 4.23 Subtractive primary colours showing the property of absorbing the primary colours of light

White light   Yellow

White light   Magenta

White light   Cyan

Source: Pira International Ltd

So far, there are only eight colours produced – obviously this is not sufficient for printing. Suppose, for example, a saturated orange is needed. The additive mixture shows that orange is produced by mixing red and green so that the proportion of red is greater than green. Depending on whether a yellow/orange or a red/orange is required, the proportion required varies. With a subtractive mixture, more red light is needed than green but no blue to obtain a saturated orange. So, a great deal of yellow is needed to subtract the blue, less magenta to subtract some green, and little cyan to subtract little of the red, hence the orange.

The same argument will apply to obtain other hues between the primary and secondary colours, so the next difficulty is to find a method of varying the amount of cyan, yellow and magenta applied. With most printing processes, it is not possible to vary the concentration (or film thickness) to adjust the red, green and blue absorption, and the amount of colour is varied by introducing the halftone principle. Thus, in order to obtain the modulation required, a halftone dot of ink is printed and the value of the halftone (or the area for AM halftones) depends on the amount of red, green or blue reflectance required.

The halftone principle enables the creation of filters with specific absorption characteristics relative to the picture that is to be reproduced. The information necessary to calculate the relevant absorption comes from the process of making colour separations.

Making colour separations

FIGURE 4.24 The principle of process colour

From top left: original; original through red filter; original through green filter; Original through blue filter; film or data separation file cyan printer cyan printer; film or data separation file magenta printer C + M; film or data separation file yellow printer C + M + Y; black file black printer C + M + Y + K

The principle of process colour is to split the original through the use of a primary filter into its red, blue and green additive components, then use this data to create a subtractive version that will be printed in cyan, magenta and yellow ink. This is now digital and the imaging software will create a black file to add detail and depth, as well as taking the chromatic impurities of printing inks into account. This is shown here, with the individual colours printed as progressives demonstrating how the full colour reproduction has been created. Most imaging software will allow images to be viewed as composite or individual separations of four colour and extended process sets.

Source: Pira International Ltd

The description of subtractive colour above shows the need for a measure of the relative amounts of RGB present in any coloured original. The process of identifying these values is called separation. Colour scanners measure the relative amounts of RGB light transmitted by, or reflected from, originals. The three datafiles generated are then passed through a colour computation that converts the description of the colour from the measured RGB into the relative amounts of cyan, magenta, yellow and black (CMYK) necessary to synthesise, on paper, a reproduction of the original.

Colour separation still refers to a set of four films, one each for the yellow, magenta, cyan and black. They may include text and other layout elements or they may be just halftones of the illustrations that will need to be planned into a final layout as a subsequent manual operation. As film use declines, the separations are electronic and can be viewed on screen as channels of the image.

Colour halftones and screen angles

In reproducing colour pictures that were originally continuous tone, printing requires to overlay the CMYK images as halftones. If the halftones are amplitude modulated (AM), they will be formed from regular patterns of fixed frequency. The need to rotate the angles of the halftone patterns comes from the fact that printing cannot precisely place down one halftone dot on top of a previously printed other-coloured dot. Commercial-quality colour printing typically has 60 dots per cm (150 dots per inch) in both the horizontal and vertical direction. A slight inaccuracy in placing four identical patterns on top of each other will result in an unpleasant moiré or screen clash. By rotating the screen patterns at 30° from each other, it is possible to reduce the frequency of the moiré to a level that is below the visual threshold – it becomes too small to be obtrusive. That reduced moiré is the pattern, which is commonly called the printing rosette.

As the halftone patterns are crossed lines at 90°, there is only 90° in which to rotate the screens before returning to the starting position. If printing with three colours, there would be no trouble since there are three 30° angles in 90° but there are not four 30s in 90 when printing with four colours, so a compromise is necessary. The cyan, magenta and black are printed at 30° apart, but the yellow, which has a low visual contrast and is difficult to see against the white paper, is rotated to only 15° difference between the cyan and the magenta. Figure 4.25 shows the relationships and the characteristic rosette that is visible, with magnification, in areas where the halftone values leave white paper uncovered.

Note that it is common for the angles of the black and the magenta to be switched. The reason for this is that skin tones are often predominantly yellow and magenta. If left with only a 15° difference between them, the chance of a noticeable moiré pattern is greater in the areas of the picture that are likely to be very important – the people!

The angle relationship between the four colours is usually fixed at 30:30:30:15°. However, the colours in this relationship may be switched. This is most usually done to overcome a clash between the yellow and another colour in a particularly important picture or tint area. In flexography, where the anilox inking roller has a 90° cell structure, the whole angle set may be rotated by 7.5° to avoid the yellow being angled precisely at 90°. Similarly, when films are made for litho-to-gravure conversion the actual angles will be different again. It is the angle relationship that is important rather than the precise angle.

FIGURE 4.25 Screen angles and the characteristic rosette

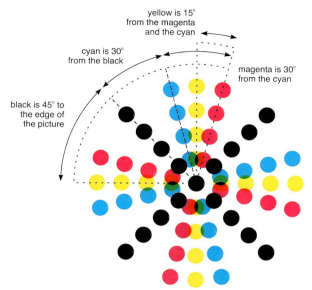

It is common for the angles of the black and the magenta to be switched. The reason is that skin tones are predominanetly yellow and magenta. If left with only a 15° difference between them, the chance of a noticeable moiré is greater in the areas of the picture which are likely to be very important – the people!

Source: Pira International Ltd

Inks for process colour reproduction

Process colour inks must be yellow, magenta and cyan, and absorb blue, green and red light respectively. Ignoring economic restrictions, an ideal ink set will reproduce as many colours as possible, to allow reproduction of the largest possible colour gamut. Figure 4.25 shows the spectral reflectance values of theoretically ideal and of real cyan, magenta and yellow inks. For the ideal set, each ink absorbs in one-third of the spectrum and reflects in the other two-thirds. Typical or real ink has spectral reflectance curves as shown on the right of Figure 4.26 (overleaf).

It is immediately apparent that inks have unwanted absorption (grey shaded areas). Relative to the ideal inks, they absorb in parts of the spectrum where they should be reflecting. The effect of the unwanted absorption is to darken the colours unnecessarily. This can be compensated for partly by colour correction. Inks could possibly be produced closer to the ideal by using more expensive pigments. In practice, the bright colours that these would permit to be reproduced are rarely encountered. Each of the real inks behaves as if they are contaminated with one (or two) of the other inks. Magenta should absorb only green but it is absorbing blue too, as if it was contaminated with yellow. Cyan looks as if it is contaminated with both yellow and magenta.

Figure 4.26 shows that the magenta is particularly deficient in the blue part of the spectrum, and cyan in both green and blue. Of the three inks, yellow is fairly satisfactory. In separations made with no correction for these deficiencies, areas containing magenta ink will be too yellow and too dark, thereby looking yellow-brown, and areas

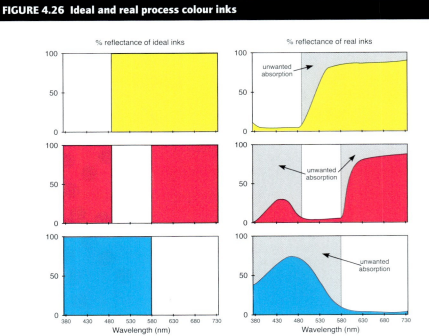

FIGURE 4.26 Ideal and real process colour inks

Source: Pira International Ltd

containing cyan too dark and too red, looking brown. Indeed, uncorrected reproductions do tend to look dirty and brown (see first frame in Figure 4.27).

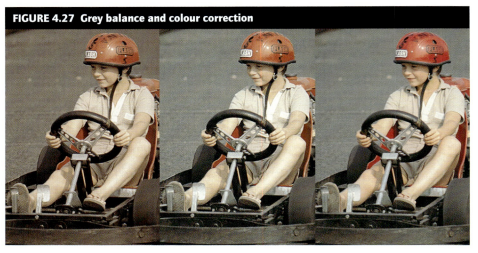

FIGURE 4.27 Grey balance and colour correction

Source: Pira International Ltd

A considerable improvement can be made relatively simply by adjusting the balance of the separations in a way so that neutrals are reproduced as neutrals. This is achieved by determining the dot sizes needed to produce greys, and adjusting the separations to achieve this. If such an adjustment is made, it not only affects the neutral colours but also the other colours in the picture. This improves the overall appearance. The result is not correct in all colours because the correction has been carried out based on equal dot areas, and will not be sufficient, for example, in colours where the magenta dot is larger than the yellow because here extra correction will be too great. This procedure is known as obtaining grey balance.

This establishes a condition where the colours are being reproduced as neutrals, but further correction is still required in certain colours that still tend to be too brown and too dark. These colours will be primarily those containing more magenta than yellow, and more cyan than yellow and magenta.

The most common causes of unacceptable reproduction are inappropriate tone reproduction and poor grey balance. Colour correction is important but the achievement of correct grey balance will go a long way to producing good colour rendition. Tone reproduction is probably the most crucial aspect since this affects whether a reproduction appears muddy, dirty or too bright.

Tone reproduction

Tone reproduction is the relative difference between levels of greys (brightness) on the original and the reproduction. If the printing process were able to match the brightness range of the original, a one-to-one relationship would be possible. However, most originals have a brightness or density range that exceeds that of printing, and tone compression has to be applied so that the relationship is no longer one-to-one. If this relationship is not correct then highlight areas may appear dirty or too bright, and shadow detail may be lost in a black mass. Precisely what this relationship should be is a matter of some debate, and is not the same for different types of original. This is still further complicated by the fact that the perceived tone reproduction is also dependent upon viewing conditions.

The relationship between tone reproduction, grey balance and colour correction is complex because we introduce the problems associated with hue and saturation of colours as well as brightness. So long as attention is restricted to a grey scale and assuming a good grey balance is achieved, then the tone reproduction is easy to define, but this reproduction will also affect the reproduction of colours. Of course, accurate tone reproduction and grey balance do not in themselves guarantee good colour reproduction. If the colour correction is inaccurate, some other colours will not be accurate, but they go a long way towards it.

The term 'colour correction' is also used to describe editorial colour changes that are used to modify or exaggerate colours in the reproduction or to correct for defective shifts of colour in poor quality originals.

FIGURE 4.28 Colour enhancement

Source: Pira International Ltd

Adding black

So far the colour theory discussed has been largely concerned with the principles of three-colour reproduction. In practice, however, black is added. This does not affect the basic theory but adds a complicating factor. The primary reason for adding black is because of the limited maximum density achieved with just CMY. The addition of black is an attempt to compensate for this.

Undercolour removal (UCR) and grey component replacement (GCR)

There are other reasons for adding black. Using undercolour removal (UCR), it is possible to replace proportions of the three process inks in the neutral and near-neutral areas of an image with one ink – black. UCR is the reduction of cyan, yellow and magenta dot areas in correct proportion to one another, as determined by the grey balance characteristic where all these are present, and printing the appropriate amount of black instead.

Grey component replacement (GCR) takes the principle further. It reduces the grey component from all colours in a reproduction (not just the neutrals), and replaces them with black ink. Both techniques (see Figure 4.29) help avoid marking and set-off difficulties associated with high areas of ink coverage. Control of the printing process is also made easier as it becomes less sensitive to changes in balance between the colours. This is particularly useful in reproducing originals containing large areas of near-neutral colour.

Adding black makes the theory and practice of colour reproduction more complex because, for many colours in a reproduction, it means there is no unique mix of colours that will reproduce them. However, it is essential to think of a reproduction in terms of a three-colour mix to obtain the correct hue and saturation rendition of colours. The black is

FIGURE 4.29 Illustration of UCR and GCR

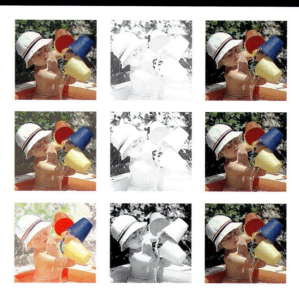

Process colour printing involves the addition of a certain amount of black ink to the cyan, yellow and magenta to provide colour depth and detail, particularly in shadow areas. Using under colour removal (UCR) or grey-component replacement (GCR) techniques allows for areas of colour that contain cyan, yellow and magenta to be replaced by black. When done correctly the observer will not notice any differences with the final reproduction, as in Figure 4.29. This provides benefits to the printer, by reducing the weight of ink laid down to minimise marking and set off, as well as replacing expensive coloured inks with cheaper black. There are also runnability benefits on press provided that the weights of colour are not reduced too much, and small colour variations become less noticeable. The relative amounts of the process inks required to reproduce the same dark brown conventionally and with GCR are show in Figure 4.30.

Source: Pira International Ltd

FIGURE 4.30 Application of grey component replacement

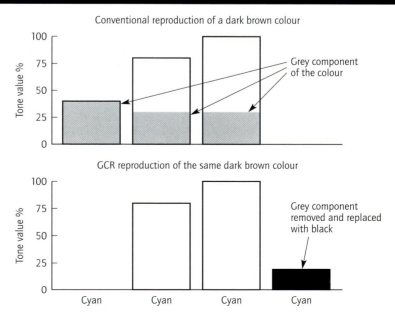

Source: Pira International Ltd

added to achieve optimum rendition of darkness, only secondly for use in replacing the process inks in greys or greyish colours. If this is not done properly, adding black can ruin a reproduction.

Preparation for printing

Halftoning (screening)

In an artist's watercolour painting, shading is created either by loading the brush more fully or by going over the same area more than once. In both cases more colour is put on the paper. The tones in the picture will be related to the quantity of paint on the paper surface. Lithography, letterpress, flexography and screen printing cannot do this; they must print ink or no ink without intermediate levels. The mechanisms by which these printing processes define image and non-image areas are capable of carrying, and transferring to the surface being printed, just a single thickness layer of ink. If a picture to be printed has tonal information, shades of light and dark, it must be manipulated before being printed.

FIGURE 4.31 In a watercolour painting the tones are related to the quantity of paint on the paper's surface

Source: Pira International Ltd

Line drawings, such as cartoons and engineering drawings, are bi-level pictures. Everything in the picture is made with solid colour, often black. For exactly the same reason, text is also bi-level information. Bi-level images, text or pictures require no intermediate treatment to make them suitable for reproduction by lithography, letterpress, flexography or screen printing.

FIGURE 4.32 A line drawing is a bi-level picture

Source: Pira International Ltd

Images that contain a range of tones, such as photographs, paintings and pencil sketches, are described as being continuous tone. Continuous tone, often abbreviated to 'contone', describes an image where the transitions from white through to black are smooth changes of grey without any distinct boundaries between the levels. Tonal boundaries that can be seen in a continuous tone picture are there because they are required by the detail of the subject rather than imposed by limitations of the reproduction processes.

Artists working in bi-level media can adopt particular techniques that, when viewed from a normal reading distance, give the impression that the illustrations contain a range of tones. For the techniques to work, the artist must exploit limitations of vision.

The human eye is not good at resolving fine detail. The generally accepted limit of normal eyesight is that from a reading distance of about 25cm (10in), differences in circles with diameters less than 0.025cm (100th of an inch) cannot be seen. Unable to identify individual points of detail, the eye will merge the points and the resulting tone perceived will be a combination of the points of detail and the background that surrounds them. Engravings and woodcuts are good examples where this principle is used. The artist arranges the detail in the illustration to be constructed from lines and patterns of different widths, spacing and areas. If the patterns are so fine that the individual elements cannot be resolved from a normal reading distance (less than 25cm), the integrated areas will have darkness value related to the ratio of the image (the inked areas) to the clean, white background surrounding them.

A European television picture is constructed of 625 raster horizontal scan lines. The scan lines are not visible when viewed from a normal viewing distance and only the total picture is seen. The eye is integrating the lines into an apparently continuous tone picture. Accepting that the illusion of greys can be created from unresolved patterns of solid black, commercial reproduction requires that the process be automated rather than rely on the efforts of individual artists. Illustrations can be constructed from flat areas of pre-defined patterns, their careful placement resulting in representational tonal changes. However, if a reproduction is to be made to look like a genuine photograph, rather than an artist's impression, the subtlety of the pattern changes must be far finer than could be rendered using areas of pre-defined patterns. The change in the pattern must be related directly to the changes in the amount of light reflected from the surface of the photograph, at every point of detail and tone change in the picture. It was in recognition of this requirement that a photomechanical method of producing the pattern was developed, the results of which are shown, greatly magnified, in Figure 4.33 (overleaf).

In the first instance, about 1850, a patterned image was produced by photographically copying the subject through the open weave of a coarse cloth. By about the 1890s this concept had developed into a commercial process using a glass screen. By the 1970s the glass screen had largely been superseded by film contact screens. It was not until the end of the 1980s that photographic methods of producing screened black and white pictures started to give way to direct electronic methods of doing the same job as a function of the RIP on the imagesetter or platesetter. Conventional printing devices use

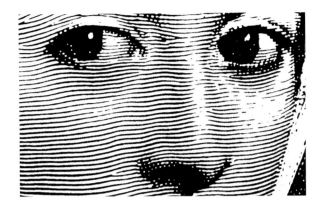

FIGURE 4.33 Artist's engraving. The similarity to TV scan lines is apparent

Source: Pira International Ltd

halftone screens to reproduce continuous tone images but digital print often applies
colourant directly as a pattern of micro dots.

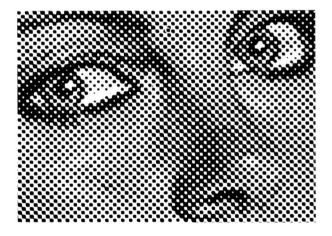

FIGURE 4.34 A halftone, greatly magnified to show the dot structure

Source: Pira International Ltd

Halftone patterns have several attributes by which they can be identified and by which
they can be chosen so as to be most appropriate for their intended purpose. The first
attribute of a halftone pattern is the method by which it carries the information from the
original to the eye of the viewer. There are two approaches for halftone patterns to
simulate tonal information: amplitude modulated or frequency modulated patterns.

In an amplitude modulated (AM), or conventional, halftone, the position of
printing dots is fixed and their size varies to carry the detail. In a frequency modulated

(FM) halftone pattern, often referred to as stochastic or random screening, the size of the individual elements of the pattern (dots) are fixed at the outset and the tonal representations are made by changing the numbers of the dots placed in an area of the image. This is the method used by many digital printing devices that do not use conventional printing dot rosettes.

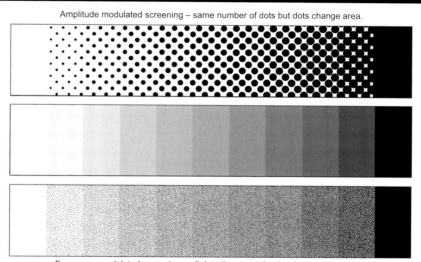

**FIGURE 4.35 Amplitude versus frequency modulated screening.
The strip in the centre shows the tints produced by either method**

Amplitude modulated screening – same number of dots but dots change area.

Frequency modulated screening – all dots the same size but the number varies.

Source: Pira International Ltd

Attributes of AM (conventional) screening

There are four attributes of a conventional screen that must be understood if halftoning is to be commissioned or approved. They are:

▶ dot percentage
▶ dot shape
▶ screen ruling
▶ screen angle.

Dot percentage

Dot percentage is a way to describe a fixed tonal value. In a given area, such as one of the sections of the scale in Figure 4.36 (overleaf), the dot percentage describes the proportion of the square that is covered by black image. In the highlight end of the scale, only a small part of the square is covered by the halftone pattern so the dot percentage value for the square is low, perhaps five or ten per cent. Conversely, at the shadow end of the scale the percentage coverage is far higher, perhaps 80 or 90%. If the paper is unprinted, it will have zero coverage; with complete coverage the halftone value is 100%. The dot percentage always refers to the image coverage on either the film or the printed result. Image processing software often provides a tool to assess the dot percentage, transmission densitometers measure dots on film while plate readers are used to measure dots on plates.

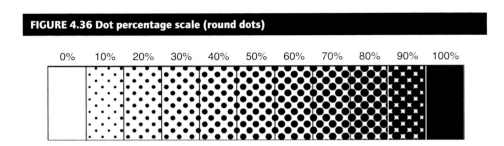

FIGURE 4.36 Dot percentage scale (round dots)

0%   10%   20%   30%   40%   50%   60%   70%   80%   90%   100%

Source: Pira International Ltd

A linen tester with an enlargement of about ×10 is a good tool for checking dot percentages on final print. However, if individual dots need to be studied for shape and formation, a dot microscope with a minimum magnification of ×30 should be used.

Dot shape

The overall shape of a halftone dot determines some of its visual and printing characteristics. There are three main dot shapes commonly used for offset printing: square, elliptical and round. The reason for choosing one shape rather than another is a combination of considerations including the purpose of the picture, the printing process and substrate involved.

Square dots are considered the most suitable for general purpose work because they provide a compromise between rendering fine, sharp detail and smooth tonal transitions. However, there is the problem that all four corners of a square dot link to all four dots surrounding it at a 50% value. This sudden link may be visible as a step in what should be a smooth tone change. Elliptical dots are better able to represent smoothly changing

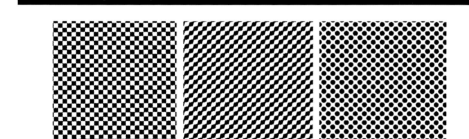

FIGURE 4.37 Square, elliptical and round dots

Source: Pira International Ltd

values in the mid-tones than square dots because their links to the surrounding dots do not happen in a single tone level. Across the long axis of the ellipse, the dots will join at about 30% but the short axis will not link until the coverage is up to 70%. The trade-off is that elliptical dots are harder to control in difficult printing conditions and can produce chains through the printed image. This is why another name for an elliptical dot is a chain dot.

Round dots are the most stable of the main dot shapes, particularly in relation to dot gain. Round dots would be the natural choice for newspaper printing because of the high dot gain associated with coldset web offset printing on newsprint. There is a trade-off in that it is difficult to keep detail open above 75% dot area coverage.

Screen ruling

The term 'screen ruling' refers to the number of halftone dots per centimetre (dpc) or lines per inch (lpi). The term is a throwback to the days when screens were made from ruled glass plates, and referred to the number of cells per linear centimetre of the screen. The screen ruling of any particular halftone can be determined by counting the dots over a measured length, using a microscope or a tester made for the purpose. The most common type of screen ruling tester is a line pattern and a scale on film. By rotating the tester in contact with the halftone and noting the interference patterns generated, the ruling frequency can be read from the scale.

The decision of which screen ruling is most appropriate depends on the printing process and the materials used. The finer the screen ruling, the more lines per centimetre and the finer the detail that may be reproduced on a high-quality paper surface. There is, however, a trade-off. The finer the screen ruling, the more sensitive the image to dot gain,

TABLE 4.6 Equivalent screen rulings

Lines per cm	Lines per inch
20	50
26	65
30	75
40	100
48	120
60	150
70	175
80	200
120	300

Source: Pira International Ltd

TABLE 4.7 Typical halftone screen rulings (dpc)

Paper type	Lithography	Letterpress	Gravure
Newsprint	48	33	48
Uncoated	50–70	33–50	60–80
Coated mechanical	60–100	40–60	60–100
Coated woodfree	60–120	40–70	70–120

Source: Pira International Ltd

and the greater the likelihood of significant tone changes occurring when the job is printed and the more difficult the job to control on the press.

In any situation where the risk of the halftone dots spreading is increased, due either to the process, as in the case of flexography, or to the materials used, as in the case of web offset newspaper printing, a coarser screen ruling will be chosen to minimise the effect of the dot change on the detail and tone range of the printed image.

Screen angle

It has been explained already that the purpose of using a halftone pattern is to simulate various levels of grey with a system that is capable only of reproducing one tone – usually solid black. The pattern of the screen should not be readily visible to the viewer. Early in the development of the use of halftone screens, it was recognised that the pattern of the halftone was less noticeable and there was an improvement in the perception of the detail of the picture when the screen pattern was angled at 45°. It is for this reason that any single ink printing, regardless of colour, that uses amplitude modulated halftones to represent tones, should be reproduced with the pattern at 45°.

Refer back to the halftone patterns in Figure 4.36. They are all at 45°. The angle always relates to the horizontal and vertical edges of the picture.

FIGURE 4.38 Conventional (AM) screening

Source: Agfa

Frequency modulated (FM), stochastic or random screening

In frequency modulated or random screening, the area of the smallest elements in the patterns, the spots, remains constant throughout the image. FM screening relies on the number of dots to simulate various tones. In much the same way that the choice of screen ruling in AM halftoning is influenced by the characteristics of the process and the substrate, so too is the choice of FM spot size.

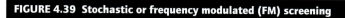
FIGURE 4.39 Stochastic or frequency modulated (FM) screening

Source: Agfa

If the calculation of the position of the FM spots was truly random, there would be instances when regular patterns would become visible. The principle of stochastic sampling is that the algorithms through which the calculations are taken reduce the likelihood of regular patterns developing. The degree of randomness and the way that the individual spots join to form larger agglomerations in the image are quite different in each of the manufacturers' approaches to FM screening. There are many FM screening software patterns on the market as part of the RIP function at the platesetter. Figure 4.40 shows two different patterns – from Agfa and Kodak Creo.

FIGURE 4.40 FM screening patterns

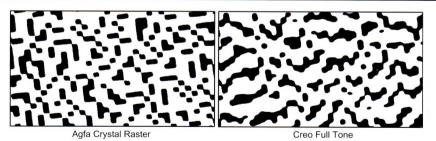

Agfa Crystal Raster   Creo Full Tone

Source: Pira International Ltd

Hybrid screening   Hybrid screening is a development of AM and FM screening, whereby different screening is applied to different parts of an image. This is particularly important for optimising the quality of flexo reproduction. AM screening is used across the midtones while FM screening is used in the highlight and shadow regions to increase the tonal range and detail. Excessive highlight dot gain and the corresponding highlight break can be significant limitations for flexo reproduction quality. Using AM screening a 2% dot on plate gains to around 15% when printed, while dots below 2% may not be held on plate at all, so giving a hard edge, or break, in highlight areas. The reverse occurs in shadow regions, with filling in. Stochastic screening can eliminate the highlight break under a wide variety of printing conditions. Stochastic screening also prints with less gain in highlight areas. The reason for this is that dots below a given percentage (e.g. 2%, depending on the specific combination of conventional and stochastic screens) the stochastic dot is actually larger than the equivalent conventional dot. Lighter tones are achieved in stochastic screening by spacing the dots further apart in a random fashion. Larger dots and wider spacing result in less gain; randomised placement results in no visible screening pattern.

Geometric or special-effect pattern screens

Users do not always need the screen pattern to be fully integrated. There are many special-effect screens available that can add interest and variety to illustrations. By definition, a special-effect screen needs to be noticed, so they are often much coarser patterns than would be used for normal screening. Simple examples, such as line screens, are often used to increase the impact of monochrome advertisements in newspapers. However, there is a wide range of alternative effects available, including circular, hessian effect and even lace. Any of these patterns can be superimposed onto a photograph to achieve a particular effect. These effects are created during origination, rather than reproduction, using software. Figure 4.41 shows a digitally generated canvas texture that easily mimics what used to be achieved with a special-effect contact screen.

FIGURE 4.41 Canvas effect generated digitally

Source: Pira International Ltd

Geometric screens produce geometric patterns rather than discrete dots; geometric line screens are often used in flexography. Relief printing has always had difficulty printing very fine detail because the image-carrier must support the printing point above the background (non-printing) level. With a conventional halftone screen this means that the dot becomes a tiny, fragile island on an open sea of plate that is easily damaged and lost. This means that the highlight detail that can be reproduced is limited. However, a line or geometric screen supports the image area along the length of the pattern. On the left side of Figure 4.42, the line pattern of the magenta ink in this flexographic print can clearly be seen, as can the line of the cyan in the green area on the right.

FIGURE 4.42 Line screen

Source: Pira International Ltd

Modern software allows different dot shapes within the same image. At different points in the tone scale, for example, they can provide optimal reproduction and improved quality for various processes.

Calibration   The predictability of halftone dot area, or frequency in the case of stochastic, is paramount to the control of the quality of printing pictures. The picture data, having passed through the halftoning algorithms, is reproduced by laser exposure on the image recorder. Whether the recorder is imaging paper, film or plates, the effect of the exposure must be controlled and consistent. When the recorder spot is projected onto the light-sensitive material, the brightness of the spot and the duration of its exposure will affect the resulting image.

If the halftoning algorithm calls for a 10% halftone, the combined effect of the lit spots in the cell must result in a given integrated density in the final image. Calibration is the means by which the consistency and predictability of the end result can be maintained. Calibration procedures involve the measurement of the effect of the variables being controlled on a test image. The known values of the test image provide the target for the recorder and the subsequent processing of the paper, film or plates. The use of a densitometer or plate reader is essential for accurate calibration. Some attributes can be judged visually, and it is often the case that calibration test formes will have elements included that accentuate visual differences.

However, for the accurate assessment of halftone predictability across the full range of the recorder's scale, objective measurement is essential. It should also be understood that calibration is an ongoing requirement. Of course, if any of the variables such as the photographic materials, chemistry or the imaging components of the recorder are changed, then recalibration is necessary, but it should also be realised that it is possible for these values to drift during normal use. All manufacturers' recommendations should be studied and their advice on calibration procedures followed. If quality is important then so is calibration.

Data compression

Data files contain gaps, empty fields and patterns that can be identified. Software can recognise the redundancy, code it and remove it. The position of its removal from the file is remembered and passed to the receiving station. Software at the receiving end then replaces the data and the file is restored to its original size. It is much more efficient to describe a pattern once and then list its occurrences than it is to describe it fully each time it occurs.

Data compression is used to reduce the size of files for short-term storage, archiving and digital delivery. Many file formats and data transmission systems use lossless compression routines without the user being aware of it. Compatibility of compression and decompression routines is an issue when transferring files between different platforms, but the incidence of problems is fairly low and many software applications recognise the routines that have been used and handle files accordingly.

Line graphics and text can be compressed to a fraction of their original size using software that recreates an exact replica of the original when it is restored. There is no loss of quality or detail (lossless). Photographs (scans) can also be compressed with lossless software but the degree of compression is small. For greater levels of compression, lossy routines such as JPEG are usually chosen. It is the lossy software that must be used with care. Raster files stored in JPEG format are small in comparison with their uncompressed equivalents, but each time they are opened, altered and re-compressed, there is an increased risk that compression artefacts will become visible in the pictures. JPEG artefacts are common in pictures on web pages simply because of the premium of having small file sizes for rapid delivery. Rarely do the artefacts detract from the value of the pictures being there. This would not be the case in a PDF destined for digital print.

Origination and prepress

5

Introduction Origination and prepress cover the stages and processes required to transform a concept into a printed item. It is the fastest changing part of the printing and graphics industries with new developments being introduced all the time. The major change that will happen over the next five years will be the requirement to prepare content for a variety of output media, as opposed to preparing a page or a document for a particular print process.

All commercially printed material will be originated electronically and this chapter will focus on this methodology. To be successful (technically and commercially) it is useful to have a good understanding of the principles of computer graphics, colour theory and communication developments, and these are included with background on the major changes that have affected prepress.

The use of digital file transfer for all printed items is virtually universal across developed markets, where PDF workflows dominate. Many printers are now unable to accept film and charge a premium if they are supplied native application files. Since the publication of the 9th edition of this manual there has been further progress. Digital prepress systems have changed the structure of the industry and specialist repro houses are becoming thin on the ground. Computer to plate (CTP) dominates the modern litho printing industry, digital cylinder engraving has long been the norm in gravure operations and laser mask CTP and sleeve engraving are being used by the flexo industry.

Distributed collaborative development is the norm, with preflight checking and a de facto standard of PDF maturing as the accepted mechanism of transferring files. Proofing has seen the widespread acceptance of digital proofs, an apparently insurmountable problem a few years ago. Low-cost, photo-realistic inkjet proofs produced on colour-managed machines have overtaken the need for print dot simulations in many sectors. Specialist high-end prepress systems have been replaced by Mac, Wintel and Linux workstations using workflow engines such as Prinergy, Taiga, ValianoRampage, ApogeeX or Twist. Font issues have been largely solved. Colour has been addressed with automatic colour management solutions that do not require colour professional input.

The trend in prepress is for creative software to handle more of the preparation activity prior to output. Adobe's Creative Suite integrates image manipulation (PhotoShop) with sophisticated drawing (Illustrator), page make up (InDesign) and output preparation (Acrobat) together with web authoring (GoLive). Version Cue manages the in-production files and Bridge provides overall organisation. Adobe products are taking market share from QuarkXPress, while non-graphic, specialist, PC-based solutions are growing, e.g. MicroSoft Publisher. The other change will be increasing use of media-independent authoring tools, based around XML. There will also be significant growth in automated page make up, with PDF on-the-fly growing in importance and more web-to-print solutions appearing on the market.

Instead of the complex series of events that have to take place, be checked and approved for a job to be printed, the prepress process will become further removed from simply printing. The aim is to create a file that will be formatted, and sent to several different output media without the need for further manual intervention. There will be intelligence built in to more elements that will allow economic automated formatting and output. This function will be similar to the hinting technology that allows fonts to be so flexible at such efficient file sizes. This means that content will be produced in a way that allows output to whatever media channel is needed effectively.

The series of prepress activities will change from a series of events and be refined into three broad areas with an overall management function encompassing the processes:

▶   Image and content acquisition

▶   Content management and editing

▶   Formatting and output.

Prepress used to be a recognisable intermediate stage between creative and printer. It had its own tools and industry structure to handle type, pictures, make-up, proofing and platemaking. Digital development and the DTP revolution blurred the creative/production boundary and changed the structure. The onward march of digitisation and the requirement to get the maximum out of the content is now changing the production/delivery interface. Printing is just one of the delivery channels to communicate with consumers and the prepress industry has to accommodate these demands. It offers great challenges to conventional print-based organisations but also great opportunities as companies discover the impacts of this huge communication change.

Conventional prepress activities are being absorbed into the creative and output ends of the digital workflow. In a few years, the role of the prepress company will be to organise and manage the digital content on behalf of customers making it easy to be served to customers as print, email, cell-phone or PDA, website, e-commerce or whatever these channels develop into. Print will still be the major delivery method for most applications but it will not be the only one. The skills required to produce good print will still be needed as the tolerances for print are more stringent than for other media.

Background and history   Before the adoption of computers, skilled craftsmen performed design and prepress operations. They used hot metal for type and photographic techniques for images. The different stages and requirements – type, illustrations, colour, proofing and platemaking – required specialist knowledge that was closely guarded. The reason for the success of digital origination is that it allows print customers to reduce the cost and complexity of producing a communication product by de-mystifying the process and making it cheaper and easier to prepare print-ready material. It is the history of the manual process that provides many of the strange names and requirements that are necessary for satisfactory print.

These serial processes took a great deal of time and money to accomplish. Printers would house these skills, but specialist companies would service the needs of customers and small printers. As mechanisation turned to early adoption of computers, the capital requirements for a scanner or photo-typesetter and front end meant high utilisation of the equipment was needed and design agencies, typesetters and repro companies became the norm. Some larger printers retained in-house origination and the majority would make their own plates, but most of the physical production of bromides, film separations and proofs would be from trade houses. The industry adopted expensive proprietary colour electronic prepress systems (CEPS) and successful prepress companies produced many pages over 24 hours to pay for the investments. Skilled operators commanded high salaries, but the final customer still had to wait for the proofs and pay a high cost for pages and corrections.

In the late 1980s, new technology irrevocably changed the industry with the desktop publishing revolution. Origination was taken in-house to publishers and many larger users of print, which used Macs and laser printers to provide layouts. Print-ready material was produced by changing trade houses (others just went to the wall), and the cost of equipment and required skill level dropped markedly as the process was opened up to the final customer. The new technology was successful because it solved a business problem of print buyers, not the printing industry. PostScript enabled the true transfer of (almost) print ready files to any printer anywhere in the world and opened up more choice for the print buyer.

The largest investment needed was a film imagesetter (and processor) and many small to medium print companies bought some Macs and an imagesetter to produce imposed pairs and then formes with larger-format devices. As the power of computers increased, the imposition of four, eight, 16 and more pages became fast and efficient. At the same time, improvements in offset plate technology allowed computer to plate systems to be fast enough to be economically viable. Printers have enthusiastically embraced CTP technology to produce high quality plates quickly with little fuss, with the users reporting significant productivity benefits of reduced make-ready and waste in the pressroom.

The software improved, font technology largely eliminated font clashes and the lower costs enabled many more users to license the technology, greatly benefiting type foundries and encouraging a massive growth in available designs. The differences between different versions (country and release) of prepress software applications gave rise to many problems that were largely overcome by the use of correctly produced PDF files. Preflight checking software allows inexperienced producers to be fairly sure that the file they produced would work at their printer.

In 2005, the majority of printed jobs – whether catalogues, newspapers, magazines, books, packaging or a more specialised sector – broadly follows a conventional workflow, detailed in Figure 5.1 (page 216).

Following the decision to commission a job, the buyer selects suppliers, a design function, final artwork producer and printer. This workflow has been in operation since the introduction of typesetting in analogue and digital form. Designers take a brief from the publisher and produce a range of dummy pages for a design approval process. These concepts and mock-ups are a key stage of the added value provided by design, ensuring that the content is legible and suitable for its purpose. Most graphic designers use programmes such as QuarkXPress, InDesign and Illustrator, running on Macs, although the Windows PC is steadily increasing in popularity. When the design is approved, the author/copywriter prepares the text, often in Word. Copy is edited and passed to make-up and the page is assembled into the defined design templates, images incorporated and a proof produced. Final native application files, with all content including fonts would be

FIGURE 5.1 Typical publishing work programme

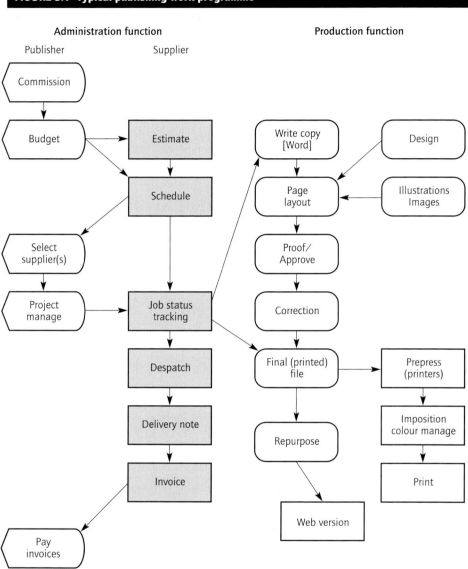

Source: Pira International Ltd

supplied to the printer for it to output, but this takes time and cost at the printer and could lead to errors. Increasingly the job is saved as a PDF with high-resolution print-ready image data and embedded font information allowing correct interpretation at any printer. The characteristics of the PDF preparation are often supplied by the printer, tailored to its particular requirements, or by a standard such as PDF/X or pass4press. When checked and approved, the files are sent to the chosen printer for output to plate and printing.

There may be several companies involved (client, agency, specialist repro company and printer), although the use of repro companies is in decline as graphic designers increasingly handle the production function for general printing. At the final printer, the supplied file will be checked and processed for output with the specific attributes needed applied according to the demands of the process involved. The screening and trapping requirements of sheetfed litho are very different to web-fed newspaper printing or flexo. A good printed job results and the administration is completed.

The key issue now being addressed is workflow – the transfer of files through the various participants to produce and approve the final result. As can be seen from Figure 5.1, the prepress function is expanding from being purely a production workflow, and it now can include parts of the necessary administration load within the files. These can handle both payment and schedule information as well as linking in to the printing process and provide methods of pre-setting equipment and reducing machine make-ready. The other change is the requirement of many customers to use their content across more than just print, adding electronic delivery channels (website, email, CD-rom, SMS text messaging) to deliver the message. Many printers are embracing the opportunities from additional distribution channels to widen the range of services they provide for clients.

When an organisation needs to distribute editorial content for different publishing channels, the selection and formatting of the content will not be the same for each channel. In the past, the solution was to rewrite or re-purpose the material, with the disadvantage that it added more steps to the editorial process and resulted in multiple versions of an item that had to be edited or updated separately. As well as the production aspects involved in the workflow elements, there are also the process and administration stages that have to be covered. Each page or spread is generally treated as a unique item with manual operator intervention and separate management.

Improving the efficiency of multiple formats is a fundamental shift for the prepress industry. Instead of having to produce a file tailored for a particular press or process, the future prepress operation will create a media-independent master file. When it is ready to be printed or delivered, the output characteristics are applied to optimise the master data for the web, digital printing, offset, gravure or flexo printing, each of which requires a different type of file in terms of colour space, resolution, trapping and colour management. As such systems develop, probably being based around a flavour of XML, the conventional proofing methods will change as relatively low-cost devices become capable of mimicking a range of printing conditions.

The role of prepress is changing from preparing plates to improving the overall process. You need to understand the characteristics of a printing press or proofing device in order to provide files optimised for it. The prepress function at printers will quantify the printing process being used to set up a colour management system to profile printing presses and proofing devices. They will then produce a simulation for the customer to examine subjectively. The devices are set up to reproduce the results under standard operating conditions.

Before considering the appearance of a printed piece it is necessary to reduce to a minimum the impact of external influences. The conditions under which the visual assessment of originals, proofs or final production prints take place must be controlled.

Standard viewing conditions

The appearance of an object can be dramatically affected by the conditions under which it is viewed. The following procedures help minimise the misinterpretation of colour matches in commercial printing. All judgements about colour and tonal value should be made under conditions that are repeatable, and every person who is involved in the print production process should use standard viewing conditions. These help the consistency of communication across all stages of design, reproduction and printing. In addition to controlling the conditions under which decisions are taken, it is also important to ensure that only people with normal colour vision should make colour decisions. It should be realised that about 8% of the male, and 0.5% of the female, population have poor colour vision (the situation is worse for ageing, white males). There are several commercially available kits to check operators' colour vision, or these can be performed at any reputable high street optician.

Standardised viewing refers to an environment where the following conditions are all controlled:

► the colour of the light sources
► the intensity of the light sources
► the degree of specular reflection and effects of glare
► the colour of the surrounding area
► the influence of non-standard, ambient light
► the visual adaptation of the observer's eye.

Conditions that satisfy the environment described above may be obtained by equipment designed and supplied in accordance with ISO 3664:2000 or 12646. ISO 3664 is being continually updated; in 2005 it is still ISO 3664:2000 'Viewing Conditions – for Graphic Technology and Photography'. It covers viewing conditions for monitor calibration and room lighting when digital image files are displayed on a computer monitor in isolation, independent of any form of hard copy. ISO/DIS 12646 'Graphic Technology – Displays for colour proofing – Characteristics and viewing conditions for originals, proofs and final printed products' was released in 2004.

A controlled working area, such as a neutral viewing booth, is recommended. These need regular maintenance to maintain the conditions demanded by the published standards. A regular maintenance schedule should include the following tasks:

► All neutral surfaces, fluorescent tubes and baffles should be cleaned weekly, using materials that will not damage the surfaces.
► The entire booth must be periodically inspected for dirt, scratches, remnants of adhesive tape and other debris. If found, they must be removed without damaging the surface finish.
► The fluorescent tubes should be replaced after 2000 hours of use.

Many commercially available booths incorporate elapsed time meters to monitor the life of the tubes. Nothing should be stuck or pinned to the inside walls of the booth because it may cause reflections or false adaptation.

One argument against the use of standard lighting conditions is that the readers of the print do not look at the final product under controlled conditions, so what is the relevance of using fixed conditions during production? Surely it would make more sense to try to simulate the end-user's viewing conditions?

There are several important factors that this argument overlooks. First, it is impractical to evaluate the elements of print under every possible lighting combination the end-user may find. Second, print production tries to co-ordinate and synchronise the input from an assortment of different people in a variety of different environments across separate companies or even countries. Standard viewing conditions ensure that all participants, wherever they are making their evaluations, do so from the same starting point. Finally, it is only during production that comparisons are being made; comparisons between original and proof, proof and production print, print and original, and print to print. In all but the last category these are comparisons between images that should appear similar but are manufactured from different materials. The end-user evaluates the print in isolation from the originals and the proofs, and the decisions the end-user makes are quite different from the requirements of production.

The only circumstance where non-standard lighting conditions should be used is when the viewing conditions of the primary environment are defined and controlled. A common example of this condition is that of a retail outlet such as a supermarket. The final evaluation of print for packaging or display materials destined for a supermarket or department store should be evaluated under the lighting conditions under which they are to be displayed.

Content acquisition
The biggest change that will be seen in prepress is the development of authoring tools that will be widely used to prepare content in a media-independent manner. The most popular creative workflows use word processing packages such as Microsoft Word to write the story. This text is then imported into a page layout program such as QuarkXPress, which positions the text onto the page and incorporates graphics together with necessary print elements such as bleeds and trim marks. This application will often generate the final PostScript code or PDF for the high-resolution interpreter (on CTP or proofing device) to output. In the event of requiring the content for other applications, such as publishing on a website or to be part of a variable data print run, additional processing and staff are needed to re-engineer the produced pages. This adds significant time and cost into the multi-media publishing process while generating the possibility of additional errors.

Traditional companies used to conducting business using print production face significant challenges from the new requirements of e-business. Competition forced companies to invest in the systems and staff needed to create and run sophisticated websites. As the internet channel matures, many companies, particularly newspaper, magazine and catalogue publishers, face a new challenge. These organisations too often operate two distinct production processes: one for print and another for the website. In many cases, these two production processes are disparate operations that run in parallel, but separate, tracks. This dual approach is inefficient, requires separate staffs, budgets and different technologies and is not affordable. Over the next few years, management will find a single solution to drive efficiencies across both channels to enable each system to make the most of the work done in the other.

By implementing asset management with neutral authoring programmes, companies can break down the technical, organisational and cultural walls that separate their website and print production teams to end up with a single solution rather than competing for finite corporate resources and building additional incompatibilities into their environments.

Any single element − picture, text, logo or document − can be instantly located, easily accessed, and quickly re-purposed by people working together anywhere in the organisation or at its agents. This will increase productivity, reduce costs and accelerate a project's time-scale. Media neutral authoring and management will help companies to maximise the return on their information and content investment.

Image acquisition

As content becomes an important asset of the publisher or corporate client it becomes an investment to acquire images; the issue is now much more than obtaining a scan for use in one publication. Most new images are from digital photography and stock images from commercially available collections and libraries, with analogue originals and scanning declining in importance. These developments make it much easier to deliver images to the creative department and then seamlessly on to production. The onward march of digitisation, with improvements in digital cameras, makes the task of getting colour-managed files to the creative department much more straightforward. It reflects the trend of creatives shooting, creating, manipulating and controlling their own images. They prefer the immediacy of doing their own colour manipulation at the desktop.

Stock photography is popular, not just for its cost, but for its ability to provide flexibility and control. Outright purchase of the rights to an image (royalty-free) will increase with a one-off payment made to the library. Faster download speeds of high-resolution images will further boost distributed image libraries across the world. Creatives will have virtually instant access to huge libraries of material. This market will grow to meet the demand from the expansion of web pages needing images. Sites must be kept fresh so web designers need to regularly update their images.

Text acquisition

One trend that is now being seen in newspaper and magazine editorial systems will have great impact across all text applications of prepress over the next few years. This is the use of media neutral word processing systems that allow great flexibility in the later use of the content. There will be many programmes appearing that will embed structure instead of format into the text stream. The software will probably be XML, or a descendent, which is being included in most office word processing applications.

There should be little additional burden placed on original authors and copywriters. One way this will happen is for software to automatically embed characteristics within the text data stream. This will allow format to be applied automatically at whichever delivery system is chosen for the content.

The use of standards and descriptive templates (schema or Document Type Definition) will greatly expand, changing and broadening the role of prepress to wider media. Authoring aids will become more widespread and easy to use and their take-up will increase as content owners understand the benefits of cross-media channels of distribution. These applications will allow real-time views of the content as it might appear in print, web or other media at the authoring stage. The other element that will make XML more prevalent is the development of software to extract XML from existing documents. Applications will extract content from legacy files to release the print-based content for re-use.

In order to transfer data between different applications, it is necessary to transform it from the data model used by one application to the model used in another, and this is becoming easier. One XML file might use a different vocabulary from the original. As XML-based electronic commerce becomes widespread, so the role of XSLT in data conversion between applications also increases in importance. Widespread use of XML will not mean the need for data conversion will disappear. There will always be multiple standards in use. For example, the newspaper industry is likely to use different formats for exchanging news articles from the format used in the TV industry. Equally, there will always be a need to do things such as extracting an address from a purchase order and adding it to an invoice, or interrogating a printing press about the status of a particular print job. So linking up enterprises for e-commerce will increasingly become a case of defining how to extract and combine data from one set of XML documents to generate another set of XML documents. Systems that are based on XML, such as JDF, are set to succeed.

Content management and editing

The biggest change that is happening in prepress (pre-media) is the development and widespread use of media-neutral content management systems. Print will still be the main medium for much material but, in addition, clients may use the same material on websites and e-commerce systems such as e-mail, or even SMS messaging to mobile phones or PDAs. The challenge for prepress suppliers lies in the fact that a printed page is technically different to a web page, even if the content is identical. The main software suppliers have added web functionality to print-design programmes, which has promoted upgrades but has also tended to make cross-media production a more limited, linear process. The print page-layout programs have provided some non-print design and export capabilities because the print was the critical medium that gave rise to re-purposed versions as a PDF or HTML file.

Increasingly companies are recognising that new media is different to print. Publishers place their titles online, corporations wish to communicate with real and prospective customers not only through direct mail and statement and billing, but also through their interactive websites and with electronic presentment and payment systems.

They see the importance of producing and editing content once, independent of the output medium, and then deliver according to whichever channel is required. The specialist applications for both print and online will exist, but cross-media production will require all publishing applications to be database clients performing appropriate formatting tasks to data. The key for this to work will be the mainstream acceptance of XML as a standard for data preparation and storage. Over the next few years there will be great strides in this area led by newspaper editorial requirements.

Currently most formatting and make-up of pages and documents is handled by operators using a suite of programmes on the Apple Macintosh. The market leader is still probably QuarkXPress although Adobe is making significant inroads with its Creative Suite (with InDesign). The latest versions of both QuarkXPress and InDesign have limited support for XML structuring.

Word processing

Word processor software now provides text design features that compete with the simpler page layout programs. There is a degree of cross-media compatibility, and the latest versions of the leading programs all include support for XML coding.

As their name suggests, word processors have always been most suitable as basic authoring and text input tools. Many publishers will provide authors and contributors with house style sheets to work with and increasingly these will allow content to be coded correctly at its inception rather than requiring later sub-editing and markup.

Proof stages

Opportunities exist for proofing at many points in the production cycle of a publication – at the word processing stage, on a made up page and in imposed pages (book-proof). Generally proof corrections become more expensive as production stages progress, and in an ideal world all correcting would be done before any of the typographic or page make-up stages are started.

Proofs at word processing stage are typically hard-copy printouts from the saved files, produced in multi-copies or photocopied as necessary. Correcting at this stage is a simple matter. Editors working remotely are sent files via e-mail. They correct them and return them the same way. In many circumstances (including the preparation of this book), the author will make corrections suggested by an editor.

Page proofs will generally be hard copy laser prints, but annotated PDFs are becoming increasingly popular. The editor can post comments electronically inside the files for query or action, and make limited corrections on the files. Imposed page proofs will be from an A3 inkjet or laser printer, either mono or colour, although colour fidelity will not be maintained.

Proof marks

All typographic proofs should be marked using the British Standard BS 5261 proof correction marks. The convention is for printer's errors to be marked in red and author's/editor's corrections in blue so that a fair allocation of cost can be made. Correcting scientific typesetting requires an additional set of marks.

FIGURE 5.2 General proof correction marks

Marginal mark	Meaning	Corresponding mark in text	Marginal mark	Meaning	Corresponding mark in text
/	Correction is concluded	None		Make space appear equal between words	between words
New matter followed by /	Insert in text the matter indicated in the margin			Reduce space between words*	between words
	Delete	Strike through characters to be deleted		Add space between letters*	· · · · between tops of letters requiring space
	Delete and close up	Strike through characters to be deleted and use mark		Transpose characters or words	between characters or words, numbered when necessary
	Leave as printed	· · · · under characters to remain		Transpose lines	
	Change to italic	_____ under characters to be altered	[ ]	Place in centre of line	Indicate position with
	Change to even small capitals	══════ under characters to be altered	□	Indent one em	
	Change to capital letters	══════ under characters to be altered	□□	Indent two ems	
	Change to bold type	∿∿∿ under characters to be altered		Move matter to right	at left side of group to be moved
	Change to lower case	Encircle characters to be altered		Move matter to left	at right side of group to be moved
	Change to roman type	Encircle characters to be altered	(move)	Move matter to position indicated	at limits of required position
⊗	Wrong fount. Replace by letter of correct fount	Encircle character to be altered	mark extends into margin	Take over character(s) or line to next line, column or page	
	Invert type	Encircle character to be altered	mark extends into margin	Take back character(s) or line to previous line, column or page	
×	Change damaged character(s)	Encircle character(s) to be altered			
under character (e.g.)	Substitute or insert character(s) under which this mark is placed, in 'superior' position	/ through character or where required		Raise words or lines*	over text to be moved under text to be moved
over character (e.g.)	Substitute or insert character(s) over which this mark is placed, in 'inferior' position	/ through character or where required		Lower word or words	over text to be moved under text to be moved
(underline)	Underline word or words	_____ under words affected	‖	Correct the vertical alignment	‖
enclosing ligature or diphthong required	Use ligature (e.g. ffi) or diphthong (e.g. œ)	enclosing letters to be altered		Straighten lines	══════ through lines to be straightened
write out separate letters followed by /	Substitute separate letters for ligature or diphthong	/ through ligature or diphthong to be altered		Push down space	Encircle space affected
	insert hyphen	/ through character or where required		Begin a new paragraph	before first word of new paragraph
	insert en dash	/ through character or where required		No fresh paragraph here	between paragraphs
	insert ellipsis		(spell out)	Spell out the abbreviation of figure in full	Encircle words or figures to be altered
	insert or substitute oblique		(out: see copy)	Insert omitted portion of copy NOTE. The relevant section of the copy should be returned with the proof, the omitted portion being clearly indicated	
	Close up – delete space between characters	linking characters			
	Insert space*			Substitute or insert comma	/ through character or where required
	Insert space* between lines or paragraphs*	between lines to be spaced		Substitute or insert semi-colon	/ through character or where required
	Delete space between lines or paragraphs	connecting lines to be closed up	⊙	Substitute or insert full stop	/ through character or where required
	Reduce space between lines*	between lines affected		Substitute or insert apostrophe	/ through character or where required
				Substitute or insert colon	/ through character or where required

*Amount of space and/or length of line may be included.

Source: Pira International Ltd

FIGURE 5.2 General proof correction marks (continued)

Alteration required	Marginal mark	Corresponding mark in text
Use Greek letter	Letter required followed by (Gk)	/ Through letter
Use German (Fraktur letter)	Letter required followed by (Ger)	/ Through letter
Use roman	Letter required followed by (Rom)	/ Through letter
Use script	Letter required followed by (Scr)	/ Through letter
Use superior to superior (e.g. '2' in y^{a^2})	Showing letter required	/ Through letter
Use inferior to inferior (e.g. '2' in y_{a_2})	Showing letter required	/ Through letter
Use superior to inferior (e.g. '2' in y_{a^2})	letter required	/ Through letter
Use inferior to inferior (e.g. '2' in y^a_2)	letter required	/ Through letter
Use figure	(fig) 1/2/etc.	/ Through letter
Use fraction made up two lines deep	2-line frac	Circle around fraction
Use text size fraction	10pt frac (according to point size)	Circle around fraction
Use decimal point	(dec)	V Where required
Space to be hair space or 2 units or either a thick space or 5 units as indcated	hair (2#) thick # (5#)	Λ Where required

Source: Pira International Ltd

Images

Originals for reproduction

The two types of digital originals are computer-generated illustrations known as vector files, and continuous tone pictures, or bitmap files. Vector images are line drawings or images in which the path of each line is defined by a computer statement rather than physical information (e.g. a line 2mm long and 2 microns thick at an inclination of 30°, starting at such-and-such a coordinate). Bitmap images are line or, more normally, tone images defined in the computer by the positions of each dot in the total physical array making up the image (e.g. all the dots covering the area of the line).

Artwork that is drawn or traced on a computer using draw packages, such as Illustrator or Freehand, can be saved in vector format. Once in this format, it can be scaled up or down in size without any loss of quality. Vector format is termed native format or application format in most drawing packages. Artwork that is scanned from a line or tone original, or is predominantly continuous tone in nature, can be saved only in bitmap format. Bitmap files (TIFF or JPEG) are editable but not as scalable as vector files.

What makes a good picture?

The correct picture sells a product or service. It illustrates a point in an article, and draws attention to the publisher's message. All originals can be reproduced and the important points to consider include:

► Will it, when printed, still deliver the statement required?
► Is the assessment of the original objective? Is it fit for the required purpose?
► Has the original been judged under the correct viewing conditions?

In the past, photographers provided prints, transparencies and negatives for reproduction and, with digital workflows, a print-ready file can be supplied. Analogue photography comes in several forms – as follow.

Colour prints

Prints should be made from the original negative or positive. Colour prints for the amateur market are made using automatic equipment, and although the consistency and accuracy of these are appropriate for the general consumer, it is unlikely that the prints will have the maximum quality of which the process is capable. Due to unavoidable losses in the graphic reproduction process, it is possible only to economically achieve high-quality print from high-quality originals. To qualify as appropriate, photographic prints need these minimum properties:

► clean and free from damage
► a gloss finish
► correct exposure
► sharpness
► neutral colour balance, within subject requirements
► the same size or slightly larger than the size of the reproduction. (Reproductions from photographic prints should not be enlarged. If enlargements are required, data conversion should go back to the original negative.)

Prints with regular, patterned surfaces, such as silk or canvas finishes, can cause problems due to the surface finish conflicting with the halftone screen pattern. This is one reason why a gloss surface is preferable. Another reason is that fine detail can become obscured by coarse surface patterns.

Original film

A first-generation photographic original is the film from the camera, either positive or negative. This represents the maximum technical quality achievable and any optical or photographic step on from the first generation will reduce the quality of the picture. Sharpness will be reduced and both the overall contrast and the fine detail contrast will be altered. The subsequent degradation is inevitable but the degree can be minimised by scrupulous attention to technique.

35 millimetre transparencies

For general illustration, 35mm transparencies are the most common film format used. The ability to record fine detail on 35mm film is limited compared with larger formats, and the small size presents more potential problems:

▶ They may be difficult to handle and remove from protective coverings before scanning without damage.

▶ They often require significant enlargement making defects such as dirt, damage, obtrusive grain and poor focus even more obvious.

Provided that the photographer has used the full area available on a 35mm, it is possible to obtain an 800% enlargement up to a full A4 suitable for magazine or general illustration. This format cannot provide suitable quality for fashion, portraiture, architecture, high-quality food shots or anything where texture and fine detail are critical issues.

Photographic technical quality

The issues concerning the technical quality of photography apply equally to digital and analogue originals (except grain, of course), although digital originals offer more scope for image manipulation.

Incorrect exposure

Professionally produced photographs should be correctly exposed. Professionals should judge the exposure required for their subject and it is industry practice to supply exposures either side of the correct one. This form of error is probably the most common defect that causes problems during reproduction with the explosion in demand for originals produced outside the control of the professional photographer.

Overexposure results in burning away of highlight, detail and a loss of saturation in the colours. Underexposure makes the image too dark and although there may be detail highlighted, the shadows remain absolutely solid where the emulsion has not received enough light for it to react and form an image. No image means no amount of subsequent image enhancement and processing will create information. Underexposure of an original colour negative allows only the brightest highlight detail to record correctly. Mid to shadow tones will be muddy and are likely to display a significant colour bias, often to green. Detail will be missing in the shadow areas and the overall contrast of the print will be low.

Non-neutral colour balance – cast

Normal colour vision is accurate at gauging neutrals as long as the reference information of the surrounding conditions is correct. Unwanted, visible colour shift is known as a cast. In most instances, the degree of shift will be slight and noticeable in shades close to grey. A colour cast may not be equal over the whole range of the image shadows and can be moved from the neutral when the midtones and highlights are correct. Incorrect exposure, poor processing, poor film storage and some product characteristics can lead to tonal colour shifts. There are three types of colour cast:

▶ *Overall colour cast.* The whole image area is affected equally by the colour defect, which is usually caused by mismatching the film used to the lighting.

▶ *Tonal colour cast.* The colour shift is confined to a particular range of tones: shadow, midtone, or highlight. There may be more than one cast of this type. There may be a different colour affecting the highlights than the shadows. To fit this description, all shadows or highlights would be affected throughout the entire image.

▶ *Localised colour cast.* Here the unwanted colour influence is confined to a particular area of the image, not a range of tones. The cast may cover the full tone range but not the whole picture. Common causes of this type of defect are unwanted reflection from a coloured object, mixed lighting (daylight plus fluorescent plus incandescent – very common in interiors or exhibition photography) or stray light from a source that may be outside the picture area.

Overall and tonal casts can be removed by global controls during scanning but the only way to remove a localised colour cast is by retouching and correcting the resultant file.

Grain

One characteristic of any photographic image is that it is made up of silver grains. Faster films have larger grains and cannot be enlarged too much without the quality of reproduction becoming poor. Once enlargement leads to the grain structure becoming obvious, reproduction will suffer and:

▶ areas of even tone become broken and granular;

▶ smooth transitions between tones may become harsh and under extremes stepped where the tone changes occur in sharp steps like the contour lines on a map rather than a smooth, continuous transition;

▶ fine detail and textures can be lost due to the false image texture imposed on the subject by the grain structure of the film.

Inadequate focusing

A camera or film enlarger is only in focus on one precise plane. In a photograph there is usually quite a wide margin that is acceptably sharp, because the eye does not resolve fine detail. This is the depth of field; it cannot be adjusted by a prepress operator. An original with poor focusing is one where the main subject is not sharp.

The use of unsharp masking (USM) cannot always solve the problem of a poorly focused original. In a fuzzy original, any enlargement may make the fault more obvious. Enlargement makes grain more apparent and while unsharp masking enhances the apparent sharpness, it can also make grain more apparent. A compromise must be chosen between these factors to produce a commercial result.

Difficult colours

Some subjects produce photographs with high colour saturations that are impossible for normal process inks to reproduce. Vibrant reds, bright oranges and deeply saturated natural greens fall outside the colour gamut of most four-colour process inks. The gamut of colours of a particular printing condition can be found from charts made from various overprinted tint values, and with the dot percentage content of each colour patch given as a reference. These give a good indication of the range of colours and maximum saturations possible from the ink-set, paper and press combination from which the chart was created. Using a visual comparison to match the problem colour in the original with the closest example to be found on the chart, and then reading off the dot overprint values, gives a guide to the target reading of the scanner meter for that colour. It will show if a particular colour in the original is too far from the achievable range that some other action must be taken to reproduce it, such as using a wider process gamut such as hexachrome or replacing one of the process colours with a special colour.

Digital photography

Digital photography is rapidly overtaking new analogue originals. This eliminates the need for environmentally damaging chemical film processing, selection and scanning of photographs to get the image into the digital prepress workflow. Scrapping these activities leads to significant cost savings and critically reduces the timescale involved in reproduction.

An enormous effort by camera manufacturers and film producers now allows almost every application, in studios and in the field, to be technically satisfied by digital photography. New camera backs allow existing lenses and associated equipment to be used, eliminating the need for Polaroids and allowing photographers to be more creative and productive.

Light-sensitive silver grains in film emulsions have been replaced by electronic devices that take advantage of the photoelectric effect. In film, a coloured image is produced when emulsion on the film's surface is exposed to light. In digital imaging, an electric signal is generated when light falls on a photosensitive site. The first technology used was charge coupled devices (CCD) linked to an external processor but integrated complementary metal oxide semi-conductor (CMOS) image sensors are being introduced.

Most digital cameras still use arrays of CCD photosites arranged in an X-Y matrix of rows and columns. Each photosite is a photodiode with an adjacent charge-holding region shielded from light. The photodiode converts light photons into charge, with the charge generated being directly proportional to the light intensity. The light is collected over the entire array simultaneously during exposure and transferred to charge transfer cells so the next exposure can be made. The next stage is to record the charge; each set of data has to be read serially, converted to voltage and amplified. This complexity makes integrating other electronics impractical. The charge is neutralised after exposure and the array is ready for re-use in timescales approaching motorised film drives for fast exposure, provided data transfer rates are high enough. Miniaturisation of CCDs has allowed high-resolution images to be captured but the separate image processing takes time.

FIGURE 5.3 CMOS and CCD sensor architectures

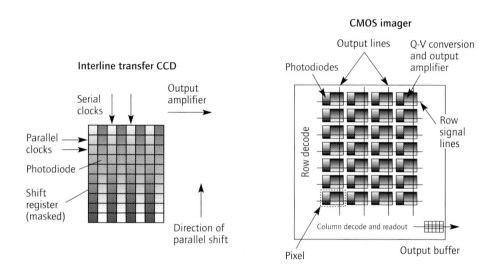

Source: Kodak Inc.

New complementary metal oxide semiconductor (CMOS) technology is replacing CCDs in digital cameras. A CMOS imager integrates the peripheral electronics, such as digital logic, clock drivers, or analogue-to-digital converters, within the fabrication process. CMOS imagers can also benefit from process and material improvements made in mainstream semiconductor technology. The CMOS sensor's architecture is arranged like a memory cell or flat-panel display. Each photosite contains a photodiode that converts light to electrons, a charge-to-voltage conversion section, a reset and select transistor and an amplifier section. This architecture allows the signals from the entire array, from subsections, or even from a single pixel to be readout by a simple X-Y addressing technique. Increasing resolution and speed of data processing and transfer is potentially much greater in CMOS technology rather than CCD, and it is likely this technology will replace CCD over time.

Benefits of CMOS technology include:

▶ lower power usage

▶ integration of additional circuitry on-chip

▶ lower system cost.

CCDs have been mass-produced for more than 25 years whereas CMOS technology has only just begun to be mass-produced.

Digital camera profiles

Camera profiling can be done using test targets but they will represent only part of the possible gamut of the subjects, and the gloss surfaces of photographic materials can cause serious problems with reflections. A good target not only has matt elements but is also designed to cover the likely gamut of natural objects. A photograph of the target is taken under the prevailing lighting and exposure conditions and analysed using their profiling software to make an ICC profile.

Camera profiling must take account of the lighting conditions in the studio as well as the specific influence of the optics and sensor of the digital camera. This raises the question: will one profile do for every subject treatment or must we develop a profile for every studio/lighting style/camera/subject/exposure combination? Clearly, if that were the case making a library of profiles would be a time-consuming and impractical approach. The photographers would have difficulty in knowing what degree of change in any one of the profile's parameters required a new profile to be made. The solution in that instance is to insist that every photograph carries its own profile. This is a theoretical solution that would double the photographer's work for every shot taken. It would be acceptable for a high value, one-off studio set but impractical in a production line, catalogue or fashion workflow.

An alternative is to use one profile that represents the camera and standard lighting values, and then use the photographer in the same role as the traditional scanner operator working from transparencies. To the scanner operator, the image values (colour and tone reproduction) held by the transparency must be optimised for the printing process. The scanner operator does that by choosing highlight and shadow points that are mapped onto the printing reproduction values by the computer associated with the scanner. That role now becomes the responsibility of the photographer. If the camera and monitor are calibrated and locked together by ICC profiles it is based on a visual assessment of the image on his screen. The intention is to treat the screen as the target, with the profiled system aiming to make the reproduction look like the screen. It does not mean that the photographer takes a picture and the ICC system makes the best reproduction possible from the file supplied. The second option requires a profile for every image but could be automated. The first option requires all photographers to adjust every file to look correct based on their screen.

Video Professional photographers have evaluated, and rejected, still video technology as incapable of providing sufficient quality for anything but screen-based presentation.

Consumers have rejected still video as a snapshot technology because they could not be convinced that a TV screen was an attractive way of viewing still photographs, but broadcast television, particularly news, represents a huge reservoir of images that sometimes must be reproduced on paper.

Capturing a frozen television picture as an original for publication is called 'frame grabbing'. The concept is not new – newspapers have been doing it for more than a decade. There are several drawbacks to using television pictures as stills, and the most difficult is its lack of detail.

The amount of information needed for a single frame of an animated sequence is considerably less than would be needed for a still picture. You would be amazed at how fuzzy and grainy a frame of big screen cine film can look, but it looks fine as part of a moving sequence. The main drawbacks are:

► lack of detail
► coarse scan lines
► interlaced frames
► easily noticeable image-processing artefacts
► easily noticeable colour artefacts.

With post-capture digital image processing, the effects of the problems above can be made better. For printing, however, video frames should be used at a very small size or considered only as a last resort, e.g. the pictures exist only as video and there is no opportunity to reshoot. The main application is for use of the dramatic image in newspapers.

Frame-grabbing boards are widely available allowing a computer to play television signals, either directly from an onboard broadcast tuner or video recording. Inputs to the boards will include composite video (as from a TV source), separate video and audio and possibly S-VHS. S-VHS keeps the colour information separate from the luminance signal resulting in less confusion between the two in the decoded signal. This makes for better pictures. To use this feature, the signal must be supplied in S-VHS format. New digital camcorders are designed to have multiple input quality standards and image processing software can optimise many images for printing.

Having displayed the video signal on the computer monitor, the frame grabber software enables you to select a frame, digitise it and save it to disk. The resolution at which the image is saved is usually the display resolution of the graphics card in the computer. Depending on the sophistication of the image processing software and, therefore, the cost of the installation, the frames can be made suitable for screen-based publications and, possibly at small size, some paper ones.

Digital conversion   Although totally digital origination is increasing in importance, there is still a major requirement to translate analogue originals, existing documents and photographs into digital form.

Optical character recognition (OCR)

Optical character recognition scanning is the process of converting printed text back into editable form without the need to re-key the characters. OCR is well established in data processing and banking (for the reading of forms and cheques). In these specialist areas both the text to be read and the scanners doing the reading tend to be designed for single tasks, although the capabilities of the systems increase regularly.

OCR for general text capture has developed to allow virtually any well-reproduced text to be scanned on a cheap desktop scanner, and the resulting raster file processed using cheap software. OCR software can recognise a wide range of different fonts and formatting, preserving the layout of the document being scanned. Specialist scanners and software are available in publishing but the emerging requirements to store content in XML format means that, for many applications, re-keying in cheap markets such as India and Mauritius are preferred. While there are many applications where OCR is useful, it still has limitations. For example, handwritten editing on typescript cannot be read and – worse – may confuse the OCR reader into misreading the printed characters. Also, 100% accuracy in reading anything but the cleanest typescript is not readily achievable and although 99% accuracy seems 'almost perfect', but translating that into the number of mistakes in a 50,000 word document means that the 1% error translates into a time-consuming editing job:

50,000 words = some 250,000 characters
99% OCR accuracy = 2500 errors = a possible 2500 words that are wrong
= 5% of the book

One of the paradoxes of text handling is that to insert corrections into previously typeset text can often take as long as re-keying the text itself. OCR for general text will always be done using spellcheckers, and for technical matter it may be worth generating specialist dictionaries. OCR is at its most useful when it is possible to present the scanner with clean, well-prepared typescript.

Image scanning

A few purists fondly remember high-end drum scanners from Hell, Crosfield and Dai-Nippon. These devices cost about £125,000 (€180,000) and a skilled operator could set up and scan between six and eight transparencies an hour, and obtain excellent reproductions. These are rare today and most scanners sold are flatbed, with limited degree of operator intervention, and capable of reproducing 20 to 30 scans an hour. High-quality machines cost around £10,000 (€14,000). Despite cost reductions and productivity improvements, the demand for scanning is dropping as the move towards digital photography and the storage of archive photography accelerates. However, the need for images has grown enormously and scanning will still be required while analogue material (photographs and artwork) has to be reproduced.

Choosing a scanner

There are many scanners on the market. Graphic arts-quality high-end models are available in rotary drum and flatbed format. Some have the copy dot option allowing the user to digitise film, although this need is rapidly waning. The use of high-quality precision optics and components means the quality achievable from these devices will be much higher than from the cheaper desktop scanners that are widely available.

A potential user must consider what he wants a scanner to do before buying one. There is no dividing line between professional and amateur scanners and much sales literature is of little help when it comes to deciding which technologies are the most appropriate for particular tasks. Tests of scanner capability, which use reproduced images for comparison, are highly suspect. Rarely is the scanner the only element in the reproduction process that has been changed. Other stages of reproduction, such as grey balance, colour correction, tone reproduction and sharpness, have such a major effect on the appearance of the final print that it is difficult to determine the precise influence of the scanner. This is particularly applicable to dumb scanners where the essential image processing, colour computations and colour space transformations are undertaken as ensuing operations rather than in real-time by the scanner. Choice of scanning equipment should take into account:

▶ the nature of the original – transparency or reflection copy and range of sizes;
▶ the resolution required – how and where the scan is to be used and at what size;
▶ the productivity needed in the environment in which it must operate – scans per hour;
▶ the availability of skill – how intelligent is the support software;
▶ the budget.

Not all scanners deliver their files equally ready for reproduction so make sure that the productivity of the system is judged from points of equivalent status rather than on the basis of mechanical speed.

Scanner specifications can be confusing. The number of subjects covered by them is large, and their names are confusing. Different manufacturers might give the same subject a different name; conversely a similar name might mean different things between manufacturers.

One of the causes of confusion is that it is not made clear which of the specs depends on the actual scanner and which is the province of the driver or subsequent image processing software. The reason it is important is that if the image is changed in software features may be lost or gained. Of all the characteristics of scanners listed in the specifications, the single biggest source of confusion is the resolution figures.

Scanning resolution

Scanning resolution describes the number of sampling points per linear measurement that a scanner is capable of recording. The higher the scanning resolution, the more pixels for a given area of original and the greater the amount of information that is captured and the larger the datafile will be. It is possible for an image to be scanned with too high a resolution for a given output requirement. Over-sampling does not enhance quality and may dramatically reduce the efficiency of the system being asked to handle the file.

For a CCD scanner, the input resolution is calculated in exactly the same way as the digital camera: the number of horizontal photosites and the vertical movements of the stepping motor. It is calculated differently for a rotary scanner and the input resolution is a combination of the digital sampling rate as the drum rotates, moving the original vertically past the scanning spot, and the incremental steps of the drive screw.

Many flatbed scanner descriptions refer to their resolution ranges under two headings:

► optical resolution
► interpolated resolution.

Interpolated resolution is much higher but the only useful information is the optical resolution, which refers to the real capture of information and the real number of sampling points. Interpolation is the process of computing intermediate values between known values. It is widely used in image manipulation software when resolution or size increases are required, and pixel data is 'invented' to fill the gaps between known points. Pixels in the area of the interpolation are sampled and, depending on the sophistication of the interpolation routine, the information is averaged, or anticipated, and additional information is inserted. In this way, enlargements can be made from rasterised information. However, this is not real information from the original and is not a good substitute for a scan at the correct resolution for the enlargement required.

X–Y flatbed scanning

Light from a point source will vary in angle and intensity over the area of a flatbed scanner. The cheapest method is point sources with an array of mirrors but more expensive movable optics in the X and Y co-ordinate provide a more consistent imaging across the bed with no anamorphic distortion of the original.

FIGURE 5.4 Flatbed scanner operation

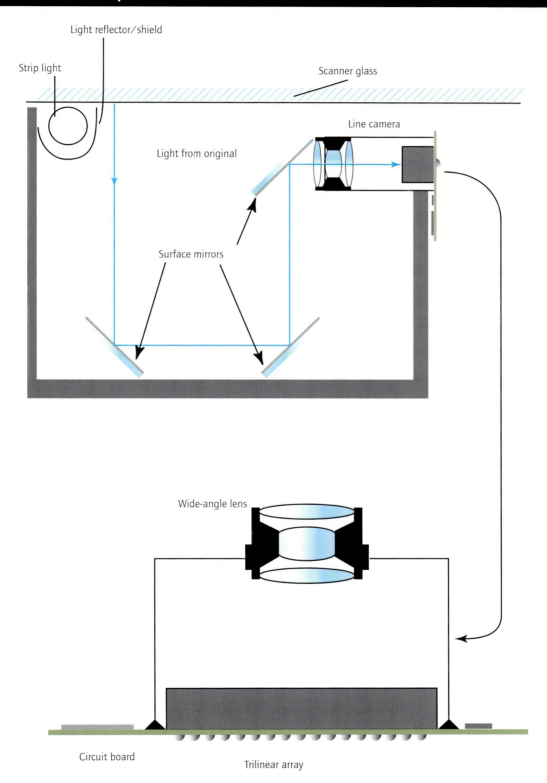

Light reflector/shield

Strip light

Scanner glass

Line camera

Light from original

Surface mirrors

Wide-angle lens

Circuit board

Trilinear array

Source: Pira International Ltd

At what input resolution should an original be scanned?

Ideally, a continuous tone original should be scanned at an input resolution that will provide double the screen ruling at which the image will be printed in conventional AM screening. Much offset colour printing uses 150 dots an inch, so scanning 300 pixels to the inch (ppi) at the final size of the reproduction is enough information for a high-quality reproduction. With higher screen rulings and FM screening, higher resolution may be required. In the past, the final destination of the scan was known and the operators would scan the original for that particular use. If it was for the front cover of a glossy magazine, higher resolutions and particular screen patterns would be used; for a newspaper, lower resolution with coarser screens was fine. Today, this approach is flawed because the image could be used in many forms that are not predicted, and it is common for an optimal scan to be produced that is suitable for multiple re-use across many publications and media.

Difficulties often arise because of confusion between input and output resolutions. The relationship between the two is quite straightforward. There is a simple formula that is used to calculate required scan resolution: $Or \times Sc = Sr$ (where Or is the output resolution, Sc is the scaling factor and Sr is the scan resolution).

EXAMPLE 1

Or = 300ppi
Sc = 60% (5in × 4in landscape transparency reduced to 3in wide)
Scan resolution = 300 × 0.6 = 180ppi

EXAMPLE 2

Or = 300ppi
Sc = 270% (2in × 2in transparency enlarged to 6in wide)
Scan resolution = 300 × 2.7 = 810ppi

It is no longer critical to minimise file sizes as communication bandwidth has increased and the cost of storage has fallen. Scanning at a higher than needed input resolution may waste scanning time, computer and network resources and storage space. It does nothing to enhance the final quality of the reproduction but it is important not to enlarge a reproduction more than the input resolution allows. If a rasterised image is enlarged too much, the pixel structure will become visible.

It is common for the resolution and reproduction ratio (scaling factor) to be calculated for the operator. All the operator has to do is indicate the area of the original that is to be scanned, key in the final size of the reproduction (in whatever units are convenient – inches, centimetres, points, etc.) and the rest is calculated by the software.

The scanner's influence on image quality

There are several factors that influence the image quality of a reproduction:

▶ resolution

▶ sharpness

▶ dynamic range

► colour resolution
► accuracy of calibration
► the operator.

Resolution

Input resolution is explained above. When deciding if a scanner is suitable for a particular type of work, its maximum optical resolution will determine the degree of enlargement achievable with that device. Dedicated scanners designed for specific tasks, like 35mm film scanners, have a relatively high resolution but limited area coverage. A 35mm film scanner will typically have enough resolution to allow a 24×36mm area (35mm format) to be enlarged to A4, which is an enlargement of slightly more than 800%.

Sharpness

Resolution and sharpness are often confused. Sharpness refers to the appearance of the well-resolved edges of detail in a photograph. The scanner will influence the sharpness of the reproduction. The sharpness of the final image will depend on five sets of unconnected variables:

► the quality and cleanliness of the scanner's optics
► the mechanical precision of the scanner, including its accuracy at focusing, the flatness of the image plane and the registration of the sensors
► the recording quality, stability and calibration of the sensors
► the scanner's unsharp masking method
► the original being scanned.

The first three items of the list above relate to the quality of the scanner's components. The price of the scanner will be a fairly reliable indicator of the calibre of the engineering and the quality of the components used.

The fourth item on the list, unsharp masking (USM), may be related to the scanner or it may be applied post-scanning by colour conversion or editing software. Unsharp masking is a means by which an image can be made to appear sharper by enhancing the micro contrast of detail edges. When colour separations were made using cameras, one of the stages of achieving this effect was to make an unsharp version of the image into a mask – hence the name. A similar effect can be achieved with a digital image by sampling and modifying the values of the pixels. Some degree of unsharp masking is required to re-establish original levels of sharpness that inevitably will have been softened by the process of scanning. So USM is a necessary part of scanning, but it cannot make an out-of-focus photograph look sharp.

The fifth category is the original. The first criterion is the focus of the original camera, but lighting contrast, type of background (textured or smooth), subject movement and whether the subject contains pastel or strong colours will all affect the appearance of sharpness.

Dynamic range

Another technical aspect of the scanner that will affect the quality of the reproduction is the scanner's dynamic range. The dynamic range describes the extremes of lightness and darkness to which the sensors (photomultipliers or CCDs) can ascribe separate values. A photomultiplier will typically have a dynamic range of 4.0, which translates into the ability to identify light differences in the ratio of 1:10,000. A good-quality scanner with a 'cooled' CCD will have a range somewhere between 3.5 and 3.9.

FIGURE 5.5 Dynamic range and density range

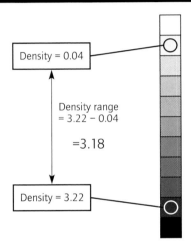

Density = 0.04

Density range
= 3.22 − 0.04

=3.18

Density = 3.22

Dynamic range describes the extremes of lightness and darkness to which the sensing device can ascribe separate values. It is a value which describes the sensor's recording range capability.

Source: Pira International Ltd

Colour transparencies have the widest density range of the photographic originals with which a scanner must cope. A well-exposed colour transparency will have a density range of about 3.4. Density range is the number that describes the difference in brightness between the darkest and lightest points in a photograph. It is the range of tones that must be encompassed if all the detail in the picture is to be reproduced. It is important that the CCD has a dynamic range well in excess of the density range of the original being scanned, particularly for recording detail in dark (shadow) areas.

One of the reasons that dark shadows of originals scanned with CCDs can be problematic is that CCDs and the associated imaging circuits can suffer from noise. Noise is caused by spurious signals that are misinterpreted as light and appear as artefacts in the image. All electronic circuits have some noise. An indication of the quality and fitness for purpose of many circuits is indicated by their 'signal-to-noise' ratio. The greater the difference, the less influence the effect of the noise will have on the end result. In the shadow part of a picture, the signal level (the amount of light) is very small and noise will be as visible as the shadow detail. If the detail is enhanced it is likely that the effect of the noise will be enhanced as well. The broader the dynamic range of the CCDs, the more likely that the detail of the photograph can be accommodated without going right into the noisy extreme of the sensor's range.

Colour resolution (or pixel depth)

Colour resolution (or pixel depth) refers to the software's ability to record colour differences. It has nothing to do with the resolution of area-related detail. The relationship between the number of grey levels or colours that a pixel can represent and the number of bits or bytes of computer memory needed to store it is listed below. The minimum requirement is eight bits per colour (one byte), but often scanners are advertised as being ten, 12 or even 16 bits per colour. Although most images are converted to eight bits per colour for storage and manipulation, sampling at a higher bit rate includes some redundancy that can be used for tone transformations optimising the results from less than perfect originals.

Colour resolution: bits per pixel

1 bit per pixel = black or white

8 bits per pixel = 256 shades or colours

24 bits per pixel = 256 red × 256 blue × 256 green = 16.7 million colours

▶ each extra bit doubles the number of tones or shades that can be expressed

▶ the software convention is an 8-bit environment

▶ 10- or 12-bit scanners = redundancy of bits for tone transformations.

Accuracy of calibration

All scanners need to be calibrated regularly. In the case of photomultiplier machines, the sensors need to be balanced to equalise their sensitivity and zeroed to white light. Although the routine is usually automatic, it has to be initiated manually. It is important that the analyse optics are focused onto a clear area of the drum when the procedure is started. Calibration will account for changes in the sensitivity of the photomultipliers due to age and will also account for changes in the colour of the illuminant as that also ages. Calibration for the light sources of CCD scanners is usually automatic, taking as a reference a scale built into the body of the scanner.

Balancing the sensitivity of the individual photosites of the sensors is a complex, fully automatic function of their control software and not something of which the operator is aware.

Operator set-up of the individual original

Every major manufacturer has control software that supports the inexperienced user. Some manufacturers describe their software as artificial intelligence: they have collected experienced operators' most likely responses to a selection of control decisions and made them available as a series of correction algorithms. Where a complex interaction of tone reproduction, colour correction and image processing settings are needed, the software will offer a pre-determined set of control functions. In this way the reproduction of a difficult original can be optimised with little understanding of the processes involved. The use of these algorithms, while being of enormous assistance to an inexperienced operator, would slow down an experienced operator. They should be considered as training aids rather than optimised operating procedures for high productivity.

Much of what a scanner operator is required to do relies heavily on subjective decisions regarding what the operator believes the client wants from the original. Issues of tone reproduction and colour correction are subjective and for that reason good or bad operators, even with the most sophisticated of modern equipment, still influence the speed and the quality of colour reproduction.

Asset management

The management of content for print is a key application for printers to add value for their customers. Printing requires large high-resolution image files with complex colour information that has long been the preserve of specialists with colour and design skills. There are many flavours and scales of systems to provide, prepare and manage a centralised asset management database, the repository for all graphic elements. Items (pictures/text/logos/illustrations/templates/documents/pages/adverts/publications) are catalogued according to customer requirements. Elements will have metadata associated with them. Metadata is simply information about information, such as descriptive (keywords, what is it, what form, what colour, etc.); physical (type of file, dimensions and file size, resolution, colour space, etc.); and workflow (is it ready for use, where is it in the production schedule, as full audit trail). These key words allow sophisticated searching on all communication material while providing maximum production efficiencies and optimal workflow, reducing lead times.

The system will provide audit trail capability for all elements and the progress of projects, defining the workflow paths often in accordance with dedicated workflow tools that perform actions when they are required to do so. Customer service agents (perhaps a helpdesk operation) and clients have direct access to their prepress material to aid the design, selection and format of their communications while following style guides. This improves quality, ensuring that customers' expectations are met. The benefits include:

► All files are catalogued with the correct, latest versions available
► Consistent prepress style and services are maintained across a distributed organisation: inter-department, inter-company and inter-country
► Redundant designs and elements are archived offline
► Electronic selection and delivery of low- and high-resolution files
► Design templates and files available for designers
► Complete library for reference is available
► Ability to update elements of design across all communications
► Useful data can be associated with the graphic (metadata), totally customisable to client requirements
► Detailed search and query capability
► PDF versions containing artwork and complete specification are available

► Complete workflow record

► Complete audit trail of prepress is available

► Individual graphics elements available as well as finished pages and projects

► Remote colour-managed proofing

► Access via any web client browser

► Total firewall security with controlled access privileges for customers and their agents

► Workflow and production management (job progress) information is available.

FIGURE 5.6 Schematic of the position of asset management

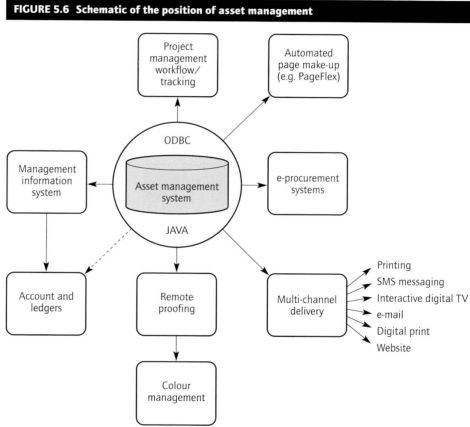

Source: Pira International Ltd

Asset management is a good business opportunity for printers, handling a task for clients that find it difficult to understand print requirements. From a print company perspective the asset management system enhances the functionality of a management information system (MIS). When a client orders printed items they can see a representation of the document or pack when they place the order. Additional information can be incorporated into the invoice, simplifying the business process. In some cases it will be possible to integrate the asset management system into the client's MIS, increasing the functionality for the client and cementing the supplier–client relationship. When all elements are tracked according to use, it is easy to use the system as a project-tracking device.

The ability to handle and manage graphic files is increasingly critical in allowing the well-organised, economical multi-channel distribution of content. When colour-managed remote proofing is offered it is important that the proofer and the press profiles are stored, and the correct transformation is applied to the file being proofed. This is stored as metadata and sent with the file for the proofing RIP to interpret.

Future digital asset management solutions will be modular, offering a flexible design across three main product components:

▶ asset management system

▶ print content management system

▶ allowing open integration with popular web content management systems.

New content will be catalogued and the system will automatically generate multiple versions of the original in several formats to simplify reuse in cross-media publishing environments. As storage capacity increases and cost reduces there will effectively be unlimited storage capacity, so the system can expand with customer growth. There will be reliable revision control to increase flexibility and simplify tracking and the relating of multiple versions of assets. There will be rights management and access control to give management control over specific assets and how they can be shared.

The system will have sophisticated security features, with identity and password protection for users, groups and the locations of company staff, clients and clients' agents. This will help to protect both production and intellectual property, maintaining confidentiality in multi-client editorial and production environments. Systems will integrate with page-layout applications, offering full drag-and-drop of content directly into a document to give users greater control over the process. In the future systems will integrate with output devices and workflows to ensure accuracy of formatting across developing workflows. There will be easy integration with business control systems used by customers to control their businesses to allow them to make efficiency gains and cost savings by sharing content between their print and web content management systems. The management of content is becoming one of the key applications for prepress providers.

Many vendors of management systems have found it difficult to convince publishers, printers and trade houses to invest in asset management solely to improve prepress efficiency. It is only as the business range has expanded to new areas that the value of the asset management system has become apparent.

MPEG-7   Use of the MPEG-7 (multimedia content description interface) standard will increase over the next few years and become an important part of an asset management system. MPEG-7 allows support for a degree of interpretation of the meaning of stored information, that can be passed to a device or a computer code. The concept is to incorporate information and details that increase the usefulness of the content as descriptors. So, a magazine article may incorporate the creation and production processes, e.g. author, title, column/article/serialisation, images included, along with details related to the usage, including copyright details, release dates and history, and syndication use. An item in a catalogue may include the product specification, instructions for use, manuals, physical stockholding, price and stock history.

MPEG-7 will develop much beyond the capabilities of metadata (a set of descriptors). The main elements of the MPEG-7 standard are description tools that define the syntax and the semantics of each feature (metadata element) and description schemes that specify the structure and semantics of the relationships between their components. These system tools can be used in a wide variety of applications, not just for print:

▶ broadcast media selection (e.g. radio channel, TV channel);

▶ cultural services (history museums, art galleries, etc.);

▶ digital libraries (e.g. image catalogue, musical dictionary, biomedical imaging catalogues, film, video and radio archives);

▶ e-commerce (e.g, personalised advertising, online catalogues, directories of e-shops);

▶ education (e.g. repositories of multimedia courses, multimedia search for support material);

▶ home entertainment (e.g. systems for the management of personal multimedia collections, including manipulation of content, e.g. home video editing, searching a game, karaoke);

▶ journalism (e.g. searching speeches of a certain politician using his name, his voice or his face);

▶ multimedia directory services (e.g. *Yellow Pages*, tourist information, geographical information systems);

▶ multimedia editing (e.g. personalised electronic news service, media authoring);

▶ shopping (e.g, searching for clothes that you like).

In practice, the standard is designed to make finding multimedia content more intuitive. For example, a searcher could draw a few lines on a screen and find a set of images containing similar graphics, logos, ideograms or charts. This might define objects, including colour patches or textures, and retrieve examples from which the objects to compose a design can be selected.

Page make-up and assembly

Once content, text and images have been created, the next stage is to assemble the content into pages and documents. The basic necessary capabilities from layout software include:

▶ importation of text from popular word processors with filters allowing retention of font definitions, line, paragraph and page instructions;

▶ search and replace on both character and format specifications;

▶ automatic numbering of paragraphs, pages, sections and illustrations;

▶ ability to define running heads and footers;

▶ ability to use pre-defined templates for the document structure and paragraph formats;

▶ ability to generate simple page design elements such as tints, rules, borders;

▶ ability to generate tables as single structures (rather than having to build them from separate paragraphs and rules) and to apply tints and rules to them;

- importing images and the opportunity to flow text around graphic elements;
- ability to rotate, crop and scale imported graphics;
- typographical freedom regarding the individual manipulation of the position of lines, words and individual characters horizontally and vertically;
- hyphenation and justification options with reference dictionaries;
- accurate presentation of the document on screen – both position and colour;
- colour definitions that relate to the operator's choice of method – RGB, CMYK, Pantone.

Some user requirements are specialised and will encourage one software to be chosen over another, one of the most obvious being transplatform document portability. Others include:

- mathematical or scientific equations;
- cross-referencing between files;
- indexing;
- hypertext linking;
- drawing functions or the ability to edit the colour and/or tone reproduction of scans;
- conversion of RGB colour into CMYK;
- the ability to apply spreads and chokes (grips) between different elements in the document;
- database referencing.

One way that third-party suppliers can enhance core layout software is through the principle of plug-ins. A plug-in is a separate piece of software code that is written so that it may be accessed as if it was part of the original program. For example, XTensions for QuarkXPress can provide some of the specialist functionality on the list above.

Plug-ins can be expensive, costing even more than the original program, although they can often be justified by the increase in efficiency that they give to the operator. It is an important management function to evaluate the difference between additional features that would be nice to occasionally use, and functions it would be a mistake to refuse.

Structured documents, SGML and XML

Increasingly, the graphic arts will use XML as a format to create, store and distribute content in an efficient manner. It is difficult to provide a clear, concise definition of XML because it allows many things to happen. It is not just for publishers and print buyers/users, but also business-to-business communication and the larger IT field. It is important to the graphics and business communities because it does two things:

- XML separates content from format, allowing repurposing for different media
- XML describes data, allowing easy data exchange between disparate computer systems.

XML stands for eXtensible Mark-up Language. It is a set of rules for designing text formats that describe data and allow it to be structured in a systematic manner. It is not a programming language; it is a language designed to make it easy for a computer to generate and read data, and ensure that the data structure is unambiguous. XML separates the syntax (structural representation) from semantics (visual rendering or other processing), and considers only syntax.

Development of XML started in 1996 as a subset of SGML, an ISO standard since 1986 that is widely used for large documentation projects. The designers of XML claim that they took the best parts of SGML, guided by the experience with HTML, and produced something that is no less powerful than SGML but more regular and simple to use. While SGML is mostly used for long, multi-input technical documentation and much less for other kinds of data, it is exactly the opposite with XML.

Standard generalised mark-up language (SGML)

SGML is an international standard (ISO 8879) that specifies a general-purpose computer language for the preparation and interchange of text-based digital documents. The use of SGML involves the acceptance of four fundamental ideas about the nature of documents. The term 'document' implies any body of content that forms an identifiable unit for some purpose, such as the creation of a publication (e.g. magazine or journal, book, article, entry in an encyclopedia). The key concept is that a document can be represented as a hierarchical arrangement of components called *elements*. Each element represents a logical unit of text, such as a chapter, section, paragraph, caption, footnote or heading. All types are defined in terms of how its content is organised. Large elements contain smaller elements, e.g. 'a chapter contains a title followed by one or more paragraphs', and the smallest elements contain simple text or in some cases have no content at all. The largest element of all is the *document* element: the logical unit representing the entire document, and containing all other elements.

Elements provide a basis for creating digital mark-up tags that are generic, and they are not necessarily tied to any specific treatment of the tagged content. While a tag that conveys the sense 'start a new page' represents a specific (probably print-based) typographic requirement, a tag that conveys the sense 'start a new chapter' does not imply any specific treatment.

Secondly, SGML information other than content may be associated with a particular element type. Such information could identify an item of text for indexing or cross-reference purposes, link a logical illustration element with a specific non-text image (in a separate file), or identify different versions of the same paragraph. In SGML an item of such information is called an *attribute* of the element.

Thirdly, every document has both an abstract, logical structure – the element structure – and a concrete, physical structure: the arrangement of objects (characters, images, flat files, database records) that are the way the document is stored digitally. The objects in this physical view are called *entities*.

Finally, definitions of element types, attributes and entities can be collected together into a formal specification called a *document type definition* (DTD). This defines everything that is needed to construct and use generic mark-up tags in preparing digital content for a specific type of document.

SGML and complex texts

SGML mark-up tags provide mechanisms for preparing content of varying complexity from simple paragraphs and headings to highly complex structures such as tables and mathematical formulae. The more complex the text structure, however, the greater the number of mark-up tags that need to be used. For this reason, it is generally not practical to use SGML mark-up tags to prepare tables or mathematical formulae, unless a special purpose SGML text editing tool is available that will display such text in a meaningful fashion, i.e. without the tags showing and with the various elements visually arranged in an intelligible manner. Some publishers have found it useful to treat tables and mathematical formulae as illustrations and not use SGML in their coding, others insist that SGML should be used for all text.

Hypertext mark-up language (HTML)

The Hypertext Mark-up Language (HTML) is the mark-up language that was developed for the preparation of documents for delivery via the worldwide web. Originally HTML was an application of SGML, with a single DTD defining the coding and use of HTML mark-up tags. Almost from the start, HTML has moved rapidly away from this model. HTML documents are generally *hypertext* documents, i.e. they can contain links to other documents, enabling a user to browse through any number of linked documents. The main drawback with HTML is the inability to render sophisticated designs within the various web interfaces. Colour and typographic control is limited, so enhancements were necessary spawning the next generation of mark-up, XML.

Extensible mark-up language (XML)

XML is a meta-language, used to define other languages. It creates documents that are well structured. This means that any data in XML is used easily across the internet because it enables businesses and their computer systems to communicate more easily. Not only does XML hold data, it can also hold the structure and even classification of the information inside a document. Using XML, the document carries information about itself because a user can define tags specific to that user.

XML is a simple, standard way to interchange structured textual data between computer programs, and it satisfies two compelling requirements.

▶ Separating data from presentation. The need to separate information (such as a magazine article) from details of the way it is to be presented on a particular device is becoming more urgent as the range of internet-capable devices grows. Publishers with valuable content increasingly need to be able to deliver them not only via print but also to PC-based web browsers (that now come in multiple versions), but also to PDAs, digital TV sets and mobile phones.

▶ Transmitting data between applications. As electronic commerce gathers pace, the amount of data exchanged between enterprises increases daily, and the need to transmit business information (such as orders and invoices) from one organisation to another without investing in bespoke software integration projects becomes ever more urgent.

It is for these two applications that XML is important. An invoice can be presented on the screen as well as being inputted on a financial application package, and magazine articles can be summarised, indexed, and aggregated by the recipient instead of being displayed directly. However, whether the XML data is ultimately used by people or by a software application, it will rarely be used directly in the form it arrives. It first has to be transformed into something else.

This has profound implications for print and publishing because XML is a text file format designed to allow the re-use of content across a variety of applications and media. When an operator makes a page up for a catalogue or magazine, he typically imports text and pictures into a standard template and edits accordingly. Text is typically formatted as it is made up. So headlines are set in semi-bold Rockwell, 36pt in 100%C/70%M, paragraph subheadings as Rockwell Light, 10pt on a 12pt body in 70%C/50%M while body text is 8pt Palatino on a 10pt body. Captions are 6pt bold Rockwell, in black running at 90° up the left side of an image. In most cases a standard template has been generated with the attributes pre-formatted and ready to receive content. Different components simply run into the available areas and the pages are made up but when a freelance operator or a busy sub-editor becomes involved, corrections may just have a style associated with them and the content loses its structure. The point with XML is to categorise these different attributes by labelling them with specific tags.

The extensibility feature means that XML may be used to create other mark-up languages such as XSL, the extensible stylesheet language. XSL is made out of XML and their relationship is important. If XML is the raw data, XSL is used to change that raw data into a usable format. XSLT, the eXtensible stylesheet language: Transformations, is a language designed to transform one XML document into another or to transform the structure of an XML document. To communicate with a human reader, this might be a document that can be displayed or printed: for example an HTML file, a PDF file, or even audible sound. Converting XML to HTML for display is probably the most common application of XSLT.

In order to transfer data between applications, it is necessary to transform data from the data model used by one application to the model used in another. To load the data into an application, the required format might be a comma-separated-values file, SQL script, HTTP message or a sequence of calls on a particular programming interface. Alternatively, it might be another XML file using a different vocabulary from the original. As XML-based electronic commerce becomes widespread, so the role of XSLT in data conversion between applications also becomes more important. Widespread use of XML will not mean the need for data conversion will disappear. There will always be multiple standards in use. For example, the newspaper industry is likely to use different formats for exchanging news articles from the TV industry. Equally, there will always be a need to do things such as extracting an address from a purchase order and adding it to an invoice or interrogating a printing press about the status of a particular job. So linking enterprises for e-commerce will increasingly become a case of defining how to extract and combine data from one set of XML documents to generate another set of XML documents and systems that are based on XML, such as JDF, are well set to succeed.

When an organisation needs to distribute editorial content through different publishing channels, the selection and formatting of the content will not be the same for each channel. In the past, the solution was to rewrite or re-purpose the material, with the disadvantage that it added more steps to the editorial process and resulted in multiple versions of an item that had to be edited or updated separately. As well as the production aspects involved in the workflow elements, there are also the process and administration stages that have to be covered. Each page or spread is generally treated as a unique item with manual operator intervention and managed separately in administration.

There are inefficiencies and much duplication of effort in providing the same content for different media channels, or even different printed versions. The content is defined along with the format of its final intended channel to reader/customer. This was fine in the past when film for a print job was the only product, but not so fine when alternative media became commercial realities. The same content is used but it is formatted differently.

One solution is to prepare content in a media-independent manner at the start of the project and use the same material for print and alternative media channels. This becomes possible by working in XML. It may mean working with different software and almost certainly in different ways to conventional prepress. Depending on the application used to create the content, the file may look like the marked up text of an old (pre-wysiwyg) typesetting system; alternatively a view of the finished page (or website or message) may be provided by the software. Often the application allows users to switch to check both structure and appearance.

There is no fixed style applied to them until the page or document is ready for output, which is performed through a specific document type definition (DTD). This allows the same content to be published in different ways. Format is applied to an XML file only when it is ready to be outputted. For print, this might involve applying different styles when a newspaper article is re-used by a magazine publisher. There is no requirement for a sub-editor to apply style as he has to just check story length and apply re-writes.

The capabilities become most useful when content is used in print and electronic media. It is possible to tag some content not to appear so that the file of the 1500 word newspaper article with five pictures on the news is sent to an SMS as a headline. At the same time, the article is expanded to 3000 words with 15 pictures on the website with links to background. For a sporting event, there may be links to websites as well as the option of buying a personalised T-shirt with your choice of picture and headline. All this can come from the same XML content, and produced once with no subsequent manual processing.

Digital workflow for print

As digital workflows have become more prevalent, so the PDF file has been accepted as the replacement of film. It works. There are many ways to produce PDFs, and printers and their customers will go through a variety of detailed tests to ensure that the quality is satisfactory and the workflow is successful. PDF offers significant benefits over film as a workable digital transfer mechanism, and acts as an improved way of getting a file into print. PDF files can be annotated with electronic sticky labels with a request for a change, or simple text corrections can be made just like film. It can be adapted, the images resized and translated into RGB and used on a website, in a way that film can't.

Using PDF remains a serial process. The industry is structured to handle that fact and there are significant improvements over transporting large amounts of film. The technological barriers were overcome successfully long before the use of PDF became mainstream. Staff had to be properly trained to understand the technology and provide safeguards to maintain quality and delivery dates. Publishers and printers organised themselves to use the technology on a daily basis and, most importantly, agree costs. Once that happened, the method became accepted and widely used. PDF is now used almost as a straight replacement for film, and the rigidity seen as a major advantage in use. The next stage will be to allow a degree of controlled flexibility into the workflow, and allow more of the benefits of technology to be used by publishers. Instead of electronic film, the use of structured XML offers the potential for electronic content.

An analogy is children's toys, where the latest must-have toy is played with for a while but then discarded. That is the situation with PDF as electronic film. It is a particular page or publication and, with a bit of effort and a developing production system, it is possible to put the file to additional use. Another toy is the Lego brick. It takes some time to assemble, gets played with and when the child gets fed up it is broken, added to the box then converted into something totally different. The Lego is XML, the instructions the DTD. The final toy is assembled on-demand to the child's specifications rather than having the fixed version (PDF) that is very good and practical for a single application.

Adobe recognised this potential limitation in PDF and the latest versions allow a degree of structure to be included through use of tags. Since version 5.0, Adobe Acrobat allows PDF files to contain logical document structure such as the title page, chapters, sections and subsections. Tagged Adobe PDF documents are designed to be reflowed to fit small-screen devices and offer better support for repurposing content, breaking the 'will read the same on any computer' strength. Reflowing capability and editability are potentially useful; there is even a plug-in that allows Acrobat files to be saved as XML. So XML is becoming mainstream. XML allows publishing to be a parallel process, offering the potential of very fast make-up. There are many tools available, some market sectors have adopted the process and it is set to increase.

Colour management   The appearance of a printed product depends on the print characteristics involved in its production. A job may reproduce quite differently between printers if these characteristics are not the same, a significant problem for advertisers. This does not only apply to printing presses. Other elements in the process can affect the result in a similar way; for example, scanners and digital cameras see colour differently. This means that if you scan the same photograph on two different machines with identical settings, different values may be recorded for the same area of the original.

Display monitors and output devices, such as inkjet printers, may also display or print colour differently. As a result, if the same file is displayed on two different monitors they are likely to appear different, and the same file sent to two different digital print engines may also look different. To illustrate one of the reasons for this, the colour limits or colour gamut of example devices is shown in Figure 5.7.

FIGURE 5.7 CIELab diagram indicating the colour gamut from a range of different devices

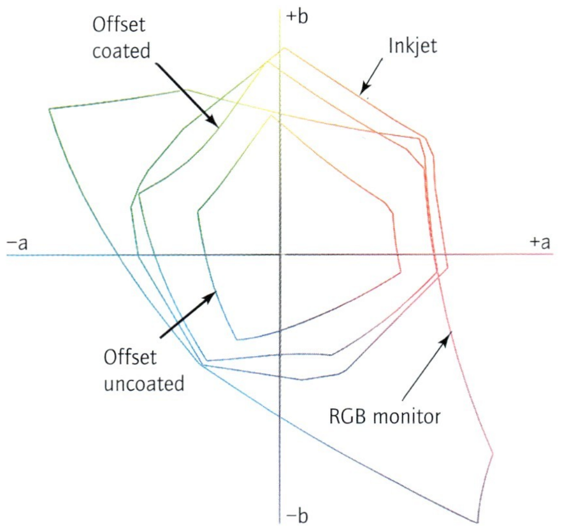

Source: Pira International Ltd

Each of these devices has a characteristic that defines the range of colours it can see or reproduce. Assuming the characteristic is reproducible and stable, it can be determined by colour measurement and communicated to other elements in the workflow, thereby allowing the appropriate translation of colour between devices. There are two ways to approach this – device-dependent transformation or a device-independent transformation. With the former approach, each device requires dedicated transformations with which it must communicate. If the workflow has to cope with numerous input, display and output devices, such an approach becomes unmanageable – as in Figure 5.8.

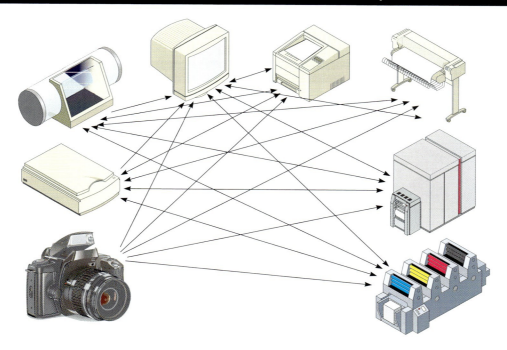

Source Pira International Ltd

The situation is more manageable and easier to maintain with device-independent transformations. This is made possible if all devices use a standard colour space to transfer to and from.

ICC colour management

For colour management to become truly device independent, it was necessary to agree a standard way for colour information to be communicated and translated between different vendors' devices. This has been the role of the International Color Consortium (ICC). Progress in the establishment of the ICC standards started in 1993, when Apple Computers joined a group of eight companies in what they called the ColorSync Consortium. Their objective was to encourage the development of vendor-neutral, cross-platform and cross-application colour communication. Today, more than 70 companies are members of the ICC.

The ICC colour management solution is based on 'device profiles', which contain the data necessary for the colour management software to translate colour values from the device-specific colour space into the standard colour space, and vice versa in the case of output device profiles (see Figure 5.9). The colour transformation is executed by software called a colour management module (CMM), which is part of the colour management system (CMS). There is a default CMM in the computer's operating system, and ColorSync is Apple's CMM, but there are CMMs from Kodak, Heidelberg, Adobe and others. The CMM accomplishes the colour transformation through a standard colour space referred to as the profile connection space (PCS). The PCS is based on XYZ (or CIELab), and assumes reflection samples viewed under illuminant (D_{50}) by a specific observer (2°), and measured with 0/45 or 45/0 measurement geometry.

FIGURE 5.9 With ICC colour-managed workflow there is a transformation to standard colour space for each device

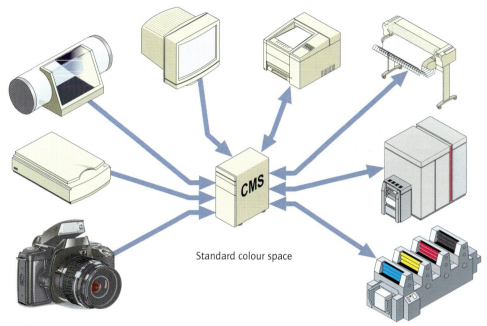

Source: Pira International Ltd

The colour management module

CMM uses profiles to provide the basis for its colour transformations. For example, it uses the input scanner profile and the profile of the computer display to convert the RGB values of the scan into a meaningful image in the RGB values of the display phosphors of the monitor. If the display is being used as a soft proof, the application will use the CMM to convert the RGB of the scan into the CMYK of the printing, and then back from that CMYK into the RGB of the phosphors to emulate the appearance of the print on screen.

Device profiles

A device profile is a data file used by CMM software to enable the transformation of an image from one device-dependent colour space into the PCS. The ICC profile format is compatible across different computer platforms. It can reside on the computer independently for use by application software or RIPs, or, depending on the file format in use, can be embedded within the file and so travel with it wherever the image goes. Profiles are typically provided by vendors of equipment (monitors, scanners, proofing systems), by software applications and for production printing as standard profiles for particular sectors and substrates. The best profiles, if produced correctly, are those produced for the specific equipment and materials in use within the print company. Profile-making software and the appropriate measuring equipment is required for this.

So, a profile is a means of characterising the device. In part this concerns the limits of the device with respect to how it sees colour (spectral sensitivity), if it is an input device, or the colour space it can reproduce if it is a display or output device. But the profiles are more than simple data tables, they contain information that defines other aspects of the transformation, and for the output profiles this also means defining the CMYK separations style.

Making profiles

The starting point for creating all types of device profile is the characterisation data, which is the relationship between defined colour data values and the device values that correspond to the equivalent areas of the image. Before this can be determined, devices must be in a calibrated and stable condition. This is a recognisable concept for scanners, monitors and digital print engines, but not something that is normally considered for production printing. It is, however, analogous to printing to a specification or reference condition.

For input devices, characterisation data is obtained by scanning a test original. This consists of a test chart (usually the IT8.7/1) imaged on the material for which the profile is being prepared, accompanied by an ASCII data file of the colour values of the image. The profile-making software compares the values in the ASCII file with the values in the image file and from that comparison prepares a profile.

Display profiles can be made using software applications that display control targets on the screen to which the user responds. The responses are captured and from this data a profile is generated. More accurate profiles are made using a spectrophotometer or colorimeter to measure a series of colour patches that are displayed on the screen under the control of the profile-making software.

The creation of output profiles follows a similar sequence, but the process is more time-consuming, particularly for production printing. For digital printing and proofing devices, a test target file is RIPped and printed. The characterisation data is obtained by measuring all the colour patches of the resulting prints. The test targets comprise many hundreds of colour patches and realistically these can only be measured with a scanning spectrophotometer, particularly for production printing, where average values from a number of prints are required. For production printing, the characterisation data must incorporate all stages, from data file to print, CTP and printing. Once the characterisation data is obtained, it is used by the profile-making software to prepare the output profile.

These are CMYK profiles, and they must also contain the specification for the colour separations related to the style of black printer that is required, levels of UCR or GCR, and the value of the maximum permitted total halftone coverage. If the production printing condition is calibrated to print to ISO 12647 standards, then the print trials can be circumnavigated by using the characterisation data for the reference printing conditions that can be found on Fogra's website (www.fogra.org) or the ICC website (www.color.org).

Prepared ICC profiles are available based on this data, but if a different style of separation is required to that chosen, the characterisation data can be used by the profile-making software with the required separation style.

Rendering intent   Colour printing, particularly on uncoated paper, cannot replicate the range of bright colours seen in a colour transparency. In such situations, where the gamut of one device is different to another, a compromise must be made. The nature of the compromise is not the same in all circumstances. In packaging, for example, it is important that the printed colour is the same as the consumer item, i.e. colorimetrically identical. In a situation where a high-quality colour original is reproduced on newsprint, colorimetrically identical rendition is impossible, so the objective will be to achieve a pleasing reproduction. ICC colour management allows the user to choose what style of compromise the CMM should use as it performs its transformation. The ICC terminology refers to these options as rendering intents, and there are four of them:

▶ absolute colorimetric
▶ relative colorimetric
▶ perceptual
▶ saturation.

Absolute colorimetric rendering defines an option where the output colours should be identical to the input colours. If the output gamut is smaller than the input, then all out-of-gamut colours are clipped, but in-gamut colours are accurately reproduced. The absolute intent is the best choice when input and output gamuts are nearly identical, and in situations where the work contains specific colours that must be reproduced with highest possible fidelity. It is also the most appropriate option where one device is being emulated by another, such as proofing for newspapers on a white-based inkjet paper.

Relative colorimetric rendering treats out-of-gamut colours the same as absolute rendering, but rescales the in-gamut colours so that the white of the original is mapped to the white point of the PCS (profile connection space). Relative intent is generally the most appropriate option when using an inkjet printer to proof images that will be used for offset printing.

Perceptual rendering attempts to preserve the appearance of an illustration by compressing or expanding the gamut of the image to fill the gamut of the destination device. This will normally mean that grey balance is preserved, but colorimetric accuracy might not be. It is the appropriate choice where the objective is to produce a pleasing picture rather than a facsimile of the original.

Saturation rendering aims to maintain the chroma of the original as far as possible. Clearly it is not possible to expand the chroma gamut of the output, the option simply enhances the chroma within the available gamut. It is the least used of all the intents and is usually an option for the reproduction of business graphics and similar charts, where impact is more important than faithful reproduction.

Outlook

At the moment, ICC colour management, as outlined in this chapter, is not universally used by the industry for the production of CMYK separations. But this will change, and the majority of printed work will be processed through an automated colour-managed workflow. For the moment, application of ICC profiles is mainly directed to the control and production of digital proofs.

Colour management will help to ensure that the correct colour is printed regardless of the press used. Proofing will use the system, allowing good-quality contract proofs to be produced remotely on relatively low-cost inkjet devices, often at the clients' office to reduce the time for approval. Colour management will be automatically applied to images to be used on the web, as it can work across all media generating lower-resolution RGB files to minimise download time. A further benefit of colour management for printers is a uniform print condition, reducing press set-up and waste, providing economic benefits that are passed on to the client.

Proofing

Proofing is changing as the costs and the time involved make many existing solutions unworkable. With the increase of distributed prepress functions and more people involved in the preparation of digital files, there is still need for proofing but not in the same way as now. This is not a technology issue and the creative community and final customers need proofs at various stages during the development of a print project. The proof validates data at a given position in the workflow. This process gives authority to the validator and defines a responsibility point for the accuracy and suitability of the data. The reference may be local and transient with no value to anyone else or it may be archival. It provides stable information that others can refer to in the event of a query arising later in the production process. While the formal proof is a communication in the process of creating print, it may not be so relevant in the wider communications area.

Colour fidelity will move to become a colour-managed system feature while proofs are used to check content rather that the contract proof as now. This will see significant growth in soft proofing, where PDF files are distributed to interested parties over the web with deadlines for comments. Systems are being developed that permit the sampling of pixel data across a web connection, with collaboration and sign-off capability or remote output if required. One such system is Kodak's RealTime Proof application.

Hard copies will be printed remotely if they are needed, probably on colour-managed inkjet printers with simulated dots – an option that will diminish. Mark-up of proofs will be electronic with comments recorded in a digital asset management system that records the development of a printed item.

Increasing use of soft proofs means that monitors will be larger, with greater colour fidelity provided by suppliers who have technology to manage onscreen colour fidelity. This will be critical for businesses that use the web for displaying and selling products.

The proofing process is rapidly changing and it will be:

► Fast, for transmission and output;

► Both accurate and consistent, achieved through colour management and calibration;

▶   Providing a hardcopy option, probably on A3 inkjets using approved substrate and inks;

▶   Both predictable and traceable. File management is needed with receipts and job tracking across all parties with full audit trail.

Proofing methods and control

In printing, the final result will be judged on the basis of how it looks. The need for subjective visual judgement is made inevitable because most reproductions are not an exact copy of the original. While it is possible to express some aspects of the relationship between original and reproduction in measurable terms, these are not capable of being interpreted as an indication of the overall acceptability of the reproduction.

An opportunity to make visual judgements in addition to measurements is, therefore, a fundamental requirement in most colour reproduction systems, and this requirement is fulfilled by the colour proof. In this context it is important that the proof mimics the final printed result as accurately as possible. This is crucial to a successful colour reproduction system.

Stages of proofing

A proof may be required at several stages in the reproduction process. Digital proofing techniques are now largely used throughout the process from mono laser iterative checks through to contract simulations of the final job. There is a wide variety of colour proofing methods and systems available, and some are more able to simulate the print characteristics than others. For convenience they are often loosely categorised into three groups:

▶   progress proofs

▶   imposition proofs

▶   contract proofs.

Progress proofs A progress, or iterative, proof is one that is cheap, fast and produced locally. It shows the information to decide if a change is needed, and it will be thrown away without concern for the budget. The progress proof is normally considered only for internal use as it has significant limitations when it comes to matching the printed result, but will be convenient to use and, hopefully, economic at the stage at which it is required.

Colour laser and inkjet printers are increasingly used and with colour management they can provide good representations of the final result, although there will be no representation of the printing dots.

Imposition proofs An imposition proof is a low-resolution representation of the printing forme, usually produced at the printing company using a large-format inkjet plotter, to check the relative position of pages on press and as a last-minute content check. It is not normally in colour.

Contract proofs The aim of the contract proof is to match the production result. It is often the means of explaining to printers what they are expected to achieve. The contract proof can form a legally binding contract between the supplier and the customer. Because of this, it should not be the subject of individual interpretation by either party. Visual assessment alone is too subjective for the results to define a contract, and the nature of this contract is that one party often has a far deeper understanding of the technological ramifications than the other does. The need for objective assessment – a meaningful control system – is one of the characteristics that separates a contract from a progress system. In digital workflows a quality standard that guarantees the integrity of the proof is a key requirement of a contract proof.

A control system and means of colour managing to an accepted standard can be applied to a cheap inkjet printer with suitable RIPs and calibration routines.

The only proof that faithfully duplicates the production print is one printed on the production press under production conditions, and with the same materials that will be used for the job. Any proof produced another way might be considered only as a target proof. So, in the context of proofing to match the production result, the terms 'contract' and 'target' are not helpful. All we can really say is that the proof should aim to achieve, as closely as possible, a simulation of the production print characteristics. What differentiates between contract and target, at this level, is the compromise accepted by the parties involved.

Methods of proofing to match the production result

Most printers still request proofs or they will generate digital proofs from the supplied files and run to that copy. Proofing has seen major changes with the development of digital workflow and the demise of film. Many commercial jobs do not use contract proofs to accompany digital jobs but use iterative proofs for content and follow colour management routines for the printer to follow standard set-up. There are two categories of proof:
▶ press
▶ off-press: analogue and digital.
Various methods or technologies are common within these three categories. Digital proofs dominate because they are fast, cheap and good simulations of the printed result with reasonable control. Some critical colour applications still require the highest quality proofs for advertising material, but these are becoming less widespread. Press proofing is still required when spot-colour mock-ups are needed.

Production press proofs A proof produced on the production press can be seen as the ultimate in so far as matching the print characteristics is concerned. Production materials can be used with the same process and possibly the same equipment. However, there are economic limitations. It is expensive, not just because of the cost of operating a production press for proofing, but also because of the plate, ink and paper costs. Although it is a short print run, it cannot be so short that the normal equilibrium print characteristics are not obtained. All this means that the timescale to produce the proof is lengthy and the results can also be inconsistent. Nevertheless, the production press proof does fulfil a need for certain products such as folding cartons. Cartons, like most packaging products, are particularly demanding with respect to colour match for spot colours and a short proof-run can be justified for the assurance of knowing that the proof can be matched.

Proofing press proofs The proofing press is more common when a printed ink-on-paper proof is required. The press is a normally single colour, flatbed rotary, plate and substrate flat, offset blanket rotary. The print is made at a much slower speed than is the case in production, and there is a comparatively long time interval between transfer of ink from plate to blanket and then paper. As most proofing presses are single colour, printing is wet-on-dry.

An accurate match to the production print characteristics is possible from most points of view. It is possible to print on the job stock as long as the weight of the paper is not too low. The inks can also use the same pigments and be similar in make-up to production inks, so that it is possible to duplicate exactly the hue and densities achieved in production. The problem comes in reproducing the production tone transfer characteristics and trapping. The nature of the process means that the dot gain is generally lower than in production and the ink trapping, being wet-on-dry, is better. It is possible to achieve production dot-gain characteristics, but this requires adjustment of the inks and printing pressure. The main problem when assessing these proofs is inconsistency, and this greatly depends on the skill of the proofer.

Note that a second meaning for the term 'trapping', is in use in page layout software. The term trapping is used to describe the process of applying grips (spreads and choked) to elements within a page or design. Here the term trapping is used in its original context to mean the degree to which an ink sticks to a previously inked substrate. If the previous ink is still wet, as would be the case in a multi-unit, litho colour press, the trapping will be lower than the wet-on-dry situation of a flatbed proofing press. The original definition and the new usage have no connection with each other and relate to completely different aspects of print and reproduction.

Digital proofing systems

The decline in the use of film has largely resulted in analogue, photo-mechanical proofing systems such as Cromalin or MatchPrint being replaced by digital methods, most based on inkjet technology. With digital proofs, the print characteristic specification is required for calibration. This information is used in the data transformation, which should then allow the proof to match accurately the production printing. It is important that the proofing system should be able to use similar substrates to production and the ink hue and gamut should also be comparable, if a customer proof is required. Other factors, such as dot gain and trapping, can be taken into account in the data transforms.

Most digital proofing systems do not create the tonal rendition with the same halftone dot structure that will be generated on the films that will be used to make the printing plates. This leads some people to ask whether a proof without halftone dots can be used to simulate a halftone print. In practice the proofs are able to produce results that match well with halftone production prints, providing that calibration has been carried out correctly.

Most contract colour digital proofs use inkjet technology with colour management and calibration to simulate various print conditions. Some offer halftone screening capability but this is becoming less important as the industry starts to lose its reliance on the linen tester.

Verification of digital proofs

In an ideal colour reproduction system, the proof supplied to the client for assessment should accurately duplicate the production printing characteristic. It is important to make the proof accurately simulate the printing characteristics. If the printer has control of proofing, this is relatively straightforward to arrange, but it may be difficult to achieve from a technical standpoint. The possibility of this happening where a third party supplies proofs depends on having good co-operation and adequate specifications of the requirements. This involves specifying a standard printing condition and ensuring all parties stick to this optimum condition.

Achieving this goal is made possible by measurement to determine the appropriate adjustments. Measurement requires a test forme to be printed and proofed. The forme should include a full range grey scale and tone scales of the primary and secondary colours. This will provide the press characterisation profile used in the colour management routine.

There has been an increase in the certification of proofs to agreed standards to ensure that the digital proof is produced in accordance with an accredited procedure to link RIP and proofing engine. A good example is the pass4press proof4press (see page 157) initiative. These provide independent verification of the quality and consistency of proofs produced from various engines.

The RIP must first output a test file satisfactorily. This is followed by a comparative visual assessment of the proofs, which are judged against certain pre-set criteria. The final check is a spectrophotometric measurement of a test strip with a maximum tolerance of $E = 2$. Then there is a compliance procedure to follow to ensure verification so that anyone receiving the proof can measure the strip to ensure it has been produced within standard tolerances. A verification set, comprising a spectrophotometer, software and a label maker to apply labels is available that demonstrates compliance.

In the case of proof4press, the Agfa Grand Sherpa and Creo Iris and Veris devices are accredited, with others to follow. Creo first launched the Veris Proofer at Ipex 2002 to succeed its ground-breaking range of Iris inkjet proofers. The Veris Proofer is a substantial tabletop device that weighs more than 100kg. It produces B2 proofs, 4 × A4 pages to view, with space for calibration strips, certification and information in the 530 × 730mm imaging area. A high-resolution proof takes around 20 minutes to output. The device uses a patented novel continuous inkjet printing technology developed from the Iris method. Creo calls it 'multi-drop array'.

Creo's Veris uses an elegant design to optimise quality and speed using a continuous drop inkjet system, rather than the drop-on-demand (DOD) approach adopted by several of its competitors. In a design reminiscent of the external drum platesetter, Creo uses a wide imaging swathe to reduce the rotational speed of the drum. The inkjet head travels slowly along the length of a rotating drum with eight heads applying aqueous ink to the paper to ensure precise placement of ink drops. This mechanism is mounted on three anti-vibration mounts to ensure that the positional accuracy of the print head to the drum is maintained.

FIGURE 5.10 Veris Proofer imaging mechanism

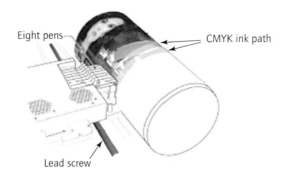

Source: Creo Inc.

There are two printing heads for each colour (CMYK), mounted together in very tight registration. Pumps in each head (Creo uses the term 'pen') deliver ink at a constant flow rate. Ink flowing out of the nozzle is broken into precise drop sizes by 1Mhz vibrations of the piezo crystal, resulting in 1 million consistent, very small 3.3 picolitre drops per second. The pen and the driving electronics can apply different electrical charges to each drop to steer them onto one of nine possible flight paths. Non-printing drops are charged to a higher level than other printing drops and deflected away from the paper before being caught by the 'knife' edge.

FIGURE 5.11 Mechanism of multi-array imaging head

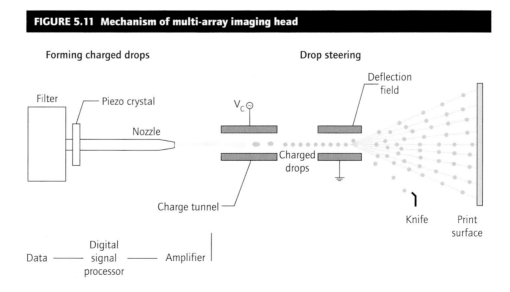

Source: Creo Inc.

Each pen writes nine lines of ink on every rotation of the drum. The multi-drop array head contains two pens for each colour, so the whole imaging head writes 18 lines of each colour (0.3mm) for every rotation of the drum.

Traditional continuous inkjet technology is unable to print at the high resolutions required for superior text and linework without being unacceptably slow. This is because each nozzle is limited to printing a single raster line per drum revolution or media advancement. In order to achieve acceptable print times, higher resolutions would require faster drum speeds, but print quality deteriorates rapidly when media is run at speed because of the air turbulence between the print head and the media. Creo claims multi-array technology solves this problem by enabling the device to print multiple image lines per drum revolution. The result, it says, generates consistent, precise drops with controlled, accurate placement.

Creo claims the result is exact colours, smooth vignettes, outstanding shadow detail and fine text clarity. Several independent industry bodies agree with Creo's claims. At the IPA Color Proofing RoundUP in June 2004, 27 digital proofing systems were evaluated to test correlation of proofs to images on GRACoL (General Requirements for Applications in Commercial Offset Lithography) press sheets. The entries were evaluated separately on colorimetric measurement using $L*a*b*$ values and ΔE correlation to CGATS-DTR004 reference characterisation. Proofers were also judged on the production of test pages to assess RIP speed, overprint correctness, spot colour, and colour management. The panel of judges included colour experts from publishers, trade shops and printers. The Veris was ranked among the top three in all categories, and top in visual evaluation. Colour standards organisations have certified the Veris system's colour fidelity with SWOP certification, Pantone qualified, SICOGIF (France) certified, Fogra (Germany) certified, and PPA (UK) accredited.

The Veris features its own RIP and provides complete ICC workflow support, including spot-colour handling. It connects to a variety of applications, and can process PDF, PostScript, EPS and DCS files. Creo emphasises the proofer is optimised for its Prinergy and Brisque workflows. These offer queue management, image preview mode, image layout and manipulation, as well as other features. It can also be connected to third-party workflow systems, including the GMG Colorproof, which consists of a colour engine, profile editor and creator, a RIP and an output module for the Veris. GMG is a privately owned software company based near Stuttgart, Germany. It develops high-end colour management solutions and has more than 5000 systems in use at advertising agencies, prepress houses, offset and gravure printers.

As part of any installation, Creo offers its Certified Proofing Process, which it has developed to provide customers with quality assurance. This creates a more secure proof that is easy for producers and their customers to use and understand. The Veris system checks that the correct process is used to make the proof. First it checks that the proofer has been calibrated recently and that the correct calibration set-up has been used. Next, the system verifies that the correct ICC profile has been selected. Finally, the system will ensure that the proof is printed with the ink and media defined for that particular proof. When the proofer has checked that each of these conditions is met, the Certified Proofing Process logo is printed on the proof. This logo ensures that everyone who sees the proof knows it has been made to a specific, defined and precisely controlled process.

While this feature is a marketing tool for Creo, it is a useful assurance for print buyers and customers requiring accurate proofs. Creo offers its own inks and media, which are necessary to obtain the certification stamp. Supplying consumables is a growing part of Creo's business and there are four grades of paper designed to give the best reproduction characteristics with the Veris. Each sheet is composed of a multilayer swellable polymer ink-receiving layer, coated onto a resin-coated photo base. Specifically formulated for Veris ProPack-GA inks, the ink receiving layer handles high ink-loading while fixing the ink dyes near the surface of the coating to achieve optimum colour performance and detail. The photo base ensures that high ink densities do not cause cockling or curling.

The sheets are edge printed on the back for easy identification, and each sheet is individually encoded to enable the Creo Certified Process. The different grades available are: Veris Pro Commercial Semi-Matte 158 and 285gsm, for woodfree art and board applications; Veris Pro Publication Semi-Matte 285gsm, for publication papers; and Veris Pro Glossy 155gsm. The water-based Veris ProPack-GA inks are formulated for optimum performance with multi-drop array inkjet imaging technology. Individual bottles are supplied with cleaning fluid and a collection bottle for fast replacement and easy handling. The proofer itself monitors and reports ink usage and identifies ink type to enable the Creo Certified Process.

Users can choose to use the job stock if required, but will need to develop a suitable profile to ensure colour fidelity. The surface characteristics of many papers (particularly uncoated) will result in too much ink spread to produce a suitable proof. Profiles for standard targets are included with Veris systems, but many users will require custom profiles to simulate unique targets. These can be developed in-house or by Creo Color Services group.

The Veris proofer can run up to 40 proofs continuously with unattended operation and the system ensures intelligent management of colour and media utilisation. The list price is £26,000 (€35,000) for the base model, which can be connected to existing Creo or other supplier's approved workflow components, or £29,000 for a standalone system with its own front-end. Various supply options are available, from a total supply contract for inks and media to a standalone installation of the equipment. Many users have installed the equipment as part of a deal to use a Creo workflow system with CTP and plates. The cost of the proof depends on the volumes involved (and the negotiating skill of the buyer), but will typically be between £1.60–2.20 for an A4 sheet, including calibration strips and certification stamps, etc.

This pricing is significantly higher than for a wide-format inkjet printer, both in terms of equipment and consumables. The time to produce a proof is also significantly longer, but the quality of the result, linked to the quality assurance tools, means there is a demanding print and prepress market willing to pay.

With digital proofing systems, the colour gamut is wider than for offset printing, and it can be controlled to manipulate the proof image to simulate the visual effect of all the print variables. The profile of the proofer can be set to match a variety of printing set-ups so one device can be used to mimic a range of production options. In some cases, the digital proofer is a digital press that can produce a prototype run of the final product, using actual materials that can be finished to provide an early run of products.

Formatting for output

The format of the content will be increasingly applied at output stage according to rules of the media involved. For print, this will mean flowing content into a range of templates and document definitions optimised for the particular print process involved. Early examples of variable document templates already accomplish these activities and follow clearly defined rules for both content selection and make-up appearance.

Automatic make-up

Developing technology will allow automatic make-up applications to create and assemble customised and personalised pages. Content can be automatically assembled into design templates with the system making up into pages or documents that have the appearance of being designed by operators. Examples of this technology are PageFlex's Mpower and .Edit, with XMPie, Wav2 and others offering templating software that allows users to create PDF files on demand and automatically create sophisticated designs.

They enable the design and automatic production of customised documents targeted to individuals or small groups. The selection of the digital content is controlled by final consumer profile information. Then flexible templates assemble this selected content into the final document for electronic or printed output. This enables the marketeer to tailor a specific message relevant to the target customer providing a better response to direct mail and improving the relations with existing customers. The content may be repurposed making it more effective.

The document content will vary according to the individual customer profile information. The template captures the overall abstract look automatically adjusting the layout according to the size and placement of the variable content. Output systems provide optimised PostScript to go to a conventional RIP or digital colour press as a PPML format to optimise the digital printing. Additionally, other formats will be supported so a PDF might be emailed or the content posted on the web or as HTML/XML data to form a dynamic web page.

The document type definition in SGML, or schema in XML, provides the same function on static documents. These will apply format to tagged content at the output stage according to the requirements of the particular print or distribution process. It will be a function of the prepress operation to obtain and prepare the correct settings for output. This will involve liaison with final printers to optimise particular settings held separately from content until the file is prepared for a particular press. In a few years' time, it will be common to receive a specific set-up to be included into the output schema as part of the specification provided by the printer.

Output file preparation – preflight checking

The principle of preflight checking recognises that most digital file preparation errors fit in a narrow range of categories (missing fonts, incorrect resolution or colour space of images, wrong trapping characteristics). Identifying and overcoming any such errors means the digital workflow will move relatively smoothly. The term 'preflighting' comes from aircraft pilots' use of a check list before take-off. Regardless of their experience, pilots perform a series of formal routines that, providing the results of each are positive, guarantee the safe state of the aeroplane before flight. The same principles should be applied to the preparation of a datafile before despatch by originator and printer to ensure smooth production saving time and money.

Early preflighting was performed manually by a skilled operator checking individual native application files. Now preflight checking of files is mostly done using commercially available software such as MakzWare FlightCheck (Figure 5.12) and EnFocus PitStop. The set-up checks for common errors and will automatically fix minor things. When passed, the file has a much greater chance of working smoothly and correctly to produce the job required without incurring additional charges Then came commercially available software integrated into the workflows and files would be dropped into hot folders and checked. Errors were reported in a log and operators would repair the files or request re-submission. The software will become easier to use and capable of handling more sophisticated errors and omissions.

The future of preflighting is integration and automation, and both relate directly to the efficiency of a digital printing workflow. It should be done either side of any point in a workflow where responsibilities for the content changes – before delivery and before accepting receipt. In that way, maximum efficiency is maintained and responsibility for errors more easily deduced.

Preflighting automates the checking and fixing of files at various stages throughout their gestation. The software is available as web-based plug-ins run by printers with their particular specification or by specialist software developers on a subscription basis. Elements, pages, templates and files (including PostScript, XML and PDF code) will be parsed and examined by the software according to the particular output requirements of the customer. Most errors will be corrected transparently to the user. In the event of a missing font, the application will source the font licence and pay the copyright owner the necessary licence as part of the agreed fees for preflighting.

5

FIGURE 5.12 Capabilities of preflight software

Source: Markzware

For printing there are six main categories that will be checked.

▶ *File* For application software files it is important to use the same version and language edition to avoid reflowing, and to check that any specialist plug-ins are present. Logos, scans, EPS design elements – are they with the document, clearly identified and in logically named folders or directories? If you had never seen the job before and you had no idea what the author was trying to achieve, could you find all the elements of the design? Is there only one version of each file being delivered? Do not send alternatives from which the printer can choose the best.

▶ *Page* Page size, orientation, bleed, extent, start point and presence of any spreads is important to know.

▶ *Print* The document's print parameters based on the settings originally chosen in the application's page setup window. This includes the print resolution, line screening, output quality, data format, registration or printer marks setting and bleed value. Additionally, whether the document will be printed in process colour, spot colour or mono, if there will be a reduction or enlargement scaling, if separations or spreads have been turned on, as well as the orientation and paper size (if known).

▶ *Font* Probably the biggest cause for concern is still use of fonts in original applications and nested within images incorporated in the document. Are they TrueType, OpenType or PostScript? Is the method by which you are ensuring that the fonts will be available legal?

► *Colours* This checks the correct rendering of spot colours used in the document or within placed images for text characters, background fills and frames of boxes, lines and paragraph rules. It will check that there is a reference to the correct specification of the colour (rather than just a default name) and ensure the correct knockout and overprint characteristics are employed.

► *Image* The images used in the document and presence of any fonts. Specific information about resolution, colour space, transparency, clipping paths and scaling factors will be checked. Ensure the image has not used lossy compression routines.

For each of the criteria, the preferred settings will be defined and the files checked against the ground rules. In some cases the software will automatically fix errors or provide a report detailing the necessary corrective action. For PDF and PDF/X supplied files, the settings will be checked against the set-up definitions. An exact duplicate of the work despatched is kept for safety and insurance reasons. If the work is lost, it can then readily be replaced but the exact duplicate can also be valuable in disputes about where something was lost or where in the process an error was introduced.

Software checking is not usually sufficient on its own because there are elements outside the datafile that are also important. Preflighting is so important to the smooth running of a digital workflow that routines combining both manual and software checking should be installed and *all* work should pass through them before being passed on to the next stage of production.

Good2Print, a Mac server-based preflight checking and error correcting workflow, claims to deliver only 'what's good to print'. It handles native application files and PDFs and can be configured to suit the needs of a wide variety of printers. Specific benefits include the use of any font with kerning pair sets, and checking any flavour of PDF, PostScript and native file format. It operates on a hot folder basis, either locally or over the web. Clients can drop a file into a folder and files are uploaded to the service provider, checked and loaded into the workflow. The system will perform a range of checks as specified, reporting or fixing them as soon as they are received. A report will be generated as soon as the file is received, providing good service for the client by identifying potential problems immediately.

This will ensure that only files fit for the purpose are uploaded. The client will get a full report directly via the system if there are any problems. Figure 5.13 outlines the workflows associated with the product; individual customers will set up the specific route and settings for their operation and equipment.

FIGURE 5.13 Good2Print workflow schematic

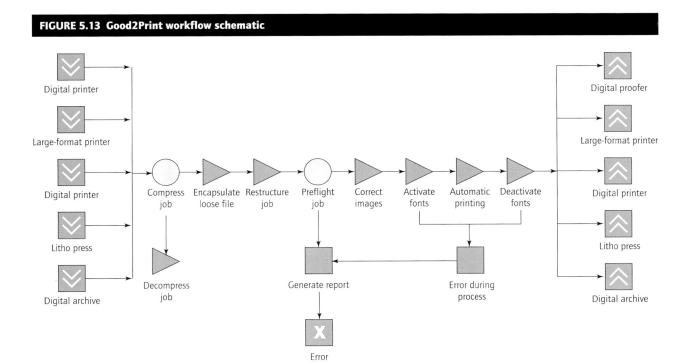

Source: ROI Distribution

The system fixes some common errors automatically, including RGB–CMYK image conversion, JPEG compression correction, font activation and deactivation, and placing jobs into the appropriate print queue. The product is being positioned as a valuable addition to the prepress function of any digital print company, replacing the need for highly skilled operators (the PostScript doctor) and always available for most jobs.

PostScript   PostScript is a page description language that describes every detail, such as text, diagrams, graphics and pictures, that could appear on a page. It is a near-English set of commands and operators, arranged in a syntax that describes a page in terms of the boundaries of the graphical elements that appear on the page. A PostScript file is generated from a front-end application program that defines the content. As a program, the PostScript file needs to be interpreted. The PostScript interpreter resides in the printer or output device, and is often called a raster image processor (RIP). The RIP will be software running on a powerful computer interpreting the PostScript file instructions into the addressable points of the output device.

Each addressable point is rendered as either to be exposed or not to be exposed. Imagine an area of electronic memory with one cell (or bit) reserved for each addressable point on the surface of the page. The PostScript file is then interpreted so as to insert a required 0 or 1 in each memory cell. The memory is then addressed to switch the laser light on (where there was a 1 in the cell) or off (0) at each addressable point, as the laser points at it, on the output medium.

A PostScript file contains the boundaries of the graphic elements, in the form of start coordinates and travel directions, as though the outline is being traced with a pointer. It also contains instructions concerning the treatment of the boundary described. The boundary can be filled in with colour (painted), or it can be stroked – painted with a set width of line – to form a visible outline on the page. This vector format makes for relatively small files when compared with bitmapped graphics. Painting can be achieved with colour or halftone to make colour-tinted elements, or with a pattern defined elsewhere in the PostScript file. For a given page, there is no unique PostScript file. Apart from the syntax requirements, the file is unstructured. There are a variety of ways in which a PostScript file can represent a page. A page described in a file made by a PostScript programmer can be quite different to the same page made by an operator working with a software application: the file sizes, orders, contents and output times can be very different, but the output pages can be identical.

Portable document format (PDF)

Adobe's PDF was developed to suit the needs of networked communities. It allowed a document created on one computer to be viewed on any other computer without the receiver having the application that created the document. PDF has been developed into an application, platform and output device-independent file structure that lends itself to transportable publishing. When created, the file is equivalent to a partly-RIPped file, containing a display list of page objects. Acrobat Reader is a utility enabling the display of the file on most computer screens, but it also adds a PostScript structure if the file is sent to a printer. The file is then RIPped in the normal way.

Since PDF aims to serve all the digital data-based graphic arts, it contains functionality that will be irrelevant to many users. As an output format for print, for example, many of the internet facilities will be academic, except that the printer may receive the document by email, or the prepress house may send it to the printer by email. The print-related functions will be of little interest to the internet community.

Font (typeface) problems currently experienced by many in the graphic arts industry will be sidestepped by the ability of PDF to incorporate the fonts for the documents within the file. The fonts will, therefore, transfer with the file but in a non-reusable way. This means that anybody can legally process the document, even without a licence for the font, because they will not be able to extract the font for their own use. To maintain a small file size, the author may choose not to include the font, in which case the receiving computer will select its best fit.

The author of the PDF file may also choose to make the file editable to allow the printers to incorporate their own fine-tuning, or to disable all editing so that the file cannot be changed at all. Both these options are required in the industry.

As an output file, the PDF overcomes the variability of PostScript by virtue of not being a program file, as PostScript is. PDF is an object-oriented format, where each graphic object carries properties and hierarchies. When the object arrives for processing as part of the

two years. Several manufacturers are offering process-less (or chemical-free) plates that are washed clean ready for use during make-ready on the press. Fuji offers a photopolymer processorless plate using controlled ablation. The laser energy weakens the bonding between the coating and the plate surface. When printing starts, the high tack of the ink picks at the coating and, where there is weak bonding, removes the coating during make-ready. The platesetter needs no special air flow because there is no ablation debris at the imaging stage and there is no requirement for special processor or expensive chemistry. Other processerless plates will be developed and will take a significant share of the CTP (and whole) print market. Early brands are charging a significant premium, up to 50%, as they are aimed at small-volume users. When they become more widely available the premium is likely to drop to the benefit of the industry. As well as the platemaking area, the preference of the printing department must be considered.

Plate handling technologies

Platesetters fall into three categories: external drum, flatbed and internal drum.

FIGURE 5.17 Rotating drum CTP device

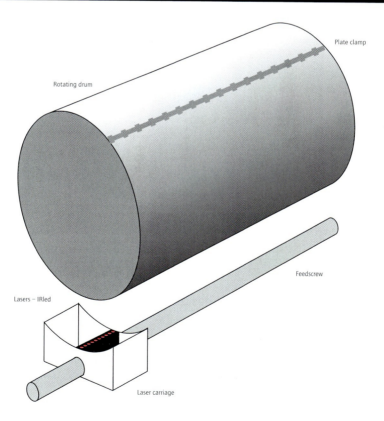

Source: Pira International Ltd

External drum

External drum imagesetters and platesetters developed from output scanners. The plate is clamped onto a drum that rotates in front of the laser source. The laser path length is short, so there is little drop off of energy. The unexposed plate is held by vacuum to the outside of the drum with the plate's light-sensitive coating facing outwards. A traversing optics head contains the exposing source and modulator. The exposing laser source can be split into a number of separate beams, thus reducing the rotational speed by imaging a wide swathe at each pass. The beams are on continuously, being interrupted by the modulator, with each acting independently under the direction of individual beam computers. These beam computers are programmed to determine the switching times of each beam according to the plate position, the required halftone dot size, the screen ruling and the screen angle.

FIGURE 5.19 Fujifilm Luxe CTP

Source: Fujifilm

Flatbed

The flatbed, rotating polygon configuration (see Figure 5.19) is widely used in newspapers where a plate is held on a flat bed that moves under a rotating polygon. This has a series of accurately ground and polished reflective faces that reflect an incident laser continuously over the surface of the medium from one side to the other. The main benefit is easy and fast plate loading and unloading allowing high numbers of plates to be produced in automated devices.

FIGURE 5.19 Rotating polygon

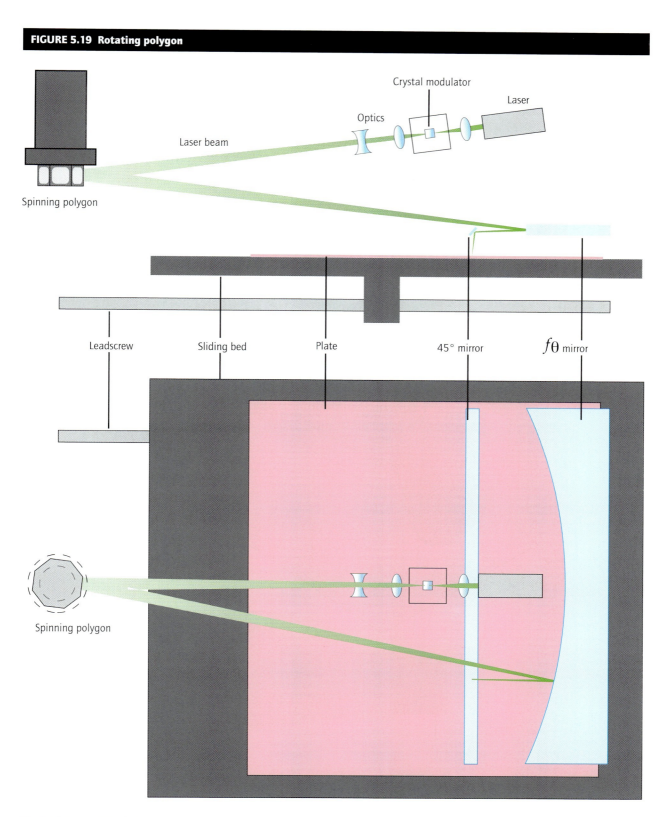

Laser
Crystal modulator
Optics
Laser beam
Spinning polygon
Leadscrew
Sliding bed
Plate
45° mirror
$f\theta$ mirror
Spinning polygon

Source: Pira International Ltd

Internal drum

The internal drum design uses rotating optics to reflect a scanning beam onto a plate held on the inside of a static cylinder. A rotating optic head is traversed axially through the cylinder, exposing the material in a helical trace. The formation of halftone dots is similar to the rotating polygon design since these devices usually use a single beam for exposure. Fairly high positional precision is assured in this design. The rotating optics design lends itself to high mechanical speed operation. The mass of the spinning optic is low, and so it can be rotated at high speed (20,000 rpm is typical).

FIGURE 5.20 Internal drum CTP

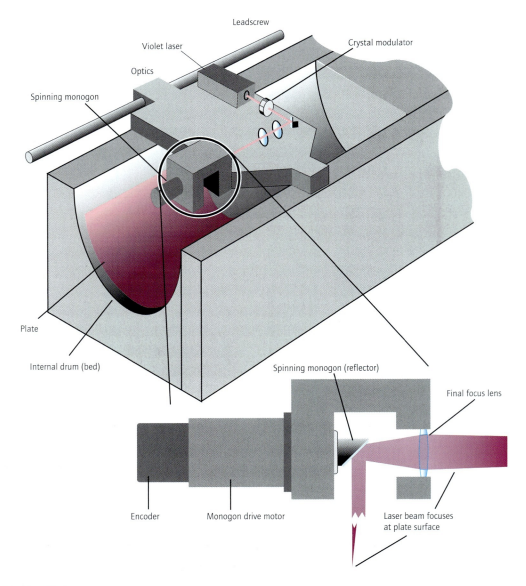

FIGURE 5.21 Internal drum platesetter

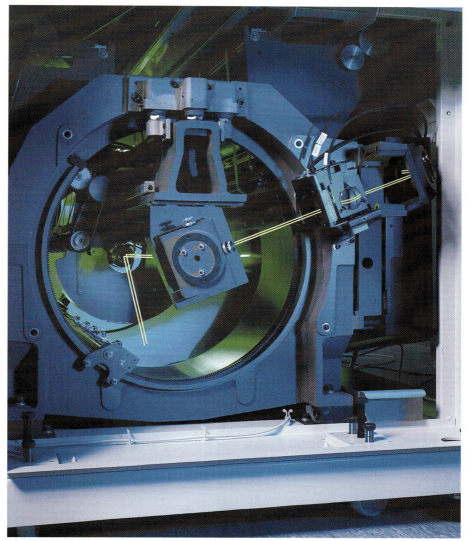

Source: Fujifilm

There are merits to all three methods. Flatbed has been accepted by the newspaper industry where large numbers of plates are required in short timescales because of the ease of handling and high levels of automation. External drum technology allows the exposure head to be close to the plate, and sophisticated beam splitting through light valves and gratings mean the rotational speed does not have to be high to achieve high speed imaging. Internal drum technology involves a fairly long beam width that suffers significant energy drop off. As more powerful 30–50mW laser expose units became available, this problem has been overcome and fast-spinning mirrors allow fast exposure. Although competing suppliers will sell the benefits of their particular technologies, all have been proven to work satisfactorily. The choice should be made on the requirements of the business, in terms of plate format, throughput and the degree of automation required.

Computer to conventional plate

Since their introduction, plate suppliers have succeeded in charging a significant premium for the supply of CTP plates over conventional types. Whether silver-based, thermal or photopolymer, the costs in the mid-1990s equated to conventional plate plus film, now the premium over conventional plates has dropped to 10–25% higher with additional developer costs. This premium can be an important issue, particularly in high-volume applications, and there have been attempts to develop exposure units that work with conventional plates. Basys Print has a number of innovative imaging systems using UV light that work with conventional plates. Inkjet CTP systems have found some success, but their penetration is still very low.

Printers put the advantage of reduced press make-ready as the key benefit for CTP, making print more efficiently. This has been a key measure of the success of CTP installations at printers. Plates are a necessary part of the offset process, and new technologies allow faster make-ready and lower wastage that greatly benefited offset printing. The cost of the special CTP plates is secondary and printers perceive use of conventional and processorless plates as not key issues.

Origination for flexography

Prepress for flexography is undergoing major change, with improvements in software, workflow, imaging technologies and materials. As flexo has grown in use, so markets for plates have grown, further fuelled by demand for shorter runs and the increasing use of colour. More suppliers of equipment and consumables are entering the flexo market, spurring on new improvements. These developments have brought about improvements in print quality and changed the economics of the process. In so doing, they have altered the structure of the industry and minimised the environmental impact of the process.

The key development for flexography over the next five years will be fully digital workflows. Digital prepress will become increasingly mainstream, with lower-cost software removing the entry barriers for printers and converters to bring prepress in-house rather than using specialist trade shops for their plates. As a result, the unit cost for press-ready plates is in decline. GAIN (the US Graphic Arts Information Network) estimates that 36% of flexo printers in Europe had digital prepress in-house in 2001; by 2006 this will be at more than 50%. Increasingly, larger printers will take prepress in-house to reduce turnaround times and increase their production flexibility, while smaller users will still use specialist trade shops to supply press-ready plates.

Most flexographic print is for packaging and label applications and uses special colours that need to be manipulated to achieve the optimal result on press. The majority of flexo plates are photopolymer based. They come in a wide range of thicknesses and hardnesses for printing onto various substrates with very different surface characteristics. Plates are still mounted onto cylinders manually, although there are positioning aids that use CCD register cameras. Plates are fixed in place using double-sided tape. There are compressible grades, which are designed to minimise air entrapment and provide a regular surface profile and hence impression pressure to improve print consistency and eliminate high spots that will wear. The use of thinner mounting tapes means plates can reproduce the original tone values more accurately. There is a trend toward imaging in the round on pre-mounted plates, and sleeves that are imaged and processed in-register ready for quick mounting on press. This reduces costly set-up time and waste in the print room.

CTP technology is coming of age in flexography. Esko Graphics announced the installation of its 500th Cyrel Digital Imager in October 2004, nine years after its launch in 1995. Initial take-up was slow – the 400th installation only took place in March 2004. An additional 100 installations over the course of the next seven months demonstrates the increased take up of flexo CTP. CTP systems for flexo have fallen in price as the technology has become more widespread. Entry level systems for narrow-web applications are available for around €100,000, down from the original €500,000 price tag. Most use laser ablation, which requires UV exposure and processing, with equipment costs starting from €50,000 depending on the plate format. Buyers can sign agreements with suppliers to amortise the capital investment costs over the life of a supply contract.

Flexo CTP exposure units give better halftone dot profiles than conventional film exposure, improving the overall quality of the final plate and increasing the print quality. These developments benefit the process and more jobs are being transferred to flexo from gravure because of the lower cost for similar levels of quality.

Specialist flexo prepress software

Offset printing has been boosted by the widespread use of low-cost graphics publishing software. Programs such as QuarkXPress, PageMaker or InDesign are used to prepare a document on a desktop computer and produce a press-ready PDF that any offset printer can use to make satisfactory plates. With flexo the situation is different. Jobs tend to be made up of many colours rather than a standardised four-colour process set, and the thickness of flexo plate is determined by the type of press, plate and mounting, which must be compensated for. The growth of shrink-applied designs on labels means the shrink factor of the printed image must be correctly predicted and compensated for. In the past this was handled by a skilled prepress craftsman, or more recently using an expensive electronic specialist workstation from a supplier such as Barco or Dalim. Now shrink-wrap software is available from suppliers such as ArtWork Systems, which markets ArtPro, a Macintosh-based programme with some 8,500 installations in operation in 2005. This is a tiny market compared with the publishing software mentioned above. This kind of specialisation brings with it higher costs. There are relatively few skilled, experienced operators compared with the publishing applications, yet the barriers to entry for printers to invest are still dropping. This type of approach will continue to grow.

A system to prepare press-ready files on a modern Mac workstation for flexo printing costs some €20,000; a comparable offset equivalent costs €4000–5000. The change will be toward a standardisation of the supply of flexo origination.

RIP technology for flexo

Every digital file has to be RIPed – converted from the editable file on the workstation to a bitmap that provides the dots and linework on the plate. There are certain features that are necessary to achieve good reproduction quality, productivity and economic use of materials. The RIP should have efficient step-and-repeat functionality to RIP a file once then assemble multiple copies in the correct position following the rules of imposition. For labels and packaging applications, the step-and-repeat function should be linked to a database of tools and die shapes to ensure that the job is correctly positioned and cannot be output incorrectly. For many applications, a further step-and-repeat function involves maximising the utilisation of plate material by placing separations in the smallest area possible. The function should group areas with ID and register marks and generate a control file for automatic cutting and mounting of ancillary equipment.

The exposure is negative, with the printed images ablated from the surface. Energy requirements are high and exposure takes time. An area-skip function increases imaging productivity by jumping across areas on the plate that do not contain information to be imaged; this is particularly helpful in the production of sleeves. The RIP must be capable of applying the correct degree of distortion to compensate for the thickness of plate and mounting, or shrink factors, for final product handling. Trapping characteristics must be set optimally to ensure good fit, particularly on older machines with limited registration capabilities.

After processing the job it is useful to have an inspection capability, allowing operators to view the job before output as a final, on-screen pre-print check of elements such as overprints, spreads and chokes, colour transpositions, screen rulings and dot shapes.

Screening techniques

The growth in CTP and the development of anilox rollers means that finer dots can be printed and held on press. Suppliers have explored the imaging process and developed hybrid screening where conventional AM and stochastic screens are merged to improve print quality. The technique uses the stochastic screening in highlight and shadow areas to ensure that detail and modelling can be maintained; conventional screening is used in midtones to provide smooth transitions between highlight and midtone – problem areas for most flexo reproduction. Solid areas can be manipulated, with dots and grooves incorporated to increase ink holding and transfer properties. All flexo platesetter and RIP suppliers can provide modified screening technology for their equipment, a further drive to improve flexo quality through the use of CTP.

Flexo plates

Flexographic plates are made from flexible photopolymer materials that cross-link under exposure to UV light; these have largely replaced rubber-based compounds. They are available in varying thickness and shore hardnesses for specific applications. The softer the plate, the better the impression on rough and uneven surfaces (such as corrugated board), but the higher the degree of squash, which leads to dot gain. Generally, harder plates are capable of higher screen rulings for continuous tone – small dots can be held to give good highlight detail. The choice of plate is a trade-off between resilience and quality.

In some cases the material is supplied in liquid form to be coated onto sheets – and increasingly sleeves – for subsequent exposure and processing. The photopolymer layer in an unexposed flexo plate contains a thermoplastic elastomer, a polyfunctional acrylate monomer, a photoinitiator and various additives. UV light activates the photoinitiator, which starts the cross-linking polymerisation. Manufacturers are continually refining the materials in use, from natural rubber to a range of compounds based around polymerising 2-chloro-1,3-butadiene (chloroprene) or styrene-isoprene rubbers with trimethylolpropane triacrylate. When exposed, the acrylate cross-links the polymer, rendering it insoluble in the washout solvents – currently mostly chlorinated solvents such as perchloroethylene, with water-washable alternatives increasingly widely used.

Conventional analogue platemaking is still used to prepare the vast majority of plates using negative film separations. Matt film is used to avoid halation during exposure, and the films are output with the images anamorphically distorted to compensate for the depth of the plate forming the relief image – the dispro factor calculated for the particular cylinder diameter and plate thickness. Platemaking involves back exposure of the reverse of the plate to create a solid base, then image exposure through a negative using low-intensity light. The plates are then processed using physical and chemical washout of the non-image area to provide the relief plate. There is movement away from chlorinated solvents toward water-wash systems, which have less of an impact on the environment. After processing, the plate is carefully dried to remove solvent and restore gauge thickness, before being post-exposed to obtain final cure of floor and shoulders before finishing. The surface is then de-tacked and the plate dried before being mounted in position on the plate cylinder, normally using double-sided adhesive tape. The elapsed time to prepare a press-ready plate will typically be a couple of hours. There are issues surrounding the capability of holdinig fine detail on the plates.

DuPont has released a non-chemical processing system for conventional and digital exposure, CyrelFast technology, where the plate is made by thermal processing. The plate is exposed through a high-powered UV-exposure unit to produce the latent image, which is then processed using heat treatment, where unexposed plate material is melted and soaked up on a developer cloth. The technology does not use solvents or chemicals and is a much faster developing and finishing method. It is likely that other non-chemical plate processing systems will be launched.

Flexo CTP Conventional flexo platemaking seems to involve a touch of the black art when compared with offset, with individual plants using their own specification for repro to optimise quality. This results in some outstanding examples being produced, but limits the choice for a customer and reduces the flexibility of the plant. The key development bringing quality improvements is the widespread use of totally digital prepress, with CTP technology being used to image plates. There are two competing technologies available, with a third in commercial production: laser ablative masking systems (LAMS); direct UV; and direct engraving.

Laser ablative mask systems (LAMS)

This form of flexo CTP is a two-stage process: the image is laser exposed onto a special coating, then exposed to light. The digital flexo plate is built from a conventional plate coated with a laser-ablative mask. This layer is a photoresistant material, originally carbon black particles, that absorbs the energy and effectively explodes, leaving a hole where the laser light has fallen. The plate is imaged by selectively removing part of the mask with a high-powered laser beam in a CTP unit. All CTP units have a debris-extraction system incorporated in the imaging head to remove the ablated mask layer. Other materials are now being incorporated that are soluble in subsequent washout solutions. The plate is then processed in the same way as a conventional plate. This two-stage process eliminates film and results in a significant improvement in quality compared with conventional platemaking. Smaller highlight dots can be held; when correctly calibrated there will be no optical dotgain on the plate and no manual exposure errors.

Flexo CTP is an external drum imaging method. Plates can be exposed when mounted onto an integral drum, or they can be pre-mounted onto sleeves, with the whole sleeve exposed and processed in a rotary developer system. The speed of imaging depends on the CTP device and the resolution required, but typically is 1–4m²/hr.

FIGURE 5.22 Luscher flexo CTP unit

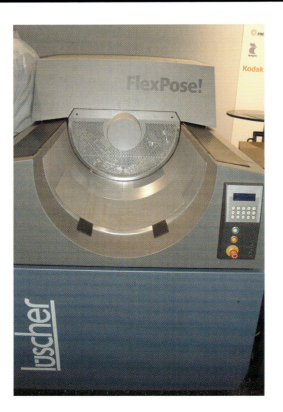

Source: Luscher

Compared with offset plates, the LAMS coating method needs considerably more power delivered to the surface. This requires specialist, solid-state lasers, with sealed CO_2, YAG (Yttrium Aluminium Garnet) and Fibre-Laser technologies in use. The market leader is the Esko-Graphics' Cyrel Digital Imager (CDI, from the first Barco/DuPont initiative from 1995), but Creo is catching up with its ThermoFlex systems, and Schepers-Ohio is also supplying machines.

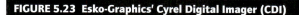

FIGURE 5.23 Esko-Graphics' Cyrel Digital Imager (CDI)

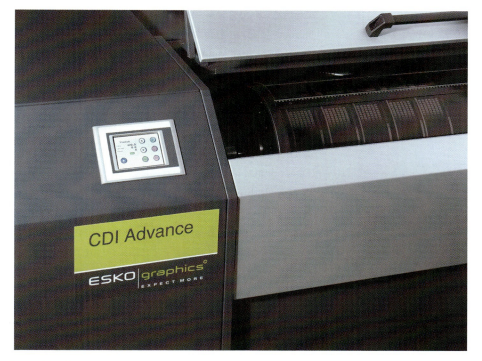

Source: Esko Graphics

The method has a couple of interesting effects on flexo. Normal plate exposure occurs under vacuum, while CTP has oxygen present at the UV exposure stage. The free-radical photopolymerisation reaction is inhibited by the presence of oxygen, so either special exposure cycles or digital exposure must be taken into account. A conventionally exposed dot will be bigger on the plate than on the film negative and flat on the top. The CTP dot will be either the same size as imaged or smaller and rounded on the top.

Exposure is digital and more controlled than scattered light exposure, so a higher screen resolution can be achieved, boosting the imaging potential of flexography by holding smaller dots, increasing the effective resolution of the plate and allowing more detail in highlights and smoother vignettes. Novel hybrid screening techniques can be used to provide enhanced quality by mixing conventional amplitude modulated screening with stochastic (frequency modulated) screening in the same image where appropriate. The dispro factors can be automatically applied and adjustments made to compensate for individual press situations. Creo offers digital plate capping, which mimicks the traditional technique where the plate surface is slightly textured by applying a pattern of small reverse dots to improve ink coverage and thus quality in solid areas.

Direct UV

This technology appeared at Drupa in 2001, when Global Graphics launched the flatbed ICG Cirrus 8. This was a modified flatbed litho plate exposer featuring a high-powered UV plasma imaging head to expose standard flexo plates. The UV system was developed with Cortron Corporation, suppliers of analogue flexo exposure units. The technology was a manual load/unload low-cost system that sadly did not live up to development hopes and never appeared commercially.

The potential for this technology is great as there is no premium for the ablative mask layer that adds cost to the plate material. But no other suppliers have announced plans to develop the technology.

Direct engraving

Direct digital laser engraving is a single-stage process in which the relief of the flexo sleeve or plate is directly ablated by the energy of a laser. The lasers are more highly powered than for LAMS, mostly sealed CO_2 lasers with acousto-optic modulation (AOM) enabling fast, accurate switching of the beam. Suppliers believe the CO_2 lasers provide the best power/cost ratio for this application and are not switching to YAG. They use a larger spot size than YAG or fibre-optic devices, but this is not seen as a barrier to the removal of material. Laser engraving is a negative process. Non-image material is removed from the surface and dots are sculpted directly on the plate material to a depth of 0.3–06mm. The plates and sleeves are then press-ready after a short water-wash and dry period. Screen resolutions above 175lpi can hold dots below 1%. The single-stage process is simpler than LAMS, eliminating the exposure, washing, drying and post-exposure stages of the process.

Most engraved material is blended elastomeric rubber with much development work undertaken to improve the durability and printability of the material. High-quality polymeric plates are an alternative. These are suitable for direct laser engraving and available from suppliers such as BASF, Jet, Toyobo, Asahi, Ligum and FullFlex. Increasingly, systems that allow the direct preparation of sleeves in-house will become available for sheeted plates and liquid photopolymer. Plates can be mounted onto the sleeve, with the join thermally sealed to allow continuous imaging where required. Asahi launched its liquid sleeve technology in 2004 with an automatic finishing system that coats a sleeve with photopolymer in less than an hour. Operators supply the base sleeve and input the required specification. The required quantity of liquid polymer is pumped from a reservoir onto the sleeve to give the desired thickness and then rotary coated; this is controlled by a doctor blade unit. Different polymers provide the shore hardness required. Once coated, the sleeve is hardened under UV light, then ground and polished ready for engraving with a CO_2 laser. The leader in this technology is Luscher Flexo (formerly Zed Instruments), which has some 300 units in the field engraving relief plates and sleeves for letterpress and flexo operations, some 40 of which are used to make flexo solely (at the time of writing). Its FlexPose!Direct uses a sealed, pulsed carbon dioxide laser ablation system that can be adapted for flexo sleeves and plates. The time to image a sleeve depends on the depth of engraving. At 0.5mm the rate is some 0.7m² per hour; the rate will increase with the use of multiple laser exposure to 1m² per hour by the end of 2005. Stork's Agrios 413X direct engraver uses a patented triple beam laser technology to burn rubber or polymer.

This compares with the 700 LAMS flexo platemaking CTP devices installed worldwide by late 2004, with a few more multi-purpose devices capable of imaging flexo plates, film and offset plates with the correct calibration. The installed base is growing but the technology is not going to become as pervasive as offset printers. The industry has a similar structure to the offset market of maybe ten years ago, with individual operations handling one part of the production process. Many flexo printers are primarily converters and extruders, long used to buying in finished plates from specialist trade shops. It is still a significant investment to bring platemaking in-house as this involves the cost of the CTP device as well as plate-processing and solvent-handling equipment.

As CTP grows in importance, suppliers will provide ever more productivity enhancements. Laser exposure heads will become faster and semi-automatic plate loading will become common, particularly for larger-format plates; it is already automatic for sleeves. Plates will be supplied in cassettes that are placed into a trolley; this is then locked into position and the job queue selects the cassette that holds the next plate to be imaged. A mechanism will present the plate onto the clamps of the exposure drum, with minimal stress and damage to the plates, and the machine's operator will carry out a final check. Once exposed, plates can be released for immediate processing, or the trolley can be filled with imaged plates and removed for subsequent UV exposure.

Table 5.1 (overleaf) summarises the issues that flexo printers need to consider when deciding which method of platemaking is best suited to their operation.

TABLE 5.1 Comparison of flexo platemaking costs

	Use trade house	Imagesetter	LAMS CTP	Direct engraving
Film production	No	Film imagesetter €100k plus €20 for film processor. Thick, matt film €25 per m²	No	No
Plate exposure	No	Manual	Direct exposure through CTP device, €100–500k depending on format	Direct exposure through CTP device, €220–400k depending on format (width)
Raw plate costs	Negotiated on volume/type	€120–200 per m²	€140–220 per m²	€100–600 per m². May buy in elastomer sleeves, sheets for mounting or liquid photopolymer coated internally. Sleeves may be stored for reprint
Plate processing	No	Yes. Equipment cost €50–100, chemicals €10–20 per m²	Yes. Equipment cost €50–100, chemicals €10–20 per m²	No
Mounting	Manual/semi-automatic on mounting tape, €25–30 per m²	Manual/semi-automatic on mounting tape, €25–30 per m²	Maybe imaged in the round or manual/semi-automatic on mounting tape, €25–30 per m²	Imaged in the round
Elapsed time for press-ready replacement plate	1–3 days	2–4 hours	1–2 hours	1–2 hours

Source: Pira International Ltd

Plate costs will be agreed commercially with the supplier – either a trade shop or supplier of consumables and equipment. The finished press-ready costs will be determined by the grade and format needed and the volume required. The decision to invest in internal plate production or to buy in finished plates will be primarily taken on economic grounds. Increasingly, service issues will become important as run lengths drop and customers demand more flexibility and shorter lead times for new pack designs and runs. When deciding which route to take, printers should formalise the process and consider personnel skill requirements as a key element of the project. Over the next five years more flexo printers and converters will invest in in-house imaging and the cost of ownership will further drop.

Market pressures will force converters to consider the time taken to get new and replacement plates as more important than simply the plate cost itself. This will boost the number of CTP installations in printers and converters.

TABLE 5.2 Transition table for flexo platemaking methods

	Main characteristics	Current trends	Key drivers	Status in 2010
Prepress software	Complex nature of packaging artwork	Software for standard computers	Need to make software simpler to use	More widespread and easier to produce plate-ready flexo plates without the need for specialist prepress personnel
Plate materials	Photopolymer compounds for plates	Move to thinner, harder plates for high quality. Move to liquid photopolymer for flexibility	Cost and processing time	More plates and sleeves prepared in-house from liquid coatings
	Elastomer plate coatings	Developments to improve printability, engraving and durability	Low environmental impact	Still used by a sector, useful with powerful solvent and UV inks
Exposure methods	Majority use matt film negatives	Increasing use of CTP	Speed of platemaking, quality of final result	Most high-quality plates will be produced by CTP or direct engraving
Assembling	Mounting onto plate cylinder with sticky back tapes	Move to pre-mounted plates and sleeves	Demand for better registration and faster turnround	Imaging in the round with no manual intervention will be common
Flexo CTP	Higher quality than conventional, fast exposure	Some 775 installations worldwide	Demand for high quality	Projected 3,500 installations imaging 60% of the total new plate usage
Plate processing	Unexposed photopolymer dissolved in chlorinated solvents	Move from use of solvents to water-wash and solvent free (e.g. DuPont CyrelFast) and direct engraving	Environmental concerns and health and safety regulations	Wash-out chemicals use will greatly decline
In-the-round imaging	Imaging and processing plates pre-mounted onto carrier sleeves	Use of sleeves is increasing to reduce manual handling	Demand to minimise press set-up time	Trend toward sleeve imaging and direct engraving

Source: Pira International Ltd

The installed base of CTP devices was around 775 in 2004, producing some 20% of all new flexo plates and directly engraved sleeves. Imaging times are 0.7–4m^2 per hour, with additional time required for final plate exposure. Pira estimates significant growth in the installed base, to almost 3500 CTP devices by 2009.

Plate mounting   Double-sided tape is used to mount plates on the cylinder prior to loading onto the press. Thinner tape grades are available with micro-channels on both sticky surfaces to minimise air bubble entrapment. The result is more uniform plate surfaces. It is important to take into account the thickness of the tape and plate when calculating the dispro factor to be applied.

For many applications, such as labels and envelopes, the technique of exposing small areas of plate material and mounting the pieces onto the plate cylinder, locating the position approximately on grids etched into the surface of the cylinder, is appropriate.

Manual plate-mounting techniques provide limited registration. There is a variety of mechanical aids that help to improve registration. These use microscopes and fine adjustment to line up cylinders in the correct position. The latest versions use CCD cameras to align plates automatically, with high degrees of precision.

Sleeve technology (in-the-round imaging)

Quick-mounting replaceable sleeves are increasingly being used to minimise printing press make-ready times. Plates are mounted before and after plate exposure and processing. In-the-round imaging has become more popular with the increasing use of CTP. Sleeve systems allow flexo printers to use their press more efficiently, reduce overall costs and enhance print quality. The mounting process fixes the sleeve in position so allowing easy registration of plates and imaging in-line. Sleeves are engineered to fit quickly over mandrels in preset positions; they slip into their lock-up position cushioned by air pressure. It is important to maintain the air supply and keep all cylinder surfaces free of moisture, oils, lubricants and ink to maintain the sleeve's long-term surface properties. Sleeves are prepared in various thicknesses for any desired repeat length to minimise substrate waste, as shown in Figure 5.24.

FIGURE 5.24 Schematic of sleeve plate-mounting systems

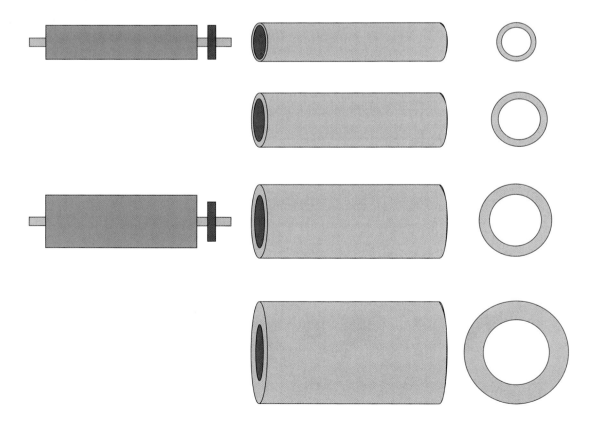

Source: Pira International Ltd

Most sleeves currently have conventionally imaged plates mounted onto them. Increasingly, pre-mounted plates will be digitally imaged in the round. Sleeves can be made from steel or carbon fibre and can be used with a variety of plate types. They are designed to provide an infinite range of cut-offs for use with gearless presses. Claimed advantages for sleeves over solid plate cylinders include:

▶ lighter, so easier to handle
▶ lower plate-making and mounting costs
▶ faster change-over times
▶ elimination of plate cylinder inventory
▶ better balanced, allowing faster press speeds

This technology is forecast to grow significantly, particularly as more new presses are installed.

Origination for digital printing

The origination function is the creative and production process that translate an idea into a print-ready format. For conventional printing, this is an expensive and time-consuming stage but there are many developments coming together to change this situation. Using sophisticated database management and flexible templating, pages that have good design can be constructed automatically. The widespread acceptance of PPML (personalised page mark-up language) allows the front-ends and RIPs of digital presses to process the data streams efficiently, further fuelling the rise of digital printing over the next few years.

Personalisation is the key technology for digital printing and, with increasing sophistication, allows targeted messages to be sent to individuals. The use of asset management databases with profiling techniques is key.

Database profiling

For automated make-up, it is necessary to profile the attributes of the recipient to ensure that the correct content is served as requested. This profile is a series of variables that initiate calls to the database storing content. For example, a 35-year-old married man with a young child, earning £25,000 will have a totally different holiday requirement to an unmarried 22-year-old woman earning £30,000. In designing a customised brochure, a travel agent needs to gather as much information on a prospective client as possible in order to provide a successful lead. It is by storing the key attributes of people or businesses that marketers can provide the useful tailored message.

The profile may come from a client that the company serves (bank, credit card or insurance customer provides great detail), from a loyalty-card scheme, or response to a questionnaire or filling in a guarantee card. Profiles result from a phone call to or from a tele-marketing call centre and increasingly from online responses on websites related to a specific product, service or activity. This information on clients is being collected and stored by corporations across the world in growing databases. Tools are developing to clean the databases (removing duplicated and erroneous data entries) and then to perform sophisticated interrogations to find prospects that match certain criteria. It is a key part of refinement of the personalisation and a central part of the developing customer relationship management tools.

Personalisation

The production (mainframe) printing and direct mail industries have been personalising documents for many years. Most new digital presses offer options for personalising that have not been possible before. These options are being sold to customers who do not have experience of complex data administration, which is traditionally more the working environment of banks and insurance companies than graphic designers and publishers. The engine manufacturers have recognised the opportunities offered by their technologies in this field and have developed various software applications to encourage its use.

Unlike conventional document design and make up, which is well understood, the success of personalised print depends not only on the relevance of the content and the appearance of the final elements but also on the management, coding format and availability of the variable data.

There are many solutions that offer a personalisation capability, from simple office mail-merge functions, through database reporting to specialised graphics rich software. Press suppliers can offer a variable data capability. Software such as Xeikon's Private Eye, HP-Indigo's Yours Truly , Nexpress' Nextreme and Xerox's AutoGraph can be used to control sophisticated elements of a graphic design – both text and illustrations. The vendors makes these applications widely available to designers as they provide a good introduction to the possibilities that variable data printing offers. However, on a larger scale, it is not the graphic design that is the crucial element. It is the data collection, organisation and filtration for the target recipient that is crucial to the success and realisation of the full potential of the technology.

Automated page make-up (PDF on-the-fly)

Digital print accounted for some 8.6% of the European printing market in 2004. This is forecast to rise to around 9.5% by 2009 (higher if jobs printed in retail outlets and offices are taken into consideration). Many new and replacement products use digital printing, all based on the premise that the the new technology allows short runs to be printed economically and quickly.

For prototype jobs and proofing, design and prepress costs are relatively unimportant as they can be assimilated into longer runs. But for many short-run jobs these prepress costs can make a project uneconomical. In effect, the cost of using a professional Mac operator to design and craft pages is difficult to bear. The latest low-cost office page make-up programmes, such as Microsoft Publisher, can make the most experienced digital print operator blanch. The files often contain incorrect settings and content that may or may not, be picked up by a preflight check, but this incurs costs and adds time, neither of which are usually available. One solution is to use variable data applications that load personal details into pre-formatted document templates before creating the final version to be printed and distributed to the recipient – a single design used many times.

The most widely used personalisation software has long been used for direct mail and transactional (billing and statement) applications. In these examples the variable content is normally limited to name, address and salutation, together with the bill, statement or certificate information, often delivered as mono-spaced font information. Many of these applications have limited aesthetic graphic capabilities, as their most important task is to present information. A similar result is achieved by the automated make-up of directories, books, catalogues and classified advertising from database publishing, which often lacks aesthetic appeal. Marketers looking for ways to improve response rates to their mailings took advantage of the opportunities offered by high-quality colour digital print by varying other portions of the content.

There was much publicity about the high added-value opportunities of variable data colour digital print, but its use was restricted to specialist applications. The software was supplied by the machine manufacturers, often with dedicated hardware to serve up the variable data at high enough speeds to keep the machine going. Early Xeikon presses used Barco's Printstreamer and Intellistream, which prepared personalised pages off-line and passed the files to the digital printer when RIPed; Indigo had Yours Truly, and these were joined by many other applications. The software offered novel capabilities but was not widely used because of its high cost and the complexity involved in structuring the jobs. Another reason it failed to find widespread use was the poor quality of recipient profile information that was generally available.

Over time, clients developed better profiles through use of their customer relationship management (CRM) programmes. Standards such as personalised page make-up language (PPML) helped by enabling common page elements to be RIPed once and stored to reduce the amount of processing required. Variable data solutions started to offer significant benefits for customers, who saw higher response rates than they would otherwise have obtained. At the same time internet bandwidth increased and web-based design software gave users the opportunity to customise a series of designs with their personal details.

The first range of widely available documents was stationery, in particular business cards. This apparently humble piece of print can be a major problem for print suppliers as recipients *always* check the spelling, and any errors are soon noticed. Using traditional proofing routines wipes out any potential profit and adds significant time to the production cycle.

The solution was to generate a master design and allow users to input their details and check the final design prior to going to print. There are many systems, with various capabilities, for the production of cards. A typical example is Goodprint, a commercial litho and digital printer based in Norfolk, UK. The company offers a range of generic designs that users can choose and personalise, then buy the cards over the web for production and despatch. Sophisticated buyers can upload content (images, logos) following instructions to create bespoke designs and choose from a variety of finishes. The user sees an on-screen proof to check before buying; the printer's system then takes the files and prints the required number of copies on demand.

FIGURE 5.25 On-line ordering of business cards from Goodprint Ltd

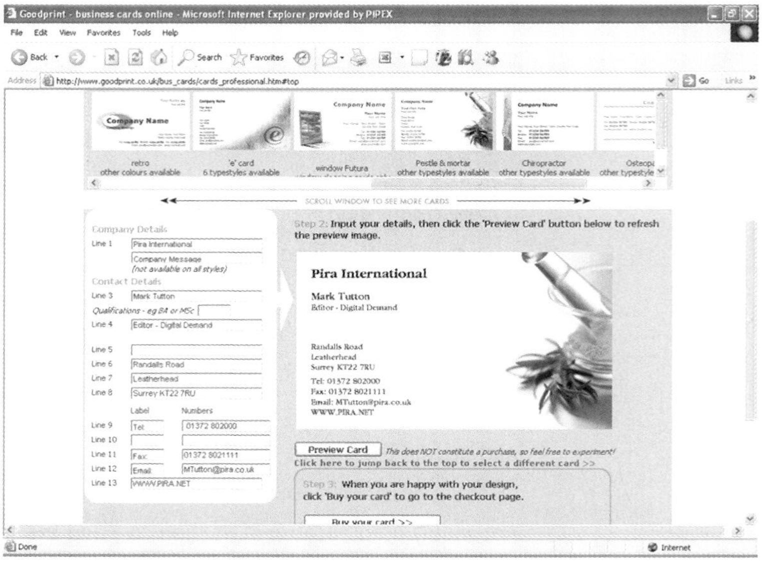

Source: www.goodprint.co.uk

Business cards are structured, templated documents that normally contain some fixed elements – company logo, background, website details – together with variable details such as name, job title, address, telephone, fax and e-mail. It sounds simple, but there are complexities involved. For example, there are some fields that may or may not be present, such as qualifications, mobile phone number, direct line or fax. These fields may be positionally linked, sometimes as groups, and vertically cascaded according to content. To make entry easy, the labels may be linked with content, so that they appear only when the field has a value. It is important for the integrity of the design that the format of the card is maintained correctly. This means more than merely the typeface and size; it may include the arrangement of the address details (number of lines), the layout of the telephone number (split between dialling code and number, international dialling rules) and the correct terminology for job titles that should follow design rules. Where customers have multiple locations, sophisticated systems may allow the user to select job title, qualification and address details from drop-down lists linked to telephone and fax details. These are useful in ensuring that users do not inadvertently make typing mistakes or use incorrect formats. Typically, users will select the correct design and number of cards required, then fill in fields for variable content. When complete, the system will normally provide a PDF of the finished card.

Business cards are not the only items that can be specified in this way. Another example is the Dream Books title *My Dream Cup Final with . . .* produced by UK printer Butler and Tanner. The plot is simple: you are playing football in the park with your pals when a football manager comes along to invite you to play for his team in the cup final. The buyer selects the team of choice and adds the hero's birthday, first and last name, name on shirt, street, town and gender, together with the names of three friends. The details are submitted over the web together with address and payment, £14.99 plus 95p P&P. The personalised details are submitted to Butler and Tanner and loaded into its XMPie PersonalEffect personalisation software to create the variable book. Several modules are used to create the original design (from InDesign), to set up the variable data aspects and to automate the merging of data, images and layout, and to generate variable data output streams that the firm's colour Xerox and Nexpress presses use to print the job.

FIGURE 5.26 Screenshot of Dreambooks' website

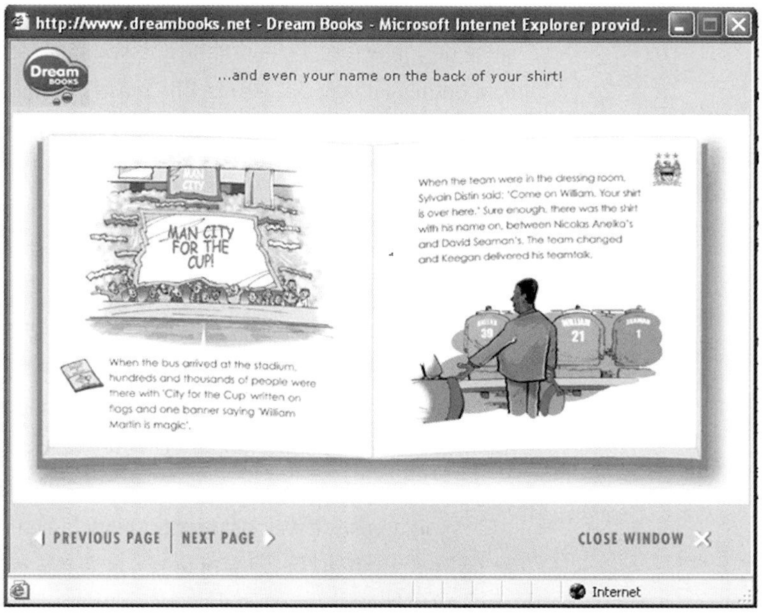

Source: Dreambooks.net

Dreambooks also offers a Spanish version, which is printed on a Xeikon press at Grafitex Servicios Digitales, in Barcelona; the company produces some 30 books each week. Once a week, Grafitex collects all the orders from the website, prepares the database, prints the multi-personalised books and takes care of the finishing and shipping. This application was runner-up in the 2005 Xeikon Diamond Awards (for creative applications giving insight into the future of digital colour printing) for one-to-one communication.

Drupa 2004 took an interesting approach to showcasing new technology with its Innovation Parc. It included a dynamic document section to showcase small specialist companies and developers. As well as XMPie, exhibitors included Assentis, Northmann, Aupus, Diron, Press-sense and Printsoft – a long-standing leader in software for formatting direct mail and one-to-one direct marketing applications with PReS and Newleaf. Kinetik Software showed iBright, which is used for the high-quality corporate design of Volkswagen and Fiat car brochures versioned for European dealerships.

German company Diron showed Diron.Newspapers On Demand, software that generates a structured newspaper automatically from any given number of texts characterised as newspaper articles, news and ads. The core of the technology is the automatic and fast calculation of the layout. An early customer is the Handelsblatt group, which offers its InvestorNewsSnap, a personal up-to-the-minute four-page newspaper focused on a user-selected topic. The content is made up and delivered to the buyer's browser as a PDF and payment is made by Micro-Payment.

cm4, part of the Bertellsman group, has an application to create a personalised document inside a workflow controlled by printers. This can be a one-to-one marketing piece or a versioned document where short runs are created for each branch – a poster for a shop or agency, or a local menu for a restaurant or hotel chain. Instead of having the same design across a chain of businesses, for example, local branches can include their own details and special events. The master design is created and the local branch can select its content as necessary, or a master database is used to merge variable details, the job printed and distributed to the local branches. The latter is useful for a business-wide promotion that could be tied into an event the company is involved with. This approach means that a single design is made and the system creates multiple versions, reducing the time and cost of each piece.

There are many other applications that provide similar functionality, including PDFlib, Isis Papyrus, Building Systems AdKit, print4media and XRalle. All enable the design and automatic production of customised documents targeted at individuals or small groups or to create book, magazine, newspaper and catalogue pages by aggregating content according to pre-set rules or instructions taken over the web.

PageFlex develops the capability of changeable templates – pictures and text can be resized or left out according to the available content. The template captures the overall abstract look and automatically adjusts the layout according to the size and placement of the variable content. PageFlex allows content to be assembled into unique, personalised documents for output as print or in PDF form for electronic distribution.

A PageFlex project is based on the principle of separating a document's form from its content. Content refers to the raw information – text, images, graphics; form refers to the design – page layout, fonts and images. PageFlex encodes a document's form into an intelligent template, capturing the look and feel of the design in an abstract way. A template consists of containers that hold the content, both static and variable. The flexible properties of a container allow it to expand, contract and reposition itself and adjacent containers to accommodate the variable contents of each different document.

A single design template contains the text, images and logos laid out as the designer requires. The example shown in Figure 5.27 is for a personalised travel itinerary; there are no fixed, recurring items that appear on every document. The content to choose from is held in a library folder. Recipients provide information on their destination and budget, together with personal details, all of which is entered into an ODBC database. When this file is linked to the project a preview can be generated, and individual records or the whole file can be processed to PDF or sent to a digital press. Other formats will be supported so, for example, a PDF might be e-mailed or the content posted on the web or as HTML/XML data to form a dynamic web page.

FIGURE 5.27 Master template and three potential designs from one PageFlex template

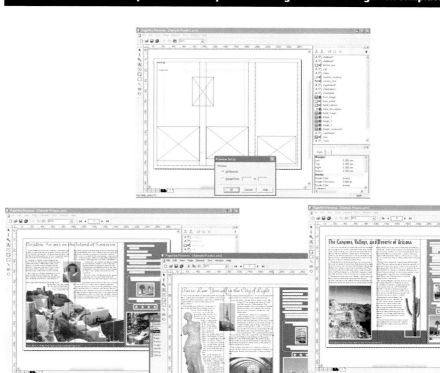

Source: PageFlex

PageFlex's power lies in its ability to change design parameters according to the profile of the recipient. In this case, the tints and fonts change as the destination changes. The main page can contain one, two or three images with captions; the images can vary in size and be either squared or cut-outs, with text flowing around the image. If one picture is not used, the others change in size so the text, which contains the recipient's details, fills the available space according to the rules and links that are set up.

A new entrant to this arena is Wave2, which proposes to offer a flexible solution to enable personalised, automated publishing. Taking a reader profile, a set of business rules and stylesheet/templates, it will query an asset management system and automatically construct a document as though it was produced by a graphic designer at a layout terminal. This can include selected editorial, images and targeted advertising/promotions.

The result is a personalised and targeted publication or document, which is generated automatically and may be printed or delivered (electronically) on demand. This will take time and cost out of creating newspaper editorial and ad pages, and offers the opportunity to produce sophisticated client-oriented content with selected, relevant advertising.

The company believes this could be a new model for newspaper publishing, where a title provides targeted content for interested local usergroups (a sportsclub, a school, a book club, the WI, marathon runners or any group with similar interests). They enter their profile and a newspaper, with bespoke editorial and targeted advertising is produced. It could be printed and distributed or e-mailed directly to recipients.

One of the company's products is Artemis. It is based on the Wave2 rules engine, a powerful object-oriented rule engine that provides expression of business rules. It is used to define the selection of content, templates and styles when creating a document. This may be controlled according to the reader profile supplied by the Profile Manager. Rules may be modified or created by system administrators. The output for print or electronic delivery is created by the formatting engine. This is a plug-in component and there is a formatting engine for each media channel supported – currently PDF, HTML and InDesign for print and electronic distribution. User interfaces are browser-based to reduce systems administration and to provide platform independence.

Artemis is different in its approach to page layout. Most other solutions are template-driven and assume structured content will be available to fill the template. Artemis is capable of handling unstructured content, such as news articles, or unpredictable content that was not originally prepared for a particular purpose. Artemis does not need the content to fit a particular template. Once given the content, it works out how many images and individual text objects it needs to place, then decides the most appropriate way to lay these out on a page (or pages). The Wave2 rules engine embedded within Artemis uses a set of styles and rules to ensure that the result is always consistent, even though the content and layout may vary considerably each time.

Applications for Artemis include automating the building of editorial pages, creating structured documents from unstructured data, and automatically paginating complex documents such as brochures and sales literature.

These software products allow real-time design of one-off documents, or multiple versioned or personalised documents with hundreds or thousands of profiles.

Future developments   More complex applications will be enabled through the use of automated document preparation; these include books, newspapers, magazines and marketing collateral, with structured layouts for new issues or versions. One-to-one marketing products will grow in use and sophistication, triggering more responses from consumers as the technology develops and profiling improves from CRM programmes. The use of websites to generate documents, making it easy to build the document and sign off the result instantly, will grow significantly. There will be increasing use of automation and PDF on-the-fly will move into the mainstream, with plug-ins for QuarkXPress and InDesign widely available at low cost. Software will become easier to use as the technology develops.

Printing processes

6

Print process recognition

A printed image has characteristics that are unique to the process used to produce it. It is useful to be able to identify the method used to print a product, particularly where it is necessary to decide on a method to be used for a new product. Identifying the printing method is possible using a process of elimination based on knowledge of the printing processes and their capabilities, and complemented by recognition based on the visual characteristics of the process. Recognising their characteristics is made easier by the use of a low-power microscope (×25), or a pocket lens giving magnification up to ×10 can serve as a reasonable alternative.

Offset lithography

In lithography, the plate is planographic, image areas are grease-receptive and water repellent, while the non-image areas are water-receptive. Both water and oil-based ink is applied to the plate. The water wets the non-image areas of the plate and prevents the ink from wetting those areas. Ink transferred to the image areas is subsequently transferred to a rubber covered blanket cylinder (offset) that transfers the image to the substrate under high pressure. The inks used are relatively thick and viscous in comparison with flexo and gravure. Printing from an offset blanket and planographic plate produces the following characteristics (as shown in Figure 6.1):

► no impression or squash is apparent at the edge of type, which is sharp even at small point sizes;

► thinner ink-film than the other processes;

► good uniform ink-coverage density in the image areas, even on rough paper;

► good uniform halftone printing with smooth vignettes, even on rough paper;

► halftone tones will normally be at a finer screen ruling than other processes on similar substrates;

► halftone dots may appear circular, elliptical or square in midtones;

► small specks of ink may be apparent in non-printing areas, but less common with CTP;

► under magnification it may be possible to see evidence of doubling (same image printed at a lower density slightly displaced from the main image);

► conventional oxidation drying inks have characteristic oil-based odour when books or brochures are opened.

FIGURE 6.1 Illustration of the characteristics obtained when printing from an offset and planographic plate

 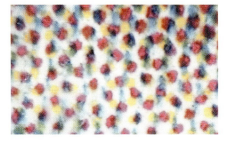

Source: Pira International Ltd

There is increasing sophistication of press format with perfecting six-colour machines (12-unit) now commonplace. This allows the use of extended process work, hexachrome printing and the use of integrated metallic and fluorescent effects. Heatset web offset results in drying out the paper and over time moisture is reabsorbed causing the print to expand in the cross-grain direction. Without very sophisticated, controlled remoistening, bound products tend to exhibit waviness and page shoot with a non-heatset cover. For perfect bound products bound cross grain there is often significant cockling as the paper expands against the fixed spine.

Flexography

Flexographic printing uses a resilient relief plate and fluid inks. The relief surface produces a squash effect like letterpress, but the halo at the edges of type and on halftone dots is less sharply defined than in letterpress.

The squash is especially noticeable on prints produced on film or foil, but if modern, thin, hard plates with kiss impression are used the effect can be reduced. Squash on halftone dots is most noticeable in highlight tones and there is typically a high level of dot gain; this makes it difficult for the process to achieve smooth vignettes.

The following points may be observed (see Figure 6.2):

► text has a fairly sharp outline but shows squash under magnification;
► the squash halo is less apparent than letterpress and line at edge is thicker;
► highlight dots in particular show noticeable squash;
► process colour shows lower screen ruling than offset, plates may be damaged and dots can be missing;
► limited highlight capability (flexo does not reproduce very small dots well) resulting in high-contrast highlights;
► tonal vignettes will not normally be smooth and the transition from substrate to the first printing tone is often quite noticeable;
► possible filling-in, particularly in shadow tones, and light tones may show bridging;
► in some circumstances, the anilox roller cell pattern may be visible in solids.

FIGURE 6.2 Flexographic print characteristics

Source: Pira International Ltd

Gravure   The gravure printing image is recessed from the non-printing surface, an intaglio process. In conventional gravure, the image is composed of a large number of small cells, the surface areas of which are similar and square in shape. Most modern gravure cylinders are engraved using a machine called a Helio-Klischograph, which uses a pyramid-shaped diamond stylus. This engraves cells that vary in depth and area depending on the strength of colour required. In both cases, the cell structure is applicable irrespective of the image, i.e. text, solid and tone.

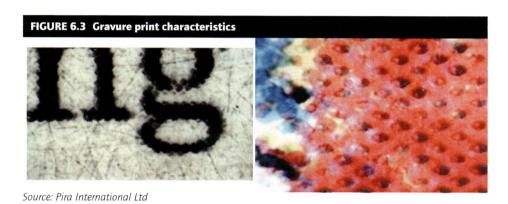

FIGURE 6.3 Gravure print characteristics

Source: Pira International Ltd

The cell pattern that is apparent in the printed image is peculiar to gravure and provides a ready means of identification. Gravure print characteristics are (see Figure 6.3):

► no embossing or squash

► irregular saw-like edge to text matter and line images

► well-defined square grid pattern on tone areas (in conventional gravure only – an elliptical pattern for engraved cylinders)

► cells in tonal areas will often have a dark edge with light centre

► good quality colour reproductions on coated paper with high colour saturation

► under magnification, the cells are normally apparent as a slight mottle in solid areas

► under magnification speckle (cell skip) will often be apparent in highlight tones, particularly on rough surface papers

► there may be entrapped solvent in bound publications, which is noticeable by the odour.

There is no wave on gravure publication properties.

Screen printing   The screen process uses a stencil image formed within a screen mesh. Medium-viscosity ink is forced through the mesh, in open image areas of the stencil, onto the substrate or container by the action of a squeegee. Screen printing generally uses greater thicknesses of ink film than is possible with any other normal printing process, and the raised ink surface is sometimes obvious. The chief characteristics are (see Figure 6.4, page 306):

► images are sharp and slightly raised to the thick ink film

► high density possible from the weight of ink applied

▶ screen mesh sometimes results in zigzag at the edge of text and line images, similar to gravure

▶ halftone work is unusual but when used, the screen ruling will be coarse

▶ dots may show a mock squash effect

▶ solids are uniform on all substrates with good covering power

▶ solids under magnification may exhibit small craters caused by entrapped air.

FIGURE 6.4 Screen print characteristics

Source: Pira International Ltd

Electrophotographic (laser) printing

The process uses a photoconductive surface that collects finely divided pigment particles and transfers them to paper by electrostatic means, and then fixes the powder image to the paper by heating. Modern, high-quality toner-based systems can easily achieve offset quality results when the right combination of front-end, prepress, substrate and engine are used. The process produces the following characteristics:

▶ often no halftone dot pattern, appearance of continuous tone

▶ powder toner laydown is not planographic, and it is possible to feel the relief effect although on the latest models this is less noticeable

▶ no impression although there may be some embossing caused by paper distortion during fusing

▶ under magnification, images do not have a well-defined outline

▶ coverage is generally good and uniform

▶ extraneous spots of pigment powder may be observed in non-image areas.

Laser printing is a digitally originated form of electrophotographic printing, and the identifying characteristics are similar if dry toner is used. Those electrophotographic systems that use liquid toner (HP-Indigo) achieve slightly sharper edge definition than dry toner and the results are similar to lithography. Unusual dot patterns may be apparent when the reproduction of photographic images is examined under magnification. This is necessary to improve tone reproduction with the comparatively low-resolution imaging.

Chief characteristics are:

▶ in halftone areas, the appearance is similar to lithography but systems using liquid toner have sharper edge definition;

▶ quite a well-defined outline, some jagged edges on type due to the comparatively low imaging resolution;

▶ halftone images appear very similar to lithography;

▶ photographic reproductions may have an unconventional dot structure.

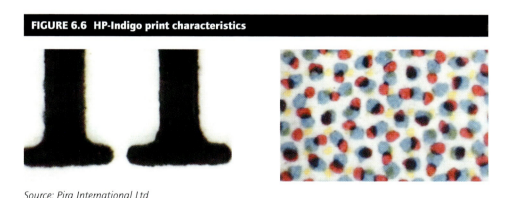

FIGURE 6.5 Xeikon print characteristics

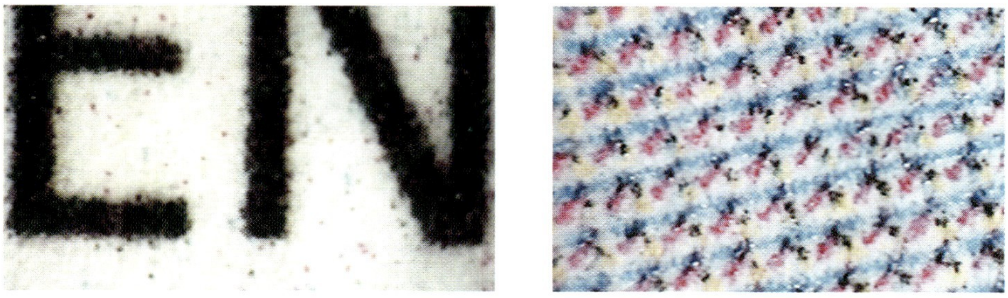

Source: Pira International Ltd

FIGURE 6.6 HP-Indigo print characteristics

Source: Pira International Ltd

Inkjet printing

Inkjet printing creates images by the controlled placement of small droplets of ink. With low-resolution systems, this will be apparent in the printing of alphanumeric characters as a coarse matrix of spots. The matrix may not be apparent with higher-resolution binary systems, but the spots should be visible under magnification and the edges of characters will be quite ragged. The reproduction of photographic images will be quite poor with low-resolution systems, but the results can appear almost continuous tone, similar to printers that have a high resolution.

New greyscale printing systems can mimic the screened result of litho, without the trapping effects, to produce high-quality results with a wider colour gamut than conventional printing. A characteristic of some inkjet systems that use traversing heads is a banding effect, which is caused by the different lay down of inks when the head moves in different directions. This happens because the head contains a fixed array of nozzles, normally side by side. So, when the head moves to the left (or up) the ink is printed in the order K-C-M-Y, while on the reverse pass in a bi-directional system it is Y-M-C-K. These different orders of ink may give rise to subtle variations in some saturated colours; in particular greens, blues and reds can appear banded. To overcome this, the printers can be used uni-directionally, which doubles the time to print, or some devices use additional colours arranged in such a way that the print order is the same in both directions.

Some inkjet printers use so-called phase-change inks, which produce an ink film that sits slightly in relief on the surface of the paper.

Chief characteristics are:

► inks are often water-soluble so will smear when wet
► heavy coverage results in paper distortion and marking, there may be strikethrough
► no impression
► irregular ill-defined outline for characters
► under magnification the ink spots from which the image is formed are likely to be visible
► photographic reproductions may have the appearance of continuous tones at high resolutions, but can be poor at low resolution.

FIGURE 6.7 Inkjet print characteristics

 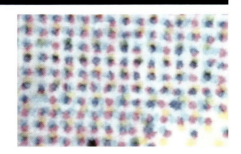

Source: Pira International Ltd

Die-stamping

Die-stamping is an intaglio process using an engraved female die and a male impression surface. The female die is charged with ink and the surplus removed from the non-printing areas by wiping with a cloth or paper. Heavy pressure is applied to transfer the ink from the engraved portions of the female die to the paper.

The process is recognised by the following characteristics:

► raised surface of the printed image with corresponding indentation on the reverse side
► feathering of the ink around the characters.

Thermographic printing

Thermography is a printing process using slow-drying ink and powdered resin. The printed image (usually lithography) is dusted with the resin and passed through a heating chamber. This fuses the resin and ink to create a raised surface similar to that produced by die-stamping.

The following characteristics identify the process:

▶ raised printed surface, with no indentation on the back

▶ usually a high-gloss effect

▶ small voids may be on the ink surface

▶ thin ink-film spread beyond outline of raised characters.

Introduction to printing processes

One of the most engaging facets of the printing industry is the range of methods that have been devised to apply colourant to substrate. Equipment suppliers are extremely innovative and are still developing new ways of printing. The first methods, applying carved blocks into an early press, have been known since Biblical times in Korea and China. The development of movable type about 1500AD boosted literacy and was one of the key sparks for the Renaissance and social development in the Middle Ages. Increased mechanisation and automation allowed the industry to boost quality and productivity of all aspects of printing. Now the computerisation and digital technologies have developed the industry from a craft into part of the high-tech communications sector.

This has made it much easier for customers to get their message into print. However, they are now faced with many decisions to ensure they get the best deal and achieve the desired result. What design and prepress? Does the job need to be on a website as well as printed? Which process – gravure, screen, flexo, web offset (coldest, heatset or UV stationery, long-grain or short-grain), sheetfed offset (which format), relief letterpress or digital? What finishing should I use? Folded, perfect bound, hard cased, side-stabbed or wire stitched? Which printing company do I use? Do I go direct, or do I use middlemen? What about e-procurement and online auctions? It is probably no longer enough to always use the same print supplier because over time, the client's requirements change, and may be better suited to different print companies with different specialisation and equipment.

These are challenging decisions and the correct choice will save much time, effort and money. The object of this chapter is to provide some guidance to the decision-making process, and to offer a brief explanation of the technology and processes involved in print production.

Today the dominant printing process is offset lithography, using sheetfed, heatset web offset and coldset web offset (including UV-curable) on a wide variety of machines from newspaper to continuous stationery presses. Globally, offset accounts for just over 50% of all print volumes. Various forecasts differ but all show the same inexorable trend. Pira International forecasts show the relative share of processes for commercial printing (Table 6.1).

TABLE 6.1 Global split of print processes			
	2000	**2005**	**2010**
Sheet-fed	19.9%	19.6%	19.6%
Coldset	14.7%	13.3%	12.1%
Heatset	18.1%	17.3%	16.1%
All offset	52.6%	50.2%	47.7%
Gravure	13.5%	12.6%	11.1%
Flexo	20.3%	20.4%	19.8%
Screen	3.9%	2.8%	2.4%
Letterpress	2.1%	1.6%	1.2%
Digital	5.6%	10.5%	15.5%
Other	3.0%	1.8%	2.2%

Source: Pira International Ltd

After litho, gravure accounts for the second highest volumes, with digital printing now accounting for some 9% of all commercially produced print by volume – higher if the amount produced in office and retail outlets, or at home, is considered.

Traditional, or conventional printing accounts for the largest proportion of all printed material. The processes are offset lithography, flexography (and some direct letterpress), gravure and silk screen printing. For the traditional printing methods, printing is accomplished by the image-carrier (printing plate, screen or cylinder) that defines image and non-image primarily by physical means. The image-carrier is produced using photomechanical methods or increasingly direct production from digital data. The traditional printing methods, with their fixed image-carrier, are ideal for printing multiple copies of the same image. They are being developed to be increasingly economic at shorter production runs. Digital printing is used for shorter runs and variable data techniques to make each copy unique. All of these methods will be considered in this chapter.

Traditional printing methods

The physical profile of the image-carrier is the most distinguishing feature defining one process from another, and it determines many of the characteristics applicable to the process. The material used to produce the image-carrier also contributes to the characteristic appearance of the printed copies, and imposes specific requirements of the ink and influences the method of ink application. It also determines the type of substrates that can be printed and influences the design and construction of the printing press. This, directly and indirectly, determines what process is most suitable for printing particular types of work.

When seen in cross-section, it is apparent how the processes define image from non-image areas. See Figure 6.8. Flexography (and letterpress) are relief processes with the image physically raised above the non-image. Gravure is an intaglio process where the image is recessed below the non-image surface of a cylinder. Silk screen is a stencil process while lithography is a planographic process, in that image and non-image are (virtually) in the same plane.

FIGURE 6.8 Physical profiles of image carriers

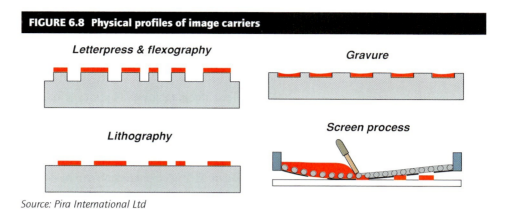

Source: Pira International Ltd

Offset lithography

The apocryphal tale of the discovery of lithography tells of Aloys Johann Nepomuk Franz (Alois) Senefelder, a Bavarian who lived from 1771 to 1834. He was writing a laundry list on a stone with a crayon. He was a playwright and had problems with printers producing copies of his work and publicity material on time and was looking for a cheaper alternative to metal type. He decided to etch a stone with acid, using the crayon to protect the image area from attack. When he inked the still wet stone and pressed paper to it he obtained a very clear image and lithography (stone writing) was born.

Lithography is planographic. The distinction between image and non-image is achieved by differences in the plate's surface chemistry, which results in differential wetting. The image areas are receptive to greasy ink and repel water, while the non-image areas are receptive to water. Both water and oil-based inks are applied to the plate. The water (actually a controlled dilute solution of various chemicals) wets the non-image areas of the plate and prevents the ink from adhering in these areas. The non-image areas that

FIGURE 6.9 The application of ink and water differentiates between image and non-image areas

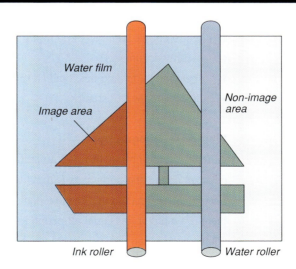

Source: Pira International Ltd

are readily wetted by water are hydrophilic (water-loving) or oleophobic (oil-hating), while the image areas repel water and are hydrophobic (water-hating) or oleophilic (oil-loving). Ink transferred to the image areas is subsequently transferred (offset) onto a rubber-covered blanket cylinder that in turn transfers the image to the substrate under pressure.

Commercial lithographic printing (except for waterless single fluid lithography) requires the application of water and ink to differentiate between image and non-image areas. The image is not directly transferred to the substrate. The main strengths of litho include:

► fine detail and good tonal reproduction can be achieved even when printing on poor surface papers;

► it is capable of reproducing clear linework and text, which enables smaller print and therefore a greater amount of information to be printed within a small area;

► fine conventional and FM screening can be used for tonal reproductions;

► relatively low prepress costs with many alternative options for platemaking;

► wide range of printing press types and formats for both sheet and web production;

► increasingly suited for relatively short production runs.

The main process limitations are:

► it places quite high demands on the surface strength of papers due to the tacky ink and the offset blanket;

► heatset web presses are normally able only to print a fixed repeat length;

► relatively high print waste due to the need to balance both ink and water.

Typical work

Offset lithography is particularly suited to printing illustrated work on a wide range of papers and it is the dominant process for most forms of printed material on paper. The main types of work are:

► promotional literature, brochures and illustrated books

► magazines, newspapers, directories and catalogues

► printed office stationery and forms

► security documents

► sheet labels, folding boxboard cartons and metal plate

► posters, maps and stamps.

Waterless lithography

Waterless litho printing also uses a planographic plate, but it is able to differentiate between image and non-image without water. The secret of the plate lies in its non-image silicone rubber coating and the ink rheology. When ink is rolled onto most dry surfaces there is a more or less equal attraction to the ink and it divides (splits) at the weakest point, which is normally within the ink itself. When ink is applied using a roller to the silicone rubber, the cohesion of the ink is greater than its adhesion to the silicone surface.

Therefore, instead of the split taking place within the ink, the low surface energy of the silicone rubber allows it to lift off cleanly from the plate.

Printing without water has the advantages of reduced start-up waste, lower dot gain and improved colour saturation. However, the absence of water means there is a significant temperature rise in the inking system during the run. This reduces the cohesive strength of the ink and, as a consequence, it does not separate cleanly from the plate resulting in scumming. It is necessary to cool the ink system and/or plate to achieve acceptable results. The silicone rubber is also rather more fragile than a conventional plate surface and is more easily damaged. However, there are an increasing number of sheetfed and web-fed printers providing this option.

Despite being available for many years, waterless litho remains a specialist niche, partly due to the lack of competition for supply of plates and the need for specialist CTP and processing, which cannot easily expose wet-offset plates. One specialist niche is on-press imaging, where the ease of use and automatic set-up and running of the press provide significant benefits.

Platemaking

There is a wide range of litho plate types and the choice will be influenced by cost, format, run length, type of work, quality requirement and continuity of supply.

The range of plates is categorised with reference to two fundamental characteristics: the base plate substrate and the imaging method.

Plate substrate

Grained aluminium is the base substrate for most medium-to-large-format litho printing plates. It is chosen because of its good litho properties and its surface is particularly hydrophilic. This characteristic is enhanced and made more durable by graining and anodising the surface. The aluminium plates are suitable for medium-to-long runs achieving run lengths in excess of one million under favourable conditions.

For demanding requirements, the plate may consist of three metals (multi-metal plates): steel electroplated with a thin deposit of copper and chrome. The image area on these tri-metal plates is formed by the copper and the non-image area by chrome. These plates are suitable for long runs but are expensive and no longer in common use, particularly as they cannot be produced in CTP systems.

Small offset presses frequently use paper or polyester-based plates. These are cheap but have a limited run-length capability (about 500–5000 impressions for paper and 5000–25,000 for polyester). They are also less tolerant in terms of ink/water balance than metal plates. Paper plates can achieve only a limited quality, which is suitable for text and line illustrations. Polyester plates can be used for colour work on small-format presses and are widely used on medium-size presses to print good quality monochrome book work. These plates provide a cheaper option to metal, if the limited run length and inferior dimensional stability can be accepted. Further take-up is due to printers adapting film imagesetters to directly expose plastic plates without need for a metal CTP installation.

Imaging methods

Litho platemaking can be accomplished in many ways: projected from rolls of film, reflected from copy, exposed through positive or negative film and directly imaged in a platesetter. Platemaking has undergone a significant revolution since the mid-1990s when powerful computers were able to quickly RIP imposed flats economically. Litho platemaking will typically be through CTP for most applications. Film use is in rapid decline but will still be covered here. Plates can be made in several ways from film: projected from rolls, reflected from copy or exposed through positive or negative film separations. More detail on the methods is provided in Chapter 5.

Film exposure

This requires film separations to be at reproduction size in an auto-imposition (step and repeat) machine, or a printing-down frame. Films are held flat in contact with a presensitised, light-sensitive plate and are exposed to a powerful source of UV light. The film must have its emulsion in contact with the plate, therefore a right-reading – emulsion side down – film negative or positive is required. On exposure to light, the plate undergoes a photo-chemical change that affects the solubility of the coating in the plate developer. Figure 6.10 shows the photomechanical processes for negative and positive working plates.

Negative working, positive working

If the film has been imaged on a large-format imagesetter it will be in an imposed form ready for contacting. However, it is possible for the imposition of film elements or pages to be combined with the plate exposure using a step and repeat machine. The step and repeat machine consists of a bed for mounting the plate, a frame or chase for mounting the films, a UV light source and a means of traversing the frame and light source accurately in $x\,y$ directions. The machine may allow the same film to have multiple exposures to the plate, as required for products like cartons and labels, and the film may be automatically changed after each exposure for magazines or books.

Projection platemaking

An alternative film-imaging system, which was widely used in books and line work applications, is a projection system using 70mm roll film negative. Here the imaging of the plate is combined with the imposition of the pages as the projector steps the pages to their appropriate location on the plate. The development of the plate after exposure is essentially the same regardless of the exposure method. The plates are processed in comparatively simple, automatic processors. A series of nip rollers transport the plate through the development bath, under a water spray, through a finishing application and then a dryer. This process will normally take between one and two minutes to complete.

FIGURE 6.10 Negative- and positive-working plates

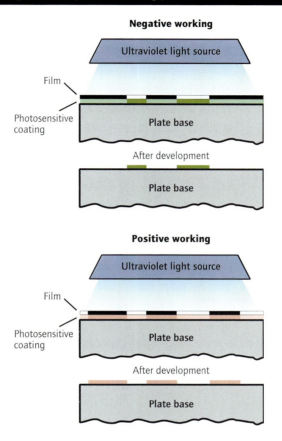

Source: Pira International Ltd

Direct production from reflection copy

The filmless production of plates from reflection copy uses dedicated, fixed-focus camera platemakers and imaging plates with silver or photoconductive coatings. This has been a common technique for the production of small offset paper/polyester plates and medium-format polyester plates for book presses.

There is a move away from these methods to some form of CTP. Most litho platemaking in developed markets involves CTP systems, with the volume of CTP plates overtaking conventional film exposure during 2002. This discussion of platemaking also describes the various methods, including:

▶ projection from rolls of film, reflected from copy
▶ exposed through positive or negative film in a contact frame or step and repeat machine
▶ directly imaged in a platesetter.

More detail on these methods is provided in Chapter 5.

Computer-to-plate (CTP)

Using a platesetter allows the plate to be imaged directly without films, reflection copy or intermediate labour. The benefits in time, cost and quality of print make CTP a compelling argument for most print operations. There are many technologies in use, from laser printing paper plates, inkjet printing onto plates, UV imaging and laser imaging (thermal and violet diode). Platesetters use flatbed, internal drum and external drum imaging arrays with a variety of formats, speeds and degrees of automation. For newspapers, a pair of machines could deliver more than 400 process colour tabloid plates, punched ready for loading onto the machine in less than an hour if needed.

Practical experience has shown that as well as the reduction in the number of stages that have to be followed at the prepress stage, users often report that CTP offers significant benefits in the pressroom. Plate quality is much higher than can be obtained by conventional exposure methods (wider range of sharp dots from 0.5–99.5% at screen rulings of 175lpi to 300lpi is common, stochastic screening being widely used), and the plates do not suffer from blemishes resulting from dust and dirt. The benefit of knowing that the set of plates delivered to the press is correct and in precise register allows press crews to reduce the time and waste in make-ready, offering significant productivity improvements.

The plates used are not compatible with conventional platemaking. They are more expensive and require different calibration and processing techniques. The premium over conventional plates is likely to remain, but the benefits outweigh the drawbacks.

The litho printing unit

The dampening system

A dampening system supplies a controlled amount of water to the plate. The one shown in Figure 6.11 (page 317) is integrated with the inking. Such systems attain ink–water balance more quickly, reducing the number of waste sheets at start-up. High waste levels are regarded as a characteristic of lithography, but this is less true with modern systems. There are other forms of dampening unit, which use rotary brushes with flicker blades and some in which the dampening solution is sprayed into the system. All systems are designed to supply an adjustable, controlled film of water to the plate.

Fountain solution

Lithography delivers water and a controlled stable emulsion of ink and water to the plate. Although the lithographic process will work for a time with water only as the dampening medium, the process works more efficiently if chemicals are added to the water and the water source is demineralised or deionised. This normally takes the form of a couple of per cent of a fount solution additive. The chemical nature of the additive is determined by factors such as:

▶ type of dampening system

▶ nature of local water supply

▶ type of ink.

Some require the use of propan-2-ol (isopropyl alcohol), although environmental pressures are gradually phasing it out. It is important to control the fount solution. Many are buffered acids and the measurement of pH is insufficient to provide the necessary regulation so measuring of specific gravity and conductivity is required.

The inking system

Litho ink is a high-viscosity, shear-resistant fluid that flows when worked. These rheological properties require an inking system with many linked rollers to break the ink down into the thin film that is applied to the plate. This presents a problem because the rollers retain a surplus of ink in those areas where it has not been removed by the image. It is necessary therefore to replenish the ink in zones to accommodate the different requirements of the image being printed. On modern presses, each zone is precisely adjusted by its own motor. This allows the adjustment to be made from a remote control desk.

FIGURE 6.11 The offset litho press

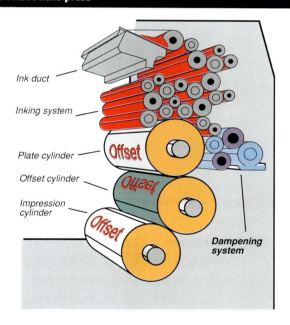

Source: Pira International Ltd

There will normally be provision for ink-zone settings to be preset, recorded and stored. The data for presetting may be obtained from a plate scanner or via a CIP4/JDF interface with the digital datafile used for plate imaging. All this could be avoided if the process was able to use a simple inking system like that used in flexography. So-called keyless presses have been developed, but this approach is currently possible only with the lower-viscosity ink that is typically used for newspaper printing and in specialist machines such as the Karat Gravuflow inking system. A thin coat of ink is applied to the single-sized ink forme roller with each rotation of the ceramic-coated anilox roller. A doctor blade then removes any excess ink from the anilox roller. This is claimed to give fast, uniform printing results, without the operator constantly having to intervene.

FIGURE 6.12 The ink wash-up system on a sheetfed offset press

Source: MAN Roland

Inks and ink drying

More detail is presented in Chapter 8, *Printing Inks*. A fundamental requirement of litho ink is to separate from the damping solution water. This is done by forming a stable emulsion of water in the ink: the correct ink/water balance that is so important to good litho production. This requirement, and the large surface area of the inking system, restricts the possibilities for ink drying. The ink must remain open on the rollers and dry only on the substrate. Conventional lithographic sheetfed inks dry by a combination of penetration and oxidation that takes some hours to complete. This is unacceptable for some printing, and radiation dryers may be used to speed the process with special inks formulated for infrared, ultraviolet and electron beam curing.

In web offset printing, the paper moves so quickly through the press that the ink does not have time to dry by oxidation. If the paper is absorbent, like newsprint, the setting of ink by absorption is normally sufficient. This is referred to as coldset printing to distinguish it from heatset, which is necessary when less absorbent papers are used. Heatset inks contain a solvent that has a low evaporation rate to avoid drying on the inking rollers. A high-boiling petroleum fraction is used and this is removed by heating the printed web through a hot air drying oven, causing the resin in the ink to crystallise and form a hard, glossy film, followed by chilling back to ambient temperatures. Other web offset uses UV-curing inks, particularly in continuous stationery presses.

Sheetfed litho presses

There is diversity of sheetfed presses designed to print on a variety of substrates, including paper, board and metal plate. Presses range in sheet size from A3 up to A0 and from single-colour to 10-colour. The most common sizes are B2 (720×540mm) and B1 (1020×720mm). To improve productivity, manufactures have introduced eight-unit perfecting machines capable of printing both sides at full press speed in a single pass. Twelve-unit presses are now common with multiple coating and varnishing units in place. Some machines now have integrated web feed, allowing printers to use cheaper reels of paper and gain efficiencies in material use.

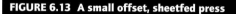

FIGURE 6.13 A small offset, sheetfed press

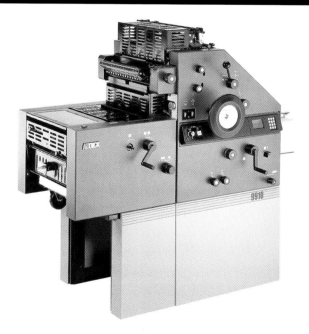

Source: AB Dick

Figure 6.13 shows a small offset, sheetfed press from AB Dick. Small offset is a term generally applied to presses that can print paper or fine card up to a maximum size of about B3 (420×297mm). This type of press is typically used by instant print shops, inplant printers and general jobbing printers. It would normally be used for short print runs of stationery, reports and similar work using paper or polyester-based plates. This press is a single-colour press, although two- and four-colour models are common. To print another colour, the inking system would have to be cleaned, the ink and the plate changed, and the sheets would then have to be passed through the press again. Most small offset presses are single colour.

Tracking problems

All litho printing presses have inking systems that require ink to be adjusted in zones across the sheet. This means inking levels have to be adjusted for individual images to obtain a colour match to the passed proof. Difficulties may be experienced where a heavy image coverage is in track with the light coverage of another, because the rate of replenishment required to meet the needs of one is too great for the other. This is referred to as a tracking problem. Tracking problems also arise if images, proofed to different specifications, are printed in the same track. Tracking problems like this should be prevented by applying tighter compliance to the standards at the proofing stage. Figure 6.14 below illustrates the two basic situations in which a tracking problem may occur.

FIGURE 6.14 Situations in which tracking problems can occur

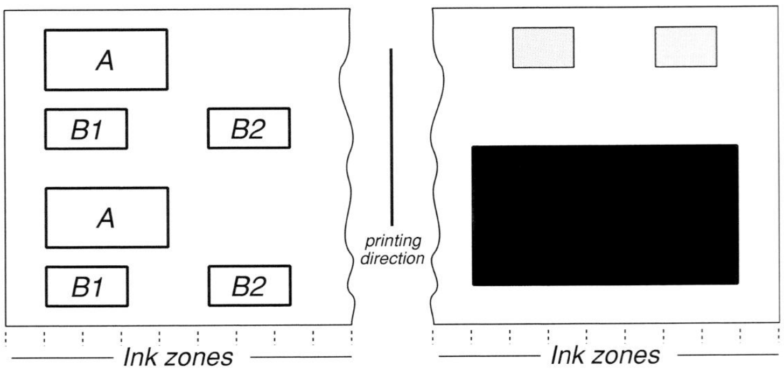

Source: Pira International Ltd

In the example on the left, images marked A have been proofed to a different specification to images marked B. When inking is adjusted to optimise the quality for the B images, the A images are too light.

If the inking is correct for A then the Bs are too dark. It is possible to adjust the inking so that A and B2 are optimised, but not both A and B1. The example on the right illustrates the condition where an area of heavy ink consumption is in track with images that consume much less ink. The high ink demand of the solid leads to excessive ink building up in the ink roller system and consequential over-inking of the lower consumption halftone images.

Multi-colour presses

Multi-unit sheetfed presses can be from two to more than 12 colours. The maximum speed of sheetfed presses depends on the make and size of press, and the paper being printed. A typical modern press is rated at 15,000 sheets an hour, with a maximum of 18,000. These presses are used to print a wide range of paper and board products such as labels, brochures, leaflets, greeting cards, periodicals and books. Typical run lengths are up to 50,000. If a printer needs to print larger quantities of sections or complete periodicals at one pass through a press, a web press would be more commonly used.

FIGURE 6.15 A ten-unit sheetfed offset press

Source: Heidelberg

FIGURE 6.16 Heidelberg Speedmaster 102 perfecting unit

Source: Heidelberg

Figure 6.16 (page 321) shows the mechanism of perfecting whereby the sheet is transferred between the grippers and turned over before being transferred to the next print unit.

FIGURE 6.17 A multi-unit sheetfed offset press with inline coating and drying units. This press has two printing units, there may be up to 12

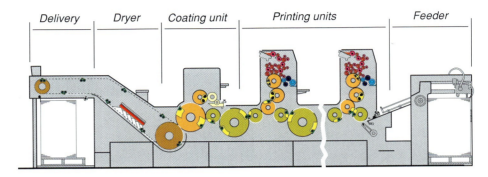

Delivery | Dryer | Coating unit | Printing units | Feeder

Source: Pira International Ltd

Presses similar to this are available as straight multi-colour or convertible multi-colour/perfector presses. In perfecting mode, the sheet is printed on one side and then tumbled over by the transfer cylinder so that the remaining units print on the other side. This is achieved by a simple adjustment and takes only a few minutes. New eight to twelve-unit presses are convertible and can print eight to twelve colours on one side of the sheet or be converted to print four/six colours on each side of the sheet. They are widely used to print short-run magazines, brochures and books. Figure 6.17 shows a medium-size, multi-colour (only two units shown) sheetfed press. The cylinders, located between each printing unit, transfer the sheet, in register and in a controlled way, through the press. It is possible to see the path that the sheet has to follow (white sheets) from the feeder to the delivery. There is no drying between the printing units except in some inter-deck UV applications for cartons and printing on plastic; most multi-colour printing in litho is normally wet-on-wet. The last unit of the press shown in Figure 6.17 is not a printing unit, but a coating unit. It applies UV-curable or water-based varnish inline with printing. The varnish may be overall or spot (if a relief plate is fitted to the coating unit).

Most multi-colour offset presses are configured in the unit-to-unit arrangement, but more compact configurations are possible using a common impression cylinder for two or more offset cylinders, as shown in Figure 6.18. This is a diagram of the Heidelberg Quickmaster DI, a waterless press with digital imaging of plates, but this type of configuration is not restricted to this machine.

FIGURE 6.18 Heidelberg Quickmaster DI, showing the four printing cylinders sharing a common impression cylinder

FIGURE 6.18 Heidelberg Quickmaster DI, showing the four printing cylinders sharing a common impression cylinder

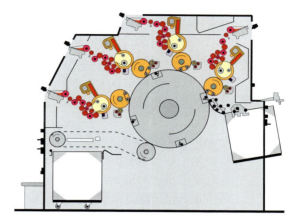

Source: Pira International Ltd

Web offset litho

Web-fed presses print from continuous rolls of paper, a cheaper source than sheetfed. They are faster than sheetfed presses and normally incorporate finishing options inline with printing. Most heatset web offset presses have an inline folder as they are widely used to print books, magazines and newspapers. Reel-fed litho offset presses are also used to print other products such as continuous forms, base stationery, labels and cartons. The speed of these presses is limited as they often have the capability of changing print units so providing variable cut-off capability to satisfy the requirement for different print lengths necessary for these products. There are also finishing units to allow re-reeling, sheeting, fan-folding and specialist in-line gluing, folding and finishing to produce complete products.

FIGURE 6.19 KBA Compacta heatset web offset press line

Source: KBA

Blanket-to-blanket units

Web offset printing units may be configured like sheetfed presses, with a plate, offset and impression cylinder, but most are used to print publications printed on both sides, and the most effective configuration to achieve this is a blanket-to-blanket perfecting unit. These may be arranged in the form of an arch with the paper being fed vertically from below or slightly offset vertically with the paper running horizontally. The arch arrangement is typical for newspaper presses, while the horizontal web path is normal for heatset commercial web presses.

Newspaper presses

A modern newspaper press comprises several basic blanket-to-blanket units. These will be configured to suit the maximum number of pages of monochrome and colour specified when it was installed. A single-width press prints on a web that is the width of two broadsheet newspaper pages. The press shown in Figure 6.20 is double width with two pages around each cylinder. The four reels of paper being printed on this press would produce a 64-page broadsheet newspaper when running in straight production mode. Presses often have heatset dryers for one or two webs, allowing higher quality semi-commercial printing capability for cover pages. These also allow the press to produce magazines and inserts at times of the day when not used for the news sections.

FIGURE 6.20 An example of a coldset web newspaper press

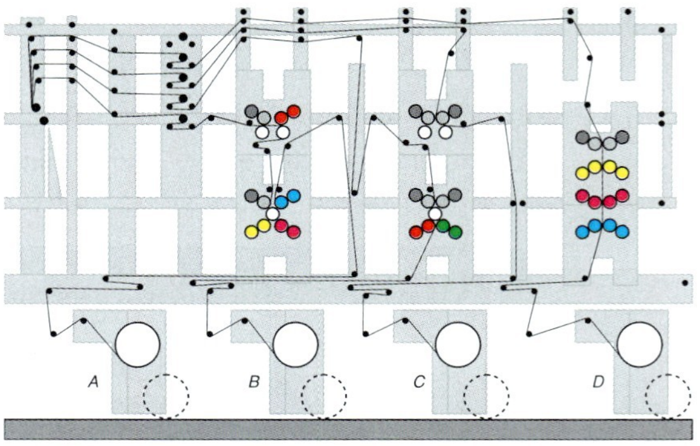

Source: Pira International Ltd

The lower units in the two left towers are convertible units. The unit on the far left is configured as a four-colour common impression satellite and the other in perfecting mode, as two blanket-to-blanket perfectors. The unit at the far right is referred to as a four-high tower, which is able to print colour on both sides of the web. Configured in this way, the newspaper will have some pages in full colour, others with only spot colour. From left to right the webs from each reelstand will print colour as follows:

Web A: four-colour process plus black and red spot

Web B: black and red spot plus black and green spot

Web C: black only on both sides

Web D: 4-colour process on both sides.

FIGURE 6.21 Alternative arrangements of cylinders in blanket-to-blanket web presses

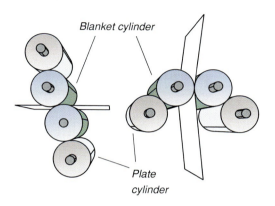

Source: Pira International Ltd

Heatset web presses

Heatset web presses normally comprise multiple vertically aligned (slightly offset) blanket-to-blanket units with the webs running horizontally. The main components of a heatset web press are as follows:

▶ The reelstand, which controls the unwinding of the reel and automatically changes to a new reel as the old one expires;

▶ The web guides, which monitor and adjust the lateral position of the web: one is positioned before the units and one after the dryer before the folder;

▶ The infeed metering, which comprises variable speed-driven nip rollers that meter and control the tension of the paper fed into the printing units;

▶ The dryer, which is a high-velocity hot-air type. The design determines the maximum speed the press will run at, often with pollution control and heat recovery systems;

▶ The chill rolls, which are water-cooled and also have a variable speed drive. Their function is to set the ink by cooling the paper and to control paper tension from the printing unit through the dryer;

▶ The silicone applicator, which consists of two rollers that apply a mix of water and silicone to the printed web. These rollers put back moisture removed by the dryer, improve slip and reduce marking;

▶ Some presses have specialist remoistening units that replace water in the paper, the technology allows controlled remoistening to remove web wave and subsequent dimensional instability;

▶ The folder, which cuts and folds the continuous web into sections. A single folder will be capable of producing a range of folded products;

▶ Some presses have a sheeter.

The number of webs and the format of the units determine the products that can be printed. The press in Figure 6.22 is capable of printing a single web in four colours on both sides but, with the addition of an extra reelstand and dryer, it is able to double the pagination throughput by printing two webs at the same time, each in two colours.

Heatset presses commonly print magazines, periodicals, books, catalogues and long-run promotional printing, and the format size and capability is typically expressed in terms of the number of A4 pages that it can produce.

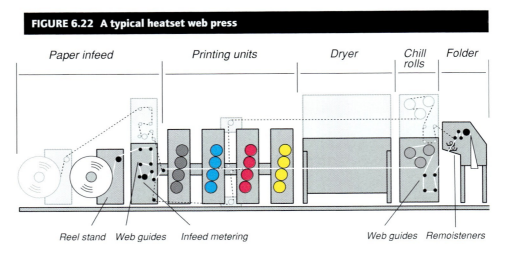

FIGURE 6.22 A typical heatset web press

Paper infeed   Printing units   Dryer   Chill rolls   Folder

Reel stand   Web guides   Infeed metering   Web guides   Remoisteners

Source: Pira International Ltd

A typical press with a web width of about 950mm will yield four A4 pages across the web with trims. The length of the printed image is determined by the circumference of the plate cylinder. When the web passes to the folder, it is cut into sections by the cutting cylinder in the folder and it is this cut-off length that identifies the press's printing size. Thus a 16-page A4 web press has a maximum web width of about 950mm and a cut-off length of about 630mm yielding eight pages to view (16 pages perfected) to each section. New microgap and gapless technology reduces the non-print area and results in a smaller circumference to produce the same product, so using less paper.

This press format produces a portrait product with the paper grain running top to bottom of the page – long grain. The long grain press presents an A4 section with suitable grain direction for adhesive binding. Many book presses and some magazine presses are short grain. A 32-page A4 model produces the same product in landscape delivery as a 32pp long grain press with the circumference of some 960mm and wider at 1180mm. A section is produced for every 960mm of paper fed through the machine rather than 1260 on the long grain model. Press crews and machine speeds are identical, and the machine offers productivity increases. With suitable remoistening, the product is fine for perfect binding. The short grain press offers some benefits:

▶   it is possible to stitch sections in the folder

▶ web speed is lower for same section output

▶ no requirement for quarter fold on A4 products, resulting in more accurate folding.

FIGURE 6.23 Short-grain and long-grain 32pp web press formats. The formats are typical maximum dimensions and the number of pages (A4) apply when printing a single web

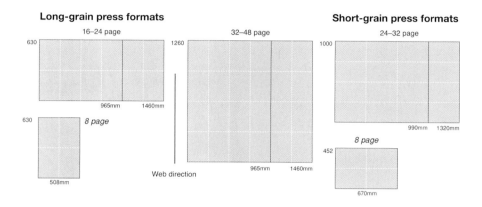

Source: Pira International Ltd

Web folding

The web folder can use the following folding methods:

▶ A former or plough fold, which is made in the grain direction while the paper is still a continuous web;

▶ A chopper or knife fold, which is made in the grain direction after the web has been cut. This is normally the last fold in a combination;

▶ A cylinder or jaw fold, which is made in the cross-grain direction after the web has been cut. Two cylinder folds made one after another are referred to as a double parallel fold.

Most web folders incorporate a combination of folding methods in sequence, but are typically categorised as:

▶ former folder

▶ ribbon folder

▶ pinless folder.

With the *former folder*, the web is directed over a triangular former (or kite) to make the first fold in the grain direction. A knife on a cutting cylinder cuts the folded web to a fixed length, the cut-off. Each cut length is folded further by a series of cylinders that contain a jaw recess into which the section is forced to complete the fold (jaw or cylinder fold). Long-grain magazine and newspaper presses will normally be fitted with a folder of this type.

FIGURE 6.24 Detail of MAN Roland double folder former

Source: MAN Roland

The *ribbon folder* is normally fitted to all short-grain presses and is also used for bookwork and high-grade multi-colour printing. With this folder, the web is slit into ribbons that are aligned into the folder by passing over angled bars. Within the folder the combined ribbons are cut and cross-folded by a series of jaw-folding cylinders. The folding of the section may be completed with a chopper or knife fold.

The *pinless folder* was developed to meet the demands for reduced trimming waste on sections. On modern magazine presses, the non-printing gap in the blanket cylinder is small and in some cases there is no gap. That means the minimum trim is determined by the need to remove the folder pin holes.

The pinless folder controls the passage of sections through the fold with tapes avoiding the use of pins and reducing the trim waste. Web press folders generally work to high standards of tolerance within their capacities. Problems that arise are most likely to be marking and set-off problems rather than the folding of the paper, although fold cracking with coated papers on heatset can be a problem.

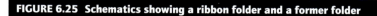

FIGURE 6.25 Schematics showing a ribbon folder and a former folder

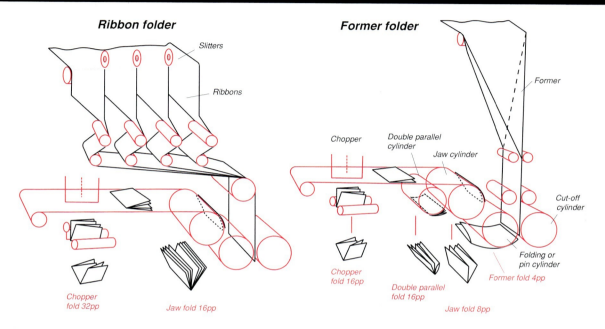

Source: Pira International Ltd

Web offset developments

The leading technological changes that have led to the substantial growth in the heatset web offset printing industry include the following:

▶ Higher pagination designs that offer productivity increases with 48pp, 64pp, 72pp and 80pp single web designs.

▶ Shaftless drives on heatset presses reduce setting and start-up time and improve register accuracy. They improve mechanical lifetime and further improve press operation and waste reduction.

▶ Variable cut-off designs using sleeve technology for plate and blanket cylinders to provide greater flexibility.

▶ Gapless sleeve blanket cylinders, such as the Sunday Press (see Figure 6.26, overleaf), enable wider machines without problems of gap-bounce vibration, increasing the productivity of new machines and personnel. This also solves a long-term problem on print quality (strikes) and improves press lifetime (wear on bearers). The most recently developed gapless presses can reach production speeds of 15msec-1 (2900fpm), while other systems like narrow-gap constructions come close to that. As well as production improvements the new formats provide significant reductions in paper waste with shorter cut off needed to yield the product.

▶ Some machines use separate servo drives replacing a single drive shaft and gears. This also reduces some press unit vibration and allows remote control of some operation functions, such as automated setting and adjustment including auxiliaries that are more integrated. New presses are software-controlled devices rather than hardware dominated.

Software can be updated to maintain performance, and maintenance controls help to keep uptime maximised through on-press targeted maintenance indicators with self-maintaining and self-repairing systems. Machine manufacturers monitor presses online because printers want to invest in efficiency, i.e. guaranteed uptime.

▶ Press auxiliaries are automatic quality-inspection and adjustment systems, tightly monitoring register, colour matching, print defects, cut-off and folding register. This allows heatset presses to process six tonnes of full-colour printed sections every hour with minimum staff.

▶ As well as high speed, presses are reducing set-up times with automatic plate loading and pre-setting from CIP4/JDF data significantly to reduce wastage.

▶ Hybrid printing, coldset presses being equipped with heatset dryers, will affect some heatset markets. These improve quality over coldset but limited compared to heatset, the quality limitations will improve in the coming years. Initial installations are on new newspaper printing lines and they may take a significant share of the magazine, catalogue or directory market.

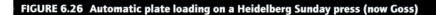

FIGURE 6.26 Automatic plate loading on a Heidelberg Sunday press (now Goss)

Source: Heidelberg

Letterpress   Letterpress is the oldest method of printing and dates from Gutenberg's invention. Its wide use has diminished with the adoption of digital prepress and the demise of hot-metal typesetting. There are now relatively few letterpress applications in developed printing markets. The process is still used to print paperback textbooks and newspapers in some countries and self-adhesive labels on narrow web presses. It is also widely used, as an offset process, to print plastic containers and metal beverage cans.

The process uses a hard printing surface, metal or photopolymer, with the image areas raised in relief from the non-image areas. Viscous low-tack paste ink is applied to the plate's surface and the inked image is then transferred to the substrate with the application of pressure. It is the hardness of the plate, nature of the ink and inking system that distinguishes modern letterpress from flexography.

The main strengths of the process are:
▶ good legibility of text even on uncoated papers
▶ low print waste even with frequent interruptions to the run.

The main process limitations are:
▶ relatively high printing plate costs
▶ poor tonal reproduction when compared with offset litho at lower, relatively coarse screen rulings
▶ low productivity in comparison to offset.

Platemaking

Some metal type is still used but most applications use photopolymer plates that are imaged by exposure to UV light through a film negative, followed by a wash-out development. The principal difference with flexography is the higher degree of hardness of the plates. Several systems are used including NAPP and Nyloprint. Letterpress uses a photopolymer plate production method and the main difference with flexography is the higher degree of hardness of the plates.

The printing unit

The basic letterpress comprises an inking system to apply ink to the relief plate with a means of generating pressure to transfer the inked image to the substrate. Conventional letterpress machines are designed on one of three principles:
▶ platen principle
▶ flatbed (cylinder) principle
▶ rotary principle.

Although it is still possible to find some examples of each type of letterpress machine, all serious modern applications use the rotary principle.

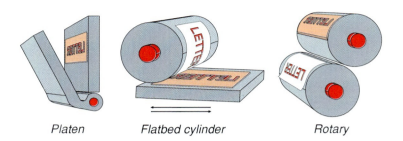

FIGURE 6.27 The three principles of letterpress printing

Platen   Flatbed cylinder   Rotary

Source: Pira International Ltd

Platen

The printing forme is held vertically. Impression is carried out by the platen, a heavy metal plate that pivots forward and upward in an arc. It carries the paper and impresses it into the surface of the forme as it reaches a position where it is vertical and parallel with the forme. Most platens are used for creasing, foil blocking and diecutting applications today.

Flatbed cylinder

The type-bed is flat and horizontal. Positioned over it is the cylindrical impression cylinder on which the paper to be printed is held. Impression is made as the bed moves in a horizontal direction under the revolving cylinder on the impression stoke; the impression cylinder lifts to allow the bed to return to its first position and the cycle is repeated.

Rotary

The printing surface is either flexible plastic, rubber or photopolymer plates that are fixed around the circumference of the plate cylinder. An impression cylinder rotates against the plate cylinder and impression is carried out as the paper (sheets or reels) is fed between them.

Inks and inking system

The viscose nature of letterpress ink, and the fact that the hard plate requires resilient rubber rollers to transfer ink, requires a roller system similar to that used in offset lithography. The inks are similar to offset litho inks and the options for ink drying are essentially the same.

Reel-fed rotary letterpress

Figure 6.28 shows a simplified view of a reel-fed rotary letterpress label machine. Starting with the reel of material, the web is passed through the printing units then on to the final operation, which in this case, is rewinding. More commonly, machines of this type would be fitted with inline diecutting and possibly foil blocking.

FIGURE 6.28 Schematic of a reel-fed rotary letterpress label machine

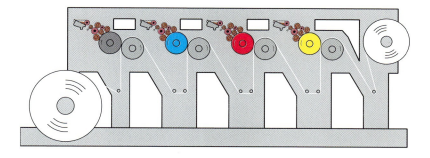

Source: Pira International Ltd

Offset letterpress

Letterpress remains an important process in package printing, but only as an offset process. It is used in this form to print plastic containers, like those for yoghurt and margarine, and drinks cans. The offset principle is needed to allow printing onto metal, but it also provides another important benefit. The different colour images that make up the design are transferred from their appropriate printing head to the offset blanket, which is attached to a cylinder common to all printing heads. A composite image is built up on the blanket and this is printed to the container in a single transfer. This avoids the problems that would be encountered in trying to register individual images to each other around the container.

FIGURE 6.29 Offset letterpress for container printing

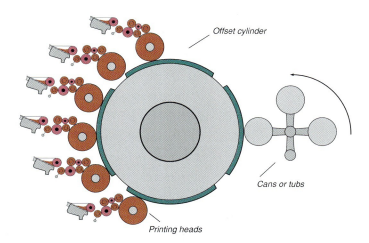

Source: Pira International Ltd

Flexography   Flexography, in its many guises, is used to produce a diverse range of products for various applications across the globe. The flexography printing process is inherently simple, making it suitable for printing onto an incredible variety of substrates and to be integrated into complex conversion lines. Because of this simplicity the printing units are relatively low cost when compared with offset and gravure equipment. The simple print mechanism means that set up is straightforward and there is relatively little make-ready and running waste. Technology advances have enabled major quality and productivity improvements, allowing flexo to demonstrate cost benefits over gravure and offset in a range of applications where it has been adopted as the preferred print process. The main types of work are:

▶ corrugated packaging
▶ flexible packaging
▶ labels
▶ cartons
▶ envelopes
▶ bags and sacks
▶ sanitary and kitchen ware (printed tissues)
▶ newspapers and some paperback books.

Flexo accounts for some 25% of the world's printing market and it is the only major conventional printing process that is increasing its market share. It is under-represented in Japan and the rest of Asia, where historical quality concerns have led converters to choose gravure rather than flexo. But this is starting to change.

Flexography is a relief printing process. It uses deformable plates made from either rubber or soft photopolymer. These plates are flexible and normally attached to the plate cylinders with double-sided adhesive tape. The image is inked with a liquid ink before being transferred to the printing stock by the application of light pressure. The basic process is very simple. Liquid ink in a duct is transferred from a pan roller to an anilox roller. The ink fills tiny pits engraved on the roller surface so a controlled volume of ink is transferred onto a relief plate. The peaks of this relief deposit the ink onto the paper.

Plate technologies are improving and reducing in cost as new suppliers join the supply side of the market. Photopolymer plate technology is growing, with major reductions in the use of solvent for plate processing as it is replaced by water-wash technology and totally chemical-free processes. Ablation mask will dominate the CTP market, with direct engraving of elastomers and photopolymers taking a significant share. Ancillary manufacturers are improving plate-mounting tapes and registration aids. Imaging in the round is growing in importance, with sleeve technology allowing very quick changeover and excellent registration on press.

In order to improve quality, more flexo presses will adopt the common impression cylinder arrangement with eight to 12 printing units. The use of direct drive, gearless presses will become standard for new installations, with retro-fits providing new life for some installed machines. These will have better control systems and the whole process will become more complex as both productivity and quality improve. The print units will be enclosed chambers, coated internally with easy-to-clean surfaces designed for quick release and replacement. Cleaning will take place off-line to minimise press downtime. Ink temperatures and viscosity will be continually monitored with additives automatically dispensed to optimise runnability. Anilox rollers will be YAG laser-engraved ceramic coatings with high-resolution cell counts and high ink-holding capability. Line rulings of 1500lpi will be widely used, with CTP plates capable of holding screen rulings of 175 or 200dpi for continuous-tone printing, using six and seven process colours to extend the colour gamut of the process.

Increasingly, radiation-cured inks will be used, the instant cure eliminating potential drying problems and reducing dot gain caused by ink spreading or being absorbed by the substrate. This will boost print quality and eliminate potential odour and taint for many packaging applications. It will also provide significant environmental benefits through the elimination of volatile organic compounds from solvent-based inks. Ultraviolet-based inks will increasingly be joined by cold electron beam curing.

As part of the conversion process flexographic printing is being joined by other processes to provide hybrid printing and inline finishing. This is particularly important in the label market where gravure, offset, rotary screen and increasingly digital units are widely available. These will be joined by integrated hot and cold foiling, mechanical and laser diecutting and specialist tag insertion, such as RFID (radio frequency identification devices).

The main strengths of the process are:
- the ink system can use relatively volatile liquids that key to a wide range of substrates and dry without requiring a lot of energy;
- the prepress costs are significantly less than for gravure, which is its main competitor in package printing;
- it is possible to print continuous repeating designs;
- the printing unit design allows for the repeat length to be easily changed.

The main process limitations are:
- tonal reproduction is poor when compared with offset litho and gravure;
- relatively coarse screen rulings have to be used because of the relief plate;
- the process has difficulty in printing smooth vignettes;
- it is difficult to print small type and halftones in combination with solids on the same plate cylinder.

Flexographic plates are flexible photopolymer materials that cross-link under exposure to UV light; they have largely replaced rubber-based compounds. They are available in varying thicknesses and shore hardness for specific applications. The softer the plate the better the impression on rough and uneven surfaces (such as corrugated board) but the higher the degree of squash, which leads to dot gain. Generally, harder plates are capable of higher screen rulings for continuous-tone imaging. They can hold small dots to provide good highlight detail. The final choice of plate involves a trade-off between resilience and quality.

In some cases the material is supplied in liquid form to be coated onto sheets and, increasingly, onto sleeves for subsequent exposure and processing. The photopolymer layer in an unexposed flexo plate contains a thermoplastic elastomer, a polyfunctional acrylate monomer, a photoinitiator and various additives. UV light activates the photoinitiator, which starts the cross-linking polymerisation. Manufacturers are continually refining the materials in use, from natural rubber to a range of compounds based around polymerising 2-chloro-1,3-butadiene (chloroprene) or styrene-isoprene rubbers with trimethylolpropane triacrylate. When exposed, the acrylate cross-links the polymer, rendering it insoluble in the wash-out solvents. Currently chlorinated solvents such as perchloroethylene with water-washable alternatives are most widely used.

Conventional analogue platemaking is still used to prepare the majority of plates, using negative film separations. Matt film is used to avoid halation during exposure and the films are output with the images anamorphically distorted to compensate for the depth of the plate forming the relief image, the dispro factor calculated for the particular cylinder diameter and plate thickness. Platemaking involves back exposure of the reverse of the plate to create a solid base, then image exposure through a negative using low-intensity light. The plates are then processed by physical and chemical wash-out of the non-image area to provide the relief plate. There is movement away from chlorinated solvents toward water-wash systems, which have less environmental impact. After processing, the plate is carefully dried to remove solvent and restore gauge thickness, then it is post-exposed to obtain final cure of floor and shoulders before finishing. The surface is then de-tacked and the plate dried before being mounted in position on the plate cylinder, normally with a double-sided adhesive tape. The elapsed time to prepare a press-ready plate will typically be a couple of hours, there are issues with the fine detail capable of being held on the plates.

FIGURE 6.30 The stages in conventional photopolymer plate production

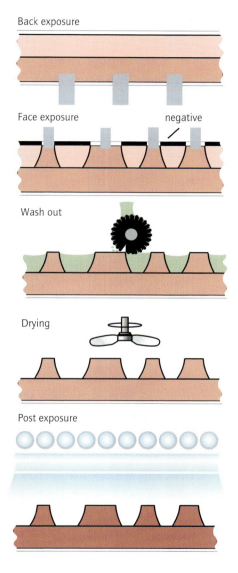

Back exposure

Face exposure   negative

Wash out

Drying

Post exposure

Source: Pira International Ltd

Conventional flexo platemaking seems to involve a touch of the black art compared with offset, with individual plants using their own specification for repro to optimise the attainable quality. This results in some outstanding examples being produced, but limits the choice for customers and reduces the plant's flexibility. The key development leading to quality improvements is the widespread use of totally digital prepress with CTP technology to image plates, as discussed in Chapter 5.

Flexo presses

The vast majority of flexo printing is web-fed, with the press often part of a converting line producing finished packs, bags, envelopes or labels inline in a single pass. Large-format sheetfed presses are available for corrugated applications. Flexo presses print webs that can be less than 10cm wide for labels and up to 2.5m wide for giftwrap and tissue applications. Rated press speeds vary greatly, from 300 to 2000ft/min (600m/min). In the past, the ability to integrate print into the converting process was the key design element; print quality was not top of the agenda for manufacturers, but this is changing as markets become more quality conscious.

Any flexo press has four basic functions that need to be optimised:

▶ substrate handling
▶ printing unit design and format for multi-colour machines
▶ drying the print
▶ delivery and processing of the printed material.

Each of the functions is being developed to overcome limitations and broaden its use in more applications. The current trends in flexo press design and technology are designed to reduce make-ready time, improve print quality and create more efficient and easy-to-use presses. Many manufacturers are looking to integrate automation and information control systems into new generation presses with increasing numbers of print units. It is common to specify machines with eight, ten or 12 print units. Relative plate position and pressure are controlled and adjusted centrally with direct drive technology as this is critical to controlling flexo image quality and making set-up easy for reprints.

Presses are computer controlled and production data can be transferred to a management information system (MIS) to provide accurate scheduling and costing information. Many print unit cylinders are being replaced with lightweight sleeve technology and manufacturers are providing trolleys and robotic aids for wide webs to aid quick changeover to different formats. Sleeve technology allows infinitely variable print lengths to optimise substrate utilisation. Each movement can be managed in sequence, by computer or manually. Automation includes changeover and cleaning. Ink units are chambered to minimise evaporation and viscosity changes, and the enclosed systems allow fast automatic ink supply and cleaning of the whole inking group (doctor blades, anilox rollers, ink pumps, ink hoses and viscosity controls). They are suitable for solvent-based and water-based inks, and specialist UV materials.

Substrate handling

The trend in all markets is towards a reduction in the basis weight and thickness of substrates, lowering the cost and weight of the packaging while maintaining strength and handling characteristics. As press speeds increase, great strains can be placed on the substrates and manufacturers are developing better control mechanisms to avoid stretch, which leads to register and material-handling problems. The unwinds are more sophisticated, with tension control and automatic splicing becoming standard, with web cleaning capabilities before surface treatment units to prepare the substrate for printing. There is increasing support of the web throughout its path; the common impression cylinder design ensures there is support between all the print units.

Press format

Flexo press formats can be stack, central impression and platform (or inline unit). The trend is for higher numbers of print units to print more colours inline, which requires better unit-to-unit registration.

Stack presses

In the stack design, the different colour units of the press are stacked over one another on one or both sides of press frame. There may be one to eight stations, with six being the most common. The arrangement of the units makes it possible to accommodate large plate cylinders and print long print repeats. These presses also offer good accessibility, which facilitates changeover, wash-up, impression setting, etc.

The stack press can be used to print almost any type of substrate but it does have register limitations when printing substrates that are extendable or of a thin gauge. With materials such as fairly heavyweight papers, thick films and laminated structures that can tolerate fairly high levels of tension, acceptable register is possible. The main drawback is poor registration, particularly on medium and wide webs where the unsupported web is prone to stretch. The simple design of the stack press makes it the lowest cost press. The web may be reversed to allow perfecting and each station is easily accessible, making changeover and maintenance easy and allowing drying units to be easily positioned.

FIGURE 6.31 A six-colour web-fed stack press

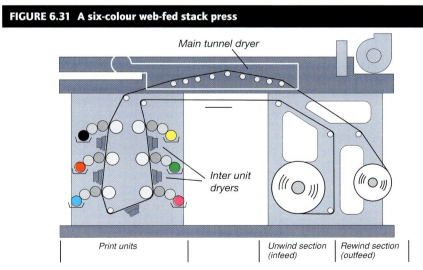

Main tunnel dryer

Inter unit dryers

Print units | Unwind section (infeed) | Rewind section (outfeed)

Source: Pira International Ltd

FIGURE 6.32 Flexo stack press

Source: Flexotecnica

Common impression presses

The central impression press, sometimes called drum, common impression or CI, positions all of its colour stations around a single steel impression cylinder. The impression cylinder supports the web and helps to maintain tight colour registration between print stations, even for lightweight film substrates prone to stretching on stack and inline configurations. There may be inter-unit drying aids for UV and solvent applications.

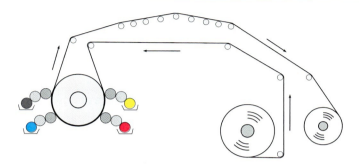

Source: Pira International Ltd

Figure 6.33 shows the arrangement of the print units on a four-colour common impression cylinder press. The greatest advantage of the CI press is its ability to hold excellent register, even when printing very thin, extendable packaging materials.

Inline or unit presses

The inline press is the only one of the major flexo press types that can be used for the printing of rigid sheet materials, such as corrugated board (although corrugated liner can be preprinted before lamination). Inline presses have the advantages of good accessibility and quick changeover. They can be manufactured with any number of colours and, since a single frame does not have to support all the print units, they can be designed to handle extremely wide web widths.

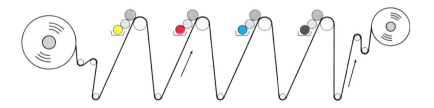

Source: Pira International Ltd

Inline presses have separate printing stations arranged in a row, horizontally or vertically in printing couples for newspaper applications. They can handle wide webs for folding carton, corrugated, multi-wall bag and pressure-sensitive and standard labels. In label presses the trend is for inline operations to be included after the flexo printing section with digital printing and coating stations, as well as rotary diecutting and liner re-reeling to produce multi-part labels. Inline presses often have inline converting operations such as bag-making, carton cutting and creasing, embossing, label or form sheeting, and so forth built in. For example, cartonboard can be fed into an inline press from a reel, printed, creased and rotary diecut at high speed in one continuous operation.

Many plastic packaging unit presses have extrusion infeeds with flexo and gravure printing and coating with a multiple laminating capability. The trend in modern label press designs is towards platform presses, where print and finishing station bases and drives can accommodate a wide range of configurations. Typical platform presses could have flexo, rotary screen, gravure or offset print modules with diecutting or foil stamping units in any print position. The technologies that enable this advanced level of press flexibility are a combination of computer controls and servomotor drives. Replacement of driveshafts with individual unit servomotors makes it easier to mix different types of printing and finishing modules on a single press. The direct drives allow precise web feeding and tension control, so extending the range of materials that can be printed on a label press, from thin unsupported films to heavy folding cartonboard.

For most flexo applications that require high quality (except for labels and newspapers), the trend is toward central impression formats to provide better control of the substrate and much improved registration.

Gearless flexo presses

Most flexographic press manufacturers now offer gearless (or servo drive) printing systems. These eliminate the mechanical components of the drive train and have allowed flexo to improve its competitive position by improving quality and reducing set-up times. Previous generation presses were designed with a powerful, large main drive motor, using one or more line shafts with gearboxes linked to plate, impression and anilox cylinder drives, with other gears, pulleys and belts to power the press line. Even when brand new and in optimal condition there are detrimental mechanical artefacts, torsional instability in the line shafts and gear backlash that cause individual sections of the press to drift in relation to each other. With increasing numbers of units and stations in the press, this will lead to print quality and converting problems. The typical result will be poor control of print registration, especially during unstable conditions such as acceleration or deceleration. Error accumulates as the drive shaft lengthens with more print units, and the number of gears in the press increases. Because the machines are designed to use interchangeable print cylinders with easy replacement the number of gears increases, so increasing the potential for error. To make matters worse, under normal operating conditions, as the gears and other mechanical components begin to wear, the error gets worse and register accuracy slips even further to show up in the printed product. To compensate for these issues the type of work that can be printed tends to self-select, either with no tight register or incorporating significant spreads and chokes in prepress, which reduces the visual quality of the result.

The gearless flexo press replaces a single large drive with a number of discrete drives for individual areas of the press. Coordination and phasing are controlled by a centralised computer taking real-time feedback from encoders to determine the relative position of each unit. Technologies such as servo and vector drives are extremely accurate, providing good position, ratio and velocity control. The control systems use high-resolution encoders (more than 5 million pulses per revolution) as an integral part of the motors; powerful computerised control can communicate and duplicate the exact position of each axis in the system. This high-precision control allows good registration accuracy, so providing improved print quality. With new plate materials and imaging, linked to more accurate plate mounting, high-resolution, full-colour flexo print quality is greatly improved.

Using more motors with smaller loads reduces mechanical wear, and the control systems mean that any wear impacts can be compensated for. Removing the gears obviously eliminates gear marking, one of the most common flaws of conventional flexo. In addition, eliminating press gears means the machine is no longer tied into standard repeat lengths dictated by gear pitch, so infinitely variable repeats are now attainable merely by changing the plate to any circumference the customer desires and punching the new repeat length in to the control centre. In practice it will be a little more complicated, but the technology offers significant reductions in set-up times, particularly important for converters involved in packaging and envelope production.

As well as offering improvements in print quality, gearless presses have other advantages. A single, large-drive motor in standard geared presses is required to overcome the build-up of friction from all of the mechanical drive components. This leads to massive power demands at start-up, a major expense when there are many presses operating in a single factory. Using gearless machines eliminates much mechanical friction; individual drives reduce the overall energy consumption as the collection of smaller motors use less power. Maintenance costs and downtime can be reduced, along with the need to hold stocks of very high value parts; it is straightforward to replace the whole motor unit in the event of a fault and repair it off-line while getting the press back into operation. With individual direct drive it is easier to add components to upgrade the press with additional print and conversion units to improve their functionality.

The drive system controllers can precisely index every axis in the drive system to a predetermined point. This precision is used to pre-position the printing plates automatically during make-ready, so reducing set-up time and waste. The dynamic registration approach can also be used to expand press capabilities by accurately registering one press inline to another press or converter unit. For reprints, the set-up details are stored for call-up when the job is next run.

Register control is better with gearless presses than traditionally driven machines using position registration and increasingly dynamic registration. Position registration is the simplest method, through the synchronisation of all drives together. It fails when the substrate is dimensionally unstable – a major problem for plastics – and there is slippage between units. Optical control is necessary to achieve the highest quality – register marks are scanned and analysed to calculate the relative position of the individual colours to a master unit (or pre-printed web). There is quick feedback to make lateral and circumferential adjustments between print cylinders to keep the register within the set tolerances.

Another impact of having to use powerful computers to coordinate and control the press is improved operator ergonomics. The user interface can make press operation very straightforward by simplifying the complex machinery. The press will be represented on a touch screen, which combines the control functions and allows the operator to focus on the entire process. The performance of the press can be downloaded into an MIS and made available in real-time to customer service personnel and clients, potentially improving customer service.

Flexo printing units

The flexo print unit is a straightforward design with a liquid ink pan containing an ink metering roller that transfers the ink to an anilox roller. The anilox has a precision surface that is engraved with many tiny cells that will hold the ink from the pan roller. Excess ink is removed by a doctor blade and the anilox is in contact with the plate cylinder. The ink is transferred to the raised surface of the relief plate for direct transfer under pressure to the substrate. This basic design is capable of high-quality, fast production using many substrates, with incremental improvements made to the ink delivery and control mechanism and the anilox roller, as well as the plate or sleeve technology.

Chambered ink units

As the pressure to improve productivity increases, one development that is becoming more widely used is the chambered ink and doctor blade unit. New designs have anti-adhesive coatings to facilitate cleaning in pressurised chambers, with electro-pneumatics to set the pressures. Special chamber doctor blades move horizontally and linearly into position, achieving an accurate setting with minimum friction. Quick-release fitments do not require

FIGURE 6.35 Controlling the inking system in the flexographic process with a doctor blade (left) or a chambered ink system (right)

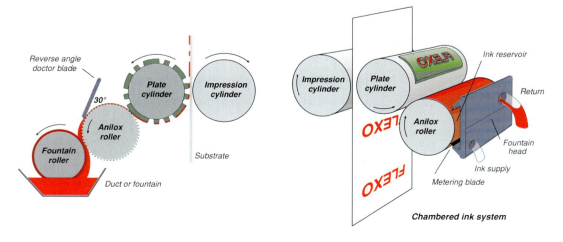

Source: Pira International Ltd

tools with trolleys to allow quick changeover. The recirculation systems use low volumes to minimise evaporation and foaming, with wash-up achieved by pumping solvent/water in using the whirlpool created inside the chamber by the higher rotation speed of the anilox roller. The expected time for a complete wash-up for one or all units is four to five minutes, depending on the ink and colour.

In attempting to control the volume of ink reaching the printing plate, the role of the doctor blade is becoming increasingly important. With harder ceramic coatings being used on the anilox, the wear characteristics of the blade are becoming an important issue to maintain consistent ink delivery. The doctor blade design is being developed, with the material and profile chosen to give a longer working life, with steel or plastic blades being replaced by more durable ceramics. Newer chambered blade systems employ double doctor blades – one on the up side and one on the down side of the doctor blade holder.

Anilox roller developments

The anilox roller picks up liquid ink in small cells engraved in the surface by capillary action when the pan roller rotates in the ink chamber. Excess ink is removed by a doctor blade so a controlled amount is transferred onto the plate surface for transfer to the substrate. Much development has aimed to improve the performance through the use of new, lightweight materials with improved surface and engraving techniques to produce high screen rulings for good ink transfer and high resolution.

New anilox roller designs have largely replaced the mechanically engraved chrome-plated steel designs. As with plate sleeves, increasingly lighter hollow steel or carbon fibre anilox sleeves are being introduced. They provide faster changeover times, greater ease of handling and storage, together with lower shipping costs when being reconditioned by the manufacturer. The rollers are coated with a layer of ceramic material applied to the surface by flame or plasma coating to provide a regular, smooth surface. The surface is then laser engraved to produce regular cells, the size, shape (normally hexagonal) and depth of which are the subject of much debate among suppliers and users.

For the best results, the higher the resolution the better. To ensure consistent coverage across all dot sizes, the anilox should be at least four to six times the screen ruling of the plate. The greater ink volume available with finer cell counts results in greater ink density delivered to the plate. However, the higher the resolution, the smaller the cell and the lower the volume of ink that can be transferred; hence the discussion and development work to refine optimal cell geometry and method of manufacture. The key issues are to ensure consistent ink transfer across all dot sizes, low wear, good release and ease of cleaning with whatever ink system is used.

The first methods used solid-state CO_2 lasers to engrave the cells. These are being replaced by YAG laser technology to take advantage of the smaller beam diameter given by the shorter wavelength. The finer beam allows smaller cells to be engraved with steeper cell walls. These deeper ink-holding cells provide higher volumes of ink at higher screen rulings, as can be seen in Figure 6.36.

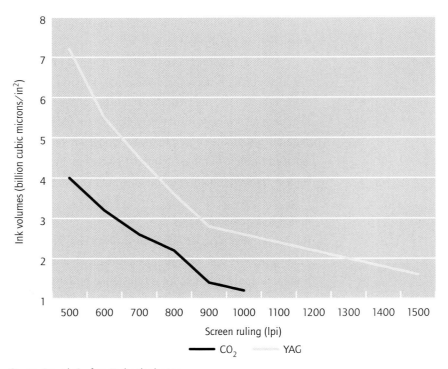

FIGURE 6.36 Relative ink volumes transferred from anilox rollers produced by CO_2 and YAG lasers at varying screen rulings

Source: Praxair Surface Technologies Inc.

YAG laser engraving significantly reduces the time to produce each cell and helps to minimise recast (the engraving process ejects vaporised material from the surface, some of which reforms unevenly around each cell), which can damage doctor blades and cause wear. The resulting smoother roll surface promises better doctoring and reduced doctor blade wear. YAG lasers are being used to produce cells that are deeper and more clearly defined. Improved ceramic coatings are also being used. These are harder and less porous, and provide new surface characteristics to improve ink release from the cells. Thermal YAG lasers can generate high-quality cells in the fine screen ranges. Each cell is thermally seared at the top of the wall to form a hard surface for the doctor blade to ride on. Fibre-optic laser technology combines the best properties of carbon dioxide and YAG lasers at high screen rulings.

Finer screen count rolls can now be used where in the past resolution was limited by available volume. Screen counts of up to 2500lpi are possible with an ink volume that makes this roll resolution viable. Printers routinely use 1400lpi, and up to 2000, up from the 1999 norm when a ruling of 800lpi was considered to be a high line count engraving. Tones print much more cleanly with these high line counts. Anilox sleeves are becoming more widely accepted in the industry.

Carbon fibre chambered systems have lighter chambers that can be handled more easily. New laser technology is being tried to replace blasting, ultrasonic and chemical cleaning systems. Laser-engraved ceramic anilox rollers are used by more than 80% of Europe's flexographic printers, although traditionalists still maintain that chrome rollers give better reproduction. Improved laser technology has given the printer an improved range of cell configurations, allowing more latitude in improving printing consistency and quality. The trend to finer screens (a greater number of cells per centimetre/inch) is forcing anilox manufacturers to meet more demanding tolerances with regard to cell volume and cell consistency. A much wider range of cell profiles and configurations is continually being demanded by printers who are fine-tuning their printing capabilities and laying down a more exact ink layer on the many substrates in use today. Gearless technology has reduced the changeover time and cost of using anilox rolls. The development of anilox sleeves should cut the weight and costs.

Inks for flexo

Presses are being configured with more print units – 10 or 12 units inline – so more colours can be printed in one pass. This places additional demands on the inks being used, which is boosting market demand for ink in terms of both volume and value. Process colour sets, some using additional inks to extend the colour gamut, are increasing, as are the number of spot colours. Base opaque white is very important in flexible packaging, and metallics and fluorescent colours are growing in popularity. More large printers are installing automated mixing and dispensing systems using computerised colour-matching technology to mix both fresh inks and inks returned from the press to give more accurate and faster colour matches, reduce waste and drive down costs.

Flexo uses low-viscosity liquid inks, pumped from a reservoir into a pan where it is picked up by a roller and transferred to the anilox roller. It is important that the viscosity is consistent and the inks are recirculated into closed chambers that reduce evaporation of solvent-based formulations and make changeovers much quicker with wash-up off-line. Modern presses use equipment to monitor the viscosity continually, with additives dosed to maintain the optimal characteristics because variation in viscosity is a major cause of colour variation. A low viscosity is needed to transfer properly, although if it is too low ink will not remain on the surface of the plate or have adequate density, and will tend to run down the sides of the image. Too high viscosity builds a halo around the printed image and can fill in halftones.

There are three main ink types: solvent based, water based and radiation drying (ultraviolet and electron beam curing). Solvent-based inks continue to dominate most market sectors; water-based and UV-curing inks are being used by an ever increasing number of printers.

Solvent-based inks give good press performance. Operators understand how to optimise productivity by adding judicious amounts of solvent to maintain runnability. The inks are fast drying on non-absorbent substrates and provide good adhesion to plastics.

The drawback with solvent inks is the environmental impact, with volatile organic compounds being released into the atmosphere and tainting of the finished product, as well as fire risks and impacts on production personnel. Ink manufacturers are developing water-based formulations that do not have the negative environmental impacts but are different to run on-press and do not give as good a printed result on many substrates.

The greatest growth is in radiation-curing inks, which is being driven by quality and productivity issues, as well as their environmental credentials. Instant-curing ink films do not spread and so exhibit low dot gain on any surface, which improves quality. Radiation-curing inks contain 100% solids; compared with water- and solvent-based inks a thinner film has to be applied to achieve the same colour. High gloss and good chemical, abrasion and heat resistance can also be achieved. Instant curing means the job can be checked for adhesion, chemical resistance and other properties immediately (except for cationic UV curing). Subsequent processing, conversion inline or rewinding will not mark, set off or block even on non-absorbent films. These properties make UV flexo especially well suited to shorter runs, where quick make-ready and low ink maintenance are key to efficient production. The latest UV flexo ink systems combine high pigmentation with low viscosity, for use with finely engraved, low-volume aniloxes of 1200lpi and higher. These inks can be pumped and are suitable for use with chambered doctor blade systems.

UV- and radiation-curing inks cost some three times the kilo price of alternative ink systems and require significant investment in lamps for curing. Generally ink mileage will be better with UV and will exhibit good press stability, with no viscosity or pH adjustment needed. UV flexo inks are normally cured after each print station, so printers must install a UV lamp at each station. Inkmakers are starting to formulate inks with tack grading to promote wet trapping on CI presses.

Heat can be a problem because much of the energy produced by a UV lamp is infrared (IR), which can be problematic for filmic substrates, causing stretch and affecting their barrier properties. Mercury vapour lamps emit less heat as infrared energy than those containing halogen compounds, but they also tend to provide a poorer cure than those with traces of metal halides. With heavy ink coverage it may be necessary to slow the web down significantly, which causes more heating.

FIGURE 6.37 Dichroic reflector system for UV curing

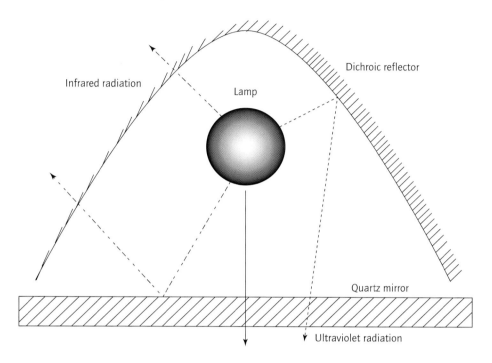

Source: Pira International Ltd

Cold-cure UV lamp systems use dichroic reflectors and quartz mirrors that remove infrared radiation from the web; these need to be well-ventilated to maintain cooling. Some CI presses for plastic film printing use special cooling impression cylinders to maintain the temperature of the film. The quartz bulb emits the IR so using a small-diameter bulb will reduce heat output; this helps placement of small interdeck curing units in presses. Cold UV curing systems to give improved results, especially with very thin extensible and delicate substrates. Press lines have a wide range of drier options, which can include cooled drums to carry heat-sensitive webs through the drying stations.

An interesting development for UV inks is the use of cationic rather than free-radical cure initiation, where polymerisation continues after the UV exposure is complete. These inks undergo little shrinkage while curing and so exhibit excellent flexibility and adhesion to many non-porous stocks. These properties would seem to make cationic UV inks ideal for flexible packaging. The raw materials used to make these inks have lower skin irritation potential than free-radical UV components and offer the possibility of formulating an FDA-compliant ink system for direct food contact applications.

Of all the inks used in flexible packaging, shrink inks have to meet some of the biggest technological requirements. They have to stick firmly to various substrates, have a high level of colour fastness and be temperature resistant as well as have shrinking properties. With all shrink inks, and the vast majority of other flexible packaging inks, however, the substrates have to be pre-treated using physical and chemical treatments such as flame, corona and plasma discharge applied to polymer surface to enhance wettability and adhesion.

Large printers are increasingly installing in-house ink-mixing systems to prepare spot colours on demand instead of relying on external suppliers and the associated high inventory costs. The systems comprise about 10–16 single pigment concentrate bases, varnish and extenders supplied in bulk linked to accurate weighing and pumped dispensers. A computer runs special colour-match prediction software with spectrophotometers to match spot colours or Pantone references that will calculate the necessary mix to achieve the desired colour on the substrate in use. A test mix of 100g can be dispensed for proofing, then production batches are mixed on demand. Use of such systems will extend as it helps the supplier secure the ink business with the converter and ensures the printer does not place unrealistic delivery demands on the supplier. In many cases an ink supplier will fund the capital cost of the system in return for a long-term contract to supply inks and additives.

FIGURE 6.38 Schematic of automatic ink dispensing system

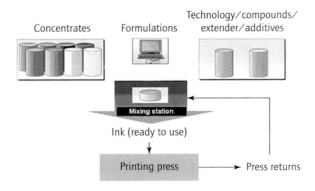

Ink supply management

Source: BASF Printing Systems

They help to minimise the inventory cost and can mix a new spot colour on demand. Less ink is wasted as only the quantity required for the job is produced, and the colour-matching system assists the printer in making the best use of left-over ink returns.

Envelope machine production

Envelope manufacture is a decoration and converting process, produced on sophisticated paper-folding and gluing machines. The printing capability tends to be secondary to the material handling, although there are developments that offer significantly improved print quality. Envelopes may be produced by converting reels of paper (web-fed) or pre-shaped litho-printed blanks (sheet-fed). During web production there are six main stages of envelope developments using variable cut-off, multi-colour flexo printing.

▶ paper is unwound and printed on both sides; first the opaque and then a number of outer colours, depending on the number of available print units;

▶ the printed web then has a window cut out and film glued into position;

▶ the shape is cut out, and the web cut into individual envelopes;

▶ seams are glued and paper folded to make the product;

▶ glue is applied to the flap, then dried;

▶ finished envelopes are delivered, counted and packed into boxes.

Gravure

Typical work

Gravure is mainly used for the printing of high-volume publications and packaging. The main types of work are:

▶ magazines and catalogues

▶ flexible packaging and confectionery wrappings

▶ folding box cartons, liquid cartons and cigarette packets

▶ postage stamps

▶ decorative coatings (wallpapers, woodfinishes).

FIGURE 6.39 Modern 4.3m publication gravure press (KBA XXL)

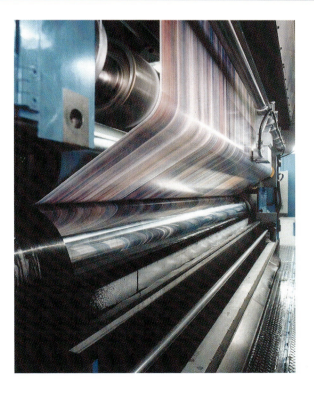

Source: KBA

Gravure is an intaglio printing process in which the image to be printed is formed by cells that are recessed into the surface of the image-carrier. Printing is achieved by flooding the surface with a liquid ink that fills the recessed image cells. The excess is scraped away by a doctor blade, leaving the surface, non-image areas, clean. The substrate is then pressed against the image-carrier's surface. Under impression, the ink in the recessed areas is drawn from the cells and transferred to the substrate.

Gravure does not have a plate system like other processes, and the image has to be formed directly in the outer copper surface of a cylinder. This makes the image-carrier expensive to produce, and the gravure process is, therefore, suited only to long production runs. Recent developments and trends have focused on digital cylinder imaging and quicker cylinder changeover on the printing machine. The main strengths of the process are:

► high-quality colour reproduction is possible on suitable substrates
► waste levels are relatively low and print quality is consistent through the production run
► the inks use relatively volatile liquids that key to a wide range of substrates and dry without requiring a lot of energy
► it is possible to print continuous designs
► high production speeds are achieved.

The main process limitations are:

► the cost of producing the gravure cylinder is significantly greater than the cost of producing plates for other processes
► the lead times for producing the cylinders are lengthy
► corrections present a problem
► the high prepress costs mean that the process is viable only for high run lengths or regularly repeating jobs in packaging
► all images have a cell pattern that is detrimental to the reproduction of line images and the legibility of text, particularly at small sizes
► print quality can be poor if paper surface roughness is not within the minimum specification.

Production of image carrier Conventional gravure is unique compared with other conventional printing processes in that it can print grey levels without using the halftone principle.

Figure 6.40 (opposite) shows an area of tonal gradation on a conventional gravure image-carrier. The printing area is divided into cells that have the same surface area but vary in depth. The variation in printed grey levels results from this depth variation: deeper cells hold more ink, printing a darker tone than shallower ones.

The methods currently used for gravure cylinder imaging provide cells that vary in area or in both area and depth. There are three options for imaging the gravure cylinder:

► chemical etching
► mechanical engraving
► direct laser engraving.

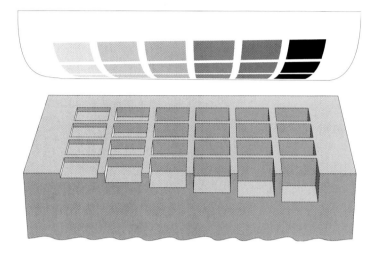

Source: Pira International Ltd

Chemical etching

The chemical etching method currently used to produce the gravure cylinder is called halftone gravure or direct transfer. It employs a photomechanical process similar to that used for platemaking by other processes and, like those, it achieves the printed grey levels by differing area (Figure 6.41). The copper surface of the gravure cylinder is coated with a light-sensitive, high-contrast photopolymer that is exposed to UV light through a film positive.

FIGURE 6.41 An image carrier produced by chemical etching – the cells differ in area

Source: Pira International Ltd

A special halftone screen has to be used to produce the dots for the film positive. It produces dots in the shadow tones and solids that never completely join together, so maintaining support for the doctor blade through to the solids. The exposure to UV light hardens the non-image areas leaving the image unaffected. On development, unexposed areas are washed away leaving areas of bare copper exposed.

The etch acts directly on the copper making the system ideal for etching machines with a one-bath etch. Some slight variation in depth does occur but the range is usually between 42 and 44 microns. The use of the halftone process simplifies and speeds up cylinder production, but sacrifices some reproduction quality associated with conventional gravure.

Electromechanical engraving

Figure 6.42 shows the basic principles of the electromechanical engraving method for producing the image on the gravure cylinder. The engraving is done by a diamond stylus that is shaped in such a way that as it digs into the rotating cylinder, it produces cells resembling inverted pyramids. Shown on the right are the inverted pyramid-shaped cells engraved by the stylus. As it is driven deeper into the copper, cells of increasing volume are produced. The stylus is followed by a diamond scraper that removes the burr produced by the gouging action. This allows 'area and depth variable' cells to be produced, as dictated by the image, at a rate normally in the region of 4000 cells per second.

FIGURE 6.42 The basic principle of the electromechanical engraving method

Stylus

Highlight

Midtone

Shadow tone

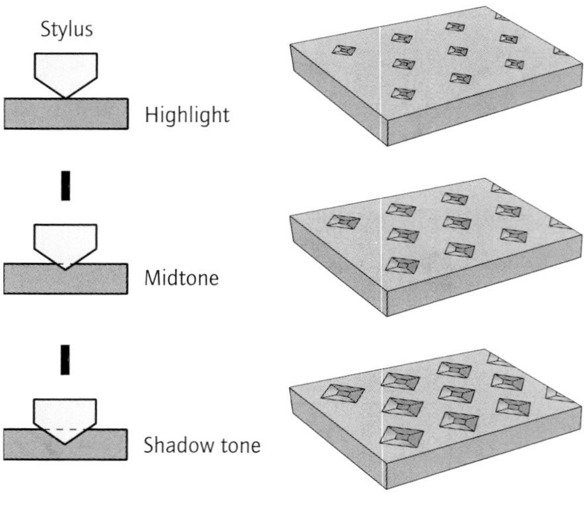

Source: Pira International Ltd

Electromechanical methods of cylinder engraving eliminate the variables associated with light-sensitive coatings and chemical etching, bringing the process of image transfer under much closer control. The engraved cells have uniform shape, with smooth walls giving improved ink transfer leading to the production of good quality prints with smooth tones.

Analogue input

This electromechanical method of cylinder imaging is commonly used with halftone screened film separations as the input. In this way it provides a form of offset-to-gravure conversion. This greatly simplifies the prepress for gravure and it allows colour proofing to be undertaken using conventional and digital prepress proofing systems.

The equipment for this comprises two cylinders, with synchronised rotation. One of these is the gravure cylinder to be engraved; the other is the scanning cylinder, on which is mounted a photographic copy of the film separations. The scanning head, containing a light source and a photocell, moves crosswise at a constant speed while the cylinders rotate. As it does so, the light beam scans the copy, and light is reflected back to the photocell. The intensity of the reflected light is proportional to the integrated density of the screened separations. After processing, these signals are used to generate electromagnetic impulses that drive the engraving head.

FIGURE 6.43 Electromechanical cylinder engraving with analysing drum

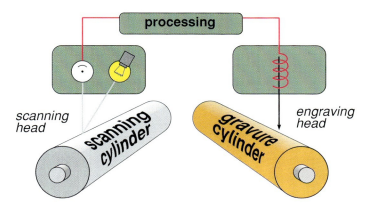

Source: Pira International Ltd

Digital input

In situations where workflow is totally digital, it is now common to bypass the analysing part of the system and feed the data directly to the engraving unit. With the wider acceptance of digital proofing, this offers a more efficient approach to gravure cylinder production.

Laser engraving of cylinders

The use of mechanical cylinder engraving has been a digital workflow that preceded litho by several years, but it still uses mechanical methods to create the cells. Many manufacturers have worked on direct laser engraving, some with plastic surfaces, with little success.

It is likely that this will change with the choice of the correct surface preparation and laser combination. Normal cylinder preparation involves electroplating nickel over the base steel cylinder, and placing a layer of copper over that. A further layer of a zinc alloy is deposited for laser engraving. This absorbs incident energy from an extremely powerful 500mW YAG laser and is vaporised, along with some of the copper underneath to produce the ink cell. After engraving, the cylinder is electroplated with a hard chrome finish, exactly like normally produced cylinders. New engravers are much faster then their mechanical predecessors and will take a share of this market.

Cylinder chromium plating

The number of copies that can be printed from a copperplated gravure cylinder is limited due to wear. It is normal for it to be chromium-plated after imaging. Under good conditions, a chromium-plated cylinder should have a life of several million impressions. An additional advantage of chromium plating is that when it does begin to wear it can be stripped off in an electrolytic bath and the cylinder replated, avoiding the need to remake. This can be done several times providing that the cylinder is taken from the printing press before the wear has extended to the copper.

Printing unit

The gravure printing unit is simple in concept. The inks are fluid and flow easily, and metering is taken care of by the volume of the cell. The gravure cylinder rotates in a liquid ink, contained in an ink duct. The cylinder then carries a relatively thick layer of ink on its surface. This layer of ink is wiped off the surface by the doctor blade leaving ink only in the cells.

FIGURE 6.44 Principle of the gravure printing unit

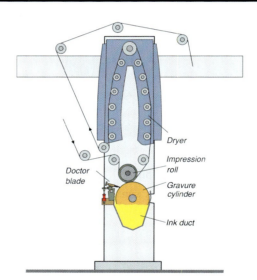

Source: Pira International Ltd

The doctor blade is normally made of thin spring steel or plastic with a thicker back-up blade behind it to provide rigidity. The edge of the blade must be perfectly smooth and free from nicks. Any nicks in the blade will leave thin streaks of ink, known as 'doctor streaks', on the cylinder that will print unwanted lines of ink on the paper. As the cylinder rotates, the doctor blade mechanism moves backwards and forwards across the face of the cylinder. This helps to spread any wear evenly over the doctor blade surface and to dislodge paper fibres or particles that may be trapped under the blade.

Pressure is needed to transfer the ink from the cells to the substrate. The substrate is fed into a nip between the gravure cylinder and an impression roller, with the cylinder and roller being squeezed together. The substrate's surface roughness and compressibility is the main factor affecting the pressure required. Unsuitable papers or insufficient pressure may result in speckle or cell skip.

To avoid or minimise this problem, a technique known as Electro Static Assisted ink transfer (ESA) is often used. This requires the rubber on the impression roll to be formulated so that it will be able to conduct an electrostatic charge. As the paper web comes into contact with the charged roller, the electrostatic field attracts the ink from the cells onto the paper.

Inks and ink drying

Gravure inks are similar to the solvent-based inks used in flexography. A wide variety of solvents can be used, the most common being toluene, xylene, petroleum fractions, various alcohols, esters and ketones. Some water-based inks are being used but not widely. Most gravure solvents are flammable and have low flash points. Safety precautions have to be taken to avoid fires, explosions and detrimental health effects. Many installations have solvent recovery or dispersal systems to remove the vapours and, where appropriate, recover the expensive solvents.

As with flexography, it is necessary to dry each ink film before the next can be printed. After printing, the paper web passes through a drying chamber where the ink is dried by removing the solvent with heated air. Rapid ink drying by solvent evaporation allows printing on non-absorbent materials without the danger of wet ink rubbing off onto rollers or sticking in the rewound reel. Thus gravure is the ideal process for a wide variety of packaging printing on films and foils. Alcohol-based inks are particularly suitable for food packaging because they are free of residual odour.

Press types

Publication presses

Figure 6.45 (page 358) shows a large gravure publication press. The paper from each printing unit passes into a drying hood where a balanced supply of air is blown onto the web to remove as much of the solvent as possible. Normally these presses consist of eight or 13 units and are used to print complete magazines or catalogue signatures. On an eight-unit press, four colours can be printed on both sides of a web of paper.

The printing cylinders can be up to 3m wide, although the most popular width is in the region of 2–2.5m. The cylinder circumferences typically provide four or six pages around the cylinder (normal circumference being about a 1000mm or 1500mm, respectively). Thus a 2.4m wide eight-unit press can print 64 A4 pages (short grain) in full-colour using a four-pages-around cylinder or 96 pages with the six-pages-around cylinder. At a web speed of 15m/s, more than 54,000 64-page magazine signatures can be printed in an hour. Larger, faster models are continually being introduced to the market.

FIGURE 6.45 Schematic of a gravure publication press

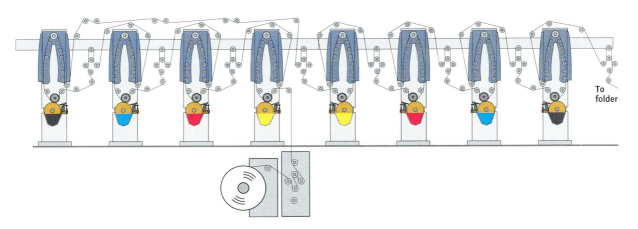

To
folder

Source: Pira International Ltd

After printing, the web is split into ribbons (in Figure 6.45 there would be eight) and folded into the correct pagination. It is then either collated, stitched and trimmed offline; or it might be stitched and trimmed inline, with the press delivering the finished product.

Packaging presses

A wide range of gravure presses is used for packaging printing. The webwidths cover a range from 350–1400mm and there are special presses built for very narrow web-widths that can be as low as 50mm. The cylinders on a gravure press are not geared together and usually the printing cylinder is the only one being driven. This means that presses can be built to easily accommodate cylinders of different diameters. This is an important point in packaging printing as it enables different print lengths to be printed on one press. For high-volume products, where the pack design does not change, cylinders can be re-used many times defraying the high prepress cost and speeding up changeover and set up.

A gravure press for flexible packaging would normally be fitted with a rewind as the product would be supplied in reel form. For carton packaging, the press would incorporate a number of additional inline finishing operations. These may include rotary embossing, rotary diecutting and creasing.

Sheetfed gravure presses

Most gravure presses are web-fed rotary. There are, however, a few sheetfed presses in use. They are mainly used for high-value speciality carton package printing and labels.

Silk-screen printing

Typical work

Screen print is a versatile printing process used for many applications not normally thought of as printing. The main types of work are:

► point-of-sale (POS) display materials
► posters, window stickers and signs
► plastic cards
► fabrics, transfers and garments
► bottles and other containers
► compact discs
► wall and floor coverings.

Screen printing is a development of the stencilling process. Images printed by simple stencilling are encumbered by the connecting links that are required to hold the elements of the images together. In screen printing, a mesh is used to support the stencil allowing the connecting links to be eliminated and a more natural printed image is achieved.

Figure 6.46 shows the basic principle employed to transfer the image. The prepared screen is placed over the material to be printed and a fluid ink poured into one end of it. The ink is spread over the screen and forced through the open mesh areas with a rubber or plastic squeegee.

FIGURE 6.46 The principle of screen printing

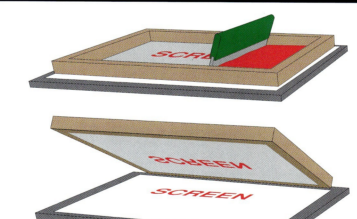

Source: Pira International Ltd

Screen printing differs from the other printing processes in a number of ways. It is the only process that prints through the image carrier rather than from it. The screen acts as an ink reservoir, or duct, for a working supply of ink, while other processes need independent inking systems preceding the printing stage.

The main strengths of the process are:

► it can print intense colours with good covering power and opacity

► it can print onto almost any substrate

► it can print onto curved, uneven and fragile surfaces

► it is possible to print thick, opaque ink films

► it can print unusual ink formulations and coatings.

The main process limitations are:

► print production speeds are slow

► it is difficult to reproduce fine detail and small type

► halftone reproduction requires coarse screen rulings.

The screen

The screen has two principal functions:

► to provide a supportive structure for the stencil

► to meter the ink film deposit.

Screens are made by fixing a fine mesh material over a wooden or metal frame. The mesh is tensioned to precise specifications before fixing using mechanical or pneumatic tensioning devices. This ensures even tension and controlled dimensional stability.

Mesh materials

Modern screen meshes are monofilament materials made from single, smooth, wire-like threads. The threads are woven together to form a regular and even gauze structure that is important for optimum ink transfer and easy screen cleaning. Nylon and polyester are the two most commonly used mesh materials. Nylon is used for many applications where dimensional stability and close registration are not critical requirements. It is extremely durable and commonly used for high volume production of single colour work, particularly in container printing and other three-dimensional objects or uneven surfaces. Monofilament polyester mesh has the same structural qualities as nylon, but it is more dimensionally stable. It is more widely used for this reason, especially in applications where fine registration tolerance in multi-colour printing is required.

The screen may also be made from stainless steel wire mesh. The relatively high cost (as much as five times that of polyester) limits its use to applications where the following requirements are essential:

► screen durability

► resistance to abrasion from inks

► heavy ink deposits

► extreme dimensional stability

► reproduction of fine image detail.

Mesh grade and mesh count

Mesh materials are classified by mesh count and grade. The selection of an appropriate grade of mesh material with a suitable thread count is important as it determines the:

- ▶ ink film thickness that will be achieved
- ▶ stencil detail that will be possible
- ▶ support given to the stencil.

The mesh count refers to the number of threads woven into the mesh. Screen mesh materials are available in mesh counts (depending on grade) from 12–200 threads/cm. As a general rule, the lower the mesh count the less support there is for the stencil detail and the heavier the ink deposit will be. The mesh grading relates to thread thickness. The grade of the thread determines the dimensional stability of the mesh and its overall calliper, that in turn influences ink film thickness. Screen meshes are available in four grades, as shown in Table 6.2.

TABLE 6.2 Mesh grades

Grade	Thread	Typical mesh open area
S light grade	thin	50–70%
M medium grade	thick	30–40%
T thick grade	thick	35–40%
HD heavy duty		20–35%

Source: Pira International Ltd

Figure 6.47 shows three grades of mesh, all with the same thread count. As can be seen, the thickness of the mesh thread determines the size of the mesh openings. As the mesh count increases the effective print area is reduced until a point is reached where the openings are insufficient to allow the ink to pass through.

FIGURE 6.47 Three grades of mesh, all with the same thread count

 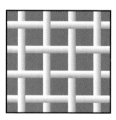 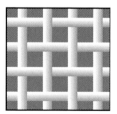

Source: Pira International Ltd

Stencil making

Stencils can be made in several ways, and the method used will depend on image and print run requirements. For simple bold line work, such as large-format signs or posters, stencils can be cut in special water or solvent-soluble laminate film. The stencil is transferred onto the screen and fixed with heat or with a water or ketone solvent. But most stencils are made using photomechanical methods that are necessary when producing images with any intricacy and fineness of detail such as fine line or halftone work. New direct digital stencil production methods are being introduced that will speed up and simplify the process.

There are a number of slightly different photo-stencil systems in current use. Choice is determined by image and production requirements such as:

▶ fineness of image detail

▶ print run length

▶ ink type.

Indirect photo-stencils

Indirect stencils are similar to cut stencils in that they are imaged and processed before being transferred to the mesh. They comprise a presensitised gelatine or polymer film coating on a polyester base. The film is exposed to ultraviolet light in contact with a film positive image. The exposure level is set to ensure that the non-image areas are made insoluble, but with a partially soluble top. When this is processed the unexposed areas dissolve into solution, leaving the exposed areas to form the stencil.

The stencil is then mounted onto the screen, its partially exposed soft sticky surface readily adheres to the mesh. After drying, the supporting film base is stripped away, leaving the stencil firmly fixed to the underside of the screen.

TABLE 6.3 The mesh count and grade for typical applications	
Mesh count and grade for typical applications	
34T to 49T: sports and travel bags, coarse fabrics, denim	
49T to 77T: rough absorbent surfaces textiles, T-shirts, flags and pennants	
77T to 100T: posters, point-of-sale display signs, large lettering, opaque inks, coarsely pigmented inks, fluorescent and metallic colours, textured or grained surfaces, overprint varnishing	
100T to 120T: halftone screens up to 26 lines/cm, fine line/lettering instrumentation, sign work, self-adhesive labels/stickers	
130T to 165M: fine line halftone up to 54 lines/cm	

Source: Pira International Ltd

Direct emulsion photostencils

This type of stencil encapsulates the screen mesh providing greater resistance to physical stressing and abrasion caused during long run production. The stencils are made by coating the screen with a photosensitive polymer emulsion. When the coated screen is dry it is exposed to ultraviolet light in contact with a film positive image. The exposed areas of the coating become insoluble in water. After exposure, the screen is sprayed with water, causing the unexposed image areas to dissolve away and leaving the exposed areas to form the non-image stencil.

Direct/indirect photo-stencils

This system offers the advantages of the two former systems by providing the durability of a direct emulsion stencil with the reproduction fidelity of an indirect stencil. Stencils are made by mounting a precision-coated polymer film onto the underside of the screen with a light-sensitive bonding emulsion. The emulsion is applied through the screen using a rounded squeegee blade. It is absorbed by the polymer film that is then drawn into the mesh. When dry, the film and emulsion become one, bonded through the mesh. The film base is then removed leaving a flat under-surface to the stencil, which allows improved printing fidelity. The screen is then exposed and processed in the same way as a direct emulsion screen.

FIGURE 6.48 Two photo-stencil making processes: indirect (left) and direct (right)

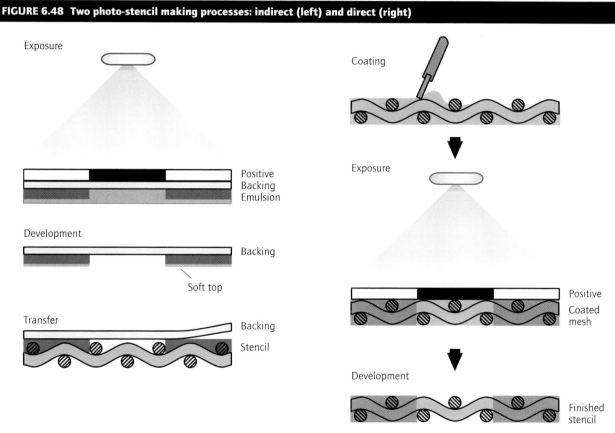

Exposure

Positive
Backing
Emulsion

Development

Backing

Soft top

Transfer

Backing

Stencil

Coating

Exposure

Positive
Coated
mesh

Development

Finished
stencil

Source: Pira International Ltd

Capillary direct film photo-stencils

This is a widely-used system that provides the qualities associated with the direct/ indirect stencil with a more simple and cheaper method of application. It comprises a precision photopolymer film coating on a polyester base. The film is hygroscopic and is drawn into the screen by the application of a fine mist water spray through the mesh. When the film is dry, its base is stripped away, and then the screen is imaged in exactly the same way as the direct/indirect screen.

Alternative imaging methods

The photosensitive stencil-forming emulsion can be exposed using other methods. For large-format stencils, which are used for posters, vehicle livery and signs, the photosensitive stencil coating can be exposed by projection. This allows cheaper, relatively small format films to be used for the imaging of big stencils.

The imaging of stencils is also possible from digital data indirectly using a data-driven inkjet printer and by direct laser exposure of the photosensitive stencil emulsion. The ScreenJet system prints a positive image directly onto the photosensitive emulsion, which was previously applied to the mesh using one of the techniques described. The inkjet printed image takes over the function of the film positive, but there is no need for a contact frame as the screen is simply exposed to a UV light source.

Printing machines

There is a wide range of screen printing machinery indicating a considerable diversity of process applications. The following classification provides a guide to the most commonly used forms of machinery.

Flatbed hinged frame

These machines are designed on the principle of the hand-bench. The screen is hinged at the rear of the flat printing base. The screen frame carriage is mechanically synchronised with the squeegee and flo-coater carriage. On all screen printing machines except rotary screen, the ink is returned to the pre-printing position by a metal scraper-blade, technically referred to as the flo-coater. It is positioned behind the squeegee. The angle, pressure and speed of both flo-coater and squeegee blade can be adjusted to suit inking requirements.

FIGURE 6.49 A flatbed hinged frame

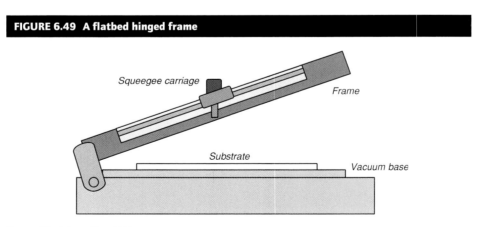

Source: Pira International Ltd

The printing cycle begins with the screen open for the substrate to be fed into the lays. The screen closes and the squeegee stroke begins, forcing the ink across the screen and through the stencil onto the substrate beneath. At the end of the squeegee passage, the blade lifts and the flo-coater drops to return the ink for the next print stroke charging the open areas of the screen as it does so. The screen opens during the flo-coater stroke for the substrate to be removed from the printing base to the dryer.

The production output of these machines can vary between 300 and 1200 impressions per hour (iph) depending on the degree of automation. A wide range of machine sizes and formats is available, from precision circuit machines with print areas of 390×510mm to the jumbo machines with print areas of 2×3m.

Flatbed vertical lift

These machines allow the screen to rise vertically from the printing base, remain horizontal throughout the printing cycle and allow for more efficient inking control. The most basic machines feature a reciprocating printing base that slides from beneath the screen to receive the substrate, back again for printing and out once more for delivery to the dryer. A more automatic version has a stationary printing base, with the substrate being picked up from a pre-register position by grippers. Output on these machines depends on the degree of automation but will range from 1000–2000 iph. Machines are available in a range of sizes and formats with print areas as small as 400×600mm or as big as 2000×4000mm.

FIGURE 6.50 A flatbed vertical lift machine

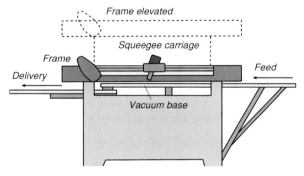

Source: Pira International Ltd

Cylinder-bed presses

Here the substrate is supported on a cylindrical vacuum bed and the screen reciprocates above with the stationary squeegee and flo-coater printing and charging the screen in sequence. The machines are usually automated with the substrate fed to the vacuum cylinder from a deep pile feeder. The suction from the cylinder holds the substrate down during the printing cycle and releases it onto the delivery tapes. It is then transported to the dryer as the vacuum cylinder receives the next sheet. These machines are the fastest sheetfed machines available. Speeds are determined by the size of the machine, with a maximum output on the smaller format machines of 6000iph and average speeds of about 3500iph. Sizes vary from print areas of 550×750mm to 1200×1600mm.

FIGURE 6.51 A cylinder-bed press

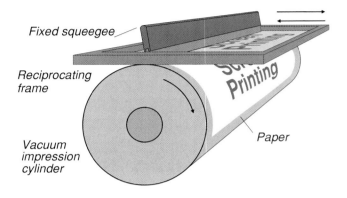

Fixed squeegee

Reciprocating frame

Vacuum impression cylinder

Paper

Source: Pira International Ltd

Container printing machines

These machines operate on the cylinder-bed principle. The curved surface of the container takes the place of the vacuum cylinder and is supported beneath by roller bearings. The printing action is the same as the cylinder press, and the screen reciprocates over the rotating container as the stationary squeegee forces the ink through the screen.

Rotary screen

These machines are used exclusively in high-volume production of printed textiles, scratch-off tickets, floor and wall coverings. Some small-format label machines have the facility for rotary print heads to be used in combination with other processes. The operational principle is different to that of conventional screen printing. Here the screen is a seamless perforated cylinder made from a light metal foil. Two metal tension rings (mandrills) are fitted at each end. These rings also accommodate the hollow squeegee carriage through which ink is pumped during the printing cycle. As the screen rotates, the stationary squeegee blade forces the printing medium through the screen apertures onto the moving web beneath.

FIGURE 6.52 A rotary screen press

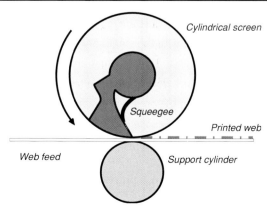

Cylindrical screen

Squeegee

Printed web

Web feed

Support cylinder

Source: Pira International Ltd

Carousel machines

Based upon the hinged frame principle, these machines were originally designed for multi-colour printing on T-shirts. They consist of multiple printing bases or garment platens that can be rotated around a central pivot. Above each platen is a printing head (also rotational). This consists of a squeegee and flo-coater integrally driven by the screen carriage mechanism. The printing cycle begins with a garment being slid over the platen. The first screen is lowered in register with the garment/platen and the first colour is printed. The screen is then raised and the second screen rotated into the printing position (registered over the garment/platen), the printing stroke completed and so on until all the colours (up to eight wet-on-wet on some machines) are printed. After printing, the garment is removed from the platen and transported to the dryer.

Screen ink drying

Ink film deposits produced by screen printing are in the order of 10–15 microns, and much thicker than for other print processes. The inks must be force dried in order to achieve reasonable production rates. The four drying methods currently employed are:

▶ wicket or rack drying – used with evaporative solvent- and water-based inks;

▶ jet air drying – used with evaporative solvent- and water-based inks;

▶ infrared drying – used with inks and textiles dyes requiring curing with infra-red radiation;

▶ ultraviolet drying – used with inks containing special reactive photopolymer resins that dry rapidly on exposure to intense UV radiation.

Hybrid printing

Until quite recently there was little overlap between different printing processes. A litho machine used litho technology; a gravure machine only gravure. In the conversion industries that use inline printing the manufacturers did not have the same attachment to a particular method of print. They developed machines that used the most appropriate technology to produce the final product, particularly in packaging and labelling applications.

The converters had to source their gravure cylinders and flexo plates from their prepress supplier. As few had the technology internally it was not a significant issue for them to mix processes where appropriate. Flexographic printing is the most widely used with other processes. Most flexo print is produced by converters for packaging, labelling and envelope applications. A key strength of flexographic printing is that it can be integrated into dedicated conversion lines to produce in a single pass. In many cases the printing is an adjunct to the manufacture and as new decoration, barrier or security functions become available they are often integrated into the line. This trend will continue and grow significantly in future as converters seek opportunities to add value to their production.

The label industry is probably the most advanced user of hybrid printing methods, with many unit presses combining litho, flexo, gravure, silk screen and digital capabilities in a single line, often with hologram and varnish application and diecutting.

Many label unit presses incorporate digital print units; Nilpeter has an integrated Xeikon unit, Mark Andy offers the :Dotrix and Jetrion 3025 inkjet engines as an optional module. These are used for narrow-web applications. Mark Andy offers all as integral parts of its unit presses, together with specialist applicators, slitters, coaters and foilers, as required. Integrating these specialist finishing features will increase with hot and cold foiling, diecutting and RFID tag insertion capability.

Hot and cold foiling

Hot foil stamping of plain and patterned foils is on the increase, with hologram applications growing as the need for security increases. Hot foiling is unsuitable for many plastic substrates and use of cold foiling is growing. The cold foiling process typically involves applying a UV-cured pattern adhesive to a film web and then pressing it against the donor web. Foil is transferred from the donor web to the pattern adhesive under pressure in a less harsh method.

Diecutting

Diecutting is important in carton, label, envelope and tissue production. The use of traditional cutting tools is being joined by lower cost foil dies for paper, where the die can be mounted in position on carrier cylinders very quickly, which reduces machine downtime during adjustment. The cutting performance is the same as for traditional tools, although they generally have a shorter life span. Laser diecutting has a number of potential advantages, including fast turnaround, no changeover time and no die costs. Unique shapes can be produced with cutting speeds of up to 150m/min. As the economics for short runs depend primarily on the changeover time taken for the cutting matrix rather than print speed, laser cutting can significantly speed up changeovers.

New technology for pattern cutting uses computer-controlled lasers with manufacturers demonstrating the capability on lightweight paper and plastic substrates. This will develop and become important in prototyping and short-run applications. The technology is still very expensive and does not work on all materials, but this will change and laser diecutting will become more widespread.

RFID and specialist tags

Radio frequency identification (RFID) tags are growing quickly in all packaging applications as there are significant logistical benefits in their use. Many flexo presses will have the capability of inserting and testing supplied RFID tags, with inline printing of RFID tags taking over from pre-printed applicators in the longer term.

In commercial printing the use of hybrid systems is growing. In litho, many sheetfed machines use flexo varnishing and coating units as well as specialist printing units, and there is a trend towards incorporating a digital printing capability. Heidelberg has a relationship with Domino to distribute inkjet machines through its sales channels in certain markets. The company, a sheetfed machine with Domino Bitjet technology, which allows variable data printing for addresses and personalising text inline. Xaar and MAN Roland have a joint collaboration to explore and develop digital inkjet printing systems for coating applications to be used in traditional offset printing presses. KBA bought Metronic, a specialist manufacturer of inkjet printing systems to expand its product range into new, high-potential markets. Web offset printers have long used Domino and Videojet heads for text printing, and wider-format Kodak VersaMark heads to offer more sophisticated inline personalisation.

Agfa is becoming a major player in inkjet printing. The company believes its inkjet strategy will give it a new platform for sustained profitable growth. Agfa made two interesting product announcements at the FESPA show in Munich at the end of May 2005. It is working with Xaar on high-quality print heads and in partnership with Mutoh for wide-format inkjet printing with the Anapurna system. The company also launched its hybrid silk screen/inkjet machine for packaging applications, the M-Press.

FIGURE 6.53 Agfa/Thieme M-Press

Source: Agfa

The M-Press is a high-speed flatbed inkjet and screen press that has been co-developed with Thieme in response to customer demand for economical, high run-length digital printing. The device is a modular design, which allows the multi-colour inkjet unit to be linked with Thieme 5000 XL series screen printing modules. The M-Press can be configured into a fully automatic hybrid printing line. A white coating can be applied by silk screen process; this can then be overprinted in process colours and varnished, or a spot colour applied, in a single pass. It is one of the first launches to offer users the versatility of screen printing and the productivity of an automatic inline solution.

Die-stamping Die-stamping is the traditional method of producing a relief image on paper or board. Its modern counterpart is thermography, but die-stamping is considered to give a superior finish, embossing both sides of the sheet. It also has the capability to be used for multi-colour images in close register. When used without printing ink (or blind) a simple embossed logo can give a unique effect to notepaper.

The process

A steel die is made photographically, or by etching, engraving or manually. Methods of die-production can be similar to letterpress blockmaking with the image intaglio and not in relief (a female die). Separate dies are made for each colour required. In the die-stamping press, the die is positioned face uppermost and the paper for printing is placed between the die and its counterpart – the male die made from card. Impression has the effect of forcing the paper into the female die; the force impression being adjusted until the male produces the finest detail from the female die. Inking of the die takes place before each impression. Power presses are fitted with automatic feed and inking, and printed sheets may be dried by an infrared unit. Blind embossing will normally be done on a cutting and creasing platen.

Applications

The normal application of die-stamping is to produce prestige letterheads, paperback book covers, packaging, note papers, envelopes, invitation cards, wedding stationery and cartons. Multi-colour work using metallic foils uses this process. The best paper and board for die-stamping contain rag fibres, but a suitable finish can be obtained on most paper substrates.

Thermography

Thermography is a cheaper alternative to die-stamping. It produces a raised image, usually glossy, but without the embossed image on the reverse of the sheet.

The process

The thermographic print is produced by dusting a freshly printed image (in the required colour) with a transparent thermosetting powder. The powder sticks to the wet ink and the rest is removed (usually by vacuum). The sheet is passed under a heater, which softens the powder and causes it to swell slightly to produce a relief image. High-gloss, semi-gloss and matt finishes are available. The amount of relief given to the image can be adjusted by selecting different size granules. The prints are normally produced by offset lithography.

Limitations

Hand dusting is the most common method used but is naturally slow and print runs are limited. Automatic systems are faster when the thermographic unit is inline with the printing press. Multi-colour thermography is in its infancy. Soft absorbent papers are not recommended. Hard-sized papers and rag-based papers hold their colour better under heat than papers containing wood pulp. This is especially true where large solids (which require more heat) are included in the image. Cast-coated papers may distort under heat, but relative success may be obtained with one-sided cast-coated board. Ivory and matt boards are recommended. Considerable difficulty has been encountered with the use of thermographed business stationery in laser printers where the heat softens the thermosetting powder. There is much development around one-set resin powder for thermography to overcome this problem.

Digital printing

The nature of printing and publishing is changing as the age of digital information develops and matures. The importance of customer service is higher than it ever has been, with consumer demands driving the move toward ever shorter runs and faster turnaround of jobs. All commercial printing is digital at some stage in its genesis until a plate or cylinder is produced to carry the image, and a growing proportion only becomes analogue after the printing process. This is produced by digital printing methods using predominantly laser printing and inkjet technologies for variable data applications, and using on-press imaging to develop offset printing.

Digital printing is now an integral component of the printing market – it is one of the key technologies used in printing today. This represents a huge shift from conventional production over the past 15 years, radically changing the nature of the printing industry. The increased computer power in imaging systems allowed this change to happen, but did not instigate it. The new technology was an enabler, allowing operations to provide additional and new products and services. Digital print is successful because it provides solutions to new consumer demands:

▶ very short run high-quality print, economically
▶ customised and personalised print.

Individual consumer demands are becoming increasingly exacting – consumers have come to expect what they want, at the lowest price, and when they want it. This is a fact of business life for all industries including printing. It is the end consumer that is driving industries to provide better products and services, faster, and at lower cost. This driver will not go away. These changes are occurring because the requirements of the end consumer are changing. Demand for customised and personalised products and services is a key driver for the future of printing. New technology is developing that allows consumers to achieve these requirements across all sectors. Conventional printing is being subsumed into a wider communications process as a result.

FIGURE 6.54 Processes involved in conventional and digital printing

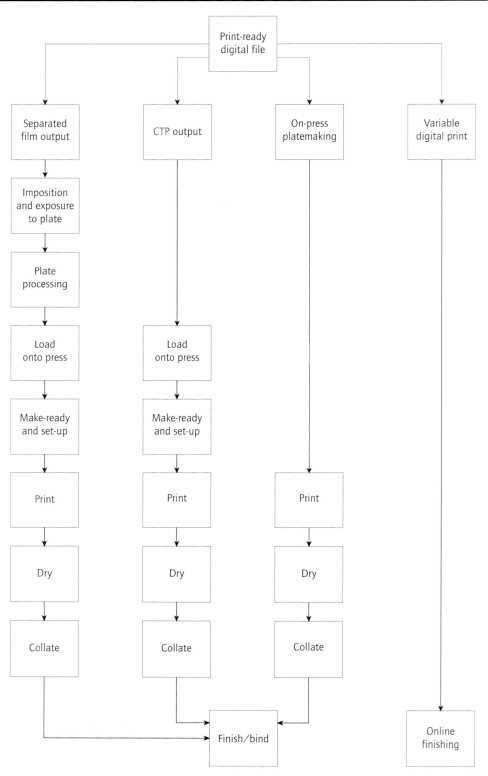

Digitisation   Creating and storing information digitally has been a fundamental change, with significant implications for every business. Information is increasingly key to both human society in general and to business. Digitisation of information – the ability to store, process, manipulate, analyse, transmit and display information via computers – is changing the way we live and work, and the way business is run and organised.

Digital printing allows the production of short-run, personalised single-copy printing to be technically and economically feasible. It is because the information to be printed is digital that the concept works. The real power of digital print is in the enabling ability of the underlying IT. When information is digitised, it becomes a resource to be used over and over again – perhaps combined with any other digital information; it can be chopped up and used in bits, and it can be distributed to any location.

Digital information can be stored, copied and transferred with no loss of quality, easily and almost instantaneously. However, the human beings who use this information have not changed quite so much. The key issue for the future is not 'how much more information' or 'how fast can it be processed', but 'how can this information be of value'. Digital printing helps add value to information for consumers in the following ways:

► movement to smaller volume, high added-value products and services

► decrease in the proportion of product value derived from 'manufacturing'

► increase in the proportion of product value derived from service

► it requires greater commitment to customer service

► it enables the supplier to provide higher added value for any product or service.

These are the key benefits driving companies to invest in digital printing technology. The significance of digital print, however, is that it encourages and enables:

► change in workflow, since it is one of the computer-to-plate (CTP) technologies;

► change in industry structure, since it simplifies operation to the point that non-printing companies may easily adopt it.

Digital printing technology is being increasingly adopted across most sectors of the printing industry. Some is a direct replacement for existing conventional technology, where digital proves more economical or offers faster turnaround. Other installations produce new products and services for their clients, opening new market opportunities.

Conventional offset litho (as well as flexo and screen printing) used film separations to produce plates. The use of film has been overcome through the widespread adoption of CTP technology. Depending on the degree of automation involved, the platesetter can prepare a punched, press-ready plate for a modern offset press to load automatically, significantly reducing the make-ready time. Other systems still require a plate to be processed and punched manually, with a normal press make-ready to set up a new job. CTP provides first-generation images to the plate, and practical experience shows the improved quality of the plate helps to reduce set-up times significantly.

With digital on-press imaging of plates there is no separate requirement for plate exposure, processing and loading onto the press; the imaging is performed in situ for all colours in a single stage, allowing the press minder to look at materials and other tasks.

The direct process sets the press and, using lithographic inks and materials, print is carried out producing the sheets in the same manner as conventional processes. Jobs dry, are folded, collated, bound and finished when all sections are printed. There are significant reductions in the different stages necessary to produce a finished product.

In the case of variable data printing (both mono and colour), all of these stages can be combined into a single operation. With the correct on-line finishing units, a collated multi-part book, including the cover, can be delivered collated and finished seconds after sending the print-ready file to the machine.

It was the potential of eliminating these costly, time-consuming stages that provided the impetus for suppliers to develop digital printing and for printers, prepress companies and even print buyers to install and use the technology. This book aims to introduce the reader to the reasons behind digital printing's success, examining markets, products, costs, prepress and the technologies involved. It provides an overview of the major suppliers and presses available, and offers some predictions about how digital printing may develop, and some of the new opportunities that digital printing provides for improving existing supply chains for some printed products.

Context of digital printing

Print has developed to produce many copies at a low unit cost. The preoccupation with unit cost has driven the industry for many years and is incredibly difficult to change. But change it must, because the market demands so. It is the wishes of the end users of printed products that drive the industry, and the end users are no longer content to be treated as part of a large group, but instead wish to be treated as individuals. The traditional strength of print may be a concern because the generic document may not be enough to engage individuals.

Conventional print has changed, with the average run length of most print jobs declining over the past 20 years. Prepress and make-ready developments have helped to make short runs economical, and manufacturers have harnessed innovative technologies to enable the single-copy print run, personalised for an individual consumer. This is the wider context of the development of digital printing, making short run and customised print economically viable.

The modern print industry is split into two camps. In one camp visionaries proclaim the death of conventional print. They are laughed at by many in the traditional, capital-intensive industry. Pundits have forecast the potential of inkjet for many years, but it has not yet replaced web offset or gravure presses. Digital print will probably not replace high-volume production, at least for many years yet, but it can be a useful addition to a printing company's armoury to increase the range of products and services offered.

Commercial digital printing developed from the invention of the laser printer at Xerox PARC (Palo Alto Research Center) in the 1970s. These mono engines have been producing enormous quantities of personalised print, driven by the IT departments of financial institutions and utility suppliers to generate bills and statements for customers. This 'production' printing is separate to the general print market. Particular emphasis is placed on document integrity and production rather than aesthetic quality of the print. The data to drive the printers are generally line text data formats of low resolution and limited typographic capability. This 'mainframe' or 'production' printing environment has seen significant change, as engines have increased in speed and quality by incorporating PDF or PostScript datastreams and increasing resolution capabilities. The graphics sector is taking advantage of the high-quality capabilities (achieving and surpassing offset) of print engines, offering economical short runs and personalisation capability.

TABLE 6.4 Timeline in the development of digital printing

1937	Chester Carlson patents xerography, electrostatic imaging
1947	Transistor developed at Bell Labs by Shockley et al.
1949	Elmquist applies for patent for inkjet
1950	First commercial xerographic equipment
1951	UNIVAC (Universal Automatic Computer) is the first commercial computer
	Siemens produces first commercial inkjet printer, Siemens Elema Oscilomink, based on Elmquist's patent
1953	IBM introduces its first computer model, the 701
1957	First dot-matrix printer
1958	Schawlow and Townes discover lasers
1959	IBM introduces second-generation computer with transistors replacing tubes
	Xerox introduces the first commercial copier, the 914
1963	Digital Equipment Corp. introduces first minicomputer, the PDP-8
1970	Xerox establishes the Palo Alto Research Centre (PARC)
1973	Xerox PARC develops the Alto, first computer with a graphical user interface, WYSIWYG editing, bitmap display, windows and mouse
1975	IBM launches laser printer
1976	IBM launches first inkjet printers
1977	Apple and Microsoft started
	First high-speed laser printer, the Xerox 9700
1981	IBM markets first personal computer
	Canon launches first bubblejet printer
1982	Adobe Systems founded and launches PostScript
1984	Apple releases the Macintosh with graphical user interface
1985	Adobe launches PostScript, with the Laserwriter and Aldus PageMaker software, forming the beginnings of desktop publishing
1986	Xerox launches first multi-beam laser
1990	Xerox launches the DocuTech
1992	First commercial on-press imaging, Heidelberg GTO-DI, installed
1993	Indigo and Agfa (Xeikon) launch competitive high-quality digital colour presses
2001	PDF workflows widely established
	Dotcom bubble bursts
2004	High-quality colour digital presses are capable of 267ppm, lower quality inkjet at 2,000ppm. High-quality inkjet for packaging capable of 1,200–2,000m²/hr
2005	Fastest inkjet system, Inca Digital FastJet, capable of 300dpi at 6,000m²/hr

Source Pira International Ltd

Over the next five years, the markets (packaging, short run, print-on-demand and personalisation) for digital print will all increase significantly. Pira market research (*The Future of European Printing*, 2005) provides the data for Table 6.5, showing the forecast market shares of the major print technologies (excluding packaging) to 2010.

TABLE 6.5 Split of print processes across Europe, 1999–2009 (%)			
	1999	**2004**	**2009**
Sheetfed	21.3%	21.2%	21.0%
Heatset	20.5%	21.0%	20.9%
Coldset	19.7%	17.9%	16.8%
All offset	61.5%	60.1%	58.8%
Gravure	13.4%	11.9%	11.0%
Flexo	12.2%	12.7%	13.2%
Letterpress	0.4%	0.3%	0.2%
Digital	7.1%	8.6%	9.5%
Other	5.4%	6.4%	7.3%

Source: Pira International Ltd

Digital print's share is higher if the volume of material printed at home, in offices and in retail environments is taken into account – a significant leakage of jobs that would previously have been printed commercially. Individual market share forecasts differ, but all follow the same general trend: digital printing will increase market share at the expense of other technologies. However, there are also new applications providing market opportunities and developing the existing, well-established production printing sector. Digital technology links printing into a continuous pyramid of quality and productivity, from home inkjet printer to high-quality contract proofers; from networked office laser printer, to high-volume mono production engines; from low-resolution inkjet marking, to high-volume colour inkjet printing; from variable colour engines approaching offset quality, to on-press imaging. Although the markets tend to be categorised differently, there is a continuum, with the same engines being used for widely different applications.

Users adopt digital printing for one of two reasons:

► to improve the effectiveness of existing processes, i.e. higher quality at lower cost with faster turnaround;

► to communicate with consumers in new ways.

In some cases both of the above may apply. If any new technology does not offer these advantages it will not replace conventional printing, which is developing to improve its competitive position. The main benefits of new technologies will be felt by the print buyer and consumer rather than by the printer himself, who will have to be increasingly competitive.

There are two categories of digital printing:

▶ CTP (computer-to-press), on-press direct imaging (DI) systems, where the plate is exposed in situ;

▶ variable data printing, where the image is formed afresh for each print; applications may be for totally variable production or for short runs.

In variable data printing there is no image-carrying master; each print is formed afresh as part of the production cycle. For short-run applications, the high-quality graphic file is prepared and RIPed (raster image processed), with data either repeatedly sent to the engine or buffered in memory for each print. A significant advantage of variable data printing is the ability to print collated and completed document sets in a single pass, rather than having to have a separate collation stage. This is particularly useful for book printing, or any application where a single pass to produce a complete product is advantageous.

FIGURE 6.55 Collation capabilities of digital printing systems

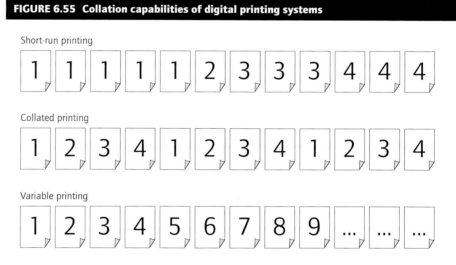

Short-run printing

Collated printing

Variable printing

Source: Pira International Ltd

Sophisticated personalisation capabilities are increasingly common: more than simply a name and salutation, they include complicated variable content in high-quality, colour products. There is much development in producing powerful, easy-to-operate front-end systems to generate variable data jobs effectively. Database systems will be linked to asset management and automatic make-up, driving powerful PPML (personalised page mark-up language)-compliant RIPs to image on fast colour presses. For straightforward text changes, variable printing systems have been used for mono and highlight colour work in direct mail, statement and billing applications for many years, using proprietary systems from the mainframe printing environment. The increases in computer power allow individual pages to be composed on the fly from a database of graphic elements.

Digital printing is a large, growing and established business. Pira forecasts estimate the European digital print market at over €10.9 billion in 2004, growing to €13.1 billion by 2009. As already mentioned, these figures are much higher when non-commercial print is considered, including wide-format signage and industrial print sectors. This significant top-line figure makes it one of the few high growth sectors of the printing market.

The main market sectors for digital printing are:

▶ financial services

▶ retailing

▶ industrial/manufacturing

▶ public sector

▶ publishing

▶ packaging.

The main products produced through digital printing include personalisation products and document fulfilment, packaging, books, magazines, manuals, corporate promotional material, stationery, point-of-sale, catalogues, labels, security print, transactional print, short-run mono and colour.

There are many digital presses available. They vary from office workgroup mono laser printers rated at more than 45ppm to web-fed devices capable of printing above 1300ppm. In colour, machines vary from office colour photocopiers through to offset-quality machines from Xerox, Heidelberg, Xeikon and HP Indigo, rated at more than 100ppm. Wide-format digital machines are taking a significant share of the signage and poster market. Additionally, there are commercial inkjet machines offering very high productivity and low page cost from Scitex Digital Printing, with new devices for packaging, books and industrial applications from Dotrix, Aprion and Spectra. Costs can vary from around €1500 to upwards of €3 million, to produce different quantities of print at a range of quality levels and unit costs.

The origination function consists of the creative and production processes that translate an idea or concept into a file suitable for printing. The installation of digital printing provides a challenge to the prepress departments of traditional printing companies. As print run lengths drop with digital print engines, the turnover of print-ready files from the prepress area must be much higher. This can cause a significant imbalance to conventional printers, where one set of plates might occupy a machine for an afternoon; with digital printing that prepress work can be consumed in a matter of minutes. Management must be aware of the changing dynamic and plan for sufficient capacity and to recover the costs incurred. In the case of a complex personalisation project there may be many months of development and prepress work necessary for a few minutes of production on a daily basis. It is necessary to understand the value to the client and to develop appropriate commercial methods to operate successfully.

For digital printing the prepress will be totally digital, with the printing itself an extension of the prepress process. That is one reason why many prepress companies invest in digital printing to develop their services as the industry changes. Unlike conventional printing presses, there are very few controls on digital machines to adjust the printed result in terms of content, position and colour on the run. It is essential that the optimum file is served to the engine first time or unrecoverable costs will be incurred and time will be lost as the prepress is corrected. This makes the smooth operation of origination absolutely critical to the success of digital printing.

Much digital print will use files submitted from customers, many using standard office- and home-use software that can be problematic in producing files suitable for high-quality print. The majority of work will be supplied as PDF files, the printer receiving the file electronically, preflighting and using a workflow system to organise the jobs.

Origination and design

Good design is critical to the success of all printed products, no matter how short the print run (perhaps a single personalised copy). The purpose of the printed product will determine the sophistication of design. An in-house document may be acceptable with low-resolution RGB (image files held in red, green, blue format rather than CMYK – cyan, magenta, yellow and black) images placed in boxes created in a word processing package, but if this is a promotional item for a prospective customer there is no substitute for high-quality images and well-set text within a clear, well-designed page.

Conventional digital prepress tends to be an expensive and time-consuming stage, but many developments are coming together to change this situation. Using sophisticated database management and flexible templating, pages that have inherently good design can be constructed automatically. More powerful RIP/servers allow high-speed variable data jobs from many sources to be handled efficiently.

Prepress workflow

Most jobs for digital printing will be submitted by the customer either as a native application file (e.g. QuarkXpress, InDesign, MS Publisher, etc.), or as a PDF. The file will be submitted to the printer or, increasingly, generated automatically using a web-to-print model, with the printer handling the processing, ensuring the file is optimised for production and handling the administration. A typical mechanism is shown in Figure 6.56.

Workflow describes the organisation of the various production stages of a print project; for digital printing the workflow will be digital. It is the various points in the process where a conversion from digits to some other form of presentation is needed that will cause most difficulty – for example, proofing. More so than any of the other printing technologies, digital printing is expected to be an automatic process by the data originators, who consider digital printing an extension of their network. Indeed with proper workflow management it is just that. This means that the need for the data to be correct when leaving the originator is greater than in any other form of printing because it will go through fewer, post-origination checking procedures. For digital printing the expectation will be that it should just run. Already designers send their work straight to the printer, and with the uptake of digital printing, it can be straight to the press itself. These industry

FIGURE 6.56 Typical prepress workflow for digital printing

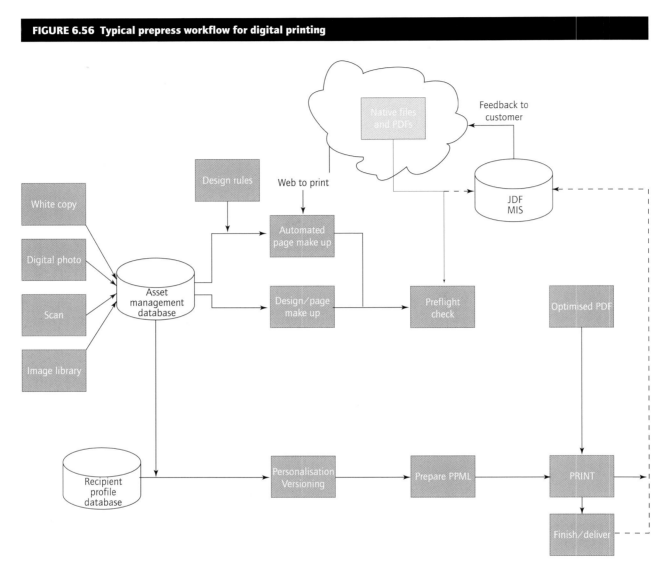

Source: Pira International Ltd

shifts will continue, as tools develop to monitor and control workflow. Effective workflow will be assembled from analysis of the specialised demands of the particular print process, including the checks and balances necessary to ensure commercial success.

There are several software tools available for printers to control their workflow. Most systems are based around the emerging job description format (JDF) that will be widely used throughout the printing industry. Workflow systems will increasingly manage the administration process as well as the production, offering benefits of reducing the process overhead costs. The scope of the tools allows new jobs to be initiated and tracks the progress of existing jobs. For digital printing the track can be set up with specific requirements for each printer.

Technology in digital printing

There are several competing technologies offered to printers and users of digital print. As a straightforward extension of offset printing, several suppliers offer direct plate imaging on-press, effectively incorporating computer-to-plate (CTP) technology on press. Totally different approaches are taken by direct imaging suppliers with electrophotographic (laser) printing and inkjet technology.

▶ on-press direct imaging (computer-to-press), where the plate is exposed in situ, to produce short to medium runs of identical copies;

▶ variable data printing, where the image is formed afresh for each print. Applications may be for limited personalisation, totally variable production or for short runs of identical copies.

These are shown schematically in Figure 6.57.

FIGURE 6.57 Schematic of the different types of digital printing

A. On-press direct imaging (DI). A plate master is imaged digitally on press; multiple identical copies are then printed offset

B. Variable digital printing. There is no master; each print is uniquely imaged on demand, with variable content, collation and layout as required

C. Industrial inkjet printing. Wide-format and web-fed signage and posters, packaging and decorating materials

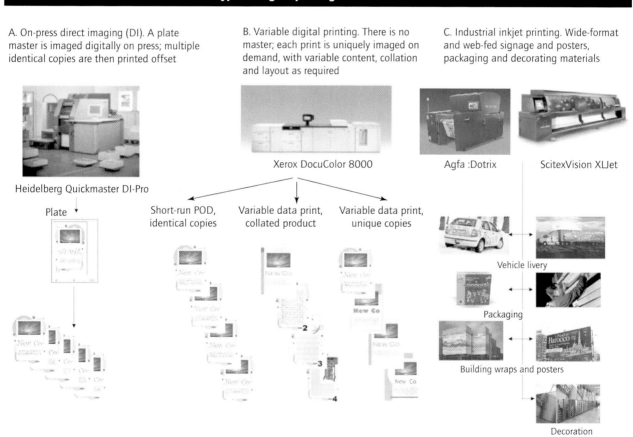

Heidelberg Quickmaster DI-Pro

Xerox DocuColor 8000

Agfa :Dotrix   ScitexVision XLJet

Plate

Short-run POD, identical copies

Variable data print, collated product

Variable data print, unique copies

Vehicle livery

Packaging

Building wraps and posters

Decoration

Source: Pira International Ltd

The different technologies and their suppliers have different criteria. For commercial printing the inexorable trend is increasing productivity (machines are becoming larger and faster) with improved quality, such that it is increasingly difficult to differentiate between process colour lithography and digital print. As the productivity increases the unit cost of production has declined so that digital is now the most effective technology for printing many print jobs. This is almost a given for mono applications, and there are signs that this is also happening for many short-run process colour applications.

Figure 6.58 is a map of the range of on-press imaging and variable data devices that are commercially available or have been demonstrated as potential systems. There are benefits and drawbacks associated with each type. This range makes some form of digital printing appropriate for most print applications, with the exception of long-run high-quality markets. The figure shows the relative positions of available technologies expressed in terms of the print quality and speed.

FIGURE 6.58 Technology map showing the relative positions of digital print processes

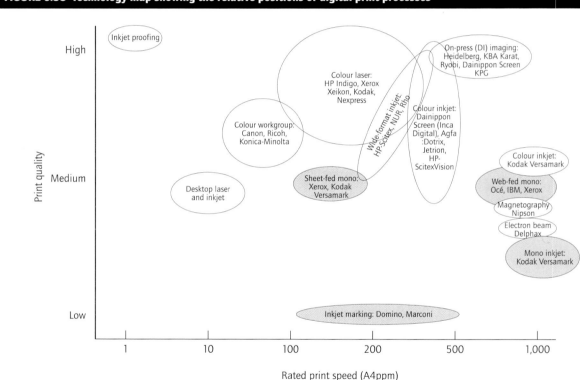

Source: Pira International Ltd

As Figure 6.58 suggests, there are systems available to print products in a wide range of qualities and quantities. Digital printing represents a continuum of devices with quality, format, capacity and speed options all well covered. The continuum is broadening all the time, making it difficult to really segment the range of available equipment. The continuum moves from personal and desktop printers for home and office use, with photo-realistic inkjet devices offering very high quality, for very low weekly and monthly usage, to workgroup and industrial-strength colour printers capable of offset quality rated at 500,000 prints per month. Beside these there is a range of inkjet systems, with heads integrated onto presses, wide-format machines and specialist lines. These use a variety of ink systems to print onto many materials from paper, board, plastics and even metal. On-press imaging is concentrated on B3 and B2 formats, although Komori has a B1 (1020 × 740mm) machine and Wifag is developing a newspaper system. These support any materials and inks that can be used in traditional offset printing.

Digital print technology has allowed print buyers and producers to respond to emerging market demands more effectively than established commercial processes. There are examples where digital printing may be more economical than conventional litho or it might provide a faster turnaround, cases where the technology competes directly with conventional and is a replacement. There are other examples where the technology allows new capabilities, such as personalisation or producing very short runs economically, so allowing incremental volume to be produced.

The increasing use of digital prepress means that most printed items have existed in digital form at some stage during production. Conventional analogue print processes are embracing digital technology to maintain and improve their competitive position. So, to an extent all print is digital. Various market forecasts show changing trends in share of print processes, but they all show relative decline in conventional processes with great increase in digital printing. Digital print is as much a service as it is a print production operation.

Buyer's checklist for investment in digital printing

Digital printing engines have evolved from devices that mimic conventional presses to those that are so fundamentally different that they offer entirely new applications. Many printers are seduced by the idea of installing the new technology they read about in journals or see at exhibitions to complement their conventional technology and offer additional services to customers. The correct investment decision is one of the most important facing any printing business; getting it wrong can jeopardise the company.

When considering investment in a digital print system, any organisation should undergo a systematic process to determine the justification for investment. There is no all-embracing model. There will always be cases where investment is determined by a client demanding a specific solution where the equipment and economics are very straightforward. When considering an investment, it is the real business benefits of these new facilities that must be considered, rather than the technological features. The most important question for any organisation to answer is 'Does the use of digital printing offer benefits for customers, both existing and potential?' But the technical questions are also important:

▶ Is the quality good enough?
▶ How productive is the device?
▶ How reliable is the device?
▶ Does the company have the correct infrastructure to provide the required service?

Printers have a tendency to concentrate on such technical details, but remain subservient to the business issues. The printing industry has long been categorised as production lead rather than market driven. The key for technical consideration is to question whether the technology will allow the company to serve its customers better and how can it provide a sustainable profitable business. As with any major investment, a detailed business case should be developed to determine if the project is feasible. The following should be considered.

Business/organisational needs:
► Market demand, budgeted achievable sales/added value;
► Impact on installed plant, will digital take volume from conventional printing presses, what is the impact on prepress/platemaking areas?
► Will the investment cope with seasonal peaks?
► What contingency is in place?

Economic justification:
► Standard financial considerations of the investment must be applied to ensure it is commercially viable. This may be hurdle rate, payback term, return on investment or NPV (net present value of cashflows), and calculations should take into account the capital, consumables and running, and maintenance costs;
► Ensure that the available capacity calculations represent achievable levels of utilisation and productive time, allowing for planned downtime.

Technical considerations:
► Quality of the product – resolution of mono engines, achievable colour reproduction, finishing;
► Front-end – RIP/server/personalisation/link to website and e-commerce systems;
► Paper/substrate handling – web- or sheet-fed, particular formats, range of basis weights that can be used, whether special grades required (as is the case with water-based ink systems);
► Finishing – how will the final product be manufactured, integrated on-line or off-line? If on-line, take into account set-up times and wastage;
► Distribution – mailing.

When complete, the organisation will have several key criteria that will be used to determine which available technology is best suited to the particular application.

TABLE 6.6 Criteria to consider in an investment decision	
Quality	What are the ongoing product characteristics, e.g. offset or copier colour, different resolution mono, finished job format, substrates, web or sheet?
Productivity	What volume of print is required per minute, per shift, per week, annually – taking into account peak seasonal workloads and real achievable production rather than maximum rated machine speed? What contingency is in place?
Cost	Capital, maintenance and per copy. Include necessary manning requirements, remembering that additional machines may not require additional dedicated labour
Peripherals	Front-end, personalisation capability, paper handling, on-line finishing, binding, mailing

Source: Pira International Ltd

When buying a digital printer it is not just the engine that must be considered. There are three elements to consider in any digital print investment:

▶ The front-end and data management

▶ The print engine

▶ Any specific finishing units, integrated or off-line.

Printing engines have evolved to provide improved quality, increased speed and lower cost. As these improvements were made, the equipment has started to move from devices that simply mimic conventional offset printing presses to machines that also offer new applications. The quality and productivity are fairly straightforward to assess, but for companies used to conventional printing the cost models of digital equipment suppliers often cause confusion.

It is the marketing and business objectives that should drive any decision to invest in digital print technology. The goal should be to serve existing customers better and/or to offer additional services and attract new customers. Users are adopting digital printing for one of two reasons:

▶ To achieve what they already do more effectively – i.e. better quality, lower cost and faster turnaround;

▶ To communicate with consumers in new ways.

If the technology does not offer benefits then it will not take the place of conventional printing. It should not be forgotten that conventional printing is also changing to improve its competitive position; the main benefits should therefore accrue to the user of print.

Digital print considerations

There are many different technologies available to apply colorant onto substrate in the digital printing of a document, book, package, newspaper, brochure, label, poster, etc. All involve at least a three-stage (often more) process, encompassing:

▶ receipt of job data;

▶ processing data – imposing pages, colour management, RIPing files, sending instructions to the imaging engine;

▶ imaging onto the substrate.

Additionally there may be a requirement to incorporate some finishing processes (cutting, creasing, folding, binding to whatever product is needed) with the imaging into an integrated line that must be controlled in tandem with printing. Digital print machines have to be able to receive files from design, prepress and office applications, and then convert these into a commercially acceptable product. In many respects, the operation of a digital press is more akin to an extension of a prepress operation rather than a print manufacturing process. There tend to be many low-value, small-quantity jobs (runs of one in the case of personalisation) being produced rather than a few large jobs. This changes the balance between prepress and printing for many conventional print businesses, making the management of workflow into the digital operation difficult.

The speed and capacity of the various systems on the market vary considerably, from a few single-sided A4 prints per minute, to 2000 good-quality full-colour duplexed pages on the fastest inkjet machines. The requirement for paper transport and control varies significantly among the machines, along with the capital cost and the ultimate printed cost of the product.

The range of uses varies from low-speed home office devices producing a few business cards and general stationery, through office and workgroup devices with faster printing and higher capacity, to machines used as print production engines in commercial companies and in-plant departments. There is a continuum of printers that range in terms of:

▶ speed – up to 2000 A4ppm, 6000m²/hr for flatbed inkjet;

▶ capacity – up to millions of pages per week;

▶ format – web and sheet to ultra-wide (5m+) and large-format flatbed;

▶ capability – from mono, spot colour, process colour and very wide gamut photo-realistic capability;

▶ quality – from low-resolution mono laser and inkjet through to offset-quality colour.

Costs range from around €100 to upwards of €3 million. Conventional offset press manufacturers have observed a growing threat to their business and have developed digital hybrids of their presses, imaging their plates in situ on-press.

On-press imaging

On-press imaging or direct imaging (DI® is a registered trademark of Presstek Inc. and Heidelberg) presses are offset presses that incorporate plate imaging within the press design. The plate technology for these presses is similar to that used in off-press CTP systems, the plates print multiple copies of the same non-variable image as conventional offset litho printing. Files are sent from the prepress network direct to the printing press, all plates are then imaged simultaneously in register.

The key suppliers of imaging systems for DI are Presstek Inc. and Kodak's Creo. The plate technology employed is laser ablation on polyester and aluminium plates that require no separate processing. Presstek's PEARLdry plate comprises an aluminium or polyester base coated with a very thin layer of titanium dioxide with a top layer of ink-repellent silicone.

The basic concept is simple and depends on an ablation process. A powerful thermal laser vaporises the uppermost image-forming layers of a printing plate to expose the ink-receptive base layer. The plate is imaged directly on press without chemicals or film. The image areas of the plate are exposed under digital control by a thermal laser source. The laser energy is absorbed by the titanium dioxide layer, causing it to ablate (vaporise) and release the silicone from the base in these areas. The residual material that is left on the plate from this process must be removed by cleaning cloths or rollers before the print run can commence. Imaging occurs with ink on the base material being repelled by the silicone surface. For DI presses using wet litho printing there are similar ablation plates from Presstek, Agfa (Thermolite) and KPG (TNPP). The residual material left after imaging with these plates is fine enough to be taken away by vacuum and the ink/dampening system of the press, so a prolonged plate cleaning cycle is unnecessary.

FIGURE 6.59 Mechanism of laser ablation for on-press plate imaging

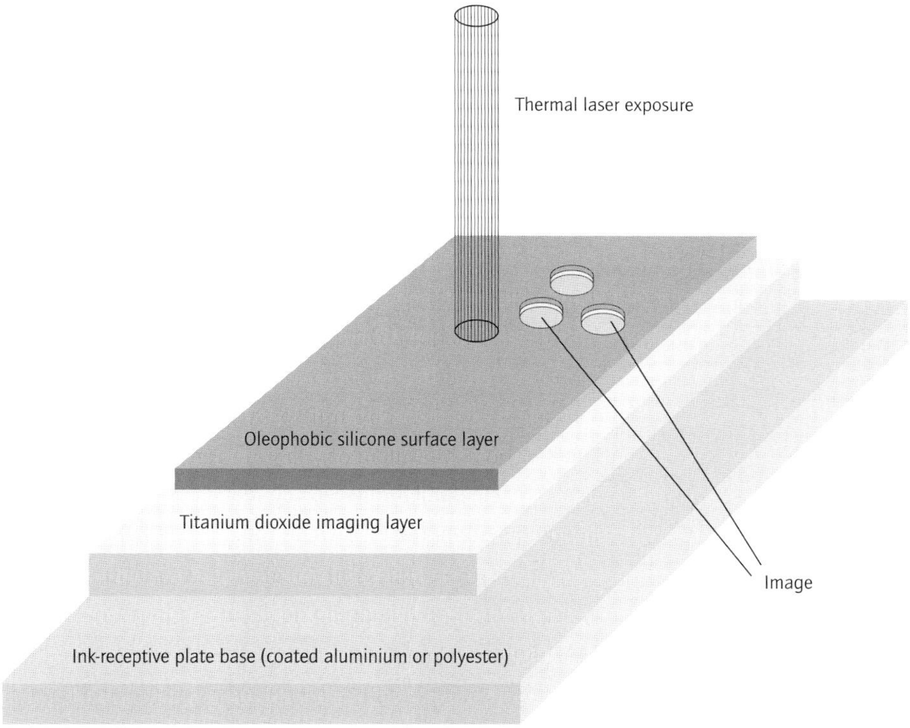

Thermal laser exposure

Oleophobic silicone surface layer

Titanium dioxide imaging layer

Image

Ink-receptive plate base (coated aluminium or polyester)

Source: Pira International Ltd

The plates used are the polyester-based TF-200 technology from Konica Minolta, which does not require separate processing or development. The 0.2mm base is coated with two layers. The first is oleophobic (water receptive), with a top layer that is a thermal-sensitive oleophilic (water-repelling) material. When exposed, the laser beam hardens the material, and when the press is run up the fount solution dissolves away the unexposed area, providing a print-ready polyester plate. This process is shown schematically in Figure 6.60.

FIGURE 6.60 TruePress plate exposure technology

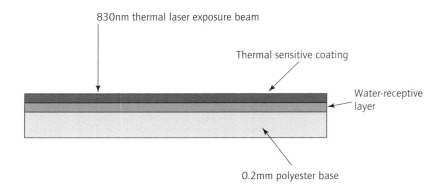

830nm thermal laser exposure beam

Thermal sensitive coating

Water-receptive layer

0.2mm polyester base

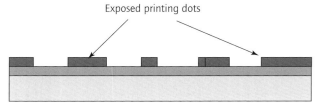

Exposed printing dots

Source: Pira International Ltd

Once exposed, the TF-200 plate allows printing to start immediately after exposure. Unlike ablation systems, no debris is produced and there is no need for special cleaning or treatment. Presstek uses modular LED exposure technology, while Creo uses its SquareSpot thermal laser exposure.

Heidelberg has led the market for DI presses since the launch of the first on-press imaging system, the GTO-DI, in 1992. Heidelberg then developed the Quickmaster DI, an original design rather than a modified conventional press, and the Speedmaster 74DI, which incorporated imaging heads on a conventional press. Other manufacturers, such as MAN Roland, Dainippon Screen and KBA Karat, have developed new concepts with significant changes to traditional offset inking and control.

On-press imaging is an area of significant development for sheet-fed offset press manufacturers attempting to increase the productivity of their machines through automating the set-up and make-ready. The large number of these DI presses in production indicates the response of the conventional press manufacturers to the development of digital printing. They are adapting their traditional machines to compete rather than trying to innovate a whole new technology strand. Manufacturers claim that DI offers the ability to make more jobs in less time, getting through a job more quickly. The process eliminates the manual production steps, labour and costs associated with plate-making, so enabling printers to be more competitive in a market that continually demands faster turnaround time, lower run lengths and lower costs, with no sacrifice of quality. A DI-enabled press can be a very cost-effective method of printing process colour jobs at run lengths of 500 to 25,000.

The claimed benefits in the DI concept include:

▶ No cost incurred with a stand-alone platesetter and, particularly, attendant operator;

▶ True offset quality and materials; some models allow spot-colour capability;

▶ No floor space requirement for platesetter;

▶ Fast turnaround time – the ability to make more jobs in less time and get through a job more quickly;

▶ Seamless integration of plate imaging with press make-ready;

▶ Images are in register without need for adjustment.

These are offset against the weaknesses:

▶ Higher cost of the press due to the incorporation of the imaging heads;

▶ The press environment is less than ideal for laser imaging;

▶ Breakdown in the imaging side means that expensive press time is also lost (not true for all presses).

It is not clear what the future for this technology is. The current installed base is quite low but it offers the potential of improving the position of litho printing. Creo suggests that plateless offset printing technology will greatly boost on-press imaging with its Digital Offset Printing (DOP) system. The plateless DOP system uses SP technology, whereby a reusable substrate is cleaned of the previous image, sprayed with a lithographic coating, laser imaged and then printed in a normal manner. For printers this technology promises significant advantages (although plate suppliers react with considerable suspicion at the idea of reusable media). First demonstrated publicly several years ago, the potential for commercial application will be determined by a marketing decision by one of the leading offset plate suppliers, calculating the potential effects on a major part of their business.

Agfa continues to evaluate the potential of this type of technology with a thermal sensitive no-process coating (Litespeed). This will be sprayed on to the plate or cylinder surface and imaged with a thermal laser source. Processing will be completed when non-image areas are removed by the inking system. This is particularly interesting for DI presses, and Komori has indicated support for it, but the system is still not yet in commercial production.

Asahi Chemicals in Japan has demonstrated a polymer-coated plate that is hydrophilic (water wetting) but has the capability to switch to being hydrophobic when imaged with an infrared (IR, 830nm) laser source. The switching is achieved by incorporating microcapsules in the polymer. These burst when exposed to the laser source, releasing chemicals that change both the colour and the water wetting of the polymer. If it can be perfected it provides an ideal plate material for DI presses.

MAN Roland has a DI press which uses an erasable cylinder system – the DICOweb (DIgital ChangeOver) – with worldwide installations in commercial heatset web presses printing up to 30,000 runs. The cycle involves the ink and previous image being removed using a special erasing solution within an integral cleaning device on completion of the job. The cylinder is then ready for the next imaging process. The new image (a polymer resin) is transferred to the plate sleeve from a donor ribbon by laser-induced thermal transfer, using a Creo thermal imaging head (shown in Figure 6.61). When the imaging operation is finished, the material transferred is fixed and made more durable by heat treatment. This is followed by a cylinder-conditioning process to enhance the hydrophilic nature of the non-image areas. Now the cylinder is ready for printing by conventional wet offset. The image is claimed to be good for around 30,000 copies, after that it can be removed and imaged again. The process can be repeated around 200 times before it is necessary to replace the seamless steel sleeve.

FIGURE 6.61 Schematic of the DICOweb imaging process

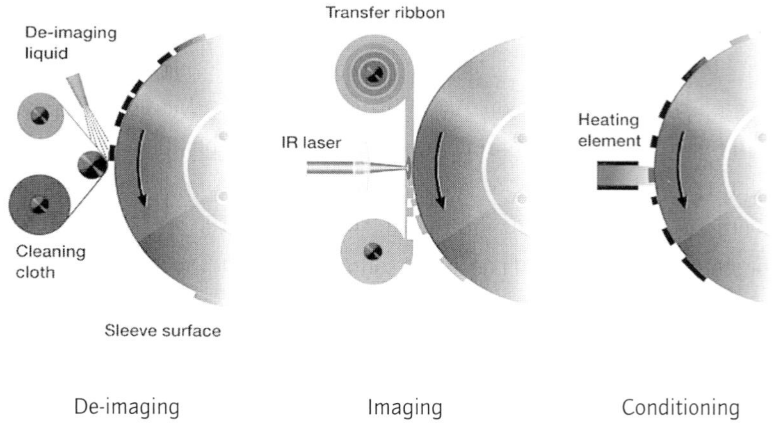

De-imaging liquid

Cleaning cloth

Sleeve surface

De-imaging

Transfer ribbon

IR laser

Imaging

Heating element

Conditioning

Source: MAN Roland

One advantage offered by the on-press technology is the proven ability for substrate conversion that offset printing provides; the difference is the plate-imaging method, rather than the inks, printing mechanism and paper transport.

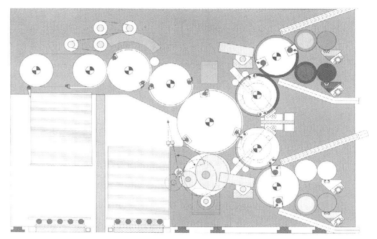

Source: KBA Karat

Printer duplicators

An interesting niche, halfway between on-press imaging and variable data printing, is offered by the digital duplicator, available from Riso and Duplo. Machines combine scanning and direct links to a digital original to produce a master, a special material that has the image produced as an array of small holes. This is wrapped around the inking drum and paper is pressed against the surface, the pressure squeezing ink through the voids created by the imaging process.

The duplicator scans the hard-copy original, or a computer-generated image is sent directly from the desktop, causing the thermal head to image a master. The master, a few microns thick and made from a polyester resin film bonded to thin, fibrous paper is wrapped around an ink cylinder. Inside the cylinder, the ink is pressed through the cylinder screens into the master. Pick-up rollers guide paper to the cylinder where the ink is transferred to the page via pressure. Colours are added by changing ink cylinders and running the copies through the printer–duplicator multiple times. While these machines produce documents directly from a PC or Macintosh connected to the system controller, they also work as stand-alone devices by duplicating hard copy read by internal scanners.

The quality is limited but the technology offers very economical production of low run lengths at speeds of 120ppm. The ink drum can be changed quickly to offer spot colours, but tight registration is impractical. Duplicators are designed to bridge the gap between the variable data printer and desktop printers for short runs where quality is not paramount, for applications such as simple forms and stationery.

Variable data printing technologies

The major technologies in use commercially are electrophotography (laser printing) and inkjet. These technologies are packaged into many commercially available systems, with alternative front-ends (RIPs and servers), paper-handling capabilities and finishing equipment. In addition there are several potential innovative alternatives – electron beam imaging (ion deposition), magnetography, toner jet and elcography – in various stages of development.

Electrophotographic technology

Laser printing is the most widely used digital printing technology for mono and colour applications. The basic operation developed from Carlson's original 1937 patents on xerography, through photocopying into digital printing. The basis of the technology is to create a latent image of electrical charge that is used to selectively attract toner, then to pass the toner to the paper. At the heart of a laser printer is a photo-receptive drum, coated with a light-sensitive photoconductive material that loses a positive charge when light falls on it. The whole surface of the drum is positively charged by a corona and laser light is shone onto the surface through an array of rotating mirrors in a series of adjacent scan lines as the drum rotates. The laser is modulated (switched on and off) by a controller that uses the pattern of incident light to expose the photoconductive drum point by point, as determined by the bitmap created from the RIPed data file to create a bitmap image to be printed. This creates a latent image of charge on the surface of the drum that rotates in front of oppositely charged tiny magnetic colourant particles.

The dry toner is a fine powder comprised of a mixture of coloured toner and magnetisable carrier particles. HP Indigo's ElectroInk, for example, comprises electrically chargeable particles dispersed in a liquid. The latent image is then developed by depositing toner particles onto the surface of the photoconductive drum. The developer (toner + carrier) is attracted to a magnetic roller and forms a magnetic brush that applies the toner to the image drum. Because the toner has a positive charge it adheres to the negative, discharged, areas of the drum and not to the positively charged non-image area. As the imaging removes toner from the development unit new toner is added by an automatic dosing system.

With the toner pattern in position, the drum rolls over a sheet of paper that moves along a belt underneath. The paper is negatively charged by a transfer corona; this is stronger than the negative charge of the electrostatic image so the paper can pull the toner powder away. By moving at the same speed as the drum the paper picks up the image pattern exactly. To keep the paper from clinging to the drum it is discharged by a corona after picking up the toner. This process is not 100% efficient, and some toner remains on the drum and has to be removed by cleaning with a static pad or charged rotating roller. Cleaning may be improved by using a pre-charged scorotron (the fine wire used to spread the charge across the photo-receptive drum) to charge toner remaining on the drum and increase its attraction to the cleaning roller. After cleaning, the drum surface passes under a discharge lamp. This bright light exposes the entire photoreceptor surface, erasing the electrical image. The drum surface then passes the charged corona wire, which reapplies the positive charge. The process is shown schematically in Figure 6.63.

FIGURE 6.63 Schematic diagram showing the mechanism of laser printing

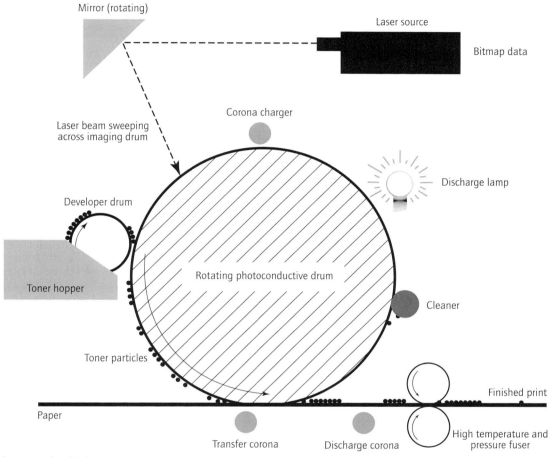

Source: Pira International Ltd

After transfer the toner is still only held on the paper electrostatically, and a final fixing process is required. This may be heat, or heat and pressure to melt the toner and fuse it into the fibres at the paper surface. Rollers will typically approach 200°C; the high temperature is necessary to cause the toner to melt quickly. There are other methods of fusing, such as the use of solvent vapour or high-intensity flash.

The first colour systems simply married four direct imaging drums together to lay down cyan, magenta, yellow and black toner. Synchronising these steps decreased speed and challenged registration, resulting in slow machines and poor image quality. Manufacturers developed indirect mechanisms of carrier and blanket transfer, individually and with a shared transfer step, to improve speed and quality. The latest Xerox iGen3 machine uses a single integrated carrier and transfer blanket. These developments, shown in Figure 6.64, have allowed improvements in colour quality, while developments in paper handling and image fixing improve productivity and product durability.

FIGURE 6.64 Schematic diagram showing development of image transfer in colour toner laser printers

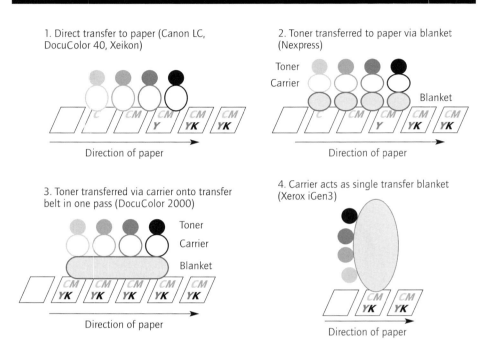

1. Direct transfer to paper (Canon LC, DocuColor 40, Xeikon)

Direction of paper

2. Toner transferred to paper via blanket (Nexpress)

Toner
Carrier
Blanket

Direction of paper

3. Toner transferred via carrier onto transfer belt in one pass (DocuColor 2000)

Toner
Carrier
Blanket

Direction of paper

4. Carrier acts as single transfer blanket (Xerox iGen3)

Direction of paper

Source: Pira International Ltd

Manufacturers are attacking the physical limitations for very fast, high-resolution electrophotographic engines. Lasers offer limited resolution: the turbulence effects of powder toners that limit their speed and the need to fuse toner to paper limits the range of substrates and may lead to curl and the need for conditioning.

Different manufacturers offer variations in terms of data handling and RIPs, laser exposure systems, toner transfer mechanism, material range and paper-handling technology. In sheet-fed mono printing Xerox Corporation is the undisputed market leader, virtually creating the high-speed monochrome, cut-sheet application. Its DocuTech and DocuPrint ranges of machines are well proven in the field and can be found in the print rooms of many commercial companies, on-demand print shops, and in printing companies specialising in the production of short-run books and manuals. They are sheet-fed machines, printing simplex or duplex and capable of being fitted with a wide range of finishing options. There are production and MICR versions, as well as the PostScript-fed flagship – the DocuPrint180, with a maximum speed of 180 A4ppm at 600dpi. At 150ppm, Kodak's Digimaster series is now providing stiff competition for high-quality work.

FIGURE 6.65 Schematic showing paper path through base unit of the Digimaster E

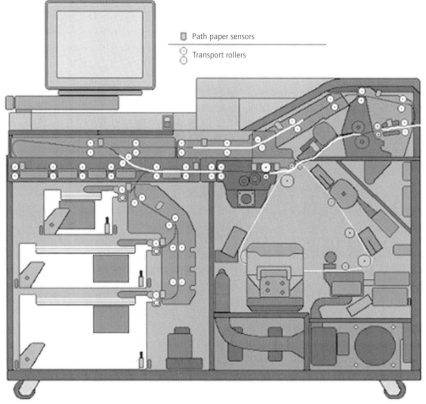

Path paper sensors

Transport rollers

Source: Pira International Ltd

Figure 6.65 shows the design of the Digimaster print engine. The imaging head places toner onto a transfer belt that circulates to transfer toner onto the paper, with fuser and delivery positioned closely together. Temperature and pressure settings are determined by the paper stock. This short, fairly straight paper path through the Digimaster contributes to its reliability, with few opportunities for paper jams. This allows heavier stocks to be printed than other high-speed laser printers – a key advantage for the device.

The Xeikon engine is a dry toner electrophotographic system incorporating variable density at each imaging point. The organic photo-conductive (OPC) drums are exposed by wide-array LEDs and each image point exposure can be at one of 16 levels, which translates as different tone densities on the drum. The variable toner density increases the range of grey levels for a given screen ruling in a halftone reproduction, and permits edge smoothing for text and line graphics.

FIGURE 6.66 Schematic of the Xeikon 5000 press

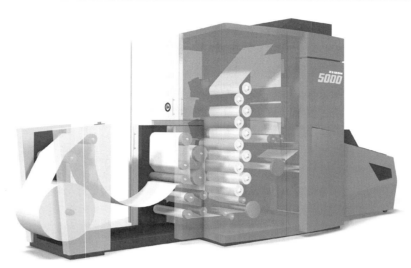

Source: Punch Graphix

Xeikon presses are web-fed, printing simultaneously on both sides of the paper as it rises vertically between two sets of drums to print the four process colours. The drums are not geared together, they rotate only by their contact with the paper web. The speed and tension of the web is controlled by an in-feed nip at the bottom of the tower and draw roller positioned after the fusing unit. The imaging of each drum is synchronised by a signal obtained from an encoder positioned on one of the drums. The process of transferring toner alternatively on each side of the paper without disturbing previously applied colours is quite complicated, requiring multiple sets of corona wires for each drum.

The fusing of toner onto the substrate takes place in a radiant fuser unit, where the paper is raised to a temperature of about 140°C to melt and fix the toner. A secondary heated nip roller-fusing unit may also be used to improve the gloss. The printed copies are normally delivered to a sheeter/stacker, although a rewind and other finishing options are also available. The printed sheet size is limited by the maximum web width in one direction, but the print length is only limited by the system's available memory. Continuous image banners of up to 15m can be printed.

The quality of the printed result is influenced significantly by the conductivity of the substrate, and since this is greatly influenced by the moisture content some pre-conditioning (pre-drying) of the paper takes place before it enters the printing tower.

The level of drying, transfer currents, fusing temperature, etc. are all substrate dependent, and to simplify this process script files are provided as part of a paper qualification process. The presses are available in two formats – 32cm and 50cm wide.

Xerox has had considerable success in selling its DocuColor 2045 and 2060 machines, superseded by the 6000 series and now by the DocuColor 7/8000 range (see

Figure 6.67). The newer machines are increasingly productive and reliable and Xerox has enjoyed considerable success with the graphic arts market.

FIGURE 6.67 Schematic of the Xerox DocuColor 7/8000 range

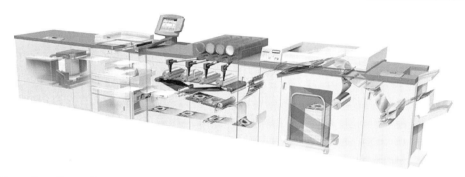

Source: Xerox Corporation

Xerox started reselling the Xeikon press as the DocuColor 70 and 100 for high quality. The success of the DocuColor 2000 series saw a decline in DocuColor 70/100 sales, contributing to the significant financial problems faced by Xeikon. These were the first machines to offer lithographic quality into the corporate office market with relatively modest monthly volumes, and have been very successful for Xerox.

Xerox followed these machines up with its iGen3, launched as the first intelligent third generation digital press, hence the name. It is designed with many mechanical and imaging enhancements to give high-quality colour output at 100ppm with a low page printing cost and good reliability. Xerox calls this SmartPress technology and the machine is covered by more than 300 patents.

FIGURE 6.68 Schematic of Xerox DocuColor iGen3 press

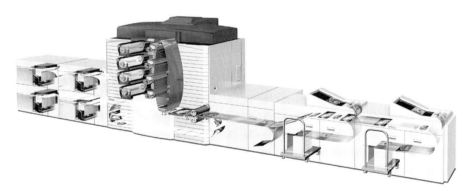

Source: Xerox Corporation

The toner (Xerox uses the term 'dry ink') comprises proprietary formulated uniform micron-size particles to offer significant advantages in colour and detail reproduction. An array of very small colour-calibration patches is imaged on the drum between every print. They control 256-level tone reproduction curves for each colour separation. This automatic calibration process provides continuous adjustment of critical system parameters to assure colour consistency while maintaining productivity.

The intelligent fusing process (termed Goldilocks – applying not too much, not too little, but just the right amount of temperature and pressure to achieve good bonding with the paper) uses details of paper weight, coating and the amount of toner to optimise the settings. Adjustments are made on the fly as the paper and coverage change. The last stop is the decurling station, where any paper curl that has been introduced is removed so the output is flat and ready for finishing. The settings of image coverage and paper type are used to adjust the decurler automatically on a page-by-page basis.

The NexPress 2100 is an A3 format dry toner, LED imaging colour press. Before printing, the paper is conditioned and carried through the press on a transfer belt to which it is electrostatically affixed. Prior to being attached, the paper is pre-registered in a similar way to that of conventional sheet-fed presses. The imaging drums are similar to other electrophotographic engines and use an LED array for exposure, but the transfer to paper is not typical of other dry toner systems, as it is offset. Offset transfer is claimed to improve the resulting transfer to less smooth substrates. The fusing unit applies a combination of heat and pressure to fuse the toner ('DryInk' in NexPress terminology).

For duplex printing the sheet is retained on the transfer belt to continue its travel to the turning section, which turns the sheet while maintaining the same lead edge. All of this is housed within a relatively large cabinet (see Figure 6.69). The conditions in the cabinet are controlled as part of the overall quality control system, which incorporates

FIGURE 6.69 Kodak NexPress 2100

Source: Kodak NexPress

closed-loop process control to monitor and adjust all process parameters continually, including the print registration.

Potential developments in toner-based laser printing

Future developments in laser printing include new laser sources, with laser diodes and edge-emitting blue lasers offering lower costs and higher resolutions. A potential drawback of laser printing has been the toner technology, with turbulence effects limiting the potential speed and the fused result showing uneven gloss and non-planographic surface, deficiencies when compared with lithography. Recent developments in emulsion aggregation, where toner particles are grown to a uniform size distribution and spherical shape, may provide better quality and productivity, while it is cheaper to make than conventional toner. The claimed benefits are sharper images and text because there are no large particles blurring edge definition. In addition, less toner will be needed as smaller but more uniform particles will cover the sheet with a thinner toner layer while still achieving the same visual result. Manufacturers claim reductions of up to 40%. Wax may be incorporated into the toner to stop sticking to the surface of the fuser rollers without using fuser oil that may leave a residue on the print. This should reduce lost time spent cleaning the fuser.

Liquid toner electrophotography

HP Indigo uses liquid toners, ElectroInk, which can be produced in a wide range of colours to allow spot-colour printing. The basic imaging principles are electrophotographic but the colourant construction is quite different to dry toner. The toner is a dispersion of very small electrically charged pigment particles suspended in an electrically insulating fluid, a paraffin-like material, and is attracted out of suspension by the electrostatically charged image on the OPC (organic photoconductive) drum; Indigo uses the term photo imaging plate, PIP. Since the toner is within a liquid, it is in some ways easier to control. As a result the particle size can be significantly less (one or two microns) than in a dry toner system, providing the potential for higher resolution on paper, sharper edge definition and thin layers of pigment.

The method of applying liquid ElectroInk to the drum is different to that of powder toners. It is sprayed directly onto the image drum, any excess is removed by a doctor roller and from here removed by cleaning blades and recycled back to the main ink supply. HP Indigo technology resembles offset in that the colourant is transferred indirectly to paper via a transfer blanket. The charged image attracts charged pigment particles to it, but the very small electrically charged colourant particles are held in suspension in an electrically insulating fluid – the patented ElectroInk.

Each separation is transferred to a hot (100°C) transfer printing blanket. This melts the pigment into a thin tacky plastic fluid, with 100% of the ink going across leaving the PIP clean, ready to be charged and receptive to the next colour. When this meets the cold paper it sticks instantly and none remains on the blanket while it cools and solidifies. As soon as the sheet leaves the machine it is dry, so there is no set-off.

This allows all colours to be printed from one print station. As one colour separation is created and printed, the next colour is output on the same print station

FIGURE 6.70 Schematic of the HP Indigo printing mechanism

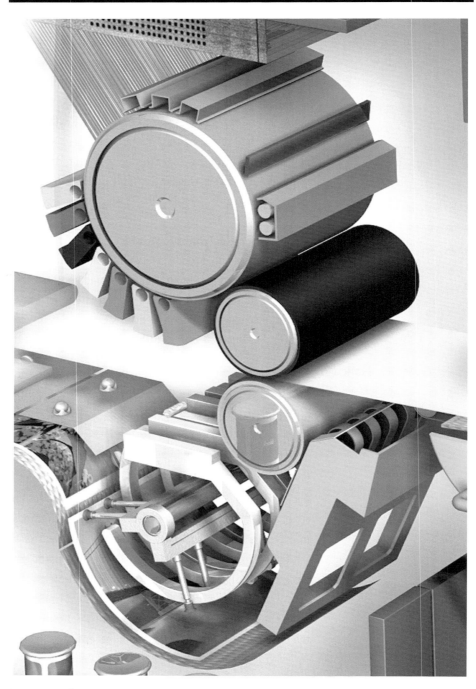

Source: HP Indigo

because the blanket transfers 100% of the previous image. To print four colours the paper stays on the impression drum for four revolutions, each revolution printing a different colour. If the paper is to be printed on both sides it is held after the first side and returns, having been tumbled, to print the reverse.

This is an elegant imaging mechanism with several definite advantages over dry powder systems. The small particle size permits higher resolution, sharper edge definition and thin layers of pigment, with planographic results comparable with offset and none of the relief effects of early toner systems. Since the toner within a liquid is in some ways easier to control, with no turbulence, it has the potential of high speed. The translucent nature and consistent gloss of ElectroInk lets the reflective characteristics of any substrate shine through, similar to the offset quality of traditional inks.

IndiChrome technology, which enables up to seven-colour printing capability, expands the colour gamut beyond the standard CMYK capabilities available in some other digital presses. A good innovation is the ink mixing station, which allows spot colours to be mixed and used. HP Indigo claims the single print station has advantages of compactness, lower hardware costs and greater mechanical accuracy. The web-fed devices allow a wide range of substrate, including flexible packaging to be printed with no fusing involved.

There are also disadvantages, particularly the regular requirement to change hot blankets and PIPs when they become damaged on the run, which can result in considerable downtime. When considering technology, downtime must be factored in. ElectroInk is patented and protected so there is no competition to drive down costs (although the same situation exists with dry toner – only inkjet has the potential for competitive supply of colourant).

Inkjet printing systems

Inkjet printing has existed for many years in a relatively simple form – it is the dominant home and small office technology. Very high quality is achievable on photorealistic imaging and the technology is widely used to generate graphic arts contract proofs on modestly priced equipment. As computer power increased, so inkjet techniques to create contract proofs expanded and the capability of direct imaging a fixed or variable data image onto the substrate developed. This involves movement of the substrate and/or inkjet head to image the area to be printed.

The goal of inkjet is to print text and colour images that rival the quality, speed and cost of conventional lithographic processes while maintaining the advantages of variable data printers. A further advantage is the capability of using spot coloured inks for corporate applications.

The principle involves directing small droplets of ink from a nozzle onto the surface to be printed. There are different methods of producing droplets, but a common feature is the control of droplet position on the substrate by its response to high-frequency digital electronic signals. Droplet formation involves the application of a controlled pressure on the liquid ink in its reservoir as it flows into the printing nozzles so that it is broken into droplets. This is achieved by applying various technologies.

There are two major types of inkjet technology: drop-on-demand (DOD) and continuous stream printing. The technologies have moved from simple low-resolution alphanumeric code printing to fast, good-quality colour printing. Manufacturers have been attracted to inkjet technology because it offers very high speed, low ink cost and is a one-step, non-contact process. Inkjet print heads are used in home and office printers, wide-format printers and in digital proofing systems for very high-quality reproductions. As the imaging units get faster they are being increasingly used in more high-volume applications.

Because the process is non-impact – only the jet of ink makes contact with the printing surface – it can be used to print on any shape or texture of substrate. In most other digital printing methods the image is pressed and fused into the substrate with heat. Inkjet printing is shown schematically in Figure 6.71.

FIGURE 6.71 Schematic of single-nozzle continuous jet inkjet printing

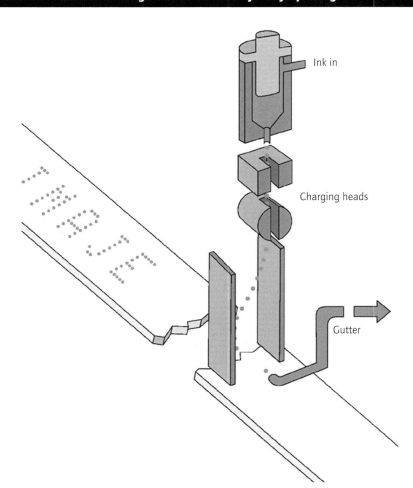

Ink in

Charging heads

Gutter

Source: Imaje

A stream of ink is forced through a narrow nozzle under pressure. The resulting high velocity breaks the ink stream into droplets. The size and frequency of droplets produced is determined by the surface tension of the liquid ink, the pressure applied and the nozzle diameter. To ensure regularity of size and spacing of droplet formation, a high-frequency pulsating pressure is applied continuously to the ink. This is achieved by applying a high-frequency alternating voltage (up to 1Mhz) to a piezoelectric crystal attached to the ink reservoir. Controlled placement of the individual ink droplets is obtained by inducing an electrostatic charge on them as they leave the nozzle. The charged droplets then pass through a set of like-charged plates that deflect the droplets to the required position on the substrate. The amount of deflection and the consequent positioning of the droplet on the substrate are decided by the size of charge induced on the droplets as they leave the nozzle. This in turn is controlled by the size of digital signal supplied to the charging plates by the digital raster file input. No charge allows the droplet to pass undeflected into the gutter, and the size of the charge varies the dot position, up to the maximum deflection. In this way the image, usually text, is defined in one dimension, with the other from the movement of the head or substrate. Single continuous jets are extensively used for inline coding, numbering and addressing systems, where they are capable of printing at web speeds of up to 20m/s or 100,000 articles per hour.

Binary inkjet

The next stage is a binary system with an array of inkjet heads each producing a stream of droplets. These have no variable charge applied to the deflection plates. The image-forming droplets are not charged, but fly straight to the substrate while unwanted droplets are charged and deflected into the gutter. The operation is therefore simpler than the single inkjet application, but the precision of nozzle assembly is considerably more demanding.

FIGURE 6.72 Schematic showing array of inkjet heads

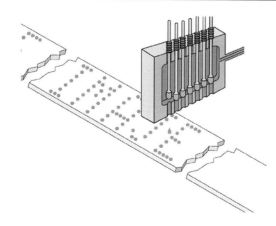
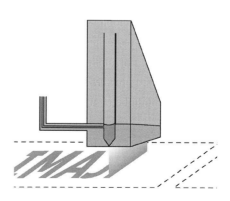

Source: Imaje

Continuous inkjet

Continuous inkjet printing involves shooting a very fine stream of ink that breaks into droplets of a predictable size, which can be individually deflected by an electrical current directly on to a substrate. Controlled placement of droplets is obtained by charging them as they leave the nozzle and passing through like-charged plates to repel and deflect to the required position. The primary advantages of continuous inkjet are extremely high speeds – systems can run in excess of 1000fpm, producing over 4000 A4ppm. They have the ability to print in a wide range of physical environments and on many substrates, including onto irregularly shaped objects in packaging. This approach is used in many binary heads, including the Kodak VersaMark technology.

Drop-on-demand inkjet

More development has been targeted at drop-on-demand, or impulse printing. In this case the pressure applied to the reservoir is not continuous, but is only applied when a droplet is needed in response to digital electronic signals from the imaging computer. Since no deflection of droplets is needed, guttering and recirculation are not required, so simplifying the design and construction of the printer. Translating the digital signal into a rapid change in pressure is achieved by heating – thermal inkjet – or using a piezoelectric effect.

In binary technologies the size of the ink droplet is fixed, the resolution determining the final image quality.

Greyscale inkjet

The highest quality inkjet is currently achieved through the use of greyscale printing. The greyscale capability is key to being able to print high-quality inkjet at high speed, by varying the drop volume. The heads used are multi-bit – eight- or 16-bit – and can eject up to seven droplets, which merge into one drop that is placed on the substrate. Drop sizes range from six to 42 picolitres. This means that at a resolution of 300dpi there are 2400 potential gradations with eight-bit drops, providing a visual rendition of linework and tonal reproduction that is much greater than the standard 300dpi. With stochastic screening and good originals, the visual results can be generally excellent.

Piezoelectric technology is growing in popularity for most forms of DOD print head, because it is one of the simplest ways to generate drops electronically. The technology makes use of the piezoelectric effect, a phenomenon whereby small electronic impulses are delivered to suitable crystalline materials, causing them to expand. When incorporated in the ink reservoir the piezoelectric effect causes pressure pulses to be created in the ink that relate to the data pulse train. Droplets are generated intermittently according to the electronic signals received. A typical construction comprises an array of nozzles, each with its own piezoelectric crystal.

Thermal inkjet or bubble jet technology, as exemplified by the Canon bubblejet printer, uses a small heating element to create pressure droplets on demand within an ink reservoir. A small quantity of ink present in each nozzle is heated by a resistive heating element actuated by the digital data stream. The ink instantly flashes to vapour adjacent to the heat source and expands to create a bubble, forcing an equivalent volume of ink droplet through the nozzle and onto the substrate. The heat is switched off, the vapour cools and contracts and draws more ink out of the tank by capillary action. It is simple and cheap to make, but the physics of evaporation and condensation limits its speed.

The heat soak effect means that nozzles have to be placed a certain distance apart, complicating attempts to improve resolution. The high temperatures that the ink must withstand also place some restrictions on the ink formulation.

Hot-melt or phase-change inkjet is similar in principle to bubblejet printing in that an impulse heater is used to create droplets on demand. The difference lies in the nature of the ink. It is supplied in solid sticks, one for each printing colour. The stick is melted into a reservoir where it is kept fluid by a heating element. The hot, liquid ink is pumped through a nozzle using thermal DOD technology. On reaching the substrate the ink solidifies and because it is not substantially absorbed by the substrate, high colour saturation with a wide colour gamut is achieved. An alternative approach has the inkjet heads creating a composite image on a warm drum, from which the image is transferred to the paper.

High-resolution piezo print head technology consists of a series of ink chambers with shared channel walls made of ceramic material. Voltage is applied to the piezo material, changing its shape, which in turn forces the ink out through a micro-orifice. Piezo

FIGURE 6.73 Comparison of binary and greyscale inkjet printing

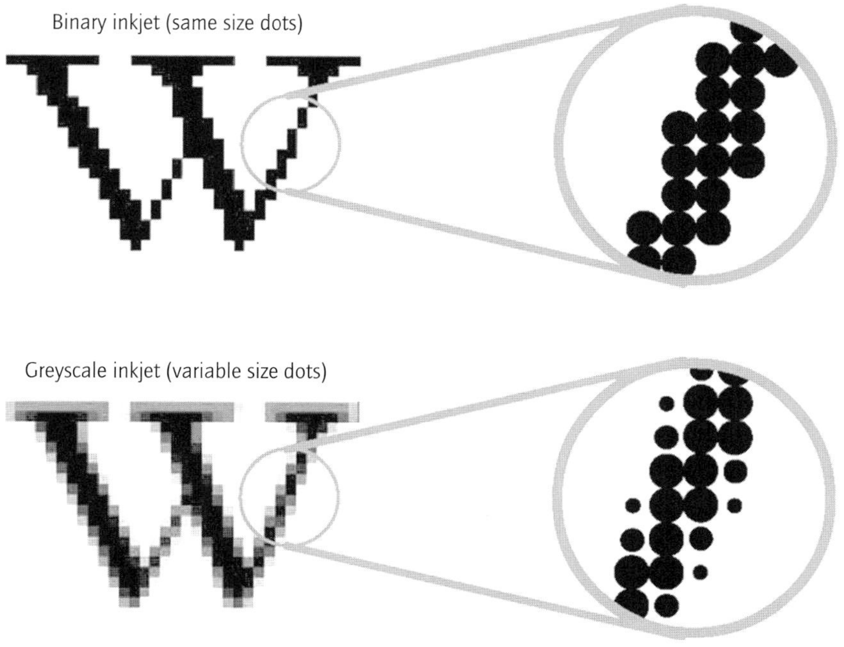

Binary inkjet (same size dots)

Greyscale inkjet (variable size dots)

Source: Xaar

technology can produce up to 25,000 drops per second and gives very high print resolution, with some 140,000 drops per second demonstrated in laboratories.

In a simplified overview, binary inkjet technology consists of ink chambers packed together into a print head, divided by shared channel walls, each with an electrode attached. By using shear mode and shared walls, highly efficient print heads provide standard single drop size printing – binary, or greyscale, on-demand, variable-sized drops for printing high-quality inkjet image solutions.

The leading print head suppliers include Spectra Inc. (a division of Dimatix), Xaar, Hitachi, Toshiba, Aprion and Kodak VersaMark. They produce a range of heads with the resolution and placement of nozzles being regularly upgraded. Actual inkjet machines are being marketed by a range of integrators who take the heads and produce units and complete machines with front-end controllers for particular markets.

The (fairly) recent arrival of Kodak (with the purchase of Scitex Digital Printing), Agfa (with the purchase of Dotrix and development of the Agfa Universal head), Dainippon Screen (buying Inca Digital) and FujiFilm (buying Sericol) will provide great impetus in the development of inkjet for commercial printing applications.

The first inroad of inkjet into commercial printing was the wide range of large-format printers used for one-off posters and signage, POS and vehicle liveries. Very low-volume, high-quality machines have transformed the proofing market. It is only in the past few years with on-press and stand-alone colour systems from Kerning Digital and Scitex Digital Printing that the promise of inkjet is being realised in graphic arts applications. The inkjet head technology has developed to a level where it can provide solutions, and these are gradually being developed into complete industrial systems. In a separate field of development, the Orphis 5500, developed by Riso-Olympus, is a high-speed colour inkjet device capable of delivering 105 A4ppm, at limited quality for an office environment.

Drupa 2004 saw the launch of significant new print heads, with original head manufacturers improving the speed and quality – the OmniDot from Xaar and M-Series from Spectra Inc. offer wider and faster heads for manufacturers to add to their printers. HP, Seiko, Aprion, Hitachi, Toshiba Tec, Konica Minolta, Epson, Trident and Canon all had developments to announce and promote.

Development of DOD piezo inkjet print heads is moving along two complementary paths. One is building print heads using micro-electro-mechanical systems (MEMS) thin-film technology, which enables rapid and lower cost manufacture. The other is creating robust print heads that can use a wider range of inks suitable for more print applications. Both approaches aim to produce cluster plates or other means to group and interlace print heads into larger and full-width arrays. However, for full-width arrays to achieve economic feasibility the cost needs to be significantly lower per nozzle than for current piezo devices. The goal is to drop the price below €1 per nozzle within two years, and subsequently €0.50 by 2008. If this comes to fruition, the increased performance/cost ratio will greatly boost the wide-format market.

FIGURE 6.74 Comparison of M-Class and Galaxy heads

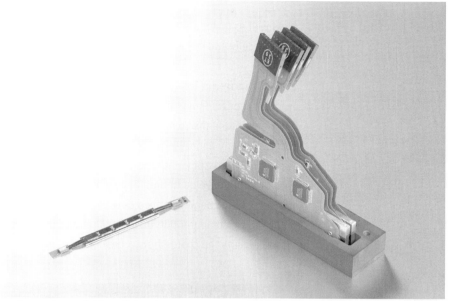

Source: Spectra Inc., a division of Dimatix

These heads can be integrated by manufacturers or specialist integrators. Spectra offers arrays of four and six colours as standard products, with a variety of widths that can be combined to produce wide-swathe printing at high speeds and quality.

FIGURE 6.75 Spectra Inc. grouped heads

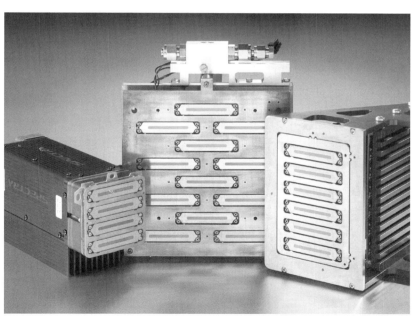

Source: Spectra Inc., a division of Dimatix

The gradual introduction of more powerful computer front ends and fast data transfer rates broadens the capabilities of inkjet printing.

Novel printing systems

As well as inkjet and laser printing there are several innovative approaches that work technically and offer interesting potential.

Electron beam imaging or ion deposition

Electron beam imaging (EBI) or ion deposition printing has been developed by Delphax. For some time the company was owned by Xerox, but in 2002 Check Technology acquired the company and changed its name to Delphax. The technology is similar to electrophotography, with the major difference being that instead of charging a photoconductive drum and then creating a latent image by exposing it to light, the electrostatic image is formed directly using an ion or electron beam source, controlled by the digital computer output. The imaging drum is a more robust, hard dielectric material that accepts the charge from a beam of electrons.

FIGURE 6.76 Direct electron beam imaging engine from Delphax

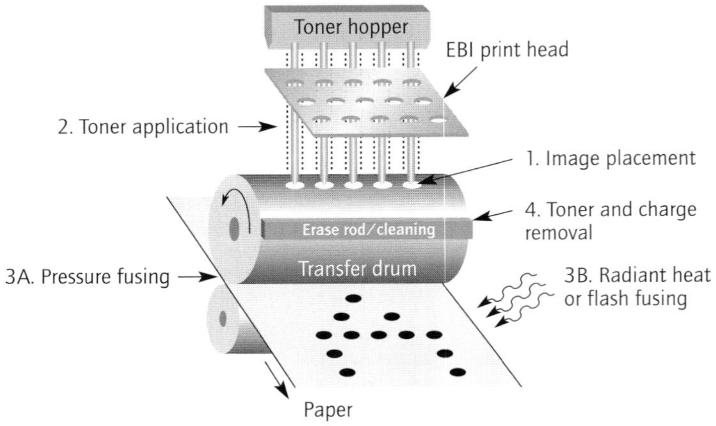

Source: Delphax Technologies

RIPed data is formatted into a matrix image and then transferred to an array of electrodes within a stationary EBI print cartridge. Information pulses provide controlled emission of beams of electrons from small holes in a screen electrode mounted on the face of the print cartridge. The beams are directed onto the hard dielectric print drum, assisted by an electric field created between the screen electrode of the cartridge and the drum's surface. A latent image with a negative charge is formed on the dielectric surface and is exposed to magnetic toner.

The toner is attracted to the charged image to form a toned image. EBI toner contains a controlled percentage of magnetite, the ingredient used in toner for Magnetic

Ink Character Recognition (MICR) printing applications. Inherent in the EBI printer engine design is the capability to produce MICR output without complex toner reformulation. A range of EBI toners are available with different characteristics to satisfy a variety of applications.

To fuse the toner into the paper, the toner is first transferred to the heated transfer belt – similar to the soft blanket used on offset presses. The toner is then heated almost to melting point before being transferred to the paper, which has been preheated to accept the liquefied toner. The entire transfusion process occurs at low pressure so the printed substrate is largely unaffected by pressure. EBI print engines easily accommodate exceptionally low paper weights and a wide variety of finishes, and no further fusing process is required. This low-pressure fusing process also provides toner transfer efficiency of over 98%; it does not require heated fusing rollers, nor does it consume silicon oil.

EBI belt technology completely eliminates the need for a developer station in the print engine. There is no downtime required to change the developer, which is a frequent maintenance issue with electrophotographic printer engines. Any toner remaining on the print drum is physically scraped from its surface by a simple steel doctor blade. The final step in the process is the erasure of electrostatic images from the print drum, accomplished with an erase rod containing an electron generator. It can use direct transfer for faster engines, such as the CR series, or indirect belt transfer in the Imaggia engine, as shown in Figure 6.77.

FIGURE 6.77 Schematic of the indirect belt transfer system of electron beam imaging

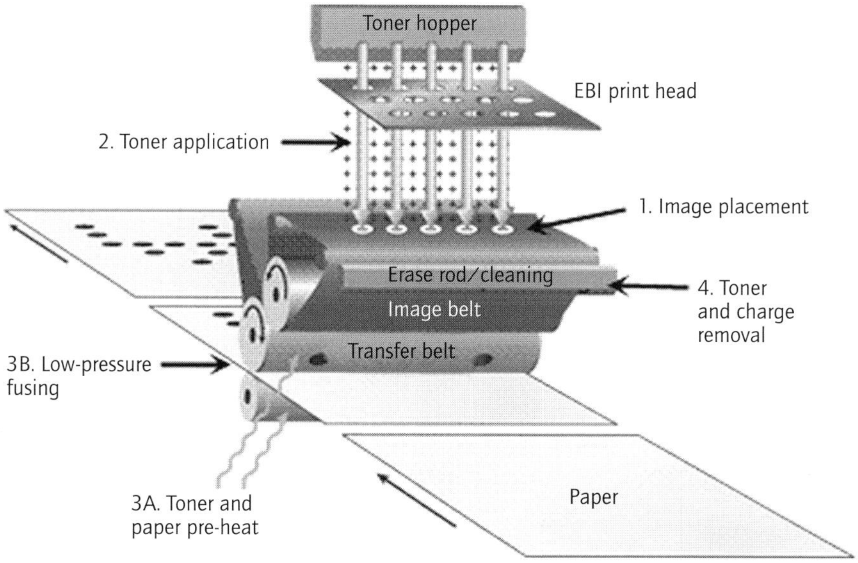

Source: Delphax Inc.

Delphax claims that EBI is more efficient than laser toner printing. The 'write black' process used means the patterns of charges are applied directly to the image belt. Compared to laser printers that have to charge an image drum surface and then remove the charge, the EBI process is a single step. This allows potentially faster, more robust engines to be produced.

Magnetography

In this application the drum has a hard magnetic coating similar to the ferro- and chrome oxide coating used on recording tapes. These magnetic recording coatings contain large numbers of minute magnetic domains that can be aligned by the strong magnetic fields created in the recording heads. In these printers the information to be printed from the computer is written with an array of tiny electromagnets selectively energised to create a latent magnetic image on the surface of the revolving drum. The magnetic write heads perform the same function that the laser performs in electrophotography. During one drum revolution, the image is developed, transferred to the substrate and then the drum is erased to prepare it for the next image. This process enables extremely fast and reliable continual printing that is ideal for high-volume, variable text and on-demand applications. The image is developed via exposure to magnetic toner particles, and the developed image is then transferred and fused to paper.

FIGURE 6.78 Schematic of the magnetography printing process

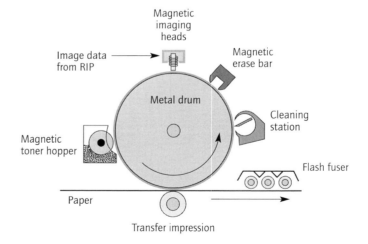

Source: Pira International Ltd

The transferring of the image to the substrate uses a combination of mechanical force (60%) and electrostatic force. The use of both mechanical and electrostatic forces yields a transfer efficiency of 80 to 85%. The current magnetographic printers use radiant heat to fuse the image on to the substrate. This method makes the black toner absorb the radiation and melt itself rather than heating the printed substrate. This renders the print quite cool compared to electrophotographic powder toner applications, so it can be used for lightweight plastic webs.

The latest models allow 600dpi resolution, providing excellent text and halftone reproduction in book printing. There are concerns over the ability to provide transparent magnetic colour toner that would be necessary for process colour; all current commercial machines are black only. A further advantage of magnetography is that the magnetic image on the drum is much more permanent than the charge appropriate to photoconductive drums, hence the possibility of producing multiple copies from one imaging operation. This may enable higher production speeds in situations where variable imaging is not required.

Electrostatic printing

Technology similar to magnetography has been brought to market by Océ in its CPS700–900 machines. These engines incorporate seven magnetographic units to lay down CMYK plus RGB colour. A print is built up by attracting toner to the surface of a rotating drum by selectively applying charge across fine wires at the drum's surface to compile a complete toner image. Coloured dots do not overlap each other. The monolayer is then pressed onto paper that could be embossed, textured or coated before fusing at a lower temperature than in laser printing, which reduces paper curl. The engine operates at a constant 25 A4 impressions a minute whatever the media. The short path is claimed to provide virtually no paper jams.

Electrocoagulation

Elcorsy is a Canadian company that operated in the photo-finishing market. The company has a multicolour printing device based on a technology called electrocoagulation. This involves pigment being precipitated (coagulated) onto the surface of a metal drum in response to electrical charges transferred from the print head. Any excess liquid ink is removed by a doctor blade, and the remaining image transferred onto the substrate. The elcography process has had a long period of development and the Elco 400 machines are now in commercial use in very small numbers.

The process starts with a conditioning system to prepare the surface of an imaging cylinder by coating it with a vegetable oil. The imaging cylinder is a simple metal-surfaced cylinder acting as the electrode in the deposition process. The imaging cylinder rotates to the inking nip where special water-based conductive ink is injected on to its surface. The print head, an array of needle electrodes, sends ultra-fast electrical charges through the ink, signifying how and where to coagulate particles on the imaging cylinder. This chemical reaction makes the dot more cohesive than the surrounding ink. This allows the next step, image revealing, where the surplus ink fluid is wiped off with doctor blades leaving the image exposed on the drum. The rubber doctor blade removes the surplus uncoagulated ink (recycled back into the injection chamber) but does not disturb the deposited image particles. The transfer of the image to paper is achieved in a cold pressure nip. A scrubber is then used to clean off any remaining image materials before a new conditioning cycle starts the process again.

FIGURE 6.79 Schematic of the elcography system

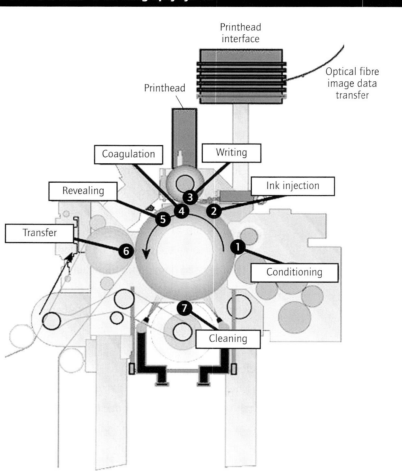

Source Elcorsy Technology Inc.

The ink system has been developed by Toyo Ink. The volume of ink coagulation varies with time so each dot can have a different thickness, which means there is no need for complex and time-consuming half-tone screening algorithms. The electrocoagulation reaction takes place in four microseconds, or writing 250,000 dots per second. At a resolution of 400dpi, the nominal writing speed is 15m per second. During the imaging process hydrogen gas is generated from the water carrier fluid of the inks, which can lead to streaks in the printed image. The vegetable oil applied during the conditioning process is incorporated to absorb the gas and avoid this defect.

Choosing the appropriate print process **7**

There are many ways of producing a print job and each offers different costs, quality levels and timescales. To the inexperienced buyer, there is a bewildering array of potential printing processes on the market. Print salesmen promote their company's capabilities to attract jobs and use capacity to earn a return on the high investment. But the messages to buyers can be contradictory as they listen to some of the almost 100,000 printing companies across Europe; this is now compounded by another set of messages from companies in the emerging markets of India and China.

There is no best printing method that applies to all businesses and market requirements. The inkjet technology used to print BT phone bills is not suitable for printing *Vogue* magazine or packaging for Kellogg's cornflakes. Gravure or offset for your catalogue? Litho or flexo for the carton? Silkscreen or offset for the credit card? Digital or litho for the short-run brochure? Long or short grain? B1 or B2? Hybrid method to speed up the turnaround and reduce costs? How can the overall supply chain be improved?

Buyers need to consider the capability, quality, run length, timescale and cost of each process that will determine which one they choose (then they come to selecting the supplier – 250 business cards will not be a job for a large magazine house). This chapter presents the choice of processes, and then looks at offset in a little more detail. This is unlikely to provide definitive answers to the absolute selection of a process but is aimed to be a guide providing some questions and issues to consider.

Project specification

The initial stage of choosing the appropriate technology is to plan the project, and its value will determine the amount of time to spend at this stage. The key considerations include:

- ► product specification (design, content, size, pagination, life-time, finishing)
- ► cost (paid to supplier, internal and overall project)
- ► quality (fitness for purpose, mono, spot, process, wide gamut)
- ► run length (single run or many small runs with updates)
- ► timescale (when needed).

The relative importance of each will vary for each project. For a financial analyst's report, the most important factor is to have the copy in the hands of the stockbroker at 8am. A make-up advertisement insert must have flawless, high-quality printing for the model's face and the plastic packaging for bacon must have the correct air barrier properties.

Product specification

The end product will determine which printing and binding combination is required, and the specification will often disqualify many processes.

For point-of-sale on a thick board, silk-screen or wide-format inkjet are the only processes capable of providing the high saturation colours required. A two-piece metal can be printed dry offset on a mandrill as part of the metal extrusion and coating process of the can manufacturing line. A cheque that has to conform to document processing specifications has to have water fugitive security inks in the background, and wet litho is not suitable. Most printed products are not so self-determining; many magazines or books could be equally well printed through digital, offset or gravure technology and some books still use flexography.

Cost
The economics of the product will be the most important factor for most print buyers, and a key element of decision making for others. It is important to consider the overall cost of buying print, and not simply concentrate on the price paid to the supplier to comply with a strategy of minimising the overall cost. This means that clients should look beyond the unit cost of production and work to reduce the costs across the supply chain.

The following table shows the broad cost implications of the main processes.

TABLE 7.1 Cost implications of printing processes

	Litho	**Flexo**	**Gravure**	**Digital**
Image master	Plates are relatively cheap and quick to produce	High cost of plate material relative to litho, longer to prepare and mount a flexo plate	Cylinder production is very expensive, long runs are needed to defray high cost of cylinder	No image master needed (except for on-press DI technology)
Run-on costs	Low, but waste is generally higher than gravure from ink/water balance issues. Sheetfed needs folding	Low, often in-line packaging or envelopes to reduce subsequent costs	Gravure run-on is lower than litho with ability to print on poorer quality paper	Highest unit cost of copy production – may change as inkjet matures
Quality	Excellent, capability of many colours and special effects	Lowest reproduction quality although continually improving. Good for spot colours	Some fuzziness of type, excellent colour reproduction even on poor quality paper	Latest machines match mono and process colour litho. Greyscale inkjet quality improving at high speed
Format flexibility	Web offset has fixed cut off and a plate gap causing process waste (except in stationery and may be introduced for commercial). Totally variable in sheetfed	Variable cylinder sizes provide optimum use for conversion products	Variable cylinder and short grain folding provides maximum flexibility for publication work	Totally variable, sheetfed limited to A3+. Web offers 'limitless' length. Inkjet wide format now an alternative
Most suitable for	Short (sheetfed) to long (web-fed) runs of most printed products	Envelopes, packaging, labels	Long publication runs, repeating packaging	Ultra short run, fast turnaround work, personalisation. Consider for products needing regular updates instead of a longer single run

Source: Pira International Ltd

Quality
Quality judges how fit the final product is for the purpose it is intended. For printed items, this involves reproduction quality, materials, printability and binding characteristics, but there is also quality of service, delivery performance against schedule to take into account. Much print quality is a subjective assessment by the customer who asks: Is it what was wanted?

Different printing processes provide degrees of printability. Characteristics of gloss, print contrast, colour saturation, resolution, consistency of solids, colour gamut, will be largely determined by the printing process. Whatever the process, the buyer must explain their requirements clearly to the supplier and maintain realistic expectations. The use of analogue quality measurement systems allowed quantitative assessment of print quality, and similar systems are being developed for the digital workflows that will aid quality across all processes.

Files should be generated following specific, or industry, guidelines, and films and proofs produced independently of the printer should comply with some form of technical specification. Many printers issue technical standards based on how their presses perform that specify the form in which they require data files to be supplied and proofed.

In addition, generic standards have been produced for specific sectors of the industry (see Chapter 3). Guidelines for digital production cover the production of application files with the necessary contents in terms of images, logos, fonts, etc. Increasingly the settings to produce suitable PDF files are also given. A good example is the pass4press standard from the PPA and FIPP (International Federation of the Periodical Press), *Practical Guide to Digital Production – Learning to Fly,* together with several PDF/X standards.

For coldset newspapers, there is *UK Offset Newspaper Specification* (UKONS) in the UK and *Specifications for Non-heat Advertising Print* (SNAP) in North America. The ISO technical committee for graphic technology has been working to develop a common set of technical specifications for the different processes. These are specified as follows under standard ISO 12647 – *Process control for the manufacture of halftone colour separations, proof and production prints*:

Part 1 (1996) Parameters and measurement methods

Part 2 (1996) Offset lithographic processes

Part 3 (1998) Coldset offset lithography and letterpress on newsprint

Part 4 (under development) *Gravure*

Part 5 (2001) Screen printing

Part 6 (under development) *Flexo Printing.*

Run length

The number of copies required is one of the most important selection criteria. The economics of initial set-up are significant for all print processes (even digital) but the subsequent running costs are relatively low, comprising materials, machinery and production time. The make-ready must be amortised across the rest of the run so the longer the run, the less important is make-ready.

The high cost of a gravure cylinder means it will be economic only for longer runs while offset platemaking is fast and cheap providing more flexibility for short to medium runs. Web printing uses more expensive machines than sheet, and wastes more paper so is used for longer runs than sheetfed. Digital printing has no separate platemaking stage, so it is most suitable for low runs and personalisation.

Timescale for delivery

In some cases, a need for immediate delivery means that the buyer will use whatever process has available capacity but, with suitable planning, the delivery time is less critical. The shorter the time available for a job, the less choice there is for the buyer. The time taken for printing, finishing and distribution depends on the processes uses. A faster process generally means the job will take less time, but the time for prepress, work in hand and the necessary stages must be considered.

The batch production nature of printing means that print companies have the best chance of optimising their work if they have reasonable lead times. There is less chance of batching similar jobs together and obtaining manufacturing efficiencies if jobs are placed at short notice.

The speed of the process will determine the time of printing. The relative speed of technologies ranges from the fastest, gravure, followed by web offset, flexo, sheetfed litho and digital. In-line gravure and flexo solutions allow parallel processing, and sometimes save the time of separate collation, folding and binding. Digital technology can allow a short time for the first complete copy in a parallel process rather than the previously necessary serial production of conventional printing. Digital printing has changed a lot of the restraints of delivery times. The capability of printing a complete job on a variable data digital press in one pass, instead of having to print different sections, means that initial quantities may be ready quickly and allow the bulk run to be produced conventionally over a longer time.

Influence of the substrate

The colour, smoothness, absorbency, substance and opacity of the substrate have a marked affect on the appearance of the final printed reproduction. White and smooth papers (e.g. coated art papers and smooth cartridge papers) will produce good image detail, colour saturation and range of tones.

Absorbent and rougher papers (e.g. matt cartridges, bonds, mechanical printings) produce a more limited tone range and colour fidelity is reduced. Inks tend to print dirtier than on coated papers because the light-scattering properties of the surface are different. Rough papers require a coarser screen to avoid excessive dot gain, which limits the fineness of detail that can be produced.

Colour separations should be made for the type of substrate to be used, which reduces some of the effects of poorer quality papers but can never completely compensate. The printing process and substrate together determine the range of tones that can be produced. Table 7.2 below gives some typical figures, expressed in density units.

TABLE 7.2 Typical density ranges of substrate/process combinations

Paper type	Litho	Flexo	Gravure
Coated	1.7–1.9	1.4–1.6	1.8–2.0
Uncoated	1.4–1.6	1.0–1.2	1.6–1.8
Newsprint	1.0–1.2	0.9–1.2	1.3–1.6
Plastic film	1.8–2.2	1.6–2.0	

Source: Pira International Ltd

A dense range will give good colour saturation and detail throughout the tone range. At lower density ranges, shadow detail will usually be sacrificed to preserve highlight and mid-tone gradation, unless instructions to the contrary are given.

Showthrough from the other side of the sheet may be significant on some papers and detract from the quality of a design. This applies particularly to periodical and newspaper printing. Large areas of light uniform tones are best avoided.

Book printing

Book printing is one of the markets that has embraced new technology, particularly digital printing, to change the economics of production. The uniform nature of the product with sections and cover makes books suited to digital printing, with short runs increasingly being produced digitally.

TABLE 7.3 Which process: books

	Digital		Offset	
	Sheet	**Web**	**Sheet**	**Web**
Run length	Single copies available, generally very short run	From short to medium, in some cases long runs	Short to medium runs	Medium to long runs. All lengths for very high pagination titles to minimise gathering during binding
Format	Non A4/A3 results in high paper waste	Totally variable cut off, width of press will determine the number of pages printed across that will affect costs	Totally variable, large format sheetfed machines to minimise number of sections in bindery	Fixed cut off and folder for particular format
Make-up of book	Mono, limited spot colour. Covers from colour machines and DI	Mono text sections or book blocks	Mono, spot and full colour with specials (metallics and varnishing)	Mono text sections, some long run standard format colour
In-line processing	Machines can be configured with in-line trimming and binding lines. Book can be imposed and printed in one pass, covers added and bound		Separate folding and binding	In-line folding, separate binding
Print-on-demand	Changing the supply chain for book production and distribution, allowing distributors and bookshops to produce single copies to order		Book printers set up specialist systems to allow simple ordering and reprints from customers, many also employ digital technology	
Issues	Publishers can reduce their print orders and maintain authors in print. Competition from electronic e-books		The industry suffers from large quantities of unsold books distributed to shops that tie up capital and have to be re-pulped. Minimum print runs make it uneconomic to keep titles in print	

Source: Pira International Ltd

Magazine/catalogue printing

TABLE 7.4 Which process: magazines/catalogues		
Sheetfed litho	**Web offset**	**Gravure**
Most versatile of the processes. Short runs of very high quality. Multi-colour capability with spot and extended process colour. Odd formats and special sections, covers and throw-outs.	Coldset and heatset possible for mono and full colour processes. Paginations from 16pp to 96pp (twin web) possible. Fixed cut off length (except for some stationery applications) mean paper wastage is higher on non-standard sizes, microgap and gapless designs reduce waste. Simple, low-cost prepress for litho platemaking with set up linked to CIP4 data. Cover presses allow additional colours and coatings to be printed with sheeters and folders providing great product flexibility.	Gravure is best suited for long runs. Quality is good on lower-quality paper than offset, and the variable cut-off allows low paper wastage. Folders are simple and allow in-line finishing and stitching so save on separate binding. Wide presses provide high pagination signatures, so high pagination (126pp) to be finished and bound; so reducing gathering stations needed for high pagination products.
Eight- to 12-unit perfecters allow single-pass production of sheets. Some machines have reel infeeds to take advantage of lower cost for web paper. Maximum speed is about 15,000sph, less for larger than SRA1 format.	Complex newspaper presses can be used for semi-commercial work, some have heatset ovens on some newer presses.	Fastest printing process allows high runs to be printed quickly reducing production schedules. Prepress tends to be lengthier than for offset with cylinder preparation and set up for variable cut off.
No significant heat-assisted drying. Grain direction can be varied to make all finished products long grain.	Typical paper surface temperatures are 100–140°C during the drying process. This dries the paper and causes waviness in the product as it takes up moisture unless sophisticated remoistening is used.	Ink drying is at lower temperature than offset on a unit basis. This allows wet on dry printing with good ink trapping. The paper does not dry out and so there is little waviness as paper reabsorbs moisture.
Water-based coatings allow silk and semi-gloss finishes, UV drying provides high gloss and capability of spot varnishing in-line.	High gloss finishes possible from heatset often demanded by advertisers.	Lower gloss than heatset, often cheaper grades of paper used to get equivalent quality.
Grain direction can be varied to make all finished products long grain.	Short grain and long grain presses mean that A3 and A5 products have different grain direction to A4 (or equivalents).	Generally short grain folding allows very fast web speeds and in-folder finishing.
Huge choice of suppliers (about 6000 in UK).	Wide choice of suppliers (maybe 100 in UK).	Limited choice in UK, more in Europe.
Higher cost of sheetfed paper although set up waste can be reduced by re-use of waste sheets.	Reels' lower cost than sheets, non-standard sizes may increase lead-time for materials.	Lower quality of paper in comparison to offset for same print quality, less uniform surface necessary.

Source: Pira International Ltd

Litho – sheetfed or web-fed? There are many sheet and web production houses competing for work as technology advances provide an ever-changing arena of competitive advantage. Assuming the priority to be the best quality for the best price, the factors that will influence the choice of process will be:

▶ longer runs of the order of 20,000 copies or more will be better suited to web offset

▶ sheetfed offers more print units for wider gamut of process colours and special effects with in-line varnishing

▶ the higher web-press speed, with its combined folding and finishing, will meet tight deadlines better than the sheetfed press

► the web press is better able to print on lower-weight papers than a sheetfed press, but is restricted on the upper limit of paper grades

► web presses offer only a limited range of standard trim sizes and folding options. Non-standard sizes and finishing processes are better handled by sheetfed litho.

The production cycle, or length of time on machine, can be crucial in establishing the cost-effectiveness of one process over the other. The web offset presses deliver perfected, folded sections, ready for finishing in one pass at comparatively high running speeds. To do the same job, sheetfed litho normally involves first printing all the sheets on one side, drying and then printing on the reverse to back them up. Folding them is a separate operation. This situation has now improved with the arrival of the eight-unit and above sheetfed perfecting presses. Folding is still a separate operation, but it does enable the sheetfed printer to compete better with the web printer, particularly for those run-lengths that are only just viable for web printing.

Sheetfed and web offset printing prices are not the same. Not only does the separate cost of folding need to be added to the sheetfed price, but also the paper can be a determining factor. Paper bought on the reel will be cheaper than the same paper bought in sheets, but web offset paper wastage will certainly be higher and the value of the paper that needs to be purchased has to enter the equation. High-volume sheetfed presses can use cheaper web paper with a sheeter at in-feed.

Where price and delivery time are evenly matched, sheet offset printing can sometimes offer more flexibility when either format or final pagination is not known until a late stage, or when there is likely to be a need to reprint in small quantities. The question of oddments in magazine or bookwork can be important. Oddments can normally be more effectively printed sheetfed, either by using a smaller machine or by printing on a smaller sheet size.

Long-grain or short-grain web offset

There are many configurations of web press, and the paginations per revolution and number of webs can be varied along with the orientation. Machines were developed to lower the unit cost of manufacture. Presses have faster paper speeds, multiple webs and wider machines to increase conversion rates. One way was to develop short-grain 32-page (16pp to view) presses. Instead of aligning A4 pages around the cylinder in portrait format, the pages are rotated by 90° to landscape orientation. Short-grain folders are generally much simpler than long-grain, using a former design rather than chopper cylinders, so allowing faster paper conversion. This results in a thinner, wider cylinder producing sections with the grain running parallel to the head rather than the spine. A 32-page long-grain press typically has a circumference of 1260mm (1248mm with microgap) and maximum width of 945mm web width for A4. The short grain press has a circumference of 890mm (878mm with narrow gap) and a maximum width of 1300mm. The mechanics of the press are similar to the conventional format with faster cylinder rotation and similar paper speeds. At the same paper speed a short-grain press yields 40% more printed sections than a long-grain machine. The investment cost is slightly higher for the larger short-grain machine, the power consumption is higher but manning and other fixed costs are the same as a long-grain machine.

FIGURE 7.1 Difference between long grain and short grain web production

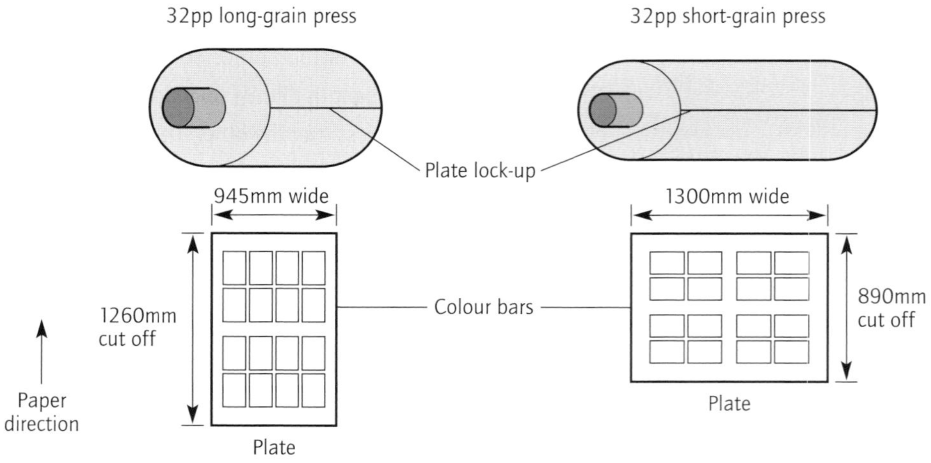

32pp long-grain press

32pp short-grain press

Plate lock-up

945mm wide

1300mm wide

1260mm
cut off

Colour bars

890mm
cut off

Paper
direction

Plate

Plate

Source: Pira International Ltd

There are now wider versions offering 48pp (96pp twin web) formats. Short grain offers potential productivity benefits over long grain. It also provides flexibility in section height by varying the width of the paper, and providing possible paper savings for some non-standard formats assuming that the page width that does not change is suitable. It is widely used for long run wire stitched products. In the case of perfect bound products, there may be significant cockling as sections reabsorb moisture post drying unless a re-moistener is used. Short grain presses can have gluing, stitching and trimming in-line in the folder to deliver finished 32pp (and 64pp in the case of twin-web machines) magazines and brochures. Short grain production should be considered for medium to high runs of wire-stitched products. The drawbacks with short grain is the grain direction of the product leading to wave across the product rather than parallel to the spine, and the need for wider reels than are used for the commoner long grain production that can cause longer lead times for paper supply.

Strengths/weaknesses of alternative printing processes

The great range of alternative processes that survive and prosper shows the way a mature industry has diversified and specialised. There are no hard and fast rules defining printing processes, and individual suppliers will provide different solutions according to their commercial pressures and the potential opportunities they spot.

Quality and technical process specifications

To get the best or even acceptable print quality, it is necessary to recognise the characteristics of a process and bear these in mind when selecting one. In situations where aspects of production or the product dictate the use of a particular process, it is desirable to consider its characteristics when the job is at the design stage. There are in fact two aspects to consider:

▶ the inherent limitations of a process, which make it more or less suitable for certain types of image reproduction;

▶ the technical specifications for the process, which define the printing characteristics and the prepress requirements.

Printing processes have different capabilities when it comes to coping with different subjects, and these fall into the following categories:

▶ type matter

▶ fine lines

▶ tone reproduction

▶ solid areas of colour

▶ process colour reproduction.

The limitations of any printing process should be considered before a design is created or films produced.

Type matter

Offset litho: Good, clear and sharp edges except for piling. Tiny type is legible, even reversed out.

Flexography: Satisfactory if delicate type styles and those with fine serifs are avoided. Small sizes that are reversed out are unlikely to work well.

Gravure: Edges are fuzzy with cell pattern noticeable, and small type is not so legible so delicate type styles and those with fine serifs are avoided.

Screen: Edge definition is poor from coarser rulings; avoid small serif faces and reverse out of heavy solids.

Digital printer: Good, electrophotography is similar to offset litho so long as resolution is 600dpi or above and type size is not too small. Inkjet is generally lower resolution and there may be character spread on some absorbent stocks.

Fine lines

Offset litho: Excellent reproduction.

Flexography: Ink squash and spread is likely to be apparent and fine lines may break up and are best avoided.

Gravure: Fine lines tend to break up, avoid if possible.

Screen: Same as gravure, screen edge effects are noticeable.

Digital printer: Good, similar to offset litho from electrographic. Inkjet suffers from lower resolution.

Tone reproduction

Offset litho: Excellent, even on uncoated papers.

Flexography: Satisfactory, but difficult to produce good gradation in light tones and smooth vignettes. Best with thin plates and UV ink systems.

Gravure: Good, but light tones will appear speckled if the paper is not well suited to the process and shadow tones are frequently mottled in monochrome reproductions.

Screen: Generally poor and requires coarse screen rulings which can be acceptable if view distance is great.

Laser printer: Good, although screen rulings and reproducible grey levels may be restricted by the imaging resolution.

All processes: Suitable calibration and adjustment is required to allow for the increase in tone transfer characteristics (dot gain) of the process.

Solid areas of colour

Offset litho: Very good on all types of substrate.

Flexography: Very good, but can be poor if a compromise anilox specification is used in order to print in combination fine tone values or text.

Gravure: Reasonably good but solids can appear mottled with some colours.

Screen: Excellent, high saturation possible, and ink surface may be like a paint surface.

Digital print: Can be good, but poor if unit is not well maintained. Early machines showed significant banding problems that have been largely overcome.

Process colour reproduction

Offset litho: Excellent on suitable paper and good results are also possible even on quite poor uncoated papers.

Flexography: Good where platemaking and press conditions have been well adjusted for process colour.

Gravure: Excellent on good paper and satisfactory on lower-quality papers if acceptably smooth, but poor on unsuitable surface papers.

Screen: Not widely used for process colour because of the coarse screen rulings required, which make it suitable only for products like posters.

Digital printer: Good, but screen rulings and reproducible grey levels may be restricted by the imaging resolution particularly in inkjet.

The main strength of flexo lies in its simplicity and relatively low cost. It is particularly suited for single colour and linework (solid areas of colour). Close registration can be difficult on envelope machines, but allowances in prepress can give improved results. Heavy ink coverage is possible but may lead to expansion and deformation of the paper.

Flexo is a direct application of ink from the relief plate to the paper. This always results in a degree of image squash. This is the identifier when examined under a linen tester. Because of the non-planographic nature of the plates, flexo cannot hold the detail available in lithography. Small dots cannot be printed and the resolution in flexo is limited compared to litho. This results in a noticeable screen pattern at 80–120lpi compared to the achievable +175lpi of litho.

TABLE 7.5 Comparison between major print processes

Flexo	Litho	Gravure	Digital
Run lengths from a few hundred to many hundred thousand. With care plate cylinders may be reused many times with just parts of the plate replaced	Used for runs between one copy to millions of copies	Generally longest runs for publication work, from 200,000 to 5m+. With packaging regular reprints of short runs are cost-effective	Generally low run lengths, personalised to low thousands. Inkjet and web mono work for longer runs
Variable cut-off available by changing cylinders	Heatset web has fixed cut-off and plate gap so may waste paper. Stationery presses can swap cylinder to provide variable depth for forms. Sheetfed has many paper and board sizes allowing best use of material	Cylinders can be replaced to provide low paper waste with no plate gap	Totally variable print depth on web machines allowing efficient use of material and ability to produce very long posters
Stack press registration capability is limited, better from common impression	Excellent multi-colour registration	Excellent multi-colour registration. Wet on dry overprinting	Electrophotography provides good registration, some front to back issues with colour duplexing that involves drying out the sheet between imaging
Specialist prepress required for well trapped files. Care when handling close or butt registered jobs. For packaging the thickness of the plate has to be taken into account	Much software development for optimising production and quality. CTP provides high-quality plates, with data to aid press set-up and make-ready	Digital workflows have been used for many years for standard publications with analogue engraving. Laser engraving now speeds up cylinder preparation even more	Straightforward to produce optimised press-ready files for variable data and on-press imaging
Plate material is expensive, some applications just place portions of plates onto cylinders to reduce cost. Plate processing is lengthy with drying of plates	Low cost plates produced via CTP very quickly	High cost of cylinder preparation	Effectively no specific prepress costs after preparation of file for printing, little make-ready required. On-line finishing allows single-pass production of saleable material
Relief plates result in image squash	Clear, crisp text and dots from planographic process. Doubling and slurring are rectifiable faults	Very good tonal colour reproduction with variable colour depth. May be some haloing of dots and type	Limited range of formats and spot colours on high-quality toner systems, text and linework may be jagged on lower resolution devices and inkjet
Limited resolution of halftone screen, frequency 80–120lpi, results in noticeable dot patterning in images	High-frequency screens (+175lpi) show no patterning. FM screening eliminates moiré patterning	Limits on mechanical cylinder engraving but no noticeable artefacts	Commercial inkjet is limited in resolution, toner-based systems provide excellent results
Minimum dot size provides limited quality in highlight reproduction and filling in shadows	Full tonal range is achievable	Wide tonal range available across lower quality papers	Excellent tonal range available from modern colour devices
Matt result, use Pantone U colours (uncoated)	Ink system can give high gloss with a sealer or overprint varnish, can match cleaner Pantone C (coated) colours	Reasonable gloss levels, spot colours either Pantone U or C	Toner-based systems provide non-planographic result with variable gloss according to coverage. Wide colour gamut allows reasonable spot colour matching but few real spot colours available except for inkjet
Six-colour machines very common for multi-colour work	Sheetfed machines with 12 units are common, five-colour web offset machines are available but most heatset is four-colour process	Publication machines are four-colour process, for packaging multiple spot colours are common	Most digital is mono and process colour, inkjet offers pigmented spot colour
Water-based inks may result in paper expansion	Few problems of paper expansion during printing; shrinkage during drying that will cause rippling when the print absorbs moisture from the atmosphere unless remoisteners are used	Very stable paper stock, liquid inks do not cause expansion	Inkjet with water-based inks may lead to paper expansion, marking and strikethrough
Limited colour saturation of inks	Denser inks available than for flexo	Widest range of density available from gravure inks	Wide colour gamut available from inkjet, toner-based systems very close to litho. HP Indigo devices provide spot colour mixing systems
Plate wear and damage can happen at any time, the printer must carefully monitor image through the run	Plate wear is rare and occurs very gradually, replacement plates are cheap and quick to produce	With good handling gravure cylinders are very hardwearing and can be re-used many times in applications such as long-run packaging or wallpaper	Imaging drums and transfer blankets are delicate and regular replacement is necessary
Ink properties vary through the run, will require viscosity monitoring and adjustment	Ink more consistent, care to avoid piling is necessary, automatic washing alleviates this	Some viscosity adjustments are made automatically on the run	Very consistent colour throughout the run and across the sheet
Plate plugging may cause problems clogging	Piling may cause problems	Dot skip may be a problem	Toner drum marking and inkjet nozzle
Many machines are integrated into conversion lines for envelopes, extrusion for flexible and barrier packaging, cartons	Web-fed machines have folders, some finishing options of stitching and gluing	Publication gravure presses have finishing in the folder, stitching, gluing and with electrostatic charge to aid flat folding	Folding, slitting and stitching available on many machines both sheetfed and web

Source: Pira International Ltd

The trend toward the use of hybrid printing systems is starting to break traditional thinking as print companies develop innovative solutions for their customers in an attempt to improve their competitive position.

Short-run colour – litho, on-press (DI) or variable digital printing

The costs of producing a printed product vary according to the chosen method of production. A common choice will be for the production of a short run of colour leaflets orbrochures where relatively new digital printing (on-press imaging or variable data) is becoming a viable alternative to offset.

The costs associated are built up as follows. Variable direct costs of paper and labour will be accounted for in a similar manner. Obviously there is no separate labour and material component in prepress as there is no platemaking stage but there are costs of data preparation and setting up the press that must be accounted for.

It is the machinery cost, consumables (ink/toner, imaging parts) and treatment of necessary maintenance that are treated differently. Digital printer vendors will supply the print engine, data handling/server/RIP and network, paper transport, finishing, maintenance as well as consumables. The ongoing relation lasts over the life of the investment that may well change with upgrades and developments as technology matures. In conventional printing, the press supplier sells and installs the printing machine. Consumables are bought on the open market from the preferred supplier and most maintenance is handled internally. Parts may be bought from the press manufacturer but they would become involved only in major repairs and overhauls. This provides the conventional printer with a wide choice of competing suppliers. There is no similar independent well-established support network for digital printers. The systems are delicate and many manufacturers will specify that branded consumables and spare parts should be used. If they are not, performance guarantees and support may not be available.

When buying a digital press, the buyer makes a contract with a supplier for the capital cost of the equipment with installation and training, and will then enter an agreement to buy consumables and maintenance from that supplier. In many cases, the vendor provides the front-end RIP and server. There are many contractual agreements available covering the capital and running costs from outright purchase, off-balance sheet lease and total cost of ownership cost per print. The three components that have to be taken care of from the supplier are:

▶ capital cost and installation of the engine (including training)
▶ consumables (toner and necessary replacement parts) and
▶ maintenance (guaranteed service response and regular servicing.

In the case of on-press DI technology, suppliers provide specialist plates to use with the imaging heads at an agreed cost, e.g. the Heidelberg Quickmaster DI plate cartridge or Screen's Konica Minolta plates, while other presses use plates from established independent plate supply channels. Some suppliers separate the capital cost of the machine from a maintenance agreement and offer a tiered price for consumables including ink/toner as well as items such as toner drums or inkjet heads. In the case of high value printing systems, the suppliers offer a range of purchase options (capital purchase, lease or total cost of ownership) with particular benefits for cash flow depending on the client requirements.

The model is fundamentally the same from all vendors. The base machine capital cost, whether leased or financed differently, including front end, paper handling, printing and finishing options is one component. Then a fixed consumable cost per print or linear length for web-fed devices (irrespective of web width or print width) is charged with a regular maintenance cost applied according to usage. Finally, there will be a charge for toner based on the average coverage involved. This represents a fixed monthly outgoing, irrespective of the volume of print. So, for a guaranteed level of usage the prints cost x, any additional volume is at a lower price so higher volumes through a press result in an overall lower unit cost, x-y. This means, in effect, that the costs payable to the supplier depend on the number of prints or length of paper printed over the period in question.

Conventional print processes have developed to provide economic reproduction of many identical copies. It is expensive to generate the first copy (although developments are helping to reduce these costs), but the cost of any subsequent copies is low. These set-up costs are amortised across the run length and, as the run increases, the unit cost of production drops. The high initial cost is made up of the prepress activities of preparing, imposing and making the plates and then the press make-ready, time and materials. Digital printing has no separate platemaking and limited make-ready on press (to choose the right file from the job queue and change to the correct paper and finishing options). This results in a low set-up cost but the cost of each subsequent print does not vary no matter what the run length. When the conventional and digital print processes are compared, there is a crossover line, at the point where digital production becomes more economic than conventional.

Comparison between short-run colour litho, on-press (DI) and variable digital printing

Table 7.6 shows how the costs of a small-format SRA3 print job, excluding the necessary prepress component, compare between conventional offset (a Heidelberg four-colour Speedmaster 52), an on-press DI machine (a Dainippon Screen TruePress 344) and a toner-based digital machine (Xerox DocuColor 8000).

TABLE 7.6 Cost build-up of a print job by production method

Run length	Screen 344	Heidelberg 52	Xerox 8000
Investment	€350k	€250k	€300k
Hourly recovery	€85	€50	N/A
Plate costs	~£10.0m⁻²	~£7.20m⁻²	N/A
Employment	1 printer	1 printer	1 operator
Platemaking	£0.04	£0.0310	£0.102
4 plates	€8.00	€5.76	2
Press set-up	5–10min, €10	10 min, €12	2 min
Total job cost			
1	€21.00	€26.16	€2.07
100	€22.21	€26.87	€9.10
500	€27.07	€29.73	€37.50
1,000	€33.14	€33.30	€73.00

TABLE 7.6 Cost build-up of a print job by production method (continued)

Run length	Screen 344	Heidelberg 52	Xerox 8000
5,000	€81.71	€61.87	€357.00
10,000	€142.43	€97.59	€712.00
Unit cost of sheets			
100	€0.222	€0.286	€0.091
500	€0.054	€0.064	€0.075
1,000	€0.033	€0.036	€0.073
5,000	€0.016	€0.014	€0.071
10,000	€0.014	€0.011	€0.071
Job elapsed time (min)			
Set-up	8	12	0
100	8.9	12.6	2.5
500	12.3	15.0	12.5
1,000	16.6	18.0	25.0
5,000	50.9	42.0	125.0
10,000	93.7	72.0	250.0

Source: Pira International Ltd

FIGURE 7.2 Total job cost comparison of conventional offset, on-press DI and variable digital print

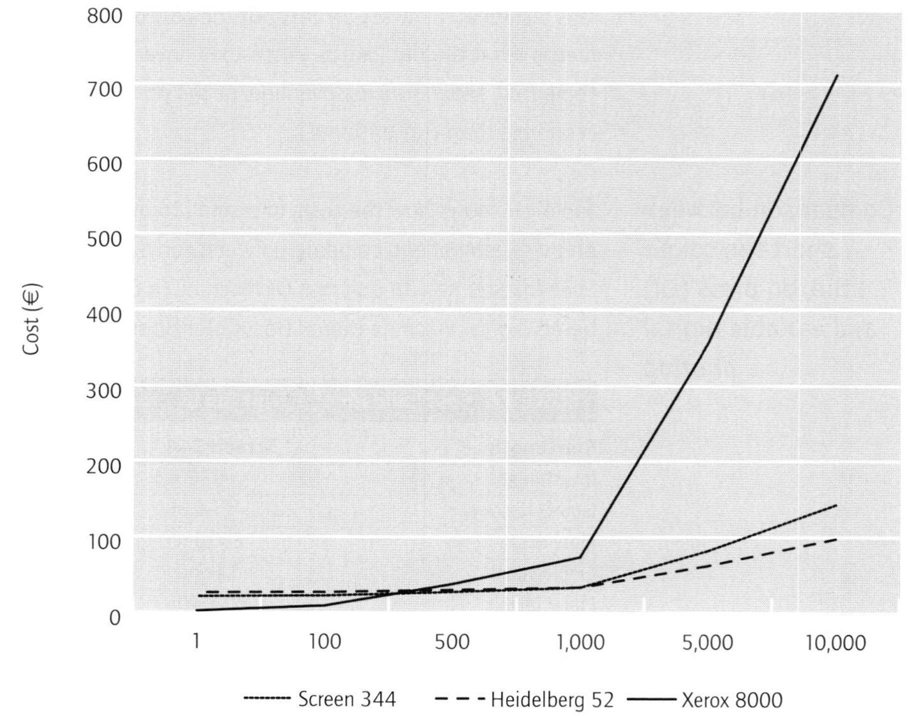

Source: Pira International Ltd

The press set-up costs for a printing an A3 colour leaflet are nominally £75 (€110) for conventional printing (platemaking and make-ready), £25 for on-press direct imaging set up and £5 for the digital press. Subsequent copy costs are set at 1p for conventional offset, 2.2p for DI and 10p for variable data digital (click charge, labour, paper, capital and overheads). In operation the actual costs may vary but the general comparison holds.

FIGURE 7.3 Unit cost comparison of conventional offset, on-press DI and variable digital print

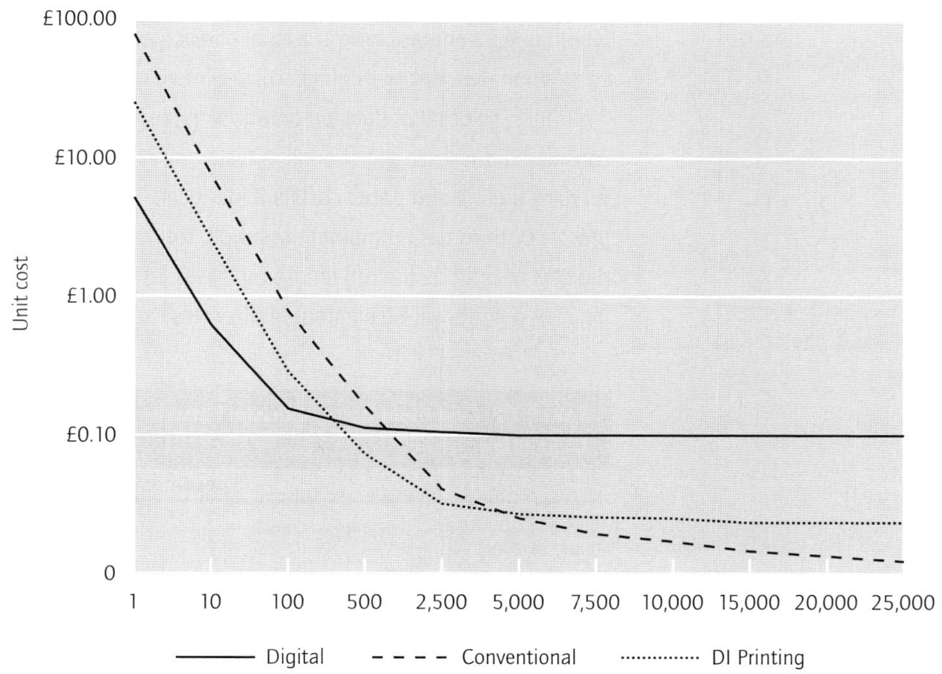

Source: Pira International Ltd

The figure demonstrates that for short runs, variable digital printing is the most cost-effective production method. At run lengths of up to 250 copies there is a crossover and DI printing is the most economical; above 3000–4000, conventional printing is more cost-effective. The figures involved are not selling prices; they are generic cost estimates for conventional and digital print production. Within organisations the internal costs are continually reviewed and refined to remain competitive and to reflect production efficiencies as they occur. If this theoretical exercise were performed over a range of alternative print products the result would be similar curves. The difference may not be so pronounced for some mono products, and the crossover point may differ within different environments.

DI press vs. litho with CTP

A long-standing criticism of DI technology is the need to buy multiple plate exposure units as part of the DI press to run consecutively, then stand idle until the next job change. With a relatively modern single CTP device there is normally sufficient capacity to keep a number of presses supplied with plates. If the press is relatively new it will have automation aids to reduce make-ready time with automatic plate loading, pre-setting of ink and water, adjustments to paper size and side-lay position, etc.

Table 7.7 shows the way costs are built up for a process colour job produced by both methods. The way these costs are apportioned vary from printer to printer, and the cost advantages will differ. In the above example a computer to plate device costing €150,000, including processor, is used to make an average of 40 plates per day. One operator runs the equipment and is paid €30,000 per annum. The equipment finance is some €60,000 per annum with €15,000 for space/power, etc., €1500 per week works out at €7.50 per plate, labour is €3 per plate, giving a total of €10.50. The DI press is more expensive than the conventional model, with plates costing more than the CTP plates.

The costs of data preparation, imposing and preparing plates for output is not considered; these do not change between on-press and off-line imaging. When the press is running the ink and paper costs are identical, the difference being the hourly rated cost. The presses both run at a nominal 12,000iph; it is the higher cost of the DI press that increases the cost of print as the run length increases. In this example the benefit of the cheaper set up, €18 per job will be eliminated after less than 15 minutes running, or 3000 copies.

TABLE 7.7 Cost build-up comparison between conventional process colour and DI printing		
	Speedmaster 74	**Speedmaster 74DI**
Investment	€975,000	€1.5 million
Hourly recovery	€150	€225
Plate costs (0.3mm metal)	~€12/m² (CTP)	~€15/m²
Employment	2 printers	1 printer, 1 assistant
Prepress from imposition	~€10 per plate (€30)	€0
Four colour	€19.20	€24
Press set-up	15 min @ €37	15 min @ €56
Costs for 4-colour process	€98.70	€80.25
100 copies	€100.20	€82.50
500 copies	€107.70	€93.75
1,000 copies	€122.70	€116.25
5,000 copies	€197.70	€228.75
10,000 copies	€347.70	€453.75

Source: Pira International Ltd

Printing inks

8

Ink is the medium that transfers a pigmented image onto the substrate in a printing process. Ink is a significant proportion of the cost of print, sometimes accounting for up to 5–10% of the cost of a finished job. Printing ink is a homogeneous mix of ingredients such as liquid or paste. It is not a particular chemical compound but a colloidal suspension of pigment in a varnish vehicle with other additives. The formula of ink is based on a coloured pigment or extender that is finely dispersed in a resinous vehicle, and sometimes with a drying agent present.

Offset, flexo, gravure, silk screen and inkjet each require different types of ink formulation. There will be many flavours of each, in many colours and coatings, to perform on different presses and equipment, to print onto various substrates, to provide security or authenticity to a product or document; or to provide a range of finishes and particular physical or chemical properties. The ink is formulated to give the final print its required characteristics, to perform well on the printing press involved and to be economic. Certain components have been found to be potentially hazardous and have been phased out of formulations. Guidelines on suspect materials are published and updated regularly, in America by the Food and Drug Administration (FDA), and in the UK the British Coatings Federation (BCF).

Basic ink formulation

Some of each of the following materials is present in nearly all inks:

▶ *pigment* – colorant (may be a dye base in some solvent-based liquid inks);

▶ *solids* – usually resins that form the binder for the pigment after the print is dry (sometimes in conjunction with the liquids below);

▶ *liquids* – make the ink fluid on the machine and may be involved in the drying process (when combined with the resins it is referred to as the vehicle because it carries the colour and other solids to the substrate);

▶ *additives* – are included in the formulation to modify press performance characteristics or to meet end-use requirements.

TABLE 8.1 Typical contents of conventional oxidation drying sheetfed ink

Ingredient	Analysis	% (by weight)
Pigment	Organic and inorganic colorants	13–22%
Vehicle	Comprising vegetable oil, alkyd and hard rosin ester	45–75%
Solvent	Petroleum distillate (mineral oil) or soya oil	10–30%
Additives	Rheological extenders	0–5%
	Wax	0–10%
	Dryers	0–3%
	Anti-oxidant	0–1%

Source: Pira International Ltd

The bulk of the ingredients are mixed together and then dispersed in a specialist grinding mill, which is normally a triple roll or a bead shot mill. The part formulation is tested and then the rest of the components, normally liquid dryers and solvent, are added to make the desired rheology. Specialist manufacturers produce a wide variety of inks formulated for their customers' processes and particular requirements. Ink users specify ink by performance characteristics and for the particular end-use print requirement.

Pigments

Pigments are obtained from a variety of organic and inorganic sources. The most common pigment is carbon-black (soot), which is used for black inks. It is manufactured by burning mineral oil with a restricted air supply. Other pigments are much more difficult and expensive to manufacture or refine and can be very varied chemically. As a consequence of this, inks of different colours can require chemical adjustments to the vehicle and additives. The result of this is that inks of different colours do not behave identically on the printing press or when drying. Their permanent characteristics may also differ.

Additionally, there is considerable price variation between colours, and some cost up to four times as much as the others for the same volume.

Vehicle

The vehicle, or varnish, will consist of oils, resins or alkyds. All litho and most letterpress inks are oil-based. Screen, gravure and flexographic inks are resin-based, but use a solvent that acts as a volatile carrier for the vehicle and, in turn, holds the pigment. There is research, due to environmental considerations, into using water as the solvent, but at present this is restricted to printing, both by gravure and flexography, on paper substrates and products such as sweet wrappers. For each process, different vehicle formulations are available offering particular features to suit different requirements. These are mostly used to meet the technical needs of the printer, but sometimes they are relevant to the end user who might want characteristics such as non-tainting formulations for food packaging.

Additives

Additives will include dryers, anti-oxidants, extenders, fillers and slip agents. The ink manufacturer will add those additives anticipated to meet most requirements, but printers often mix in other additives to obtain characteristics to meet particular or unusual requirements. The most common additives are the following:

Dryers

Different mixtures are formulated depending on the printing process used, substrate, speed of drying, additional production processes and the end use. Paradoxically, excessive addition of drying additives can slow, or prevent, satisfactory drying. Additionally, with the litho process, excessive dryers can react with fount solution chemicals and cause printing problems.

Extenders

Extenders are inorganic substances that increase the area covered by the pigment and improve transfer. Materials include whiting, barytes, aluminium hydrate, blanc fixe.

Distillates

These are high-boiling hydrocarbons that alter the rheological characteristics of an ink to enable it to flow more freely.

Anti-oxidants

These modify the open-time of the ink on the press and the subsequent drying on the substrate.

Waxes

These are used mainly in packaging grade inks to improve the slip and scuff resistance of the finished sheets. On no account should inks with wax additives be used when sheets are to be varnished or laminated subsequently.

Printing process requirements

All of the traditional printing methods use inks that need to be fluid on the printing machine but become solid when on the print. Each process also requires specific qualities and properties that are appropriate to its individual needs.

Offset lithography

Offset litho inks are relatively viscous with high tack for good transfer, and a high pigment concentration. This is needed because the printed ink film thickness in offset litho is much less than in other processes. The ink film thickness of dry litho ink is not normally more than two microns. Conventional lithographic inks must be oil-based to enable the planographic process to work, and the inks must function and print well in combination with the fount solution. The fount solution must be able to emulsify with the ink, but not excessively, and this should not hamper the performance of the ink. To avoid drying on the roller system, the inks must not contain readily evaporating components.

Gravure

Liquid ink is needed to enable the millions of minute cells of the gravure cylinders to readily transfer ink and replenish with ink. Gravure ink is often supplied at a higher viscosity than is required on the press, and the viscosity is reduced with additional solvent before printing. Gravure deposits a greater ink film thickness on the substrate compared with offset litho, and is similar to that for letterpress. The small, enclosed ink system enables relatively volatile materials to be used in these inks, although there is much environmental pressure to minimise the use of toluene and other volatile organic compounds (VOCs), despite the fact that the driers are efficient at recycling solvents. There is growth in the use of water-based inks, as well as radiation-cured varieties, as gravure moves out from just solvent-based inks.

Flexography

Flexographic printing uses low-viscosity liquid ink. The ink is pumped from a reservoir into a pan where it is picked up by a roller and transferred to the anilox roller. The viscosity of the ink must be consistent. It is recirculated into closed chambers that reduce evaporation of solvent-based formulations and make changeovers much quicker, with wash-up taking place off-line. Modern presses use equipment to monitor the viscosity continually, with additives dosed to maintain the optimal characteristics because a change in viscosity is a major cause of colour variation. A low viscosity is needed to transfer properly, but if it is too low the ink will not be dense enough and will tend to run down the sides of the image; too high a viscosity results in a halo around printed images and infill of halftones.

There are three main ink types: solvent based, water based and radiation drying (ultraviolet and electron beam curing). Solvent-based inks dominate most market sectors; water-based and UV-curing inks are being used by an ever growing number of printers.

Solvent-based inks perform well on-press and operators know how to optimise productivity by adding judicious amounts of solvent to maintain runnability. The ink is fast drying on non-absorbent substrates and provides good adhesion to plastics. The drawback with solvent-based inks is the environmental impact of volatile organic compounds (VOCs) being released into the atmosphere and tainting the finished product. Fire risks and any impact on production personnel also have to be taken into account. Ink manufacturers are developing water-based formulations, which do not have these negative environmental impacts, but they are different to run on-press and do not give as good a printed result on many substrates.

The greatest growth is in radiation-curing inks, driven by quality and productivity issues as well as their lower environmental impacts. Instant-curing ink films do not spread so they exhibit low dot gain on any surface, which enhances quality. Radiation-curing inks contain 100% solids; compared to water- and solvent-based inks, a thinner film has to be applied to achieve the same colour. High gloss and good chemical, abrasion and heat resistance can also be achieved. Instant curing means the job can be checked for adhesion, chemical resistance and other properties immediately (except for cationic UV curing). Subsequent processing, conversion inline or rewinding will not mark, set-off or block, even on non-absorbent films. These properties make UV flexo especially well suited to shorter runs, where quick make-ready and low ink maintenance are key to efficient production. The latest UV flexo ink systems combine high pigmentation with low viscosity for use with finely engraved, low-volume aniloxes of 1200lpi and higher. These inks can be pumped and are suitable for use with chambered doctor blade systems.

As flexo presses are being configured with more print units – 10 or 12 units inline – so more colours can be printed in one pass. This places additional demands on the inks being used. Process colour sets, some using additional inks to extend the colour gamut, are increasing, and there are many spot colours. The opaque white base is important for flexible packaging, with metallics and fluorescent colours growing in popularity. More large printers are installing automated mixing and dispensing systems using computerised colour-matching technology to mix both fresh inks and inks returned from the press to give more accurate and faster colour matching, reduce waste and drive down costs.

Screen Screen inks are usually semi-liquid with good flow characteristics to allow for free passage through the screen/stencil apertures. Consistency can vary from gel inks with thixotropic properties to the longer-gloss finish inks. They are not usually supplied in a press-ready condition and require reducing with an appropriate thinner to provide the correct viscosity for printing. The range of inks available is large. One major supplier lists more than 50 different types, which reflects the diversity of the process. Inks can be formulated to provide specific properties related to the application. There is significant growth in the use of UV-curing inks.

Digital printing

Variable data digital printing uses two major technologies: toner and inkjet. Dry toner system comprises a mixture of pigmented toner and magnetisable carrier particles while liquid toner from HP Indigo comprises electrically chargeable particles dispersed in a liquid. Developments of emulsion aggregation, where toner particles are grown to a uniform size distribution and spherical shape, may provide better quality and productivity while it is cheaper to make than conventional toner. The claimed benefits are sharper details, as there are no large particles blurring edge definition, while less toner will be needed as smaller, but more uniform particles, will cover the sheet with a thinner toner layer and still get the same visual result. Wax may be incorporated into the toner to stop sticking to the surface of the fuser rollers without using fuser oil, which may leave a residue on the print.

HP Indigo's electroInk comprises toner pigment that is suspended in an electrically insulating fluid. Since the toner is in a liquid, it is in some ways easier to control than a dry powder. As a result, the particle size can be significantly less (1–2 microns) than in a dry toner system giving the potential for higher resolution on paper. The wide range of inks now available for the Indigo presses appears to indicate that the toners for these inks may be easier to manufacture and produce a wider range of pigments.

Inkjet ink has developed considerably from the use of dyes in water or solvents and care is needed to avoid drying up and clogging the nozzles. Pigmented systems are now in use with fine dispersions enabling more lightfast and resistant print. Water-based, solvent (including less aggressive 'eco-solvents') and fast-growing UV-curing formulations are broadening the scope of inkjet while improving the reliability of the process.

Ink drying mechanisms

The basic drying methods are chemical (polymerisation) and physical (the deposition of a dry film by solvent removal). Almost all drying mechanisms are based in some way on these either singly or in combination. The choice is to a large extent dictated by the printing process and the need to maintain press stability on the one hand, and adequate drying on the other.

Chemical drying methods

Oxidation

Oxidation is the chief way by which sheetfed offset and letterpress inks dry. The ink vehicle takes oxygen from the air in a chemical reaction that causes it to harden (polymerise), and binding the pigment with it. The reaction is slow and it takes several hours to achieve a rub-proof ink film.

Polymerisation – heat assisted

The oxidation polymerisation process can be speeded up by heat, and IR driers are used on sheetfed offset presses for this purpose. There are also two component ink formulations that are designed for this method of drying.

Polymerisation – UV assisted

Ultraviolet curing inks and clear varnishes contain a photoinitiator and use ultraviolet light to cause almost instantaneous polymerisation. The inks are 100% solids with acrylate and urethane monomers and oligomers that polymerise in the presence of free-radical or cationic photoinitiators. These ink systems can be used only with specially equipped printing presses. The method is commonly used in sheetfed offset litho and is becoming more widely used in screen and flexography. The dry ink film is hard, scuff-resistant and is favoured for packaging applications.

Polymerisation – electron beam assisted

Electron beam curing uses similar ink formulations to those of UV but it is bombardment with electrons that initiates the curing mechanism. The capital cost of drying equipment is high but it is being accepted more widely, particular in web carton printing.

Physical drying methods

Penetration (or absorption)

In the simplest form of penetration drying, the ink does not become solid but is taken into the pores of the paper. This achieves a dry print but it is not rub-proof, and it is only possible on absorbent papers. The method is used mainly for newspaper printing by letterpress and web offset litho where it is referred to as coldset. It can be recognised by ink rubbing off onto a newspaper reader's fingers.

Quick-setting

Penetration is the first stage of quick-set drying inks. The second stage is oxidation. Quick-setting inks contain two oil components: a thick resinous/drying one and a thin one. They are blended to be stable on the press and in the tin. When printed onto coated papers, the thin phase is quickly drawn into the fine pores and the resinous portion is left set on the surface. This finally dries by oxidation. Quick-setting inks are widely used in sheetfed offset and letterpress. High-intensity short wave IR drying units are often used to accelerate both the penetration and oxidation process on sheetfed presses.

Heat-setting

Inks containing significant amounts of aliphatic hydrocarbons – in a boiling range of 85–120 °C – are dried by passing print through well-ventilated ovens to flash off the solvent and crystallise the resin out of solution, binding the pigment to the paper surface.

Evaporation

Solvent removal by evaporation is used in gravure, flexo and screen. As there is only limited opportunity for evaporation on the press, compared with litho and letterpress, fast-evaporating solvents can be used. In inks formulated to dry by evaporation, the solvent is evaporated away either naturally or using high temperatures to leave a resin film that sets, or polymerises, on the substrate and binds with the pigment. Some web offset inks dry by evaporation and then by oxidation. The solvents have to evaporate more slowly to avoid drying on the litho inking system. Evaporation takes place at a higher temperature, and this requires significantly greater amounts of energy than is required for flexo and gravure inks.

Precipitation

This method relies on the fact that some liquids are liquid only in certain circumstances. The main examples of this are vehicle systems that exist and remain stable only while the system is alkaline. As the water evaporates and/or the system is neutralised by the paper, the resin bonds the pigment on the paper surface. This method of drying is mainly used by flexography, but also in gravure and some inkjet.

Particular properties may be required either to meet the technical requirements of the printing process or press. There may also be particular features of the graphic design or requirements of the end user that may require modifications to the ink. It is vital that the end user explains to the printer any special features that are required otherwise the inks used may ultimately be unsuitable.

Specific ink properties
Special characteristics that might be required by the process or printer could include:
► ink colours for wet-on-wet printing may be tack graded to ensure that there is good transfer when one ink overprints a different colour ink as it passes through a multicolour press;
► inks that will dry well on the stock to be used. For instance, cartridge, art and cast-coated stocks require different ink formulations (although the addition of special dryers may often be adequate);
► inks that will dry hard enough to resist scuffing in subsequent operations, such as folding and binding. Matt-coated papers and boards have a deceptively abrasive surface, particularly when calcium carbonate has been used extensively in the coating mix. Elimination of scuffing problems can never be guaranteed;
► special inks that will give optimum results with fine screen halftones or FM screening;
► special inks that will produce particularly dense solid areas. The requirements of an ink for halftones and for solids are different: solids and halftones in the same forme should ideally be printed as separate impressions. In high-quality process colour work, this difficulty is sometimes overcome for black solids by printing a tint of the cyan in register to increase the density of the black;
► special inks that are compatible with subsequent varnishing or film lamination. Some colours give few problems, but others either bleed, change hue or mottle. Purples and

reflex blues are perhaps the most susceptible, and tests should always be made to be certain of avoiding problems. In particular, wax additives (which are used frequently in carton work) should never be added to inks that are to be subsequently varnished or laminated.

Often the end user's requirements will be the same as the printer's. For example, the end user may also want good scuff resistance so that a carton or the cover of a brochure does not easily get scratched in use.

Additional special characteristics include:

► particular colour hues. These are best specified by referring to one of the internationally recognised colour matching systems such as Pantone. The process colours are specified by ISO for the litho process. It should be noted that ink colour varies considerably depending on the paper used with coated papers giving rise to less variation than uncoated papers. Additionally, metamerism can be a problem. This is a phenomenon where colours can shift considerably in hue under different lighting. Ink manufacturers try to minimise this characteristic by an appropriate choice of nonmetameric pigments. When colour requirements are critical, it is sensible to match ink colour under the same lighting conditions as will eventually be experienced rather than under printers' standard lighting. Supermarkets frequently have their packaging colour-matched under lighting conditions the same as in the stores. Where inks must match under a wide range of lighting conditions, it may be necessary to consult the ink manufacturer. Manufacturers have a wide range of non-standard pigments available, but these may be more expensive than the standard range or less satisfactory in other respects;

► different tones of black are available. Most usually, neutral-toned or blue-toned blacks are used, but others such as brown-toned and bronze-toned are available. Pantone does a special black that is neutral-toned and of the correct pigmentation to give the anticipated result when used in a colour-mixing formula;

► high-gloss or matt finishes. Inks are available that cover the full range of finishes. Those at the extremes generally have other disadvantages and are not so easy for the printer to use. Consequently, the printer may make an additional charge for their use to take this into account as well as to recover their higher cost. When printing special colours, additional charges may also be made for the same reasons and also because the ink consumption of some colours may be higher than average due to the differing specific gravity of each colour;

► any printed item that is liable to be exposed to direct sunlight or other ultraviolet radiation should have lightfast inks specified. Lightfastness is measured on the blue wool scale of which eight is the highest for printing inks. The minimum level for exposure to daylight for a few days is six. Cyan and black are usually at least this, but magenta and yellow may not be. Most ink manufacturers offer a colour set of greater lightfastness;

► food grade inks may be required for certain packaging or insert leaflets to avoid contamination by toxins or odour;

▶ resistance to finger marking may be needed. Some ink colours (such as reflex blue)
react particularly strongly to finger moisture and grease, and so are best avoided for
covers and for packaging. In all cases, varnishing or lamination will considerably help
the maintenance of unspoiled work;

▶ specialist inks such as fluorescents and metallics are available for most processes.
Note, however, that a key colour or primer frequently needs to be underprinted to
achieve a satisfactory result (in much the same way as a tint of cyan is often printed
under a black solid). That means allowance may have to be made for an additional
print working when using such inks.

Health and safety

All inks and printing mediums must conform to UK and EC health and safety regulations.
They must be clearly labelled, and any hazardous substances contained in them must be
indicated on the label. Inks used for printing children's clothes and toys must conform to
the United Kingdom Toy (Safety) Regulations 1974. Product liability legislation is also
relevant in this context, especially with regard to packaging.

Possibly the most significant emphasis is now on environmental considerations.
The Environmental Protection Act is one instrument affecting the printer but increasing
pressure is coming from new and impending EC legislation. Both printers and publishers
need to be aware of the listings of many hazardous substances (including inks and some
chemicals used in printing) that must not be discharged into rivers or sewers. It is wise to
assume that most of the inks and chemicals used in printing or prepress departments
should not be discharged into public waterways.

Printers' criteria for ink selection

Printers will categorise ink according to the following criteria:

▶ *Ink type.* Which printing process is involved, e.g. gravure, silk screen, UV curing,
flexography, heatset, coldset, offset lithography, waterless offset, letterpress? Each
process requires different ink in terms of pigmentation, viscosity and vehicle formulation.

▶ *Ink drying mechanism.* How does the wet printed ink form the permanent film on the
substrate surface? In some cases the ink does not chemically dry, and in coldset
lithography the ink is absorbed into the paper surface and typically shows low rub
resistance. A more sophisticated method involves a physical separation process where
low viscosity ingredients are absorbed into the paper causing a crystallisation effect of
the rest of the ink formula as it sets. This setting may be speeded up by exposure to
infrared radiation. In heatset and some metal printing, the low viscosity mineral oil
component is driven out of the ink by heating the print in an oven. Much sheetfed ink
dries by a conventional oxidation chemical reaction over quite long time spans.
Instant ink drying is available when radiation curing ink systems are used, using
either ultraviolet or electron beam radiation. Cross-linking ink systems have been
developed for the new generation of Indigo digital offset presses.

▶ *Colour.* The shade of an ink is probably its most important property after cost. The hue
is compared with a colour sample or to defined colorimetric values and strength, the

pigmentation and transfer characteristics on press. Standard four-colour process inks may be specified to match international standards such as BS 4666 or DIN/16538-9.

▶ *Spot colours* may be specified to match an accepted colour communication system such as Pantone, and allowing final colours to be accurately determined by the graphic designer. Alternatively the client may supply a coloured sample for the ink supplier to match, and provide laboratory prints on a particular paper or substrate for the client to approve.

▶ *Mileage.* Ink mileage is a measure of the amount of print per unit quantity of ink. Purchase price is a poor determinant of value for printing ink, and more expensive ink will often provide better value. If the ink has a higher pigment loading and good transfer characteristics, the desired colour may be achieved from a lower film weight. This means that the ink will produce more copies. Ink should always be costed as price per 1000 sheets of printed work rather than a price per weight or volume.

It is relatively straightforward to compare the mileage of alternative spot colour inks of the same shade on press by working out the number of sheets per unit weight of special colour. It is more difficult to accurately measure the mileage of a process ink in publication work. Here the pages continually change between sections and ink is often pumped to the duct automatically from a central store.

▶ *Performance on press.* The ink industry is competitive and suppliers spend much time and money improving the performance of inks. There should be no cases where ink performance significantly reduces the press productivity by slowing running speed or causing repeated press stops. If this does occur, the first reaction should be to clean the press and dampening system and check the mechanical order. If a problem persists, contact the ink supplier or try an alternative manufacturer's product.

▶ *Environmental criteria.* Some inks are formulated to minimise their impact on the environment. This may involve replacing mineral oils with a renewable source such as vegetable oils, or reducing the solvent levels to reduce emissions, and creating water-based inks for flexography or gravure.

Designing ink to perform well on press without the need for potentially damaging press chemicals and cleaners might also provide benefits. Much of the offset industry would like to run with no isopropyl alcohol in the dampening, and reducing the use of cleaning solvents will lower cost and improve the environmental performance.

Ink packaging should be designed to minimise waste. Bulk supply of inks and varnish may be pumped into holding tanks at the printer or in reusable containers. Small quantities should be provided in recyclable (after cleaning) containers, which are designed to minimise waste at the printers. Conventional oxidation drying ink should be sprayed with anti-oxidant and packed in vacuum-sealed tins rather than having a paper or plastic skin across the surface. These skins are classed as special waste.

▶ *Final print properties.* Most applications demand that the final print must show some special properties. There are many British and International Standard Test Methods to determine the printed ink performance properties. These include:

- ▶ print gloss
- ▶ degree of lightfastness (BS1006 or ISO 787/15)
- ▶ degree of heatfastness
- ▶ suitability for subsequent laser printing
- ▶ rub resistance (BS 3110)
- ▶ slip
- ▶ low mar properties, resistance to finger marking
- ▶ physical degradation (BS4321)
- ▶ water/soap/alkali/oil and grease/chemical resistance (BS 4321/BS560)
- ▶ suitability for subsequent lamination or varnishing
- ▶ odour and taint (BS3755)
- ▶ print to not be organoleptic in food packaging
- ▶ permanent record
- ▶ security applications
- ▶ release properties
- ▶ heat seal resistance
- ▶ adhesion to substrate, scuff, scratch and peel resistance
- ▶ flexibility (elasticity and plasticity)
- ▶ photochromic or thermochromic properties
- ▶ opacity
- ▶ glueability (hotmelt or PVA adhesives)
- ▶ suitability for blister packaging
- ▶ suitability for deep freezing
- ▶ conformity to Toys (Safety) Regulations (BS 5665 pt3, EN 71 pt3)
- ▶ recyclability and deinkability.

The printer must notify the final requirements to the ink maker who will ensure the correct formulation. In many cases, a sample print may be necessary for the final user to test.

Ink manufacture controls

Ink makers rigorously control their ingredients and manufacturing to produce a stable, consistent product. Many are accredited to ISO9000 and there should not be significant variation between batches of ink within limits agreed with the printer. The available test methods characterise many ink properties in a laboratory but may not directly correlate to press performance. During the formulation and manufacture of paste inks, inkmakers will test the key ink properties of:

Shade and strength

The pigments used in ink are the most expensive raw materials involved. Using modern spectroscopy-based colour match prediction systems, the ink maker has the tools to provide the most cost-effective blend of pigments for the printer. Information on the particular lighting conditions that a colour will be viewed under must be provided to avoid unwanted metamerism effects. The ink maker will keep master samples of the approved ink together with test prints for subsequent comparison, providing inks within agreed colour difference, ΔE, values.

Ink hue may be compared visually and colorimetrically with standard samples and test prints to test the consistency of different batches. Strength is checked in a bleach test where an amount of ink is diluted with opaque white (with yellows a weak opaque blue) until it matches the strength of the diluted standard.

Tack

Tack is the stickiness of a paste ink; a resistance to splitting of an ink-film. Tackmeters measure tack by distributing a fixed volume of ink over two temperature-controlled rollers rotating at a fixed speed. A third small roller attached to a pressure transducer is placed on the rig and the force exerted in the standard rotation is measured. The higher the force, the higher the tack. Different instruments and conditions of speed and temperature mean that inter-instrument comparison is not possible.

Normally the tack measurement is recorded when the ink is evenly distributed and the reading stabilises after about one minute. The change in tack over time is a good indicator of press stability. An unchanging tack reading over some 10 minutes indicates a stable ink, which is normally an important contributor to trouble-free press performance. The press stability may result in slow initial setting and then drying on paper, however. Tack measurement may be made more sophisticated by adding fount solution to the ink on test and then monitoring the tack over time to determine stability of the emulsified ink on rollers. Low tack ink is used with uncoated paper to avoid picking and linting problems. In four-colour printing, ink makers may tack-grade the process set so that the first ink printed has the highest tack. This should aid ink overprinting and avoids contamination of inks by colours that are already printed. It is important in waterless or dry offset, but in lithography the key property is the tack of the printed ink-water emulsion.

Rheology

The viscosity of paste inks is their resistance to flow when a force is applied. Viscosity will determine the ink performance on the high-speed rotating roller chain on press. Plastic viscosity and yield value may be measured on falling rod, cone-and-plate, axial or concentric cylinder viscometers. In gravure printing, the ink viscosity is adjusted on press by adding solvent to the supplied ink to optimise transfer from cylinder to paper.

Fineness of grind

Printing ink is an homogeneous mixture of raw materials, and part of the formulation may be a fine powder of pigment, extender or wax. Good dispersion to avoid aggregates and adequately wet the powder with ink vehicle is needed for good performance on press. Ink makers will test for the physical size of particles present using a steel Hegmann gauge. This takes a sample of the ink onto a graduated groove and draws it down the channel with a steel blade. As the channel becomes shallower, any particle will be pulled through the ink fluid showing lines in the ink. The gauge has a depth indicator, and normally an offset ink should not contain any particles above 4–5μ.

Water pickup

This is the amount of water, or fount solution, that an offset ink will absorb quickly when forming a stable ink-water emulsion under agitation in the laboratory.

Flow

The flow of a paste ink is tested by letting a fixed volume flow down a vertical plane after agitating the ink to overcome any thixotropic properties. It is important to transfer on press and vital to avoid blockages in any central ink pumping to the duct system.

Ink setting and drying characteristics

Ink may dry by radiation curing, heatsetting or oxidation drying on a glass slab with a slowly moving pointer disrupting along the film until it dries. The setting characteristic of a conventional drying ink is measured by pressing paper against a print over time and observing how much wet ink is transferred from the printed film.

Ink makers will test samples against a master standard to ensure consistency between batches. Tests are designed to simulate printing. The main limitation to ink testing in laboratories is the lack of dynamic conditions in which fresh ink is continually replenishing the ink being used. In cases where ink makers test on their own press, the conditions will rarely match those used commercially. The printer must test the ink on the press under normal production conditions to determine its initial press performance (printability and runnability) and the final print properties. If satisfactory, extended ink trials will determine longer-term press runnability and allow the buyer to conduct a commercial evaluation.

Manufacturers may lower the raw material cost of ink by reducing the amount of pigment present, and lowering the selling price. An apparently attractive price may result in higher costs for the printer if a higher ink film thickness is necessary to match the required density. This may cause problems with drying as well as resulting in increased usage. Every job in commercial printing is different so obtaining an accurate comparison of four-colour process ink mileage from different suppliers is difficult. Comparing the relative costs of different suppliers is necessary if the printer wants to ensure the best value.

A simple test to compare process ink mileage between two ink suppliers is necessary. Choose a suitable long-run job and run the first 40% of the job with ink from supplier A. Towards the end of this part of the run, allow the ducts to empty and then, during the middle 20% of the run, change to ink from supplier B. It is important to achieve a similar result so ensure comparable density and dot gain readings as well as the visual comparison. Then run the final 40% of the job with the second supplier. Note the quantity of each colour from each supplier used together with the total number of sections produced. It is then possible to compare relative ink mileage as use per 1000 copies or as a percentage of the standard ink from the main supplier. Then compare relative costs from each supplier and make a purchasing decision on the relative amounts to buy on the true cost basis.

There are several formulae used to calculate the correct amount of spot colour ink to order for a particular job. For offset lithographic sheetfed printing the formula is:

$$\text{Kg required} = \frac{N \times A \times F \times S \times I}{178}$$

where: N = number of sides of paper

A = area of print, expressed in square metres (m²)

F = format of print. Solid colour = 1, reverse out lettering = 0.7, mostly illustrated = 0.4, normal illustration = 0.3, heavy type = 0.2, light text = 0.15

S = type of stock. Art paper = 1, coated mechanical = 1.2, super calendered = 1.4, newsprint = 1.8, carton board = 2, cartridge = 2.2

I = type of ink. Black = 1, machine overprint varnish = 1 other colours = 1.1, ultraviolet curing ink = 1.1, fluorescent colours = 1.4, opaque colours = 1.5, metallic inks = 1.6, opaque white = 1.8.

This formula is a start, and a more accurate method will come from a good relationship between the printers' estimators and ink supplier to develop the correct estimating measure for the particular plant. The use of in-plant colour mixing from single pigment base inks means that problems of over- or under-ordering quantities can be overcome as special colours are mixed on demand at the printer. In some cases printers allow ink makers to supply a technician to take control of ink handling for the plant.

Digital colorants   The rapid growth of digital printing through toner (powder and liquid) and inkjet technologies has opened up significant new markets for inkmakers. Home and office inkjet printers use specially packaged inks that can cost up to €1300 per litre or kilo. Unsurprisingly many major ink manufacturers have entered the market.

Laser toners   Laser printers use a proprietary electrostatic toner to create an image. The toner is often supplied by the equipment manufacturer as part of a deal that involves a click charge. It is important that the correct toner is used as the imaging and fusing conditions vary from printer to printer.

New emulsion aggregation technology is changing the way toner is manufactured. Traditionally the ingredients would be mixed together and then ground into a fine powder with a wide distribution of particle sizes. The new technology allows very consistent toner shapes and sizes to be produced, providing better quality, sharper images, according to the manufacturers.

Toner technology has been a drawback for laser printing, with turbulence effects limiting the potential speed and the fused result showing uneven gloss and a non-planographic surface – deficiencies when compared with lithography. Recent developments in emulsion aggregation, where toner particles are grown to a uniform size distribution and spherical shape, may give better quality and productivity, while being cheaper to make than conventional toner. The claimed benefits are sharper text and images because there are no large particles to blur edge definition, and less toner is needed as smaller, more uniform particles cover the sheet with a thinner toner layer to give the same visual result. Manufacturers claim reductions of up to 40%.

HP Indigo uses liquid toners. Its ElectroInk can be produced in a wide range of colours including spot colours. The basic imaging principles are the same as for dry toner, but the toner construction is different. The toner pigment is suspended in an electrically insulating fluid, typically a paraffin-like material. It is attracted out of suspension by the electrostatic charged image on the OPC drum. As the toner is in a liquid, it is in some ways easier to control. As a result the particle size can be significantly smaller (1–2 microns) than in a dry toner system, giving the potential to produce higher resolutions on paper.

Inkjet inks   There is a wide range of inks available for inkjet machines – for home and office use, through industrial applications such as coding and marking, to flatbed, narrow and wide-format machines. Ink manufacturers are increasing their R&D effort. Several are partnering equipment manufacturers, suppliers and end users to develop new solutions. In 2005 the inkjet ink market is worth some €14 billion, 80% of which is accounted for by non-commercial home and office printing. For many equipment suppliers, ongoing consumable contracts are their major revenue earners with strong growth forecast in all applications.

For home applications it is not unusual for a replacement ink cartridge to cost the equivalent of €1300 per kilo or litre; hence the strong interest from ink manufacturers. There are four categories of ink in use:
► solvent based
► aqueous
► oil based
► UV curable.

For both continuous and drop-on-demand inkjet the common method of differentiation is the ink category that is used. Early single head continuous inkjet printers used dye-based solvent inks, with aggressive organic solvents such as MEK (methyl ethyl ketone). With the advent of array technologies, alternative ink formulations were developed that used mineral and vegetable oils, water-based systems and UV curing. Optimal performance is achieved using low-viscosity inks. Dye-based colorants were later joined by pigmented inks, which offered improvements in the lightfastness and durability of the final print.

Inkjet inks use reactive, disperse, direct, cationic and acid dyes. There are also other dye groups that offer potential in inkjet applications, in particular metal complex dyes. Inkjet geometry generally requires that pigment particles used in inkjet inks are no larger than than 100nm in order to fit through nozzle orifices without clogging. To achieve colour brilliance all pigment particles must be of a similar size. Since pigment particles tend to flocculate, ink chemistry uses electrostatic and steric mechanisms, and other treatments applied to pigment particle surfaces to keep them dispersed in suspension so they do not group together and precipitate.

FIGURE 8.1 Technology map of industrial inkjet technology

Source: Pira International Ltd

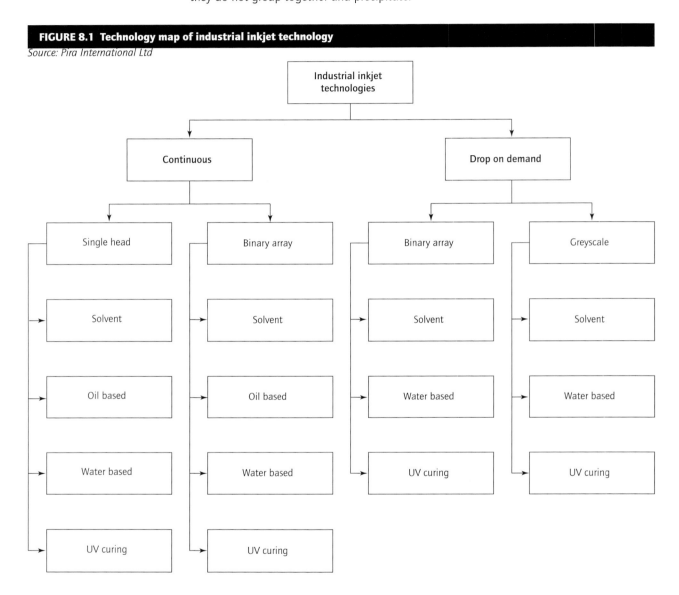

Pigments and dyes carry chromophores as part of their molecular structures. The chromophore will have one or more ring structures that absorb portions of the electromagnetic spectrum in the visible range. After light passes through a chromophore, it will appear as the part of the colour spectrum that the chromophore did not absorb. High levels of electromagnetic radiation, such as that found in the ultraviolet spectrum, can energise a chromophore's ring structure with sufficient energy to disrupt the atomic connections holding it together. As the ring opens, it loses its ability to absorb wavelengths of light, which causes fading. As dyes are dissolved in their surroundings, they float alone as single molecules vulnerable to radiation. Pigment particles, on the other hand, are clusters of thousands of molecules and are better able to absorb UV energy without losing their chromophore rings.

In addition to base or solvent pigments and dyes, inkjet ink formulations include other chemicals to enhance ink performance:

► surfactants to control wetting and absorption

► humectants to prevent premature drying

► dispersants to keep pigment particles in suspension

► resins and binders for ink adhesion and durability

► biocides to prevent bacterial growth, particularly in aqueous inks

► buffers to control pH

► chelating agents to keep heavy metal ions in solution

► antioxidants and co-solvents.

TABLE 8.2 Comparative table of inkjet ink systems	
Ink type	**Drying mechanism**
Water based (dye or pigmented)	Evaporation and absorption
Oil based	Absorption and oxidation
Solvent based	Evaporation
Eco-solvent (lite-solvent)	Evaporation
UV curing	Polymerisation

Source: Pira International Ltd

Users have a wide range of print heads and ink systems to choose from when they consider inkjet. They offer a variety of speeds, qualities and formats to cater to different markets.

Industrial applications have moved from coding and marking into signage and poster printing using large- and grand-format roll-fed printers with a traversing head that prints incremental stripes to make up the final print. Initially the quality was poor, which was not an issue where large-format posters were concerned. Early devices were quite slow, both in terms of data manipulation and the printing speed, but again this was relatively unimportant as the job was sent and left to print unattended. This changed the economics of signage printing and made short runs and personalised versions possible.

Each of these requires a different formulation of ink to optimise the printing process and the properties of the final print. Outdoor applications may require good lightfastness, but other important properties include adhesion, physical and abrasion resistance, high gloss, high and low temperature stability, and chemical resistance.

TABLE 8.3 Comparison of ink characteristics			
	UV curing	**Solvent drying**	**Water based**
Purge requirements	Low	Higher	High
Nozzle failure	Low	Higher	Higher
Flammability	Non flammable	Flammable	Non-flammable
VOC emissions	None	High	Negligible
Drying rate	Instant	Variable	Slow
Solvent resistance	High	Lower	High
Energy requirements	Low	Higher	Very high
Ease of use	Very easy	Operator involvement	Operator
Application window	Very wide	Wide	Narrower

Source: Pira International Ltd

Pigmented oil-based inks

Oil-based inks are low-odour, low-volatility pigmented inks designed to give rapid drying times on porous substrates such as paper and card. The products are designed for outdoor use and with a suitable substrate should withstand one year-plus exposure. All pigments are lightfast with a Blue Wool Scale rating of 7+. The inks are particularly suited to wide format and coding and marking applications. Oil-based inkjet inks do not dry easily in print head nozzles, they do not cause deterioration in the adhesives that hold print heads together, and they do not corrode print head circuitry. But they have limited application due to their slow-drying characteristics.

Oil-based inks may find a use, but up till now they have only been used in some coding applications and the Riso–Olympus Orphis 5500 colour printer, as few ink suppliers can provide the low-viscosity formulations required. Oil-based inks are not widely used in inkjet colour applications as it is difficult to produce optimal viscosity with reasonable pigment loadings.

Water-based inks

Water-based inks do not generally dry very quickly, but they are environmentally friendly. However, they require media that have been treated with a receptor coating. They are in wide use in desktop and wide-format inkjet printing machines. Water-based inks can corrode conductive circuitry and undermine some epoxy adhesives that adhere layers and parts in some print heads. A typical wide-format aqueous ink will consist of about 4–5% pigment or dye, about 2–3% polymeric dispersant, 18–19% diethylene glycol and 74–75% water. In order for the aqueous ink to dry, the substrate absorbs the water and/or the water evaporates. The flow of air and heat can help produce evaporation. As production speeds of water- and solvent-based printers increase, printer manufacturers will also increase the capacity of on-board printer heating and venting systems.

Water-based inks present major problems for high-volume printing as significant quantities of moisture have to be removed. In many paper and board applications unwanted absorption of water may result in cockling and marking. As a result, solvent-based inks, including eco-solvent formulations that use less volatile or toxic components (and are also less costly), are widely used. These present potential flammability hazards, so they must be stored safely and the solvent must be removed after printing, which requires ventilation and, in some cases, solvent recovery. These inks are formulated to dry quickly when printed through evaporation of the solvent. This gives them the unwanted property of drying in the head, which can lead to significant downtime and a need to purge nozzles when they become clogged.

Dye-sublimation inks

Dye-sublimation inks are low-volatility, dye-based inks designed to transfer from coated paper onto polyester-containing substrates through the application of heat and pressure. The ink can be printed directly onto some grades of polyester and heat-treated ex situ. The products can be used outdoors following the application of a suitable overlaminate. Dye-sublimation inks are particularly suited to wide-format applications.

Solvent and eco-solvent inks

Solvent inks are pigmented inks designed to dry rapidly on common vinyl substrates through the application of heat. The inks are designed for outdoor use and can withstand exposure for one year-plus when applied to a suitable substrate. The inks are particularly suited to wide-format applications. Solvent-based inkjet inks use:

▶ alcohols such as ethanol and methanol;
▶ ketones such as methyl ethyl ketone (MEK), acetone or cyclohexanone;
▶ aliphatic hydrocarbons;
▶ esters, including ethyl acetate, ethyl butyl acetate, ethyl glycol monobutyl ether acetate and isopropyl acetate;
▶ glycols and glycol ethers, including ethylene glycol, methoxy trigylcol, tripropylene glycol monomethyl ether and diethylene glycol ethyl ether.

The colouring agent in ink is usually dye and/or pigment. Dyes are soluble at a molecular level in their medium or base. Pigments are insoluble in the medium that surrounds them and are dispersed as small particles, i.e. clusters of molecules.

Non-volatile solvent ink is a black-pigmented ink specifically designed to give good contrast on cardboard in coding and marking applications. Solvent-based inkjet inks generally use pigments or a combination of pigments and gamut-enhancing dye. Solvent-based sublimation inks act like pigmented particulate inks during inkjet printing and like dyes during heat transfer. They evaporate their solvent and can dry in print head nozzles if they are not used and maintained regularly. A typical pigmented solvent-based ink for grand-format inkjet printing will contain about 8% pigment, 7% vinyl acetate resin, 10% cyclohexanone and 75% ethylene glycol monobutyl ether acetate (EGBEA), also known as 2-butoxyethanol acetate.

A major problem with solvent inks in high production systems is the need to remove significant quantities of solvent, either water or volatile organic solvents. In 2005 the fastest device is the Inca FastJet. In beta testing the 1m wide machine had a maximum throughput of some 6000m²/hr. At this rate, printing four-colour process, the FastJet could consume several tonnes of ink an hour. With solvent loadings of 30–50%, extraction is a major problem. For a water-based ink the energy requirements to vaporise 1kg of water is 2260kJ, while its specific heat capacity is 4.1kJ per degree Celsius. Even with high-volume warm air flows to aid evaporation, the load may be 300–400MW/hr, at considerable cost and only achievable with the aid of a significant drying unit. The energy required to remove more volatile organic materials from solvent-based inks is lower, but the environmental considerations in terms of protecting workers and avoiding discharge to air and water are considerable. This is a major consideration in environmentally aware regions such as Japan, the US, Canada and the EU, where the additional costs of extraction, recovery and treatment add to the cost of the process. In the developing markets of China, India, south Asia, South and Latin America, and central and eastern Europe, where environmental regulation is less pronounced, solvent-based machines are popular.

UV-curing inkjet inks

UV inks use focused UV light to initiate free-radical polymerisation of acrylate chemistry. UV-cured inkjet inks involve oligomers, monomers, photo-initiators and pigments or dyes, as well as surfactants and other components. Most UV-cure inkjet inks contain little or no evaporative material.

The use of UV inks is growing rapidly for a number of reasons:

▶ environmental pressures will continue to force reduction of solvent-based ink usage

▶ demand to increase productivity and speed while reducing equipment downtime

▶ UV inks can be used to decorate a wider range of uncoated media

▶ printers need greater production speeds and print performance.

These factors suggest continued growth in the use of UV ink technology. These are important developments for UV inkjet, and the introduction of white and metallics into ink sets will broaden the number of potential applications.

UV-cured inks are abrasive and can cause print head wear. For free running, pigment particle sizes should not exceed 10% of the nozzle diameter (preferably not above 2%), which makes it difficult for the highly reflective plate structures of many conventional metallic and pearlescent pigments.

Developments in ink technology will be key to future prospects for the UV inkjet market. These should concentrate on:

▶ Reducing the ink selling price by reducing the cost of the ink components as the market grows, although the final selling price will remain a marketing decision by inkmakers. At the same time increased demand for petrochemicals, limited refining capacity, and supply disruptions may increase ink costs.

▶ Further cost reduction will be achieved through reducing the amount of ink required, lowering volumes by calibrating data handling and prepress, and using higher pigment loadings.

▶ Improving the final print performance adhesion and resistance properties.

▶ Improving the brightness and brilliance of the final print product – attributes that score poorly in comparison with many solvent applications.

▶ Cationic curing will grow for specialist applications.

▶ Print head performance – higher viscosity formulations at higher temperatures.

There is the potential for electron beam curing to replace UV curing in some applications as the technology offers a more complete cure at low temperature for opaque and metallic ink formulations.

General advice on the use of inkjet

The following show how critical inkjet ink performance is in terms of production performance. These apply equally to all inkjet manufacturers.

▶ The *quality* of the inks and fluids used has a direct impact on the digital imaging system's output and performance. Inks are carefully formulated for purity, consistency and compatibility with the print heads being used.

▶ *Purity* ensures that no contaminants are allowed into the ink manufacturing process. Impurities can cause clogging in the imaging system, damage to the ink and print head systems, and below-par imaging performance. Hence the relationships that have been established with raw material vendors to further ensure this purity, and to enable consistent performance over longer periods of time.

▶ *Consistency*. It only takes one inferior batch of ink to bring a production line to a halt. In order to prevent this, inks, fluids and supplies are manufactured to the most stringent quality standards. Continual testing of critical ink parameters throughout the production process is essential to provide customers with some assurance about ink performance.

▶ *Compatibility*. While off-brand supplies can clog printers and affect production output, vendor inks are formulated, tested and manufactured to offer maximum efficiency and performance. Inferior or incompatible inks can cause internal metal corrosion and deterioration of plastic/rubber parts in any inkjet printer. Mismatched fluids can adversely affect application performance such as adhesion, dry time, maintenance intervals or other parameters key to reliable printer operation. These can cause systems to fail with the consequential high hourly costs of interrupted production. The message is clear enough – ensure that inks, print heads and substrates are all fine-tuned to achieve a quality inkjet printed result. If you plan to use (cheaper) third-party inks as replacements, make sure that they are not going to damage the print heads or the ink supply lines.

Paper

9

For runs of significant length, paper is the largest cost of most print jobs and it will define the characteristics of the finished printed product. In future, good printability and runnability of paper will become even more important. The ideal printability characteristics of paper are a smooth, strong surface, maximum whiteness and brightness with maximum opacity. Better and more widely used measures will develop at specific printers and generally in the industry. The range of papers available will still provide a rich choice for specific publishing needs. A fashion magazine, child's annual, annual report, business form and a 2000-page catalogue each has different needs from different types of paper. A newspaper selling colour advertising will look for whiteness and brightness unlike a financial section printed on a pink sheet. In the future, the methods of choice will be more quantifiable.

The paper-making process

Fibrous components

Paper is sometimes defined as a felted sheet of fibres formed on a fine screen from a water suspension. Apart from fibres, paper contains fillers or extenders, such as clay or chalk, and surface coatings made from a range of materials. Vegetable (mainly wood) fibres are the major source of raw material although some man-made synthetic fibres are used in speciality or security grades. Vegetable fibres include:

▶ stem fibres, e.g. woods (softwood, hardwood), basts (flax, hemp, jute, bamboo), grasses (esparto, straw, bagasse)

▶ leaf fibres, e.g. manila, sisal

▶ fruit fibres, e.g. seed hairs (cotton), pods (kapod) and husks (cour).

Of all vegetable fibres, wood provides the main source of fibre for making paper. The figure is about 90% worldwide and about 98% in the UK and North America. The leading non-wood fibre is straw, followed by bagasse and bamboo that are used principally in China, India, Pakistan and Mexico.

Wood fibre can be divided into:

▶ softwood fibre from coniferous trees, e.g. fir, pine, spruce

▶ hardwood fibre from deciduous trees, e.g. oak, beech, birch, eucalyptus, maple.

Wood fibres are made into a pulp in the course of making paper and the resulting softwood or hardwood pulps have different qualities. The main characteristics of softwood pulps are:

▶ long fibres

▶ high strength.

The main characteristics of hardwood pulps are:

▶ short fibres

▶ good bulk and opacity.

Most papers contain a mixture of pulps depending on the qualities of the grade required. Apart from wood, the other important source of raw material for making paper is waste paper: white waste (sometimes called pre-consumer waste, or broke), or printed waste (post-consumer waste).

Fibre obtained from trees to be made into pulp is known as virgin fibre or primary fibre; fibre obtained from reusing paper is known as secondary fibre. In their natural state, wood fibres consist of long, narrow tubes composed of three main compounds:

> ▶ cellulose

> ▶ hemicellulose, a compound similar in nature to cellulose

> ▶ lignin, a resinous compound that binds the fibres together.

The cellulose-based constituents are required for making paper, and the lignin constituents are impurities that must be removed during pulping. The aim of pulping is to separate the fibres in the raw material and allow the cellulose fibres to form a free suspension in water.

Pulping   Three basic methods of pulping wood fibre can be used:

> ▶ mechanical

> ▶ mechanical/chemical

> ▶ chemical.

Mechanical pulping removes the lignin from the fibres by physical means. Mechanical/chemical pulping removes it by a mixture of physical and chemical means and chemical pulping by entirely chemical methods.

Mechanical pulping

The most basic form of mechanical pulp is produced from coniferous softwood trees only (mainly spruce). After felling, the trees are selected, cut into suitable lengths and debarked in a rolling open drum called a tumbler drum debarker.

The debarked logs are forced against a revolving grindstone in hot water. The resulting mix of pulp and water is sent over a series of increasingly fine screens that remove any remaining lumps or splinters – shives – until the final mixture is completely dispersed. Plain and basic mechanical pulp produced this way is known as stone groundwood pulp (SGW) to differentiate it from the purer mechanical /chemical pulps (below). Process variables include the stone surface, speed, pressure, temperature, consistency and type of wood.

Advantages of this process include an extremely high yield with low effluent level. The resulting pulp cannot be used on its own to make printing paper but is the principal component of mechanical publishing grades, which are used for low-cost news and magazine papers. It has good opacity, high bulk, good printability and is cheap.

The disadvantages include low surface brightness and shade, lack of strength and durability, rapid discoloration and weakening with age due to the high residual lignin content.

Mechanical/chemical pulping

Several processes have been devised to produce mechanical pulps that are purer than the basic SGW product. They differ from SGW in that they use wood chips as the starting point of the process rather than whole logs. The first common step in the process is that, after cutting and debarking, the logs (or wood scraps) are fed into a chipper that reduces them to chips a few millimetres long.

Refiner mechanical pulp (RMP)

The chips are suspended in water and passed continuously through a series of disc refiners. The discs shear the chips into smaller and smaller pieces until they form a pulp that can be screened and bleached in the same cycle of operations as for conventional SGW pulp.

Advantages: wider range of woods can be used, waste wood and sawn timber scraps can be used, and a slightly purer pulp results.

Disadvantages: as for SGW, but slightly reduced discoloration with ageing and slightly stronger tensile strength.

RMP is also known as refiner groundwood pulp (RGP).

Thermomechanical pulp (TMP)

The chips are steamed at 135°C to soften the lignin before they are passed through a system of disc refiners. This allows the lignin to be separated more easily and causes less damage to the fibres.

Advantages include stronger pulp, use of a wider range of trees, faster drainage and reductions in debris. The smoothness and porosity of finished papers is improved, and there is less discoloration with age.

Disadvantages include lower yield, lower brightness and opacity and softer surface resulting in increased risks of linting or fluffing when printing.

Chemi-thermomechanical pulp (CTMP)

In a process one stage beyond TMP, a chemical stage is added that dissolves the lignins in the wood chips before they are refined. The advantages include: in finished papers, quite close in quality to many woodfree grades, long fibre length, good strength, good brightness and a high yield (sometimes called high-yield pulp).

The disadvantages are that it is expensive to produce, often little cheaper than woodfree pulp and finished papers are liable to some discoloration.

Biochemi-thermomechanical pulp (BCTMP)

This is a variant of CTMP using biological and chemical processes. The advantages and disadvantages are similar to those of CTMP, but it is easier to dispose of effluent and fewer chemicals are used.

Chemical pulping

The aim of chemical pulping is to reduce or dissolve the lignins in the wood by chemical rather than physical means. In this way, the fibres separate more cleanly from each other and fewer impurities remain in the final stock. Chemical pulping yields the purer and stronger forms of pulp known as woodfree (i.e. free of groundwood pulp). The absence of mechanical forces that tear and bruise the fibres means fibre lengths can be maintained and a stronger, more resilient paper can be made.

Two main processes are used: the sulphate (or alkaline) method, and the sulphite (or acid) method. Most modern pulp mills run the more environmentally friendly sulphate method, and the sulphite method is the older traditional method.

Sulphate process

An alkaline process, sometimes known as the kraft process, it can be used for both softwoods and hardwoods. Caustic soda (sodium hydroxide), sodium sulphide and sodium sulphate are cooked with a continuous feed of wood chips inside a continuous digester (Kamyr digester). After two to three hours, the fibres separate easily and maintain their full lengths yielding a pulp that will form strong, well-formed paper. The process yield is high and effluent disposal relatively easy.

Sulphite process

This is an acid process associated particularly with softwoods, especially spruce. Calcium bisulphite and sulphur dioxide in water are introduced into a digestion tower filled with wood chips. The chips and the liquid are cooked together for between six and 24 hours to remove the cellulose fibres. Compared with the sulphate process, the yield is low. A variant of the sulphite process is the bisulphite process in which the calcium bisulphite is replaced by sodium, magnesium or ammonium bisulphite.

The advantages of chemical pulping include stronger and longer-lasting papers with better colour and brightness. The disadvantages are that it is much more expensive than mechanical or mechanical/chemical pulping, the yield is lower, there are more effluent problems and reduced choice of tree stock.

Bleaching

The next stage in making paper – and the final stage in pulp making – is bleaching. The object of bleaching is to whiten, purify and stabilise the pulp without too much damage to the fibre. This can be done continuously or in batches. Most modern bleaching is carried out as a multi-stage process. Two main sets of chemicals are used in bleaching: those based on chlorine, and those based on oxygen, ozone or hydrogen peroxide. In many countries, environmental laws prevent the use of chlorine for bleaching. Oxygen and hydrogen peroxide bleaching processes are more environmentally friendly and are growing in use.

The degree of bleaching that a pulp will undergo is affected by the qualities required in the final paper. Processing variables include: dwell time, bleach temperatures and the condition of the unbleached fibre.

Stock preparation

Stock preparation embraces the whole sequence of final processes that must take place to redisperse the pulp, add to it any chemicals or other loadings or fillers needed and bring it to the final furnish (recipe) and consistency required for the paper making machine.

In an integrated pulp and paper mill (i.e. one in which the pulping and paper making facilities are on the same site), finished pulps are kept liquid and pumped to the stock preparation area of the paper mill.

In non-integrated pulp mills, the final slush pulp mix is drained over a wire gauze-covered cylinder or series of drying screens, pressed out, and is sheeted for transport in bales to the paper mill.

Breaking

Breaking is the process of returning the pulp sheets to liquid form. It is carried out in a hydrapulper or slusher, a large circular metal tank in which the baled sheets of pulp are dispersed in water using high-shear blade mixers. This is the point at which other ingredients will be added.

Sizing agents

These are added inside the furnish to improve a paper's water-resistance and prevent ink from feathering on its surface when the paper is printed. The quantity of size used varies with the grade of paper being produced:

▶ unsized, e.g. blotting paper

▶ slack sized paper gives fast ink penetration, e.g. newsprint

▶ medium sized paper is a compromise between excessive absorption and speedy drying, e.g. uncoated book stock

▶ hard sized, e.g. offset litho cartridge papers.

The traditional sizing chemistry uses rosin, alum and casein. Alum (aluminium sulphate), however, is mildly acidic and several synthetic, chemically neutral sizes (also known as alkaline sizes) have been developed as alternatives. (One chemical family of synthetic size is known by the abbreviation AKD, standing for alkyl ketene dimer.)

Loadings and fillers

These are minerals or compounds added to the stock to improve the opacity, formation, printability, dimensional stability or other characteristics in the finished paper. Printings and writings may contain up to 30% fillers. The most common are:

▶ china clay gives a smooth surface for printing (especially for illustration printing) and accelerates ink drying. It has a unique combination of firm, smooth, pliant properties;

▶ calcium carbonate gives hardness, opacity and whiteness. It is an increasingly common alternative to china clay, principally in conjunction with alkaline sizing, to give properties of brightness, light fastness and opacity, but it tends to be more abrasive than clay;

▶ titanium dioxide is used for opacifying, but it is expensive. It reduces the efficiency of any optical brightness agents (OBAs) present and is usually used in conjunction with china clay or calcium carbonate. Titanium dioxide is used where already high filler levels reduce runnability – lightweight publication/magazine grades demand high strength with opacity;

▶ optical brightness agents (OBAs)/fluorescent whitening agents (FWAs) are chemical compounds used to improve whiteness and fluorescence;

▶ Wet strengths are chemicals used to improve wet strength. They include formaldehydes, polyamides, and sulphuric acid (greaseproof).

Chemical additives

▶ Antifoamers are used to disperse the froth or foam produced during stock preparation.

▶ Retention aids are used to keep the fillers in the paper from falling through the wire of the paper-making machine. These include sodium silicate and gum.

▶ Slimicides are chemicals used to keep down the presence of slime producing microbes. These include chlorine and chloramines.

▶ Colouring materials – pigments and dyes – are used for colouring/whitening.

Refining (beating)

From the hydrapulper, the stock is pumped through a series of cone refiners. These are enclosed conical containers holding a series of metal blades that rotate from a central shaft against static blades built inside the outer casing. The fibres are mechanically modified: they are teased apart, separated and fibrillated so that their walls collapse and become fragmented. The purpose of this is to make the fibres spread and absorb more water, as this will enable them to bond more readily on the wire of the paper-making machine at the next stage.

The time allowed for the refining stage is critical in determining the characteristics of the finished sheet:

▶ prolonged refining reduces the length of the fibres dramatically and beats water into them so that they will bond without air and produce a paper like greaseproof paper on the wire of the paper machine;

▶ excessively short refining will not fibrillate the fibres in the pulp enough to allow them to mesh tightly on the wire, and the result will be a soft, bulky sheet like blotting paper.

The paper-making machine

After stock preparation, the treated liquid suspension is ready to be released onto the paper machine. The design of machine used for practically all paper production (as opposed to card or board production) is the Fourdrinier (see Figure 9.1, page 457). These machines have two main process areas: a wet end consisting of a wire section and a pressing section, and a dry end consisting of a dryer section and a calender section.

Wet end

At this stage the stock is 99% water, and 1% fibre and filler. It is delivered uniformly onto a moving mesh belt through a head box (flow box).

Head box

Many types include an open head flow box, hydraulic flow box, pressurised flow box and vacuum flow box. The flow box keeps the fibres dispersed and prevents them from flocculating (clogging together) so that a consistent and even formation can be achieved.

9

FIGURE 9.1 Schematic of a Fourdrinier paper machine

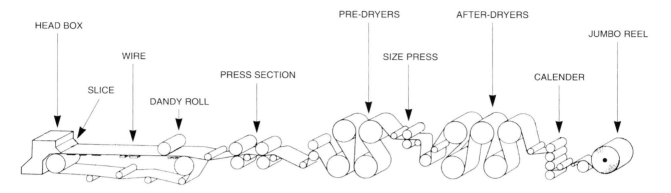

Source: Pira International Ltd

Slice

A gate slice, or projection slice, projects an even amount of fibre onto the wire in its cross-direction. Adjustments affect the substance and bulk of the finished paper. Fibres tend to align in the direction of flow giving a paper its characteristic grain or machine direction. (The direction at 90° to this, across the wire, is known as the cross direction.)

The wire

The wire is a moving belt across which the fibres have been distributed. The stock flows along the wire and the excess water (white water) drains through to leave the web of paper forming on its surface. Types of wire include:

▶ phosphor bronze, the original types

▶ synthetic, which have replaced phosphor bronze wires and are now used for almost all grades.

The wire is the drainage and forming element of the machine. Synthetic wires are used because of greater stability, better control over de-watering, reduced wire mark and longer life. Drainage is helped by table rolls, foils and suction boxes that draw the white water down by suction. The two surfaces of the newly forming paper have visually different characteristics:

▶ the wireside (also known as the underside or wrong side) is the underside and it has a poorer, rougher surface due to the drainage of the excess water in the stock through the machine wire;

▶ the topside (also called the felt side or right side) is the upper side, and is often smoother since the longer (denser) fibres tend to settle first.

Dandy roll

The dandy roll is a hollow roll with a variety of possible coverings, but usually metal wire. Its main functions are:

▶ to consolidate the sheet by compacting the fibres
▶ to apply a watermark
▶ to give a flatter top surface and improve the distribution of the fibres.

Dandy roll coverings (supported sleeves) give finish characteristics to this side of the web, e.g. wove, laid, watermark.

Press section

At the end of the paper wire, the partly formed paper web is drawn off the wire into the press section of the machine. It is transferred to an endless felt belt that passes through a series of rollers that compact the fibres and remove as much water as possible. In this process, the moisture content is reduced to 60–70%. The amount of pressure and the dwell time in the press section affect both the bulk and the finish of the paper. Open, bulky, book antique laid and wove grades need less wet pressing; smooth machine finish (MF) printings need more.

Drying section

The web passes through graded steam-heated drying cylinders with low temperature cylinders initially and high-temperature cylinders further down the line. If the early banks of cylinders become too hot this can cause problems such as picking, cockling and dye migration. The web is supported around the cylinders by further belts made of felt. At the end of the drying section, the moisture content is down to a final 2–8%.

Additional operations during the drying process may include:

▶ *surface sizing*. This involves the application of size, using a size press, to the surface of the paper (as distinct from into the furnish, where it is added at the breaking stage). This is done to control the absorbency and porosity of the surface. A coating mixture containing pigment may also be added at the size press. Size presses used to consist of a simple bath with two rollers forming a single nip, but now they resemble coating heads in their design and sophistication;

▶ *machine calendering*. This is the use of polished steel rollers at the end of the paper machine to give a smooth finish known as MF;

▶ *machine glazing (MG)*. A smoothly polished, steam-heated cylinder gives a smooth, glazed finish to one side of the paper.

Finishing

A variety of off machine options are available after the base paper has been made.

Supercalendering

This is different from machine calendering. The finished web is passed through further polished steel and fibre-packed rollers, which give it a polished, smooth surface. Papers treated in this way are known as SC papers.

Coating

Coating a paper increases its opacity, improves surface smoothness and ink hold out (important for litho printing, and especially for illustration printing), and enhances ink gloss. The two main coating pigments used are china clay and precipitated or ground calcium carbonate (chalk). China clay is smooth, hard but pliable; calcium carbonate is bright and white, but more abrasive. An alkaline substance, it is seldom used in acid papers that contain alum/rosin sizing. China clay is inert and can be used in papers with any furnish. Binding agents include casein, starch, synthetic resins or latex compounds (now most common). These allow the coating mix to be thicker but still flow easily, and provide a flexible coating receptive to a good gloss with calendering. Other additives may include pine oil or silicone-based defoamers, preservatives and wax-based chemicals to enhance gloss.

Coating processes

The different coating methods possible give a range of options in coat weight, coat density (which affects the rate of ink penetration), the degree of smoothness achieved, and in the degree of print gloss and density. Coating may be carried out on or off the paper-making machine. Some common methods are:

▶ *roll coating.* A light coating is transferred to the paper by roller, and usually followed by air-knife smoothing;

▶ *blade coating.* A faster process that produces good print quality with less coating. A thin steel blade spreads the coating to produce a flat, even surface. It is either left as a matt finish or supercalendered to produce a gloss finish. It combines good quality with reasonable cost and is the most common coating method;

▶ *air-knife coating.* The coating is levelled and the excess removed by a stream of compressed air (air knife). It can produce high coating weights. With a good base paper, it produces good print quality with minimum supercalendering. It is a faster process than brush coating and has replaced it for producing art paper;

▶ *brush coating.* The coating is distributed over the base stock by a series of brushes, some stationary and some oscillating. Replaced by other methods except in specialist applications;

▶ *cast coating.* The coating is dried by passing the coated paper under pressure over a hot, polished cylinder leaving it with a perfectly smooth, high-gloss surface without the need to compact the coating by supercalendering. Produces excellent ink receptivity.

Slitting

Paper reels of the full deckle (paper machine width) are slit and rewound to the desired width and diameter for the printing press.

Sheeting

Sheeting is usually performed by paper mills but can be handled by specialist paper converters. The two main methods are:

► *rotary trimming*. A rotary trimming machine cuts the web at predetermined intervals;
► *precision sheeting*. A more accurate, often computerised, version of rotary trimming that has now largely replaced it.

Mill converting and packaging

All mills are now able to control accurately the moisture content of paper so, immediately after production, the mother reels are slit and wrapped before shipping or being sent for sheeting. Slitting and sheeting is carried out under controlled atmospheric conditions to prevent dimensional changes occurring due to gain or loss of moisture.

Packing specifications

Packets

Where possible, specify moisture-proof wrappers strong enough to avoid splitting when handled. Sheets are usually packed in multiples of a thousand or parts of a thousand depending on the quality and weight of packet. The size, substance and weight of each packet should be clearly labelled.

Pallets

Pallets must be strong enough to carry the load required, should allow four-way entry by a standard fork-lift truck and have feet strong enough to allow safe stacking. The pallet base should be flat and even and be slightly bigger than the sheet size to avoid edge damage. Binding straps should not be too tight in order to avoid distortion or damage. Waterproof wrappers or shrink wrapping should be used around the outside of the finished stack.

Reels

Reel covers should be secured to the flat ends and reels should be moisture proof wrapped. Seasoned wood or plastic core plugs should be fitted to prevent damage if dropped. Reels should be stored on their end to avoid distortion.

Markings and protection

A full description on all packets/pallets/reels is important and should include:
► quality
► quantity (weight, number of sheets or length in the case of a reel)
► size
► grammage
► colour
► making order number
► grain direction
► on reels, it is important also to indicate the unwind direction and whether the reel is wound topside in or out (i.e. whether the feltside as opposed to the wireside faces inward or outward).

Transportation loads should be adequately protected from the weather and thoroughly secured.

Hand-made paper

Hand-made paper for specialist use is made sheet by sheet with the wire immersed in a hand-held wooden frame (deckle). It is generally of special furnish, traditionally rag content. The resulting properties include permanence and durability.

When making hand-made paper, it is usual for the deckle edges to be left uncut (feathered edges) and for traditional characteristics such as watermarks to be included. Its manufacture requires craft skills that are extremely expensive. It is feasibly specified only for top-quality specialist purposes such as craft printing and binding, or for artists' paper. Hand-made paper is traditionally made in three finishes ranging in decreasing smoothness, from hot pressed (HP), through not hot pressed (NOT) to rough.

Boardmaking

Board is usually defined as paper above an agreed substance (220–225gsm in UK, and 250gsm in many other countries). It can be single-ply or multi-ply. The multi-ply structure consists of top liner, under liner, middle and back liner. Much of the making process is similar to paper. Points to note include:

Furnish

Basically the same as for paper, and ranging from high-quality bleached pulps down to recycled waste paper. Stock treatment is basically the same as for paper. If waste paper is used, more cleaning and screening may be required. Board is generally given a lesser degree of beating/refining in order to ensure efficient drainage.

The liner plies are often given conventional beating and refining to develop their strength while the middle stock is hardly given any mechanical treatment and just simply broken then lightly refined.

Manufacture

In multi-ply board, the plies may be combined on-machine or off-machine. In the case of on-machine boards, either Fourdrinier or vat process machines may be used. In the case of the Fourdrinier manufacturing process, the board is built up on the wire from a series of Inverform units each of which contains a head box depositing successive layers on each other. The vat boardmaker consists of several vats or cylinder units, in-line containing a revolving large hollow cylinder. Each cylinder picks up a layer of stock and deposits it on the underside of a moving felt that carries the first ply of board. The layers are built up progressively, and at the end of the wire the board is removed for drying.

In the case of off-line finishing, the resulting boards are known as pasted boards to distinguish them from the homogeneous product that comes off a single machine. A number of webs of board are unreeled in parallel to each other; adhesive is applied to the top surface of all but the top sheet, and a pressing cylinder finally brings all the reels together to create a single reel of thicker board. The edges are slit to provide flush edges to the new reel.

Finishing

The range of operations in finishing corresponds to those for paper and can include: calendering, supercalendering, coating, slitting, sheeting, conditioning and, finally, packing for despatch.

Choosing a suitable paper

Three factors need to be taken into account when choosing a suitable paper:

▶ the characteristics of the paper

▶ the requirements of the printing process

▶ knowing the variety of papers from which to choose.

Paper characteristics

Those characteristics formed during the paper-making process are shown in Table 9.1.

TABLE 9.1 Paper characteristics

Characteristics	Formed by	Desirability of characteristics
Brightness	▷ Type of pulp ▷ Degree of bleaching ▷ Amount/type of chemical additives (eg optical brightening agents also known as OBAs)	Essential for white printings and writings
Opacity	▷ Type of pulp ▷ Degree of beating/refining and type of loading, e.g. clay, precipitated calcium carbonate (pcc) or talc	Printings, book paper, writings
Tensile strength	▷ Type of fibre ▷ Degree of beating/refining	Packaging papers, map papers, web offset grades
Wet strength	▷ Degree/type of wet strength agent used	Packaging papers, label papers, map papers
Permanence	▷ Type of fibre, paper chemistry, ▷ Type of sizing	Share certificates, legal documents, archival papers
Dimensional stability	▷ Method of forming ▷ Amount of beating/refining ▷ Amount of sizing, fibre orientation and type of drying	Laser printing grades, business forms, litho printing papers, label papers
Rigidity	▷ Type of pulp (high bulk) ▷ Amount of stock preparation	Positive feeding and delivery on printing machine, ease of converting, creasing and laser printing
Ink hold-out	▷ Type of coating, sizing and calendering	High-quality printing papers
Sizing	▷ Degree/type of sizing agent added	Prevents water-based inks from feathering, improves pick resistance
Picking resistance	▷ Binders used in the coating mix	Printing papers, especially litho
Caliper/tracing paper	▷ Type of fibre, beating/refining ▷ Degree of compression	Greetings card board, bulky book, tracing paper
Gloss	▷ Type of coating ▷ Degree of calendering	Glossy magazines, art papers etc.

Source: Pira International Ltd

Paper varieties (furnishes)

These are the main varieties of paper available defined by the paper maker's recipe (furnish):

Bulky mechanical

Mechanical pulps are the cheapest pulps and are produced by grinding debarked thinnings from forestry management. After grinding, the wood fibres are bleached and refined, and chemical or mechanical processes are used to produce grades such as CTMP (chemi-thermomechanical).

They are used for low-cost paperbacks, newsprint and wallpaper, and can be printed letterpress, web offset litho, gravure or flexo. Mechanical papers have high bulk, good formation and dimensional stability and quite good opacity, but tend to be weak, lose strength and colour on ageing. They can be bleached to approximately 80% brightness.

They can also be coated for use in magazines and as low-cost printing paper. Substances (grammage) available are normally right through the range.

Part mechanical

These are used for cheaper printings and writings (e.g. telephone directory) and are somewhat stronger than papers made from 100% mechanical pulps. Part mechanical papers contain a significant percentage of sulphate (woodfree) pulp to give them added strength, and they may be printed litho as well as letterpress and gravure. The proportion of woodfree to mechanical pulp in a part-mechanical paper varies with the grade required. Part-mechanical papers can also be coated to improve ink hold-out and produce an improved print finish.

Recycled

Environmental groups and European legislation have encouraged the use of recycled fibre. Apart from the traditional uses in the production of boxboard and fluting, recycled fibres are now a principal component of test liner, newsprint and even office copier and business stationery. The early problems of inconsistency, dusting and fibre pick have now been overcome and, in many cases, the recycled papers perform as well as virgin grades.

Woodfree

These are papers that contain only chemically produced pulp or less than 10% mechanically produced pulp. The properties of the papers vary according to the type of pulp used, amount of stock preparation, type and quantity of additives and the finish that the paper might receive. Environmentally friendly grades include ECF (made with pulp chlorine bleached using environmentally approved methods) and TCF (made with pulp bleached without the use of chlorine).

Esparto

Esparto has high bulk and opacity, good smoothness and dimensional stability, good formation and good compressibility. It is mainly used for high-quality printings and for coating base. Softwood pulps or rag fibres are often included in the furnish to improve strength.

Manila

Manila has strong fibres producing very strong paper. It is mainly used for envelopes and wrappings.

Cotton (rags)

This is used to impart softness, permanence, durability, dimensional stability, bulk and opacity. Now used mainly for banknote paper, and formerly in durable papers and high-quality writings. Cotton linters (from the flower part of the cotton plant) have largely replaced rag-based pulp in machine made papers.

Eucalypt

Eucalypt is widely grown in managed forests in South America and the Iberian peninsula. The pulp from eucalyptus trees has unique paper making properties enabling the production of smooth, bulky, uniform papers without the need for heavy refining.

Paper ordering

A formal order form is preferable if ordering paper regularly. Publishers ordering paper for delivery to a printer should always confirm the printer's requirements.

TABLE 9.2 Paper ordering		
Specifying sheets	**Specifying reels**	**Specifying markings/delivery**
▶ Title of job	▶ Maximum diameter of reels	▶ Marking: you will normally want paper
▶ Paper name	▶ Maximum reel width	name, substance, weight/quantity, reel
▶ Quantity of sheets	▶ Maximum reel weight	number, direction of winding. Name of
▶ Substance	▶ Substance	publication or publisher, if appropriate
▶ Caliper	▶ Caliper	▶ Delivery notes should carry all information
▶ Long/short grain	▶ Meterage on the reel	marked on the sheets/reel. Time and date
▶ Printing process	▶ Splices – normally no more than two	of delivery should be arranged with printer
▶ Number of colours to be printed	per reel, taped both sides, and giving	
▶ Packing – ream wrapped or packed	parallel edges after the join	**Imperfections**
on pallets	▶ Winding – normally wireside out, tight and	There should be no cuts, nicks or edge
	even, with no baggy centres or edges	damage and the surface should be free
	▶ Wrapping: normally wrapped in	from slitter dust.
	waterproof paper with ends protected	
	by cardboard, suitable for vertical	
	stacking if necessary	

Source: Pira International Ltd

Paper finishes

Mechanical, recycled or woodfree papers have a number of finishes that include:

Machine-finished (MF)

This is a paper that has been dried in contact with the drying cylinders on the paper-making machine to create smoothness and uniformity on both sides.

Matt-coated

The base paper is coated with a coating mix that usually contains a mix of latex/starch and ground calcium carbonate/china clay. The best matt-coated papers give a smooth non-reflective surface with low abrasivity and good ink hold-out. Typical descriptions are velvet, silk or matt art.

Gloss-coated

Paper that has received this type of finish is also known as gloss art paper. The coating is applied, and then the web is passed between two rollers. One is highly polished steel and the other is fibre packed. This gives the paper a smooth surface with a high-gloss finish. Most high-quality art papers are coated at least once, and sometimes three times, on each side.

Machine-glazed (MG)

A paper that has been dried against a polished drying cylinder. This gives one side of the paper a smooth, glossy appearance while the other remains relatively rough.

Chromo paper

A paper that is coated and then supercalendered (polished) on one side only. Used for greetings cards and label stock.

Cast-coated paper

A paper that is coated in the conventional way but with the coating dried by passing the wet-coated web around a highly polished drying cylinder. This form of coating gives an improved gloss finish to the surface of the web. A variant of this process is known as Trulux, which uses a calendering process in which the soft coating is encouraged to flow under pressure and heat.

Specialist papers

Kraft (bleached or unbleached)

Produced from sulphate wood pulp, it is the strongest of all papers. It is used mainly for wrappings but kraft pulp can be added to other furnishes to increase strength.

Hand-made paper

The furnish is usually cotton, and in the form of rags or cotton linters. Hand-made paper has good dimensional stability, random fibre orientation with good permanence and durability. It is extremely expensive to make and is mostly used by artists for watercolour painting or for other specialist jobs.

Carbonless paper (NCR)

NCR (no carbon required) produces copies when pressure is applied to the top sheet of a set. The set is made with special coatings on the appropriate sides of the sheets. Coated front (CF) is a receptive clay while coated back (CB) contains microcapsules that break under pressure releasing a colour former that reacts with the clay to form an image where the two coatings are in contact. It is used in multi-part business forms for delivery notes, invoices, order forms and pads.

Heat-sealable paper

This uses a coating of heat-activated adhesive. Activation can either be instantaneous or delayed (useful where direct heat may damage the surface or product). It is used for labels.

Pressure-sealable paper

Pressure-sealable paper uses a special polymer coating that is printable but bonds under pressure. It is used for mailers.

Self-adhesive paper

Applied to a silicone-coated backing sheet from which the permanently sticky paper can be peeled off when ready to be stuck down.

Gummed paper

This type of paper is coated with an adhesive that is activated by water. There are two types: conventional gummed paper and dry particle gummed. The former is cheaper but suffers from severe curling problems. In the latter, the particles of adhesive are suspended in an emulsion before coating and drying resulting in a flatter product. Gumbreaking involves passing the gummed paper over a static bar at a sharp angle to craze the gum and reduce the tendency to curl. An ingenious particle-gummed paper is produced by a form of rotary screen printing.

Boards

Unlined chipboard

This is made entirely from waste paper and is relatively cheap. Grey and used where appearance is not important, it contains a large amount of shive and is usually used for tube winding and ridged boxes.

Lined chipboard

Types include white-lined chipboard, Kraft-lined chipboard, mottled (white) chipboard and test-lined chipboard. Test liner contains a mixture of virgin fibre and recycled waste board.

Straw board

Straw board is produced from unbleached straw pulp by light chemical treatment. Digestion is usually with slaked lime (calcium hydroxide). Its applications include envelope-backing postal stiffener material and boards for hardback books.

Pulp board

Made completely from chemical wood pulp, sometimes on an inverform type machine. This grade can be uncoated or coated depending on the end application. Uncoated grades might be used for food packaging while coated grades might be used for paperback covers, brochures and greeting cards. Thickness generally ranges from 0.19–0.41mm. Pulp board can also be castcoated to use with high-quality products such as cosmetics and toiletries.

Coated board

The coating is usually confined to white-lined chipboard and carton boards. The coating is carried out on the board by blade or air knife. The usual amount of coating applied varies from 8–18gsm. It can be used for board games and shop displays.

Artboard

This is made in the same way as art paper except that board weights usually start above 220–225gsm.

Alternative substrates

In addition to paper-based substrates, there are many alternatives used for more specialist printing applications such as metals, plastics, glass and foils. These often have particular surface characteristics that require special inks, treatments and printing processes to ensure good printability and adhesion of the final print to the material. Plastic films are widely used in packaging, labelling and card production. Flexo, often using specially formulated low-odour and taint inks, is the most common print process for these applications. To ensure good bonding of ink on the surface, the film is often corona discharged at the entrance to the printing press. Exactly what occurs during the process is a matter of scientific conjecture but one effect is to raise the free surface energy of the surface. This will gradually decline after treatment, hence the benefit of an in-line application. The energy can be measured with Sherman dyne-treatment liquids. These are a range of mixtures of liquids with varying surface tension. A little is dabbed onto the material and the energy level is indicated when a continuous film is formed with no beading.

Litho printing on plastic, metal and glass

PVC and polypropylene sheets are widely used in plastic card and specialist labelling markets. The packaging industry uses plastic containers that are usually printed in the final shape while metal printing can be done on a flat sheet or the finished product. There are several problems associated with this printing. The surface is not absorbent and ink drying has to be totally chemical with oxidation drying and UV curing the principal methods. Water remains on the surface so the level of damping has to be minimised when printed. Relief and waterless offset are often used.

The inks have to be formulated to adhere well to the substrate. This is often the most important property of the ink over printability and runnability considerations. It is necessary to stop and clean the presses regularly and to develop accelerated adhesion tests to check the quality of the product.

Problem types and testing methods

There are occasions when paper faults cause printing problems.

Printing defects associated with paper

Hickeys can occur with any of the main printing processes. They are random spots on the printed surface, and each consists of a dark spot surrounded by a white halo. They are caused by solid particles of ink skin, paper debris, damper roller lint or debris from the ink rollers that attach themselves to the printing surface.

Depending on the cause and severity of the problem, the remedies may include changing the ink, changing the damper covers or fitting a hickey removing device. A quick fix is often to run the paper through the first unit blind (to remove lint) or change the paper.

Linting (debris piling) mainly occurs with letterpress and litho, and usually when running uncoated grades. Loose fibres on the paper surface are picked up by the blanket, which in turn breaks up the print reproduction on the following sheets. Remedies: decrease ink tack, check fount concentration, reduce press speed, use vacuum brush on press feedboard and increase water feed to plate.

Surface picking can occur on letterpress and lithographic printing process. The fibre or the coating of the paper is lifted from the surface and can be due to too high an ink tack or insufficient binder in the paper stock. Remedies: reduce ink tack, reduce press speed, increase impression cylinder pressure, use a harder blanket, increase water supply to the dampers or change paper stock.

Chalking occurs mainly with letterpress and litho printing and coated papers. The dried print can be easily smudged when rubbed. This problem occurs because the ink vehicle drains into the paper leaving the pigment with insufficient binder to hold it together. It is a characteristic of highly absorbent papers having an open pore structure, e.g. cast-coated papers. Not to be confused with matt rub (see below).

Cheesy drying is a similar effect but is caused by over-emulsification leading to a soft ink structure after drying, particularly when too much alcohol is added to the fount. Remedies: change ink or reduce ink tack, reduce water supply to damper, reduce acidity of fountain solution, use correct fount concentration, check and correct water or fount conductivity. A sealer or varnish may provide a fix.

Mottle can occur on any printing process. The print, especially in solid areas, appears to be blotchy and can be due to uneven absorption characteristics of the paper stock, or poorly formulated ink. Remedies: increase ink tack, reduce supply of ink, increase blanket to impression pressure, and change the ink or the paper.

Set-off can occur on most printing processes. Traces of the ink on the printed side of a sheet are transferred to the back of the following sheet in the delivery pile. Possible remedies include: reduce delivery stack height, use quick-set inks, use a paper with higher absorbency characteristics, use an anti-setoff spray or a delivery pile spacer.

Ink-rub or *matt-rub* is particularly associated with illustrated work printed on matt art paper. The ink on the sheet is abraded by the paper surface with which it is in contact. This causes a form of set-off known as micro rub, or smudging, either in the delivery pile or in the later stages of the finishing/binding process. Some papers are worse than others in this respect. Remedies include: change ink to a full oxidation drying grade, or one formulated for matt papers, use anti-set-off spray, use a varnish/sealer, reduce delivery pile height, reduce quantity of ink, check for overemulsification or incorrect fount addition, allow more time for drying and change paper to as near a neutral pH paper as possible.

Show-through is when the printed image can be seen through from the opposite side of the sheet due to the opacity of the paper being too low for the job being printed.

Strike-through is similar to show-through, except that it is caused by ink penetrating through the sheet. Remedies: use a less absorbent or porous paper, reduce the printing pressure, adjust the ink supply or use quick-set ink.

Ghosting mainly occurs in litho printing processes and on gloss-coated grades. The printed image on one side of the paper appears as a ghost on the printed image of the other side. This is due to chemical ingredients in the first print affecting the wettability characteristics of the reverse side of the paper. It often appears after varnishing or lamination. There are no remedies. For prevention, air the stacks thoroughly before printing the second side; or print the second side with minimum delay.

Blade scratches occur only on blade-coated papers and are caused by dirt or coating mix getting caught under the coating blade and causing a series of fine channels to be formed. It is usually detected at the mill, and is unlikely to affect a large proportion of a making. Remedy: change the paper reel or try another pack.

Distortion can appear in the form of wavy or tight edges in a stack or reel of paper:
▶ wavy edges are caused by the stack having a lower moisture level than the surrounding atmosphere. Paper expands in the cross machine direction when it picks up moisture, and the longer edges are accommodated by the development of edge wave;
▶ tight edges are caused by the stack having a higher moisture level than the surrounding atmosphere. The paper releases some of its moisture to the atmosphere, which causes the edges of the sheets to become tight and the centre of the sheets to become baggy.
Remedy: don't unwrap paper until ready for use, but keep it in the press room for at least 24 hours before use. Protect it from atmospheric moisture in between successive print runs by using film wrap or stack hoods.

Creasing occurs when an uneven moisture content in the sheet causes creases at the edges and back of the printed area. If the edges are wavy, creases tend to occur on leave edge corners; if tight, they tend to occur in the centre of the sheet. Remedy: packed paper should be left to adjust to room temperature before opening.

Tail end hook is caused by the paper sticking to the blanket too tightly when pulled off by the delivery grippers. Remedy: use of a heavier paper or make adjustments to ink tack, blanket or dampers.

Reel defects

Web breakage can be caused by too much tension on one or both edges due to loss of moisture and shrinkage, wrinkles, slime spots, or any type of rupture or poor splicing.

Burst reel is caused by the reel having been wound with too much tension. Remedy: remove outer laps of the reel or if the burst is too deep, reject the reel.

Telescoped reel is due to the reel being wound with insufficient tension.
The only remedy is to have the reel rewound.

Reel out of round is caused by the reel being stored on its side. It can cause misregister when printing due to the variation in tension that will occur. The only remedy is to make sure reels are stored correctly on end.

Web wrinkles appear due to compressive forces in the cross machine direction, which are caused by uneven moisture profile or a misalignment of rollers on the paper machine or in the conversion process.

Chain marks are caused by uneven caliper from one edge to the other. The reel will be travelling at slightly different speeds from one edge to the other causing the paper to slightly twist and cause a distortion in the form of chain marks.

Testing methods

Paper tests

Most of the characteristics of paper that are routinely checked during its manufacture are described below, and the procedures that are in use for doing this. Standard testing conditions are 23°C at 50% relative humidity (RH). Note: RH is the ratio of the absolute humidity (actual amount of water vapour in the atmosphere) to that of air saturated with water vapour at the same temperature and pressure.

Apparent density
(BS3983 1982) Apparent density is the weight of 1cm^3 of paper or board expressed in grams per centimetre cubed. Formula: (units g/cm^3)

grammage / caliper (μm) of one sheet

Ash content
(ISO 2144, 1987/BS3631, 1994) Ash content is the amount of loading or filler in a paper. The residue left after combustion of the paper is expressed as a percentage of the original weight of the sample. The paper sample is put in a crucible, placed in a furnace at 575°C and burned until only a white ash is left. The average ash content from an uncoated cartridge paper may be between 10% and 15%, but the quantity of filler that is used tends to vary widely as paper makers strike a balance between strength, opacity and freedom from dusting or linting.

Bulking thickness

Also known as caliper (BSEN 20534 1994) or the thickness of a single sheet, bulking thickness is tested by measuring the thickness of a number of sheets with a static load applied. The instrument used is a precision dial micrometer and measurement is expressed in micrometres (μm), e.g. a 50gsm sheet may have a caliper of 65 μm. Formula for bulking thickness:

reading on micrometer / number of sheets measured

Brightness (whiteness)

(BS4432:2 1995) Brightness is the reflectance factor of a paper at an effective wavelength of 457mm using a D65/10 degree illuminant. The instrument used is the Elrepho 2000, which uses a conversion factor to calculate the reflectance. The result is expressed as an ISO brightness factor. A typical reading for a 80gsm bond sheet might be 85 ISO.

Burst

(BS3137 1995) Burst is measured by the maximum pressure in kilopascals that can be sustained by a circular area of paper immediately before rupture. Instruments used include pneumatic testers (e.g. Schopper, Dalen) or hydraulic testers (e.g. Mullen). The results are expressed in kilopascals or pounds per square inch. If the result is expressed in lb/sq. in. it may be converted into kPa by multiplying the result by 6.895. A typical result for an 80gsm bond sheet might be: 25lb/sq. in. or 172.4kPa.

Fibre content test

The fibre content test measures the type and amount of fibre in the furnish of a paper or board. It can only be done by microscopic analysis. A sample is prepared on a slide and stained to enable fibre identification. The slide is placed under a microscope and the following points noted:
► length of fibre
► width of fibre
► type of lumen (the hollow central channel within the fibre)
► type of fibre end
► any surface marking
► any other marking.
Where more than one fibre is in the furnish, a fibre count (ISO 9184 BS 7463 1991) will be necessary to determine the percentage of each type of fibre.

Folding endurance

(BS ISO 5626 1993) Folding endurance is measured by the number of double folds required to cause rupture in a strip of paper 15mm wide. This test should be carried out in both machine direction and cross direction. The instrument used is known as the Schopper. The result is expressed as the number of double folds before fracture.

Formation

The two extremes of formation are described as wild or even, and it is assessed by holding the sheet up to a light source and viewing it. A wild formation is where there are clumps of fibre, and the sheet appears uneven and patchy. An even formation is where the fibres are distributed evenly throughout the sheet.

Furnish determination

Phloroglucinol solution is used to determine whether a paper has a woodfree or mechanical furnish. If the paper remains yellow when the stain is applied, it is said to be woodfree, i.e. only chemically produced pulp has been used in the furnish. If the paper is stained red, the paper contains mechanically produced pulp. The depth in shade of the red stain indicates the percentage of mechanical fibre present. This is a comparative test only.

Gloss

(TAPPI T480 OM-85) This test is usually carried out on supercalendered art paper/board. It is determined by the intensity of an angled beam of light (typically 75°) that is reflected from the sheet of paper/board. The result is expressed as a percentage. The usual result for a glossy board should be 60% or more.

Grammage

Also called basis weight (BS ISO 536 1995), or substance, it is defined as the weight in grams of a sheet one square metre (gsm). A sample is cut to a known area, usually 10x10cm and weighed on a balance under standard test conditions. The formula for determining grammage (g/m², or gsm) is:

$$1 \text{ sq. metre} \times \text{weight of sample} / \text{area of sample}$$

In North America the basis weight is the weight of one ream (500 sheets) of a given paper cut to its basic size, given in pounds (lb).

Strictly speaking, substance weight is the basis weight of bond paper (500 sheets of 17 × 22in), but the terms basis weight and substance weight are often used interchangeably. Note that a ream of some tissue and wrapping grades is considered to be 480 sheets.

Internal tearing resistance

(BS EN 21974 1994) Internal tearing resistance is measured by the mean force, expressed in millinewtons, required to continue tearing of an initial cut in a single sheet of paper. Four sheets with the same grain direction and cut to a specific size are usually torn together. The initial cuts are of a specified length and made on a specially designed hand guillotine supplied with the tear tester. This test is carried out in both machine and cross direction. An average result for a typical 80gsm bond sheet might be 440–490mN.

Moisture content

(BSEN 20287 1994) All paper naturally contains a certain amount of moisture, typically about 3–7% in printings and writings and as much as 10% in newsprint. The moisture content is determined by taking a representative sample, placing it in a sealed container to be weighed. The sample is placed in an oven for a minimum of four hours at 105°C, and then replaced in the same sealed container and reweighed. The difference in weight (i.e. the moisture content) is expressed as a percentage of the original weight:

loss in weight × 100 / weight of original sample

Opacity

(BS 4432:3 1996) Opacity is the ratio of the reflectance of the surface of a single sheet of paper with a black backing, to the reflectance of a wad of the same paper thick enough to be completely opaque. The instruments used are the EEL Opacimeter (obsolete) and the Elrepho 2000. The result is expressed as a percentage; 91–93% is typical.

TABLE 9.3 Typical opacity readings														
Paper	**Newsprint**			**Bank**			**Bond**			**Matt coated**		**Supercalendered**		
Substance (gsm)	49	45	60	70	80	90	100	115	135	170	90	100	115	135	170
Reading (%)	91	70	80	83	87	91	93	95	96	98	90	92	94	95	97

Note: Readings may vary by + or −1%, eg for a 100gsm supercalendered paper 91–93% would be typical
Source: Pira International Ltd

Porosity (Bendtsen)

(BS6538:2 1992) Porosity (Bendtsen) is measured by the flow of air in millilitres per minute through an area of 10cm² at an overpressure of 150mm water column. The apparatus consists of a clamp holding the paper securely, a means of applying a steady air pressure difference across the sheet and a means of measuring the rate of flow of air through the test piece. The instrument usually has two or three measuring tubes on it so that a wide range of measurements can be obtained. The average result for an 80gsm bond sheet might be 380ml/min.

Porosity (Gurley)

(BS6538:3 1995) Porosity (Gurley) is a measure of the time taken to displace 100ml of air through a circular area of one square inch. The instrument consists of an outer and inner cylinder. The outer cylinder is filled with a given quantity of special lightweight oil. The inner cylinder is open ended and has a clamp at the top end to hold the sample tightly against the inner cylinder. The inner cylinder is graduated in 100ml and the result is expressed in seconds.

pH value

(BS2924 1983) The pH value is the degree of acidity/alkalinity of a substance. The pH scale ranges from 1–14 with seven being neutral. Below seven is acidic, and above seven is alkaline. The pH of a hot or cold water extract of the paper is the most accurate method; surface pH in a water drop can be measured using a flat electrode attached to a pH meter. A quick comparative method is to use a smear of indicator solution, but generally this will give a reading 1–2 units lower than the extract method. Most European papers are now neutral or alkaline giving an extract pH of 6.5–8. This is because synthetic neutral sizing has replaced the traditional acid-sized papers. The acidity of a paper was usually associated with slow ink drying, but now the main need for pH checks is partly to confirm whether a paper has archivability.

Roughness (Bendtsen)

(BS4420 1997) Roughness is measured on the same instrument as Bendtsen porosity but with a different measuring head. It is the extent to which the surface of the paper deviates from a plane. The measuring head, when placed on a smooth plane hard surface, will allow no air to escape. When it is placed on the surface of the paper, that will be rougher, the amount of air that escapes is measured in millilitres per minute. This test must be carried out on both top and wire side as the results may differ. A possible result for an 80gsm bond sheet might be 400/420ml/min.

Sizing degree

(BSEN 20535 1994) Sizing degree is measured by the Cobb test using a short metal cylinder with a cross sectional area of 100cm² and height of about 5cm. The sample is clamped between the metal cylinder and the rubber base, and 100ml of water is poured into the cylinder. After 45 seconds the water is poured off and after one minute the sample is blotted to remove any water remaining on the surface and the sample is weighed. The result is expressed as the amount of water in grams taken up by one square metre of exposed surface in one minute. The figure obtained determines the degree of sizing, i.e. 30+ soft-sized; 20–30 medium-sized; 0–20 hard-sized.

Stiffness

(BS 3748 1992) Kenley instrument. Stiffness is measured by the force required to bend a 5cm test length through 15°.

Surface strength

Dennison wax pick (TAPPI T459 om-93) This test determines the highest numerically designated wax that does not disturb the surface of the sheet when it is applied to the sheet and then pulled away. The waxes are graded according to the degree of tack that they have with 1 being the least tacky and 23 having the greatest tack. A paper that would be suitable for four-colour litho printing would have a Dennison wax figure greater than 11.

IGT pick test

(BS 6225:2 1982 (1995)) ISO 3782/3 IGT is the Dutch manufacturer of the testing instrument. The test determines the printing velocity at which surface picking occurs using a complicated procedure involving a low viscosity oil and a special printing unit applied at an accelerating speed. Four-colour litho printing would normally require no picking at a minimum reading of 135cm/sec.

Tensile strength

(BS EN ISO 1924:2 1995) Tensile strength is a measure of the minimum force, in newtons, required to break a strip of paper 180mm long and 15mm wide clamped at both ends. A tensile tester is used and tensile strength is measured in kilonewtons per metre. The formula for tensile strength is:

$$kN/m = tensile\ reading\ (N)\ /\ 15$$

Wet strength retention

(BS2922 1995) The paper is burst (using a hydraulic burst tester). The sheet is then submerged in water for 15 minutes, the excess water is blotted off and the sample is again burst. The result is expressed as a percentage of the wet burst to the dry burst. A wet strength paper should have a minimum reading of approximately 50%.

Board tests

Board is tested mainly by the same methods as paper. Additional tests that are carried out include:

Scott Ply Bond

(TAPPI UM 403 1991) Scott Ply Bond is measured by delaminating the board using double-sided tape and two plates that are separated at high speed.

Creasing

Creasing tests are carried out on carton boards with a creasing rule to evaluate the creasing qualities in both machine and cross direction. The test determines the extent to which the board is likely to crack when creased then folded.

Environmental commentary

Forest management

The paper industry is not a net consumer of trees but a net provider. Trees for making paper are grown, harvested and replanted like any other crop. In most western European countries at least two trees are planted for every one cut down. In Finland and Sweden, the rules stipulate three. Further, reforestation programmes seek to increase biodiversity and maintain sustainability of wood production. The result is that in virtually every country in Europe, tree coverage is steadily increasing rather than decreasing. Some 15% of the world's annual wood consumption is used for pulp and paper and very little native forest is cut down specifically for this purpose.

Tropical and temperate natural forests are being cleared to provide living space, to secure grazing land for cattle, and provide timber for furniture and construction. Replanting of hardwood forests to provide wood for making paper is now common in countries such as Brazil, Chile, Thailand and Indonesia.

Pollution

Pulp and paper makers are aware of the environmental effects of their production processes and are seeking to reduce emissions to air, water and land. An example is the pulp industry's change to chlorine-free bleaching processes reducing the possibility of generating potentially toxic by-products. Natural shades (off-whites) of paper require less bleaching chemicals than are required to achieve bright whites and have now gained acceptance.

Recycling

In western Europe and the US, virgin pulp derived from trees accounts for just under half of all fibre used for paper. The remaining fibre is derived from recycled paper, mostly post-consumer waste. In the UK, the figure was 62.3% recycled fibre ('Mill consumption of waste paper – pulp equivalent 3,674,600 tonnes', Paper Federation Reference Statistics for 1996).

The paper industry has always made use of recycled fibre in the form of broke generated from paper production and converting. This is known as pre-consumer waste. In countries with insufficient virgin fibre sources, such as the UK, Germany and Japan, historical use has also been made of post-consumer waste paper. The use of post-consumer waste has, therefore, been driven traditionally by market forces. In recent years, further increases in use have been stimulated by government policy resulting from environmental concerns, particularly to reduce the use of landfill and to reduce consumption of energy and resources.

The global waste paper recovery rate was 40% in 1994 and this will continue to grow within the limits set by collection and sorting costs, effects on paper quality and the environmental impact of de-inking technologies. New developments in de-inking technology have resulted in the recovery of high-grade fibre that is used to produce high-quality printing and writing grades.

Energy conservation

The reduction of energy consumption is a priority for paper makers. An example is the co-generation of electric power and low pressure steam. There has also been an increase in the amount of energy generated internally from waste.

Water conservation

Much progress has been made in recycling the water used in paper making. Most mills are aiming to produce closed systems that continuously recirculate water within the paper machine system.

Measurements and calculation

Sheets are usually specified by either an internationally agreed range of the International Standards Organisation (A, B, C series) or a range of metric variations on the old imperial sizes (mostly for bookwork).

The international ISO range

British Standard BS4000 1983. The International ISO range is based on three series of interrelating sizes, which are designated A, B and C. The sides of the sheet are always in the ratio $1:\sqrt{2}$, the subdivision from one size to the next one down is denoted by a higher numeral and is made by halving the length of the longest side (e.g. A2 is half of A1).

Trimmed size is defined as the final dimensions of a sheet of paper.

Untrimmed size is defined as the dimensions of a sheet of paper, untrimmed and not specially squared, sufficiently large to allow a trimmed size to be obtained from it as required.

A series

The A series comprises trimmed sizes designed for standard printing and stationery needs: $A0 = 1m^2$; $A1 = 0.5m^2$ and so on.

RA sizes are for normal trim work.

SRA sizes are for bleeds or extra trim.

B series

The B series comprises trimmed sizes falling between A sizes that are designed for large items, e.g. wallcharts.

C series

The C series comprises sheets for envelopes and folders to take A series contents.

Useful metric units and symbols

Area	square metre	m²
Dimensions	millimetre	mm
centimetre	cm	(1cm=10mm)
metre	m	(1m=100cm=1000mm)
Grammage	grams per square metre	g/m² or gsm
Mass	gram	g
kilogram	kg	(1kg=1000g)
tonne	t	(1t=1000kg=1,000,000g)
Thickness	micrometre, micron	µm
millimetre	mm	(1mm=1000µm)
Bursting strength	kilopascal	kPa
Internal tearing	millinewton mN	strength
Temperature	degrees	Celsius °C
Relative humidity	percentage	%

Sheet count standard ream 500 sheets

Machine direction indicated by symbol (m) e.g. 640 × 900 (m) long grain sheet, 640 (m) × 900 short grain sheet

Paper sizes

TABLE 9.4 A sizes

Sheet size	Millimetres	Inches
4A	1682 × 2378	66¼ × 93⅝
2A	1189 × 1682	46¾ × 66¼
A0	841 × 1189	33⅛ × 46¾
A1	594 × 841	23⅜ × 33⅛
A2	420 × 594	16½ × 23⅜
A3	297 × 420	11¾ × 16½
A4	210 × 297	8¼ × 11¾
A5	148 × 210	5⅞ × 8¼
A6	105 × 148	4⅛ × 5⅞
A7	74 × 105	2⅞ × 4⅛
A8	52 × 74	2 × 2⅞
A9	37 × 52	1½ × 2
A10	26 × 37	1 × 1½

Source: Pira International Ltd

Figure 9.2 (opposite) shows the progressive reductions down from A0 to A5 and each size is half the previous one. In the diagram on the right, it is clear that each size has its sides in the same ratio of $1{:}\sqrt{2}$. (1:1.412)

FIGURE 9.2 A series size relationships

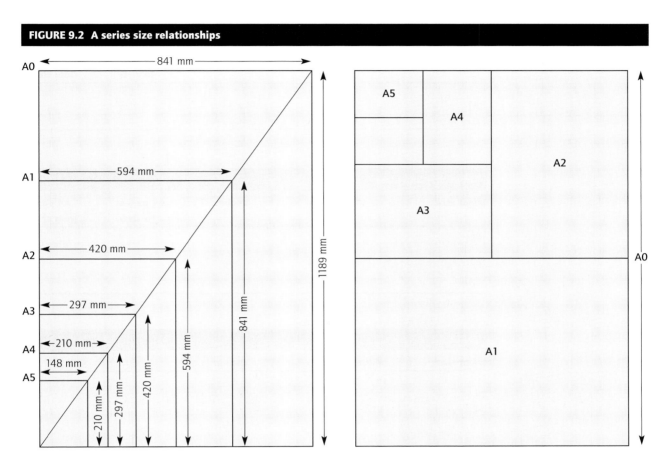

Source: Pira International Ltd

TABLE 9.5 C series			
Sheet size	**Millimetres**	**Inches**	**Common use**
4A	1682 × 2378	66¼ × 93⅝	
C0	917 × 1297	36⅛ × 51	
C1	648 × 917	25½ × 36⅛	
C2	458 × 648	18 × 25½	
C3	324 × 458	12¾ × 18	
C4	229 × 324	9 × 12¾	takes A4 sheet flat
C5	162 × 229	6⅜ × 9	takes A5 sheet flat
C6	114 × 162	4½ × 6⅜	takes A5 folded once
C7/6	81 × 162	3¼ × 6⅜	takes A5 folded twice
C7	81 × 114	3¼ × 4½	
DL	110 × 220	4⅜ × 8⅝	takes A4 folded twice

Source: Pira International Ltd

TABLE 9.6 RA sizes				
Sheet size	**Millimetres**	**Inches**	**A4 pages to view**	**A4 pages from sheet**
RA0	860 × 1220	$33^3/_8$ × 48	16	32
RA1	610 × 860	24 × $33^7/_8$	8	16
RA2	430 × 610	$16^7/_8$ × 24	4	8

Source: Pira International Ltd

TABLE 9.7 SRA sizes				
Sheet size	**Millimetres**	**Inches**	**A4 pages to view**	**A4 pages from sheet**
SRA0	900 × 1280	$35^3/_8$ × $50^3/_8$	16	32
SRA1	640 × 900	$25^1/_4$ × $35^3/_8$	8	16
SRA2	450 × 640	$17^3/_4$ × $25^1/_4$	4	8
SRA3	320 × 450	12 × $8^1/_2$	2	2

Source: Pira International Ltd

TABLE 9.8 B series		
Sheet size	**Millimetres**	**Inches**
4B	2000 × 2828	$78^3/_4$ × $111^3/_8$
2B	1414 × 2000	$55^5/_8$ × $78^3/_4$
B0	1000 × 1414	$39^3/_8$ × $55^5/_8$
B1	707 × 1000	$27^5/_8$ × $39^7/_8$
B2	500 × 707	$19^5/_8$ × $27^7/_8$
B3	353 × 500	$13^7/_8$ × $19^5/_8$
B4	250 × 353	$9^7/_8$ × $13^7/_8$
B5	176 × 250	7 × $9^7/_8$

Source: Pira International Ltd

Substance

Paper weight or *substance* is defined as the weight in grams of one square metre of one sheet of paper (i.e. an A0 size sheet). It is reported as grams per square metre (abbreviated to gsm).

Volume

Paper *volume basis* (a measure of caliper or thickness) is the measure of thickness in millimetres of 100 sheets of the paper in 100gsm. As a unit of measurement, it is referred to as *volume* and abbreviated to vol, e.g. for a vol 16 paper, 100 sheets of 100gsm of the paper will have been measured as 16 mm thick. Alternatively, the caliper of a single sheet can be measured in *micrometres* (also called microns) and for which the symbol is µm.

Board, however, is always sold by thickness rather than weight and this is normally measured as the thickness of a single board in micrometres, although it can sometimes be measured in millimetres. Standard stock thicknesses are 200, 230, 250, 280, 300, 400 and 500µm.

Weight and volume (metric system)

Derived from Imperial sizes, they allow for a 3mm trim at the head, foot and fore-edge of the page. Standard sheet sizes are as follows:

TABLE 9.9 The metric range of book publishing papers					
Name	**Trimmed page (mm)**	**Untrimmed page (mm)**	**Quad sheet (mm)**	**Pages to view**	**Pages from sheet**
Metric Crown 8vo	186 × 123	192 × 126	768(m) × 1008	32	64
Metric Crown 4to	246 × 189	252 × 192	768 × 1008(m)	16	32
Metric Large Crown 8vo	198 × 129	204 × 132	816(m) × 1056	32	64
Metric Demy 8vo	216 × 138	222 × 141	888(m) × 1128	32	64
Metric Demy 4to	276 × 219	282 × 222	888 × 1128(m)	16	32
Metric Royal 8vo	234 × 156	240 × 159	960(m) × 1272	32	64
Metric Royal 4to	312 × 237	318 × 240	960 × 1272(m)	16	32
Reels: sizes are usually made to order, the width determined by the requirement of the printing machine.					

Source: Pira International Ltd

BS4000 also recommends the following for printer's board and cover paper.

TABLE 9.10 Recommendations for printer's board and covers		
Sheet size	**Printer's board untrimmed stock sizes (mm)**	**Cover paper untrimmed stock sizes (mm)**
SRA2	450 × 640	485 × 640
Royal	520 × 640	520 × 780
Postal	570 × 730	640 × 970
SRA1	640 × 900	

Source: Pira International Ltd

Calculating the number of sheets required for a job

$$\text{sheets required} = \frac{\text{pages} \times \text{print run}}{\text{pages per perfected sheet}} \text{ plus allowance for overs}$$

Calculating the weight of paper in the job

1.
$$\frac{\text{length (mm)} \times \text{width (mm)} \times \text{gsm}}{10^6} = \text{kgs/1000 sheets}$$

Example: the weight of 1000 sheets of 120gsm paper size RA1 is

$$\frac{610 \times 860 \times 120}{1,000,000} = 62.95 \text{ kg}$$

2.
$$\frac{\text{kgs/1000} \times \text{sheets required}}{10^6} = \text{weight of paper in the job (tonnes)}$$

Example: the weight of 16,500 sheets of the above paper is:

$$\frac{62.95 \times 16,500}{1,000,000} = 1.039 \text{ tonnes}$$

Calculating the cost of paper for the job

Weight of paper in the job × tonne rate = cost of paper in the job

Example:

8000 copies of a 128pp monochrome book trimmed size 216 × 138mm, printing 32 to view on 888 × 1128, 80gsm paper at £600 per tonne:

(i)   Sheets required = $\dfrac{128 \times 8000}{64}$ = 16,000 + 4% overs = 16,640

(ii)   Weight of paper = $\dfrac{888 \times 1128 \times 80}{10^6}$ = 80.1 kgs/1000

then $\dfrac{80.1 \times 16,640}{10^6}$ = 1.333 tonnes

(iii)   Cost of paper = 1.333 × 600 = £799.80

Calculating the weight of a magazine or book

$\dfrac{mm \times mm \times gsm \times \frac{1}{2}\ pages}{10^6}$ = weight (grams)

Add 20 grams for a paperback cover. Add 100 grams for a hardback case.

Calculating the cost of paper in a magazine or book

$\dfrac{Weight\ of\ paper\ (grams) \times tonne\ rate}{10^4}$ = cost (pence)

Number of sheets in a tonne

$\dfrac{10^6}{kgs/1000}$ = number of sheets in one tonne

Number of copies of a job obtainable from a given number of sheets

$\dfrac{sheets\ available \times pp\ per\ perfected\ sheet}{pages\ in\ job}$ = copies, less allowance for overs.

Calculating sheet size required

Always check with the printer before finally ordering paper in your calculated sheet size. The allowances given below are averages and may vary up or down according to the needs of the particular printing machine being used and the working methods employed.

1.   Establish the maximum sheet size of the machine you plan to use.
2.   Take the trimmed size of the job (article/magazine/book).
3.   Add 6mm to the depth dimension and add 3mm to the width dimension to give the untrimmed size.

4. Multiply the depth by 2/4/6/8 width by 2/4/6/8 to get the nearest depth and width figures to the maximum sheet size.

5. a) If the job is *monochrome unbled*, no further allowance is needed.
   Round up the figure you now have to the nearest 10mm in both directions.

   b) If the job is *monochrome bled* add the following and *then* round up to the nearest 10mm in both directions:
   15mm on the leading edge for grippers,
   12mm on the leave edge for handling,
   6mm on each side edge for handling.

   c) If the job is *four-colour bled* add the following and *then* round up to the nearest 10mm in either direction:
   15mm on the leading edge for grippers,
   30mm on the leave edge for colour bars,
   6mm on each side edge for handling.

Example:

Colour book trimmed size 251 × 203 mm bled to be printed on a Roland Ultra 5:

1. Maximum sheet size Roland Ultra 5 = 890 × 1260
2. Trimmed size of book = 251 × 203
3. Untrimmed size of book = 257 × 206
4. Nearest approx. sheet size = (257 × 4) = 1028
   (206 × 4) = 824
5. Short dimension: 824mm + 45mm = 869mm
   Long dimension: 1028mm + 12mm = 1040mm
   Rounded up = 870 × 1040mm sheet size

Calculating the meterage required for a job

1. Meterage for one section = machine cut-off (m) × print run plus allowance for overs.
2. Meterage for whole job = number of sections in the job × meterage per section.
   Calculating the weight of this meterage

   $$\frac{m \times m \times gsm}{10^6} = \text{weight of paper in the job (tonnes)}$$

   Calculating the cost of this paper
   Weight of paper in the job × tonne rate = cost of paper in the job

Example:

80,000 copies of a 128pp colour book, trimmed size A5, printing on a web with a reel width of 640mm and cut off 450mm. 80gsm paper at £550 a tonne:

a) 1. Meterage for one section = 0.45 × 80000 = 36000.

Plus 15% overs = 41400

2. Meterage for whole job = 8 × 41400 = 331200 metres

b) Weight of this meterage =

$$\frac{0.64 \times 331\,200 \times 80}{10^6} = 16.957 \text{ tonnes}$$

c) 16.957 × 550 = £9326.35

TABLE 9.11 Spoilage allowances			

Sheetfed work

Add 2% per colour to the printer's allowance for multi-colour work

Printing quantity	printer's allowance	binder's allowance	total spoilage allowance
1000–2500	4.0%	2.5%	6.5%
2500–5000	3.0%	2.0%	5.0%
5000–10000	2.5%	1.5%	4.0%
10,000+	2.5%	1.0%	3.5%

Web-fed work

Add 3% per colour to the printer's allowance for multi-colour work

Printing quantity	printer's allowance	binder's allowance	total spoilage allowance
10,000–15,000	11.0%	1.0%	12.0%
15,000–25,000	9.0%	1.0%	10.0%
25,000–75,000	7.0%	1.0%	8.0%
75,000+	5.0%	1.0%	6.0%

Reference should be made to the printer for the exact figures he requires. However, typical figures for monochrome sheet- and web-fed litho are shown here.

Source: Pira International Ltd

Calculating the weight of a magazine or book

$$\frac{mm \times mm \times gsm \times \frac{1}{2} \text{ pages}}{10^6} = \text{weight (grams)}$$

Add 20 grams for a paperback cover. Add 100 grams for a hardback case.

Calculating the cost of paper in a magazine or book

$$\frac{\text{Weight of paper (grams)} \times \text{tonne rate}}{10^4} = \text{cost (pence)}$$

Calculating bulk where the volume of a paper is known

$$\text{Bulk (mm)} = \frac{gsm \times volume \times \frac{1}{2} \text{ pages}}{10^4}$$

Calculating caliper

$$\text{Caliper (microns)} = \frac{\text{gsm} \times \text{volume}}{10}$$

Calculating volume where caliper and substance are known

$$\text{Volume} = \frac{\text{caliper (microns)} \times 10}{\text{gsm}}$$

US measurement and calculation

Most of the world uses the metric system of grams and metres outlined above. The main exception to this is the United States of America, whose system retains much in common with Britain's old Imperial system.

The standard units of measurement for weight are: pounds, hundredweights (100lbs) and tons (2000lbs). Paper size is measured in inches and quantity in reams (500 sheets unless otherwise specified).

Weight and size information

Substance is identified by *basis weight*.

Basis weight = weight (lbs) of a ream of paper cut to its *basic size*.

A paper's basic size depends on its grade. The basic sizes for the common paper grades are:

Paper	Basic size (inches)	Equivalent in mm
Cover boards	20 × 26	508 × 660
Newsprint	24 × 36	610 × 914
Book papers	25 × 38	635 × 965

A book paper of basis weight 60lb is written as 25 × 38–60(500).

Caliper calculations

Grammage and basis weight conversion

Convert from one to the other using a multiplying factor. See Table 9.12.

Note that different multiplication factors are applied to each basic size.

For rough calculations with the most common 25" × 38" basic size papers the factors to retain are:

lbs to gsm : multiply by 1½ (the exact factor is 1.4800)

gsm to lbs : multiply by ⅔ (the exact factor is 0.6757)

Substance number

The term 'substance number' is sometimes used as an alternative to basis weight, particularly for bond or writing papers. For example, a bond paper with basis weight 20lb can also be called substance 20.

M weight

Basis weight is often converted into the weight of 1000 (M) sheets (instead of a ream or 500 sheets). So a book paper with a basis weight of 60lb has an M weight of 120lb. For a book paper of basis weight 60lb this would be written as:

25 × 38–120(M) (instead of 25 × 38–60(500)).

Prices

Usually expressed as dollars per 100lb (divide by 100 to give price per lb).

Calculations

Price per 1000 sheets

M weight × price per lb

Weight of paper required when using paper in its basic size

$$\text{lbs} = \frac{\text{M weight} \times \text{number of sheets required}}{1000}$$

TABLE 9.12 Conversion factors for basis weights and grammage		
Basic size (inches)	**to convert from gsm to lb/ream multiply gsm by**	**to convert from lb/ream to gsm mutiply lb/ream by**
17 × 22	0.266	3.76
20 × 26 (cover boards)	0.370	2.70
20 × 30	0.427	2.34
22 × 38	0.438	2.28
22½ × 28½	0.456	2.19
25½ × 30½	0.553	1.81
23 × 35	0.573	1.75
24 × 36 (newsprint)	0.614	1.63
25 × 38 (book papers)	0.675	1.48

Source: Pira International Ltd

Weight required using non-standard (not basic) sheet size

First calculate the M weight of the non-standard size:

1. $$\text{Weight of 500 sheets} = \frac{\text{non-standard size} \times \text{basis weight}}{\text{basic size}}$$

Example:

Weight wanted of non-standard size 23 × 29 using a 60lb book paper:

$$\text{Weight of 500 sheets} = \frac{23 \times 29 \times 60}{25 \times 38} = 42.1\text{lbs (round up to 42)}$$

Then apply the M weight to the formula for calculating paper in its basic size.

2. M weight = 2 × basis weight

Calculating weight in reels

The formula for reels is essentially the same as for non-standard sheet.

Calculate the M weight as 1000 sections where the dimensions of one section are defined as the reel width by the machine cut off:

Example:

Weight of a 40lb book paper in reels with a width of 34½" and a machine cut off 23⁹⁄₁₆":

$$\text{Weight of 500 sections} = \frac{23^{9/16} \times 34^{1/2} \times 40}{25 \times 38} = 34\text{lbs}$$

Therefore M weight = 68lb

Now apply the formula:

$$\frac{\text{M weight} \times \text{number of sections required}}{1000} = \text{total weight in lbs}$$

Linear footage on a reel

$$\text{Linear footage} = \frac{\text{reel weight} \times \text{basic size} \times 500}{\text{reel width} \times \text{basis weight}}$$

$$\text{Number of sections out of a reel} = \frac{\text{footage on a reel} \times 2}{\text{machine cut-off (inches)}}$$

Thickness

Thickness of paper and board is measured by one of two related methods:

► bulking number = number of sheets that will bulk to one inch under test conditions.

► per inch (ppi) = twice the bulking number (because one sheet = two pages).

Standards for testing are laid down by TAPPI (Technical Association of the Pulp and Paper Industry), PO Box 105113, Atlanta, Georgia 30348, US.

TABLE 9.13 Weight (lb) per 1000 sheets of standard sheet sizes and weights of book papers

Sheet size (inches)	Basis weight (lb) 25 × 38" ream (Equivalent gsm)									
	30	35	40	45	50	60	70	80	100	120
	44	*52*	*59*	*67*	*74*	*89*	*104*	*118*	*148*	*178*
17½ × 22½	25	29	33	37	41	50	58	66	83	99
19 × 25	30	35	40	45	50	60	70	80	100	120
23 × 29	42	49	56	63	70	84	98	112	140	169
23 × 35	51	59	68	76	84	102	118	136	169	203
24 × 36	54	64	72	82	90	110	128	146	182	208
25 × 38	60	70	80	90	100	120	140	160	200	240
28 × 44	78	90	104	116	130	156	182	208	260	312
32 × 44	88	104	118	134	148	178	208	238	296	356
35 × 45	100	116	132	150	166	198	232	266	332	398
38 × 50	120	140	160	180	200	240	280	320	400	480
42 × 58	154	179	205	230	256	308	358	410	512	614

Source: Pira International Ltd

TABLE 9.14 Weight (lb) per 1000 sheets of standard sheet sizes and weights of cover boards

Sheet size (inches)	Basis weight (lb) 25 × 38" ream (Equivalent gsm)					
	50	60	65	80	100	130
	135	162	175	216	270	351
20 × 26	100	120	130	160	200	260
23 × 35	155	186	201	248	310	402
26 × 40	200	240	260	320	400	520
35 × 46	310	392	402	496	620	804

Source: Pira International Ltd

TABLE 9.15 American book sizes

Name	Size (inches)	Name	Size (inches)
Medium 32mo	3 × 4¾	Medium 12mo	5⅛ × 7⅔
Medium 24mo	3⅝ × 5½	Demy 8vo	5½ × 8
Medium 18mo	4 × 6⅔	Small 4to	7 × 8½
Cap 8vo	7 × 7¼	Broad 4to (up to 13 ×10)	7 × 8½
12mo	4½ × 7½	Medium 8vo	6 × 9½
Medium 16mo	4½ × 6¾	Royal 8vo	6½ × 10
Crown 8vo	5 × 7½	Super Royal 8vo	7 × 10½
Post 8vo	5½ × 7½	Imperial 8vo	8¼ × 11½

Note that the American usage is to express the width dimension of the book first. The sizes quoted are not absolute and may vary slightly.
Source: Pira International Ltd

Choosing the correct paper

So which paper should be used, and how should the choice be made? The paper must fit the publisher's cost and quality requirement and should represent the most cost-effective choice for the printer. Paper can be specified in terms of three categories of properties:

▶ *Service properties* Properties designed into the paper by the manufacturing mill

▶ *Performance properties* How the paper performs at the printer

▶ *Commercial Properties* Agreed between paper supplier and customer.

These criteria can be used to determine the best choice. A publisher (the term is used to refer to any client of a printer) will consider the service and commercial properties of a paper while the printer has to assess all three types of property.

Individual printing companies will assess paper performance on their machines, using measures of runnability to determine their acceptance of a particular grade. Modern paper machines make large tonnages of paper extremely quickly and consistently, but they may spoil the effort through poor finishing, presentation and delivery techniques damaging the paper before it gets to press. Mills and suppliers should work more closely with printers to understand better how they use the paper and so to improve performance. The batch-to-batch consistency of paper is vitally important and will be more so in future. Printers will no longer be able to offer out-of-specification print to customers, or afford the consequences of poor runnability. Printers will work with their preferred suppliers to develop the process for the benefit of each other to give publishers a better service.

Service properties of paper

These properties are the design and manufacture of paper at a mill. A mill will choose the ingredients and method of manufacture of their paper taking the economics, performance on the paper machine and finishing line, subsequent performance on printing press and final product properties into account. It is the balance between the paper machine and printing press performance that sometimes causes problems between the supplier and printer.

Paper is a complex organic material made of an enormous number of cellulose fibres, coating and various bonding elements. Papers vary through raw material selection, method of manufacture and type of paper machine, surface coating and finishing. The service properties determine the end use of paper and may be used as a method of classification. It is the overall mix of properties that determines the suitability for any particular publishing application.

Each property will affect how a printer can treat the substrate on the press. The list can act as a check list for buyers to consider when placing a paper order. There are more than 50 British Standard test methods to determine the service properties of paper. In the US, the Technical Association of the Pulp and Paper Industry (TAPPI) publishes methods for testing paper and board, and individual laboratories in mills, merchants and printers use a variety of these tests, together with particular routines they have developed to characterise paper samples.

There is little correlation between the instruments used in different laboratories in mills and printers, and certainly not between different countries, although several bodies are working to calibrate to a standard. PIRA International offers a calibration service that is helping standardisation. The Confederation of European Paper Industries (CEPI) offers a range of calibrated test materials and protocols to laboratories to calibrate their instruments. Despite these initiatives, at present there is no absolute result and the recorded numbers from different testing sites cannot be directly compared. Providing quantitative comparisons of available papers can be a useful marketing tool for printers to give the publisher an informed choice of the particular grade.

There are many paper mills manufacturing and selling into the well-developed global paper market, and they often use local paper merchants as part of the distribution channel. West European and Scandinavian paper suppliers have served the UK well and are being joined by suppliers from America and eastern Europe. There are many grades of paper, from uncoated newsprint to triple-cast coated woodfree grades. Each is designed and manufactured to have different properties for a wide range of end uses. There is no standard paper nomenclature system to define the type and grade of paper, so a lightweight coated (LWC) from supplier X may be mediumweight coated (MWC) from Y.

| **TABLE 9.16 A list of service properties of paper and board** | | |

▶ **The paper grade**
Which type of paper or board, see Table 9.17.

▶ **Raw material content**
The major ingredient of paper is cellulose fibre, mostly pulp from farmed softwood or other plants. As well as fibre, paper will contain mineral fillers, sizes and chemical additives such as alum, retention aids, dyes or optical brighteners. If the paper is coated, the coating may contain pigments, adhesives, dispersants, hardeners and preservatives.

Pulp may be recycled from used paper and board, or from virgin fibre. There are two main grades of pulp: mechanical, where the fibres are physically separated by grinding up logs and wood chips under great pressure in water; woodfree pulp is manufactured in a chemical refining process that dissolves the lignin present in wood. Woodfree pulp is more expensive than mechanical. It gives the paper greater strength and shows less tendency to yellow in sunlight. The pulp will be bleached during manufacture using traditional chlorine or more modern oxygen bleaching. The chlorine content is a live issue and important for environmental awareness concerns, and chlorine-free paper is often a successful marketing ploy.

▶ **Method of manufacture**
Most printing paper is made on large, fast-running machines based on the Fourdrinier design. This is a wet method where the raw material ingredients are mixed in a suspension in water, the furnish. This carries the raw material to be distributed evenly into a thin film on a moving belt that forms the web of paper. This web is then dried by filtration, pressing and evaporation to give a dry product with a moisture content normally between 3–7%. The paper may be surface treated during the drying stages. It may be sized to improve surface strength and render it resistant to penetration by water, or have one or more pigment or polymer coatings applied to impart a particular smooth glossy or matt finish. The jumbo paper reels may then be calendered to improve the smoothness before being slit and wound into smaller reels for printing or sheeted then packed, labelled and despatched.

▶ **Basis weight**
This is the weight of a known area of the paper. In Europe it is expressed as grams per square metre (gsm), and pounds per ream (1,000 square feet), normally referred to as lbs, in North America. Paper is traditionally sold by weight so accuracy in basis weight is important for the printer to ensure that sufficient sheets or length of paper for the job is delivered. There is a trend that printers and publishers should encourage to specify quantities of paper by the number of sheets or metreage of reels. Modern winding and sheeting equipment at paper mills are able to provide accurate measures of length or number of sheets in a package.

The lower the basis weight of paper, the lower the cost of printed product distribution through the postal service. Lowering the basis weight increases the unit cost of paper, and may incur higher printing costs through slower running. At close to 225gsm, paper becomes board. Web printing is rare on paper above 200gsm with the product sheeted rather than folded.

▶ **Caliper**
Is the thickness of a sheet, and normally measured in microns (μ). Paper bulk is the ratio of thickness to grammage, Bulk = Caliper (μ)/gsm. The bulk determines the volume of paper reels, sheets and printed product. The higher the bulk, the greater the number of reels and pallets that will affect the logistics and warehousing needs.

Knowing the caliper is necessary to calculate the final spine thickness for a book at the design stage to allow for cover dimensions and to adjust page imposition in thread-sewn and wire-stitched products to allow for the effect of page creep.

▶ **Dimensions**
The size of sheets, reel width and diameter of reels are important to ensure that the minimum of waste is produced. Normally, the smallest size paper that will produce the product is best. In some short run sheetfed printing, the extended make-ready involved in setting a new size of paper may make it economic to use a small range of standard sizes to reduce make-ready. Sheets must always be square to allow good feeding through press and folder.

▶ **Grain direction**
This is the alignment of the long dimension of most fibres that occurs during paper manufacture on a Fourdrinier machine. When paper absorbs moisture, it expands much more across the grain than in the direction of the grain. For this reason it is preferable to run long-grain (grain parallel to the axis of the press cylinder) during offset multi-colour printing of large sheets to minimise fan-out misregistration. In binding, the grain direction affects performance in finishing machines and the properties of the final product.

▶ **Moisture content**
Paper typically contains between 3–7% water by weight when supplied from the mill. Paper is a hygroinstable material and its dimensions change when the water content changes. Individual fibres absorb water from the atmosphere when the relative humidity is higher than the paper. This causes them to swell in thickness and the dimensions of the sheet change. When in a reel or a stack, it is the paper at the edge that is affected first as the bulk of the paper acts to insulate the interior from the outside.

Reels and sheets are wrapped with waterproof material before shipping. The printer should allow paper to come to the temperature of the pressroom before unwrapping and then use it immediately to avoid uneven absorption of moisture causing tight or slack edges to piles or reels. In heatset printing, the sections may shrink too much if the base paper has a high moisture content. Often sections may require re-moistening to avoid problems of web-wave, especially when perfect bound with the grain direction perpendicular to the spine. Using paper with a suitable moisture content may overcome such problems.

Moisture may be determined by drying paper in an oven and measuring the weight loss, using short-wave spectroscopy or with a sword hydrometer in a stack of paper.

TABLE 9.16 A list of service properties of paper and board (continued)

▶ **Gloss**

Gloss is a measurement of light reflection from both sides of a flattened sheet using a specular gloss meter. Generally it holds that the higher the unprinted paper gloss, the glossier the colour printed result.

▶ **Opacity**

Opacity Is the transparency of the paper. It is measured by comparing the intensity of a light source with and without the paper placed between the source and analyser. The higher the opacity, the more difficult it is to see the print on the reverse side and next page in a magazine or book.

▶ **Internal bonding (Scott Bond)**

For paper manufactured on a twin-wire Fourdrinier machine and for any coated paper or board, the Scott bond is the force required to split a single sheet apart.

▶ **Surface smoothness**

This is typically determined by an air leakage measure between the paper surface and a flat ring or an optical scatter measurement. The smoother the surface, the more uniform is the lay of printed ink although uneven absorption may affect the printed appearance.

The smoothness will affect the slip of the printed sheet, determining the stability of piled sheets in a stack and the performance of cartons in a filling line.

▶ **Water absorption**

Water absorption is the amount of water absorbed by the paper when a known area is in soaked in water and then dried after a set time. Low water absorption is important for lithographic printing and in end use applications where the print may be in contact with moisture, such as in packaging frozen goods. Papers used in these ways will contain sizing agents.

▶ **Oil absorption**

This is the time taken for the paper to absorb a drop of oil placed on the surface. There is some correlation with strike through, where ink from one side of the paper penetrates the paper to show on the other side. The speed will indicate the relative setting speed for conventional oxidation drying inks. If the ink sets too fast, the film may chalk and show rub or scuff and, if too slow, there may be drying problems.

Uneven absorption may lead to an uneven ink lay and an appearance of mottling. Mottle may be due to uneven coating and can be tested by applying a coloured liquid to the paper surface and examining the pattern after some time. This is done either visually or with some form of image analysis.

▶ **Shade and brightness**

The absolute shade is a colorimeter or spectrophotometer measurement of the paper surface using a particular quantitative colour space. For example, CIELUV, CIELch or the more widely used CIEL*a*b* where:

$L*$ = lightness (0 = black, 100 = white);

$a*$ = green/red −120 = green, +120 = red;

$b*$ = blue/yellow −120 = blue, +120 = red. In both $a*$ and $b*$, 0 = neutral grey. When taking an absolute colour measurement, the angle of observer and illuminant of the calibrated instrument must be defined. Paper makers use the ISO brightness measurement that is rigidly defined by ISO standard 2469 for paper that does not contain an optical brightener. Fluorescence under UV light tests for the presence of optical brightening agents. This can be visually compared with a range of standard samples to give a quantitative measure. Examining paper under ultraviolet light often clearly shows patterns and unevenness in the paper surface that may contribute to printability problems.

The brighter the paper surface, the higher the maximum ink contrast that will give a brighter looking printed result.

▶ **Strength**

Paper strength may be expressed by measuring the resistance to burst, tensile, tear resistance, stiffness and fold endurance. All except burst are markedly different in grain and cross-grain direction. Paper strength is a function of the choice of furnish and the amount of beating the pulp undergoes, and so more refined, woodfree pulps give better strength than mechanical grades. The amount of fibre in the paper is also critical, and generally the strength increases with increase in grammage.

There is some relationship between strength and performance on press. Often the higher the strength, the better the runnability for a web although there is no direct correlation. Strength measurements may provide a good idea of the consistency of the paper making within a batch or across many makings.

▶ **Stretch**

Stretch is the amount of distortion that a test piece of paper of known dimension undergoes when a constant rate of load is applied in a tensile tester before the paper ruptures.

▶ **Surface strength**

The tendency for the surface to break up may be tested by coating with a tacky fluid on the IGT printability tester and examining any surface disruption, or by the wax pick test.

▶ **Special coatings**

These include impregnating the surface with waxes or plastic to produce impenetrable barriers for liquid packaging materials, or thin plastic foils for particular colour and appearances.

Source: Pira International Ltd

TABLE 9.17 Some of the many available printing papers	
Newsprint	Uncoated paper containing 80% mechanical pulp Uses – *newspapers*
Improved newsprint	Newsprint with the surface finished on machine Uses – *newspaper, colour supplements*
Super calendered	75% mechanical sized uncoated paper between 45–90gsm. Different grades (SC/WSOP) are designed for offset and gravure, the surface is smoothed by calendering Uses – *magazines, brochures*
Film coated	Low coating weights applied on a non-blade coater part mechanical paper Uses – *catalogues, magazines, brochures*
Bulky mechanical	High bulk coated or uncoated papers Uses – *children's annuals, comics, paperback books*
Short dwell coated	Mechanical paper with low weights of on-machine coating Uses – *bulky magazines*
Lightweight coated	Mechanical with between 7–10gsm coating weight on each side of (LWC) the paper in a final weight range between 45–65gsm, glossy or matt finish Uses – *magazines, brochures*
Mediumweight	Higher weight range coated mechanical, 75–100gsm Uses – *glossy magazines*
Super LWC	Double (or Triple) coated mechanical, 60–115gsm Uses – *high gloss magazines/brochures*
Fine paper	Woodfree (by definition a woodfree paper contains less than 10% mechanical pulp) paper for writing, drawing and printing between 40–150gsm
Woodfree lightweight (Bible papers)	Thin papers, coated or uncoated that may contain rag pulp up to 40gsm Uses – *applications requiring low weight and bulk, catalogues, timetables*
Art	Woodfree coated paper, matt (smooth) or glossy Uses – *high quality colour books*
Cartridge	Woodfree uncoated paper Uses – *books*
Cast coated paper	Woodfree, heavily calendered, smooth, glossy paper Uses – *paper labels*
Cast coated board	Heavier version of the paper, often cast coated only on one side Uses – *glossy covers, folders*
Carton board	Wide range of heavy, often multi-ply, thick board Uses – *Magazine and brochure covers, packaging*

Source: Pira International Ltd

Many other papers are made for non-printing applications from lightweight cigarette paper, to sanitary application, greaseproof paper and heavy corrugated kraft liner board. The feel and appearance of these grades differ. People respond differently to the same information printed on various papers. Researchers in Finland put forward the concept of characterising paper as an information carrier. This develops the idea that the paper surface determines how a human observer understands and absorbs information printed on it. The optical properties of contrast, reflection, colour and light diffusion are important in the presentation of information. For example, many advertising agencies prefer a white, bright, high-gloss paper in mass circulation glossy magazines to get their message across to readers. Generally, as the paper quality improves (and increases in price), so the information capacity increases. Figure 9.3 (opposite) schematically represents the relation between information capacity and grade price for typical publication papers.

The information capacity is a difficult property to quantify and is probably outside the scope of most printers to use on an everyday basis. The boundaries of the different grades demonstrate the limitation of particular grades, and so newsprint can never carry as much easily understood information as a coated woodfree art grade. For specific marketing purposes, such measurements are useful when making a publishing decision on the grade to use. This type of measure may be important to print and paper when comparing its performance against new electronic media.

A printer or publisher may construct a simple database of service paper properties to allow interested personnel access to this information. Paper suppliers will do this for their product portfolio, but they are reluctant to release to the market their internal comparisons with competitive papers. It is important that a consistent system of paper coding is in use, to identify paper by:

► Paper trade name

► Paper grade

► Grammage

► Manufacturing mill

► Supplying agent or merchant.

Recording the laboratory measurements of service properties means that papers can be sorted according to any service criteria. This means the glossiest, most opaque lightweight coated paper from the myriad available may be quantitatively chosen for print tests if that is the clients'

FIGURE 9.3 Schematic representation of the information capacity of a range of publication printing papers

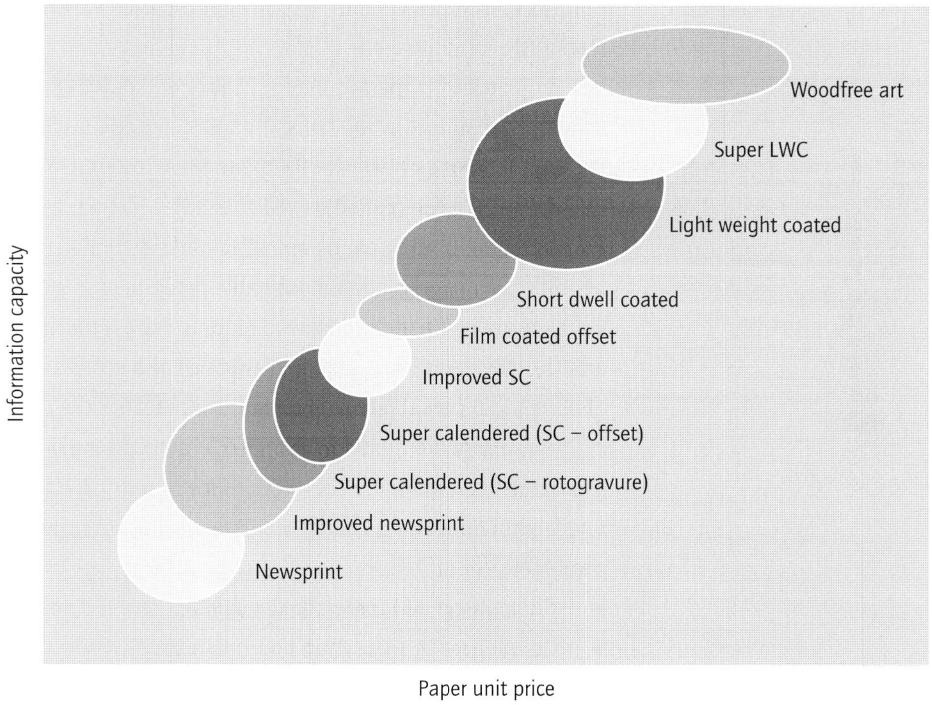

Information capacity

Woodfree art

Super LWC

Light weight coated

Short dwell coated

Film coated offset

Improved SC

Super calendered (SC – offset)

Super calendered (SC – rotogravure)

Improved newsprint

Newsprint

Paper unit price

Source: Pira International Ltd

requirement. Such information can be a useful marketing tool for the printer, particularly when the customer's experience of paper is limited. The mechanisms of selling paper often involve merchants' re-branding paper. In some cases this involves taking papers from different sources and giving it the same name, which leads to confusion on press. It is the original mill and finisher that determine the paper's characteristics, and not any subsequent labelling for marketing and distribution purposes. When service properties and performance measurements are made, the identity of the paper involved is required to ensure validity of the data.

Properties to put on a database include:

▶ Grammage, particularly to compare with the quoted value
▶ Caliper
▶ Presence of mechanical pulp
▶ Gloss
▶ Surface smoothness
▶ Opacity
▶ Surface shade and fluorescence
▶ Moisture content
▶ Burst strength
▶ Tear resistance
▶ Tensile strength and stretch.

All these service property tests are on discrete samples of paper, and typically using just a few A4 pieces. The results are useful in defining a type of paper and then checking inter- and intra-batch consistency. If problems occur at the printer, examination of the service properties is useful in troubleshooting. Any changes from the standard may suggest some manufacturing problem.

Service properties may indicate the expected printability of a paper, but do not define it. Laboratory simulations of printing provide useful guidelines using apparatus such as the Prufbau, Duncan-Lynch or IGT printability testers. Only the printed result on the machine that the job is to be printed on will adequately define the printability. Printability is simply the perception of the print by an individual and is influenced by many factors. Crucially, a person's perception is not a measurable property as it is determined by the brain's response to visual stimulus. The individual who matters most is the customer. However, being the graphic arts, everybody else who sees the result will also express an opinion. A commercial definition of acceptable printability is: The result that satisfies the customer for every copy.

There are problems involved in quantitatively defining printability. The visual characteristics determine the appearance of print so it is important that it is examined under suitable viewing conditions. This will ensure consistency when considering characteristics of:

▶ Comparison with proofs and originals
▶ Colour gamut, saturation and balance
▶ Highlight and shadow detail
▶ Print sharpness

▶ Spot colour definition

▶ Gloss

▶ Print contrast.

These are reasonably easy to define, measure and quantify using a densitometer, colorimeter or spectrophotometer. It is less easy to measure the more intangible properties of lift, life, thin and zing, which are terms commonly bandied about.

Printers listen to what the customer is looking for on press. There are ways of altering standard conditions to achieve the result. These involve the application of skills developed by the pressman over time but are ultimately down to empirical trial and error. These take time and waste materials. The trend for print personnel is to marry the strengths of craft skills with a more technical approach as there is not enough time and money in a job to allow leisurely experimentation on press.

Good printability results from a consistent, even paper surface. Different grades of paper have very different surfaces that alter the appearance of the print through dot sharpness. Smooth, glossy paper receives ink readily to give a sharp result. Uncoated paper has a rougher surface that, on a micro scale, is full of hills and channels. To get good ink lay, a heavy squash with compressible blankets is necessary. This engenders high dot gain. Different ranges of dot gain are not problems. They are process phenomena that should be recognised and taken into account during the repro stage and particularly the proofing process chosen. High dot gain limits the printability of the rougher grade in achieving high print contrast, colour saturation and sharpness.

The shade of the paper governs the maximum contrast a halftone dot can achieve. Ink on paper printing is a subtractive colour process with the ink pigmentation removing part of the incidental light that is reflected back from the paper surface. If the stock is dull and yellowy-grey, then the range of reproducible colours is limited and the printability is poor. Improved printability comes from smooth, white, opaque paper.

The combination of surface properties of shade, smoothness and opacity enables some grades of paper to produce a more pleasing printed image to most people. When a bright, white, smooth opaque paper is used, the print has bright colours, a wide dynamic range, maximum saturation in the shadows with open mid-tones and detailed highlights. The printer tries to achieve the most pleasing result on every stock he uses. Customers complain when they see variation through the job or that the print does not match the proof. The most common complaints concerning printability refer to inconsistencies between (and within) batches of paper. Invariably a consistent grade of paper with inferior service properties will produce an overall better job than an inconsistent 'better' grade.

A workable solution to define and determine printability for most printing jobs will develop. Probably there will be a multitude of solutions for the different printers and requirements across the world. The key factors are mid-tone and shadow dot growth with the balance of cyan, magenta and yellow. Whatever monitoring system is in use, regular measurement throughout the run will ensure more consistent printability.

Performance properties of paper

How the paper performs at the customers's site Paper runnability through printing presses will become an increasingly important issue between printer and paper supplier in the future. Service properties tend not to correlate well with the press runnability. Paper mills tend to concentrate on the paper machine spending a great deal of money on monitoring and control systems to increase the productivity and consistency of the jumbo intermediate reels. Paper finishing seems too often to be the poor relation with performance of the slitter, winder or sheeter and wrapping stations overlooked. Delivery to the printer may result in reels and pallets being handled many times with the risk of damage. The printer will expect and demand paper to be in perfect condition upon delivery.

In reel-fed printing, paper is stressed as it passes through the press. Web tension will vary in the reelstand and infeed (particularly when a festoon reelstand is in use), between the printing units, through the oven, over the chill rolls in the case of heatset; and in the folder. Roll-fed paper has an inherent strength with areas of weakness. There may be obvious defects such as a slime hole, a crease, or a nick in the edge. An area of paper may contain slightly less fibre but more coating. Perhaps the reel has an imperfect edge from an unsharpened knife or maybe uneven tension from the winder. A fast unwinding roll containing more imperfections will be more likely to break than a perfect one. A modern web press will print paper with tacky ink and water at speeds of up to 3000ft a minute. The paper path may be through many additional guide rollers and any slight imperfection may result in a break, losing press time for the printer.

Like printability, runnability is a widely used term with many interpretations depending on individual perspective. The areas of interpretation concern what is good, acceptable or unacceptable runnability, with disagreement between the printer and paper maker not unknown. The runnability of paper is simply the actual production speed of the job through the press to the agreed specification.

There are micro and macro paper properties. A paper reel may be considered as a mass of potential imperfections. The higher the incidence of imperfections in a reel, the more likely a web break is. Tests on discrete samples cannot detect these imperfections. Traditional test methods may not be relevant to develop paper suitable for printing at higher speeds. Paper makers should consider alternative methods based on performance at the end user.

Press statistics will provide the information on which grades to use for printers, and the best performers with least problems. As in many other manufacturing industries, statistical process control techniques will provide the basis for runnability improvements. Quantitative runnability measurements of the running speed of the press, waste, metres (or sheets) of paper per break or per wash can be calculated from shopfloor data. This requires the total number of copies (Nt), the number of good copies (Ng), the press running time (Tr), time taken for paper related problems (Tp), and the number of press stops for breaks and washes. Shopfloor data collection systems can automatically record these data or it may be manually entered on a machine docket.

The key information to process is a measure of gross running speed, which is defined as:

Gross Speed = Ng / (Tr + Tp)

Gross speed is a quantitative measure of runnability to rank and assess papers. The higher the gross speed, the better the paper. This allows a company to place a value on the runnability, which is used in determining which paper is used for any job. This measure can also be used to improve the productivity and reduce the waste by eliminating papers with the lowest gross speeds. Manual collection and assessment of this information is time consuming and difficult. With automatic shopfloor data collection into expert management information systems, more data can be processed to information and intelligence.

The paper problems will be breaks, jams and stops for washes. The biggest runnability problem in web printing is the paper break. The press stops and between 20 minutes to an hour of production time is lost together with up to 2000m of paper on a twin-web press. This is irrecoverable dead time. During one month in a factory with five web presses, there was an average of three breaks on every press per day. At a generous allowance of 20 minutes a break, this represented more than 4% of standard press time. This equates to another two extra full press weeks each year, for each press, of production capacity lost. It is an enormous amount of potential revenue and equivalent to 10 weeks of press running lost through poor runnability.

It is sometimes possible to determine the cause of the break. The minder pieces together the two ends and finds a slime hole, a cut edge or a poorly prepared mill splice. The printer later presents these to the mill as evidence of poor paper. On other occasions, there are other clear reasons for the break: improper preparation of the reelstand splices, mechanical fault in the folder or tar from the oven cause breaks that are internally due to the printer. The largest category of breaks falls into the no evidence bracket. There is no clear evidence of a paper fault or a press problem but the break occurs and press time and paper is wasted as a result. The gross running speed does not differentiate between causes of break and downtime, but it is the gross speed that concerns the printer.

The other major contribution to both sheetfed and web press downtime caused by paper is through the gradual build up on the blankets and plate. This piling will affect the printed image and must be removed by washing blankets, and sometimes plates, to clear the build-up and debris. Manual or automatic blanket washing wastes time and paper. The solvent and cleaning agent used may contaminate the fountain solution, affecting the lithographic performance and causing more wastage and downtime. Blanket build-up should be avoided wherever possible by judicious choice of paper and control of press ink and water chemistry. The most common cause of paper-related piling is poor adhesion of the paper surface. It can be physically pulled onto the sticky ink-covered blanket, in extreme examples a linting problem. When samples are scraped off the blanket, the presence of fibres or coating material proves the poor surface properties to be at fault. On web presses, ink from the first unit often builds up on the final blanket. High oil absorption of the paper may cause a phase separation of the ink leaving a tacky residue that picks off onto the final blanket. In such cases, paper is a contributory factor to poor runnability.

The paper may conform to the manufacturer's specification and perform particularly well on other jobs and presses at other printers – it invariably does. It just does not suit particular conditions and the printer will exercise his right of choice to use a paper that does perform well. When paper is bought by a publisher and supplied to a printer, there must be a mechanism for all parties to agree on acceptable performance.

Commercial properties of paper

Conditions of supply negotiated between supplier and customer The BPIF publishes a booklet, *British Paper and Board Trade Customs*, that covers trading terms and conditions for the supply of paper (see Chapter 3). The publisher promotes this as '*A compilation of the customs and practices that have been found by individual British mills to be practical and valuable in handling their sales*'. These terms may not be so valuable to their customers and have not helped a great deal of conflict between printer and supplier over the years. Particular areas of concern include the amount of paper to be delivered compared to the order and actions in the case of dispute or poor performance. The printer requires the precise amount of the particular paper to be delivered on time in perfect condition. Anything less is not acceptable.

Most printing companies are small, buy small quantities of bespoke paper from merchants and the situation is generally well served. With larger printers or publishers ordering larger quantities, however, the merchants' terms are less beneficial to the customer, particularly a jobbing printer using a wide variety of different types and sizes of paper. A look in the warehouse of most large print houses shows an area of redundant stock containing part reels and pallets of sheets left over from completed jobs. It may be possible to use this paper up for make-ready, in a similar later job, or to sell it to a waste merchant or broker at a significant loss. Either way, it ties up capital in slow moving stock costing money.

Paper has traditionally always been sold by weight and the terms and trading conditions reflect this. However, paper is always printed by area (length for web and number of sheets for sheetfed). Gross reel weight includes packaging and the core incorporating some 1–2% by weight into the paper wastage of the printer. This must be taken into account when calculating the required amount of paper for a job. Reducing paper waste is a major thrust for printing companies, typically placing much effort on the actions of pressmen but less on the administration support. Two major areas that immediately reduce waste are buying by area and specifying exact quantities for delivery.

It is impossible to manufacture paper so that the basis weight is totally consistent. Paper machines have sophisticated control systems and paper weight varies about a mean level, and when sold by weight the tendency is for paper to be slightly above the nominal weight. Paper that is 58gsm instead of the nominal 57gsm inherently includes almost 2% of waste. This is outside the scope of any pressman to recover. On a sheetfed application, overweight paper results in a shortfall in sheets available for use; in web, the paper may run out before the last section is completed.

For a specific job, an estimator or account handler will calculate the amount of paper required according to the systems of the particular plant. It is interesting occasionally to check the quantities that different personnel come up with, and check with technical and production the smallest quantities they require. A source of paper saving is to use a slightly narrower reel if possible. When ordering paper, the supplier will supply a quantity close to the ordered amount, typically to a tolerance of ±2%. Printers rightly fear under delivery to their customers, and so they typically allow a comfort zone of extra paper to be delivered.

The printer cannot print on this hidden source of waste and even the best-run printroom cannot save this waste. More stringent contract review and agreement can eliminate the problem quickly. The paper supplier can use precise basis weight and quantity delivered as a source of competitive advantage to sell a major benefit to the printer and increase their market share.

The paper should arrive at the printer in the same perfect state that it left the mill. A printer must take into account that paper supply is a global market and paper often travels vast distances before being delivered. Paper should be checked before printing and any damage identified and claimed back from the supplier or haulier. With exact quantities and working to strict deadlines, there may not be enough time for re-supply in the event of problems. It is vital to eliminate damaged and out-of-specification paper to gain the economic benefits of precise quantities and timely delivery.

Papers for digital print

To obtain the optimal printability and runnability from a digital printing system, it is important to use the correct substrate. As the manufacturer most often supplies the colorant, the choice of paper is critical, particularly for the new inkjet machines. Paper of guaranteed quality can be provided by using materials accredited by the equipment manufacturer. Users want a wider range of papers, and the ability to use heavier grades and more prestige branded woves.

On conventional printing presses, there is virtually no limit on the type of paper that can be used. On digital presses, the paper impacts performance. Coated stocks are a serious problem in electrographic printing because the paper has to hold an electrical charge. In coated paper the clay used is an inert insulator and coated stocks don't always work well. Moisture level affects the toner transfer efficiency; too much moisture causes the paper to leak charge and if it is too dry, the paper is too resistive and does not accept toner as designed. Manufacturers are reformulating many papers to accept toner. Some are plastic-based, using fillers that combine pulp and plastic to provide the feeling of coated stock without having the problems of coated stock. Older digital printers were limited on the weight of stock that they could handle, but the new generation of printers that use carrier blankets can handle up to 400gsm card.

There are several issues to consider when deciding which paper to use: presentation (sheet size and reel dimensions), properties (paper is an inherent part of the printing process in digital printing, it is advisable to always use a properly accredited source), the packaging of the paper to prevent moisture loss or uptake, and the particular finishing requirements to avoid scuffing, cracking and waviness.

Ideally, a paper should be matched to a particular printer. In the case of dry toners, the sheet should be smooth and free from curl. It is difficult to make a fast sheetfed machine because the higher the speed, the more likely that there will be jams. Operators are needed to feed paper and clear the jams. Most sheetfed machines print on one side of the paper, turn it over and run it through again. The second pass uses paper that already has fused toner on it and there is a possibility of curl that can cause a jam. Sheetfed machines have inherent limitations on the speed of paper. The more toner applied, the higher the likelihood of problems.

Much work is being performed to produce coated papers and films that are suitable for digital printing. The major press suppliers operate an approval system for stocks (Pira International acts as an independent qualifier on behalf of the Xeikon web press range) to test substrates for printability (image quality, fastness) and runnability properties. The effect of the substrate on the mechanism of printing is particularly important. A slight lint build-up may be only a slight annoyance for offset, but will block inkjet nozzles, requiring expensive refurbishment of the head. It is important to consider the impact of the stock on the operation of the press.

Other major concerns include the effects of fusing on drying out the sheets, causing cracking, and of the build up of static on sheets at delivery. As well as adversely affecting the subsequent handling of the material, there is the concern of damaging the press in some way. As the volume of paper converted increases, there will be more problem solving by the paper makers and press manufacturers to overcome these issues.

Papers for inkjet systems have particular requirements because of the use of water-based ink that leads to paper-related strikethrough, dimensional instability and subsequent ink marking. This is particularly acute for heavily inked duplex jobs and requires the use of specially coated papers. Such papers are significantly more expensive than standard grades, and are necessary to obtain consistently good results while optimising print quality and runnability. As the technology becomes more widely used, the cost premium for inkjet will fall. Users test a range of papers from many suppliers for suitability and imaging system in tandem, rather than looking at individual components with their inks, analysing performance and cost to select the most appropriate paper.

In applications with heavy coverage, it is necessary to use graphics prepress and colour skills to minimise ink coverage through under colour removal (UCR) techniques to replace neutral colour areas of CMY with black ink. This example is one of the few where traditional prepress skills brilliantly complement the data handling skills necessary for delivering digital data streams. Because of the data format and offline RIPping before printing, there is no possibility of adjusting colour at the production stage, and the result is totally independent of the operator. This means that the colour settings and control have to be determined at the design stage of the job. Early inkjet jobs have required much prototyping and testing; as more experience is gleaned the quality obtainable has improved significantly. The best quality and productivity results will be produced from the correct combination of paper, colourant and print engine.

Binding and finishing

10

Most products need to be finished after printing before they are ready for sale or use. Some printing machines and systems offer online finishing but the diversity of products means that most finishing remains offline using specialist cutting, folding, gathering and binding equipment. Applying ink or colourant onto paper is only a small part of the issue.

Postpress has long been considered the Cinderella of the print industry – it has not enjoyed the radical technological changes that have taken place in prepress and printing, nor those currently affecting administration. However, there have been a few developments to increase the automation and pre-setting of various finishing machines for cutting, creasing, folding and binding, and some suppliers are offering JDF-enabled equipment where it is considered worthwhile to do so.

Current trends in finishing

There have been significant improvements in finishing and distribution, due primarily to digital and computer applications. Digital printing has sparked a wave of inline finishing developments such as inline saddle-stitching, perfect binding and three-side trimming options. New systems support variable sheet-count and variable information jobs with full integrity, because the sheets never leave the system.

Binding, folding, gluing, and stitching are the primary finishing services offered by printers, while more sophisticated and specialist finishing services such as lamination, diecutting, embossing and foiling are often outsourced. Increasingly, print companies are broadening the range of services on offer, with warehousing, mailing and fulfilment services becoming increasingly popular.

In 2005 the main trends affecting finishing and postpress include:
▶ automation
▶ materials handling
▶ selectivity/targeting
▶ personalisation and labelling
▶ onserts and inserts
▶ gimmicks
▶ distribution, enclosing, mailing and fulfilment
▶ customer service.

Although these are still key trends in finishing, over the past five years they have been modified to include a focus on the human resource aspect of finishing. Following reported labour shortages, much attention is now being given to the acquisition, training and retention of finishing personnel.

Fulfilment is a significant growing added-value service offered by printers and finishers. This involves many different services, including the ordering, sorting, managing, assembly and dispersion of product through warehousing and stock management such as kitting, providing personalised customer packages of a product, or multiple products.

Guillotining and cutting

Guillotines

All cutting machines have the same basic components and are used in both productive (i.e. print) and non-productive (i.e. white paper) guillotining. They range from small, single-knife guillotines for cutting white (i.e. blank) paper for small offset presses to large, computer-controlled, robotic-aided machines capable of cutting large quantities of work to a higher standard.

White-paper cutting machines range up to 150cm in length (the length of the cutting area) and are used for trimming or cutting flat sheets before printing. Robotic equipment may help the loading of the guillotine (using a flying carpet system) for cutting large quantities of paper such as cut sheets for office use. Increasingly, this is carried out at the paper mill with automated slitting, cutting and wrapping from jumbo reels to reduce handling and processing costs.

In the productive area, guillotines range from small hand-operated machines to large-format automatic and programmable models. The size of the guillotine is the measurement taken across the table between the side frames or side gauges, and the size range is from 52cm upwards. The machines have many uses including cutting half sheet work (multiprint covers and leaflets), stationery items, promotional material and labels.

Label cutting is a specialist field and requires a machine capable of cutting large quantities of work with great accuracy. It is essential that machines be fitted with a computer capable of storing and reproducing data relevant to the work. The computer holds the required label sizes in the memory allowing the machine to reproduce them in sequence for fast, accurate production in a competitive field.

Programmable machines are common as the volume of work, even of a general nature, requires the accuracy and speed of which these machines are capable. Many programs can be stored at any time and repeated when the same format is finished.

The main parts of a cutting machine are:
▶ the clamping mechanism
▶ the knives
▶ the cutting sticks
▶ the back gauge
▶ the side gauges.

All guillotines will have sophisticated guarding and control mechanisms to improve the working conditions and safety of the employees. Infrared beams in the cutting area will stop the machine when any movement is detected, and the clamp and knife operate only when at least three buttons are pushed simultaneously (two hands at either side and a foot).

Clamping mechanism

The aim of the clamp is to hold the substrate firmly during the cutting cycle. Too little clamp pressure will allow the work to be pulled forward causing undercut on the pile being cut. Too much clamp pressure can cause indentation on the top sheets. These sheets will be wasted (and sometimes waste can be too high in relation to work).

Hydraulic clamping mechanisms permit a variation on the pressure applied to suit either a soft (easily deformed) paper or a hard (coated or hard-sized) paper.

Knives and knife action

Most guillotines are fitted with a double-action knife mechanism. The knife beam descends at an angle and becomes parallel only at the bottom of its stroke. This puts less strain on the beam and enables the machine to be less bulky in its structure.

The knives are made of mild steel with hardened steel fused on the back edge (the only part that makes contact with the substrate) to provide the cutting edge.

The knife bevel has an angle of 19–24°, according to the types of papers being cut. The standard bevel for general work is considered to be 22°; a finer bevel of 19° is used for soft papers, and coarser bevels are used for hard papers and boards. Double bevels are used to provide resistance to chipping. Blunt knives are changed as required to maintain accuracy and re-ground.

Cutting sticks

Single-knife guillotines work by making a cut through the substrate into a solid piece of material. This material is made from either plastic or compressed paper and is designed not to blunt the knife.

Back gauge

The back gauge is power-operated to push the material into the correct cutting position. It is serrated to intermesh with a matching grid in the clamp face. This allows the back gauge to be drawn in to about 25mm for strip cutting. A clamp plate is normally attached to prevent marking of the top sheets.

Side gauges

Side gauges are used to position the substrate before cutting. They are set at right angles to the knife and allow the paper to be positioned for accurate cutting either manually or to push the material into the final position.

Book trimming machines

Where there is a requirement for a large number of books to be cut, single-knife guillotines are not capable of satisfying the production needs and specialist book trimming machines are employed.

Three-knife trimmers Three-knife trimming machines use a double clamping action. The primary clamp receives a pile of books, feeds it into the cutting position and goes back for the next pile. At the cutting position, a secondary high-pressure clamp holds the books while the cutting takes place. The cutting is also double-action, and the head and tail are cut in one action and the fore-edge in a subsequent action. This pile is then ejected and the next takes its place in a continuous process.

Systems that are linked to an adhesive binding line have the highest capacity and obtain 15–20 piles a minute (depending on the thickness of the book), which may translate into as many as 14,000 books an hour. Freestanding machines are capable of 10–15 piles a minute while manual machines achieve 4–5 piles a minute.

Single-copy trimmers Single-copy trimmers are designed for coupling to other units and completing insetted saddle-stitched products. After stitching, the books travel on the transfer unit and are usually cut singly, some machines gather and trim two or more at once, and are then finished. Production is timed to the capacity of the insetting and stitching unit.

Saddle-stitched books are usually processed with a shearing action of the top knives and fixed lower knives. The books are fed into the cutting unit by chains or belts, clamped and cut – head and tail, then fore-edge. Some machines reverse this cutting process (fore-edge first), but handle two books within the cutting unit. Output of up to 18,000 copies an hour is possible depending on the thickness, type of work, size and length of run. Most machines can be fitted with an extra knife for splitting two-up work.

Folding machines

The folding scheme and the imposition of the printed pages on a sheet are interdependent. Most trade houses would use standard impositions of eight, 16 or 32 pages with all folded at right angles, i.e. each fold at 90° to the preceding one. The industry does have a standard imposition scheme introduced by the British Printing Industries Federation (BPIF). It is used in book-finishing houses and is an essential tool in the planning process of multi-page books and magazines. Detailed knowledge of the folding process and sheet travel will ensure the imposition is laid down correctly allowing the pagination to follow sequentially.

Folding machines are produced in many types, sizes and configurations, but the three main types of machine are:
► knife-folding
► buckle-folding
► combination folding.
Of these the latter two are the more common.

Knife-folding machines

The knife-folding principle is fairly basic. The sheet to be folded is taken by tapes to the folding position where it is aligned by a gripper or wheel into a side-lay against a back gauge. After positioning, a knife (a thin piece of metal, normally with a serrated edge) descends and pushes the sheet between the nip of reciprocating (inward rotating) rollers. The rollers emphasise the fold and direct the sheet to subsequent folding positions until the desired folding scheme is completed.

Knife folders are relatively slow (1000–4000 copies an hour) but accurate. Since they also use sheet controllers to avoid deformation and perforators, and slitters to aid the folding process and expel excess air, they are suitable for folding very thin stock (bible, manifold, airmail). With adjustment to the machine, thick papers can also be accommodated.

FIGURE 10.1 The principle of knife folding

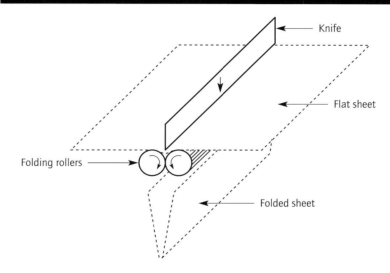

Knife

Flat sheet

Folding rollers

Folded sheet

Source: Pira International Ltd

Buckle-folding machines Sometimes referred to as plate folders, the principle of buckle-folding machines is to encourage the sheet of paper to fold or buckle at its weak point. The sheet to be folded is guided over to a side lay, either on rollers or tapes that then take the sheet between a pair of revolving rollers. The gripped sheet is then directed into a fold plate (like a metal envelope). The sheet enters the fold plate and is driven forward by the gripping rollers until the front edge strikes the fold gauge (which has been set to the required position). As the front edge of the sheet cannot now travel further into the fold plate, the sheet distorts (buckles) at its weakest point, i.e. where it is not supported. The sheet is then directed (from the point at which it has buckled) into another pair of reciprocating rollers and is folded. Where a fold plate is not required, a deflector is put in its position and the sheet is directed through the bank of rollers to the next folding position.

Deflectors are often attached to the plate for easy changeover of folding imposition. A much wider range of impositions is possible on an all-plate or buckle machine, and a bank of up to six parallel plates is not uncommon. It is also possible to get a number of folding positions into a small space, unlike with the knife folder.

The buckle folder is at its best folding middle-range, 80–120gsm substances. To help the folding processes, creasing and perforating wheels are positioned within the bank of rollers. This breaks down the fibres especially in the cross-grain direction. Good production is possible on these machines as the sheet is always in motion.

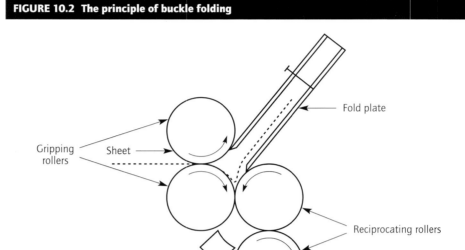

FIGURE 10.2 The principle of buckle folding

Fold plate

Gripping rollers

Sheet

Reciprocating rollers

Deflector

Source: Pira International Ltd

Combination folding machines

Combination folding machines use both the knife-folding and bucklefolding principles on one machine. They have the advantage of speed through the first-fold folding plates and accuracy when folding at right angles and cross-grain. A typical layout would be three to four plates in the first position followed by two knives at right angles to the plates and each other. When using the knife on a combination machine, it is essential to have some form of timing device or microswitch so that the sheet to be folded arrives under the knife when it is in the up position.

Combination folding machines can be used for folding straightforward sections but will also handle a wide range of paper stock and more complicated folds for brochures and maps. They are capable of perforating, creasing and slitting two, three or multiple printed sections.

Quality control in folding machines

Due to the nature of the substrate, ensuring accurate usable sections requires sheet control measures and operator awareness. Various faults reoccur during the folding process and it is necessary to check the work. Chief among these are:

► Creasing of the sheet during its travel through the roller train can occur at any time because of the hydroscopic nature of the material. This requires diligent checking by the operator to ensure consistent quality;

▶ Inaccuracy of the finished section due to folding out of square. With every printed job, the finishing department follows the grip and side lay used on the press. If the back-up varies, or the press is not consistent in its production, this will be emphasised during the folding process;

▶ Another source of inaccuracy is in not having enough sheet control mechanisms in place. The paper will often distort under the speed of the process and the optimum speed will depend on the grammage and nature of the substrate.

Computer controls

The latest technology involves computer control of the setting sequence. This enables repeat jobs to be stored, and microprocessors reset the various parameters of plate setting and side lays. These are expensive additions and are a consideration only on the more expensive equipment.

Print enhancement additions

It is becoming increasingly possible to adapt folding machines for a range of other finishing processes. The following are among the more common print enhancement additions.

Thread sealing

Folding machines can be adapted to do thread sealing, where thread is inserted into the spine of a printed section to strengthen the binding. The purpose of the thread is to act as a binder for the adhesive (usually hot melt) when making book bocks. The resulting bond is stronger than perfect or unsewn binding where the complete spines of the sections are removed.

Burst binding

Burst binding is used, like thread sealing, to strengthen the binding. This process involves inserting a serrated rotary knife into the last set of folding rollers and has the effect of removing small slots of the paper, called bursts, in the back of the fold. During the binding process, the bursts allow the adhesive to penetrate further into the spine and produce a stronger bond.

Section gluing

Section gluing can be used for binding a small number of pages (up to 16). It entails placing a gluing unit in front of the first folding position where a thin line of glue is drawn down the sheet. The glue application is timed to ensure that only the area for attachment is covered. After folding, such products can be finished on the machine by the addition of knives and slitters.

Direct mail requirements

Many of the processes required by direct-mail publicity material can now be accomplished in the folding process. Manufacturers offer perforating, strip or side gumming, coating and inkjet printing on specialist folders. The input can be reels into a sheeter or sheets and in some cases it may be carried out in-line with printing.

Pressing units

Sections can be reduced to an even thickness with the addition of a pair of heavy metal rollers, positioned after the last folding position, and applying pressure. This is an essential aid for many subsequent binding operations and will increase productivity in those areas where bulk uniformity is important.

Noise limitation

The recognition that ear defenders are required ensures that manufacturers reduce the decibel level of the folding operations. High-speed folding machines are equipped with noise hoods over the folding plates that ensure that the levels of noise are at acceptable standards.

Gathering

Gathering is the placing of folded sections in the correct sequence on top of each other before binding. Small quantities can be produced by hand, and volume production will require the assistance of expensive and complicated equipment. Gathering machines work on the conveyor-belt principle: piles of sections of the same sort are placed in stations called hoppers along the belt in section sequence, and one of each section is fed on the belt sequentially to make up one copy of the job when completed. There is often a control mechanism that monitors the thickness of a gathered product and rejects the product when an error is detected. The control will automatically switch the gatherer off when multiple errors are detected.

Collating

The term collating can be used in two different senses. Traditionally, collating is the process of checking gathered sections to ensure they are in the right order. This is done visually with the aid of printed marks. The marks can be back marks (most usually) or they can be added to the folio (page) number on the first page of a section.

Back marks are printed step marks about 5mm high and printed in a pre-determined position so that they are visible on the back when the section is folded. When all the sections are gathered correctly, the black steps fall in a regular and unbroken progression down the back of the spine (for which reason they are also known as black steps or back steps). If gathered incorrectly, the sequence is broken or out of line. Marks added to the first page number of a section are usually in the form of a letter A on the first section, B the second and so on, but leaving out the letters I, J, V and W to avoid confusion. If the book exceeds 22 sections, the sequence restarts with AA, BB and so on. In more sophisticated collating operations, the use of a star indicates that sections have to be insetted into each other before gathering, e.g. A*, A**, A*** would show that section A consist of three pre-insetted sections before gathering.

With the development of sheet-collating machines, the term may now simply mean 'gathering'. Such machines gather single leaves for multi-part form sets, pads, carbonless sets and other sequential repetitive work. Some have crash numbering or inkjet printing to allow personalisation of the sets.

Numbering

Some business forms and sets are sequentially numbered to give each document a distinct identity. Great care is needed when ordering new stock to ensure that the supplier provides the correct numbering sequences as the numbering can include alpha-numerics, or machine-readable forms, either MICR or barcodes. The technology is developing beyond crash numbering into variable data digital printing to print barcodes and sequences involving modular check digits, and to offer guaranteed validation of the sequences supplied (often to multiple locations). These techniques can offer valuable additional services to the label, ticket and voucher markets.

Insetting

Insetting (or inserting) is the placing of sections inside each other in the form of a V before saddle-stitching. Normally the larger, and therefore thicker, sections, e.g. 32/48pp, are placed inside the thinner 8/16 pp sections.

Inserting

Inserting is the placing of material – promotional advertising, reply cards and schedules – into the finished product. Inserting imposes no restrictions on the binding method of the finished product and the insert may have been saddle stitched. Material can be inserted randomly or, should the customer so require, it can be placed within a particular section or after a specified page, but at greater cost. To distinguish the operation from insetting, it is sometimes referred to as loose inserting.

Bundling

Bundling is the compression of folded sections under controlled pressure to ensure bulk uniformity. On high-speed web and gravure machines these will be handled robotically with accurate counts and automatic palletising.

Books

Bundling is necessary in the production of case-bound books when the cases (hard covers) are to be drawn on to the book blocks offline. Consistency of the book block ensures that the spine thickness of the case will meet quality criteria and permit mechanisation of the process.

Magazines and newspapers

Bundling is particularly necessary in high-production inline insetting, stitching and trimming lines where the speed of the operation requires automated loading procedures. The compressed sections can either be placed end-to-end to form a log about a metre long, or they can be positioned around an inner wheel and rolled into a circle. A roll can hold up to 500,000 pages and is unrolled into the hopper or box on-demand. The log system employs a similar principle with flat-feed conveyors transporting the sections into the hopper. Only high-volume production can exploit this production technique, as the initial installation cost of the system is very high.

Tipping

This expression covers both tipping-in and tipping-on. Tipping-in refers to the fixing of a single leaf (a tip or tip-in) inside a section by pasting a strip along the back edge of the tip and pressing it in position inside the section. This may be a planned operation – a frontispiece, for example, or an illustration that must appear next to a specific reference – or, more commonly, an unplanned operation to correct a mistake. Tipping-in almost invariably has to be done by hand. It is laborious (and consequently expensive) if the fold between the relevant pages needs to be slit before the tip can be fixed in. Tipping-on refers to the fixing of a single leaf to the outside of a section: endpapers are tipped on to the front and back section of a book before gathering and, unless the run is very short, the operation is usually done by machine.

Guarding

A guard is a strip of stout liner, usually a strong paper (such as manila) about 5mm wide, which is used either for attaching to the edge of a single leaf that is then wrapped around the outside of a section and sewn on with it, in order to secure the leaf into a book, or as a reinforcement to be attached to the folded back of a section in order to strengthen it.

In the case of a single leaf, guarding is an expensive but secure alternative to tipping-on but does depend, of course, on the position of the tip being on the outside of a section. In the case of section, guarding is often used to reinforce the first and last sections of dictionaries and encyclopaedias where there is considerable stress on these two sections when the book is frequently handled.

Punching and drilling

Round holes can be produced either by punching or drilling. Sheets to be placed into ring binders are invariably drilled due to the volume required and smaller jobs might be punched (especially if the drilling machine is set for production runs). Shaped holes can be punched by using a shaped steel upper and lower casting or steel-forged dies. Dies can be of any shape. The pre-cut material is forced against them under pressure and the sharp die edge cuts away the undesired waste leaving the required shape, e.g. bottle labels.

Creasing and scoring

Thicker material, such as card, is easier to fold if the fibres have been 'pre-deformed' or creased. This can be achieved either by using a creasing rule fitted to a carton-making die against which the carton is impressed, or by a rotary action using an upper and lower creasing wheel. Thick paper or board covers are creased prior to attachment to the book block, resulting in a crisp edge to the finished product. Other reasons for creasing are to assist folding of card, e.g. birthday cards etc.

Scoring requires a definite cut into the top third of the material. Economies of scale in box-making processes often result in cross-grain work and the only method of ensuring a definite fold across the grain of a box is to score the substrate and then cover the offending feathered edge with another material. This is not uncommon in the fancy box making industry where quality work and specialised production is the norm.

Perforating

The need to be able to perforate and separate sheets as part of a production process is becoming more common. Where high-volume production is required, perforation can be carried out inline with the printing process, e.g. postage stamps. Pinhole perforation and slit-perforation are offline alternatives. In pinhole perforation, an upper male die is contacted with a female die below through about five sheets of 100gsm paper, in a treadle operation. In slit perforation, a circular wheel with a serrated edge runs between two lower wheels and perforates a sheet of paper passed between. Production of slit perforation can be reasonably high with a skilled operator.

Index cutting

Index cutting, as the name suggests, is the cutting of a pre-printed leaf or series of leaves to indicate sectional divisions within a printed product. A thumb index is where a semi-circular, thumb-shaped recess is cut at the required page, e.g. in dictionaries, bibles.

A stepped index is used in the production of telephone directories or address books to indicate the start of an alphabetical section. A tabbed index extends from the page and is used to signal the start of a new section or area (e.g. catalogues, motor manuals, part works).

Banding and counting

To ensure the customer receives the correct print quantity, it may sometimes be necessary to band and count. With, for example, a very large order of labels in the packaging industry, multiple printed sheets are counted before cutting. After cutting, the individual labels are banded using strips of paper in a designated number.

Padding

Padding is a cheap form of binding that is used to produce notebooks, writing pads and sets of NCR forms. Loose leaves of paper, either printed or plain, are collated and glued with a board at the back and drawing on, i.e. positioning, a cover on the front. The binding permits the individual sheets to be torn from the top without wrecking the glued spine.

A lot of padding is a manual operation that involves preparing a pile of individual sheets, collated with a heavier board inserted at designated intervals to act as a backing and cover material to provide stability. The pile is jogged to create a smooth edge before applying liquid glue, which is normally painted on manually. The stack is then weighted and sometimes clamped in a padding press until the glue is thoroughly dry and individual pads are separated with a sharp knife to produce the final product.

Automated, carousel hot-melt glue systems are highly productive. They include a collator to produce the pads, which are individually clamped, and the spine is glued in a similar manner to a hot-melt perfect binder, often drawing a separate cover on to the glue before it dries.

Soft cover binding

In most cases, one of two methods is commonly use to bind a magazine, pamphlet or paperback book:

▶ insetting and saddle-stitching

▶ gathering and adhesive (perfect) binding and other forms of sequential binding.

The techniques have remained fairly stable on the surface but the impact of computerisation has seen significant increases in productivity and capability in the bindery. The set-ups of repeating jobs can be stored allowing reduction in make-ready with presetting of stream feeders and trimmers. A popular trend in North America that is starting to impact in Europe is the use of selective binding techniques, where a product is made from a selection of available sections chosen according to the profile of the end recipient. Journals, magazines and promotional catalogues are developing into dynamic means of communication. The selective make-up of printed products with varying degrees of personalisation inkjetted onto sections and covers, inserts and glued in merchandise samples and order cards make the product more useful, but place greater demands on the production methods.

Saddle-stitching

Saddle-stitching is a fast, effective and relatively cheap form of binding. Folded sections are placed inside each other in the form of a V and are bound with wire staples. There are constraints on the thickness (extent/volume) of the finished product if bulging at the spine is not to occur, and if the book or magazine is to open flat without the reader having to crease the spine or the pages. Although thin books and lighter-weight papers (70gsm and lower substances) will allow the books to open flat, thicker books and heavier papers will require creasing by the reader to get them to open flat.

The operation might be performed manually with small runs. However, the nature of machine design means that runs of less than 500 copies, and up to six sections, can be economically produced by machine. Of course, large production runs have to be completed on high-speed machines and in-line combination units are necessary.

Stitching machines are configured in-line, consisting of:

▶ feeding boxes or hoppers for sections and covers

▶ transfer and stitching

▶ trimming

▶ inserting

▶ inkjetting (may be on some feeders)

▶ stacking and wrapping

▶ palletising.

Quite complex configurations are possible with multiple cover stations and feeders providing flexibility of pagination and maximum speed to push two streams into one trimmer. A relatively new innovative design combines several gathering and stitching units in a rotating drum configuration, allowing fast operation of multiple lines.

Feeding boxes or hoppers

Up to 12 boxes may be fitted for the initial insetting of the sections, with the inside text placed in the first hopper and the cover in the last. The sections are fed over a continuous chain where lugs, known as 'flight bars', head up the sections to ensure accuracy. There is no theoretical limit to the number of sections that can be insetted, but the thickness of the paper and the number of pages in each section are a limiting factor.

On thick books, the outside sections require the imposition to allow for the thrust of the V formation around the inner sections. Pages should be shingled (centre margins reduced for sections away from the centre). If this is not taken into account, there is the possibility of trimming into the text or illustration area on the inner sections. The magazine or book will normally have been imposed and folded so that the thicker sections are placed inside the thinner ones to minimise this danger. The cover can be folded and placed over the chain or can be left flat, and creased and folded on a special folder feeder hopper. This is a great advantage when finishing cover-board or substrates heavier than 160gsm. Most machines allow a card or glue attachment hopper to be positioned anywhere on the insetting line. A simple hoist system removes the selected hopper and places the card/glue attachment into the desired position.

Transfer and stitching

Insetting completed, the books are positioned under a caliper device before saddle-stitching. On high-production machines, the speed of operation requires section control detectors to minimise incorrectly insetted sections being stitched. These devices eject the incomplete books into a reject tray. The incomplete books can be taken apart and the sections redistributed into the appropriate hoppers. The stitching operation places two or more staples, depending on the size and make-up of the book, into the spine before directing into the cutting unit.

Today, the wire used tends to be stainless steel of a varying thickness to suit the books being stitched, but aluminised wire, plastic (Teflon) coated and copper wire are all available should the product destination demand. Due to the high cost of the combination unit, computers are necessary to reduce non-productive time and waste.

Trimming

Stitched books are accurately positioned under the cutting area. The book is clamped firmly and trimmed in a double operation with the head and tail being cut first followed by the fore-edge. On some machines this process is reversed but the end result is the same. Some machines gather the books in pairs before trimming, allowing the speed of the action to be halved and so ensuring accurate finishing. Two-up work is also possible within the parameters of the machine enabling the speed of production to be almost doubled.

Inserting and inkjetting

The product can be opened after trimming, and loose inserts placed between the open leaves. There is control of the opening, and inkjet print heads can be placed to put a subscription address onto the cover or to personalise the inserts. Catalogue personalisation and subscription renewal notices for magazines are high value operations performed on the binding line.

Stacking and wrapping

High-volume production requires delivery to match output. A compensating stacking device equalises the swell on the spine of the books due to the wire thickness. Piles of books are ejected into a wrapping unit where they can be labelled automatically before despatch. High-volume magazine production is generally carried out on linked machines that are capable of outputting more than 20,000 copies an hour (cph). The speed of production depends on many factors: the age of the equipment, the competence of the operator, the weight of the paper, the number of sections and the number of copies to be produced. For any job, the machine will be set to an optimum speed determined by the particular combination of these factors.

Note that whereas in magazine work it is common practice to complete all the operations of insetting, saddle-stitching and trimming in-line, it is not uncommon where small runs of small products are being processed for each of these operations to be carried out individually on free-standing, unlinked equipment.

Binding methods similar to saddle stitching

Thread-stitching is much like saddle-stitching except that cotton thread is used instead of wire. The process is used for children's books where the staple could cause injury and for some short-run prestige books.

Saddle thread-sewing or *singer-sewing* is an alternative, less common, binding method more favoured on the Continent than in the UK. The endpapers are frequently wrapped and sewn with the printed pages of the book rather than tipped-on to the book block.

Gathering and sequential section binding

Thicker magazines and books require an adhesive binding. This method is also known as perfect binding or, in book binding, as limp unsewn binding.

Quality control in any form of limp unsewn binding should include checking the even application of the adhesive, and ensuring that the covers are drawn on square.

Note that a significant enhancement in quality can be made by specifying that the adhesive is applied to the book block in a strip about 4mm wide of the spine on either side. The cover is scored with corresponding lines 4mm to either side of the spine lines.

When the cover is drawn on, a glued 4mm hinge is thus formed at the front and back, which gives the binding extra strength at no extra cost.

The sequence of production is as follows:

► gathering
► adhesive binding
► cover application
► inkjet personalisation (may also be done on the feeders)
► inserting
► trimming
► wrapping/sealing
► palletisation.

Gathering

The folded sections are gathered together on top of each other to form a pile. Gathering can be performed manually for small runs, but mechanical feeders or hoppers are used in high-volume production. In mechanical production, the sections are loaded into a line of feeders, last section furthest from the binding operation, which deliver them to a chain. The chain collects the sections and forwards them to the binding operation.

Adhesive (perfect) binding

In the adhesive or unsewn binding operation, the book block is fed into the binding area by a clamp. The gathered book is jogged to ensure the heads and spines are positioned before final clamping. The book block is then introduced to a circular cutting disc that grinds a pre-determined amount from the spine (usually 3mm) leaving an uneven spine that can easily take glue. This milling operation is omitted (by removal of the cutting disc) when binding sections that have been thread-sealed or burst-folded. During the milling operation, the spines are roughened to ensure greater coverage of the adhesive. The book block spine then travels over the glue application roller or rollers that apply a film of adhesive, either cold glue (usually synthetic polyvinyl acetate PVA) or hot glue.

The hot glue or hot melt is almost universally synthetic and is either hot PVA or ethylvinylacetate (EVA). Stronger polyurethane adhesives are available but, due to their toxic nature, have to be carefully contained with the fumes treated before being expelled. To obtain an adequate bonding on certain materials (thick board or coated stock), a two-shot method can be employed, providing that the machine is adapted for this. In this process, a film of cold glue (water-based PVA) is first applied and dried using infrared dryers. Another film of hot PVA or EVA is applied in the binding line sealing the original bond. This ensures a strong bond of water-based adhesive while maintaining high-speed production due to the quick-drying properties of the hot melt. Hot melts can have varying open times – the length of time the adhesive will be tacky enough to attach the book cover and after which the book can be handled – of between eight and 16 seconds.

Hot melt glues cool quickly on application and then crystallise over the next couple of days so gaining maximum binding strength after the binding is finished. Most binders tend to err on the safe side and apply more glue than is necessary. This leaves a thick film at the spine that may start to thread during trimming, and may crack at cool temperatures when the product is opened. Highly glued titles do not lay flat at opening. They have a tendency to close and the reader often forces the book open resulting in a broken spine. New adhesive technology based on polyurethane resins (PUR) provides for a much thinner film of flexible glue. These reactive hot melts polymerise in a chemical reaction when they come into contact with water in the atmosphere and in paper fibres. The result is a stronger bond and a book that is easy to open, even in the case of cross-grain titles. For the binder, a different pre-melt system is needed to keep the adhesive dry before use. A short pot-life makes housekeeping more important and keeping bound copies stable over a few days, to develop the maximum bonding before testing the books, is a change to traditional methods.

Covering and trimming

After binding, the cover is fed to the book block by a timing mechanism. The cover feed usually presents the pre-creased cover to the book block within a few seconds of the application of the adhesive, depending on the speed of the machine. The covered product is then either taken from the delivery hopper and manually trimmed on a single-knife machine (for small runs), or fed into a three-knife pile trimmer (longer runs). In high volume production, the binding line is combined with an automatic trimmer that takes the books in pre-determined piles to the pile trimmer. The trimmer cuts first the head and tail of the pile, and then the fore-edge.

It is common in paperback book production to impose print and bind books two-up (head to head to minimise the plate requirement). This effectively doubles the speed of binding by producing two books from each cycle and incorporating a book saw or splitter to separate the final products. In some cases, two separate titles may be produced together if the quantities and pagination are identical, and a sophisticated conveyor system to keep the two streams separate is then required. The pile of books is then ejected for delivery to the inserting, inkjetting, stacking and wrapping unit, as in the high-speed saddle stitching operation.

Limp sewn binding

Limp sewn binding is a common specification for paperback books that require greater durability than perfect binding allows. The most common specification is section-sewn continuous, where the cover is drawn onto the sewn book block. The main operations are the same as for limp unsewn binding except that the sections are sewn together rather than milled away at the spine before the covers are drawn on. The drawing-on operation is often performed on an adhesive binding machine in which the milling unit has been disconnected.

Since the objective in section-sewing a limp book is to achieve extra security in the binding, factors that will influence this choice are:

▶ the use of matt-coated or gloss art papers
▶ particularly long extents (multi-section)

> ▶ types of book that will have frequent handling (e.g. reference, works, dictionaries)
> ▶ where the period of use will be over many years.

Note, too, that books containing illustrations laid over double-page spreads will normally require sewn binding (or special imposition for unsewn binding). Sewn binding helps a book lie flat when opened. Unsewn books will tend to resist opening wide and are opened flat only by creasing the pages, or by wrenching the book open and jeopardising the glued binding. Section-sewing is always more secure than adhesive binding, but is correspondingly more expensive.

Stab- or side-stitching

With stab-stitching or side-stitching, the books are gathered into book blocks and stitched by driving a wire staple through the spine area about 3–4mm from the edge. The books are then wrapped (a cover is attached) and trimmed. There are major drawbacks with the process that outweigh the fact that it is the strongest, most permanent and secure form of binding:

> ▶ the book make-up has to allow wider back margins for the spine to take the wire stitches, losing page area;
> ▶ the book will not open flat and so will be difficult to handle;
> ▶ the wire stitches (even though flat wire is available) will inevitably show through the cover with the subsequent loss of appearance;
> ▶ the stitching process is slower and less suitable for volume production.

The advantage of the process lies in the strength of the binding; it is used for the products in which pages becoming detached would be unacceptable, e.g. chequebooks, bank passport books, some catalogues.

Side-sewing

The side-sewing process is the same as side-stitching except that thread, rather than wire, is used as the bonding agent. The operation requires special equipment and it is a relatively slow one, but the appearance of the finished product has merits in the production of children's books, especially in the US.

Selecting the process

A decision to either inset and saddle-stitch or gather and adhesive bind must be made before production, as the imposition of the pages on the printed sheet will differ between saddle-stitching and perfect binding. Of course, beyond a certain thickness, the decision can only be to adhesive bind. The advantages it carries are that the cover spine can be printed and used for promotional purposes, and the book opens out and lays almost flat for ease of reading. Also, the adhesive book product is perceived to have more coffee-table appeal, but it should be remembered that the cost of perfect binding would normally be higher than saddle-stitching.

Hardcover (cased) binding

Conventional production line bookbinding is sometimes known as edition binding. Leather binderies or small specialist hand binderies cater for more expensive or specialised bookbinding requirements, whereas edition cased binding imitates the true bound book in appearance but not in structure. The true bound book has the boards attached to the body of the book; the cased book has the hard case made apart from the book and assembled with the text only at the final stage. Cased binding can be either sewn or unsewn and, as with limp binding, there are options within each. Unsewn encompasses adhesive-bound/burst-bound/notch-bound while sewn may be section-sewn continuous/thread-sealed/side-sewn.

It is important that the following aspects of cased binding should be monitored:

▶ *Folding* Check that the folding is square and if it does not appear to be so, check the back-up and imposition of the printed sections;

▶ *Rounding and backing* Rounding is often inadequately carried out on sewn work, and is notoriously difficult to do effectively with unsewn work;

▶ *Backlining* Check the quality of linings used. Occasionally only one lining is used, which both weakens the backs of the sections and allows the risk of glue seeping through and causing the backs to stick to the case hollow;

▶ *Case-making* Check bubbling or smearing underneath the case material, and check the case hollow for strength;

▶ *Boards* Take precautions against warping in more quality-conscious work;

▶ *Blocking* Inaccurate application of heat or pressure can cause imperfect transfer of the foil to the material. Particularly rough or heavily embossed materials can benefit from a run of 'blind' blocking before foil blocking in order to ensure that the surface will accept the foil properly;

▶ *Casing-in and forming* Check that the shoulders, grooves and hollows are properly formed. A square-back, shoulderless case should always be avoidable;

▶ *Jacketing* Check that the jackets are trimmed correctly – 1–2mm less than the depth of the board prevents the risk of scuffing the jacket at top and bottom – and that jackets are wrapped around the books accurately;

▶ *Packing* Cased books are best packed with spines turned alternately left and right, which allows space for shoulders and joints.

Sequence of events

Conventional section-sewn cased binding is the most common specification, and these are the operations:

1. The printed sheets are folded (off press) to a predetermined imposition.
2. The folded sections are bundled.
3. The first and last sections in the book are separated out and have the endpapers tipped-on.
4. The sections are gathered on a gathering machine into book order.
5. The gathered sections are collated.
6. The collated sections are thread-sewn on either semi-automatic or automatic sewing machines. The standard section-alongside-sections sewing method is known as French sewing, continuous sewing or section sewing, to differentiate it from inset singer sewing and from side sewing.

7. The books are divided off according to the collation marks, and at this stage they are called book blocks.

8. Each book block is forwarded on for final back-lining and then casing in, using either in-line equipment or freestanding equipment, generally following this pattern of operations:

    (a) Nipping (crushing, smashing) to remove air from the sections.

    (b) Glueing – a light coating of glue is applied to the sewn backs to secure the sewing threads.

    (c) Three-knife trimming to give correctly trimmed blocks.

    (d) Rounding and backing to put a round into the shape of the book block and a joint below the shoulder. The name of this operation is often abbreviated to R&B (rounding and backing), or R&J (rounding and jointing). Rounding is performed by an oscillating former bar and the backing (or jointing) is carried out by two nip bars.

    (e) First and second linings are applied to the glued and sewn spines – the first lining is of expandable mull and the second of stout kraft paper as a stiffener.

    (f) Head and tailbands are added if specified.

    (g) Casing-in – where the endpapers are glued up, and the bookblocks are fed inside the pre-formed cases and then pressed.

    (h) The cased books are jacketed by hand or by a jacketing machine.

    A number of linked systems bring in line all the later operations of bookbinding as outlined in stage 8 above.

Cased binding – variations on the sequence of events

Thread-sealing techniques, when used in edition cased binding, replace the conventional section-sewing process at stage 6 by thread-sealing each section in-line with folding at stage 1. Stages 7, 8(a), 8(b) and 8(e) are then omitted.

Side-sewing techniques can be used to replace the conventional section-sewing process (stage 6) when extra durability is required. This specification is uncommon (and expensive) in the UK and Europe, but much more common in the US.

Unsewn edition cased binding follows the same general principles described above, with the exception that instead of being sewn, the book block is perfect-bound and backlined using a flexible mull lining at stage 6, and stages 7, 8(a), 8(b) and 8(e) are omitted.

Burst-binding and *notch-binding* techniques are also used in cased binding. At stage 6, the burst or notched book-blocks are adhesive bound and lined, and again stages 7, 8(a), 8(b) and 8(e) are omitted.

Case-making

Cased binding

Saddle wire stitching, and particularly saddle thread sewing, can also be specified in cased binding. In this process, the main text is saddle-stitched or thread-sewn, endpapers are added to the stitched book block and the whole is then cased in exactly the usual way.

Saddle-thread-sewn, or singersewn, case-bound children's books are quite common in the US and on the Continent, but less so in the UK. Cases are made on a case-making machine. Such machines are set up to stick the pre-cut binder's boards to the chosen covering material in the prescribed positions for the size of the book. The pre-made case is usually blocked using a copper or zinc binder's brass (die). This uses heat and pressure to impress coloured foil (usually silver or gold) onto the case to form the lettering. The blocked case is affixed to the endpapers to complete binding at stage 8(g) above.

Materials

The material used to cover the boards in the making of the case for a hardback book is known as the covering. The covering used in most edition cased books will be a dyed, embossed and reinforced paper rather than a cloth. In roughly ascending order of cost and durability, the options are:

► non-woven materials – paper or plastic-coated paper
► woven materials – starch-filled or nitrocellulose-filled woven cloth
► leathers.

Non-woven materials

► Plain fibrefelts: dyed embossed and reinforced papers, from 105gm-2 upwards
► Over-printed fibrefelts: base paper similar to plain fibrefelts, but in heavier weights up to 155gsm
► Pyroxilin-coated fibrefelts: reinforced and lightly plasticised papers
► Over-printed, pyroxilin-coated fibrefelts: pyroxilin-coated fibrefelts with over-printed patterns
► Vinyl-coated papers: papers with a tearproof, washproof surface
► Plastic-coated fibres: heavy duty, embossed, 'imitation leather' finish.

Woven materials

► Whiteback cloth: cotton filled with starch, dyed and coated on one side only, calendered.
► Leather-cloth: plasticised cotton, dyed-through, calendered
► Art canvas: loose wove, strong cotton with a tissue lining
► Buckram: heavy duty, stiff, dyed-through and coated cotton-base.

Leathers

► goat hides
► pig skins
► calf skins
► vellum
► sheep skins
► forels
► reconstituted leather.

Most non-woven and woven materials are supplied in 100m rolls about 1m wide, and are charged per running metre. The more expensive non-woven materials are heavier in substance, have more expensive overprinting and are coated with nitrocellulose or other plastifiers to give surface protection and extra strength.

Woven materials cost more according to the fineness of the cotton weave, and the degree of dyeing, filling and coating applied to the base cloth. Note that man-made fibres, particularly rayon, now replace cotton in some of the woven-cloth qualities and provide a characteristically uniform, precise and even base surface for dyeing and coating.

Leathers are charged according to area and quality of hide. Expert advice is recommended when ordering leather. Production runs in these materials are rare.

Boards

The usual types of boards available for case-making are:

▶ chipboard or thamesboard – the cheapest form of board, made from waste paper

▶ Eskaboard or grey board – a cross-grain board designed to prevent warping

▶ millboard – waste paper furnish with some flax or hemp for extra strength.

Chipboards are usually provided to one of the following specifications, listed here with approximate equivalents:

>1700 microns 0.070" 1200gsm
>
>2000 microns 0.080" 1400gsm
>
>2300 microns 0.090" 1600gsm

Warping is the main problem associated with boards. While this risk can never be eliminated, the following precautions will minimise it:

▶ Specify that all boards should be cut long grain (i.e. with the grain direction parallel to the head-to-tail dimension of the book);

▶ Specify that the grain direction of the covering material must be parallel to the spine, and also the endpapers, if possible;

▶ Use the heaviest weight and best quality of board consistent with the budget;

▶ Allow boards time to mature both before production and afterwards in transit. Pack books in porous materials, not plastic, if manufacturing with high humidity (e.g. the Far East) for sale in an area of lesser humidity (e.g. Europe).

Specialist bookbinding

Note that the methods and costs involved in true hand-binding bear no relationship to the method and cost structure for conventional flow-line edition binding, and true hand-binding is normally viable only for single or low-quantity presentation copies, prestige monographs and specialist limited editions.

Certain categories of work combine both flow-line methods and hand methods, notably bible binding and account book binding. In these cases, folding and sewing might well be conventional, but extra strength and attractiveness is brought to the binding by (for example) edge-gilding, the use of marbled endpaper and an attractively blocked leather-covered binding case. The cost structure here will depend on the quality of materials specified and the proportion of hand to edition work, but it may well be viable for production quantities where a high selling price can be obtained.

When dealing with hand-bound editions it is important to take specialist advice. Hand-binding operations include the following:

Folding is often done by hand using a bone folder to make especially sharp folds.

Sewing Traditional hand sewing might be specified as either on tapes or on cords. Such sewing is carried out at a sewing frame that carries tapes or cords. The pages of each section are sewn through and to each other incorporating the tapes/cords in the structure of the sewing. A hand-sewn book on tapes/cords is extremely tough.

Endpapering Endpapers in traditional hand-binding are made tough by using a double-fold sheet reinforced with cloth. This is sewn in with the main book block instead of being merely strip glued, as in cased binding. Marbled endpapers are often used.

Forwarding A typical sequence of operations might be:
1   Trimming the book-block
2   Gilding or edge-colouring: gilding might use real or imitation gold leaf applied by hand or machine; edge-colouring can be done either by the application of a dye with a sponge or by spraying
3   Rounding, done by hand with a hammer
4   Backing or jointing, again done by hand with a hammer and a range of special tools.
5   Backlining with strong mulls and kraft papers.

Casemaking The case is attached to the book block, not just by the endpaper-glueing process, by securing the boards to the book block using the ends of the tapes or cords used in the sewing. Where cords have been used, the boards are drilled and the cords are laced into the holes. Where tapes have been used, a split or made board is slit through for about one-third of its width and the tapes are secured inside the slit.

Covering A typical covering might be leather or partial leather. The leathers most frequently used in bookbinding are:
▶   goat skin – probably the most commonly used leather, and also called Morocco – Niger Morocco (Nigerian goat), Turkish goat, crushed levant and ordinary levant are the more usual qualities;
▶   pig skin – very durable, but also stiff and inflexible so it is suitable only for large, heavy books;
▶   calf – less durable than either goatskin or pigskin. It has a naturally smooth surface and great flexibility;
▶   vellum – made from the inside of calfskin, it has a beautiful surface but is expensive and difficult both to handle and to tool;
▶   sheep skin – soft and smooth-surfaced with reasonable durability;
▶   forels – split sheep skin, less expensive and less durable;
▶   reconstituted leather, which is available at the cheaper end of the range.

Finishings are elaborate hand-tooled and decorative effects achieved by using onlays or inlays of skivers – thinly pared leathers – in contrasting colours or by impressing gold or coloured decorations the surface of the leather covering. Special hand tools are required.

Quarter-bound and half-bound styles are commonly adopted. In the quarter-bound style, the spine is covered in one material (often leather) while the sides are covered in another (often cloth or marbled paper). The half-bound style adds to this with leather edges at the top and bottom corners of the book.

Mechanical binding

The major forms of mechanical binding are:
► plastic comb binding
► spiral binding
► wire 'O' binding
► ring binding
► plastic welding.

All mechanical binding is relatively slow and labour intensive. The requirement for mechanical binding is to reduce the pages to single leaves. Folded sections may be trimmed all round after gathering, depending on the finished size and the printing method. The binding style then requires the drilling of holes along the spine: typically two or four holes for ring binding, a succession of holes for plastic comb, wire 'O' or spiral binding. Spiral and wire 'O' tend to be used where permanency is required – calendars, office manuals. Plastic comb and ring binding are used when the publication is likely to be updated on a continual basis.

Plastic comb binding

Plastic comb binding uses a comb of plastic circles (unjoined down one edge) that is opened along the length of the book and inserted through the pre-punched holes of the contents.

Spiral binding

Spiral binding uses a malleable wire. A mandrill within the binding machine shapes the wire, and the soft wire is then inserted into the pre-punched holes of the contents.

Wire 'O' binding

Wire 'O' binding uses multicoloured plastic-covered wire. It is extensively used for calendars with the machine design enabling a continuous process of gathering, drilling, inserting the wire and hanger, and closing. Also in some books where the ability to open flat and fold back on the spine is important, e.g. road atlas titles.

Ring binding

The ring binder is the simplest form requiring two or four 6mm holes to be drilled centrally on the pages. The drilled pages are then placed into a pre-manufactured binder.

Plastic welding

Plastic welding is another form of specialist binding used on ring binders, cases, wallet covers and other containers. A plastic welding machine uses a high frequency band that generates heat between opposing electrodes. The material is fused together under pressure to form a strong bond. Both clear and opaque PVC is available in various calipers and finishes, and can be welded and heat creased at the folds or joints. The PVC can also be foil blocked or screen printed.

Varnishing and laminating

Varnishing and lamination are generally treated as alternative finishing techniques, although combinations of both can be specified – matt lamination with spot varnishing, for example. Varnishing is sometimes seen as merely a cheaper alternative to lamination, but this is to underplay the merits of a good gloss-varnish finish.

Varnishing

Varnishing is normally performed by running the printed sheets through varnishing rollers that may or may not be in-line with the printing machine. Varnish can be applied either to the whole sheet, or to particular areas (spot varnishing) in the same way as printing inks. Special care needs to be taken with drying.

Note that varnish offers scuff resistance and gloss (in varying degree depending on the process) but, in contrast to lamination, adds no extra strength to the substrate. Printing inks must be chosen which are suitable for the type of varnish that is to be used.

There are different grades of varnish for different purposes:

▶ machine varnish
▶ water-based emulsion sealing varnish
▶ ultraviolet varnish.

It is common for an all-over finish or spots to be applied on a standard printing unit of a conventional offset lithography press (often using the damper system to achieve maximum thickness), or through a specialist coating unit. In five- and six-unit presses, the last unit can be given over to the varnish in the same way as the other units are given over to a particular colour of ink.

The varnish may be formulated like transparent, unpigmented ink, or a specialist material. This will be an oleoresinous alkyd-based material providing a thin film, relatively low-gloss material. Water-based acrylic emulsion varnishes applied through coaters are increasingly common. These are available in various levels of gloss and, when printed over conventional ink, can replace anti set-off spray powder, drying quickly to allow fast turnaround of work. Warm air dryers further speed the drying allowing additional high gloss UV coatings to be applied in-line. Ultraviolet curing varnishes have an acrylate base that polymerises under ultraviolet radiation. The formulations vary to provide different degrees of gloss, resistance and specialist finishes.

Coating machines typically apply varnish by a roller over the sheet. Spot patterns may be applied from a relief plate, and care is needed to ensure the varnish does not affect the plate. An alternative is to use silkscreen to apply the patterned varnish.

Lamination

Originally introduced in the 1940s, developments in the methods of application of both the adhesive and the film laminate have laid the ground for increasing usage. Laminating is now used extensively on book jackets and covers, CD covers, magazines, postcards and publicity material. In the production process, both webs and sheets can be laminated. It should be noted that with sheet lamination, the printed sheets are overlapped slightly as they are applied to the reel of laminate that may cause a slight indentation in the back edge. Film laminates are thin plastics, cellulose acetate, polyester (mylar and melinex) or orientated polypropylene (OPP), supplied in reels. They can be either gloss or matt finish. The film can be applied to the substrate by wet or dry lamination.

In plastic card production, a surface laminate is often part of the manufacturing process. Typically these are thin sheets of transparent PVC that are glued and heat sealed under pressure to the printed surface.

However the process is carried out, lamination has a significant effect on the printed appearance. There are physical, chemical and optical effects that result in significant tonal dot gain and colour shifts during the process. This change must be accounted for at the printing stage. Small test laminating devices are available that will allow proper evaluation of the print; a quick and dirty method of assessing the effect is to place some clear adhesive tape on the surface.

Wet lamination

Wet lamination is by far the most extensively used process. Both webs and sheets can be laminated. The process first involves the application, through a coating head, of adhesive to the film laminate. Solvents or water-based adhesives may be used, depending on the film type and the requirements of the finished laminate.

The solvent or water is next removed from the adhesive by passing the film web through a drying tunnel where the heat causes the solvent to evaporate and the adhesive to become tacky. The tacky film web travels to the nip of the laminating pressure rollers, where it meets the printed web/sheets. Together they are passed under high pressure between the heated rollers to ensure total contact.

Although dry enough for light handling immediately afterwards, the adhesive needs to cure for up to 24 hours to give a permanent, non-detachable bond between the film and substrate surface. Insufficient curing can lead to problems. Guillotining, creasing or embossing laminated sheets immediately after lamination may lead to delamination or lift of the film from the substrate. UV lamination, in which a UV adhesive is cured by exposure to ultraviolet light passing through the laminating film after nipping to the substrate, is used for high-speed processing of long-run work.

Dry lamination

Dry lamination is achieved by using film that has been pre-coated with either a heat seal synthetic resin or a pressure-sensitive adhesive. The film is contacted to the printed sheet and bonded by heat or pressure. Dry lamination is mostly used for small-scale production or when technical problems prevent wet lamination being used. The film, which is considerably thicker than that used for the wet process, is more expensive because it has been pre-coated with the adhesive. Maps, documents, warning signs and identity passes are typical examples of its uses.

Specification and choice of materials for varnishing and laminating

When choosing varnishing or film lamination, there are several technical factors that should be taken into account in the selection and processing of materials for the job. These are:

► sheet/reel allowances
► quantity allowances
► paper and board quality
► the use of set-off spray in the printing process
► ink formulation
► proofing.

Sheet/reel allowances

No extra margins are required for UV varnishes applied by roller coating as the web or sheet is completely covered with varnish. Lamination does require extra margins around the image area for technical reasons and to ensure that any bleeds are fully covered by the laminate. When sheets are laminated, they are overlapped slightly where they are to be gripped, as they are fed into the machine. The film runs off the trailing back edge of each sheet and contacts onto the leading edge of the following one after a small gap caused by the overlap. The front (gripper) edge of each sheet stays unlaminated and each trailing edge is liable to carry a small indentation at the point where the following sheet tucks under it. The two side edges of the sheet must also be left free of film for the side-lays (see Figure 10.3). No extra margins are necessary at the head and foot of the image area for reel lamination, but at least 5mm is required for each side margin, so the maximum width of lamination coverage is 10mm less than the full width of the web.

FIGURE 10.3 The extra margins required when laminating sheets

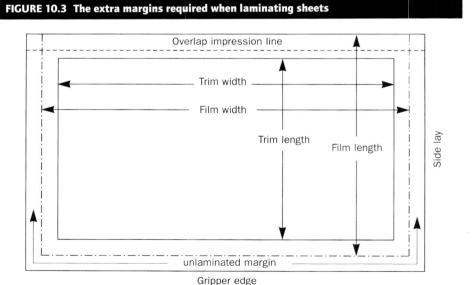

Source: Pira International Ltd

Quantity allowances

It should be remembered that additional meterage or sheets would be required by the varnisher or laminator to set up the equipment before starting the full production run. Typical allowances are:

- ▶ up to 5000 sheets 5% overs
- ▶ 5000–50,000 3% overs
- ▶ 50,000–100,000 1% overs
- ▶ over 100,000 between 0.5% and 1% overs.

Paper and board quality

The quality of a UV-varnished surface will depend on the smoothness and absorbency of the board or paper. Paper and board for varnishing should have good varnish hold-out and a surface oil absorbency test (SOAT) result in more than 60 seconds.

Film lamination is a little more tolerant. Most types and calipers of paper and board can be laminated successfully if supplied flat and at a stable moisture content (relative humidity 50–55%). However, the quality of substrate chosen will have a bearing on the quality of the final finish. So, whenever possible – and especially when pre-grained, rough or absorbent boards are selected – a proof is advisable.

Anti-set-off spray

Where varnishing or laminating is taking place offline, the laminate operator can improve matters by tapping the sheets, end-on, to dislodge the loose particles before placing the sheets in the in-feed. If this fails to produce the desired result, the only option may be to clean each sheet by hand, which is an expensive and time-consuming solution. It is also an impractical one on long runs. Avoiding the excessive use of set-off sprays is by far the cheapest solution, or using water-soluble materials.

Excessive use of anti set-off spray in any area of the printed sheet will be highlighted both by varnishing and laminating causing a silvery appearance. In the case of varnishing, too much anti-set-off spray will prevent good laydown and result in a poor and uneven finish. To minimise the problem, the smallest amount of finest grain spray and even application should be ensured. The best results can be obtained by printing with UV-cured inks, or using an emulsion coating in place of the anti-set-off spray. The emulsion coating should be chosen carefully after discussion with the UV varnisher.

Ink formulation

The choice of printing ink should always be made with regard to the type of finish that is to be applied to the print. The printer can choose inks that are formulated for use with varnished or laminated products and do not compromise printing quality. Such inks should have the following characteristics:

- ▶ drying quickly on the selected substrate and with low residual solvent content;
- ▶ no anti-slip and scuffing agents, e.g. wax, polythene, silicone;

► strong pigment so that application and the use of anti-set-off spray can be minimised;

► pigments should be resistant to solvents used in the lamination process (as defined by BS4342 Test method 4).

Metallic inks carry with them specific technical problems and should be approached with great caution. There are two main problems:

► migration of lubricants to the ink's surface causes reticulation in varnishes and prevents laminating adhesives adhering properly;

► poor cohesive bonding between the flakes of metal in the ink causes poor scratch resistance in varnishes and delamination of laminates.

Fluorescent ink always cause problems and it is advisable to see proofs wherever metallic or fluorescent inks are part of the specification.

Proofing

Proofing is recommended where an exact colour match is required as both UV varnishing and lamination do alter the optical qualities of an ink's surface, and can produce an apparent colour shift by highlighting the dominant colour value of the ink pigment.

Blocking and embossing

Embossing and plate sinking

Embossing, or die-stamping, and plate sinking are ways of making a printed area stand in relief. Both are common in the production of paperback fiction books. Embossing is achieved using a raised die and a hard base produced from embossing powder.

The reverse process is used for plate sinking. The effect in both cases is the same: the substrate is distorted around the image giving a three-dimensional effect. Pre-printed sheets can have the important area – image, title, and author – highlighted for greater impact. There are hand-operated machines for small runs and semi-automatic cutting and creasing machines, fitted with the male and female dies, for larger-scale production.

Hot foil stamping (blocking)

For cased books, the processes of machine blocking, or hot foil stamping, imitate to a large extent the earlier hand-tooling processes of bookbinding. For paperback books, blocking can also be used in conjunction with embossing to enhance the raised image. Security printing applies holograms to high-value paper documents, currency tickets and plastic cards in a similar manner using specialist holographic foils.

The process uses either a metallic or pigmented foil that is produced in rolls of various widths. The foil is brought in contact with the substrate under heat and pressure, and releasing the pigment onto the surface in a permanent bond. The foil or pigment is covered by a film consisting of four elements: the carrier, wax releasing agent, adhesive and the pigment. Under the influence of heat and pressure, the block that is placed in the machine impresses the foil or pigment onto the substrate.

Blocking can be done in more than one run and in more than one colour. Blocking designs for case covers need to be reasonably bold, as the process is not attuned to the transfer of fine detail.

Making the block

The block can be made of any hard-wearing material, but commonly zinc or brass, and can be re-used many times if the setting operation is carried out with care. Spine blocks, or chemacs, are made photomechanically from artwork supplied as film or increasingly from digital files. The image is exposed onto a light-sensitive coated copper plate, and the sensitive surface hardens where the light falls. In development, the plate is washed to remove the soft coating while the hard coating covering the image remains in place. The surface of the copper plate is next etched with acid. In the image areas, the coating protects the metal from the acid, and the image stays unbitten. In the non-image areas the acid eats away the metal to leave the image standing proud.

Packaging: carton and box making

The packaging industry is huge and diverse, and its requirements result in an input in the print finishing arena. Carton and box making is usually the manifestation of much creative design, planning and printing and finishing, and plays an important role in much point-of-sale promotion. Main areas of production can be identified:

▶ corrugated and fibre board containers;

▶ rigid boxes;

▶ carton manufacture;

▶ plastic materials in packaging and polystyrene mouldings, vacuum formed platforms, flexible wrappings and laminates are also commonplace.

Corrugated and fibreboard containers

Corrugated and fibreboard containers offer the maximum protection for packing glass and other breakable goods, and for the transport of large objects. They are also widely used as a final pack for moving quantities of small goods to stores and shops.

The principal method of production is to feed the container blanks into a machine that combines printing and slotting. Rubber stereo plates are the usual printing medium used, in conjunction with alkaline inks, and the sheet of printed material then passes directly into the slotter unit. Here, a series of adjustable rotary punches and counterparts set across a shaft cut away the material to form slots that give the shape to the flaps of the finished container. At the same time, creasing discs put the lateral creases in and form the sides. Speeds of up to 15,000 blanks an hour can be achieved depending upon the quality of substrate. Make-up in this section of the industry includes folding and partial closing of the construction by gluing, wire-stitching or taping using suitable hand-fed or automatic methods.

Rigid boxes

There has been little growth in the market in recent years but rigid boxes are still in great demand in sectors of the packaging industry. The boxes are made and stay rigid and offer maximum protection for smaller objects, e.g. jewellery boxes, gift presentation packs for the cosmetic, perfumery and confectionery industry and in the shoe-making area. The point-of-sale properties of goods can be greatly enhanced by using high-quality covering papers. The four stages in the manufacture of rigid boxes are:

▶ cut and score blanks;

▶ corner cut;

▶ corner stay;

▶ cover with paper.

Cutting and scoring the blank is usually done on a rotary cutting and scoring machine with a series of rotary drivers set along a shaft to the various measurements required. A sheet of board is fed into the rollers and, as it passes through it, is cut and scored to the required dimensions. The machine is reset (if the box is not square) and the other measurements cut. For larger quantities, a double-rotary machine with right-angle cutting and scoring assemblies produces finished blanks in one pass through the machine.

The unwanted corners are next cut from the prepared blank. Powerful machines will process one or two corners simultaneously, four to six blanks thick. The third stage requires that the blank be erected to its three-dimensional shape and held there by gummed tape at the corners. The tape may be glued, water reactivated or heat reactivated using a thermoplastic adhesive and is processed one, two or four corners at a time.

In a mechanical method of box covering, a wrapping machine is used, the glue being previously applied to the cover by a sheet-gluing machine. A specially prepared block is mounted on the machine and will fit exactly into the open rigid box that has the glued cover correctly positioned to its base. The movement of the machine pushes the box and cover downwards, with the cover being drawn over, tucked in and ejected.

Cartons The carton sector is one of the main sectors of packaging. Everyday household items such as toothpaste, soup, tea, sugar, cereals and cosmetics are bought in a carton, and the sector continues to grow.

A carton usually starts its life as a hand-made sample into which will fit the object that the customer wants to pack. At this stage, details need to be studied carefully to ensure that the customer will get the most suitable and economic carton. Factors include the weight of goods to be packed, style of the carton best suited to the needs of the product, economics in relation to sales, printing method to be used and the quality of the board suitable for the process.

Having studied these points and decided the style of carton required, a suitable caliper and quality of board is selected and a carton made. This will be of the correct size for the measured object and other items that may have to be included such as leaflets. Making best use of the grain direction, the complete shape of the carton is drawn in reverse on the back of the board to be used and the lines indicating creasing area are creased by using a rule and stick. The shape of the carton blank is cut out with a knife and, where necessary, pieces of cutting rule are bent to specific shapes. Technological advances allow the production of samples digitally with CAD systems linked to a plotting table. The printed material may be produced on a digital press, along with short-run promotional packs. The blank is then checked for size and assembled. The goods are fitted in and, if satisfactory, the sample is submitted for approval. The sample maker will keep a register showing size, style, board used and sample for future reference. Once the carton style is approved, a one-off master cutting forme is prepared to the exact sizes. Samples are cut from this forme, and accurate drawings are supplied to the artist to prepare the artwork. A pilot test run may be cut from this same forme to check the carton's suitability for automatic packaging machinery. When finally approved, the job goes for platemaking and printing. Proofs are produced in colour on the correct material, cut to shape and a complete printed carton presented for approval. A layout sheet can now be prepared showing the number of cartons to be on the sheet correctly in position and this should agree with the original estimate.

Most cutting and creasing dies are still made as a wooden one-piece die. The carton shape is drawn onto plywood and this has to be repeated for the complete number of cartons on the sheet. This means that if a particular job is 20 cartons on a sheet, then all 20 cartons are drawn onto the surface of the wood by hand, correct to size and in position to fit the printed sheet. To prevent the plywood from breaking into several small pieces when the rule slots are sawn, small areas (bridges) are left and the position for these is now selected and marked. Drill holes are made at strategic points to enable a jigsaw blade to be inserted into the wood and saw around the drawn shape.

Rules are then cut to size, shaped, bridged and inserted into the wood. As bridges have been left at the side, top and bottom of each block, the rules will be slotted or bridged to allow a good fit over the uncut portion of the wood block. Rules are made in many varieties and thicknesses. There is a standard height for cutting rules but the height of the creasing rule is governed by the caliper of the paperboard to be used. The thickness of the cutting, and particularly the creasing rule, are also relative to the caliper of the paperboard from which the carton is to be made.

Much die-making still requires the use of a jigsaw machine, normally with circular saw and rotating drill attachments. The accuracy of the die relies entirely on the skill of the die-maker, and there no adjustable gauges that can be used to assist in following the required shapes. The digital methods are encroaching with dies produced by a CAD system linked to a laser operation. A metal guillotine for cutting the rule to random or repeat sizes is followed by various small machines for bending, bridging and lipping as required. A grindstone is used for small adjustments with the assembly being completed on a composing surface. Tolerances of less than 0.4mm are needed to ensure that the cartons run smoothly through packaging machines.

At this stage, the prepared die is rubbered up. A specially prepared rubber is placed alongside the cutting rule in steps about 6mm wide and 1mm above rule height. The rubber is compressed when pressure is applied. As the pressure is released it will resume its normal height and, in doing so, will force the board away from the rule.

The main types of cutting and creasing machines are as hand or automatically fed platen, cylinder and autoplaten. The platen is used mainly for short runs and is usually hand-fed. This machine will produce approximately 600–800 impressions an hour on stocks up to and beyond 2000 microns caliper. Showcards are also cut on the larger type platens.

The cylinder machine is usually fitted with an automatic feeder and runs up to a speed of 3500 impressions an hour. It is used for longer runs on medium-caliper materials while an autoplaten has the platen in a horizontal position and is fully automatic at speeds of 6000–10,000 impression an hour.

The preparation and make-ready varies on each type of machine, to apply a patched-up sheet to level the cutting impression and to ensure that all cutting knives are cutting evenly. A stencil matrix provides the female part that allows the creasing rule to crease the board. After the sheets have been cut and creased, the cartons have to be broken or stripped. In this operation the cartons can be stripped out by hand leaving the waste area behind. On autoplaten machines, it is possible to completely strip and separate cartons while the sheet is passing through the machine but this is dependent mainly on the length of run and set-up time.

The stripped cartons are then ready for the make-up operations of gluing, stitching, window patching and waxing. In the case of a carton to hold a tube of toothpaste, the side seam is glued on the carton-gluing machine. First, the glue flap of the carton is folded over 180° and brought back to the flat plane while simultaneously the third crease is similarly treated.

The glue flap receives a line of glue as it passes over a glue wheel and creases two and four are folded by bars and belts so that the glued flap half is stuck to the inside of the side panel. A belt ensures that the glued joint is under pressure while the glue sets, the belt travels much slower than the previous part of the machine and the cartons are delivered on top of each other and slightly staggered. As the cartons are delivered at the end of the machine, they pass through a collection system that automatically slows them down and directs them into the outer cases ready for delivery to the packaging machine.

Material handling and finishing for digital printing

There is some movement away from a highly labour-intensive process into more automated approaches through the use of on-line and near-line finishing equipment for digital printing. The trick is to maintain product flexibility at the same time. The type of automation that has been used on litho presses is migrating into the finishing department, with collators, binders and folders automating set-up to reduce make-ready, especially for repeat or same format jobs. Many digital users are looking to broaden their range of products. Further push for this trend will come from health and safety concerns that unskilled labour contracts repetitive strain injuries from handling high volumes of part-finished products.

The most significant changes are taking place with materials handling systems being integrated with the digital printing systems through partnerships of engine supplier and specialist finishing equipment. To be successful and provide fast turnaround, digital printers will increasingly handle the finishing and mailing in-house. This will include developments in the job ticket controlling the operation, or at least the set-up, of folders,

collators, inserters, cutters and binding equipment. Such automatic flow lines significantly increase capacity on guillotines and folders with reduced manning levels.

Finishing equipment   There are many differing requirements concerning finishing, which determine whether work can be completed on- or off-line. The following are significant:

▶   binding method – perfect binding, sewn binding, and/or booklets

▶   monochrome books or in combination with colour pages

▶   on-demand or simply short run

▶   cover lamination – varnish or as is

▶   getting the product right (a particularly important consideration if on-demand) correct cover with content, correct size, sending to the right customer.

The range of on- and off-line finishing equipment is quite comprehensive but is often quite restrictive in terms of formats. The range of operations dealt with by specialist equipment includes the following:

▶   perfect binding with separate cover

▶   booklet making with separate cover – includes collation, saddle stitching and folding

▶   three-edge trimming

▶   stackers

▶   sheet rotation

▶   book block banding.

For mailing operations there are many systems to cater for a variety of requirements and volumes so the digital press can have its web output directly fed into an inserter, together with sheet-fed flyers and inserts to feed into a mailpack. Total integrity can be maintained using systems from manufacturers such as Bell and Howell, Böwe and Pitney Bowes.

Mailing, packing, distribution and freight

11

Printed products have to be distributed to customers and then on to the final user or consumer. It is important that the products arrive in good condition and on time. Stock products will be warehoused and distributed as needed while bespoke items will go straight into the distribution systems. As well as using a vehicle to deliver products to the client warehouse, some printers have developed specialist distribution to ensure their magazines arrive on the newsstands early, or have mailing experience; others are content to allow specialist logistic and distribution companies or the postal systems to distribute their products.

Printing and inserting

There are many systems to print base stock, personalise, fold and insert into envelopes for all types of communication from document factory, direct mail, transactional mail, subscription and fulfilment. The content may be generic or highly targeted and personalised to an individual. Digital printing is increasingly important, with overprinting starting to be challenged by complete full-colour inkjet personalisation.

Specifying bulk packing

Packing is best specified with reference to the parcel size required, the method of transport to be used (or distance involved) and the conditions available for storage.

Typical specifications for bulk packing of printed material might include:
► packed in binder's parcels (brown waterproof paper)
► properly labelled
► shrink-wrapped in specified parcel sizes
► cartoned in cardboard boxes strapped on pallets
► strapped loose on pallets with board coverings at the head of stacks
► palletised and containerised.

Parcels

Parcels should be specified by reference to the number of copies required per parcel up to a maximum size, normally recognised as 13kg. The British Post Office will not handle more than 22.5kg in a bag.

Pallets

Where work is to be palletised, the exact sort and size of pallet should be specified to ensure that pallets can be handled both at the binder's and the customer's warehouse.

The European standard (Europallet) pallet size is 1000×1200mm, four-way entry. A maximum pallet weight of 1000kgs (just under one imperial ton) and a maximum height of 1219mm (4ft) are commonly specified. A pallet of this size might typically carry 1000–1250 books of average 8vo size (say 216×138mm), or about 2000 96-page A4 magazines (typical weights about 500kgs a pallet).

Containers

Containers are of two standard sizes: 20ft×8ft×8ft (6.10m×2.44m×2.44m) and 40ft×8ft×8ft (12.20m×2.44m×2.44m) Typically, a 20ft container will contain 24 pallet-loads (six pallets lengthwise, two pallets widthwise and two layers); and a 40ft container will contain double this amount. A typical 20ft container load might be 30,000 books of average 8vo size, or 50,000 A4 magazines (a weight about 12–13 tonnes on each container).

Book packing for postal distribution

With the advent of important internet retailers (e.g. Amazon), direct distribution to individuals has significantly increased. The choice of packing for single copies of books to be mailed depends almost entirely on the facilities available in the publisher's or printer's warehouse. Large publishers will have their own preferences for the use of boxes and/or envelopes and kraft wrapping, and will often have manual or automatic lines constantly wrapping to a set specification.

A universal method of despatch for books and other printed material needing protection is the Jiffy Bag, an envelope in which lightweight protective material is sandwiched between the inner and outer paper layers of the envelope. These are available in a variety of sizes.

Corrugated board is also widely used for protection inside envelopes or other forms of wrapping, as are book-sized boxes. Books are sometimes shrink-wrapped individually but usually to protect them before sale rather than for mailing purposes. Specialist distributors often shrink-wrap books (with other products) onto a corrugated board and pack into boxes with bubble-wrap to protect the contents in transit.

Magazine and brochure wrapping for postal distribution

There are five main methods of wrapping and labelling magazines for postal distribution:
► conventional paper and manila envelopes with a label fixed on the address side with magazine and PPI (Printed Postage Impression of the mail-house) printed on the envelope
► wrapping in kraft paper and labelling on the outside
► polywrapping in plastic film with the label on the outside or the inside
► inserting in plastic envelopes with the label on the outside or the inside
► mailing without wrapping but with the address label fixed to the front or back cover of the magazine, or inkjetted onto cover.

Paper envelopes

With extended runs for magazine printing, escalating costs and the advent of automated wrapping techniques, this conventional method of preparing magazines for mailing is declining. The main disadvantages are the additional weight of the heavier substance of paper forming the envelope compared with paper wrapping or plastic film, which leads to higher postal costs. There is automation that can be applied to the process of inserting A4 size range magazines, but it is still rarer than C5 and Dl inserting.

Some publishers still regard conventional envelopes as the most authoritative-looking form of wrapping especially for serious material such as academic journals, and there is debate over the additional protection afforded compared with other methods. Where confidentiality is important or where the product is sensitive, a conventional envelope is still often the only practicable medium, although opaque polythene is available.

Paper wrapping

Kraft paper is usually used for wrapping, but strong printed white sheets are sometimes preferred for aesthetic reasons. Automatic wrapping on a machine will either involve folding an A4 magazine in half or wrapping it flat. A5 sizes are wrapped flat. The magazine is delivered from the machine in a sleeve of paper which encloses it tightly and which will not float off in transit.

Labels are fixed to the outside of the paper wrap manually or by machine, but direct inkjetting onto the package is increasingly replacing separate production and application of labels. Manual wrapping usually involves rolling the magazine rather than folding it and is sometimes preferred to a folded wrap since there is no crease for short subscription runs.

Plastic wrapping

Plastic wrapping is increasingly replacing the paper wrapping business. The use of transparent plastic polywrapping for magazines and brochures is widespread. It is the most cost-effective as volumes have increased and specialist automated machines have been introduced.

Plastic wrapping from rolls of film is normally automatic and speeds of up to 15,000 units an hour can be achieved. Leading machine suppliers include Sitma and Norpak. The technique is broadly the same. Wrapping lines can be specified to a variety of requirements depending on the work. Printed items travel along a conveyor belt and are then enfolded in a sleeve of plastic film that is heat sealed along the centre join by a heated rocker element. A cross-sealer cuts and seals the plastic across the length at pre-set intervals finishing the total enclosure of the product.

Labelling is mostly inkjet, either onto the product, onto a carrier sheet or outside of the mailer into pre-determined positions. Plastic for wrapping is available in different gauges, which provide varying degrees of strength but have different weights. Unless unusually bulky, A4 magazines of average extent are often mailed in 35 micron gauge film, while a heavy, glossy mail-order catalogue may use 80 micron gauge. A high-density plastic is available down to 18 microns and although this may work out no cheaper than 35 micron on an area calculation, the reduced weight can make significant differences in mailing costs on long runs.

The polythene can be overprinted with one or more colours, and a 3in white strip is mandatory for most European postal systems. Many clients will print promotional material on the wrap.

Plastic envelopes

Plastic envelopes or bags such as Polylopes are more expensive than polywrapping for long standard runs. They tend to be used for complicated requirements or shorter runs. Inserting can be automatic or manual and sealing can be by machine or self-sealing by hand. They are available in a variety of sizes and as units or on reels for automatic feeding. Like sheet film, plastic bags can be made in a range of gauges and strengths. Most are preprinted and can be addressed by inkjet or application of a sticky label.

Direct labelling

Direct labelling is increasing in America and most European post systems will accept the method. Labels are applied or inkjetted onto the front or back cover and the item is posted without wrapping. Sometimes a sticker is applied to stop the title opening and becoming damaged in the post.

The advantage is there is no additional weight created by wrapping materials. The disadvantage is that the magazine is unprotected on its travels. There are two further considerations for the publisher to take into account:

▶ the label either obscures part of the front cover design or part of the back page which, if it is an advertisement, may be unacceptable to the advertiser;

▶ this method precludes the sale of loose inserts that would fall out.

Postal distribution services

The commercial activities that are being carried out by postal systems in different countries are rapidly changing. Most have been privatised and de-regulated by national governments, and there is increasing competition between service providers. The inevitable result will be consolidation of national providers (certainly across Europe), with new services providing better deals to mailers. The opening of markets to competition is occurring with many distribution companies looking to attack some of the traditional markets for national postal providers. The consequence of this is that there are new products and services being introduced, so it is necessary to keep in contact with developments. Here we consider UK postal options in greater depth.

Pricing in proportion

From 21 August, 2006, UK postage pricing will change to take into account size as well as weight. Mail weighing up to 1kg will fit into one of three categories: small letter, large letter or packet.

▶ small letter, up to C5 (240×165mm, maximum thickness 5mm up to 100g);

▶ large letter (up to 353×250mm, maximum thickness 25mm, four price bands according to weight);

▶ packets (where one dimension is greater than 353×250mm, or it is more than 25mm thick, price bands according to weight).

The postal suppliers justify these changes because it costs more to sort, handle and deliver larger envelopes and lightweight packages. As mail service providers become increasingly commercial they want their prices to reflect their costs. Currently large, lightweight items of mail cost more to process than the price of the postage. They claim this is a consequence of increasing competition and the opening up of the market, otherwise private companies could cherry-pick services while ignoring the universal delivery.

Magazine distribution

There are significant implications for magazine publishers and companies that post brochures and mail order catalogues. In the UK the distribution of magazines and newspapers is under scrutiny from the Office of Fair Trading (OFT), which has found that current distribution mechanisms to newsagents, garages and supermarkets may be anti-competitive. This poses significant dangers for small, specialist titles.

In May 2005 the OFT published a draft opinion providing guidance on the compatibility of newspaper and magazine distribution agreements with UK competition law. The OFT concluded that newspaper distribution agreements which provide wholesalers with 'absolute territorial protection' are compatible with the Competition Act 1998, but indicated that similar territorial protection in magazine distribution agreements would not be compatible with the Competition Act.

In 1995, the US magazine supply chain underwent a rapid transformation, following the consolidation of major retail chains. Safeway announced that it would stop dealing with dozens of small wholesalers and focus on one distributor at a national level. Other large retailers, including Walmart, followed suit, creating an intensely competitive environment in which wholesalers battled with each other to see who could offer retailers the cheapest deal. The result has been major consolidation of the wholesale market – down from 180 distributors in 1995 to only a handful, with four major wholesalers controlling more than 90% of magazine distribution. According to the PPA, around 2000 US titles closed and more than 20,000 retailers went out of business.

Although the UK market differs from that in the US, which is more subscription based, the publishing community believe the same or worse may happen in the UK. Only time will tell.

Posting printed items

The main distribution services for printed items are listed below. Detailed information on these and the whole range of postal services, both inland and overseas, may be obtained from sales representatives of postal systems. By doing part of the work of the postal distribution system, the mailer can gain the benefit of significant discounts on price.

Inland services

Mailsort

Mailsort is the name for the range of postal services offered by Royal Mail to organisations that produce or handle large volumes of mail for delivery within the UK. It is a range of discounts against standard postal tariffs by the mailer handling some of the work of the postal service. This is mainly connected with the sorting and presentation of mail that would otherwise be undertaken by the mail service provider. The level of discount achievable depends on the service required. Similar operations are offered by all other major postal authorities across the world. In the UK the range of products and service levels include:

Mailsort 1400

Mailsort 1400 (for letters and packets) involves sorting the mailing into approximately 1400 selections, based on UK Delivery Offices. It does not generally involve any level of machine sorting by Royal Mail.

Mailsort 700

Mailsort 700 for letters involves only sorting the mailing into about 700 selections based on the requirements of our mail centres' automated sorting machines. To do this, mail items must have an approved customer barcode applied.

Mailsort 120

Mailsort 120 for letters involves sorting the mailing into approximately 120 selections based on large geographical areas. To do this, mail items must have either a customer barcode applied, or use an Optical Character Recognition (OCR) font for printing the address, as well as meeting clearly defined design criteria. Unlike Mailsort 1400 and Mailsort 700, Mailsort 120 is available only as a first or second class service.

Presstream

Presstream is a periodical distribution service that is tailor-made for publishers who regularly mail large volumes of magazines and journals. Presstream is a two-tier service with Presstream 1 targeted at next-day delivery for periodicals published and posted ten times a year or more frequently, and Presstream 2 aiming at delivery within three working days for periodicals published and posted at least twice a year. Like Mailsort 1400, Presstream involves sorting the mailing into approximately 1400 selections based on UK delivery offices. It does not generally involve any level of machine sorting by Royal Mail. It is available as a first or second class service. All Presstream services are exclusively for publications.

Walksort

Walksort is designed for large national mailings, letters or packets, or those destined for a high number of addresses within a specific area. It involves sorting the mail right down to the level of individual postal walks (of which there are about 80,000 in the UK). It does not involve any level of machine sorting. It is available as a first or second class service.

Service levels

Products that provide discounts for distributing direct mail and individual printed matter offer a range of service levels.

▶ Mailsort 1/Walksort 1 are for letters and packets targeted for delivery the next working day after posting. They are discounted against the cost of first class postage.

▶ Mailsort 2/Walksort 2 are for letters and packets targeted for delivery within three working days after posting. Discounts are against second class postage rates.

▶ Mailsort 3 is for letters and packets targeted for delivery within seven working days. Higher discounts than service 2 are available.

▶ Presstream 1 is for publications targeted for delivery the next working day after posting.

▶ Presstream 2 is for publications targeted for delivery within three working days after posting.

▶ Presstream Premium is a specialist service for delivering publications in certain urban areas. It allows you to deliver items to the Royal Mail as late as 12.30am for delivery same day, Monday to Saturday.

▶ Mailsort 3 Deferred Delivery option is available only for Mailsort 3. This lets a client prepare and lodge a mailing with the postal service for delivery within a five-day time window enabling it to coincide with other media exposure, such as a TV or newspaper campaign. The complete mailing must be lodged between seven and 28 days before the commence delivery date, and the entire posting handed over within 20 working days.

The mailing will then be completed four working days after the commence delivery date. The key for all the discounted services is to pre-sort the mailing into post office distribution centres. This can be done by pre-sorting the address file against the Postcode Address Finder (PAF) file of addresses and then printing the delivery labels in the appropriate order. When the envelope or package is fulfilled, the mailer sorts them into individual tagged mailbags that are caged and picked up to go straight into the postal distribution system.

There are two categories of mail in any mailing: directs and residues. These are the numbers of items that postal services will offer discount against, currently in the UK this is 25 items for letters and five for packets. Each location has its own mailbag, and for a direct this will contain at least 25 letters. If there are fewer (or there is no post code) the mail is categorised as a residue that carries a lower discount. To obtain the maximum discount, there should be a minimum of residues normally achieved by maximising the run to provide the highest number of pieces for each area. In the UK a mailing of 10,000 pieces may achieve only 4% directs while a 100,000 mailing will be at some 96% directs.

International services

Sorted contract service (for pre-sorted printed matter)

Sorted Priority

This services offers:

▶ full airmail service to all countries, five to seven days delivery outside Europe, three to five days for Europe

▶ for direct bag consignments, see the M-Bag option

▶ zonal rates on a per kg basis or item and kg

▶ percentage discounts available for large-volume users.

Sorted Standard

Available to 90 destinations outside Europe for the despatch in bulk of printed paper items, this service offers both speed and economy by combining air and surface transport. Sorted Standard provides a much faster delivery service than can be achieved by using normal surface post, but at a charge often considerably below the standard airmail rate. It also offers:

▶ the M-Bag option (see box) for direct bag consignments

▶ zonal rates

▶ discounts for large-volume users.

Sorted Economy

This service offers:

► worldwide service with delivery as for ordinary letters and printed papers, i.e. one to three months

► zonal rates

► discounts for large-volume posters.

Unsorted Service (letters and print without pre-sorting)

This is an airmail service for customers sending more than 2kgs of international letters and printed papers abroad per collection. The service is worldwide and ideal for correspondence, financial mail, travel schedules, reports and personalised mailshots. It has a simple price structure based on a two-stage weight step and a two-zone (Europe and Rest of World) geographical split. Payment is in cash or on account using postage paid impressions and there are collection facilities.

General conditions are:

► mail to be sorted into the two zones described above

► items must have airmail/*par avion* labels

► items to be bundled and bagged (the materials are provided)

► weights and dimensions are the same as for ordinary letters

► standard of service as for ordinary airmail letters.

The M-Bag option

The M-Bag service can be used to send newspapers, magazines and books to the same address, and offers significant cost savings. M-Bags cannot be used for personalised mail or mail containing enclosures of commercial value. This is a special service to customers who regularly send large numbers of printed papers to a single address (for example a distributing agent or bookseller) in another country. Available to all countries, it allows for complete bags to be forwarded to a particular addressee abroad (known as the agent). M-Bags cannot, however, be sent to HM Forces addresses or HM Ships overseas.

A made-up M-Bag constitutes one postal item and must not contain any items to a person other than the agent to whom the bag as a whole is addressed.

Most of the necessary materials (bags, labels, forms) are provided by the Royal Mail, and the poster (the service user) then packs and labels the bags and presents them to the Royal Mail ready for despatch abroad in conformity with international postal requirements. The Royal Mail instructs customers' staff how to do the job.

Although not essential, it is recommended that the contents of M-Bags be made up into individual packets addressed to the agent, so that the packets can be safely sent on their way even if the outer bag labels become detached or if the contents become separated from the bag. Where individual packets are made up, the normal limits of weight and size for printed papers given in the Royal Mail International Service Guide may be ignored, but in these circumstances particular attention should be given to the standard of packaging.

M-Bags may be used in any Sorted Service stream, i.e. Sorted Priority, Sorted Standard and Sorted Economy, depending upon the speed of the service required. Charges are assessed on the total weight of the bag and the service used, with a minimum bag charge for 1–3kg. Maximum weight is 11kg.

M-Bags cannot be accepted for registration or insurance. All bags are associated with, and consigned as, part of the ordinary letter mails being despatched by the Post Office to the respective destination abroad, as appropriate.

Airsure

The Royal Mail offers online tracking and tracing with Airsure. The items leave on the first available flight and they receive priority handling abroad, and with Airsure your mail is electronically tracked all the way to its final delivery address. Airsure is available to a limited number of countries although Royal Mail will continually add destinations. It currently costs £4 an item on top of the airmail postage.

Swiftair express letter service

Swiftair is an international express letter service with signature on delivery available to all countries. The service caters for airmail letters, printed papers and small packets. The weight limits are: 2kg for letters, small packets and most printed papers, and 5kg for certain books and pamphlets.

Swiftair items receive special handling in the UK and express delivery in those countries of destination, which operate an express delivery service. Items must either be handed over a Post Office counter or included in firms' collections (but kept separate from other correspondence to ensure proper handling). Each item must bear a Swiftair label and this should be fixed to the top left corner of the address side.

A fee must be paid in addition to the normal postage. Items can also be recorded, registered or insured to most countries on payment of the appropriate additional fee. (For all these fees see the Postal Rates Overseas leaflet or compendium.)

A Certificate of Posting will be supplied free of charge on request at the time of posting.

Because of the special treatment in this country and also in many countries abroad, the Swiftair service cuts down on delay risk. Royal Mail International aims for Swiftair items to be flown to the country of destination on the day after posting (subject to availability of flights) and delivered at least one day earlier than the ordinary airmail services.

Outside the EU, Swiftair items containing merchandise must bear the small green Douane CN22 label. If the value of the merchandise is more than £270 (€391), the CN23 form must be used.

Airsure and Swiftair prepaid plastic self-seal envelopes for a range of pack sizes and weights can be bought from any Royal Mail post office or online.

Parcelforce International Datapost

This is a guaranteed timetabled express delivery for documents and merchandise to more than 239 countries. It features:

▶ reliability backed by comprehensive insurance (up to £5000 per item for loss or damage, plus consequential loss insurance from £100 up to £5000 per consignment)

▶ competitive prices, generous size and weight limits

▶ versatile accounts facilities.

For on-demand collection and full details of prices and services available to specific destinations, phone free on 0800 224466.

International Direct mail

Direct mail is a popular and cost-effective direct marketing tool available to the international marketer. Advantages are:

▶ campaign effectiveness can be easily measured

▶ target audience can be accurately selected

▶ mailings can be personalised either by name or job title

▶ it is flexible in size, content and timing

▶ it enables database building

▶ it is a versatile means of advertising, e.g. mail order, sales lead generation, customer loyalty building, fund-raising, market research, product launch, conference and exhibitions promotion.

Reply facilities

To encourage quick responses to mailings, an International Business Reply Service is available to most countries. From the UK, the Royal Mail will provide continually updated lists. This facility enables overseas customers to reply to mailings without them going to the expense of paying postage. The advantages are:

▶ it stimulates response

▶ replies are returned by airmail to the designated UK address

▶ it is easy to use – the customer has only to post the pre-printed, reply-paid envelope or card

▶ the single design for all participating countries saves on print and organisation costs

▶ it is simple and economical – a single fee covers the cost of the annual licence and the first 1000 responses in that year

▶ it facilitates measurement of campaign effectiveness and database building.

Alternatively, International Reply Coupons (IRCs) can be sent (available from larger post offices). These are exchangeable by the respondent for stamps representing the minimum international postage payable for reply to the UK.

International Admail

International Admail offers a reply-paid device that is pre-printed with a local address. This perceived local presence, especially when used with the Direct Entry service, can break down customers' reluctance to replying overseas and boost response rates. Royal Mail will supply the local design specifications so your reply device matches local postal designs.

Export distribution

Shipping

As a general rule, sea freight is usually the cheapest method of getting large quantities of printed matter distributed overseas; air freight is usually the most expensive.

Sometimes trucking can be the best method of getting goods to specific destinations in Europe, especially if good consolidation services are available. Before making a decision, it is advisable to consult a freight forwarder who has the strength of service in the area of Europe where you need to send your goods.

Distribution charges can vary wildly, even within the particular modes. The reasons for the variations are complex. Be aware that prices obtained one month will almost certainly be out of date a few months later. When goods are exported, it is essential to ensure that all documentation satisfies the importer's government's regulations. In general, books have a zero rate of import tax (duty) and customs clearance depends only on having the correct documents with the customer (or his agent) by the time the consignment arrives.

Sea freight rates are nearly always quoted per cubic metre of cargo, which then has extras added – normally fixed charges relating to port congestion and oil prices.

Sailing frequencies to small countries can be erratic, and vessels can often be bound for one particular port but unload the cargo at another port for onward transmission to the original destination. This is done when there is little cargo for one particular port and the economics do not warrant the vessel calling there.

Apart from the main commercial routes, schedules can vary from those advertised and often changes are not notified until the last minute. Consequently, if shipments are to be made to infrequently served ports, or are made on vessels with many ports of call, it is advisable to try and get the goods to the customer at least two months before he actually requires them in order to allow for shipping delays.

Air freight

The speed at which air cargo travels means that documentation must be meticulously prepared. Customs regulations often require an invoice to be sent with the goods so that they can be immediately cleared at the destination.

Air freight rates are usually quoted in sterling or US dollars per kilo and often there are break points on the scale charges, which differ from airline to airline. Consignments of less than 45kg are usually penalised quite heavily, but a sliding scale reduction can usually be obtained for those of more than 100kg. In addition to the freight rates, there are minimum customs clearance charges and inland transport charges. These are fixed additions to the freight costs and vary from country to country.

As a general rule, anything under 20kg or a low-value consignment is better sent by air-parcel since these fixed charges do not apply. Valuable consignments of less than 20kg can often be sent cost-effectively by courier who will provide full tracking and tracing of the consignment, normally over the internet.

In addition to the normal freight rates, more companies are offering consolidation services that operate on a periodic basis – usually once a week at the weekend. The rates that can be obtained if a consolidation service is used can dramatically reduce the cost of air freight. However, there is a price to be paid in time.

Having the correct documentation is essential for any exporter, and documentation starts when the order is taken. The following is a check list of points that should be gone through to ensure that the final documentation will be correct:

▶ If there are any import restrictions in a particular country, ensure that the customer has the necessary documentation such as, for example, the necessary import licence or foreign exchange allocation licence;

► Be aware of customs regulations and banned or prohibited items. Some countries require a certificate of origin (CO) and/or a consular invoice to accompany the goods, in addition to any other documentation. A certificate of origin may need the involvement of the local chamber of commerce. A consular invoice needs the commercial invoice to be sent to the importer's consulate for stamping and approval before the goods are despatched;

► Ask if there is a requirement for the shipment to be inspected before it is shipped. This is known as obtaining clean report findings. This process can take anything up to three weeks from the time that the goods are packed and ready to be shipped until clearance for shipping is given, and you will need to have all invoices and shipping documents ready at the time of inspection. Note that when an inspection before shipment is known to be a requirement, a pro forma invoice will always have to be raised before the official order being given;

► If the country is remote, check on vessel frequencies before promising delivery dates;

► If the transaction is by letter of credit, ensure that the expiry date is well behind the shipping date.

Common documents are listed below.

Air waybill

An air transport term for the document made out on behalf of the sender as evidence of the contract of carriage by air freight; it is also called an air consignment note. The air waybill contains the following details:

► the place and date of execution
► the place of departure and the place of destination
► the name and address of the consignor
► the name and address of the first carrier
► the name and address of the consignee
► the nature of the goods
► the number of packages, type mark and numbers
► the weight, quantity, volume or dimensions of the consignment
► the name and address of the party who is liable for the payment of the freight and incidental charges.

Documentation

► if the goods are sent for payment cash on delivery, the price of the goods and, if necessary, the amount of expenses incurred;
► where required, the value specially declared for insurance by the carrier;
► where required, the amount of the value declared to the carrier increasing the liability;
► the number of parts of the air waybill;
► a list of the documents handed to the carrier to accompany the air waybill;
► the time fixed for each completion of the carriage and a brief note of the route to be followed;

▶ a statement that the carriage is subject to the rules relating to liability established by the Warsaw Convention;

▶ the freight, incidental expenses, date and place of payment.

Bill of lading

A bill of lading fulfils three important functions:

▶ it is the receipt issued to the exporter by or on behalf of the shipping company for goods accepted for carriage;

▶ it is evidence of a contract between two parties and will include an undertaking from the shipping company to deliver the goods in the same condition as they were received;

▶ it is a document of title to the goods.

Usually prepared by the exporter or freight forwarder, the bill of lading should contain a description of the goods, terms of carriage, name of the vessel and the port of discharge.

It is then signed by the shipping company and issued in sets of one or more, known as negotiable bills of lading.

Any one set gives title to the goods, the number of copies comprising a full set being shown on each. If the carrier receives the goods in apparent good order, a clean bill of lading will be issued. If, however, the shipping company considers there is a defect in the goods or their packing, the bill of lading will be claused to this effect. These bills are known as claused or dirty bills of lading and may provide the buyer with contractual reasons for refusing to accept the goods.

Importers will normally require an exporter to produce bills of lading as evidence that goods have been shipped on board. When a bill of lading merely states 'received for shipment', there is a risk that the goods are lying on the dock waiting for the next vessel.

Title to the goods passes on endorsement and delivery of an original bill of lading.

The shipping company will release the goods at their port of destination against presentation of the first original bill of lading – it is, therefore, essential that proper control be exercised over these title documents. Non-negotiable or unsigned bills of lading – not forming part of a set – are sometimes supplied for statistical purposes.

When goods are shipped on cost, insurance and freight (CIF) or on cost and freight (CFR) terms, it is important to ensure that freight is paid and that bills of lading are marked accordingly.

Carnet

This is an international customs document allowing temporary duty-free import of certain goods into certain countries. There are two types: ECS for commercial samples, and ATA for exhibitions. Carnets are obtainable from the major chambers of commerce.

Certificate of origin

The certificate is completed by the exporter and then submitted with copies of the commercial invoice to the chamber of commerce for authorisation. In the case of Arab countries, there is an Arabic version of the form that must be certified by the Arab/British Chamber of Commerce in London.

Methods of payment

Certified invoice

Some countries insist on all invoices being certified by an authorised person. The most common form of certification is: 'We hereby certify this invoice is true and correct and the only one issued by us for the above goods'.

Consular invoice

An importing country may insist that goods are accompanied by an invoice that is certified by its own consul in the exporting country.

Inspection certificate

Certain countries, notably African countries, require inspection of consignments (usually when the invoice value is over a certain amount). On receipt of an order, a pro forma invoice is raised and sent to the importer. The importer obtains an import licence (sometimes called an import declaration form (IDF)), which prompts the inspection company in the UK to raise a request for information (RFI) form that must be completed before an inspection can be carried out. Once inspection is completed, the order can be despatched. The exporter must then submit a copy of the final commercial invoices and details of despatch, at which point a clean report of finding (CRF) is issued. Without a CRF, customs clearance cannot be completed.

Collection system

The seller collates all the documents that are required by the buyer. The documents are entrusted to the seller's bank (the remitting bank) with detailed instructions of the action the bank is to take. The bank sends the documents to its correspondent bank in the buyer's country repeating the seller's instruction.

The correspondent bank (the collecting bank) approaches the buyer and attempts to collect payment, holding the documents until payment is received. When payment is made, the documents are released to the buyer and payment remitted to the seller.

The handling of collections by banks is in many cases regulated by rules drawn up by the International Chamber of Commerce (ICC). Anyone entrusting documents to a bank for collection is recommended to obtain and read a copy of these rules. However, the system is well established and, providing that full instructions are given to the bank at the beginning of the process, there is little risk of error as long as the buyer is willing to take up the documents.

Bill of exchange (B/E)

Documents sent for collection of funds are frequently accompanied by a bill of exchange (sometimes referred to as a draft or a bill for collection), which is distinguished by being a negotiable instrument, i.e. title to the money that the bill represented can be transferred to another party by simple endorsement to the bill. The time at which a bill is due for payment is known as the tenor of the bill:

▶ Immediately at sight draft
▶ Future date at usance payment.

Immediately at sight draft

Where payment is made on sight of documents, a bill of exchange serves little useful function. It may be advisable to dispose of it in the drawee's country – it may be liable to stamp duty.

Future date at usance payment

Where payment is to be made some time in the future, a bill of exchange provides a way of allowing buyers to take possession of the documents and, therefore, the goods that they represent while giving sellers an assurance that they will receive payment when it is due. This is done by requiring drawees to accept bills by writing words to that effect on them and signing their acceptance.

The addition of an acceptance to a bill of exchange imparts an existence completely separate from the documents to which it relates. It also separates it from the underlying trade transaction and enables bill holders to take advantage of the protection of the extensive legislation governing the operation of bills of exchange (in the UK this is based on the Bills of Exchange Act, 1882). If the bill is not paid after being properly presented at maturity, the holder is able to sue its acceptors as well as any or all of the previous holders of the bill. This extends right back to the original drawers. The security afforded by this right has facilitated the development of the bill of exchange as a financial instrument.

For exporters, the use of a bill for collection means that they may safely part with documents relating to goods despatched overseas. This may include the bill of lading, which represents actual title to the goods, as the documents will be released to the buyers only when they have either paid for the goods or given a solemn undertaking by acceptance of a bill of exchange that payment will be made at a future date.

If payment or acceptance is not forthcoming, the seller's documents remain in the hands of the banks acting as their agents. In this way, control over the goods can be maintained and steps taken for their protection pending resale or return. For this reason, it is important to give full instruction to remitting banks when entrusting collection to them for details of what to cover in these instructions.

CAD

CAD stands for cash against documents 'c/o bank'. Goods and documents are sent to a bank with instructions that they are to be handed over to the buyer only in exchange for the sum due.

Letter of credit (L/C)

There are many forms of letters of credit, but basically it is a letter addressed by a bank in the importing country to a bank in the exporting country authorising the latter, under certain conditions, to advance a sum of money.

The only form providing a complete security of payment to the exporter is the confirmed irrevocable letter of credit. This letter of credit carries the absolute guarantee of the issuing bank and is confirmed (guaranteed) also by the home bank acting as the agent of the issuing bank. It cannot be cancelled (revoked) or amended without the consent of the beneficiary (the exporter), the opener (consignee) and the two banks concerned.

The exporter will be advised by the home bank acting as agent for the issuing bank of the terms of credit. These will usually state that certain specified goods must be despatched by a stated date and must be accompanied by specified documents. On presentation of the necessary documents, the exporter receives immediate payment.

Documents required under a letter of credit are usually:

► a bill of lading

► an insurance policy (or certificate)

► a commercial invoice.

In addition, other documents, such as a consular invoice and certificate of origin, may be required to meet customs requirements. There are a number of points to be watched carefully when a letter of credit is received, among the more important being:

► Is the letter of credit irrevocable? Is it confirmed by a recognised bank?

► Are the names and addresses of opener and beneficiary spelt correctly?

► Do the expiry and shipping dates give sufficient time to assure payment?

► Is the L/C amount sufficient to cover the order plus all charges?

► Is the description of the goods correct?

► Is the quantity correct?

► Is trans-shipment prohibited where this is physically impossible?

► Are part-shipments forbidden when there are likely to be several consignments?

► Is shipment permitted from any port in the UK, or only one named port?

► Does the L/C request a certificate of insurance or insist on a policy?

► Can properly executed documents be obtained in time to conform to the letter of credit, e.g. the consular invoice, certificate of inspection and certificate of origin?

In the event of any discrepancy being found, the matter should be taken up immediately with the bank and the customer requesting the necessary amendments. Rarely will a bank accept documents that do not conform exactly to the requirements of a L/C (letter of credit). Points in the journey are identified by contractual terms called incoterms.

Ex Works (EXW)

Goods simply need to be placed at the disposal of the buyer at a named place of delivery. This is usually the seller's premises, but it should be noted that the seller has no responsibility for loading the goods or ensuring that they leave the factory or warehouse grounds.

Free carrier (FCA)

The seller must deliver the goods into the custody of the carrier named by the buyer at the specified terminal. This often refers to an inland depot in the UK that might be a

Customs clearance depot, or, in cases where the goods are a full load direct from the exporter's premises, the point at which the goods are loaded onto the vehicle provided by the buyer or are handed over to the carrier. This term is appropriate to all modes of transport, that is:

▶ *Sea*. Container base or a full container load taken over by the sea carrier

▶ *Air*. Airport

▶ *Road*. Carrier's depot or full load loaded on buyer's vehicle

▶ *Rail*. Goods or loaded wagon handed over to rail carrier.

Free alongside ship (FAS)

The seller must deliver the goods alongside the named vessel at the named port of shipment. This is quite unusual in the UK.

Free on board (FOB)

The seller must deliver the goods on board the vessel named by the buyer and bear the risk of loss or damage until the goods cross the ship's rail at the port of shipment. While it is common for the seller to actually book the shipping space, it should be noted that, technically, it is the buyer's responsibility. The expression 'FOB with services' describes the situation in which the seller arranges the space booking.

Cost and freight (CFR)/cost, insurance and freight (CIF)

When goods are sent CFR, the seller must arrange and pay for the carriage of the goods to the named port of destination. When goods are sent CIF, the seller must also arrange the cargo insurance of the goods to the named port of destination.

Terms of trade

However, in both of these cases, the risk of loss or damage to the goods passes at ship's rail at the port of shipment, in exactly the same way as with an FOB contract. While this might appear to be a contradiction, it is possible for an overseas buyer to make a claim on the insurance taken out by the exporter, in that there is a transfer of insurable interest at the ship's rail, port of shipment. Thus the terms CFR and CIF are definitions of who pays for what, rather than who is responsible for what.

Carriage paid to (CPT)/Carriage and insurance paid (CIP)

With goods sent CPT, the seller arranges and pays for the carriage to the agreed point, which will invariably be a depot at destination. When goods are sent CIP, the seller also arranges and pays for cargo insurance to the agreed point. In both of these cases the risk of loss or damage to the goods passes at the same point as in a CFR contract, i.e. when the first carrier takes over the goods, which will be at the UK depot or where the full load is taken over. Just as with FOB, CFR and CIF contracts, in which the risk passes at ship's rail, port of shipment, the same logic applies to FCA, CPT and CIP and the risk passes when the first carrier takes over the goods.

Delivered ex ship (DES)

The seller arranges and pays for the carriage to the named port of destination, and must place the goods at the disposal of the buyer on board the vessel.

Delivered ex quay (DEQ)

The seller arranges and pays for the carriage to the named quay at destination and must place the goods at the disposal of the buyer, cleared duty paid.

Delivered at frontier (DAF)

The seller arranges and pays for the carriage to the named point of delivery at the frontier. There is no obligation to arrange cargo insurance and risk passes at the frontier.

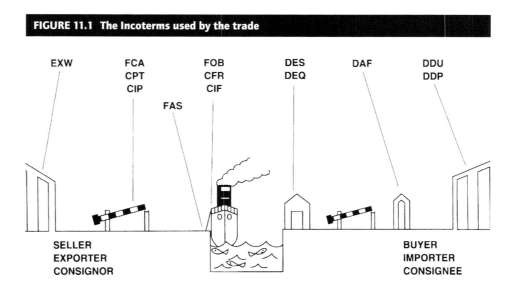

FIGURE 11.1 The Incoterms used by the trade

Source: Pira International Ltd

Delivered duty unpaid (DDU)

The seller arranges and pays for carriage to the named place of destination. There is no obligation for insurance and the import clearance charges are the responsibility of the buyer.

Delivered duty paid (DDP)

The seller must make all arrangements, and pay the costs, of delivery to the specified destination. There is no obligation to arrange insurance. In the cases of DDU and DDP, the specified destination is often the buyer's premises.

An examination of these terms will reveal immediately that an ex works contract is much easier for the exporter than a DDP contract. However, the seller must consider what the buyer might prefer in terms of a package deal rather than simply take the easy way out by quoting ex works.

Also, the exporter should appreciate that for several of these terms, the obligations for transport and insurance, often to overseas destinations, differ from the point at which the risk of loss or damage passes from the seller to the buyer.

The final point to make about the selection of appropriate trade terms is relevant to the introduction of the relatively new terms of FCA, CPT and CIP. Their introduction reflects the increased use of electronic messages rather than paper, and the changing nature of international movements. The traditional port to port transit of goods, where the ship's rail was an important point in the journey, has given way to the depot to depot movement of unitised (mostly containerised) loads.

What this leads to is the, almost heretical, statement that FOB, CFR and CIF are actually obsolete for the majority of exports and imports. The fact that they are still the most commonly used terms is somewhat unfortunate.

The function of a freight forwarder can vary from a comprehensive service including packing, full documentation, customs clearance, pick and delivery – all from non-technical instructions by the customer – to a specialised service covering any part of the freight operation, e.g. customs clearance of a package at an airport and its delivery to a recipient at the other end.

The customer is buying both information and service, and may need one or other or both in varying degrees. Functions can, therefore, cover packing, delivery and associated clerical activity, or only a particular complicated part of a limited consignment.

Freight forwarding: agents and services

Freight forwarders specialise either in market areas, types of commodity or methods of freight and it is important to find a company with the right interests.

Choosing a freight forwarder

The Institute of Freight Forwarders has lists of members, but membership is not compulsory and the Institute has no legal responsibility to the customer. The best method is to seek quotations for specific and typical tasks, and compare costs and methods. Ask for detailed explanations on procedures and methods of freighting.

A customer whose needs are specific and limited might well find a small forwarder that specialises in the type of business required; a customer without their own shipping department, but with widely varying and continuous demands, is likely to need one of the bigger international forwarders to provide a flexible range of services.

There are about 3000 freight forwarders in the UK, but more than a third are small operations with only a few customers, serving limited markets. The larger agents with international connections advertise widely but often still specialise, so comparative costing of services is essential. A useful additional test is for the customer to ask the forwarder for the names of similar customers and ask their views on the service provided.

Functions of a freight forwarder

A customer with diverse needs may be well advised to use different freight forwarders who specialise in different markets or methods of despatch. Air freight and sea freight, for example, involve vastly different disciplines, and a company based at Heathrow which spends most of its time arranging customs clearance on air freight of weekly magazines may not be the right operator to organise the containerisation of loads of books from Hong Kong to Southampton. Equally, freight shipments to west Africa and the Middle East have very specific requirements in terms of documentation and logistics that require an experienced company. In an enquiry, specify clearly whether you want a packing service, whether you need transport arranged at every stage or only in part, whether or not you need total help with documentation and how important deadlines are to your delivery.

Consolidation

A freight forwarder should be able to advise on whether consolidation is feasible, but some have much better access to consolidation arrangements than others. Broadly, consolidation consists of arranging groups of freight from different customers into economic units. There may be delays in waiting for the consolidation unit to be arranged, but there may be substantial savings. Air freight and sea container consolidations to popular locations are quick, effective and are widely used by all types of manufacturer. Some of the bigger printers are now able to offer consolidation services, especially those who have started mailing and despatch operations which tie-in with their production facilities.

Insurance

Never assume that a transport company insures its freight for the client's benefit. Transport companies and agents involved in the transport of freight often do have insurance cover, but normally it is to protect their own liability and rarely covers the case of the client who will want to make a claim on his own behalf. A good starting point, therefore, is to discuss with the agent, freight forwarder, or transporter whether he has insurance and, if so, whether it serves your purposes. Frequently it will not.

Insurance through the freight forwarder

There is some advantage in establishing whether it is possible, or sensible, to arrange insurance through your freight forwarder. Although this may not immediately appear to be the cheapest form of insurance (one would expect the extra work caused to the freight forwarder to be charged in some way), it is often the most economic alternative in the long run for a variety of reasons. First, the freight forwarder knows (or should) the insurance market from having traded extensively in the sort of transport involved. Second, he has the advantage of an established trading relationship with a broker or insurance company and this is likely to make quotations and claims easier. Third, he is likely to have the advantage of a volume of business and can use his buying power to negotiate competitive rates.

Insurance through a specialist broker

Alternatively, use a specialist insurance broker that has knowledge of with transport insurance. This is likely to be a sensible route for a company transporting small amounts of freight (especially in the UK) without the help of a freight forwarder. Such a company is unlikely to have extensive contacts in the insurance industry, but can be assured of a sensible proposal by obtaining competitive quotations from brokers. Dealing direct with an insurance company is, of course, possible and in many cases desirable, but it may be costly in terms of time and effort spent in identifying the most suitable company and the most competitive quotation. Many big printers and publishers deal direct with insurance companies and have found this the most cost-effective system, but that is because they are transporting large volumes on a constant basis and have great experience of the market.

Premiums are normally calculated as a percentage of the total sum insured and it is, therefore, necessary to be pragmatic if you are to avoid unduly large premiums. It is impossible to give advice for all circumstances, since much depends on your assessment of the scale of the disaster if something goes wrong with the shipment. This may range from total bankruptcy, say in the case of a very large order being delivered by a small company, to an annoying hiatus, say in the case of a small order and a large company. A common form of cover is known as CIF plus 10%, which embraces the insurance of the goods at manufactured cost, the insurance cost and, of course, freight plus 10% of the total to cover other items.

Print supply chain impacts

Printers and their customers are increasingly looking to save time and money across all areas of the print supply chain. Examining areas outside the design, prepress, printing and finishing arenas offers opportunities to save hidden costs by doing things differently. Printers may broaden their service offerings to manage stock on behalf of a client, allowing them to manufacture in as efficient a method as possible. Others take the opportunity to produce in a different manner to provide overall improvements across a whole chain.

Business process re-engineering opportunities through the use of digital printing

As well as the technological developments, digital printing will allow suppliers to change the supply chains of several industries. Many digital print users are moving from being a manufacturer to a service provider. Two markets where the application of technology will change the shape of part of the supply industry are books and packaging. In both these sectors the position of printing in the supply chain is set to change as publishers, brand owners and retailers act to improve their profitability.

Packaging/POS industry change

The development of inkjet machines offers the possibility of decorating irregular shapes and surfaces. Using print-on-demand techniques, with printing an integral part of the filling or packing line, can provide radical change for the typical supply chain. There are great potential savings from minimising warehousing costs (of product and packaging) that would be balanced against the higher unit cost of the digital print. The technology has considerable appeal to marketers in providing significant savings of cost and time in developing new products and helping them lower their time to market. This might involve changing product ingredients at short notice to take advantage of changing commodity prices or on-pack promotional offers.

An early example is the integration of inkjet printing at Philips Lighting's fluorescent tube production lines in Roosendaal (in the Netherlands). The solution was developed by Belgian distributor Elink, using HSAJet printers from Danish machine manufacturer HS Automatic, incorporating Xaar's XJ126 and XJ500 print heads. Philips wanted to have the flexibility to print barcodes, customer logos, images and marketing messages onto product packaging while reducing costs and lowering product lead times. The line was designed to print advertising campaign materials and co-branding, as well as allow changes to packaging designs at short notice and without incurring additional printing costs.

FIGURE 11.2 Xaar heads positioned in the Philips Lighting line in Roosendal, the Netherlands

Source: AD Communications

Before installing the integrated inkjet printers Philips outsourced its printed label requirements for packaging, buying pre-printed labels that were attached to the packaging. This was costly, had no variable data capability and required considerable inventory for multi-language packs across the variety of brands. The company felt conventional methods were unable to accommodate customers' changing requirements for more flexibility and customisation. Philips explored in-house coding and marking, which led to it looking at ways of printing in full colour.

Elink provided a tailor-made, fully automated two-stage variable printing process integrated into Philips Lighting's main production line; the system went live in August 2003. The first printers in the line print full-colour graphics and text on the product's primary packaging sleeve. The other heads then apply a single colour logo directly onto the secondary packaging – cardboard boxes that wrap around the outer casing. They can also mark the tubes directly if required.

The integrated line allowed Philips to reduce its packaging stock references from 6000 to 200, so the company no longer has to order large volumes of pre-printed labels. Software controls the coding and marking applications for each product line. The machines enable the specification of different packaging materials late in the packaging process, through their ability to print on different substrates. The variable data printing capability has lowered Philips' dependency on external suppliers. This has significantly reduced business costs, and thus justified the investment.

FIGURE 11.3 Secondary printed boxes

Source: AD Communications

FIGURE 11.4 Primary sleeves printed on the integrated inkjet line

Source: AD Communications

Retailers looking to reduce their costs and time are showing considerable interest. In the conventional carton printing process there are five points of stock storage before any product gets to the retailer (Figure 11.5).

FIGURE 11.5 Outline of conventional carton packaging supply chain

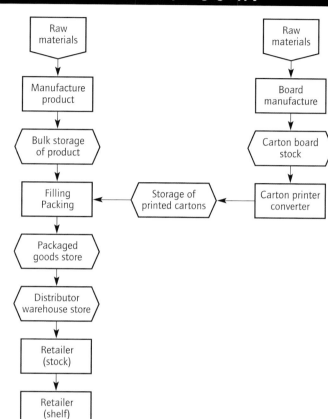

Source: Pira International Ltd

To eliminate these stock holdings, a digital on-demand carton printing operation might be set up, either at the product manufacturer or at a contract filling/packing operation. In both instances, the printing process is integrated into the filling operation. Product is packed only in response to an order from the retailer and directly despatched to the store for shelf filling and selling. This dramatically reduces the turnaround time and eliminates need for stocks of printed cartons, packed goods and stocks in the distribution chain.

When product is filled at the manufacturer, a further efficiency may be gained by manufacturing product to order instead of distributing stock, as well as the packing/filling. This eliminates the bulk storage of product. There may be an option for a digital printer to work with the manufacturer to operate and install the digital print line in partnership as the manufacturer is unlikely to have the core skills.

FIGURE 11.6 On demand manufacture of product and carton/filling supply chain

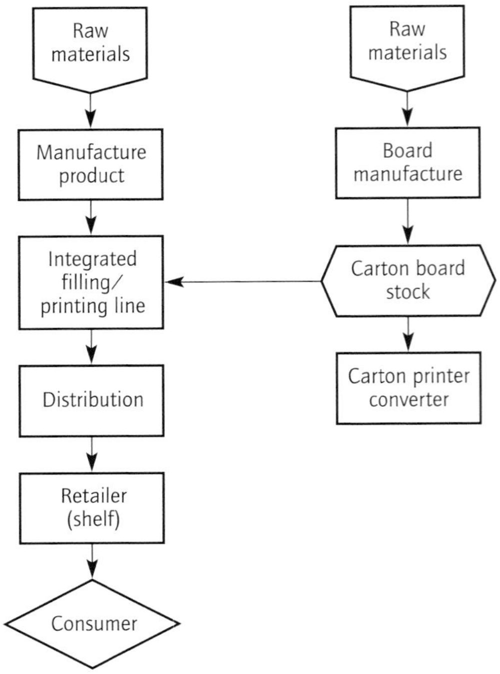

Source: Pira International Ltd

Taking this further, a retailer may choose to operate an in-store manufacture and pack system, or have the product delivered in bulk and fill on demand. This scenario allows potentially significant efficiencies for large retailers but places new demands on the printing/filling operation. The line should require a very low (ideally zero) skill operation, running at relatively low speeds with no need for maintenance. To be widespread, such lines will also be low capital to provide the distributed operation.

FIGURE 11.7 In-store printing and filling operation

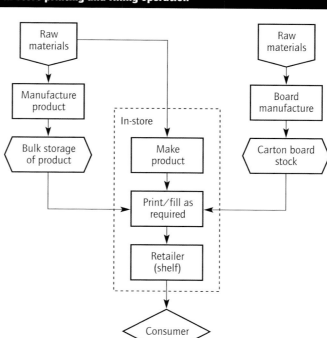

Source: Pira International Ltd

The main driver for change in the production of packaging is growing competition in the retail market. The lead time for new product launches is increasingly shorter, with more launches of specialist, niche products that need short-run packaging. Some sectors, such as pharmaceuticals, are looking to incorporate more information on the primary packaging. In the case of multi-size and multi-language packs the range of packaging is significant and managing the supply chain effectively can be very complex. Brand owners are demanding reduced lead times and smaller batch sizes to allow them to supply their goods off the shelf whenever their retailer customers place an order. This presages a change from make to batch, with its low productivity levels for short runs, and interrupting batches, because the time demanded by customers for changeover and reconciliation procedures may be disproportionate to the time actually spent producing packaging. Many packaging suppliers are moving to a make-to-stock system, using developments in inkjet printing technology to make changing design and decoration fast and easy.

These demands from the customers of packaging producers are the key factors driving the need to manufacture based on forecast. This will have a significant impact in the package printing industry, from secondary packaging applications, such as case-coding, to full-colour imaging directly onto primary packaging. Inkjet printing is poised to be accepted alongside established printing methods, and, in some applications, may replace them altogether in time. The range of inks and equipment makes direct inkjet printing possible on a wide range of substrates, e.g. paper, boards, plastic, foils and metal.

The above examples involve considerable cooperation between printer, publisher or product manufacturer and retailer. These changes have occurred in other supply chains; look at the demise of mass bakeries following the installation of in-store breadmaking. Twenty-five years ago that was unthinkable; now it is commonplace. Digital printing offers packagers the potential for producing personalised products and a variety of standard pack designs. In pharmaceutical carton manufacture, end user details might be incorporated onto the box, perhaps in large print for an elderly patient making the carton more secure.

Book publishing change

Books are a very successful application of digital printing in the commercial printing sector. Many book printers have embraced digital printing in order to offer publishers very low print runs, so allowing more titles to remain in print. There are two business models for printing books digitally:

▶ In the on-demand model, the publisher or self-published author pays a fee to get a book into the system, and then pays a much smaller printing fee for each copy of the title. Books are printed when needed, possibly singly, by distributors and book sellers. Ingram's Lightning Source is the most advanced example of centralised on-demand printing by a distributor. Transactions with the book buyer are handled by a bookstore passing orders to Lightning Source, or via web e-procurement. For printing on demand at book shops, a distributed system with printing and binding equipment is needed. It must be a compact system to produce the textbook block, colour cover, perfect binding and trimming. It must be easy to use by retail personnel and low investment in order to justify the production of a few copies a day.

▶ The short-run scenario involves printing small batches of books, perhaps 20–500 copies, as a standard order placed by the publisher and the printer. From the publisher's perspective, there is no operational difference between short-run digital printing and ordinary offset runs. In both cases, books are shipped to the warehouse or the distributor where they wait until orders are received. The advantage of digital printing is that less working capital is tied up in the print run than if offset is used, although the unit cost of each book is higher. Most are produced as part of the manufacturing capability of a book-printing company or group as a short-run arm.

One of the key benefits offered by digital printing is improved efficiency in the supply chains of printed products through reduced costs and time saved in the overall process. The book publishing market, where the cost of unsold books and maintaining lists in print are major problems, is one of the early adopters of digital print. There are now several well-publicised examples of print-on-demand (POD) applications replacing conventional book manufacturing.

The area of greatest change – enabled by digital printing – is the printing and manufacture of books. The abandonment of the net book agreement and the arrival of

new retailers, supermarkets and internet booksellers has impacted this market. The
conventional chain is shown in Figure 11.8.

FIGURE 11.8 Conventional book supply chain

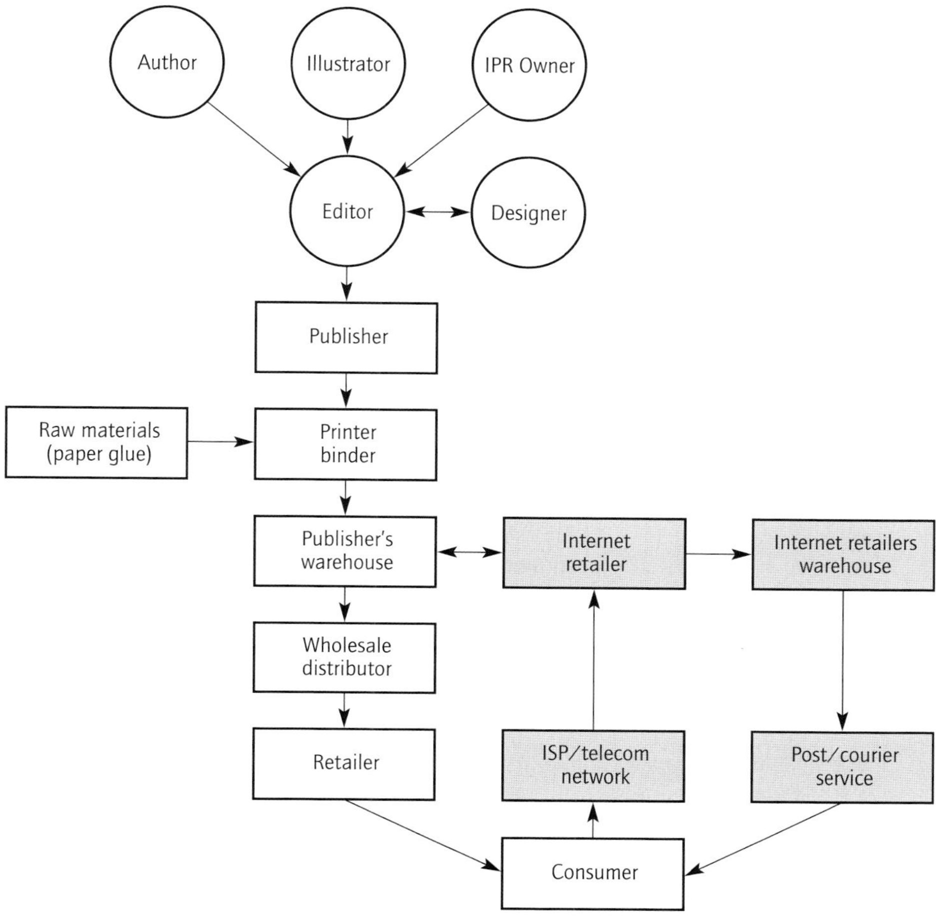

Source: Pira International Ltd

Traditional book manufacturing used mostly offset litho printing and binding. The
books are made for stock, which is supplied into publishers' warehouses and then distributed
to the retail bookshops. Internet booksellers are now established retailers, often having their
own warehouse and using courier services or the post to deliver titles to consumers.

With digital printing technology, the concepts of the virtual warehouse and in-
store production become reality. In the virtual warehouse printing is still centralised but
books are digitally printed on demand. For these books there is no stock and no need for
warehousing. Systems such as Océ's Bookstore are being offered to allow the virtual
concept at printer or distributor. They can receive files and orders remotely to satisfy clients

regardless of location. Printing may be at a printer or somewhere in the distribution chain – as is the case with Lightning Print – eliminating the conventional printing stage and the need to transport books to the distribution centre. They claim a mutually advantageous situation for customer, bookseller, publisher and author. The loser is the conventional printer and warehouse.

Amazon.com bought US POD specialist Booksurge in 2005 as part of its strategy to control the future supply channel and produce titles that are difficult for customers to access. Amazon will take an increased share of the value chain by producing titles internally and developing new revenue streams to enable lower book prices. Booksurge has international print facility partnerships in Europe, South America, Australia and Canada. The company will continue to fulfil and distribute book orders around the world, printing from one to 1000 copies. Bookforce, in Grantham, UK, is Booksurge's UK partner and provides trade paperbacks and binding, in addition to author sales support and distribution throughout the UK. Amazon is getting direct access to specialised content in preference to direct competition.

With on-demand printing there is reduced waste. Evidence suggests that up to 30% of stock in the chain remains unsold and may have to be repulped. As many books are supplied to retailers on a sale-or-return basis there are clear opportunities to increase efficiency with the print-on-demand model. Publishers then produce only books that have been ordered. Taking this one stage further leads to in-store production shown in Figure 11.9. In this scenario a low-cost, easy-to-operate, digital print-and-bind system is housed within the bookstore to produce a book for the customer while he waits.

FIGURE 11.9 In-store production for books

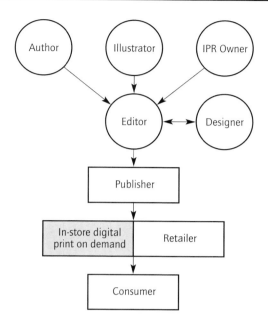

Source: Pira International Ltd

Digital printing offers a better way of doing some things. It may well take over from conventional printing in the long term, but in the medium term it is more likely to be used in combination with conventional technology. Hybrid systems are becoming increasingly popular in commercial printing. In litho many sheetfed machines use flexo varnishing and coating units as well as specialist printing units and there is a trend towards incorporating a digital printing capability. This first appeared in the label sector with Mark Andy and Nilpeter adding laser and inkjet technology to their unit press designs. Agfa and Thieme developed their hybrid inkjet/silk screen line, the M-Press, which joined other hybrids used in the label sector. Mark Andy has long offered the dotrix inkjet head for use with its flexo, gravure, offset and screen units, configured as the customer requires. Chromas Technologies is a flexo press manufacturer that offers a variety of printing technology solutions. The Argio 75 SC is an optional assembly using Spectra inkjet heads that can be integrated into its product line to create a hybrid flexo/inkjet system.

Heidelberg has a relationship with Domino to distribute inkjet machines through its sales channels in certain markets and showed a sheetfed machine with Domino Bitjet technology with a variable data printing capability for addresses and personalising text in-line at Drupa in 2000. Spectra has a long-term licensing relationship with Heidelberg. Their first links were shown at Drupa in 2000 with the page-wide VDP 921 imprinting unit integrated with an A3 Quickmaster press. Xaar and MAN Roland have a joint collaboration to explore and develop digital inkjet printing systems for coating applications to be used in traditional offset printing presses. In 2004 KBA bought Metronic, a specialist manufacturer of inkjet printing systems to expand its product range into new, high-potential markets. Web offset printers have long used Domino Videojet heads for text printing, and wide-format Kodak VersaMark heads for more sophisticated in-line personalisation.

In 2005 Müller Martini announced a hybrid version of its Concepta variable size web offset press, where the machine links four-colour offset printing with two VersaMark inkjet units. The press is capable of printing at speeds of up to 1000ft/min with in-line customisation for the direct mail and other commercial printing markets.

The likelihood of using hybrid technology is high with the impact of the development also significant as printers look at ways to increase productivity. The main developments over the next ten years will be the integration of digital printing, particularly the more flexible inkjet, into conventional sheet and web machines. This will allow multiple versioning and personalisation applications to be produced more efficiently in a single process.

Production control systems

12

Production control of printing is changing through the introduction of computer-integrated manufacturing (CIM) techniques, many based on job definition format (JDF), to link a management information system (MIS) to specific pieces of production equipment. In 2005 it is still the technology leaders and early adopters that have working systems in place with many others examining the potential for their businesses. The industry as a whole is in transition from analogue to digital control. Digital offers significant rewards in terms of major productivity increases, but the main change will be increased customer communication leading to more process transparency and control for the print buyer.

Printers are offering more ways for their customers to communicate with them. Sales contact, telephone, letter, fax, e-mail are being joined by e-enabled systems to handle the process of obtaining estimates, selecting the supplier then managing and tracking the production process. The methods of dealing with printers may be changing, but the reasons and topics to be handled remain the same.

It is important that customers provide the most detailed information when making an enquiry. Previous versions of this manual have reproduced various forms used in the genesis of print projects, which were aimed primarily at publication work. Several of these have been updated and retained.

They have been printed on unnumbered pages with no running heads so that you may photocopy or reproduce them if you wish, and add your company name where appropriate. No permissions or fees are necessary.

Alternatively, you may adapt them for other purposes. It is impossible to cover every type of product or every production process, and you are free to modify the forms, convert them to electronic files or use them as you wish. Over time, there will be greater use of electronic versions – based on a print production standard, probably JDF – with expert help available to specify and track any print project through its development.

The reason for having analogue or electronic forms is to provide a check list of actions to ensure that all aspects of managing a print job are covered. There are three basic stages to follow:
► commissioning
► manage production
► project completion and performance monitoring.
Individual companies will have their own internal budgetary procedures, and the following is offered as a generic catch-all.

Commissioning It is important organisations check that a proposed print project is justified financially where it is appropriate (a published item will recoup costs, a marketing piece provides maximum benefit for expenditure). The first details of an intended project should provide estimates of costs and, where applicable, revenues to determine an outline cost-benefit for the project. Potential marketing revenue is offset against editorial, production and distribution costs, perhaps in several alternative quantities or specifications. This provides the information to determine the viability of the project, and the approval to proceed is given.

PRINTING SPECIFICATION / ENQUIRY FORM	Ref number
	Order number
	Date

To   _____

                  _____

                  _____

                  _____

                  _____

Author and Title _____

Trimmed page size _____

Extent _____

Quantities _____

Text   COPY PROVIDED _____

        PRINTING _____

        PAPER _____

Covers COPY PROVIDED _____

        PRINTING _____

        MATERIAL _____

        FINISH _____

Binding style   _____

                      _____

Packing specification _____

                      _____

Price for _____ copies CIF _____ = _____

Price for _____ run-on copies CIF _____ = _____

Quotation valid for all work completed before _____

                           Signature _____

| **COMPANY:** |

PAPER ORDER

Ref number
Order number
Date

To _____
_____
_____
_____
_____

Author and Title

Paper specification Quality _____

Sheets/Reels Quantity _____

Size _____ Long/ Short Grain

Substance gsm _____ Volume/Caliper _____

Note: paper purchased on reels is subject to the specifications issued by the printer to whom delivery is to be made.

Printing process Litho/Letterpress   1 colour/2 colour/4 colour

Delivery to _____
_____
_____

Delivery Date _____

Packing Guillotine trimmed/precision cut
Reels/Sheets/bulk packed on pallets/reamwrapped

Price _____ Signature _____

Special Instructions

Important Ensure that the outer wrapping of the paper is marked with quantity, substance, size, description, name, order number and author/title.
Inform immediately of any alteration to the delivery date.
Notify consignee of despatch in advance.

COMPANY:

AIRFREIGHT INSTRUCTION FORM
for attention of freight forwarding company

Ref number
Order number
Date

From	Contact	Telephone No.

INSTRUCTION TO ARRANGE AIR FREIGHT DESPATCH OF THE FOLLOWING CONSIGNMENT BY
CONSOLIDATION/DIRECT IATA SERVICE/CHARTER SERVICE

COLLECT FROM _____

MARKS AND NUMBERS	NO OF PKGES	DESCRIPTION	GROSS WEIGHT	DIMENSIONS OF PACKAGES	FOB VALUE	VALUE FOR CARRIAGE

CONSIGN TO

CHARGES PAYABLE BY: (Delete as required)	
DOMICILE CHARGES	SHIPPER/CONSIGNEE
AIRFREIGHT	SHIPPER/CONSIGNEE
FOB. CHARGES	SHIPPER/CONSIGNEE
INSURANCE	SHIPPER/CONSIGNEE

INSURANCE: IS/IS NOT REQUIRED. AMOUNT £

ALSO NOTIFY

DOCUMENTS ATTACHED

OTHER INSTRUCTIONS

RESTRICTED ARTICLES DECLARATION - TO BE COMPLETED
AND SIGNED FOR ALL CONSIGNMENTS
(DELETE INAPPLICABLE SECTION)

THIS CONSIGNMENT CONTAINS MATERIAL OF A HAZARDOUS
NATURE AND IS SUBJECT TO THE CURRENT DANGEROUS
GOODS REGULATIONS.

THIS CONSIGNMENT DOES NOT CONTAIN ANY HAZARDOUS
MATERIAL AND IS NOT SUBJECT TO THE CURRENT
DANGEROUS GOODS REGULATIONS.

NOTE: AN AIRWAYBILL IS NOT NEGOTIABLE

Indicate if consignment is under any form of Customs Export
Control   YES/NO

Signed

**No insurance is effected except upon express
instructions given in writing above.**

ISSUE OF EEC/T DOCUMENTS

Issue T2L forms on our behalf. We declare that the goods
are in free circulation and eligible for EEC preference.

Signature

Signed

COMPANY:

GENERAL PRINTING ENQUIRY FORM

For the attention of:	Customer Full Name and Address, new prospects include TEL, FAX & POSTCODE	Date
Salesman / Div		Quote Required By

Quantity	Form Title/Reference Number:	No. of Makings	No. of Deliveries

Sprocket Punched	Cut Sheet	Book	Pad	Cut Sets	Others: please describe

Depth	Width	No. to View	Parts Per Set	Sets Per Pad/Book	Previous Reference

Part	Material (state if for Laser use)	Ink Front	Reverse (Pantone Ref, if available)	Perforations Horizontal	Vertical	Special Features Punches, etc.

Numbering Details

Collating Details - Continuous Stationery

Bindery Details

Special Notes

Marketing/Pricing Information

The next stage is to provide more accurate costing information along with the timetable of events and changeovers needed. This defines the specification of the piece in detail, possibly requesting alternatives for quantity and paper weight. There should be a formal method of comparing quotes and reaching a decision about the approved supplier. Orders for design, prepress, printing, finishing and distribution can then be placed.

Manage production

Design and prepress work is placed with a record of transmission of any digital files maintained (this is a significant benefit for asset management systems that incorporate a full audit trail). Text, images and make-up must be signed off and approved, with final files being finished and preflighted according to the printer's requirements, and files transmitted along with any hard copy proofs. This formal record serves as a materials hand-over note so that both parties have a record of what has been sent in the event of query. It is important to allow enough time for checking proofs and, if necessary, taking corrective action.

The acceptance of estimates and placing of orders provides a base specification, but it is important to record and agree any variations to the specification, and agree any charges that may result as they occur. The paper order lays out the details needed by a paper merchant or mill to fulfil the paper requirement.

Clear delivery and despatch instructions are necessary along with proof of delivery. When preparing material for export shipping, it is vital to have to hand the details of how the material is packed and how the forwarding agent should proceed with the job. The airfreight form serves as a check list of what is needed to communicate effectively with the freight-forwarding company.

Project completion and performance monitoring

The final invoice amounts should be compared to the estimate, together with an assessment of the on-time delivery and quality, to assess the performance of the suppliers. An actuals v. estimates record will use the information from the detailed estimate to compare with the invoice, and highlight any changes. The use of a formal performance record allows objective comparisons of suppliers to be made over time.

Events and activities, together with tracking and budgetary information, will typically be held as a computerised record. Often the buyer and supplier will have specialist systems to manage these events; the current trend is for such systems to communicate with each other, which provides significant productivity boosts for the administration functions associated with print supply chains.

Electronic methods of production control

The natural progression from using paper-based forms to manage print jobs is to use electronic versions. At the very least these have the benefit of eliminating a great deal of duplication, avoiding the need for administration staff to re-enter data into an internal MIS. Making such systems work is not easy and will involve changing working practices but when properly implemented print suppliers will see significant productivity improvements.

Most suppliers must learn the particular requirements of their customers, as these can vary greatly. But instead of using manual sales and customer services time to understand these requirements there are tools that can help smooth out the complexities of the print supply chain. A better understanding of these requirements will make it easy for clients, and sales and administrative staff to provide the necessary information to complete a project smoothly. These systems offer real-time access to up-to-date information and the other great benefit of electronic production control is that it generates a total audit trail, detailing all activities carried out.

Use of management information systems

The base of an MIS is the collection and analysis of data to manage a function better. Printing and publishing involves a huge amount of detail, and using a computerised system allows the data to be tracked and sorted. This can be used to improve the productivity of staff and the efficiency of the plant.

The printing industry adopted these systems in the late 1980s and used a variety of specialist software suppliers to provide management tools. The particular requirements of printing, a batch manufacturing process involving many inputs and production stages, can be complex. The first suppliers were specialists to the print industry and created computerised estimating and costing systems to handle the requirements of individual print businesses. These were largely successful and the larger printers readily accepted the high cost and drawn-out implementation plans that were needed. It was the larger printers that both needed and could afford systems, but their complexity led to a raft of solutions being available.

The capabilities improved as computers became more powerful and software improved. Printers could buy specialist modules to help the various facets of their businesses such as raw material purchasing, stock control, production planning and scheduling, finance functions, tracking customers and leads. Shop floor data collection systems allowed real-time monitoring of machinery activity, from prepress to the bindery. Tools to allow management control became easier to use and justify financially.

Each of the available modules was developing and becoming a useful tool for the business to control itself. The next change, which is still maturing, was the arrival of the internet and the need for the real-time sharing of information, not only within a printing plant but also with customers, suppliers and partners. Each module not only has to be able to communicate with sister modules, but also with a myriad of other systems. Early integrators provided links to specific systems, often at great cost and time to allow suppliers to link in to their larger customers. These integrations are fraught with difficulty as there is far more to consider than a simple mapping of like-for-like fields across two databases. Early pioneers had degrees of success but quickly faced the prospect of expensive multiple work that needed to be done quickly. When the customer is large and security conscious, such as a financial institution, the costs of compliance can outweigh the benefit of the business. The way to develop compatible systems, and make integration a straightforward process, is to adopt a standard method to which all systems should comply.

Most installations are of products that are specific to the printing/graphic arts industry. These are from dedicated software houses that now have much experience of printing and a list of leading suppliers is provided at the end of this chapter. In addition, there are two other competing sources: major enterprise resource planning (ERP) software houses such as SAP, Oracle, PeopleSoft, Baan, JD Edwards, Lawson, and from equipment vendors that offer network control over devices within a workflow solution. It is possible to link these systems as communication standards emerge from Heidelberg, MAN Roland, Fujifilm, Agfa and Creo.

There has been significant consolidation among MIS suppliers over the past few years, particularly with the fall-out of e-commerce dotcom suppliers who joined in the late 1990s. The big thing that is happening now is the requirement for systems to communicate with clients, suppliers and partner organisations. Such systems will move from providing internal management and cost control support into supporting business development by providing additional services for customers and potential clients.

Print-specific MIS suppliers

These companies have developed software to help management effectively run printing companies. Most offer a range of scalable modules for specific parts of a print business. Users select the modules they need (often after a consultation process) and implement them with plant-specific production statistics and cost information. The range of choices broadly encompasses the following:

Administration/customer service
Job specification and job planning
Request for quotation
Estimating
Works instructions/job bags
Job costing and invoicing
Sales analysis
Order processing
Financial reporting
Budgeted hourly rates
Multi-divisional accounting
Accounts or accounting link
▶   Accounts receivable
▶   Accounts payable
▶   General ledger
▶   Nominal ledger
Inventory management
Payroll/personnel

Purchasing
Vendor qualification
Purchase orders
Purchase ledger
Materials

Outwork

Services

Sales

Request for quotation

Contact management , CRM capability

Order entry

Pricing targets

EDI and links to customers' systems

Sales analysis

Sales ledger

Sales management and marketing

Production

Production control

Stock control

Schedule

Job tickets

Time and cost

PDF workflow tools

Loading and scheduling

Shop floor data collection

Direct machine interface and data collection

Section tracking

Finished goods

Inventory control

Warehousing

Despatch

Shipping

MIS functions

Security

Performance reporting

Management report writer

Executive information system.

The best system for any business is the one that accomplishes the designated tasks. When considering an MIS and reasonably high-tech installations, project planning is key to a successful installation, as planning and implementation are critical. The business process will change during implementation, so changing people's jobs and tasks, typically the most difficult aspects to manage. When choosing a system, do not underestimate the costs involved and the time it will take to implement.

A list of some of the leading MIS suppliers is provided at the end of this chapter. In addition to helping maximise internal production efficiencies, the role of systems has developed, and particularly over recent years. The MIS is no longer a stand-alone tool used within a print company; it is now part of a wider system allowing fast access for remote sales staff, customers and suppliers through e-commerce.

Electronic methods of production control

There have been many examples of electronic specification, quotation, ordering and tracking of jobs, but it is only recently that these have worked effectively enough to benefit both buyer and provider. The early examples of the dotcom printing vendors were largely unsuccessful; not because the technology did not work, but because it did not provide sufficient control over the jobs and allow a relationship to develop that gave both parties confidence. It is true that most suppliers have to learn the particular requirements of their customers, and these needs can vary greatly. Instead of having to spend the manual sales and customer services' time and effort in understanding requirements, there are tools that help smooth the complexities of the print supply chain. These make it easier for clients, sales and administrative staff to provide the necessary information for smooth project completion. There is real-time access to up-to-date information and the other great benefit that is provided by electronic production control is a total audit trail detailing the activities carried out.

Using e-commerce to improve procurement efficiency

E-commerce is simply a tool to help users increase the efficiency of the print supply chain. It applies to customer, printer (print manager) and suppliers to the printer. It is a range of tools to describe and control the administration associated with specifying, costing, producing, storing and distributing printed items.

Print procurement is becoming more efficient. In the UK this has been led by the sophisticated purchasing departments of organisations that have realised they could gain a competitive advantage by buying better. The technology enabler was the internet, with specialist purchasing and ERP systems being used to help control logistics. It met with an unreceptive set of producers in the print industry, as early buyers got burnt on the open market and forged relationships with proven suppliers on closed sites.

There was a great fall out and retrenching, and the useful tools were largely those that improved the relationship and communication between buyer and seller. The capability was enthusiastically embraced by print management companies which used systems to reduce the cost of administering printed jobs, consolidating a wide variety of work on behalf of clients who could deal with a single supplier. They spent much time researching the capabilities of the market and had access to the trade-only sector, which is important in the business forms sector where manufacturers require precise instructions. They concentrated on manufacturing rather than sales development.

Most printers today have websites; a smaller number have interactive sites that are integrated into an internal MIS. In some cases the functionality is supplied by the MIS as an additional module, otherwise there are many suppliers of e-commerce solutions that can be used, either stand alone or after integration into the MIS. There are two main flavours of e-commerce: e-auctions and workflow sites.

e-auctions

e-auctions have a chequered history in the procurement of print. They were one of the features offered by the first wave of dotcom companies, launched in a wave of publicity that promised to change the print industry. In fact they did not offer real benefits to buyers – who were reluctant to place important jobs with suppliers they did not know – and sellers were concerned about the potential for erosion of their margins.

e-actions were shown to work in other fields and were tried in print in a significantly different form where buyers worked with known, proven suppliers.

Advocates of e-auctions claim that they work well and offer benefits to both parties when conducted properly. The buying function comprises two components:
▶ Sourcing – analysing the capabilities of the market and selecting potential suppliers
▶ Procurement – awarding the contract, getting the goods, paying invoices, etc.
In traditional print purchasing the buyer will spend maybe 20–30% of their time sourcing and determining the capabilities of suppliers, and 70–80% of their time placing and administering print orders. For buyers the sourcing takes time but when done effectively it creates value because they have found the most effective suppliers. With e-auctions the balance of a buyer's time is reversed – the procurement process taking only a few hours when an auction is in progress.

Opposition to e-auctions is considerable. Many printers avoid or choose not to do business in this way primarily because it turns printing into a commodity pricing environment and eliminates the value and personal service element of a particular job. Some print buyers have reported considerable success in reducing their print spend by using e-auctions and pre-qualified suppliers for more standard items.

In 2005 one of the leading print suppliers in the UK, Communisis, announced that it would use e-auctions as part of its print procurement strategy. The company developed a web-based system that takes each supplier through a series of defined bidding stages. A pre-qualification process ensures that suppliers have the core criteria required to participate in the e-auction process. Each approved supplier then takes part in an e-auction and competes on price for nominated lots of products that are relevant to their capabilities and capacities.

Workflow sites

Workflow sites that are used to handle several functions of the print supply chain are more popular among printers. These give customers access to suppliers over the web, making it easier for them to work with the printer. There are many functions and features on offer. Systems can handle several or all of the following:
▶ catalogue of stock items for call off
▶ preparing a specification

▶ producing an optimised specification to improve functionality or to minimise cost

▶ estimating the costs

▶ placing an order

▶ submitting, checking and optimising files for print

▶ aiding the design, prepress and manufacturing processes

  ▶ web-to-print

  ▶ dynamic documents (PDF on-the-fly)

  ▶ asset management

  ▶ remote proofing

▶ job tracking/job status

▶ stock management

▶ distribution

▶ reporting.

Workflow sites are the natural development of internal MISs. They provide external customer links to open up the print supply chain. Innovative printers will start using their systems to generate activity and they will become revenue generators rather than internal control mechanisms.

The following images demonstrate some of the functions that are widely available for printers to improve their communications in 2005.

FIGURE 12.1 Client on-line print ordering screen for standard and bespoke jobs

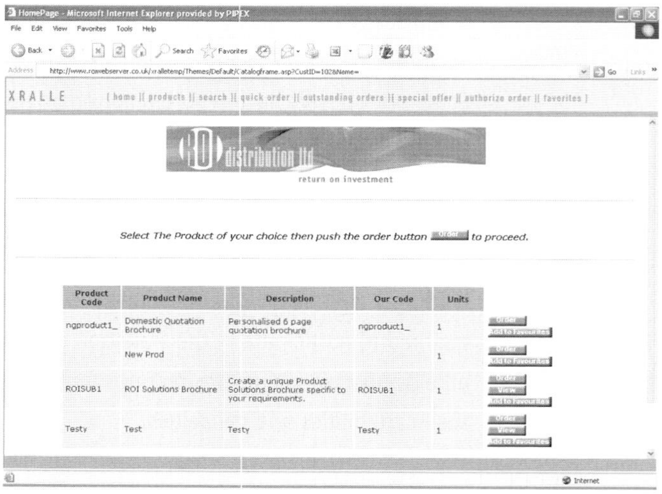

Source: ROI Distribution

There are many successful suppliers offering this service. Each print project can be specified afresh, or as an amendment to a previously ordered job. A detailed specification containing as much detail as is necessary is generated that defines the job.

FIGURE 12.2 Typical outline specification

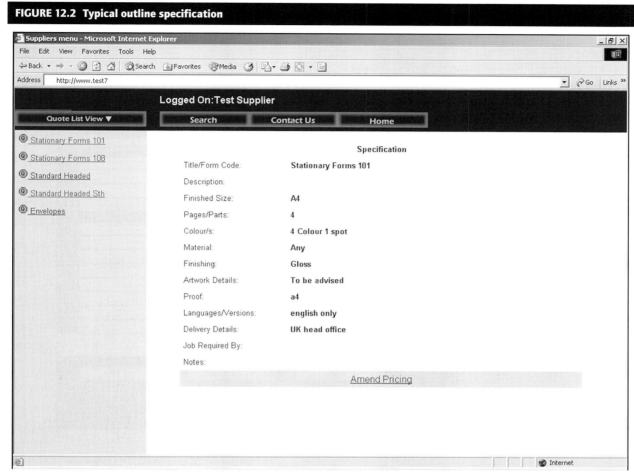

Source: Pira International Ltd

According to the level of complexity, suitable suppliers capable of meeting quality and delivery would be chosen to quote.

FIGURE 12.3 Estimating screen from supplier

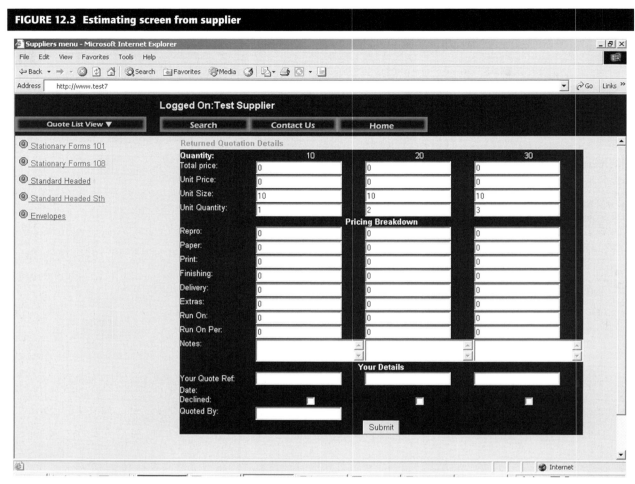

Source: Pira International Ltd

They would fill in details from standard estimating systems according to the request for quotation. When a successful estimate is accepted, the job goes live with the system monitoring the transmission of files and meeting of production schedules.

The first types of print product to benefit were standard business stationery documents such as letterheads, envelopes and business cards. Suppliers would provide a standard template that would allow customers to enter their personal details to instantly generate the document and allow the client to approve and order the job.

12

FIGURE 12.4 Business card ordering routine, selecting correct template

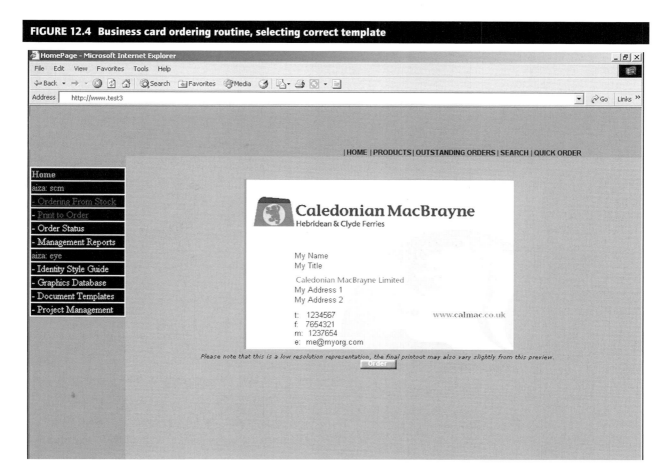

Source: Pira International Ltd

This shows the approved artwork for a client's business card. It is set up so that the personal details can be changed by simply typing the correct information into a range of forms.

FIGURE 12.5 Entering personal details into form

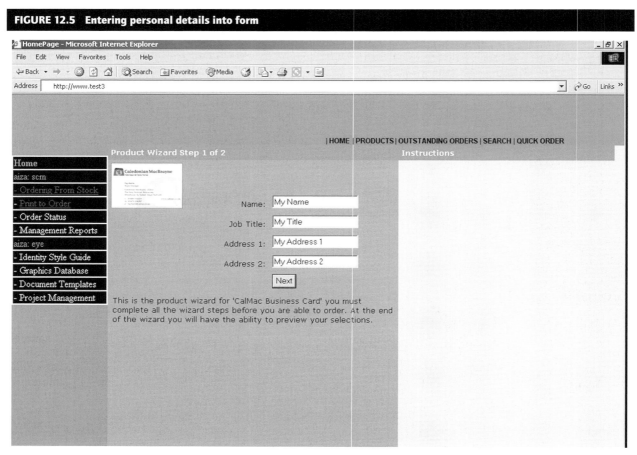

Source: Pira International Ltd

When all the data is entered, the user selects a preview option to display a proof of the finished card. Users do not need any graphics experience or knowledge of print technology to create their product.

FIGURE 12.6 Viewing personalised card details

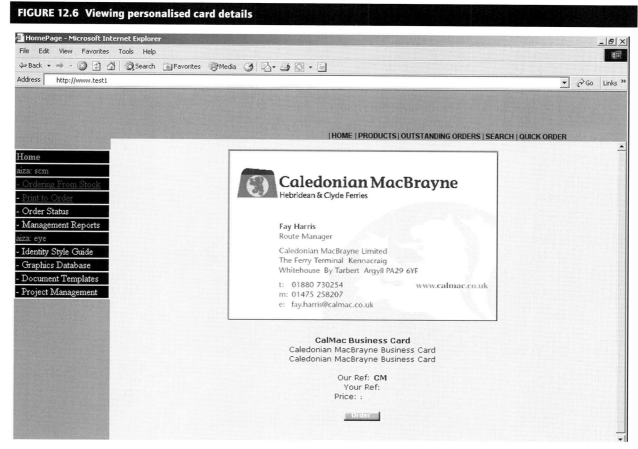

Source: Pira International Ltd

Business cards can be complex, so vertical justification may be needed if the individual does not have a business mobile, or additional fields like direct phone or fax can be positioned correctly. When satisfied that the information is correct, the order button is pressed and an order produced.

FIGURE 12.7 Sending approved order to supplier

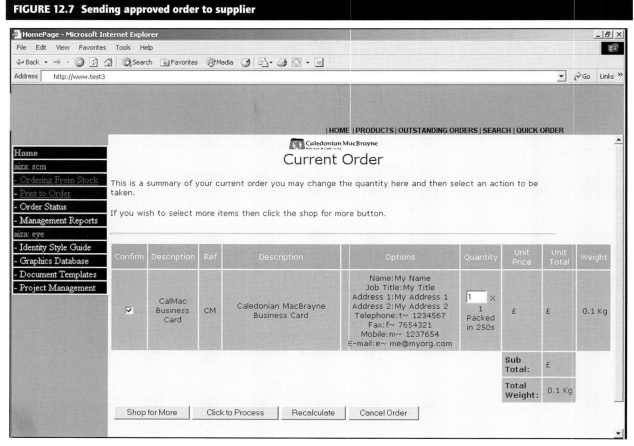

Source: Pira International Ltd

The details are presented and, provided the user has the correct level of authority, the order is posted. At the same time, the systems automatically generate the printable file (generally a PDF) that is sent directly into the imposition system, and taking time out of the prepress and administration at the printer. With online asset management systems, the degree of sophistication of products can extend far beyond stationery requirements. The identity style guide can be made available with the correct typefaces and logos provided in standard document templates to preserve the corporate identity. Project management is the setting up of complex checks for actions to happen within a timetable, and ensuring that the most complex and repetitive tasks do not slip through the net. There are many potential competing systems available.

As well as improving communications and the supply chain externally with customers, the other significant change is the combining of production and administration data to control the overall printing process. This means that print companies with the appropriate equipment can develop efficiencies through computer-integrated manufacturing (CIM) techniques.

Applying JDF

As run lengths decline the key issue for printers changes from being able to achieve the quality demanded by a customer to producing the desired result far more efficiently. Computerised MISs have long been important in helping printers manage their businesses more efficiently. Generally they comprise a specialist relational database that contains details of a company's production capabilities and materials. There are many types available, from low priced estimating aids through to complex systems with bespoke hardware and software. These are aimed at large organisations, involve long implementation periods and can cost well in excess of £1 million. The range of features in general use has broadened from estimating and costing, through production control to sales and marketing aids. The latest offer customers, suppliers and sister organisations direct access. They can provide remote access across the web, with the systems often operating interactively through real-time queries on all aspects of the print supply chain. The latest must-have is a JDF-enabled system, which opens up the possibility of CIM.

Developments in printing technology have extended the range of products and services available to print buyers. Costs have been lowered through increases in the efficiency of equipment and methods used across the supply chain, many resulting from better decision making based on information provided by an MIS. More printers are investigating the use of CIM techniques in their production and administration processes. These methods are used to link different pieces of equipment and transfer information to help in the set up of presses and finishing equipment. At first press manufacturers used these developments to reduce make-ready time and waste. Plate scanners were used in litho printing to measure ink profiles and automatically adjust ink settings on press. These devices were successful at reducing set-up time on press and demand for them grew. As computer to plate (CTP) became more widespread the need for scanning diminished as the RIPed data was directly parsed to provide the ink profile. The benefits of passing data from one device to another were recognised and further developments were undertaken where appropriate, mostly between pieces of equipment from the same manufacturer with compatible computer control mechanisms. This was fine when the same supplier provided all the equipment but largely impossible where there were mixed suppliers, as the equipment could not communicate. The potential of integrated manufacturing went largely unrealised until the CIP3 (Committee for the Integration of Prepress, Press and Postpress, later upgraded to CIP4 with the addition of Process) consortium developed its standard for information exchange, the job definition format (JDF).

JDF describes print jobs electronically, permitting the exchange of information between different applications and systems used by the graphic arts industry. A JDF file contains the management and production details of a job. In a true JDF environment, this digital job ticket would be used to adjust each piece of equipment involved. It might control the RIP settings for plate exposure in a CTP device or set the parameters of the press and finishing unit, as well as providing real-time production information to an MIS. The JDF job ticket is capable of much more than saving operators from having to make a few adjustments to a machine. It is designed to provide a means of monitoring and controlling a job from the point at which a customer makes an enquiry, or places an order, to delivery of the finished work and completion of the invoice. A fully working JDF MIS system would automatically check and order paper and supplies for a job, if required. The information for the job ticket would come from the details held in the original enquiry and quotation, a facility already offered by many JDF-enabled MIS suppliers. JDF-enabled workflow encompasses administration as well as the design, prepress, press and finishing areas. The JDF job ticket can be updated automatically, even via an on-line e-commerce function, as the job progresses. It gives management the ability to reduce costs by improving automation in production and administration.

Just as PostScript revolutionised prepress by reducing the time and costs involved for all parties and improving the competitive position of printing, JDF has the capacity to improve print production. The range of functions covered by JDF that are currently available is shown schematically in Figure 12.8.

FIGURE 12.8 Schematic of the links currently available through the use of JDF

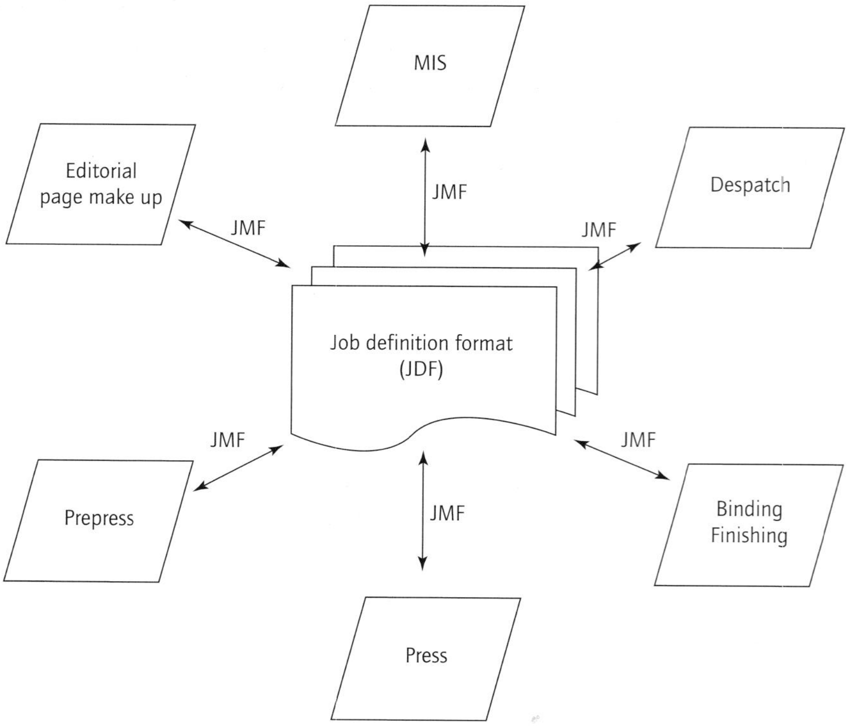

Source: Pira International Ltd

JDF is being developed by CIP4, a standards body located in Switzerland. CIP4 exists to encourage computer-based integration of all processes in the graphic arts industry. In 2005 CIP4 had some 200 members; of these over 120 were equipment vendors with all major MIS, prepress equipment, press (conventional and digital) and finishing manufacturers represented. These suppliers are investing heavily to build open, non-proprietary and productive process automation into their software, systems and equipment.

The areas of concern at present relate to the way jobs are described and handled by different parts of the print process. When does an enquiry get translated into being a definite job? Are the materials available? What is the confirmed quantity and pagination? How does outwork become included? When will the proofs be approved? With more suppliers working together these problems will be solved as more experience is gained and linked systems are used.

There are three fundamental parts of JDF:

▶ the JDF job ticket
▶ the job messenger format
▶ the packaging

The job ticket provides two views of the job: the product view (or product intent) and the process view. The product view provides a snapshot of the finished product from the perspective of an end user. For example, it describes a 32-page A4 section folded to A5 and saddle-stitched, with two-colour text on 100gsm paper, and a process-colour front and back cover on 150gsm coated card. The product view takes no account of the size of press sheets or how the job will be imposed, trapped, bound, etc. The process view contains company specific settings, parameters and dimensions to allow the automatic set-up and execution of a job on various machines. The step-by-step flow of a job through the plant is defined in great detail, even including the physical movement instructions of materials between production stages. Every action taken by each system or system operator is logged into the JDF, providing a time-stamped audit trail that means a job can be analysed later in an MIS.

The JMF is the means of moving JDF data between systems. JMF is a series of standard XML commands and queries that the sender and the receiver write and read to understand the same thing. Examples range from the 'SubmitQueueEntry' command that inserts a job into the input queue of the receiving system to the 'Resource' query, which demands a report of the current state of a particular resource, be it paper, ink, employee, etc.

An MIS or production control system can register signals from the various systems in a factory. Whenever a particular event occurs, such as a digital printer going off-line because the paper tray is empty, the printer's JDF interface sends a signal to inform the MIS or production control system of its status. Rather than relying on an operator to look for blinking beacon lights on the shop floor, the systems send a help message proactively. Real-time job-costing data can be sent in the same manner, allowing the MIS to create a constantly updated financial picture of the job as it progresses.

JMF uses http as its transport protocol, which makes it straightforward to install on a standard network with firewalls and other security devices. To send a job to a platesetter or press, the user selects it from a drop-down menu in the prepress application, and off it goes. The action is the same, whether the job is destined for the machine in the next room or on the next continent. The fact that JDF and JMF are created and routed through multiple systems is completely transparent to the user.

The third aspect of the JDF standard is the packaging mechanism that allows everything needed for the job, or sub-job, to be bundled up and sent. JDF references the various assets, such as a PDF, or an ICC profile using URLs like those used on web browsers. This allows the receiving software to know which files to use as inputs, how to name files and where to put the files it creates. When everything is grouped into a package, this link must be retained. Packaging of JDF will show up in graphic arts applications as a check box, probably called something like 'Submit all JDF files'.

To make JDF more workable the CIP4 work groups are defining various interoperability conformance specifications (ICS) such that two applications that comply with a given ICS will communicate meaningfully, generally with the MIS at the hub. The MIS group will establish the interfaces between the MIS and the various components of the print workflow. These will include:

▶ customer – input to and output from an MIS for product description, enquiries and quoting;
▶ production planning – interface between an MIS and a production scheduling, tracking and planning system;
▶ prepress – interface between an MIS and a prepress production system;
▶ pressroom – interface between an MIS and the pressroom, including both digital and conventional printing;
▶ postpress – interface between an MIS and finishing and binding.

Until these are defined and agreed integration will often require bespoke modification, which may result in a significant drag on the widespread acceptance and use of JDF.

JDF solutions offer the ability to control parts of a print job, and the ability to link MIS with production, or both. JDF provides the mechanism to control all of the processes in print production from job submission through prepress, press and postpress. It does this by translating each process step in a job into a node; the entire job is represented by a tree of nodes. All of the nodes taken together describe the desired printed product and the workflow of its production.

Each node is a process that is defined in terms of inputs and outputs. The inputs consist of the resources it uses and the parameters that control it. So a cover will include the completed PDF, inks, the paper, the plates, final untrimmed size for binding together with parameters detailing the required quantity. The output of the process node using these particular inputs will be a set of printed press sheets. Resources produced by one process will then be consumed by subsequent processes, so these sheets become the input resource for some set of finishing operations, such as folding and cutting. The finished sheets that are the output of those operations become the input resource for, say, binding, until the finished product is ready for the final operation, despatch from the plant.

The job can be defined as a hierarchical network of processes, linked through the consumption of inputs and the production of outputs. The end result is a combination of outputs that produce the desired finished product. The system is set up with a job defined as a network of nodes, each of which describes a process.

FIGRE 12.9 Schematic showing the hierarchy of nodes in a simple job

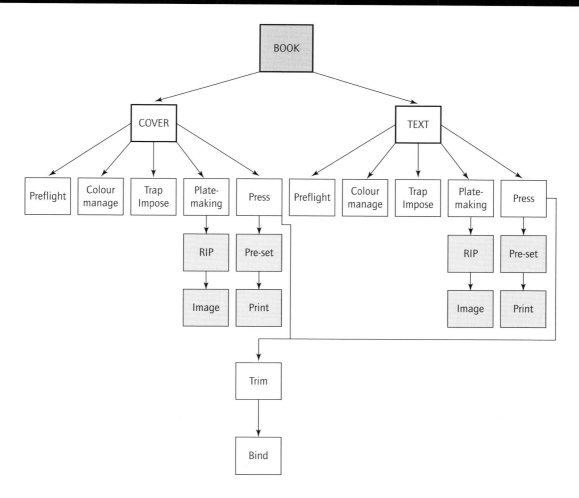

Source: Pira International Ltd

Processes are executed by devices, and devices are grouped together in work centres. A print production control system controls the devices in a work centre. The system communicates with the devices to control the flow of jobs through the work centre, to monitor the process of individual jobs and to detect and correct exception conditions. JDF's role is to specify a messaging architecture to enable communication between the controller and the devices in the work centre. JDF supplies a messenger service to run between the MIS and the production machinery. As each process in a job is completed the results are recorded in the JDF file to facilitate the tracking of each aspect.

FIGURE 12.10 Communication between MIS and production

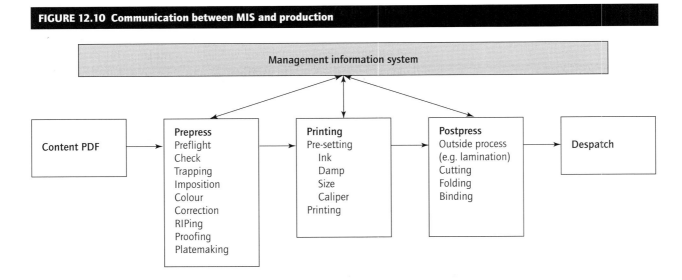

Source: Pira International Ltd

This messaging capability is provided by the job messenger format (JMF). It can be none, uni- or bi-directional. The most basic level of support is notification where a device will inform the MIS when it begins and completes processing of certain procedures for a job; it may also notify the MIS of any error conditions. The next level of communication supports queries. Devices that support queries respond to requests from the controller by communicating status, such as current JobIDs, queued JobIDs or current job progress. The most sophisticated and useful is support for commands where the MIS can interrupt the current job to restart a job or to change the priority of jobs in a queue. JDF gives the MIS the ability to collect performance data for each process and pass that information to a job-tracking system for use by the job accounting system.

The JDF name and logo are becoming commonplace on new equipment, be it for traditional print and finishing, digital print and finishing or the MIS used to control them. Most trade magazines and journals contain gushing praise and alarming technology descriptions, with case studies demonstrating how company *X* gained major benefits from implementing a particular solution. All this sounds compelling but one reads more about the potential for JDF than actual practical applications. From the publicity and hype it would seem that the industry had whole-heartedly embraced the technology, but there are issues. Most print workflows involve multiple pieces of equipment with separate interfaces in the same plant. Not all equipment offers the same functionality and the JDF compliance of different vendors may apply to different elements. Two pieces of equipment may be JDF compliant yet still unable to communicate with each other.

Late in 2004 the CIP4 consortium asked vendors to give details of their installed base of JDF-compliant equipment to see how the market was developing. CIP4 believes there were some 1700 installations of JDF-compliant systems worldwide at the end of 2004, with another 1500 on order, awaiting installation. This is a drop in the ocean considering there are some 300,000 printing companies worldwide, but it is a start. So JDF is not a universal panacea at present. It offers the promise of integrating MIS and production equipment. There are some 100 vendors offering around 200 products that could be usefully linked. The number of products will grow with new launches and increased functionality. Not all devices need to communicate directly, e.g. there is no benefit to be gained from a RIP talking to a wire stitcher. There are now some 20,000 potential pairings – not all of them proven – and this number is growing strongly. There are practical pitfalls to be overcome until all the ICS are finalised and implemented, particularly if the MIS is to act as the hub for data transfer and recording.

JDF is getting a trifle top heavy. With so many companies involved, satisfying all parties becomes difficult across the range of activities from customer enquiries to stocking and delivery. One development that is helping to speed things along is the Creo lead networked graphic production (NGP) initiative, which aims to define, develop, test and deliver JDF-based integration between systems. NGP is smaller than the CIP4 group. It has some 40 members, including 20 MIS suppliers. To ensure good integration between multi-vendor equipment, NGP members have agreed to define and use a standardised set of JDF-based interfaces. The NGP partners have developed more than 140 pairs of integrated solutions to provide a seamless flow of job and production data across the entire production process.

Leading MIS and system suppliers

Data Design Services
Lakesbury Mews, Hiltingbury Road
Chandlers Ford, Eastleigh
Hants SO53 5SS
UK
T +44 (0)23 8024 0470
www.ddssoftware.co.uk

DiMS!
Eschpark 5–7, PO Box 165
7130 AD Lichtenvoorde
The Netherlands
T +31 (0)544 396600
www.dims.net

EFI
303 Velocity Way
Foster City, CA 94404
US
T +1 650 357 3500
www.efi.com/products/printMIS.fhtml

Hiflex GmbH

Rotter Bruch 26a

D-52068 Aachen

Germany

T +49 (0)241 16830

www.hiflex.com

Imprint Business Systems Ltd

Poplars, High Easter

Chelmsford, Essex CM1 4RB

UK

T +44 (0)1245 231670

www.imprint-mis.co.uk/

i-teba

Pride Court

80–82 White Lion Street

London N1 9PF

UK

T +44 (0)20 7841 3300

www.iteba.com

Optichrome Computer Systems Ltd

Maybury Road

Woking

Surrey GU21 5HX

UK

T +44 (0)1483 740233

www.optimus202.com

Prism

50 O'Dea Avenue Waterloo

Sydney, New South Wales 2017

Australia

T +61 (0)2 9313 8346

www.prism-world.com

12

Radius Solutions Ltd

Manor Farm, High Street

Dronfield, Derbyshire S18 1PY

UK

T +44 (0)1246 290331

www.radiussolutions.com

ROI Distribution Ltd

Unit 1, Norwood Road Industrial Estate

Norwood Road, March

Cambs PE15 8QD

UK

T +44 (0)845 602 3558

www.xralle.co.uk

Sanderson

Sanderson House, Poplar Way

Sheffield S60 5TR

UK

T +44 (0)1709 787787

www.sanderson.com

Shuttleworth Business Systems

Graphic House, Club Street,

Kettering, Northants NN16 8RB

UK

T +44(0)1536 316316

www.shuttleworth-uk.co.uk

Technique Business Systems

Turing House, Milshaw

Leeds LS11 8LZ

UK

T +44 (0)113 383 6000

www.technique-group.com

Telekinesys Software

Clayton House, Warfield Park

Bracknell, Berks RG42 3RA

UK

T +44 (0)1344 886620

www.telekinesys.co.uk

Tharstern Limited

RB House, Greenfield Road,

Colne, Lancashire BB8 9PD

UK

T +44 (0)870 720 2080

www.tharstern.com

General reference tables

13

Metric table multipliers

In communications, electronics and physics, multipliers are defined in powers of 10 from 10^{-24} to 10^{24}, proceeding in increments of three orders of magnitude (10^3 or 1000). In IT and data storage, multipliers are defined in powers of 2 from 2^{10} to 2^{80}, proceeding in increments of ten orders of magnitude (2^{10} or 1024). These multipliers are shown below.

Prefix	Symbol(s)	Power of 10	Power of 2
yocto-	y	10^{-24}	--
zepto-	z	10^{-21}	--
atto-	a	10^{-18}	--
femto-	f	10^{-15}	--
pico-	p	10^{-12}	--
nano-	n	10^{-9}	--
micro-	μ	10^{-6}	--
milli-	m	10^{-3}	--
centi-	c	10^{-2}	--
deci-	d	10^{-1}	--
deka-	D	10^{1}	--
Hecto-	h	10^{2}	--
Kilo-	k or K **	10^{3}	2^{10}
Mega-	M	10^{6}	2^{20}
Giga-	G	10^{9}	2^{30}
Tera-	T	10^{12}	2^{40}
Peta-	P	10^{15}	2^{50}
Exa-	E	10^{18}	2^{60}
Zetta-	Z	10^{21}	2^{70}
Yotta-	Y	10^{24}	2^{80}

** note case difference, $k = 10^3$ and $K = 2^{10}$

Examples of quantities or phenomena in which power-of-10 prefix multipliers apply include frequency (including computer clock speeds), physical mass, power, energy, electrical voltage and electrical current. Power-of-10 multipliers are also used to define binary data speeds. Thus, for example, 1kbsec^{-1} (one kilobit per second) is equal to 10^3, or 1000 bits per second; 1Mbsec^{-1} (one megabit per second) is equal to 10^6, or 1,000,000 bits per second. The lowercase k is the technically correct symbol for kilo- when it represents 10^3, although the uppercase K is often used instead.

When binary data is stored in memory or fixed media such as a hard drive or CD-ROM, power-of-2 multipliers are used. Technically, the uppercase K should be used for kilo- when it represents 2^{10}. So, 1KB (one kilobyte) is 2^{10}, or 1024 bytes; 1MB (one megabyte) is 2^{20}, or 1,048,576 bytes.

The choice of power-of-10 versus power-of-2 prefix multipliers can appear arbitrary. It helps to remember that in common usage multiples of bits are almost always expressed in powers of 10, while multiples of bytes are almost always expressed in powers of 2. Rarely is data speed expressed in bytes per second, and rarely is data storage or memory expressed in bits. Such usages are considered improper. Confusion is not likely, therefore, provided one adheres strictly to the standard usages of the terms bit and byte (1 byte = 8 bits).

Length

10 ångström	=	1 nanometre
1000 nanometres	=	1 micrometre
1000 micrometres	=	1 millimetre
10 millimetres	=	1 centimetre
10 centimetres	=	1 decimetre
10 decimetres	=	1 metre
1000 metres	=	1 kilometre
1000 kilometres	=	1 megametre

Weight

1000 milligrams	=	1 gram
10 grams	=	1 dekagram
10 decagrams	=	1 hectogram
10 hectograms	=	1 kilogram
1000 kilograms	=	1 tonne

Area

100 sq millimetres	=	1 sq centimetre
1000 sq centimetres	=	1 sq metre
10000 sq metres	=	1 hectare
100 hectares	=	1 sq kilometre

Capacity

1000 millilitres	=	1 litre
100 litres	=	1 hectolitre
10 hectolitres	=	1 kilolitre

Volume

1000 cu millimetres	=	1 cu centimetre
1000 cu centimetres	=	1 cu decimetre
1000 cu decimetres	=	1 cu metre
1000 cu metres	=	1 cu decametre
1000 cu decametres	=	1 cu hectometre

Computer memory

8 bits	=	1 byte
1012 bytes	=	1 kilobyte (k or kb)
1012kb	=	1 megabyte (Mb)
1012Mb	=	1 gigabyte (Gb)
1012Gb	=	1 terabyte (Tb)
1012Tb	=	1 petabyte (Pb)
1012Pb	=	1 exabyte (Eb)

Conversion metric to imperial

	Metric	*Multiplication factor*	*Imperial*
Length	centimetres	0.3937	inches (in)
	metres	3.2808	feet (ft)
	metres	1.0936143	yards (yd)
	kilometres	0.62137	miles (ml)
Weight	grams	0.03527	ounces (oz)
	kilograms	2.20462	pounds (lb)
	tonnes	0.984207	tons (2240lb)
Area	sq centimetres	0.155	sq inches
	sq metres	10.7639	sq feet
	sq metres	1.9599	sq yards
	sq kilometres	0.3861	sq miles
	hectares	2.47101	acres
Capacity and volume	cu centimetres	0.06102	cu inches
	litres	1.7598	pints
	litres	0.2200	gallons
Velocity	kilometres per hr	0.62137	miles per hr
	metres per sec	3.2808	feet per sec
Temperature	degrees Celsius	× 5/9 (+32)	degrees Fahrenheit

Conversion of paper basis weights, metric to North American

North American	Metric	Metric
35lb		54gsm
40lb		60gsm
45lb		70gsm
50lb	74gsm	90gsm
55lb	81gsm	120gsm
60lb	89gsm	300gsm

Typographical measurements

Points and Picas (Anglo-American standard)/Didots and Ciceros (European standard)

	Inches	Millimetres
Anglo-American point	0.013837	0.351
Pica	0.166044	4.218
Didot point	0.0148	0.376
Cicero	0.1776	4.511

Conversion factor Picas to Ciceros
1.069596 (1.0696)

Conversion factor Ciceros to Picas
0.9349324 (0.9349)

Conversion table: points to inches and millimetres

	Anglo-American		Didot	
Point size	Inches	Millimetres	Inches	Millimetres
1	0.0138	0.351	0.0148	0.376
3	0.0415	1.054	0.0444	1.128
6	0.0830	2.109	0.0888	2.256
7	0.0969	2.460	0.1036	2.631
8	0.1107	2.812	0.1184	3.007
9	0.1245	3.163	0.1332	3.383
10	0.1384	3.515	0.1480	3.759
11	0.1522	3.866	0.1628	4.135
12	0.1660	4.218	0.1776	4.511
14	0.1937	4.920	0.2072	5.263
18	0.2491	6.326	0.2664	6.767
24	0.3321	8.435	0.3552	9.022

Screen rulings

Lines per inch	Nearest equivalent lines per cm	Paper surface
65	26	newsprint
85	34	newsprint
100	40	MF
120	48	MF/matt coated
133	54	MF/matt coated/art
150	60	matt coated/art
175	70	art
200	80	art

Paper sizes

Stock sizes for normal trim work

Sheet size	Millimetres	Inches	A4 pp to view	A4 pages from sheet
RA0	860 × 1220	33.9 × 48	16	32
RA1	610 × 860	24 × 33.9	8	16
RA2	430 × 610	16.9 × 24	4	8

Stock sizes for bleed trim work

Sheet size	Millimetres	Inches	A4 pp to view	A4 pages from sheet
SRA0	900 × 1280	35.4 × 50 .4	16	32
SRA1	640 × 900	25.3 × 35.4	8	16
SRA2	450 × 640	17.8 × 25.3	4	8

A series sheet sizes

Sheet size	Millimetres	Inches
4A	1682 × 2378	66.3 × 93.6
2A	1189 × 1682	46.8 × 66.3
A0	841 × 1189	33.1 × 46.8
A1	594 × 841	23.4 × 33.1
A2	420 × 594	16.5 × 23.4
A3	297 × 420	11.8 × 16.5
A4	210 × 297	8.3 × 11.8
A5	148 × 210	5.9 × 8.3
A6	105 × 148	4.1 × 5.9
A7	74 × 105	2.9 × 4.1
A8	52 × 74	2 × 2.9
A9	37 × 52	1.5 × 2
A10	26 × 37	1 × 1.5

B series for posters

Sheet size	Millimetres	Inches
4B	2000 × 2828	78.8 × 111.4
2B	1414 × 2000	55.7 × 78.8
B0	1000 × 1414	39.4 × 55.7
B1	707 × 1000	27.9 × 39.4
B2	500 × 707	19.7 × 27.9
B3	353 × 500	13.9 × 19.7
B4	250 × 353	9.8 × 13.9
B5	176 × 250	7 × 9.8

C series for envelopes

Sheet size	Millimetres	Inches	Common use
4A	1682 × 2378	66.3 × 93.6	
C0	917 × 1297	36.1 × 51	
C1	648 × 917	25.5 × 36.1	
C2	458 × 648	18 × 25.5	
C3	324 × 458	12.8 × 18	
C4	229 × 324	9 × 12.8	takes A4 sheet flat
C5	162 × 229	6.4 × 9	takes A5 sheet flat
C6	114 × 162	4.5 × 6.4	takes A5 folded once
C7/6	81 × 162	3.3 × 6.4	takes A5 folded twice
C7	81 × 114	3.3 × 4.5	
DL	110 × 220	4.5 × 8.6	takes A4 folded twice

Metric book and sheet sizes (quad sheets)

Name	Trimmed page (mm)	Untrimmed page (mm)	Quad sheet (mm)	Pages to view	Pages from sheet
Crown 8vo	186 × 123	192 × 126	768(m) × 1008	32	64
Metric Crown 4to	246 × 189	252 × 192	768 × 1008(m)	16	32
Metric Large Crown 8vo	198 × 129	204 × 132	816(m) × 1056	32	64
Metric Demy 8vo	216 × 138	222 × 141	888(m) × 1128	32	64
Metric Demy 4to	276 × 219	282 × 222	888 × 1128(m)	16	32
Metric Royal 8vo	234 × 156	240 × 159	960(m) × 1272	32	64
Metric Royal 4to	312 × 237	318 × 240	960 × 1272(m)	16	32

Imperial book and sheet sizes (quad sheets)

Name	Trimmed page (mm)	(inches)	Quad sheet (mm)	(inches)	Pages from sheet
Crown 8vo	184 × 124	7.3 × 4.8	762(m) × 1016	30 × 40	64
Crown 4to	248 × 187	9.8 × 7.4	762 × 1016(m)	30 × 40	32
Large Crown 8vo	197 × 130	7.8 × 5.1	813(m) × 1067	32 × 42	64
Demy 8vo	216 × 140	8.5 × 5.5	889(m) × 1143	32 × 42	64
Demy 4to	279 × 219	11 × 8.6	889 × 1143(m)	35 × 45	32
Royal 8vo	248 × 156	9.8 × 6.1	1016(m) × 1272	40 × 50	64
Royal 4to	311 × 251	12.3 × 9.8	1016 × 1272(m)	40 × 50	32

Other imperial book and sheet sizes

	Trimmed octavo mm	inches	Trimmed quarto mm	inches	Quad sheet size mm	inches
Foolscap	165 × 105	6.5 × 4.1	210 × 168	8.3 × 6.6	686 × 864	27 × 34
Largepost	203 × 130	8 × 5.1	260 × 206	10.3 × 8.1	838 × 1067	33 × 42
Medium	222 × 143	8.8 × 5.6	286 × 225	11.3 × 8.9	914 × 1168	36 × 46
Imperial	273 × 187	10.8 × 7.4	375 × 276	14.8 × 10.9	1118 × 1524	44 × 60

Typography

14

Typography is the balance and interplay of letterforms on the page, a verbal and visual equation that helps the reader understand the form and absorb the substance of the page content. Typography plays a dual role as both verbal and visual communication. As readers scan a page they are subconsciously aware of both functions: first they survey the overall graphic patterns of the page, then they parse the language, or read. Good typography establishes a visual hierarchy for rendering prose on the page by providing visual punctuation and graphic accents that help readers understand relationships between prose and pictures, and headlines and subordinate blocks of text.

Good typography depends on the visual contrast between one font and another and between text blocks, headlines and the surrounding white space. Nothing attracts the eye and brain of the reader like strong contrast and distinctive patterns, and you can achieve those attributes only by carefully designing them into your pages. If you cram every page with dense text, readers see a wall of gray and will instinctively reject the lack of visual contrast. Just making things uniformly bigger does not help. Even boldface fonts quickly become monotonous, because if everything is bold then nothing stands out boldly.

When your content is primarily text, typography is the tool you use to paint patterns of organisation on the page. The first thing the reader sees is not the title or other details on the page but the overall pattern and contrast of the page. The regular, repeating patterns established through carefully organised pages of text and graphics help the reader to establish the location and organisation of your information and increase legibility. Patchy, heterogeneous typography and text headers make it hard for the user to see repeating patterns and almost impossible to predict where information is likely to be located in unfamiliar documents.

Good design is paramount for maximum impact and easy assimilation of a message, whether printed or on-line, based on sound principles of typographic layout.

Measurement and terminology

Systems of measurement

All printing measurements derive from the term 'point', which was the base unit of measurement used in the early days of printing to describe the common sizes of type. In those days, it was used with no particular sense of precision. Founts were cast in 6 point size, 10 point size, 24 point size and so on, but were known more commonly by name: the 6 point size came to be known as Nonpareil, 8 point as Brevier, 10 point as Long primer and the commonly used 12 point size as Pica. The common names and approximate sizes are shown in the box (page 607). Of these names, only the point and pica have survived to the present.

A disastrous fire in a Chicago type foundry in the 1870s led to a call for standardisation and the point was defined at 0.013837 inches, the pica at 0.166044 inches. These subsequently became the accepted – and exactly defined – units of measurement for all typographical purposes in America and Great Britain.

In Europe, a similar move to standardisation had already been under way using a slightly different definition of the point as its standard – the didot point – and its equivalent to the 12pt pica, the cicero. This system – called the Didot system – continued and has become the standard system used in Europe. Didot points and picas are some seven per cent larger than Anglo-American points and picas.

▶ Anglo-American point = 0.013837 inches (0.351 mm)

▶ Didot point = 0.0148 inches (0.376 mm).

All modern DTP and typesetting systems can be set up to Anglo-American points/picas, Didot points/ciceros, inches or millimetres. The important Anglo-American measurements to remember for quick calculation purposes are:

Point size	Inches	Millimetres
1pt	0.014 (72 per inch)	0.35mm
12pts (1 pica)	0.166 (6 per inch)	4.2mm
72pts (6 picas)	1.000	25.4 mm

Table 14.1 gives the exact conversion table.

TABLE 14.1 Conversion table: Anglo-American and Didot point sizes to inches/millimetres				
	Anglo-American		**Didot**	
Point size	**Inches**	**Millimetres**	**Inches**	**Millimetres**
1	0.013837	0.351	0.0148	0.376
3	0.041511	1.054	0.0444	1.128
6	0.083022	2.109	0.0888	2.256
7	0.096859	2.460	0.1036	2.631
8	0.110696	2.812	0.1184	3.007
9	0.124533	3.163	0.1332	3.383
10	0.138370	3.515	0.1480	3.759
11	0.152207	3.866	0.1628	4.135
12	0.166044	4.218	0.1776	4.511
14	0.193718	4.920	0.2072	5.263
18	0.249066	6.326	0.2664	6.767
24	0.332088	8.435	0.3552	9.022

These figures are derived from the measurements as they were originally defined:

1 Anglo-American point	= 0.013837in
1 pica	= 0.166044in
1 didot pt	= 0.0148in
1 cicero	= 0.1776in

The conversion factor from Anglo-American to Didot is 1.069596.

The conversion factor from Didot to Anglo-American is 0.9349324.

The conversion factor from inches to millimetres is 25.4.

TABLE 14.2 Old Anglo-American names for type bodies and their approximate sizes

Name	Point size	Name	Point size
Minikin	3.5	Two-line brevier	16
Brilliant	4	Great primer	18
Diamond	4.5	Paragon	20
Pearl	5	Two-line small pica	22
Agate (or Ruby)	5.5	Two-line pica	24
Nonpareil	6	Two-line English	28
Emerald	7	Four-line brevier	32
Brevier	8	Two-line great primer	36
Bourgeois	9	Two-line paragon	40
Long primer	10	Two-line double pica	44
Small pica	11	Canon (or four-line pica)	48
Pica	12	Five-line pica	60
English	14	Six-line pica	72

Source: Pira International Ltd

Terminology

Much of the terminology used in typography derives from the days of metal type. A single letter, numeral or other component in a type alphabet is known as a 'character' or 'sort'. The parts of a metal type character are shown in Figure 14.1.

FIGURE 14.1 The parts of a metal type character

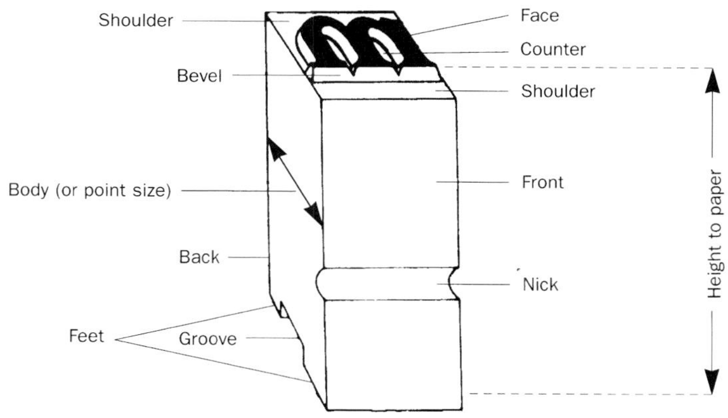

Source: Pira International Ltd

Each point is positioned on a cartesian co-ordinate system that has its origin on the character's base line (the line on which letters without descenders rest). The horizontal distance between the origin and the leftmost edge of the character is called the left side bearing (it may be negative, positive or zero). All characters have a width, and this is the distance from the current character's origin to the origin of the next character. The distance between the right edge of the character and the width is called the right side bearing. The size of a type character (e.g. 10pt) is the size of the body of the character, its top-to-toe dimension. Solid lines of 10pt type, therefore, measure ten points from the top of capital letters to the bottom of such characters as 'g' or 'y'.

Extra vertical spacing between lines of type is known as 'leading'. This is because in the days of metal setting, lead rules of 1pt, 2pt, 3pt thickness were inserted between each solid line of type in order to space out the lines.

Type that is set without leading is known as 'solid' (e.g. 10pt Times solid). Type that is leaded is described either as leaded or as 'on' another particular body: e.g. 10 pt Times, 2pts leaded; or 10 on 12pt Times (usually written as 10/12pt Times).

The width of a type character is known as its 'set'. The set-widths of characters within an alphabet vary enormously but, in all except the more eccentric fonts, 'm' is the widest character, 'n' is the average character and 'i' is the narrowest character.

Different manufacturers approach the allocation of set-widths to characters within the alphabet in different ways, but usually they choose measurements by reference to the width of the 'm' (the widest letter) in the font. For example, where the 'm' is given to be 1000 units, the smallest unit might be one-thousandth part of this; the 'n', that is classically half the 'm', will be 500 units; the 'i', 300 units.

Because the 'n' is the average character in width terms for any composition font, single characters of setting are often loosely referred to as 'ens'. In an average 11pt book-setting typeface, an 11pt en will be about 5pts wide (0.07in or 1.75mm), which works out at about 14 characters for each linear inch. Standard Courier-style printout (identified as 'typewriting') is designed to either ten characters to the linear inch (Pica) or 12 characters to the linear inch (Elite). Book typography, therefore, tends to be much more economical word-for-word than typescript.

An em is double the width of the en. As well as describing the type character 'm', the term em on its own, or 'pica em,' is also used to mean 'pica' or 12 points. This rather confusing shorthand comes about because the width of the em in the commonly used pica size (12pt) was itself 12 points wide, and the use of the term to mean 12 points has stuck. An 'em of set', on the contrary, means the width of the em in the particular font concerned, but this term is rarely used.

A character like 'g' or 'y' extends below the baseline, and is called a descender; a character like 'k' or 'l' extends above it, and is called an ascender. Most Latin (and Greek and Cyrillic) fonts have certain standard heights: the height of a lower case letter (without an ascender) is called the x-height, the height of a capital letter is called the cap-height and the height of the ascenders is called the ascender height (some, but not all, fonts have the ascenders and capitals at the same approximate height). Usually these will not be exactly the same for all characters; the letter 'O' is usually slightly taller than the letter 'I', but they both are within the range of the cap height for the font.

The font itself has an ascent and descent associated with it. In the old days of metal type, nothing could ascend above or descend below these values but now accents and ascenders may reach above the font-wide ascent and descenders below it. However, the concept is still a convenient one to retain. It is true that in almost all cases, the characters will not ascend above or descend below the font-wide ascent and descent. The sum of the ascent and descent is the size of the font. The point size of a piece of metal type was determined by this value (essentially the height of the metal block holding the character). In a PostScript font, the local co-ordinate system is independent of the final size at which the font will draw. By convention in PostScript, the sum of the ascent and descent is 1000 units, while in TrueType it is usually a power of two, and often 2048.

Fonts and type families

Font, or fount as it used to be in British spelling, is a word whose definition has changed in recent years to accommodate computer technology. In the days of metal type and the early days of phototypesetting, a fount referred to a single weight, a single size and a single design (plus italic) of a typeface: 12pt Plantin medium roman with italic, for example, was a fount; 14pt Plantin medium roman with italic was another fount. In today's usage, 'font' is often synonymous with 'typeface', meaning the main version of the typeface in its medium upright version – properly called 'roman'. All sizes are obtained by computer enhancement. The design variants, such as italic and bold, generally have to be ordered separately.

The basic components of the roman set of characters will comprise:

► an upper case alphabet

► a small caps alphabet

► a lower case alphabet

► ligatures, dipthongs, figures, punctuation marks, signs and symbols.

Here are the Plantin roman designs for these (set in 10pt):

Caps: ABCDEFGHIJKLMNOPQRSTUVWXYZ

Small caps: ABCDEFGHIJKLMNOPQRSTUVWXYZ

Lower case: abcdefghijklmnopqrstuvwxyz

Ligatures: Æ, Œ, æ, œ

Dipthongs: fi, fl

Figures: 1234567890

Punctuation marks: , . ; : ? ¿ ! ' ' " " – – —

Reference marks: * (asterisk), † (dagger), ‡ (double dagger),
¶ (paragraph), § (section) | | (parallel)

Miscellaneous signs: ( ) (parentheses), [ ] { } (brackets), & (ampersand)

Accented letters: á é í ó ú (acute) à è ì ò ù (grave)

â ê î ô û (circumflex)

ä ë ï ö ü (diaresis)

ç (cedilla) ñ (tilde)

Mathematical signs: + ÷ = < > ≤ ≥ ± ° / |

Commercial signs: % @ © ® £ $ € ¢ ¥ ™

Not all typefaces will be supplied with a specially designed or truecut small caps alphabet (that will differ from the same alphabet two sizes smaller by having slightly strengthened character strokes to reflect the look of the main type size more accurately).

Figures (numerals) may be:

► 'lining' (also known as aligning or modern), in which the numerals sit on the baseline with the other characters;

► 'non-lining' (also known as hanging or old-style), in which the numerals extend either side of the baseline.

Few typefaces are supplied with non-lining figure designs. Ligatures may not always be provided. Punctuation marks will distinguish the hyphen, the en-rule and the emrule.

In addition to the roman characters, versions of most characters will be supplied as italic designs and as bold designs, but normally without truecut small caps. A basic type font will therefore comprise three designs and seven alphabets:

► roman caps, roman small caps, roman lower case

► italic caps, italic lower case

► bold caps, bold lower case.

Here they all are in 11pt Plantin:

Roman caps: ABCDEFGHIJKLMNOPQRSTUVWXYZ

Roman small caps: ABCDEFGHIJKLMNOPQRSTUVWXYZ

Roman lower case: abcdefghijklmnopqrstuvwxyz

Italic caps: *ABCDEFGHIJKLMNOPQRSTUVWXYZ*

Italic lower case: *abcdefghijklmnopqrstuvwxyz*

Bold caps: **ABCDEFGHIJKLMNOPQRSTUVWXYZ**

Bold lower case: **abcdefghijklmnopqrstuvwxyz**

Beyond the medium, italic and bold designs of a typeface, other variants, whether in weight or set-width, stretch out in all directions. The whole agglomeration of weights and widths from a basic design is sometimes called a type family.

Weights traditionally progress as follows:

► ultra-light

► extra-light

► light

► semi-light

► medium

► semi-bold

► bold

► extra-bold

► ultra-bold.

Some typefaces are supplied as designs with these names (e.g. Helvetica Light, Rockwell Light). Others can be made by digitally altering the medium or bold versions in the output device.

Design variants: weights
Light
Medium
Bold
Extra-bold

Widths traditionally progress as follows:

► ultra-condensed

► extra-condensed

► condensed

► semi-condensed

► medium

► semi-expanded

► expanded

► extra-expanded

► ultra-expanded.

Again, some are supplied (e.g. Helvetica Condensed); others can be created digitally.

Setting to a measure

Type is set to a measure (line length) expressed in picas (ems or pica ems), millimetres or inches. Lines can be:

► ranged left (or unjustified, ragged right)

► justified, in which all lines are the same length

► centred

► or ranged right (or ragged left).

Ranged-left setting (unjustified or ragged right) is indicated in the following way:

'10/12 pt Plantin R/L × 18 picas'

> This is an example of 10 on 12pt Plantin typesetting ranged left (unjustified or ragged right) across (a measure of) 18picas. This is an example of 10 on 12pt Plantin ranged left.

Justified setting is specified:

'10/12pt Plantin × 18 picas justified'

> This is an example of 10 on 12pt Plantin across (a measure of) 18 picas justified. This is an example of 10/12pt Plantin across (a measure of) 18 picas justified. This is an example of 10/12pt Plantin across (a measure of) 18 picas justified.

Centred setting is indicated:

'10/12pt Plantin centred over 18 picas'

> This is an example of 10 on 12pt Plantin centred across (a measure of) 18 picas. This is an example of 10 on 12pt Plantin centred across (a measure of) 18 picas.

Ranged-right (unjustified, ragged left) setting is indicated:

'10/12pt Plantin R/R × 18 picas'

> This is an example of 10 on 12pt Plantin typesetting ranged right (ragged left) across (a measure of) 18 picas. This is an example of 10 on 12pt Plantin type ranged right.

Design variants: Set-widths
Ultra-condensed
Extra-condensed
Condensed
Semi-condensed
MEDIUM
Semi-expanded
Expanded
Extra-expanded
Ultra-expanded

Word spaces within a line may be:

► fixed (unjustified setting)

► variable (justified setting).

The standard fixed word space is the mid space, half the width of the average en character (and a quarter the width of the em). The standard variable word space starts at a 'thin', around 20% of the em, and may extend out as far as an em or more. Traditionally, word spaces were described in fractions of an em:

► hair space 6 to the em 17%

► thin space 5 to the em 20%

► mid space 4 to the em 25%

► thick space 3 to the em 33%

► en space 2 to the em 50%

► em space 1 to the em 100%.

While this terminology is still used in a loose sense, all modern DTP and typesetting systems offer infinitely smaller increments.

Figure 14.2 shows the features that are used to describe typefaces and styles.

Typeface characteristics

Typefaces are distinguished from each other by the following characteristics:

► *Weight* – the general density or colour – that may be spindly or robust

► *Character fit* that may be loose or tight

► *Proportions* – the relationship of the x-height to the cap height

► *Appearing size* that may be large or small

► *Stress* – the angle of shading in the letter strokes may be:

  ► oblique (diagonal, stressed at 45°)

  ► vertical (upright, stressed at 90°).

Diagonally stressed letter forms look more calligraphic and relaxed. Vertically stressed letter forms look mechanical and formal (see Figure 14.3).

► *Serifs* A typeface may or may not have serifs. If it hasn't, it is termed 'sans serif'; if it has, the serifs may be 'bracketed' or 'unbracketed' and oblique or horizontal in angle. The weight of the serifs in relation to the main strokes of the letters can be distinctive:

  ► hairline (thin) at one extreme,

  ► slab (thick) at the other.

► *Earmarks* – quirks or distinguishing features. The letters Q, f, g, j, w, are often very distinctive. Note, however, that each typeface company has patented its own interpretation of the traditional classic typefaces, and each one differs in a number of ways, subtle or otherwise, from the interpretation of his competitors. Similarly, each manufacturer will take a popular design, remodel it to a greater or lesser degree, and, for copyright reasons, might market it under a new name. This element of creative reinterpretation sometimes alters the earmarks as well as other basic characteristics, so a certain amount of judicious interpretation is sometimes needed.

FIGURE 14.2 Typeface terminology

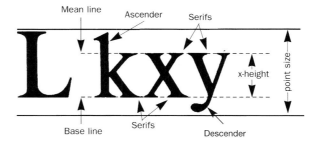

Source: Pira International Ltd

Typeface classifications British Standard 2961, drawn up in 1967, offers nine classifications.

1. Humanist
2. Garalde
3. Transitional
4. Didone
5. Slab serif
6. Lineale
7. Glyphic
8. Script
9. Graphic

FIGURE 14.3 Stress can be oblique or vertical. With obliquely stressed letterforms, the serifs are generally oblique; with vertically stressed forms they are horizontal

Source: Pira International Ltd

The traditional nomenclature in operation before BS2961 is used, however, and is annotated alongside the British Standard classification where the two coincide. A few examples of each typeface are given, set in 11 pt, with a note of the particular earmarks that distinguish them.

Humanist

Traditionally known as Venetian typefaces, examples include: Centaur, Cloister Old Style, Horley Old Style, Kennerley, Veronese. Features:

▶ light in weight, oblique stress, calligraphic in origin;

▶ bar of lower case 'e' inclined as in script handwriting;

▶ bracketed serifs.

Centaur

abcdefghijklmnopqrstuvwxyz

ABCDEFGHIJKLMNOPQRSTUVWXYZ

abcdefghijklmnopqrstuvwxyz

ABCDEFGHIJKLMNOPQRSTUVWXYZ

Centaur: Small x-height, long ascenders and descenders. Italic cap Q and italic lower cases are very distinctive.

FIGURE 14.4 The weight of serifs in relation to the main strokes of the letters can be distinctive, ranging from hairline at one extreme to slab at the other

Hairline   Slab-bracketed   Slab   Blunt

Bracketed   Chamfered   Sans serif

Source: Pira International Ltd

Horley Old Style

abcdefghijklmnopqrstuvwxyz

ABCDEFGHIJKLMNOPQRSTUVWXYZ

abcdefghijklmnopqrstuvwxyz

ABCDEFGHIJKLMNOPQRSTUVWXYZ

Horley Old Style: Open bowl on roman lower-case g. large upper loop on italic lower-case k.

Garalde

Traditionally known as 'Old Face' or 'Old Style'. Many of the most popular traditional bookwork typefaces come into this category. Examples:

Bembo, Caslon, Ehrhardt, Garamond, Old Style, Plantin. Features:

► less calligraphic in appearance than Humanist styles

► oblique stress, but with horizontal 'e' bar

► traditional bookwork appearance.

Bembo

abcdefghijklmnopqrstuvwxyz

ABCDEFGHIJKLMNOPQRSTUVWXYZ

abcdefghijklmnopqrstuvwxyz

ABCDEFGHIJKLMNOPQRSTUVWXYZ

Bembo: Extended upper stroke in roman lower case f. Cap height lower than ascender line. Distinctive italic lower case y with foot serif.

Caslon

abcdefghijklmnopqrstuvwxyz

ABCDEFGHIJKLMNOPQRSTUVWXYZ

abcdefghijklmnopqrstuvwxyz

ABCDEFGHIJKLMNOPQRSTUVWXYZ

Caslon: Rather loose fit and light in colour. Apex of roman cap A has a double point. Cap Q in roman and italic have tail in a horizontal position below the O.

Ehrhardt

abcdefghijklmnopqrstuvwxyz

ABCDEFGHIJKLMNOPQRSTUVWXYZ

abcdefghijklmnopqrstuvwxyz

ABCDEFGHIJKLMNOPQRSTUVWXYZ

Ehrhardt: Rather narrow appearance. Distinctive looping serif on roman lower case g. Curved bar on roman cap A. Distinctive backward-springing italic lower case w and y.

Garamond

abcdefghijklmnopqrstuvwxyz

ABCDEFGHIJKLMNOPQRSTUVWXYZ

abcdefghijklmnopqrstuvwxyz

ABCDEFGHIJKLMNOPQRSTUVWXYZ

Garamond: Serifs on roman lower case m and n are dish-shaped. Roman cap T has heavy serifs at each end of cross-bar. Italic letterforms are irregular. Note particularly inward-curling lower case h.

Plantin

abcdefghijklmnopqrstuvwxyz

ABCDEFGHIJKLMNOPQRSTUVWXYZ

abcdefghijklmnopqrstuvwxyz

ABCDEFGHIJKLMNOPQRSTUVWXYZ

Plantin: Large x-height, rather dark in colour. Roman lower case k has no foot serif. Roman cap P has unclosed bowl.

Sabon

abcdefghijklmnopqrstuvwxyz

ABCDEFGHIJKLMNOPQRSTUVWXYZ

abcdefghijklmnopqrstuvwxyz

ABCDEFGHIJKLMNOPQRSTUVWXYZ

Sabon: A modern design based on Garamond. Characteristic roman lower case f. Italic lower case f is very condensed with straight tail. Italic lower case j has straight tail.

Transitional

These are typefaces based on Plantin's types of the mid-18th century in Britain. The transitional aspect is between the oblique, calligraphic inspiration of Garalde/Old Style faces, and the more mechanical, vertical stress of the Didone/Modern faces (see below). Examples: Baskerville, Caledonia, and Scotch Roman. Features:

▶ axis of curves now vertical in stress. Rather more engraved in appearance

▶ bracketed oblique serifs (as Garalde).

Baskerville

abcdefghijklmnopqrstuvwxyz

ABCDEFGHIJKLMNOPQRSTUVWXYZ

abcdefghijklmnopqrstuvwxyz

ABCDEFGHIJKLMNOPQRSTUVWXYZ

Baskerville: Lower case roman g has unclosed lower bowl. No serif on middle peak of roman w. Curly cross-bar on italic cap T.

Didone

Traditionally known as 'Modern' typefaces. Examples: Bodoni, Corvinus, Modern Extended, Walbaum. Features:

► abrupt contrast between thick and thin strokes

► axis of curves completely vertical in stress

► horizontal top serifs, sometimes unbracketed hair-line.

Bodoni

abcdefghijklmnopqrstuvwxyz

ABCDEFGHIJKLMNOPQRSTUVWXYZ

abcdefghijklmnopqrstuvwxyz

ABCDEFGHIJKLMNOPQRSTUVWXYZ

Bodoni: Strong thick/thin contrast. Horizontal foot serif on roman lower case b. Horizontal serif on roman lower case q. No bracketed serif on roman lower case t.

Walbaum

abcdefghijklmnopqrstuvwxyz

ABCDEFGHIJKLMNOPQRSTUVWXYZ

abcdefghijklmnopqrstuvwxyz

ABCDEFGHIJKLMNOPQRSTUVWXYZ

Walbaum: Open, light, square in appearance. Roman lower case g has backward-springing joining stroke. Roman lower case w is an unusual and distinctive design.

Slab-serif

Otherwise called 'Egyptian'. Typefaces have heavy, square-ended serifs, with or without brackets. Examples: Cairo, Century, Clarendon, Egyptian, Playbill, Rockwell.

Egyptian

abcdefghijklmnopqrstuvwxyz

ABCDEFGHIJKLMNOPQRSTUVWXYZ

abcdefghijklmnopqrstuvwxyz

ABCDEFGHIJKLMNOPQRSTUVWXYZ

Egyptian: Very black, monoline, with thick, unbracketed serifs. Mainly used for display. Cap R has a very rounded tail.

New Century Schoolbook

abcdefghijklmnopqrstuvwxyz

ABCDEFGHIJKLMNOPQRSTUVWXYZ

abcdefghijklmnopqrstuvwxyz

ABCDEFGHIJKLMNOPQRSTUVWXYZ

New Century Schoolbook: Closely related to slab-serif typefaces but with slightly slanted serifs and some old-style letterforms. Roman lower case t has thick bracket to cross-bar. Italic lower case f has an almost straight tail.

Rockwell

abcdefghijklmnopqrstuvwxyz
ABCDEFGHIJKLMNOPQRSTUVWXYZ
abcdefghijklmnopqrstuvwxyz
ABCDEFGHIJKLMNOPQRSTUVWXYZ

Rockwell: Many related weights and condensed/expanded versions. Distinctive horizontal serif over cap A in roman and italic.

Lineale

Typefaces without serifs, otherwise known as sans serif. Four distinctions are made:

▶ Grotesque
▶ Neo-Grotesque
▶ Geometric
▶ Humanist.

Grotesque

Lineales with 19th century origins. Rather angular and gothic in appearance. Examples: Grot 215, Headline Bold, Sans No. 7.

Grotesque

abcdefghijklmnopqrstuvwxyz
ABCDEFGHIJKLMNOPQRSTUVWXYZ
abcdefghijklmnopqrstuvwxyz
ABCDEFGHIJKLMNOPQRSTUVWXYZ

Grotesque: Many variations available on the basic design. Angular, upright in appearance. Roman lower case f has an abrupt curve at the head. Roman lower case t has sheared-off main stroke. Roman and italic lower case a retain bowl and top-stroke rather than plain bowl design.

Neo-Grotesque

Later designs, more rounded, open and monoline in weight. Examples: Helvetica, Univers.

Helvetica

abcdefghijklmnopqrstuvwxyz
ABCDEFGHIJKLMNOPQRSTUVWXYZ
abcdefghijklmnopqrstuvwxyz
ABCDEFGHIJKLMNOPQRSTUVWXYZ

Helvetica: Many weights and versions available. Lower case y in roman and italic has curly tail, roman cap G has vertical down stroke outside bowl, roman cap Q has angled tail going through bowl.

Univers

abcdefghijklmnopqrstuvwxyz
ABCDEFGHIJKLMNOPQRSTUVWXYZ
abcdefghijklmnopqrstuvwxyz
ABCDEFGHIJKLMNOPQRSTUVWXYZ

Univers: Many weights and versions available. Lower case y in roman and italic has straight tail, roman cap G has no down stroke, roman cap Q has tail horizontal to baseline.

Geometric

Lineales constructed on simple geometric shapes, e.g. circle or rectangle.
Examples: Erbar, Eurostile, Futura.

Eurostile

abcdefghijklmnopqrstuvwxyz
ABCDEFGHIJKLMNOPQRSTUVWXYZ
abcdefghijklmnopqrstuvwxyz
ABCDEFGHIJKLMNOPQRSTUVWXYZ

Eurostyle: Square, mechanical appearance. Roman lower case t has unusual design. Roman cap Q has distinctive appearance.

Futura

abcdefghijklmnopqrstuvwxyz
ABCDEFGHIJKLMNOPQRSTUVWXYZ
abcdefghijklmnopqrstuvwxyz
ABCDEFGHIJKLMNOPQRSTUVWXYZ

Futura: Lower case j and t are a single straight down-stroke. Lower case q has no top-stroke.

Humanist

Based on the proportions of Humanist or Garalde lower case, with shading and stroke contrast. Examples: Gill Sans, Optima, Pascal.

Gill Sans

abcdefghijklmnopqrstuvwxyz
ABCDEFGHIJKLMNOPQRSTUVWXYZ
abcdefghijklmnopqrstuvwxyz
ABCDEFGHIJKLMNOPQRSTUVWXYZ

Gill Sans: Available in many weights and versions. Lower case g has two-bowl form. Italic lower case p has thin stroke commencing bowl to left of main stroke.

Optima

abcdefghijklmnopqrstuvwxyz
ABCDEFGHIJKLMNOPQRSTUVWXYZ
abcdefghijklmnopqrstuvwxyz
ABCDEFGHIJKLMNOPQRSTUVWXYZ

Optima: Clean lines with notable thick/thin contrast. Lower case f has thickened stroke at head. Lower case g has two-bowl form and horizontal serif. Cap J extends below baseline.

Glyphic

Typefaces based on a chiselled rather than a calligraphic form and used in display sizes. Each design is distinct from all others and is best identified by direct reference to a type catalogue. They are blunt, elephant-foot serifs. Examples: Albertus, Chisel, Festival, Latin.

Script

Typefaces that imitate cursive writing. Two distinctions are made:
► Formal, examples are Marina and Palace Script
► Informal, examples are Flash, Mistral and Pepita.

Graphic

Typefaces that appear to have been drawn graphically rather than written. Examples: Cartoon, Klang, Libra, Old English.

Hybrids

The traditional category of '20th-century' book faces are mainly hybrid in origin and are defined under BS2961 by reference to their double origin, e.g. Humanist–Garalde, Garalde–Didone. Examples: Goudy Old Style, Lectura, Melior, Photina, Pilgrim, Spectrum.

Goudy Old Style

abcdefghijklmnopqrstuvwxyz
ABCDEFGHIJKLMNOPQRSTUVWXYZ
abcdefghijklmnopqrstuvwxyz
ABCDEFGHIJKLMNOPQRSTUVWXYZ

Goudy Old Style: Note roman lower case f, g, i, j; roman cap Q; italic lower case throughout is distinctive.

Palatino

abcdefghijklmnopqrstuvwxyz
ABCDEFGHIJKLMNOPQRSTUVWXYZ
abcdefghijklmnopqrstuvwxyz
ABCDEFGHIJKLMNOPQRSTUVWXYZ

Palatino: Note roman lower case t; roman cap Y; all italic lower case is very calligraphic.

Perpetua

abcdefghijklmnopqrstuvwxyz
ABCDEFGHIJKLMNOPQRSTUVWXYZ
abcdefghijklmnopqrstuvwxyz
ABCDEFGHIJKLMNOPQRSTUVWXYZ

Perpetua: Note roman lower case a, f, r; extremely small appearing size; italic lower case f, g.

Times

abcdefghijklmnopqrstuvwxyz
ABCDEFGHIJKLMNOPQRSTUVWXYZ
abcdefghijklmnopqrstuvwxyz
ABCDEFGHIJKLMNOPQRSTUVWXYZ

Times: Note thickening of stroke on lower case; long, straight stroke on roman cap G; italic cap Q.

Typographic design and specification

In clockwise order from the left-hand side of the page, the margins round a type area are called the back margin, head margin, fore-edge margin, and foot margin. The two inside margins that make up the white space across the gutter on a double-page spread are called the combined back margins or combined backs.

In specifying margins, it is conventional to state only the back margin and head margin along with the measure (length of line) and depth of page, so letting the fore-edge and foot margins make what they will.

A suitable type measure (line length) for a conventional book or magazine page is:

▶ 70–75% of the total width, remaining white space divided in the proportions 1:1.5, back to fore-edge margin

▶ 75–85% of the total page depth, remaining white space divided in the proportions 1:1.5, head to foot margin.

Example: apply this to a 216 × 138mm Metric Demy 8vo page:

Width of the page is 138mm = 33 picas
Therefore a suitable type width is between 23 and 25 picas.
If 23 picas: back margin 4 picas, fore-edge margin 6 picas
If 25 picas: back margin 3.5 picas, fore-edge margin 4.5 picas.

FIGURE 14.5 Type area and margins

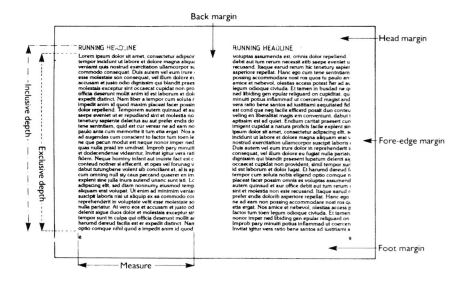

Source: Pira International Ltd

When the calculation leaves scope for two back-margin options, it is often better to go for the larger of the two. This allows more tolerance in the folding and binding processes and is particularly important in cross-grain books (see Chapter 10).

Depth of the page is 216 mm = 51.5 picas

Therefore a suitable type depth is between 38.5 and 44 picas.

If 38.5 picas: head margin 5 picas, foot margin 8 picas

If 44 picas: head margin 3 picas, foot margin 4.5 picas.

When specifying type depths on a page, it is important to make clear whether the depth is the inclusive depth or the exclusive depth (referring to the running head). This is an example that avoids ambiguity:

10 on 12pt running head + 12pt white line + 42 lines 10 on 12pt (504pts) + 12pt white line +10 on 12pt foot folio.

When the calculation leaves scope for two head margin options, it is often better to go for the smaller of the two. This is to avoid the visual risk of the text falling off the page. Visual centring of type on a page is surprisingly high (about a third of the way down). In a well-balanced page, the back margin will tend to be similar to the head margin, or slightly smaller than it. Clockwise from the back margin, the following proportions work well: 2/2.5/3/3.5. In the example above the proportions of the larger margin version would be 2/2.5/3/4, which is reasonably close to this.

Choosing typefaces

Selecting a typeface for a job is often a question of personal taste more than anything else, but there are several practical factors worth considering as well.

Standardisation

Consider the following:
► The typeface range/collection held by the supplier or yourself. Do you want or need to add to it? Some publishers and typesetters aim to standardise on a particular range of fonts or font supplier's collection – Bitstream, for example – for reasons of economy and of output standardisation;
► Updating requirements. A standard collection is desirable so that files can be rerun with no possibility of font clash or error;
► Special requirements. Maths and science setting makes heavy use of special mathematical symbols and characters. Many of these are designed in Times, so sticking to Times for the main text is sensible;
► Typographic niceties. Not all fonts are supplied with true small caps, for example.

Type of publication

Sans serif faces are notoriously hard to read for long periods, and are best avoided for long magazine articles, book work or other publications that demand continuous reading. Italic styles too are hard on the eye for continuous reading.

Paper

The paper to be used for the job should have an influence on your choice:
► a delicate, spindly typeface will fare badly on a bulky news or antique wove;
► a heavy, high-contrast face will look dazzling on art paper;
Recently designed faces often work better in integrated illustration formats than the more classic old-face styles.

Set-width and appearing size

Set-widths and the appearing sizes of typefaces can vary dramatically. It is most important never to specify 10 on 11pt, or whatever, without specifying the precise typeface (and even a particular manufacturer's design of that typeface). In isolation, 10 on 11pt means very little, and guarantees only that the baseline of each line of type will be 11pts away from its fellows. Font designs for the same nominal size can differ enormously, and 10 on 11pt in one face might have the appearing size of 9 on 11pt in another or 11pt solid in yet another.

Not only will the appearance of the page be affected, but also the castoff content. For example, a page containing 45 lines of 10 on 11pt type set across 24 picas renders 540 words in Linotype Perpetua, but only 425 words in Linotype Melior – a 25% difference.

Design variants

Manufacturers' designs of the same nominal typeface can differ considerably. All manufacturers have their own versions of Times, Plantin, Garamond, Helvetica, Univers, and so on (sometimes called by that name, sometimes given a different name), and each has subtle – or sometimes not so subtle – design alterations made for copyright reasons. That is why it is important to see samples of the typeface you are specifying in the particular version you are to use.

Readability

Generally speaking, what matters more than the choice of any particular typeface is:

► how the type is arranged on the page
► the proportions of leading and measure to the appearing size of the type
► the way white space is used
► the way a double-page spread looks.

Typefaces do set a general mood or look but, by and large, positioning, colour and layout are much more important to the reader, and to the success or failure of a design.

Specifying magazine and book work

In designing magazine or book work, house style or series requirements often play a part. When this is not the case and a typographical design needs to be built from scratch, the following notes may be helpful. By and large, they represent conventional wisdom.

When an outside supplier does the typesetting, the typesetter will expect a complete type specification that may be usefully provided either as a form completed by hand, a word-processed template (highly convenient for books of similar format) or an instruction to follow a publication of similar style.

If files are being supplied, some or all of the formatting information may already be in the files, in which case the instructions will be mainly to do with confirming finished type sizes and styles and with page make-up requirements.

When a manuscript is being supplied for keying, the typesetter will need to create all the formats at the time of keying.

Appearing sizes

Monotype Bembo: Font designs for the same nominal size can differ enormously, and '10 on 11pt' in one face might have the appearing size of 9 on 11pt in another, or 11pt solid in yet another.

Monotype Perpetua: Font designs for the same nominal size can differ enormously, and '10 on 11pt' in one face might have the appearing size of 9 on 11pt in another or 11pt solid in yet another.

Monotype Plantin: Font designs for the same nominal size can differ enormously, and '10 on 11pt' in one face might have the appearing size of 9 on 11pt in another or 11pt solid in yet another.

Structure

It is necessary in book work to specify all elements of the book, and the order in which they should run. The following list gives the conventional order and positioning (recto/verso).

Prelims

▶   half-title page opening recto

▶   advertisement verso

▶   title page recto

▶   copyright page verso

▶   dedication recto or last verso of prelims facing the first page of main text

▶   acknowledgements verso

▶   contents list recto

▶   list of illustrations verso/recto

▶   list of abbreviations recto/verso

▶   foreword recto

▶   preface recto

▶   introduction recto.

Main text

▶   part recto

▶   section or chapter

▶   sub-section

▶   main text ... repeated.

Endmatter

▶   appendix/appendices recto

▶   notes recto

▶   glossary recto

▶   vocabulary recto

▶   bibliography recto

▶   index recto.

Body text setting and subsidiary text setting

The basic page specification, type area and margins should be specified and described as explained previously. The size of type should be appropriate to the type area.

The most commonly used typefaces for continuous body text are serif faces such as Baskerville, Bembo, Century, Garamond, Plantin, and Times.

Sans serif faces – Helvetica, Univers and so on – are harder to read in continuous text and are generally not advised for long stretches of type.

The old adage 'Never set type to longer than half its point size in inches' may be useful to remember, but this does allow an extreme case even so: for a Demy 8vo book, with a type measure of 24 picas or 4in, for example, the adage would allow the smallest continuous-text size to be 8pt, whereas in practice anything much denser than 9 on 10pt would test the reader's patience. More normally 10pt, 11pt or even 12pt would be correct.

Leading is best judged by the character of the typeface itself: fonts with small appearing sizes (e.g. Bembo, Perpetua) need little leading, while fonts with large appearing sizes (Melior, Plantin, Walbaum, Times) need at least one or two points in composition sizes.

Extracts

Extracts inside the main body text are frequently set one or two sizes smaller than the main text size. Conventionally, extract text may be any combination of the following:
▶ marked by space above and below
▶ set in a reduced type size/set solid/set in italic
▶ indented at the left/indented at both left and right.

Footnotes/endnotes

Footnotes are generally set two or three sizes smaller than the body text and, ideally, are set at the foot of the page containing the reference mark. Depending on the complexity of the text or the deficiencies in the page make-up software, footnotes can, if necessary, be relegated to the end of the chapter containing the reference or to the end of the book (in which case they become endnotes), but this is generally less satisfactory from the reader's point of view.

Captions

When specifying picture captions, bear in mind that the length of the average entry might best determine the general style. If a roman font is chosen, the amount of space separating caption from body text is crucial if the reader is not to confuse caption with text.

If files are being transferred, the main text type and extract, footnote and other subsidiary types should have been marked electronically to help identification and typesetting to the correct finished sizes. If a manuscript is being supplied for keying, these elements should have been sidelined in the manuscript for the typesetter.

Display headings

Composition sizes (up to 14pt) are normally expressed in points and picas, but specifying larger sizes of type or specifying type that floats inside a given area is often more conveniently done in:
▶ x-height
▶ cap-height
▶ inches/millimetres.
Display heads are normally specified by giving the drop from the head of the page (i.e. including the margin) to the baseline of the first line of type, or in lines/picas/millimetres off the exclusive type area to the baseline of the first line of type.

In the case of chapter heads followed by text, the number of lines of main text to appear on the chapter opening page can also be specified along with the space between the baseline of the heading and the first line of text. Display heads can be ranged left, right or centred in the same way as headlines, and it is common practice to let headline and heading positionings echo each other.

Part openings are often treated typographically in much the same way as the title page. Part openings are normally announced on a new recto (right-hand) page with the backing verso (left-hand) page blank. Section or chapter opening pages might start new pages, right-hand pages only, left- or right-hand pages (as they fall) or they might simply run on from the body text of the previous section/chapter (separated by a few lines of space).

Subheadings

If files are being transferred, all subheads should have been marked electronically to make identification and typesetting to the correct finished sizes easier. If manuscript for keying is being supplied, all subheads should have been marked A, B, C and so on in the manuscript for the typesetter.

Subheads are conventionally typeset as either:

▶ cross-heads, which straddle the main type measure. Usually centred over the measure, they are used for greater emphasis than a boxed head

▶ boxed heads, which are ranged left on the main type measure. There are two types:

    ▷ shoulder heads, which occupy a line alone and text starting either flush or indented below. Shoulder heads are frequently used to break up text into subsections. They are often set as text bold, and balance well with about two to three times as much space above as below;

    ▷ side heads, which have the main text running on in the same line. Side heads are often set as text caps or italic and are normally subsidiary to shoulder heads.

The conventional levels of importance in headings, in descending order, are:

▶ display heading (chapter or part)

▶ cross-head

▶ shoulder head

▶ side head.

Headlines and folios

A headline is the phrase or word that runs over the top of book pages to indicate position inside the book. A running head is a headline that is repeated, unchanged, throughout (usually the book title). Headline or running head text should not be supplied inside text files but left to the typesetter to generate in accordance with the type specification.

Page make-up programs generate folios (page numbers) automatically; running heads are only semi-automatic, and in degrees depending on the sophistication of the program and the variability of the headline. Conventional arrangements in book work differ depending on whether the work is fiction or non-fiction. When it is desirable to have headlines in fiction, the most common arrangement is to have the book title on all verso pages (so the verso headline is unvarying throughout the book) and the section or chapter title on the recto (varying between chapters). If there are no section/chapter titles, the book title might then be the running headline both verso and recto.

Small format paperbacks commonly have no headline. Likewise, a non-fiction title with a fairly simple structure might carry the book title as a headline on the verso and the section/chapter title on the recto. More complicated works might carry the section/chapter title on the verso (varying between chapters) and the next level of subheading on the recto (varying between pages). Dictionaries and encyclopedias would carry the name of the first entry on the verso and the last entry on the recto (varying page to page).

Conventional positioning of headlines might be:

▶ centred
▶ ranged to fore-edge margin, or indented 1/2/3/4 picas in
▶ ranged to back margin, or indented 1/2/3/4 picas in
▶ separated from text by one line space.

Note that less than one line space below is frequently sufficient separation from the main text.

Typographical arrangements that work include:

▶ italic, either text size or one size larger
▶ letter spaced small caps of the text face
▶ fine rule between headline and first line of text.

Note that small caps (letter-spaced) may often be visually preferable to text-sized caps.

Folios are conventionally either ranged with the headline at the head of the page, or placed alone at the foot of the page, and separated from the text by a line space (a half-line might sometimes be adequate) at the same size.

Whether figures are lining or non-lining will depend on the general style of the publication and the typeface being used (note most typefaces do not carry non-lining figures as a matter of course).

Conventional positioning of headlines with folios might be:

▶ folio ranged to fore-edge margin with the headline centred on the text measure
▶ ranged to fore-edge margin, separated from headline by 1 or 2 picas
▶ ranged to back margin, separated from headline by 1 or 2 picas.

Where folios are separate from running heads, at the foot of the page it is usual to range them in the same manner: both centred, ranged with fore-edge margin.

Prelims and endmatter

In design terms these are often best tackled last. Any of the main prelim matter, if extensive, can be set one or even two sizes down. If this is done, it is good practice to reduce the type measure a little on the pages affected and scale down the sizes of the headings in proportion. This is particularly true for the contents page. The same thing applies in the endmatter: notes, glossaries, vocabularies, bibliographies and indexes often benefit from being set one or two sizes smaller.

The title page needs special care, and should reflect the general look of the rest of the book (centred or ranged-left style, same use of italic, bold). Any text to be centred visually on the page needs to be placed quite high. Remember that the visual centre of a page is around two-thirds the way up.

Detailed points of typographic style

There are many points of typographical nicety that can also be specified, some of which might reasonably form part of a house style. The following is a set of detailed instructions for book work setting and page make-up that you may find useful to choose from.

Punctuation setting

▶ *Quotes* Use single quotes and double within single unless otherwise instructed. In quote-within-quotes, use hair-space between double and single quote marks.
▶ *En-dashes* used parenthetically should be word-spaced.
▶ *Em dashes* might be set either close-up to previous word or word-spaced according to context – follow copy.
▶ *Full points*, commas, colons, semicolons to be set closed-up to preceding word. Followed by word space.
▶ *Ellipses* Three dots or four, according to context (the fourth dot is a full point that might precede or follow the three-dot ellipsis. Follow marked copy. Whether three- or four-dot, the spaces between dots should be fixed with a thin space. The space on either side of the ellipsis should be word-spaced, except where the first dot is the full point.

Spacing parameters

▶ No more than two successive lines of text to begin or end with the same word
▶ Phrases or groups of words that appear in successive lines must not be set in the same position in both lines
▶ Paragraph indent one em of set
▶ No extra word space after punctuation
▶ Word spacing: minimum 17% of the em, average 22–28% of the em, maximum 100% of the em
▶ Letter spacing within text not allowed. For display caps and small caps: narrow – 5% of the em of set extra; medium – 10%; wide – 15%
▶ Kerning of relevant cap combinations (LY, YA etc) permitted
▶ Feathering (vertical justification) not allowed.

H&J/word breaks

▶ As a general principle, divide words in the same way as they are split into syllables when pronounced
▶ Place a single vowel before a hyphen rather than after, so allowing the second part of the broken word, beginning a new line, to start with a consonant, e.g. rumi-nate not rum-inate; tele-vision, not tel-evision; commu-nism, not commun-ism

▶ Compound words such as milli-metre should be split only at the logical breakpoints

▶ Minimum stub to be three letters

▶ Dates, initials and names not to be split unless in extreme cases

▶ For general rules, follow (one of):

   ▷ Hart, *Hart's Rules for Compositors and Readers at the University Press Oxford*

   ▷ Butcher, *Copy-editing. The Cambridge Handbook*

   ▷ Collins, *Authors' and Printers' Dictionary*

▶ No more than two successive lines to end with hyphens; then no further hyphens allowed within two lines

▶ Prelims: use roman numerals; then arabic numerals begin with first page of main text unless otherwise indicated on individual typescript

▶ Paragraphs: set first line of opening paragraph or section within a chapter full out. Indent first lines of subsequent paragraphs one em of set

▶ No widows at tops of pages (or if absolutely unavoidable, accept a limited number per book provided the lines are at least half full). At no time are two widows on the same spread acceptable

▶ Last word on a right-hand page must not be hyphenated.

Page depths must be equal across each spread (or, if absolutely unavoidable, spreads may be left one line long or short, but facing pages must always be equal).

▶ At least four lines of text must appear on the final page of each chapter.

▶ If a new run-on chapter or section within a chapter falls near the foot of a page, at least two lines and preferably three must appear at the foot of the page. It is not acceptable for the last line of a new section/displayed extract to appear at the top of a page

▶ If line spaces marked in the copy fall at top/foot of a page, insert an asterisk, centred on the measure, at the foot of the previous page.

Headlines and folios

▶ *Headlines* In main text, set book title on versos, chapter title on rectos, unless otherwise instructed; in frontmatter/endmatter sections set section title (e.g. preface, index) on both rectos and versos

▶ *Folios* No folio on part titles or versos, or on opening pages of sections/chapters. Always set folio on chapter ends and final page of book.

Typography for the web

Although the basic rules of typography are much the same for web pages and conventional print documents, type on screen and type printed on paper are different in crucial ways. The computer screen renders typefaces at a much lower resolution than is found in books, magazines and even pages output from inexpensive printers. Most magazine and book typography is rendered at 1200 dots per inch (dpi) or greater, while computer screens rarely show more than about 85dpi. Also, the usable area of typical computer screens is smaller than most magazine and book pages, limiting the information you can deliver on a web page without scrolling.

The most distinctive characteristic of web typography is its variability. Web pages are built on the fly each time they are loaded into a web browser. Each line of text, each headline, each unique font and type style is re-created by a complex interaction of the web browser, the web server and the operating system on the reader's computer. The process is fraught with possibilities for the unexpected: a missing font, an out-of-date browser or a peculiar set of font preferences designated by the reader. You should regard your web page layouts and typography as suggestions of how your pages should be rendered – you'll never know exactly how they will look on the reader's screen.

Typefaces

Each typeface has a unique tone that should produce a harmonious fit between the verbal and visual flow of your content. With the first versions of HTML, web authors had no control over typefaces (fonts in personal computer terminology). Fonts were set by the browser, so pages were viewed in whatever font the user specified in his or her browser preferences. The more recent versions of HTML and cascading stylesheets (CSS) allow designers to specify the typeface. This is useful not only for aesthetic reasons but also because of the differing dimensions of typefaces. A layout that is carefully designed using one face may not format correctly in another.

In specifying typefaces you should choose from the resident default fonts for most operating systems. If you specify a font that is not on the user's machine, the browser will display your pages using the user-specified default font. Bear in mind, too, that users can set their browser preferences to ignore font tags and display all pages using their designated default font.

Legibility on screen

Some typefaces are more legible than others on screen. A traditional typeface such as Times Roman is considered to be one of the most legible on paper, but at screen resolution its size is too small and its shapes look irregular. Screen legibility is most influenced by the x-height (the height of a lowercase 'x') and the overall size of the typeface.

Adapted traditional typefaces

Times New Roman is a good example of a traditional typeface that has been adapted for use on computer screens. A serif typeface like Times New Roman (the default text face in most web browsers) is about average in legibility on a computer screen, with a moderate x-height. Times New Roman is a good font to use in text-heavy documents that will probably be printed by readers rather than read on the screen. The compact letter size of Times New Roman also makes it a good choice if you need to pack a lot of words into a small space.

Designed for the screen

Typefaces such as Georgia and Verdana were designed specifically for their legibility on computer screens; they have exaggerated x-heights and are very large compared to more traditional typefaces in the same point size. These fonts offer excellent legibility for web pages designed to be read directly from the screen. However, the exaggerated x-heights and heavy letterforms of these fonts look massive and clumsy when transferred to the high-resolution medium of paper.

The most conventional scheme for using typefaces is to use a serif face such as Times New Roman or Georgia for body text and a sans serif face such as Verdana or Arial as a contrast for headlines. We generally set our text-laden web pages in Times New Roman because it produces a reasonable balance between density of information and overall legibility. Most readers expect a serif font for long blocks of text and find Times New Roman comfortable to read off-screen from paper print outs. Various studies purport to show that serif type is more legible than sans serif type and vice versa. You can truly judge type legibility only within the context of the situation – on screen – as users will see your web page. The most useful fonts that ship with the latest web browser (Microsoft Internet Explorer 5 in 2005) include:

andalemo.ttf	Andale Mono
ariblk.ttf	Arial Black
comic.ttf	Comic Sans MS
comicbd.ttf	Comic Sans MS Bold
georgia.ttf	Georgia
georgiab.ttf	Georgia Bold
georgiaz.ttf	Georgia Bold Italic
georgiai.ttf	Georgia Italic
impact.ttf	Impact
trebuc.ttf	Trebuchet MS
trebucbd.ttf	Trebuchet MS Bold
trebucbi.ttf	Trebuchet MS Bold Italic
trebuci.ttf	Trebuchet MS Italic
verdana.ttf	Verdana
verdanab.ttf	Verdana Bold
verdanaz.ttf	Verdana Bold Italic
verdanai.ttf	Verdana Italic
webdings.ttf	Webdings

Source: Microsoft

This means that when creating websites and pages using these fonts the design aesthetics are likely to be retained for the project.

Glossary of printing/publishing terms

3D Three dimensional, will be an important subset of inkjet printing for prototyping and modelling

A The A series is an international ISO range of paper sizes reducing from 4A at 1682×2378mm through A0 at 841×1189mm to A10 at 26×37mm, with subsidiary RA and SRA sizes. Each size folds in half to preserve the same proportions of 1:√2 at each reduction. See also B, C.

A&I Abstracting and indexing. The act of making summaries and indexes for books or journal articles.

A format paperback Mass market paperback of trimmed size 178×111mm.

A/D conversion See analogue to digital conversion.

a/w See artwork.

ablation mechanism of imaging plates by vapourising surface material using a laser (see **DI printing**).

abrasion resistance Measured resistance of a material surface (e.g. paper) to abrasion.

absolute humidity Quantity of water vapour in a unit volume of atmosphere.

absorbency The degree to which paper takes up contact moisture measured by a standard test. In optics, a transparent material's degree of suppression.

absorption Absorption or penetration is one of the four principal ways by which inks dry; and is associated most readily with coldset web-offset printing on newsprint. The other three methods are oxidation, polymerisation and evaporation.

abstract Short summary of the contents of an academic paper or scientific article.

AC Author's correction. See **author's corrections**.

accelerated ageing Testing of paper to determine strength loss through ageing.

accents Marks added to letters in some languages to indicate stress, e.g. é (acute e) in French.

acceptance testing The process by which a manufacturer tests a new system to demonstrate that it works. See also beta testing.

access The ability to retrieve data from a computer storage medium or peripheral device.

access fee Fee charged by a museum or gallery for the facility of photographing items in its collection. Also called a facility fee.

access provider See internet service provider.

access time The time taken to retrieve data from a computer storage medium or a peripheral.

accession number Serial number used in a library indexing system that shows when the new book was first acquired.

accessions New books added to a library.

accordion fold Parallel folds in paper, which open like an accordion bellows, each in an opposite direction from the preceding fold.

accordion insert Periodical insert with accordion fold.

achromatic colour An intermediate grey level in the monochromatic grey scale in computer graphics.

achromatic separations Colour separations produced by CCR (complementary colour removal). The black printer carries more detail than with conventional separations and the tertiary, or complementary, elements of any colour hue are removed. Also called ICR (integrated colour removal) or GCR (grey component replacement).

acid resist Acid-resisting coat on printing plate.

acid-free paper Generic term to describe paper that is free from acid-producing chemicals which reduce longevity. See permanent paper and neutral sized paper.

acknowledgements page Page of a book in which the author gives his list of sources and references.

Acrobat A technology produced by Adobe Systems Inc. that allows documents created on one computer system to be read and printed on other systems. The technology uses portable document format (PDF) files, which are produced either directly as a print option in the source application or by running PostScript code through a program called Acrobat Distiller. All formatting information is embedded in the compressed file and graphics and font information can also be included. If the fonts in the document are not present on the system where the document is viewed, 'Multiple Mastering' technology is used to simulate those fonts. Acrobat can be used for proofing (particularly in conjunction with **ISDN**) and for electronic publishing, although the facsimile of the printed page is not always an ideal format for viewing onscreen.

across the gutter Printed over the **gutter** margin of a book.

acrylic A polymer based on synthetic resin and used for surface coatings among other applications. Acrylic coatings are tough, flexible and waterproof.

ADAR Air-dried all rag paper.

ADC See **analogue-to-digital converter**.

add-on board An expansion board (or card) that is inserted into one of the computer's expansion slots to provide additional features such as additional memory, communications or graphics.

addendum Late addition to book after printing, often as a pasted-in slip.

additive colour The production of colour by blending different colours of light. Colour (**RGB**) computer monitors and television sets use additive colour. Blending equal amounts of red, green and blue light gives white light and other combinations give other colours. This should be contrasted with the way in which we normally see, using white light, when the colour perceived is made up of the wavelengths reflected by an object, with those absorbed or subtracted.

Subtractive colour is used in printing (see **CMYK**).

additive primaries Red, green and blue that when added together as light appear as white. Known also as the **light primaries**. Their complements or 'opposites' are known as the **light secondaries**: each one is made up of two colours out of the three, taken in turn. They are cyan (i.e. minus red), magenta (i.e. minus green), yellow (i.e. minus blue).

additives Substances added to ink to control such things as drying and permanence.

adhesive binding Binding style for books and magazines involving the application of a hot-melt adhesive to the roughened or ground back to hold the pages and cover

together. Also called **cutback binding, perfect binding, thermoplastic binding, threadless binding**.

Adobe Inc. Californian software company that developed PostScript. Important font supplier and responsible for PDF development.

Adobe PhotoShop See **PhotoShop**.

ADSL Asymmetric Digital Subscriber Line is a two-way voice and data communications channel allowing up to 8Mbps download and 256Kbps upload. It is asymmetric because the download speed is different to the upload speed.

advertorial Magazine article written by an advertiser with the aim of boosting a product or products.

against the grain Folding or cutting at right angles to the grain of the paper. Contrast **with the grain**.

AFM Atomic force microscope, a type of scanning probe microscope.

AGV Abbreviation for **automatic guided vehicle**, a driverless or robot cart that travels round a factory floor carrying materials/finished products. Used extensively in modern newspaper printing plants and automated warehouses.

air bar Bar on a web offset press that conveys the web of paper. Tiny holes in the bar float the web on a minute cushion of air, preventing set-off.

air knife coater Device that applies a jet of compressed air to the coating on a web of paper to achieve a smooth level film while fluid.

air knife cooling Cooling using jets of compressed air.

air shear burst Break in paper reel caused by trapped air.

air waybill Air transport term for the document made out on behalf of the sender as evidence of the contract of carriage by airfreight. Also called an **air consignment note**.

air-dried paper Paper is dried by passing the web through warm air with only minimum support rather than on steam-heated cylinders. Used for high-quality production.

air-dry pulp Pulp with a standard moisture content of 10%.

alcohol damping The use of isopropanol as a component chemical in the damping solution in a litho press.

alcohols Solvents used in some inks.

algorithm An arithmetical computer routine in the form of programmed instructions that perform a recurring task.

aliasing A possible result of displaying or printing an **analogue** or continuous image in a **digital** format so that the image is split into cells. This can create a jagged or pixellated image and is particularly noticeable on low-resolution devices and in fine detail. (See also **anti-aliasing**, **moiré**).

align To line up type, horizontally or vertically, using a typographical criterion, e.g. **base alignment.**

aligning numerals See **lining figures**.

alkali resistance Quality in paper that resists staining or discolouration by alkaline materials.

all rag paper Paper made from rag pulp.

alpha test Early testing of a software package before a **beta test**.

alphabet A set of all the characters, digits and symbols used in a language or work.

alphabet length Length of a lower case type fount.

alphabetic character set One that contains letters, but not digits, but may contain control and special characters.

alphanumeric Relating to the full alphabetic and numeric character set of a machine.

alphasort To sort data into alphabetical sequence.

altar fold Also called gatefold or windowfold where a sheet is folded so that two flaps are formed that can be opened from either side.

alum Aluminium sulphate. One of the main components in papermaking **size**.

AM See **Amplitude modulated screening**.

ambient conditions Those conditions pertaining to the surrounding medium (temperature, noise).

ambient noise level A random and uncontrollable noise level in a circuit or at a location. See **noise**.

American National Standards Institute (ANSI) A body that creates standards for a wide variety of industries, including computer programming languages. Important Committee for Graphic Arts Technologies Standards (CGATS) for print-related activities.

American Standard Code for Information Interchange (ASCII) A data transmission coding standard designed to achieve compatibility between data devices. Each symbol in ASCII code consists of seven data bits and one **parity bit** for error-checking purposes. This combination allows for 128 code combinations. If the eighth bit is not used for parity checking, a total of 256 code combinations is possible.

ampersand Symbol (&) for the word 'and'.

amplitude modulated screening Where variably sized dots in fixed positions make up the image, referred to as conventional screening.

analogue Information that can vary in a continuous fashion (e.g. loudness of sound), containing no discontinuous elements. (See also **digital**)

analogue proof Proof produced by mechanical means from physical materials, (e.g. Cromalin proof produced from film) as distinct from a **digital proof** produced from a computer file.

analogue-to-digital conversion Conversion of information from **analogue** form to **digital** (so it can be represented in a computer), e.g. scanning.

analogue-to-digital converter (ADC) A device that produces digital output from an analogue input, e.g. a scanner.

analyst A person who defines problems and suggests procedures for their solution.

anamorphic distortion Scaling in which one dimension of a subject is reduced/enlarged to a different proportion from the other dimension.

anchor A marker for the beginning or the end of a hypertext link to indicate where a graphic or other imported information is linked to the main document text flow.

angle cutting Web sheeting at an angle rather than cutting horizontally to the machine direction.

aniline ink Volatile ink that dries very quickly. Used in **flexography**.

anilox roller Mostly laser-engraved chrome or ceramic-coated metering roller to meter a controlled film of ink to the plate. The volume of ink is affected by the cell resolution and the shape and depth of the cell.

Anilox system The flexo inking system consists of an elastomer-covered fountain roller running in the ink pan, adjustable against a contacting engraved anilox metering roller with the two as a unit adjustable to the printing plate cylinder. Ink is flooded into the engraved cells of the anilox with any excess doctored off by a blade with ink in the anilox cells transferred to the printing plate surface.

animal-sized paper Paper treated by passing it through a bath of animal size (gelatine).

anodised plate Printing plate used for offset litho and specially coated to prevent oxidation.

ANSI See **American National Standards Institute**.

ANSI character set The character set adopted by **ANSI** as the standard for computers; also the character set used by **Microsoft Windows**. Unlike the **ASCII** character set, ANSI uses all eight bits, so that the character set comprises 256 characters. The printable characters of the ASCII character set have the same code in both the ANSI and ASCII character sets. ANSI characters that are not displayed on the keyboard are accessed using the 'alt' key on a PC keyboard and the 'option' key on a Macintosh keyboard. In Windows the characters can also be accessed using the Character Map utility.

anti set-off powder Fine spray sometimes applied on litho printing machines at the delivery to prevent **set-off**.

anti-aliasing Ways of improving the display of **analogue** or continuous images in digital formats by reducing the pixellated appearance or reducing the creation of artefacts when the **colour resolution** is low. Can use either **dithering** or **grey levels**. (See also **aliasing, jaggies, hinting**)

anti-halation backing Coating on the back of photographic film that prevents **halation**.

anti-oxidant Ingredient in an ink that extends the **open time** of an ink on press.

anti-rust paper Paper with additives that protect metal surfaces against rusting.

anti-tarnish paper Paper with additives that protect bright metals against tarnishing.

antique A printing paper with a rough finish but good printing surface that is valued in book printing for its high volume characteristics. Also called antique wove.

AOM Acousto-optical modulation is a fast and efficient mechanism for modulating an exposing laser beam used in anilox engraving and CTP devices.

APACS Association of Payments and Clearing Services. The UK trade association of banks and building societies that exchange payments for customers. It also has responsibility for the cooperative aspects of money transmission and other payment-related developments.

aperture Lens opening on a camera, expressed as an **F number**.

apochromatic Lenses that focus blue, green and red in the same plane.

apparent density Weight of paper per unit of volume.

apparent specific gravity See **apparent density**.

appearing size The physical size of a type, as opposed to its nominal point size. Two typefaces of the same point size can have very different appearing sizes.

appendix Addition to a book or document following the main text.

Apple Computer Inc. Manufacturer of the **Macintosh** range of computers.

applet See **Java applet**.

application software Programs that are applied to solve specific problems such as business systems.

aquafuge water-soluble inks used in security printing

aquatint Type of print using 'mottled' areas designed to resemble water-colour painting.

aquatone Form of **collotype printing** using a finescreen gelatin-coated plate and offset printing.

arabic figures The numerals 1, 2, 3, 4 and so on, as distinct from Roman I, II, III, IV. Evolved from Arabic symbols. Arabic figures can be typeset as **lining** or **non-lining figures**.

arc lamp Lamp that produces light by a current that arcs across two electrodes, usually of carbon (thus, carbon arcs). Used as a light source in photography or plate-making.

architecture The design or arrangement of components in a microprocessor.

archival paper A paper with long-lasting qualities, usually with good colour retention. See also **permanent paper**.

art canvas Loose wove, strong cotton with a tissue lining. Used in bookbinding.

art paper Paper coated with china clay and polished to a high finish.

artboard Woodfree board coated to a high finish for fine printing of halftones.

artificial parchment A paper that simulates parchment.

artwork Original illustrative copy or typesetting ready for reproduction at pre-film stage.

ascender The part of a letter extending above the **x height**, as for example in b, d, h, k and l. (See also **descender**)

ASCII American Standard Code for Information Interchange.

ash or **ash content** Residue of paper after incineration, gauged by standard test. Represents the amount of **loadings** and **fillers** (mineral content) in the paper.

aspect ratio The ratio of width to height. Common uses are to describe a **pixel**, display screen or a **graphic**. Although square pixels (1:1) are considered preferable, most displays use aspect ratios of about 5:4. The aspect ratio of graphics will not always appear to be the same on paper as it does on screen (partly because the pixel aspect ratio is not 1:1).

assembly Bringing together film separations to make up rows of pages and produce final imposed foils for platemaking. Also called **planning**. **asterisk** Star-shaped symbol (*) often used as a footnote reference mark.

ATS Animal Tub Sized Paper sized after manufacture with animal gelatine.

attribute Property or characteristic. Within the **DTD** (see **document type definition**), attributes may be defined for **SGML** (and **HTML**) tags or elements, as well as possible values for an attribute. Within a **document instance**, a tag may include a particular value for an attribute. Attributes are also used within SGML to define the position of cross-references and their targets. Within typography, attribute is used to mean type style, such as italic or bold; in **paint** and **draw programs**, attribute refers to line weights, colours and styles, as well as to the colours and styles of fills.

audit trail In workflow management, the facility to keep track of all successive versions of documents with information on when changes were made and by whom.

authentication Verification of the identity of a person or process. In a communication system, authentication verifies that messages really come from their stated source. (See also **digital signature**, **encryption**)

author's corrections Corrections made by the author on proofs and changing the original copy, as distinct from **printer's errors** or **literals** made by the typesetter. Author's corrections are by convention marked in blue; printer's errors or literals are marked in red.

author-date A bibliographical reference system comprising the author's name and date of publication, e.g. Smyth, 2003.

automatic error correction Referring to the detection and correction (usually involving retransmission) of transmission errors. The degree of correction will be dependent on the error checking codes employed and equipment configuration.

automatic feeder Device on a printing or folding machine that draws paper into the machine.

automatic heading The positioning of a heading on consecutive pages by means of a generic instruction at the start of a project. Common on modern page make-up systems.

automatic pile delivery System on printing machines that jogs printed sheets into an orderly pile and gradually lowers the accumulating stack.

autopaster See **flying paster**.

autotracing The conversion of a **bitmap** to a **vector** or **outline** image.

azerty Keyboard arrangement used in France as alternative to the standard **qwerty** keyboard arrangement of characters. Accommodates **accents**.

azure laid Blue-tinted laid paper, usually used for stationery.

azure wove As **azure laid** but without characteristic laid lines.

B The **B series** is an international ISO range of sizes designed for large items (wall charts, posters) and falling between the **A series** sizes.

B format paperback Mass market paperback of trimmed size 198×126mm.

B2B Business-to-business transaction. A transaction (may be in e-commerce) through which businesses can offer and market their products and services to other businesses.

B2C Business to consumer, often e-commerce business process where consumers can buy goods and services online.

B/W Black and white.

back 1. The binding edge of a book. The back margin is the space between the type and bound edge. 2. In binding, to form a shoulder on each side of the spine. See **backing**, **rounding** and **backing**.

back exposure UV light exposure through the back of a flexo plate that sensitises the plate and sets the floor.

back lining Strip of paper or fabric glued to the spine of a book to give reinforcement strength. See also **first and second linings**.

back margin The margin of a book nearest the spine.

back number Copy of a previous issue of a periodical.

back swell A build-up of thread or glue at the spines of books during binding causing the spines to swell undesirably.

back-edge curl Distortion of the back edge of a sheet of paper usually caused by heavy solids too close to the back edge. Also, **tail-end hook**.

back-of-book Pages in a periodical following the editorial; often classified advertising.

back-up The act of duplicating data for security purposes.

back-up ad Advertisement published in conjunction with an insert or editorial announcement.

backbone The primary connectivity mechanism of a hierarchical distributed system.

backer card Display card fixed to back of dump bin or stand.

background processing Low-priority tasks, in a multi-tasking environment, that are performed when higher-priority programs are inactive. In word processing, performance of a task such as printing while the operator completes other tasks.

backing In binding, the operations that form a shoulder on each side of the spine. Also known as **jointing**. In paper the carrier sheet for a peel-off stock **release paper**, often silicone coated.

backplane The wiring and connecting units that allow a computer to be connected to its peripherals.

backs Combined **back margins** of a book.

backslant Backward sloping **typeface**, i.e. opposite to italic.

backwater Liquid containing dissolved ingredients in papermaking process, that passes through the **wire** when stock is deposited. Also known as **whitewater**.

bad break Undesirable end-of-line **hyphenation** of a word.

bagasse Fibre sometimes used in papermaking obtained from sugar cane.

baggy paper Loosely wound **web**.

balanced score card Provides an enterprise view of an organisation's overall performance by integrating financial measures with other key performance indicators around customer perspectives, internal business processes, and organisational growth, learning and innovation.

band strapping Enclosing a stack of printed material with a strong, thin plastic band to secure it. The machine is a band strapper.

bandwidth Technically, the difference, in **hertz** (Hz), between the highest and lowest frequencies of a transmission channel or the range of frequencies required to transmit a signal. However, as typically used, the rate at which data can be sent through a given communications circuit.

bank Grade of lightweight writing and printing paper used for correspondence, multi-part sets. Weights over 60**gsm** are known as **bonds**.

banner 1. Large headline on advertisement or newspaper story. 2. Poster or cloth strip containing an advertising message.

barcode A horizontal strip of vertical bars of varying widths, groups of which represent characters. There are various different standards but each symbol typically contains a leading quiet zone, start character, data character(s) including an optional check character, stop character and a trailing equate zone. In addition to conventional barcodes, there are also radial and two-dimensional coding systems, that are used for specialised applications such as automatic warehousing.

barrier resistance The property of a plastic packaging material to stop particular gases (e.g. oxygen or carbon dioxide) getting into a sealed pack.

baryta Heavy grade of coated paper sometimes used for reproduction proofs.

base alignment Aligning characters of different sizes on the same line.

base paper Paper to which a coating is to be added. Also called **body paper** or **body stock**.

baseline The line on which characters are based, that is, the line along the bottom of characters, such as a, b and c, that do not have descenders (as in j, p, q and y). Line spacing is measured between baselines. **Leading** is extra

spacing added, based on the strips of lead (the metal) that compositors used to add between the blocks of type.

Base-T ethernet Network on standardised twisted pair cable, 10-, 100- and 1000- versions are available with the numbers relating to Mbits Sec⁻¹ of **bandwidth**

basic size American paper term for the specified sheet size used to define **basis weight**. Different papers have different basic sizes: the basic size applied to book papers is 25×38in; for bond papers it is 17×22in.

basil Grade of leather produced from sheepskin and used in the production of account book bindings.

basis weight or substance 1. The weight of a material, usually paper, defined in grammes per square metre. 2. (US) Weight in pounds per ream of paper cut to **basic size**. Typical US weights for book papers are 50lb (equivalent to 74**gsm**), 55lb (equivalent to 81gsm), 60lb (equivalent to 89gsm).

bastard progressives Set of progressive proofs showing every possible colour combination of the four process colours.

bastard size Non-standard size of any material or format.

beard Distance from the bottom of the **x-height** of a piece of type to the bottom edge of the body.

beater (beating engine) Large vat used midway through the papermaking process to refine liquid pulp. Replaced in modern papermaking by the **cone-refiner**.

beater-sized pulp Paper making furnish to which the size is added during beating rather than at a later stage in the process. See **internal sizing; engine sizing; sizing**.

beating Part of the papermaking process where fibres are mechanically treated in a cone-refiner (beater) to modify their characteristics to those required by the desired paper quality in manufacture. Also, refining.

Bekk smoothness Measurement of smoothness of paper surface using the Bekk instrument.

benchmark test A routine designed to evaluate the performance of a device under typical conditions.

bespoke software Software written for a specific application for a single customer. Also, **custom software.**

beta testing The stage at which software is tested under real conditions before general release. See **acceptance testing**.

Bézier curve Geometric curve whose shape can be defined through a series of intermediate points called control handles.

bf Bold face. See **bold**.

bible paper Very thin, strong, opaque printing paper used where low bulk, or weight, is needed. Originally made for bibles and prayer books, also used for dictionaries and air-mailed publications.

bibliography List of books and articles relating to a written work, usually given at the end of the work. Each item in the list may include details of author, title or publisher.

bill of exchange A common payment instrument for exporters, defined as 'an unconditional order in writing, addressed by one person to another, signed by the person giving it, requiring the person to whom it is addressed to pay on demand or at a fixed and determinable future time, a sum certain in money to the order of a specified person, or to bearer'.

bill of lading A statement of goods being carried by sea, used as a document of title by the consignor, and as a receipt by the shipping line.

bimetal plate Lithographic plate where the printing image area base is usually brass or copper, and the non-printing area is usually aluminium, stainless steel or chromium. Used for long runs.

binary system (base two) A method of working with numbers based on only two digits, 1 and 0. Used in all **digital** computing systems because 1 and 0 can represent on and off, or connected and disconnected. All data input into computer systems and transferred over communications links is therefore converted from the everyday decimal system to binary. **Octal** and **hexadecimal** systems (based on 8 and 16) are also widely used in computing, essentially because they are based on powers of 2.

binder 1. Device for holding loose-leaf sheets. 2. Person who does bindery work.

bindery Place where binding is carried out.

binding 1. The process of fastening printed sheets together and securing them in a cover. 2. The bound part of a publication, i.e. cover, stitching.

binding board or **binder's board** Board used in the covers of a case-bound book. Usually good quality and single-ply. See **case board**, **grey board**, **millboard**, **unlined chipboard**.

BinHex A **Macintosh format** for representing a **bit.** An acronym for **binary** digit, the smallest item of information that a computer can hold, being either 1 or 0, essentially representing a switch being open or closed. More meaningful information is handled by using combinations of bits, called **bytes**. In **serial communications**, bits are transferred one at a time.

bit rate The rate at which digital information can be sent across a communications system, measured in **bps** or kbps or Mbps.

bitmap A two-dimensional array, in which pixels are either on or off, i.e. black or white, or 1 or 0. Can easily be stored in a computer. Often used to describe the image itself. Unlike **vector graphics**, bitmaps cannot be resized without loss of quality. If a bitmap represents a coloured image, there will be more than one bit for each **pixel**, i.e. each colour will have its own bits. (See also **raster**, **1-bit**, **8-bit** and **24-bit** colour.)

bitmap font (raster font) A **font** in which each character is stored as an array of **pixels** (or a **bitmap**). Such fonts are not easily scalable (see **aliasing** and Figure 1), in contrast to **vector** or **outline fonts** (like those used in **PostScript** and **TrueType**). In practice, bitmap fonts need to be stored in all the sizes required, that not only limits their functionality but also takes up space on the storage medium, particularly at large sizes. Of course, all fonts are bitmapped when displayed on-screen or printed. The difference between outline and bitmap fonts is that the bitmaps for outline fonts are created **on the fly**.

bitmapped font A typeface generated as a **bitmap** rather than a **vector outline** and of a fixed point size.

bits per second (bps) A measure of **bandwidth** or data transmission speed.

black and white Single colour black only originals or reproductions as distinguished from multicolour. Sometimes called **mono** or **monochrome**.

black letter Also called **gothic**. A type style based on a style of handwriting popular in the 15th century.

black printer The black plate in four-colour reproduction used to give correct neutral tones and detail.

black-step collation Method of ensuring sections of a publication are gathered in the correct sequence. The outer fold of each section is printed with a rectangle or short thick rule. The position of the rule on each section is such that when the spine of the complete publication is viewed, the rules form a stepped pattern. See also **collate**.

Blackberry range of mobile computer devices that allows users to stay connected with secure, wireless access to email, corporate data, phone, web and organiser features.

blackening Paper defect associated with calendered paper where areas darken. Can be caused by paper being too damp when calendering.

blad Sample pages of a book produced in the form of a booklet and used for promotional purposes.

blade coater Machine for **blade coating**.

blade coating Paper coating method where a surplus of coating is applied to the web and then levelled and controlled by a flexible steel blade.

blade cut Paper defect where a **blade scratch** cuts deeply into the web.

blade scratch Paper defect where there is a hair-like indentation in a coated surface running in the grain direction. Caused by a particle lodged behind the blade during coating.

blade streak Paper defect that is similar to a **blade scratch** but larger and caused by a larger particle.

blade-coated cartridge See **coated cartridge**, **blade coating**.

blanket A rubber-surfaced sheet clamped around the cylinder of an offset litho printing press that transfers the printing image from plate to paper. Standard DIN 16621 sets out the requirements for 'blankets for indirect lithographic printing (offset printing)'.

blanket contamination Occurs where undesirable material becomes attached to the litho blanket and interferes with print quality.

blanket cylinder The cylinder around which the blanket is clamped.

blanket-to-blanket Printing configuration where two blanket cylinders act as opposing impression cylinders printing both sides of the sheet or web simultaneously.

bleach-out Underdeveloped bromide print used as a basis for a line drawing. The bromide print is bleached away after the drawing is finished.

bleaching Part of papermaking process where chemical treatment is used to purify, whiten, brighten and improve permanence of the pulp. Treatments include exposure to chlorine, chlorine dioxide and alkalis.

bleed Printed matter running off the cut edge of a page. The bleed allowance beyond the trimmed size (see **trim**) is usually 3mm to ensure a clean cut-off.

blind 1. Blocking or stamping of covers or jackets without metallic foil or ink resulting only in an indentation or embossing. 2. Used to describe a litho plate where the image has lost its ink receptivity.

blind blocking Blocking or stamping of covers or jackets without metallic foil in order to smooth down, indent, or emboss the surface. Also called **blind stamping**.

blind embossing A paper processing stage in the print process where male and female dies are used to generate an impression in the paper under high pressure. Embossing with raised motifs is known as high embossing and embossing with sunken motifs as deep embossing. High embossing can also be simulated by applying and melting special powder, see **thermography**.

blind keyboard Typesetting keyboard with no visual display (e.g. screen or marching display) or hard copy of keying.

blind stamping See **blind blocking**.

blind stitch The stitch that joins the books together in the sewing process. It is this stitch that is cut to separate one book from the next. See also **kettle stitch**.

blister Paper defect usually occurring during heatset drying of coated papers where clearly defined bubbles form on both sides of the web.

blister cut Paper defect resulting in a web cut often diagonally to machine direction.

blister pack Packaging method using a sheet of plastic holding bubbles of air that form a cushion of protection.

blister packaging object packed in front of a printed card and heat-sealed in by clear plastic.

block Transmitted information regarded as a discrete entity, often identified by starting and ending delimiters.

block-pull Proof of a printing **block**.

blocking 1. Binding operation to impress a design or lettering into a book cover, often filling the impression with metal or pigment **foil**. 2. Fault where stack of printed sheets stick together as the ink dries.

blocking fee See **holding fee**.

blog See **weblog**.

blogging system Technology to allow easy posting of weblogs to the internet from a PC or mobile phone (see **mo-blogging**).

blottings Grade of highly absorbent papers.

blow-up To enlarge photographically; or a print so made.

blue wool scale Scale of light fastness for inks. Eight is the highest for printing inks. Six is the minimum level required for exposure to daylight. Yellow and magenta inks tend to be less light fast than black and cyan.

blurb Brief description of a book, usually for the jacket.

board General term for paper above 220**gsm** (although sometimes applied to substances down to 200gsm). The term includes numerous grades ranging from those of one finish throughout, to those made from combining several plys of the same or different furnishes. Boards may be uncoated or coated one or both sides. See also **case board**, **paperboard**.

board hollow In case-making, a spine hollow made of the same board as the front and back boards. Used particularly in children's books.

body 1. Typesetting term for the size of the body of type, e.g. 12pt = a 12pt body. 2. Ink making term describing the viscosity of the ink.

body copy or **body matter** Text pages as distinct from prelims, endmatter, index.

body paper See **base paper**.

body size Same as typesetting term **body**.

body stock See **base paper**.

body text The main text of a book.

body type The type used for text, rather than for headings, usually between eight and 1pt. Conventionally, a **serif** typeface, but this is not always the case in modern typesetting. For electronic publications, there is much controversy over the most effective type sizes and styles for screen viewing.

bold Heavier version of a typeface, as distinct from light or medium. Sometimes abbreviated to **bf** (bold face).

bolle-a Letter 'a' with a small circle over it used in a number of Scandinavian languages.

bolt Folded edge of a printed section (other than the binding fold) that is removed in final trimming.

bond Range of heavier substance printing and writing papers often used for letterheads, invoices. Similar papers of lighter substance (under about 60gsm) are known as **banks bonded ink** One suited to **hard-sized** papers, drying by oxidation rather than penetration.

bonding strength Measurement of a paper's resistance to picking and delamination when printing.

book block Book at the binding stage after sewing or perfect binding but before **forwarding** operations have been carried out.

book jacket Protective wrap-around to a book, usually made of paper.

book paper Paper with characteristics good for book printing but also used more generally.

book proof Page proofs paperback-bound in the form of the finished book.

bookmark A mark to indicate a position in a document (used, for example, in **Acrobat** files). Also used to describe a **URL** to a document, that may be on the same server or a different one. Web browsers save a file of bookmarks and thus allow quick location of pages and frequently referenced documents.

bookplate Printed (and often specially designed) label glued onto the fly-leaf of a book to show who owns it.

books on demand Books not printed in a production run with a fixed length, but produced and shipped individually on the basis of orders. This uses digital print and will cut the cost of short runs because the expense of storage and unsold copies is eliminated. It can be used to compile customised books from pre-defined content.

bookwork Production of books.

Boolean search A search formalism using logical operators such as AND and OR.

boot or **bootstrap** Computer term for necessary instruction procedures where programs are loaded and activated prior to operating.

borders Decorative designs usually edging the page or type.

bottom up An approach to building things by combining smaller components; important in nanotechnology. Opposite of the **topdown approach**.

bound books Term sometimes used for books where the coverboards are attached to the book before applying cover material or affixing endpapers. Much stronger than cased books and expensive to produce.

bounding box A rectangular space on the page that is defined by dragging the mouse diagonally. Type can be placed or typed into it.

bowl Typographical descriptive term for enclosed part of a letter, as in a, p or o. Also known as a **counter**.

boxboard Card used in carton-making.

boxed heading A ranged-left heading, as distinct from a **cross head** that is centred.

boxhead ruling Space at head of a ruled column where headings are to be inserted.

BPIF British Printing Industries Federation.

BPM Business process management.

BPOP Bulk packed on pallets. Refers to consignments of sheets.

brace Form of bracket { }, mainly used in tables.

brackets Pairs of marks ( ), [ ], used in text. Also called **parentheses**.

BRAD British Rate and Data. Publication listing all UK publications and their advertising specifications and requirements.

brass A die made from metal and used for blocking, e.g. spine brass that is used for blocking the spine of a case prior to casing in. A true 'brass' is made by engraving the metal, brass, mechanically. The normally used brass is produced photomechanically on copper or zinc. See **chemac**.

break-line Term for the short last line of a paragraph. See also **club line**, **paragraph**, **widow**.

break-up Pull apart a letterpress **forme** and distribute the type.

breaker (breaking machine) Vat used in the first stages of papermaking to break down the crude pulp and dissolve it in water. Replaced in modern papermaking by the **hydrapulper**.

breaking length Measurement of the limiting length of a uniformly wide strip of paper where the strip held by one end breaks due to its own weight.

breaking strength Paper measurement to determine comparative strengths.

breve Symbol placed above a vowel to show it is pronounced short.

brevier Obsolete type size, about eight point.

brightness A measure of how much light is perceived by the eye. The more correct term is luminance, but brightness is important in some methods of representing colour in computer graphics.

bristol board Good paperboard comprising three or more layers, where the outermost layers are woodfree, while the inner material may contain wood. It is not coated, durable and produces good results in offset printing and finishing. Typical applications include postcards, envelopes and packaging.

British Standards Institution British national coordinating body for technical standards in industry.

broadband High-capacity data transfer network, over 4Mbps.

broadcast A transmission either addressed to two or more stations at the same time or a transmission to multiple, unspecified recipients. (The terms **narrowcast** and **personalcast** have been coined to describe more focused transmission)

broadcast quality video Flicker-free video (more than about 30 frames per second) at a resolution of about 800 × 640 pixels.

broadsheet Newspaper size approximating to A2 when folded.

broadside Traditional 'standard' sheet size from which the sub-divisions of quarto, sexto, octavo derive.

brochure Promotional booklet about a company or product, often produced to a high quality to create an image of success.

broke Defective paper discarded during manufacture and usually re-pulped. Usually marked xxx. See also **retree**.

broken ream Part of a ream of paper left after use.

bromide Photographic light-sensitive paper used in photographic reproduction or phototypesetting, producing a positive image.

bronzing Process for obtaining a metallic printed effect. Metallic or bronze powder is applied to printed sizing ink while the ink is still wet giving a metallic lustre.

brown mechanical pulp Mechanical paper pulp produced from boiled or steamed wood.

browser A program for displaying web pages

brush coating Method of coating a web of paper where the coating mix is distributed by a set of stationary and oscillating brushes.

BS Number given to a British Standard published by the **BSI (British Standards Institution)**.

buckle folder Machine for sheet folding where the sheet is bent or buckled by a metal plate. Also called a **plate folder**. The main alternative folding method is knife folding on a **knife folder**.

buckram A heavy and strong binder's cloth made from woven textile stiffened with size.

bug Computer term for a defect interfering with a computer operation (non-documented software feature!).

bulk Paper term used to describe the degree of thickness of paper. Measured by **caliper**, **volume** or **ppi** (**pages per inch**) (American).

bulk basis Obsolete paper term describing the thickness (32nds of an inch) of 320 pages in 60lb quad crown (68**gsm**).

bulk between boards The total thickness of a **book block** without counting the thickness of the front and back boards.

bulk wrapping Wrapping several copies of a periodical, as distinct from individual wrapping.

bulking dummy A blank book to show the paper being proposed and the bulk that this paper will achieve.

bulking index American paper measurement of bulk formed by dividing the thickness of a sheet (in inches) by its **basis weight**, or the inches of thickness per pound of basis weight.

bulking number American paper measurement of the number of sheets that bulk to one inch in thickness under standard pressure. Multiply bulking number by two to give **pages per inch** (**ppi**).

bulky mechanical Grades of paper made predominantly from mechanical pulp to a specific and high bulk, e.g. as often used for cheap paperback books.

bullet A large dot used for display and ornamentation.

bulletin News sheet.

bulls eye See **hickey**.

bump exposure Photographic term describing method of increasing highlight contrast when producing a halftone by removing the screen briefly to remove any dots in the highlight area.

bundling Compressing the folded sections at the beginning of the binding process in a special bundling press that squashes the sections flat and expels the air from them prior to further processing.

burst Rupture of a paper web due to one of a variety of causes, e.g. the reel being too tightly wound or air trapped into the reel when winding.

burst binding A form of unsewn adhesive binding where the sections are 'burst' or punched along the spines, typically on a web printing press, thus giving extra adhesion between sheets as well as sections when the sections are bound. Also known as **punch binding**. See also **notch binding**.

burst factor A measure of the **bursting strength** of a paper.

burst index A measurement of paper bursting strength relative to grammage under standard test conditions.

bursting strength The strength of a paper to resist a uniformly distributed pressure under test conditions.

business press Periodicals directed to the business and professional sectors.

byline Writer's or journalist's name on an article or newspaper story.

byte A combination of eight **bits**, generally used to represent a character. There are 256 permutations of the eight 1s and 0s and, therefore, 256 characters can be represented in a byte. Bytes, kilobyte (1kb = 1024 bytes), megabyte (1Mb = 1024kb), gigabyte (1Gb = 1024Mb), terabyte (1Tb = 1024Gb) and petabyte (1Pb = 1024Tb) all used to describe the size of computer memory. Bandwidth is given in **Mbits per second**.

C 1. A high-level programming language. 2. The **C series** is an international ISO range of sizes for envelopes, designed to accommodate stationery in the **A series sizes**.

C format paperback Paperback of trimmed size 234×156mm.

c&sc Capitals and small capitals, i.e. words that begin with capitals and have the other characters in small caps the height of the lower case body size.

C1S Paper coated on one side.

C2S Paper coated on both sides.

cache To store documents or images, usually locally, after they have been accessed over the **internet** in order that future access can be achieved more quickly. If a document or image is not available in the cache, the **browser** has to return to the internet to retrieve it. Cache is also used as a noun describing the place where the files have been **cached**. In computing generally, cache has the meaning of storing temporarily, usually to allow other information or programs to be loaded into memory.

CAD/CAE Computer-aided design/engineering.

CAD/CAM Computer-aided design/computer-aided manufacture.

calcium carbonate Chalk pigment used as a filler in some papers and as a white coating mix.

calcium hypochlorite Used for bleaching paper.

calender A set of rollers on a paper machine that give a smooth finish to the web as it passes through by applying pressure. Calendered paper has a smooth, medium gloss finish. See also **supercalender**.

calf Leather of high quality used in bookbinding.

calf cloth An imitation leather binding material.

calibration The task of coordinating devices to ensure correct operation. Important that input and output devices, monitors, proofing, presses are calibrated to test how colours reproduce to operate colour management effectively.

caliper The thickness of a sheet of paper or board, measured with a micrometer and usually expressed in thousandths-of-a-millimetre (microns).

caliper shear burst Web break during winding caused by variations in roller nip.

calligraphy Art of handwriting or script drawing (from the Greek *kalos* = beautiful, *grafein* = writing).

callout Text to point out/identify parts of an illustration.

camber Convex surface of a roll of paper.

Cameron belt press, book-o-matic A web book press that, linked to a binding line, can print, gather and bind a substantial book in one pass. Used primarily for paperbacks.

cancel 1. To remove a leaf in a book and replace it with another. 2. Reprinted sheets for replacing cancelled leaves.

canvas Bookbinding cloth of good strength. Also known as **art canvas**.

canvas note A type of embossed stationery that simulates canvas.

cap height The height of the capital letters in a particular **typeface** or **font**. (See also **x-height**.)

capillary rise The distance liquid travels vertically up a strip of paper, measured by standard test.

caps Capitals. Upper case letters, e.g. A, B, C and so on. See also **lower case**.

capstan imagesetter Imagesetter that uses a capstan roller to advance the film.

caption Text accompanying and describing an illustration.

carbon black Intensely black pigment used in ink manufacture.

carbon paper Light paper coated on one side with transferable colouring agent for producing copies by impression onto an underlying sheet.

carbro Continuous tone colour print.

card See **board**.

cardboard Any stiff sheet of card, usually comprising several layers of paper pasted together.

carding Thin spacing of lines of type.

caret Proof reader's mark indicating an insertion.

carriage paid Refers to a deal where goods are delivered with the freight element paid by the sender. See also **cif**.

carrier sheet Sheet of paper inside film wrapping that carries the address label.

cartography Map production. Special problems include the correct determination of ground elevations (topography) and the most realistic possible rendering of the curved surface of the earth on a planar map. By nature, only compromises are possible in this connection. Aerial views taken from satellites have largely replaced the complex and arduous methods of terrestrial surveying.

carton Cardboard box for packing.

cartouche Decorative box framing a piece of text.

cartridge Printing or drawing paper with good dimensional stability, high opacity and good bulk. Often used in bookwork.

case Refers to whether letters are capitalised (upper case letters) or not (lower case letters). The term comes from the days when typesetters used metal type and stored the letters in wooden type cases: the capitals were usually kept in the top, or upper, case; the small letters were kept in the bottom, or lower, case.

case board Board used for case making, typically Dutch grey board or unlined chipboard. Typical caliper/**gsm** ranges are from 1725 microns/1120gsm at the lower end up to 3000 microns/1750gsm.

case material The material, or imitation cloth, that covers the case boards to form the case of a hardback book.

case-bound Referring to a book with a hard case. Also described as 'cased'. See also **limp-bound**.

casein glue Near-acid-free glue used in book binding and in making coated papers.

cassie Damaged paper at the top and bottom of a **ream**.

cast coated Paper given a high gloss by pressure from a polished, heated cylinder before the coating dries.

casting 1. The process of forcing molten metal into a mould to create a character or slug of type. 2. Producing **stereotypes** in newspaper printing. A casting box is used for this purpose.

casting off Calculating the number of pages a given amount of copy will make when set in a given type face and size to a given area.

Category 6 (5e/7) cabling developing standard for the performance of network wiring overseen by the telecommunications industry association (TIA)

Cataloguing in Publication data A system operated by the British Library offering classified entries that publishers can print on the imprint pages of their books to facilitate library cataloguing, bibliographical compilation. The equivalent in the US is the **Library of Congress (Lib Con) number**.

catch line A temporary heading on a manuscript or proof for identification.

catch-stitch See **kettle stitch**.

catch-up, scumming Ink/water balance problem on a litho printing plate resulting in a colour filling in or being removed.

catchword(s) Word or words highlighted in some manner, such as first and last words on dictionary pages repeated in the headline.

cathode ray tube Video screen activated by **electron gun**.

CCD See **charge-coupled device**.

CCI See **computer-controlled inking**.

CCR Complementary colour removal. See **achromatic separation**.

compact disk read-only memory (CD-rom) A data provision using the same physical format as audio **compact disks**. Up to 650 Mbytes of data can be stored on one CD-rom.

compact disk-recordable (CD-R) Type of compact disk on which data can be overwritten (compare **CD-rom**). The disk combines magnetic and optical technology so that during the writing process a laser melts the surface of the disk, thereby allowing the magnetic elements of the surface layer to be realigned.

CeBIT Centrum für Büro und Informations-Technik (Centre for Office and Information Technology). Huge IT exhibition that takes place every spring in Hannover.

cell A fixed length of data for transmission, as used in **asynchronous transfer mode**. Also used in other ways, for example to describe parts of tables or spreadsheets.

cellulose Complex fibrous substance forming the walls of plant cells, and the prime raw material in pulp and paper.

central processing unit See **CPU**.

centre To position type centrally in a given measure.

centre notes Notes placed between columns of a page.

centre spread The two facing pages at the centre of a **signature**.

centrifugal cleaner Device that removes unwanted material from paper fibres by centrifugal force.

cerfs (kerfs) Grooves cut into the backs of sections into which the thread cuts.

certificate authority A body that attests to or confirms the identity of a person or an organisation and issues digital certificates. Used in secure communications.

certificate of origin A certificate stating details of where a commodity has been manufactured.

CGATS see Committee for Graphic Arts Technical Standards.

chad The waste punched out of paper tape or cards.

chain lines The wider watermark lines that run at right angles to the narrow laid lines on **laid papers**.

chalking Powdering of ink that has not adhered properly to paper or plastic. It indicates a lack of cohesion in the ink due to insufficient binder, over-dilution or incorrect formulation for printing on the material in question.

chancery Style of italic such as Bembo.

chapter drop White space between the head of the chapter title and the head of the type area of a book.

chapter head Chapter title and/or number.

character A representation of a single unit of meaningful data, e.g. a letter or a number, usually using **ASCII** or **ANSI** coding.

character code Numeric representation of a character. See, for example, **ASCII**.

character compensation Global reduction or expansion in character fit by adjustment to the normal set width values resident in a typesetting system's computer. Also called **track kerning** or **tracking**.

character count Total number of characters and spaces in a piece of copy.

character entity A way of describing a character, using only **ASCII** characters, that is used in **SGML** and **HTML** (see **entity**). The character is usually delimited by '&' and ';' so that, for example the Greek letter alpha (Éø) might be represented as 'α'. The **delimiters** can be changed in the **SGML declaration**. **character fit**. Space between letters that can be reduced or expanded.

character formatting The application of a format or style (including such factors as typeface, typestyle, indents, space before and after) to a single character, or group of characters in a **desktop publishing system** or **word processor**. Compare with **paragraph formatting.**

character recognition Reading characters by machine, often for digital storage. Also, **optical character recognition, OCR.**

charge-coupled device (CCD) An array of light-sensitive transistors, arranged across a **scanner** head, one for each **pixel** or unit of resolution. They convert the reflected light signal into **bitmap** information. Sensors may be only **bilevel** or they may measure **grey levels.**

charting Transforming numbers into graphical representations (pie charts, bar charts).

CHC paper Paper impregnated with cyclohexylamine carbonate, used to deacidify old books.

check bit, digit An extra digit calculated automatically from other digits in a data item and used to check its accuracy.

chemac A copper die used for **blocking**. Made by photochemical methods, unlike a true **brass** that is engraved on brass by hand.

chemi-thermomechanical pulp (CTMP) Thermomechanical pulp that undergoes further chemical bleaching, resulting in a pulp not far below the quality of woodfree pulp. The very best quality of mechanical pulp made.

chemical ghosting Ghost images on sheets caused by the chemical reaction of inks.

chemical pulp Pulp obtained from wood or other plant sources by chemical removal of impurities rather than mechanical processing.

chemically pure paper Acid-free paper used in preserving old books or maps.

cheque paper Special paper used for cheques and having a surface that betrays attempts at alteration.

chill roll Cooled roller, used for setting ink after drying in a web-offset machine.

china clay White clay used for loading and coating paper.

china grass A fibrous material which is obtained from the subtropic nettle plant, ramie. Its high purity and strength make it ideal in the production of banknote paper.

chinese white Paint used in re-touching artwork.

chip or **microchip** 1 An electronic component containing extensive logic circuits. 2. Woodchip used in pulp making. 3. Trim (US).

chipper A machine that chips logs after debarking.

chlorine bleaching The bleaching of wood pulp using **chlorine dioxide**.

chlorine dioxide A gas used in the bleaching processes of chemical pulp. Environmentally dubious, and being steadily superseded by hydrogen peroxide bleaching processes.

chlorine-free paper Paper bleached without the use of environmentally harmful chlorine compounds.

choke See **trapping**.

chroma Purity of colour.

chromatic aberration The inability of a lens to bring light of all colours to a common point of focus. See also **apochromatic**.

Chromo paper Includes woodpulp or woodfree stocks coated on one side. The coating is always waterproof and designed for maximum embossing, varnishing and bronzing performance in offset environments. Chromo paper is used mainly to make labels, wrappings and cover paper.

Chromolux A brand name for a high-gloss, cast-coated board that is white on one side.

CI Common impression cylinder press, where the substrate is guided around a central cylinder with print units positioned around as satellites with the capability of interdeck drying. Gives excellent registration and hence print quality in flexo.

cicero The basic typographical unit of the **Didot point system**. (See **font size**.)

CIELab colour space Defined by the Commission Internationale de l'Eclairage (CIE) in 1976 and represents a three-dimensional, rectangular coordinate system. The vertical coordinate L specifies the lightness of a colour, the two horizontal coordinates *a* and *b* represent the hue and the saturation on red/green and blue/yellow axes respectively. It is ideal for representing colour differences, ΔE, as geometric distances in the colour space approximate the intuitive colour differences.

cif Carriage, insurance and freight. A price quoted cif includes all charges up to delivery at the quayside at the port of destination. Contrast **FOB**.

CIM Computer-integrated manufacturing, automation system allowing computers to control production equipment to increase efficiency

CIP data See **Cataloguing in Publication data**.

CIP3/4 International Cooperation for the Integration of Processes in Prepress, Press and PostPress Standard for the transfer of job information from administration systems to production equipment, allowing automated set up to reduce make-ready. Controls the JDF standard.

ciphertext Encrypted information, that will require a **password** or **key** to decrypt. The converse of ciphertext is **plaintext**.

circular Printed leaflet distributed to prospective purchasers.

circular screen Halftone screen that can be rotated to obtain proper screen angles for colour halftones.

circulation Total copies of a publication distributed.

CIT Conductive ink technology.

citation A mention or reference in an academic or journal paper to a published work. The status of academic journals is assessed on the number of citations their papers receive in other journals.

citrix A client server computer architecture that delivers a suite of software products and services to provide access to any device, over any network to any application or information source.

classified Advertisements for job vacancies, articles for sale set in columns and sorted by classification.

clay See **china clay**.

clean Correct a proof, or a list of names and addresses.

clean line An electrical power line dedicated to one machine and therefore not subject to **spiking**.

clean proof A printer's proof in which there are no errors.

Cleartype A system to generate the clearest possible typeface on-screen, achieved by anti-aliasing to smooth lines and edges that have a staircase-like appearance due to the pixels of the monitor. Cleartype is intended to improve the legibility of fairly small fonts such as those used for laptop computers and e-books.

cleat binding A method of binding single leaves using a form of **side-sewing**.

click-and-drag Pressing a button on a **mouse** (or other **pointing device**), holding it down and dragging the mouse to the required position before releasing the button. (See also **drag and drop**.)

clickable image An image displayed on a screen, that when pointed at with a **mouse** and the mouse then **clicked**, initiates some action on the computer.

client application In Windows, an application whose documents can accept linked or embedded objects.

client-server A mode of network computing in which a **distributed computing** system is split between one or more **server** tasks that accept requests, according to some protocol, from (distributed) **client** tasks, asking for information or action. There may be either one centralised server or several distributed ones. This model allows clients and servers to be placed independently on nodes in a network. Client-server computing allows more effective use of computing resources, higher performance, greater flexibility, simpler upgrades and (for some applications) greater reliability and data integrity. See **citrix**.

clip art Computerised art, often copyright-free, that can be used in both conventional and electronic publications. A successor to the book of clip art, from which illustrations really were clipped.

clipboard A temporary storage area to which text and/or graphics can be **copied** or **cut** and from which the stored material can be **pasted**. In most systems only one item can be stored at a time, but there is software that allows more items to be stored on a longer-term basis.

clipping path Outline or silhouette around an illustration or shape that determines the cut-out area or printing boundary for that illustration.

clock A regularly occurring signal that provides a timing reference for a transmission and is used to synchronise reception of a data stream.

close up Reduce spacing between characters of type or other elements on a proof.

closed user group A sub-group of users on a **network**, who can communicate only with other members of the sub-group.

closing date See **copy date**.

cloth binding The use of cloth to cover the boards of a case-bound book.

cloth joint A strip of cloth that strengthens the joints of a bound book (usually attached to the endpapers).

cloth lined paper Paper backed with linen or muslin for additional strength.

cloth-centred paper Paper with a linen centre, often used for maps when much refolding is anticipated.

clothings Pieces of leather or cloth fixed at the backs of stationery books for strengthening.

club line Strictly, the short last line of a paragraph at the bottom of a page. But also used frequently as a synonym for **orphan** too, and therefore by extension to mean any short line at the foot of a page.

CMOS, complementary metal oxide semiconductor integrated circuit fabricated in a single pass containing multiple components, including photoreceptors for digital photography.

CMYK Abbreviation for colour processing based on the four process printing colours: **cyan**, **magenta, yellow** and **black** (the key K distinguishes black from blue).

CNT Carbon nanotube.

coat weight The amount of coating on a base paper expressed as dry weight on a given area, i.e. **gsm**.

coated cartridge Dull-finish coated paper, normally blade-coated, and commonly used for printing colour books.

coated paper Paper coated with china clay or similar to give a smooth surface suitable for halftone reproduction.

coat weight is the amount of coating on the base paper, expressed as dry weight on a given area, i.e. in **gsm**.

coating 1. Light sensitive surface applied to litho plate. 2. Clear protective varnish applied to printed surface for protection. 3. china clay mixture used on paper. See **coated paper**.

coating binder That part of a coating formulation whose purpose is to bind the pigment system to the body stock and to obtain many of the desired properties of the final coated paper, such as pick and water resistance, ink receptivity, flexibility, gloss and blister resistance. Binders are obtained from natural sources like starch, casein and soya protein or can be produced synthetically.

coating mix or **coat mix** or **coating slip** White suspension of china clay or calcium carbonate and other pigments, that is applied to base paper by blade or roller and when dry forms the matt or gloss coat.

coating slip See coating mix.

coaxial cable (coax) A cable with a solid or stranded central conductor surrounded by insulator, in turn surrounded by a cylindrical shield, that is solid or woven from fine wires. It is used to carry high-frequency signals such as television, video, radio and other telecommunications transmissions. The shield is usually connected to electrical ground to reduce electrical interference.

Cobb size test A measurement of the sizing of paper by water absorbed under specified conditions.

cocked-up initial Initial letter in a new line that is larger than the characters in the rest of the line, but which sits on the same baseline as them. Compare **drop initial**.

cockle Puckered finish to a sheet of paper created during the drying process to add crispness.

cockling Wavy edges on paper caused by unstable atmospheric conditions.

code A character string or line of symbolic instructions to a computer.

code conversion The process of altering the numeric representation of one group of characters to that required by a different system, language or process.

cold colour colour containing blue tones.

cold melt An adhesive such as **PVA** that is applied for binding purposes at room temperature.

cold start The act of starting a computer after the power supply has been switched off before. At this stage the device has no operating programs in memory and these have to be loaded from backing store or ROM.

coldset Web printing in which the ink is allowed to dry by penetration on an absorbent paper without heat. See also **heatset**.

collage Image comprised of a number of items collected together as a visual whole.

collate Loosely used to mean 'gather'; but, strictly, to check the gathered sections to establish that they are in the correct sequence. **Collating marks** on the back folds assist in this.

collating marks Black marks on the back folds of sections in sequential positions used for checking that the sections are in the correct order after gathering.

collotype printing A short-run, screenless printing process using gelatin-coated plates to produce continuous tone reproduction.

colophon A printer's or publisher's identifying symbol, printed on spines and title pages.

colour Colours are usually represented on screen using the additive **RGB** system, in which either a colour image may be stored as three separate images (one for each of red, green and blue) or each **pixel** may encode the colour using separate **bit** fields for each colour component. Subtractive **CMYK** and/or **Pantone** representations of **spot colours** are used for printing.

colour bars Coloured strips on four-colour process proofs showing densities across a sheet and revealing other printing characteristics.

colour blanks Printed sheets with illustrations only but no text. Produced in this way typically in expectation of language changes for co-editions.

colour breaks The separate colour overlays for each overlay in a four-colour set (US).

colour cast An excess of one shade or hue in a subject for reproduction or in a printed subject.

colour gamut The range of **colours** that can be produced in **subtractive colour** printing by combining inks of the **process colours** or can be displayed on a screen using additive **RGB**. Note, however, that there are some bright, strong clean colours that cannot be made up of a mixture of inks or light, as well as fluorescents and metallics.

colour guide Instructions on **artwork** indicating colour requirements.

colour management Refers to the control of colour reproduction in a digital graphic production process. The various input and output devices from **scanner** to the **printing press** support different **colour spaces**. In order to standardise the way colours appear throughout the production process, **colour profiles** are generated for the devices and processes involved. The combination of these profiles makes it possible to calculate the coefficients necessary for data conversion. Those colours in a given colour space that cannot be displayed in another are approximated as closely as possible.

colour profile Of an input or output device (scanner, monitor, printer, printing press, etc.) is an element of colour management which indicates how the colour information supplied by the device behaves with respect to a superordinate, device-neutral colour system, e.g. CIELAB colour space. Manufacturers supply colour profiles with professional devices. To ensure high-quality results, profiles need to be created individually using special measuring instruments. This procedure may need to be repeated at regular intervals.

colour proof Used for a binding, advance check of the colours of a printed product.

colour resolution The number of **bits** per **pixel** in a colour image. (See **1-bit, 8-bit and 24-bit colour**.)

colour separation Separating **full colour** into the **four** (or more) **process colour channels**

colour sequence The order in which the four process colours are printed.

colour splits Instructions for the allocation of correct printing colours to individual components of a piece of integral artwork.

colour swatch A sample of a specified colour.

colour transparency A full-colour photographic positive on film.

colour-matching system Method of colour specification by matching the colour required to one in a swatch of colours provided as a set. Each colour in the swatch has its ink-mix formula described. An example is the **Pantone matching system (PMS).**

coloured edges Dyed edges on a book block.

coloured tops Dyed tops on a **book block.**

column 1. Vertical area of print comprising lines of the same measure. 2. Regular newspaper article.

column balancing The automatic adjustment of columns to create a visual evenness.

column centimetre See **column inch**.

column guides The dotted, vertical, non-printing lines that mark the left and right-hand edges of the columns of text to be created. See also **margin guides, ruler guides**.

column inch A newspaper measure of text space: one column wide and one inch deep.

combination folder A machine combining a **buckle** and **knife folder**.

Comdex Computer and communications trade show and exposition held in Las Vegas.

coming and going An imposition in which two copies of a book result from one set of plates.

command A computer instruction specifying an operation.

commercial register Colour printing to a register tolerance of plus or minus one row of dots.

Committee for Graphic Arts Technical Standards (CGATS) The organisation tasked with creating standards for the graphic arts industry in the US by ANSI.

commodity papers White general-purpose papers produced in enormous quantities by the larger paper mills.

communication The electronic transfer of data between different hardware. Also known as 'comms'.

communication system A system or facility providing information transfer between persons and/or equipment. The system can consist of a combination of individual communication **networks**, transmission systems, relay stations and tributary stations, together with terminal equipment capable of interconnection and interoperation, that forms an integrated whole. The individual components must serve a common purpose, be technically compatible and employ common procedures and protocols; they must respond to some form of control and generally operate together.

communications protocol A set of signals that computers can use when they want to exchange data. These signals make it possible for computers to send and receive information and to check that the information has been transmitted and received correctly. There is more than one set of protocols and a computer, or group of computers, may use different protocols in different situations.

communications speed This is normally specified in **bits per second** (bps) or multiples such as kbps or Mbps. Often described as the **bit rate**.

comp 1. To **compose**. 2. A **compositor**. 3. **A comprehensive layout** (US): a layout showing everything in position.

comp list List of periodical subscribers receiving complimentary copies.

compatibility The ability of two pieces of electronic hardware to emulate each other and to communicate with each other.

composition sizes Types under 14pt in size. As distinct from **display sizes**.

computer graphics The use of computers to display and manipulate images and drawings. Images can be stored as either **raster** (**bitmap**) or **vector graphics**. Computer graphics are used in a wide range of applications, as well as in publishing.

computer output on microfilm (COM) (Or computer output micrographics) Direct output from computer onto microfilm or microfiche.

computer to plate (CTP) System that exposes plates by laser or thermal imaging techniques directly from data supplied from a computer

computer to press (CTPr) Direct digital imaging engine

computer-controlled inking The use of equipment that sets and monitors correct in kflows on the press and makes automatic adjustments for make-ready and during running.

concordance Index listing the main words used in a large work in alphabetical order, giving reference points and explanations.

condensed type A typeface with narrow characteristics.

conditioning See **mature**.

cone refiner In paper making, the cone-shaped piece of machinery into which the stock is pumped from the **hydrapulper** in order to undergo further beating or 'refining'. After this stage, the stock is cleaned in a series of **centrifugal cleaners** and finally pumped to the **headbox** for the beginning of the **Fourdrinier** process.

configuration The arrangement of peripherals into a computer system.

conformability The degree in which a paper surface will change shape to contact ink on the press.

connected dot Halftone dots joined together.

connector Connectors are the parts on the ends of cables that actually make the connection to another piece of hardware. Both the part on the end of the cable and that on the hardware that it plugs into are called connectors, and they are described as either male or female.

constat Short for continuous stationery.

consumable textbook A book that can be written in by the student and therefore can be used only once.

consumer press Periodicals circulating widely among the general public (as distinct from trade and technical press).

container boards Boards used in manufacturing box containers.

Content All elements of published material including text, graphics, sound and video clips.

contents page Page of a book or magazine explaining the contents and where they appear.

Continuous Acquisition and Lifecycle Support (CALS) Note that what the acronym stands for has changed several times. Originally a US Department of Defense standard for electronic exchange of data with commercial suppliers. Now, more generally, a global strategy intended to bring about more enterprise integration through the streamlining of business processes and the application of standards and technologies for the development, management, exchange and use of business and technical information. Includes **SGML** for the documentation aspects; a CALS **Document Type Definition** has been defined. This gives particular attention to coding tables and is widely used outside CALS applications themselves.

continuous pulping Pulp produced in a constantly running digester.

continuous stationery Reel stationery used on computer printers and other automatic machines.

contone, continuous tone An uncountable range of colour variations or shades of grey such as occurs in a photograph or painting, that cannot be directly reproduced. All such images must go through a halftone process in order to be reproduced. In the **halftone** process the image is broken up into a series of discrete dots that, when printed, give the illusion of continuous tone.

contract proof Colour proof or set of colour proofs that define the expected standard for the printed job and which are used by the printer as the accepted match for quality. There is a lively debate between publishers and printers on whether **digital proofs** can be viewed as contract proofs, since the technologies of digital proofing and wet printing are so far apart.

contraries Unwanted material in paper or stock.

contrast Wide range of tonal gradations.

contrast ratio opacity Paper opacity measured by the **TAPPI** method of gauging reflectance from a backed sheet.

controlled circulation Magazine or newspaper distribution free to selected names or groups of readers.

convertible press A press that will print either one colour on each side of the sheet in one pass, or two-colour on one side of the sheet in one pass.

converting Sheeting, re-reeling or changing the format of sheets or reels of paper. The person who carries this out is known as a '**converter**'.

cookie Internet mechanism through which servers can obtain information stored on the client side, usually as part of a **browser** implementation. Storage of such information is an automatic process that occurs as the Web is accessed. A common use of cookies is to identify registered users of a website without requiring them to sign in each time they access that site.

cooking Treating pulp with heat, water and chemicals.

copier paper Paper used in photocopying machines.

copy To transfer a copy of text and/or graphics to the **clipboard**, while leaving the original in place. (See also **cut**.)

copy date Scheduled date for delivering copy to a publisher or printer.

copy prep Copy preparation. Putting instructions on a manuscript to ensure understanding of the requirement.

copy-dot scanner Scanner designed to capture pre-screened page films digitally so they can be included in the data going into a **CTP** or similar all-digital system.

copyboard Holding frame for material being photographed for reproduction.

copyfitting Determining the typographical specification to which a manuscript needs to be set in order to fill a given amount of space.

copyholder Proof reader who reads aloud to a colleague who checks text.

copyright The exclusive legal right of the author of a work (or whoever he or she transfers that right to) to make and distribute copies, prepare derivative works, and perform and display the work in public.

copyright page Title page verso of a book containing bibliographic information. Also known as **biblio page**.

cording Putting cord into stationery as a form of loose binding.

corona treatment A method of rendering surfaces more receptive to adhesives or decorative coatings by subjecting them to a high voltage corona discharge. The corona discharge oxidises the surface through the formation of polar groups on reactive sites.

corona wire Thin wire in a laser printer that gives a charge to the powdered toner particles as they cross it.

corrugated Packaging grade of cardboard made by sandwiching fluted kraft paper between sheets of cardboard to absorb any impact.

corruption An unsatisfactory alteration of data during transmission or while held on a backing medium.

cotton content paper See **rag paper**.

cotton linters Cotton seed-hair fibres used in fine paper.

couch End of the wet end of a paper machine where the web is passed to the press section.

counter Centre part of a letter enclosed by strokes, such as the bowl of an o. Also, **bowl**.

counting keyboard Keyboard that has logic for justification purposes.

country code A two-letter abbreviation used for a particular country. The codes are based on **ISO** 3166 and used as the top-level **domain** for internet hostnames in most countries, although the code for the US, us, is hardly ever used.

cover Outer section of a periodical, bearing its title.

covering 1. See case material. Non-woven materials, woven materials and leathers comprise the most commonly used coverings. 2. The fixing of a book cover to the spine and endpapers.

covering power The opacity achieved by a printing ink.

cpi Characters per inch. Unit of measurement of type in a line.

cpo In direct mail, cost per order.

CPU Central processing unit. The computing unit in an electronic system.

cracked edge Broken edge on a web of paper.

crash 1. Serious hardware or software failure in a computer system. 2. Muslin cloth or mull as a first lining on the spines of the sections in a cased-bound book.

crash finish Linen-look finish on imitation cloth.

crawler See **spider**.

crawling Contraction of ink on paper when it has not penetrated the surface.

crease 1. Impress an indented line across a sheet of paper or board to assist folding. 2. A folding fault that leaves a crease in the sheet, hence 'creasing'.

creep 1. Blanket movement during printing. 2. The effect of the back margins of the outer pages in a printed section becoming narrower than the back margins of the inner pages, due to the thickness of paper across the fold. Needs to be compensated for in imposition by **shingling**.

creping Crinkling paper to create a soft, elastic sheet.

critical path The sequence of events that takes the shortest time. Analysis of the critical path ensures that events on the path are never delayed, while events on less critical paths may be if necessary.

CRM Customer relationship marketing, methods of segmenting and developing communications to encourage customer response.

crocking Dry ink rubbed off after printing.

Cromalin DuPont's proofing technology. Originally analogue and now digital, using inkjet. General term for contract proof.

crop Cut back part of an illustration to give better effect or achieve better fit.

crop marks Marks printed on a printed sheet, that indicate the edge of the intended physical page. They can also act as **registration** marks if more than one colour is to be printed.

cross direction Across the web of paper.

cross fold A fold at right angles to the direction of the web.

cross grain Used to denote that the grain of the paper in a book runs at right angles to the spine, not parallel to it (which is preferable). Also used to refer to endpapers as book-covering materials in which the grain is at right angles to the spine.

cross head A sub-heading ranged centrally over text. As distinct from a **boxed head** which is ranged left.

cross sealer Blade in film-wrapping machine that cuts and seals ends of wrapping.

cross-machine tension burst A paper break at the winding stage.

crossmarks See **register marks**.

crown Standard size of paper measuring 384×504mm.

CRT Cathode ray tube.

crushing Paper defect affecting a small area and showing as a visible surface fault.

cryptography The study of **encryption** and **decryption**. Usually involves taking **plaintext** and applying various encryption algorithms to produce encrypted **ciphertext**. The security of a cryptosystem usually depends on the secrecy of (some of) the keys rather than on the algorithm itself.

crystallisation Condition of an ink layer that will not accept a second ink overprinting.

CSWO Coldset web offset.

CT Continuous tone.

CTP Computer to plate.

CTPr Computer to press.

CTMP See **chemi-thermomechanical pulp**.

cumulative index An index that combines several other indices.

curl Sheet distortion leading to a tendency to roll up.

cursives Typefaces that simulate handwriting without joined characters.

cursor The screen symbol that indicates where the action initiated by the next keystrokes or **mouse click** will take effect. Cursors in **character-based interfaces** are either a block or an underline (sometimes flashing), while in a graphical user interface **(GUI)** the cursor can consist of any icon chosen by the software developer or the user.

curtain coating A paper coating system in which the coating is injected horizontally across the web.

custom Non-standard, or specially commissioned.

cut To copy text or graphics to the **clipboard** but, unlike **copy**, also to delete the original from the current file.

cut and paste Areas of text or graphics are defined and stored for subsequent insertion into another area, page or file.

cut flush Binding style with the cover cut flush with the pages.

cut marks See **crop marks**.

cut-back binding See **adhesive binding**.

cut-in index Divisions cut into edge of book to indicate alphabetical steps.

cut-in notes Notes in an outside margin of a page but which the text runs round to some degree.

cut-line Mark left on negative or printed copy by failure to spot out a shadow left by an edge of patched-in artwork on CRC.

cut-off The web press measure of length of sheet cut, determined by the plate cylinder circumference. Measured in inches or millimetres.

cut-out Illustration with background painted out or removed by process work.

cut-size paper Small-sized paper sheets for stationery.

cut-through index See **step index**.

cut-to-register Paper with a watermark in the same position on each cut sheet. Compare **cutting ahead**.

cutscore Blade in diecutting that scores for folding.

cutting Sheeting web paper.

cutting ahead Cutting watermarked paper regardless of watermark positions. Compare **cut-to-register**.

cutting marks Marks on copy that indicate cutting lines.

cwt Hundredweight. The short cwt (US) equals 100lb, the long cwt (UK) equals 112lb.

cyan The blue colour used in process printing.

cyberspace Term to mean all the information available on computers worldwide that is available through networks and the internet.

cylinder In printing, the structure that carries the printing plate or blanket on the printing press.

cylinder dressing Sheets of paper around the impression cylinder of a letterpress printing machine that improve the definition of the print by providing a cushioned impression.

cylinder machine 1. A paper machine that makes paper on a mould revolving in pulp. 2. A letterpress printing machine that uses a revolving cylinder to make the impression.

cylinder mould machine A paper machine that makes high-quality mould-made paper by forming the paper on a cylindrical mould that revolves in the stock.

cyrillic alphabet The Russian alphabet.

dagger Dagger-shaped symbol † used as a footnote reference mark. Usually follows the asterisk in order of use.

dailies National daily newspapers.

damper Roller on a litho press that transfers moisture to the plate prior to inking.

dancer roller Roller on a web offset press that controls the tension of the web.

dandy roll Cylinder on papermaking machine that impresses patterns and watermarks on the surface.

dash A character, similar to but longer than a hyphen. An en dash is the width of 'N' in the **font** being used and an em dash the width of 'M'. While the hyphen has clearly established uses, how em and en dashes are used depends on the style of a publication and on the country in which they are being used.

DAT See **digital audio tape**. The abbreviation is also used within computing generally to mean dynamic address translation.

data Information recorded in a quantifiable, i.e. **digital**, manner. Data is the plural of datum (Latin for 'given') but is today almost always used as a singular collective noun.

data compression Techniques used to reduce file size in order to cut down either the amount of storage needed for a given amount of data or the time taken to transmit it over a communications link. Often (but not always) this data is text.

Data Encryption Algorithm (DEA) An **ANSI** standard identical to the **Data Encryption**

Standard (DES) data encryption key (DEK) Used for the **encryption** of text and to calculate integrity checks (or digital signatures). (See **cryptography, EDIFACT**.)

Data Encryption Standard (DES) The **encryption** algorithm developed at the US National Bureau of Standards. It operates on 64-bit blocks of data and is based on a 56-bit key. DES is identical to the **Data Encryption Algorithm (DEA)**. DES has been implemented in both hardware and software.

data integrity The degree to which data can be trusted or assumed correct.

data protection legislation Legislation that seeks to protect persons from three potential dangers: the use of personal information that is inaccurate, incomplete or irrelevant; the possibility of personal information being accessed by unauthorised persons; and the use of personal information in a context or for a purpose other than that for which the information was collected. The legislation usually covers only personal data in digital form and is concerned with three general categories: factual data about an individual; subjective judgements and expressions about an individual (judgemental data); and statements of intent, rather than statements of opinion (intention data).

data transfer rate or **data rate** The speed at which data travels from one device to another. This can vary greatly, in that data transfers within computers using internal **buses** are very fast, while transfers via **modems**, over **analogue** lines, can be much slower.

data transparency Transmission such that a signal is not modified by the communications system in any way.

data validation The process of checking that data corresponds to agreed criteria.

database A structured container of data of any type. There are several different types of database that are more or less appropriate for different applications.

database query language A language in which users of a **database** can (interactively) formulate requests and generate reports. The best known is **SQL**. Such requests will often be made over a **network** using a **client-server** approach.

database server A computer in a **network** that holds and manages a **database** (the back end), while the user only manipulates data and applications (the front end). Database servers should be distinguished from file servers in that with **file servers** it is necessary to download large parts of the database to the user or **client** because the database software has not been designed for a network. It was the development of later, network-aware software that allowed the use of the database server.

day glow Proprietary name for fluorescent inks.

DDAP Digital Delivery of Advertising for Publication. An association of ad agencies, prepress companies, publishers, printers and their vendors aiding the acceptance of digital delivery of advertising material for magazines.

dead white A white with no modelling tint.

debarking Stripping bark from logs prior to their being pulped.

debris Used to describe paper dust or edge dust that finds its way onto the offset printing blanket.

debugging The detection and correction of errors in a computer program before it goes into use.

deciduous trees Hardwood trees that shed their leaves every year.

deck Term used in multi-unit web offset imposition, where a section is being formed from running one web under another into the folder. After cut-off the two sheets are folded together to form a section (typically two 16pp sheets folded one inside the other to yield one 32pp section). 'A' deck is the top side of the top web, and 'B' deck is the lower side of the top web; 'C' deck is the top side of the lower web and 'D' deck is the lower side of the lower web. Colour locations may appear in different positions according to the configuration used. See **colour fall.**

deckle The width of a papermaking machine's web. Deckle boards retain the stock on the wire. Deckle edge is the untrimmed feathering edge of paper. Deckle frame is the rectangular frame that contains the stock on the wire in handmade paper.

decryption To restore information that has been encrypted, i.e. to restore **plaintext** from **ciphertext**. (See **cryptography, encryption**.)

dedicated An item of equipment or electronics used for only one type of application and maybe only running one program.

dedication Inscription by the author dedicating a book to an individual. Carried among the **prelims**.

dedupe or **deduplicate** In data-processing, running a program that identifies and eliminates duplicate entries in a database (typically in a mailing list).

deep-etch plate Litho printing plate made from positive film in which the printing areas are recessed below the surface. Used for long runs.

default In computing, the parameters defined by the designer or programmer that will be used in the absence of alternative input by a user.

definition The degree of detail and sharpness in a reproduction.

deforestation The depletion of natural forest resources by indiscriminate felling.

degradation The deterioration of communications signal characteristics.

dehumidification Removal of humidity from the air.

deinking Removing ink and other unwanted chemicals from printed waste paper to recover and re-use fibre content.

del Delete. Proof reader's instruction to erase text or other matter.

delamination Separation of surface from paper by ink tack or separation of film laminate from its substrate, often caused by impurities trapped between the film and the substrate.

delimiter The character used at the beginning and end of **SGML/HTML tags**. In the **reference concrete syntax** (the usual way of encoding using SGML, also used by HTML), the opening delimiters are '<' for a **start-tag** and '</' for an **end-tag**, while the closing delimiter is '>' for both start and end-tags.

demodulation The extraction of information from a modulated carrier signal.

demographic edition Edition of a publication designed for a specifically targeted sector of the readership with advertising limited to that edition.

demy Standard size of paper 444×564mm (metric system).

density Measurement of the tonal value of a printed or photographic area. Density is the light stopping, or light-absorbing, ability of an object. In mathematical terms it is the reciprocal (opposite) of 'transmission' or 'reflection', and it is measured by the formula, incident light divided by transmitted (or reflected) light expressed as a logarithmic value (power of ten). Logarithmic values are chosen to reflect the fact that perceived density proceeds in steps of 'twice as much as last time', not linearly. In practice this means a measuring scale of 0.0 at the lightest end of a subject measured by a densitometer (100% transmission/ reflection of light) up to 3.0 at the farthest end (0.1% transmission/reflection of light).

density range The range of contrast between the lightest area and the darkest area of a piece of artwork or photograph (see **density**). A good transmission density range in a transparency for reproduction should be between 1.8 to 2.4, with no less than 0.3 in the highlights and no more than 2.7 in the shadows as the outer parameters.

densometer Instrument that measures the air resistance of an area of paper.

depth of field Area that remains in focus between close and distant objects in a photograph.

descender The part of a letter extending below the character **baseline**, as for example in j, p, q and y. (See also **ascender**.)

desensitise Treat an offset plate with chemicals to ensure that the non-image areas do not retain ink.

designation marks Identifying letters at the foot of each signature of a book that confirm the sequence. See also **signature**.

develop Use chemical or other process to produce an image on photographic paper or a printing plate.

developer Material used to remove unexposed coating on a litho plate.

DI Direct imaging technology in which printing plates are imaged in situ on press

diacriticals Marks above and below letters, such as accents or the cedilla.

diagnosics Programs designed to trace faults in a system or program.

dial-up A temporary, as opposed to dedicated, connection between machines that is established over a **public switched telephone network**.

diaresis Two dots over a vowel to indicate stress, for example ë.

dichroic reflector Reflective housing around UV lamps designed to allow the passage of infrared radiation, which helps to cool the substrate.

dictionary A file used by a word processor or frontend system to check spelling or hyphenation. A dictionary can be a true dictionary, that contains all words that can be hyphenated with their hyphenation points, or an exception dictionary that lists only exceptions to logical rules, and is used to hyphenate words in conjunction with a hyphenation logic program.

Didone Group of typefaces previously know as **Modern**, e.g. Bodoni.

Didot The European measure of type. Based on a point of 0.376mm (0.0148in) Abbreviated to **D**.

Didot point system A method of measuring type size, used in Europe. (See **font size, cicero**.)

diecutting The cutting of paper or card with steel rules on a press to give cut-outs or folds in printed material.

die-stamping An **intaglio** printing process from a steel die giving a relief surface on the paper.

die case Monotype matrix case.

digest-size A page size the same as *Reader's Digest*, i.e. 5×7in.

digester The container in a chemical pulping system in which wood is processed with chemicals to extract the fibres.

digit A character that represents a whole number.

digital Meaning 'coded as numbers', digital signifies the use of two states – on and off, low and high, black and white – to encode, receive and transmit information. Should be contrasted with **analogue**, that implies continuous variation.

digital audio tape (DAT) A format for storing music, in **digital** form, on magnetic tape.

digital camera A camera that records images in **digital** form rather than on photographic film. There are both video digital cameras and still image digital cameras.

digital data service (DDS) The class of service offered by telecommunications companies for transmitting digital data as opposed to voice.

digital display A display that shows discrete values as numbers (as opposed to an analogue signal, such as the continuous sweep of a hand on a clock).

digital papers Papers specially formulated to be used with digital presses.

digital printing (DP) Printing directly from computer data, electrophotography and inkjet are the leading technologies.

digital proof Any proof produced directly from a computer file rather than a via a physical medium such as film or bromide.

digital signature Data at the end of a message that both identifies and authenticates the sender of a message. Uses public-key **encryption**. With a one-way hash function the sender generates a hash-code from the message and then encrypts this with his or her private key. The receiver decrypts the received hash with the sender's public key and compares it with a hash code generated from the data. If the two hash codes are the same, this confirms that the sender is who he or she claims to be and that the message has not been **corrupted**.

digital video (versatile) disk (DVD) Successor to the CD, which is single-sided and contains only one layer. The DVD can be dual-layer and double-sided. Its maximum storage capacity is 17 Gbytes, equivalent to four full-length feature films.

digital workflow system Prepress system for managing the flow of made-up pages from creation through proofing to imposition on plate.

digital-to-analogue conversion (DAC, D/A conversion) Conversion of information from a **digital** form (as information is held in a computer) to **analogue** form (such as sound), for example in a **modem** for transmission over analogue telephone lines.

digital-to-analogue converter A device that converts a digital value to a corresponding analogue form. Compare **analogue-to-digital converter (ADC)**.

digitise To convert an **analogue** signal, such as video, graphics or sound, into a digital format so that it can be input, stored, displayed and manipulated by a computer or transmitted over a **digital** communications system.

diluent The material used to reduce the viscosity of (or thin) a liquid ink.

dimensional stability Ability of paper to retain its shape despite variations in moisture content or mechanical stress.

DIN Deutsche Industrie Norme. The German standards institute. DIN paper sizes, now renamed **ISO**, have been adopted as the European standard. See also **A series**.

dingbat A term for typographical characters, such as arrows, stars, hearts and snowflakes also called **ornaments. Zapf Dingbats** is a symbol font that is provided as standard with most **PostScript** printers.

dip coating Coating method in which the web is passed around a roller immersed in coating solution.

diphthong Letters placed together as in æ, œ. Contrast **ligature**.

Direct selection A group of postcode districts (or sectors) for sorting **Mailsort** mail. It allows bags to go unopened to a local area delivery office, rather than be sorted at an intermediate office.

direct litho Litho press system that transfers the image direct from the printing plate without offsetting it to a blanket first.

direction of travel Direction in which web moves through a paper machine or press.

directory An index file containing details of all other files held on disk.

dirty 1. Typesetting with many errors introduced at the keyboard. 2. Copy with many handwritten amendments.

disc refiner Machine that refines pulp by rubbing fibres between vertical rotating discs.

disc ruling A method of ruling stationery with metal discs.

discrete speech In voice recognition technology, speech that contains short pauses between words to improve the recognition process.

discretionary hyphens Hyphenation points for words, either held in the hypenation exception dictionary of a front-end system or introduced while keyboarding new text. They indicate where a word may be broken if it needs to be hyphenated at the end of a line. Discretionary hyphens will overrule any logical hyphenation program in use.

disk drive A device that writes information to or reads information from a magnetic disk. See **disk**.

dispersion An ink or other type of coating in which a solid constituent that is not soluble in the liquid medium is pre-ground so that the particles are fine enough to remain in the suspension fluid.

display adapter Also called **graphics adapter** and **video controller**, that part of a computer circuitry that interprets data so that it can appear on the screen as text or graphics.

display ads Advertisements 'displayed' to occupy part or all of a page rather than set in columns.

display face A typeface designed for display sizes rather than for **composition sizes**.

display matter Typography set and displayed so as to be distinguished from the text, e.g. headings. Hence display sizes are sizes of type from 14pt upwards.

Display advertisements Those using **display faces**.

display papers and boards Papers and boards used for point-of-sale or exhibition purposes.

Display sizes Sizes of type larger than 14pt, i.e. used for display rather than text.

display tube See **cathode ray tube**.

display type Type used for headlines or title, rather than for text (see **body type**). These typefaces are usually 14pt type or larger. Some typefaces are designed specifically for this use, while other **expert sets** have special versions of particular typefaces intended for use as display faces.

dispro Intentional around-cylinder compensation of the image to address flexo plate printing characteristics.

dissolving pulp Highly-processed and pure chemical pulp.

distortion A corruption of a signal as a result of changes to the waveform.

distributed computing (distributed data processing, DDP) The dispersal of computing power, storage and applications throughout a number of computers connected through a **network**, rather than concentrating computing on a mainframe. (See also **client-server**.)

distributing rollers Rollers on a press that distribute ink from the duct to the inking rollers.

distribution See **diss**.

dithering A technique used in computer graphics to create the appearance of additional colours and shades of grey. As a **bit** can only be on or off, depending on the **colour resolution** (bits per **pixel**) or number of **grey levels**, there will be a limit to the number of colours (or grey levels) that can be displayed. However, as the dots that make up a conventional **halftone** illustration are much larger than a pixel, pixels are grouped in ways that fool the eye into thinking that it is seeing more shades of grey (by using pixel groups making up different shapes) or additional colours (by combining pixel combinations of different colours that the eye integrates). Dithering is also used in **anti-aliasing**.

ditto Typographic symbol („) for 'repeat the above matter'.

doctor blade A thin flexible blade mounted parallel to and adjustable against an engraved anilox roller to scrape off excess ink in flexo and gravure printing.

document Any printed piece or communicated content.

document architecture Rules for the formulation of text-processing applications. These are may be used in conjunction with SGML to control the structure and semantics of a document.

document reader An input device that reads marks or characters, usually on specially prepared forms and documents, such as cheques.

Document Style Semantics and Specification Language (DSSSL) An **ISO** standard (ISO 10179) that defines how to transfer information about the presentation of an **SGML** document to formatting software, associating **style sheet** information with a **document instance**. SGML, by definition, says nothing about how a document is to appear, either on paper or onscreen. DSSSL is intended to formalise the process of associating appearance information with the SGML structure.

Document Type Definition (DTD) The definition of a document type in **SGML**. This is a formulation of the hierarchy of the document and the definitions and relationships of the **elements** that make up that hierarchy, together with their **mark-up tags** and their **attributes**, the rules for applying the tags and definitions of **entities**. The DTD actually forms part of an SGML document, but in many SGML applications is not seen by the user, for example in **HTML**, that is defined by a DTD. Other well known and widely used DTDs are the **CALS** DTD and the American Association of Publishers (AAP) DTD, which has been revised and published **as ISO 12083**.

DocuPrint Leading sheet-fed high-speed laser printer family from Xerox.

dog-eared pages Corners of pages that are inadvertently folded over during processing. When the book is trimmed and the corners corrected the untrimmed portions protrude.

domain A group of computers on the **internet** whose hostnames share a common suffix, the **domain name**. Domains often indicate a country, e.g. .uk, or a type of organisation: .com (commercial), .edu (educational), .net (network operations), .gov (government). Within the .uk domain, there is the .ac.uk subdomain for academic sites and the .co.uk domain for commercial ones. Other top-level domains may be divided up in similar ways.

domain address The name of a **host** on the **internet** that is part of the **hierarchy** of internet **domains**.

dongle A hardware security component sold with a software package and without which the package is rendered unusable. The dongle is inserted into the computer's serial port, external expansion port or internal expansion slot.

dot 1. The individual element from which a halftone reproduction is made up. 2. Synonym for **pixel**. Dots per inch (**dpi**) is the standard measure of resolution, expressed as dots or pixels, for faster image output systems.

dot gain The increase in the size of the dots in a halftone illustration when they are printed on the paper (using a printing press, rather than a computer printer). The magnitude of the dot gain will depend on the characteristics of the press, the paper and the ink. If there is cooperation between the originator of the artwork and the printer, it is possible to use software to adjust the colour curves and even dot size to obtain the image that is desired. New calibration routines are necessary for use with **CTP**.

dot slurring Elongation of dots at their trailing edges.

dot spread Unacceptably enlarged dot size formation during printing.

dotless i An 'i' available in some photocomposition founts for the purpose of accommodating ligatures.

dots per inch (dpi) The **resolution** of a printer or scanner is measured in dots per inch. For a printer it is the number of dots of toner placed on the paper (in both directions), while for a scanner it is the number of **charge-coupled devices** per inch.

double black In printing four-colour process illustrations and heavy black solids together, refers to printing the black twice: once for the halftone, and once for the solid. Permits better control of ink weight and **tracking**.

double elephant Drawing paper measuring 27×40in.

double roll A second press roll over the printing surface when extra inking is required.

double spread Print going across two facing pages.

double tone ink A printing ink that creates an extra tone on drying, due to spreading.

double-black duotone A duotone created from two black plates. Used in very high-quality work to extend the ranges available.

double-click To **click** twice on the button of a **mouse**. While single-clicking usually means selecting an icon, double-clicking almost always means that the command associated with the icon or with a file name should be executed. If a file name is double-clicked, then this is equivalent to (single-) clicking on the name to select it and then (single-) clicking on the 'OK' button.

double-coated Coated paper that is given two coats either side instead of the normal one. Gives increased smoothness and consistency to the sheet.

double-duty envelope Envelope that can be reused by the recipient.

double-page spread Facing pages in a book or periodical.

double-tone halftone A colour plate printed slightly out of register to create a duotone effect.

doubling A second out-of-register image produced during a single impression. Caused by the ink on the blanket remaining wet after impression and transferring back from the blanket cylinder to the following sheet. If the following sheet is out of register it appears as a double image.

doughnut hickey A **hickey** with a white 'halo' around it.

DOVID Diffractive optically variable image device: a hologram is the most common example.

down-time Non-productive time when a printing machine is being maintained or made ready.

download To transfer data from a distant computer to a local one. The opposite of **upload**, although the distinction between downloading and uploading is not always clear, except that downloading often refers to transfer from a larger 'host' system (especially a mainframe) to a smaller 'client' system.

Downcycling the effect of deterioration suffered by cellulose fibres during a recycling process, this limits the number of times paper can be recycled.

downloadable fonts Fonts that can be sent to an imager's memory from an outside storage source rather than being resident on the printer's own fount cartridge or in ROM.

DP See **digital printing**.

dpi See **dots per inch**.

DPS See **double-page spread**.

drag To move the **mouse** cursor while holding down the mouse button and then, at a new position, to release the button. Used on scroll bars, to move icons, to resize drawings, to select text and for many other tasks.

drainability The rate at which paper stock parts with water when drained.

draw down A thin film of ink spread on paper with a spatula to evaluate its shade.

draw program A program used to create and edit objects (lines, circles, squares) using a **vector** approach, such as Bézier curves. Should be contrasted with a **paint program**, that is used to edit and manipulate **bitmaps**. It is usually possible to import bitmap graphics into **draw programs**, but not to edit them. If a bitmap is **autotraced**, then a **vector graphic** is produced that can be edited in the draw program.

draw-in Binding method in which the section threads are pulled through cover boards and glued.

draw-type graphic A graphic created from a series of geometric elements stored in memory as distinct from a graphic created by invoking x-y coordinates. Also known as an **object-oriented graphic** or **vector graphic**. Contrast **bitmap graphic**.

drawn-on cover A binding style in which the cover is glued directly onto the spine. Also known as 'wrappered'.

drier A mechanical device, such as a gas oven, used to dry ink on **heatset** web machines.

driers Additives in printing ink such as cobalt, manganese and resinates that accelerate drying.

drilling Perforating a pile of sheets with holes for special binding methods, such as loose-leaf.

driography (waterless offset) Litho plate making process in which the non-image areas are silicone rubber.

drop cap(s) Drop capital. A letter or letters at the beginning of a paragraph that extend beyond the depth of the rest of the text line. Also called **drop initial(s)**. Compare **cocked-up initial**.

drop guides Guides on a printing machine that position the sheet ready for the grippers.

drop heads See **dropped heads**.

drop-out halftone Halftone in that the highlight areas have no screen dots and simply show the white of the paper. Also known as a **deep-etch halftone**.

dropout Characters lost in data transmission for whatever reason.

dropped heads Chapter headings positioned a few lines below the top of full text pages.

drum scanner Scanner with cylindrical platen for mounting transparencies to be scanned, as distinct from a **flatbed scanner**.

DRUPA A major printing technology exhibition held in Düsseldorf (hence DRUck PApier) every four years.

dry back The loss of gloss of an ink as it dries.

dry indicator size test Method of measuring paper's water resistance. See also **Cobb size test**.

dry picking resistance The picking resistance of paper in dry conditions.

dry pulp Pulp in dry sheets.

dry transfer lettering Sheets of typographic characters which can be transferred onto paper by rubbing.

dry-mounting A method of photographic mounting that uses pressure-sensitive backing.

dry-up See **scumming**.

drying section The last part of the papermaking machine, after the press section, which completes the drying of the web.

drying time Time taken for the ink on a printed sheet to dry enough for further work to be done on the sheet, e.g. binding or extra printing.

DSSSL See **Document Style Semantics and Specification Language**.

DTD See **document type definition**.

duct Ink trough on a printing press. The duct roller regulates the amount of ink released.

dull finish enamel An enamel paper with a low gloss.

dummy Mock-up of a book or other piece of printing to indicate specifications.

dump bin Point-of-sale container for easy stacking of goods.

duoformer The duoformer paper machine has an additional wire running on top of the normal machine wire, which draws water from the topside of the web, producing an evenly formed sheet. As distinct from the **twin-wire** process, which has two separate webs of paper which are brought together before pressing.

duotone A black-and-white photograph (or other artwork) that is reproduced using two colours, both near to black. Two halftone images are generated, one of which is slightly underexposed and the other slightly overexposed, and they are printed one on top of the other. The effect is to give a more striking image, together with more control to the designer, who can vary the proportions of the two images. **Tritones** and **quadtones** are also possible.

duplex cutter A sheeting device that cuts two different sheet lengths from the web simultaneously.

duplex paper Paper with a different colour on each side.

duplex printing Double-sided printing.

duplicator Small office machine for short-run reproduction from a stencil.

duplicator paper Special absorbent paper for duplicating from a stencil master.

dust jacket Paper wrapper of a book carrying the title and author's name.

dusting Accumulation of powdered paper on the non-printing areas of a blanket.

DVD See **digital versatile disk**

Dvorak Keyboard layout in which the keys are positioned so as to be most readily accessible to the fingers that most often use them. Contrast **azerty**, **qwerty**.

dye A soluble colouring matter (pigments are insoluble).

dye mask Special sort of colour film used when colour separating transparencies by camera to assist with colour correction. See also **masking**, **trimask**.

dye transfer Photographic process producing colour prints with dyes that are selectively absorbed.

dyed through In bookbinding, a dyed-through cloth is dyed on both sides, not just on the surface. Contrast '**whiteback**'.

dyne testing See **Sherman tester**.

e- Prefix indicating a process changed by being conducted electronically via computer (email, e-procurement, e-book, e-commerce).

EAN European Article Number. See **barcode**.

earmark Particular characteristic or feature of a typeface that distinguishes it from all others and assists recognition.

earpieces Small advertisements on either side of a newspaper's mast-head.

easer Printing ink additive used to reduce tack.

EB Electron beam curing of inks and coatings.

EBCDIC See extended binary-coded decimal interchange.

ECF Elemental chlorine free. Relates to pulp and paper manufacture. ECF pulp is one stage less pure than **TCF**, totally chlorine free, pulp.

ECM Enterprise content management.

edge cutters Water jets on a paper machine that 'clean off' the edges of the web on the wire.

edge decoration Coloured dyes, marbling transfers or gilding on trimmed book edges.

edge gilding Gold-leaf edging on a book.

edge tear Broken edge of web.

edge tearing resistance Resistance of paper to the further development of a small edge tear.

edgeboard connector The most common method of connecting add-on printed circuit boards to computer hardware.

EDI See **electronic data interchange**.

EDIFACT See **ISO 9735**.

edit Check, arrange and correct data or copy before final presentation.

editing terminal Visual display unit capable of retrieving a file and editing the contents prior to processing.

edition All the copies of a printed work from the same set of type or plates.

edition binding Conventional, production line, casebound binding.

editor A software utility employed to aid the production and modification of source programs.

editorial 1. Publication's formal views on a subject expressed in a special column. 2. The editorial matter (as distinct from advertisements) in a publication.

edutainment The integration of interactive education and entertainment services or software.

eggshell antique Bulky paper with a slightly mottled surface, like that of an egg.

Egyptian Type style with a squared serif.

Ektochrome Alternative name for transparency.

elastomer Artificial rubber compounds, used to make printing sleeves. The material can be stretched and deformed greatly, but will revert back to its original shape without permanent deformation when the force is released.

elastomeric Flexible and resilient.

Electrocoagulation Digital printing process from The Canadian Elcorsy company, .a potential technology that has yet to take off.

electronic data interchange (EDI) (Or electronic dissemination of information) The exchange of certain business documents – such as orders, invoices, bills of lading – in standard format between organisations, using **electronic mail**. Can include **electronic funds transfer**.

electronic dissemination of information (EDI) See **electronic data interchange**.

electronic document Any **document** that is held in electronic, as opposed to print-on-paper, form.

electronic journal (e-journal) The electronic equivalent of a paper-based journal or magazine.

electronic mail Transfer of documents of messages between computers.

electronic mark-up Generic codes inserted into a text being sent on disk or down the wire that identify headings, different levels of text. The generic codes can be converted into typesetting commands by means of a look-up table at the time of output. See also **generic mark-up** and **ASPIC**.

electrophotography Leading digital printing technology involving incidence of laser or the reflection of light from an original onto an electrically charged drum. Areas affected by the light lose their charge. **Toner**, retained by the charged areas, is fused to paper, thereby creating an image. Laser printers use this principle for output.

element A structural part of an **HTML** or **SGML** document. The name and usage of an element, together with its **attributes**, are defined in the **Document Type Definition**. Elements are coded within the **document instance** by using **tags**. For example, within this glossary, the element for 'SGML' defined as 'entry' would be coded as '<entry>SGML</entry>'. (See also **start-tag**, **end-tag**.)

ellipsis Three dots ... indicating an omission.

elliptical dot Elongated dot giving a smoother gradation of tone in midtones.

em 1. Width of the body of the lower case 'm' in any typeface. 2. Standard unit of measurement (also called 'pica'). One em equals 0.166044in.

em dash An elongated hyphen (the width of capital 'M' in the **font** in use) that is used within printed (and electronic) documents as a form of punctuation. Different publishers and different nationalities have different conventions about how the em dash and **en dash** should be used. (See **dash**.)

embossed finish Surface pattern pressed in paper.

embossing See **blocking**.

emulsification Dispersion of water into another liquid, e.g. when water soaks into the ink on a litho plate and degrades the image.

emulsion Photosensitive coating on film or plate. Hence, 'emulsion side'.

emulsion varnish see **water miscible coatings**

en Half the width of an **em**. The width of the average type character, so is used as the basic unit of measurement for casting off copy.

en dash An elongated hyphen (the width of capital 'N' in the **font** in use), that is used within printed (and electronic) documents as a form of punctuation. Different publishers and different nationalities have different conventions about how the en dash and **em dash** should be used. (See **dash**.) There are two almost universal uses of an en dash. The first is to indicate a range, as a substitute for the word 'to' (or 'through' in the US), for example 'pp 20–30' (pages 20 to 30), while the second is to denote a relationship, for example 'speed is a time–distance relationship'.

enamel paper Paper coated on one side with a very high finish.

Encapsulated PostScript (EPS) A **graphic** created using **PostScript** code.

enclosure Contents of a mail shot.

encode To code groups of characters.

encryption Conversion of a **plaintext** file to **ciphertext**, so that it can be used or understood only by those who have the information to decode or **decrypt** it.

end of file (EOF) The physical termination point of an amount of data or the mark used to indicate this point.

end or **end leaf** See **endpaper**.

end-of-line decisions Decisions on hyphenation or justification made either by the operator or automatically by the typesetting system.

end-tag The tag that indicates the end of an **element** in S.

GML or **HTML**. For example, this entry could be represented as '<entry>endtag</ entry>', where '</entry>' is the end-tag. Although this syntax is that usually used, it can be modified in the SGML declaration, if so required. The logical structure of a document may mean that end-tags are not always necessary, because they are implied by the next **start-tag** or another end-tag. Whether or not end-tags should be included for particular elements is defined in the **Document Type Definition (DTD)**.

endmatter The final parts of a book after the main text: appendices, notes, index.

endpaper Strong paper used for securing the body of a book to its case. Endpapers may be plain, coloured, marbled. and should be specified with the **grain direction** parallel to the spine.

endsheets Endpapers (US).

engine sizing Sizing paper in the beating machine or refiner rather than at a later stage in manufacture.

engine-sized pulp See **beater-sized pulp**.

English finish Smoothly calendered book paper.

engraving A relief pattern that has been cut in or incised into a printing surface by mechanical, etching or laser exposure processes.

entity A code used in **SGML** and **HTML**. There are two types: the first is the **character entity**, used to code **non-ASCII** characters using ASCII coding, while the second use is as a kind of macro and inclusion facility. The second use is not currently implemented in HTML.

envelope paper Paper made for high-speed envelope diecutting machines.

envelope-stuffer Mail shot promoting or advertising products or services, sent out in an envelope.

EOL End of line.

EOT End of tape.

epigraph Quotation in book prelims.

epilogue Closing section at the end of a novel or play.

EPS See **Encapsulated PostScript**.

equilibrium moisture content Moisture content of paper at the same relative humidity as its environment.

ERA The European Rotogravure Association headquartered in Munich was founded in 1956 and is an association of European gravure printers with manufacturers from the industry as associate members.

erasable storage Storage medium that can be erased and reused as required, i.e. a floppy disk.

ERP Enterprise resource planning system; computerised control system.

erratum slip Slip of paper pasted into a book and containing list of author's post-press corrections.

error correction See **error detection and correction**.

error detection and correction Detection of errors in transmitted or stored data and the correction of them.

escrow Deposit of information with a third party for safe-keeping. The practice is used for the deposit of software source material to ensure that it will be available should the supplier cease to trade. It is now being used for deposit of **encryption** keys by the US government.

esparto Long-fibred grass used in pulp for papermaking. The stock is extremely opaque and, thanks to its low moisture pick up, features relatively high dimensional stability.

esquisse Rough layout or design.

Ethernet A **local area network technology**

EtherTalk An implementation of **AppleTalk** on an **ethernet LAN**, allowing a Macintosh to connect into ethernet networks; the Macintosh must have an ethernet interface card installed.

ETO Ethylene oxide.

EUPRIMA European Print Management System Association is an association of MIS suppliers, formed to promote the electronic exchange of data between manufacturers, customers and suppliers using JDF.

even small caps Small capitals without full capitals.

even working A total of pages in a publication that can be produced entirely by printing sections of the same numbers of pages (16s, 32s). See also **oddment**.

everdamp paper Transfer paper for laying down images on lithographic plates.

exception dictionary Computer store of words that do not hyphenate in accordance with the machine's rules of logic. See also **hyphenation**.

exception dictionary and **discretionary hypens**.

exclusive type area Type area exclusive of headline and folio. The type area inclusive of headline and folio is known as the **inclusive type area**.

expanded type Typeface with characters wider than the normal fount.

expert set (Or expert collection.) A **font** with an extended **character set**, including such characters as true small capitals, non-aligning (or old-style) numerals and additional accented characters. The term 'expert set' is used by monotype while Linotype and Adobe use 'expert collection'.

export To copy out from one program into another, typically from a word processing program to a page make-up program.

export filter A program that converts text from one format and code structure into another.

expose Image a film, plate or cylinder with the print material.

extended ASCII An alternative term for **high-level ASCII**.

extended binary coded decimal interchange (EBCDIC) An eight-bit character code set, a number of variants of EBCDIC are used but more generally **ASCII** is the standard.

extended type See **expanded type**.

extenders Ink additives used to increase coverage. Typical extenders include whiting, borytes, blanc fixe.

eXtensible Markup Language (XML) A simplified version of **SGML**, developed under the auspices of the **W3 Consortium** with the aim of enabling SGML to be 'served, received and processed on the **web** in the way that is now possible with **HTML**'. XML has been designed for ease of implementation and to be interoperable with both SGML and HTML. One area in which XML has an advantage over SGML is that it is designed to handle international character sets corresponding to **ISO 10646**.

extensible paper Paper that has tear-resistance due to stretching properties.

extent Length of a book in pages.

extract Quoted matter within a text, often set indented and in a smaller type size.

extranet The extension of an **intranet** to allow access to other, authorised, users and organisations.

F number Defines the aperture of a lens at different settings, and is obtained by dividing the focal length of the lens by the diameter of the aperture. Also referred to as **f-stop**.

f&g sheets Folded and gathered sheets of a book.

f-stop See **F number**.

face 1. The printing surface of a piece of type. 2. A style of type, i.e. typeface.

face-down feed When the side of the sheet to be printed faces downward on the feed board.

facing Lining of fibreboard.

facing editorial Appearing opposite editorial pages. A special position used when ordering advertisement space.

facing pages Pages that face each other in an open book or magazine. Also **double-page spread**.

facsimile (Latin *fac simile* = to make similar) 1. Exact reproduction of a document or part of it. 2. Machine that copies and transmits documents by telecommunications. Hence **facsimile transmission**.

facsimile transmission or **fax** Method for the electronic transmission of printed material by means of special transmitting and receiving equipment. The document to be transmitted is scanned at a resolution of around 200 lines per inch; the signals are sent along conventional dial-up telephone lines; at the receiving end, a thermal imaging head writes a facsimile of the transmitted message: Group 1 defines analogue transmission taking four or six minutes per page; Group 2 defines analogue transmission taking two or three minutes per page; Group 3 defines digital transmission taking less than one minute per page; Group 4 defines digital transmission over **ISDN**. While Groups 1 to 3 are for black and white only, Group 4 will also handle colour.

fade-out See **ghosting**.

fair copy A correction-free copy of a document.

fair dealing A provision in copyright law that permits the copying of an otherwise protected work for the purposes of criticism, review, or private study.

fake duotone Imitation duotone obtained by printing the halftone in one colour (normally black) over a flat screen tint of another colour (lighter). Contrast **duotone**.

fake process Colour separation achieved by means of the artist producing separate overlays.

family A series of founts related to the basic text roman face.

fan-out Moisture-distorted edges of paper on the press, creating waviness in the sheet.

fanfold A web of paper folded into connected sheets by alternate folds across the web.

fanning-in The condensing of the image on the trailing edge of a sheet caused by the sheet stretching temporarily on the press.

FAQ Frequently asked question(s). Selected, sometimes summarised and specially listed to help newcomers to a particular topic.

Fast ethernet A **networking** protocol that provides bandwidth of 100Mbps, as opposed to the 10Mbps of original **ethernet**, being superseded by gigabit ethernet.

fastback binding See **tightback binding**.

fastness Resistance of colour to fading under physical or chemical attack. See also **lightfast ink**, **blue wool scale**.

fax See facsimile transmission.

FDA Food and Drug Administration, the US agency responsible for giving approval for products suitable for contact with food and drugs.

FED Field emission device. A device that ejects a stream of electrons in response to an applied electric field. A major application is likely to be flat panel displays. Carbon nanotubes are good field emitters.

feathering 1. In printing, ink-spread on inadequately sized paper. 2. In typesetting, the addition of fractional parts of a point of leading between all lines in a page to 'stretch' the text to a predefined depth. A form of **vertical justification**.

feature 1. Newspaper or magazine article. 2. Specially promoted item of merchandise or characteristic of that item.

FED Field emission device. A device that ejects a stream of electrons in response to an applied electric field. A major application is likely to be flat panel displays. Carbon nanotubes are good field emitters.

feed board The surface over which paper is passed to the printing mechanism of a press.

feed edge Edge of a sheet presented to the lays of a press. Also called **gripper edge**, **leading edge**, or **pitch edge**.

feed holes Holes in paper tape used by the sprocket on the mechanical reader to feed the tape in.

feeder The mechanism on a press that separates and lifts sheets into the printing position.

feet The base of a piece of metal type.

feint ruling Horizontal pale blue lines running across stationery.

felt finish A finish to paper created by felts with special weaves.

felt-side Top side of paper formed on a paper machine **wire**. As distinct from the underside or wire side.

festoon In web offset printing, an arrangement of long loops at the paper feed that allows paper to be tensioned during autopasting on the fly using a **flying paster**.

FET Film effect transistor.

fibre The cellulose constituents in wood pulp.

fibre cut Damage to the web on a papermaking machine caused by a bundle of fibres.

fibre optic cable A protective glass or plastic cable containing a pure fibre of the same material, used to transmit light from LEDs or lasers in the communication of signals.

fibre optics The technique of communicating data by the transmission of light through plastic or glass fibres.

fibre puffing Coated paper surface roughening caused by heatset drying on a web press.

fibre-optic transmission A high bandwidth transmission method that uses modulated infrared or visible coherent light, which is transmitted down multiple optical fibres.

fibrefelt Another name for **imitation cloth**.

fibrilla Part of cellulose fibre separated during the refining process.

fibrillation In papermaking, the process of roughening the outside of the fibre to increase bonding capabilities.

field A predefined area of a computer **record**.

FIFO See **first in first out**.

figure 1. A line illustration referred to in the text of a book. 2. A numeral, either in **Arabic** or **Roman** form.

file Text, or any collection of related records held on a computer in structured form.

file compression The **compression** of **data** in a file, usually to reduce storage requirements or transmission time.

file conversion The process of changing either a file medium or its structure, usually required because of the introduction of new software or hardware.

file management An established procedure for the creation and maintenance of files.

file server A computer in a **network** that holds files that can be accessed by users on the network. File servers often also act as **print servers**, while **database servers** provide database intelligence such as transaction processing, indexing, logging, security and so on. Storing files on a file server means that it is unnecessary to have multiple copies stored on individual computers, which saves disk space and makes controlling and updating files easier.

file transfer Copying a file from one computer to another computer over a network or a direct connection.

File Transfer Protocol (ftp) A **client-server** protocol that enables a user on one computer to transfer files to and from another computer over a **TCP/IP** network (often over the **internet**); ftp is also used to describe the client program that the user executes to transfer files.

fill The pattern and the colour inside an object produced in a **draw program**. The parameters controlling the fill are almost always handled separately from those controlling the **outline** of the object.

fill character A character, typically a space, that is added to a set of characters to make the set up to a given size.

filler advertisement Advertisement used to occupy redundant space rather than booked for insertion.

fillers Pigments added to the furnish of paper to improve the printing or opacity characteristics.

film polyester based material coated with light-sensitive, silver-based emulsion that is opaque when developed. Still in wide use by imagesetters but quickly being superseded by digital production methods.

film processor Machine that automatically develops, fixes, washes and dries exposed film.

film recorder An output device that captures data and records it onto film, usually at high resolution. (See **imagesetter**.)

film wrapping See **plastic wrapping**.

filter An electronic or optical device that removes unwanted frequencies from a signal. A program which converts one file coding structure into another. A control within a **firewall machine** that blocks transmission of certain kinds of traffic.

filter factor The extra exposure necessary to counteract the light-reducing effect of a filter.

Finder The file and memory management system generally used in the Apple **Macintosh**. Finder allows only one program to be run at a time.

fine papers High-quality printing and writing papers.

fine screen A screen with ruling over 120 lines to an inch.

fines Small fragments of fibre remaining after refining.

fingerprint A method of software protection in which a unique signature is written to a floppy disk. When the program is run, a test sequence checks for the presence of the signature and disables the program if it is absent.

finish The type of surface on a particular grade of paper, e.g. machine finished or supercalendered. Also, varnish or lamination on a cover or jacket.

finishing Bindery processes taking place after a job is printed and bringing it to its final form ready for despatch, i.e. folding, stitching, cutting, inserting.

FIPP International Federation of the Periodical Press.

firewall A security barrier to prevent external access to a system, by hackers. The firewall is intended to protect other machines at the site from potential tampering via the internet.

FireWire A fast data transfer standard for use with Apple computers, capable of transferring data at 400Mbps.

FIRST Flexographic image reproduction specifications and tolerances, a set of procedural processes to provide flexo benchmarks, specifications and tolerances developed by the **FTA**.

first and second linings The two linings applied to the back of the book in case binding. The first lining is normally **mull**, a form of muslin cloth, the second lining normally **kraft**, a strong form of brown paper.

first and third Printed sheet that contains pages one and three after folding. See **outer forme**.

first colour down The first colour printed on a sheet when more than one colour is being used.

first proof The earliest proof used for checking by proofreaders.

first revise The corrected proof made after errors noted on the first proof have been re-set.

first-level heading First (and most important) level in a series of headings in a book.

fit Space between letters that can be reduced or expanded. See **character compensation, character fit, kerning**.

fixed back Book back glued directly to the back of the pages. Also **fastback, tightback binding**.

fixed length record A record that is of the same length as others with which it is associated.

fixed position Set location for an advertisement within a periodical, often specified by reference to other material, e.g. facing leader page.

fixed space The amount of space between letters and words which cannot be varied for justification needs. Contrast **variable space**.

flag In general, a variable or quantity that can take on one of two values (often 'on' or 'off'). May be a **bit** (within operating systems) or a **byte** in some programs. In communications bit-oriented protocols, a unique bit pattern used to identify the beginning and end of a frame.

flat Lacking contrast when printed.

flat artwork Artwork that is drawn on a solid base and that cannot always be directly scanned.

flat ASCII A text file that contains only **ASCII** (seven-bit) characters and uses only ASCII-standard control characters. Thus it includes no (eight-bit) embedded codes specific to a particular program or output device, and no **meta characters**. Also called **plain ASCII**. **SGML** files are flat-ASCII in that all non-ASCII characters are represented by **character entities**. (See also **flat file**.)

flat back Bound with a flat back (as distinct from 'rounded'). Also, **square back**.

flat etching Etching of a plate in a tray of solution.

flat file A representation of a database or tree structure as a single file from which the structure can be rebuilt. The file will often be in **flat ASCII** form, but may also contain accented characters represented by eight bits.

flat plan Diagrammatic scheme of the pagination of a magazine or book.

flat wrapping Wrapping a magazine with film or paper without folding it.

flatbed A press with the printing surface flat rather than curved as on a rotary press.

flatbed proofing press A litho flatbed press designed to produce machine proofs from colour separation plates in limited numbers.

flatbed scanner A scanner with a flat platen, rather than a rotating drum.

flax tow Linen fibres used in paper making.

fleuron Typographical flower ornament used for decorative purposes, a **dingbat**.

flexiback binding Binding with reinforced spine using paper or fabric lining.

flexography (flexo) Relief printing process using flexible, deformable **plates**.

flexstabil binding Binding method used for heavy books and catalogues. A centre portion of the back of the book is scooped out, flooded with glue and resealed, prior to the cover being drawn on. Extremely durable binding method.

flier Promotional leaflet or handbill.

float Centre a piece of artwork in an area which is too large for it.

floating accents Accents that are not tied to a given character in type fount and can therefore be positioned over any letter.

flocculation Ink-mixing fault caused when pigment floats as particles in the ink vehicle rather than dispersing smoothly. Solid areas have a spotty, pimply appearance.

flooding Excess of ink on a printing plate.

floppy disk Small flexible plastic disk used for storage of information on computers. The standard size disks are 3.5in.

floppy disk drive A device into which a floppy disk may be loaded and from which data may be read or written.

flotation de-inking Removing ink from recycled paper by creating a 'froth' which can be skimmed off.

flow The spread of ink over press rollers.

flowchart The sequence of steps in a computer program.

fluff Loose surface fibres on paper. Also, **lint**.

fluorescent ink Ink with extreme brightness qualities which react to ultraviolet light. Fluorescent papers have fluorescent pigments added. Fluorescent whitening is included in pulp to add brightness to paper.

flush centre, **left** or **right** alignment of text to the centre, left or right of the column or page. (See **justification**.)

flush cover A cover trimmed flush with the pages of the text of the book.

flush left/right Type aligned with either the left or right-hand margins.

flying paster Pasting mechanism that joins a new reel of paper to that currently running out on a web press without stopping the press.

flyleaf Plain sheet in a book next to the covers. Usually pages 3–4 of the front **endpaper**.

FM Frequency modulated screening technique where dots of the same size are positioned randomly to create the image; often called stochastic screening.

FOB Free on board. Carriage paid only up to the point of placing goods on board a vessel at the departure port. Contrast **cif** which includes carriage payment up to the point of placing goods on the quayside at the arrival port.

focal plane The plane where light entering a lens forms a sharp image.

focus Sharpness of definition in photography or in projection of a product or service.

fog Unintended light penetration of photographic materials.

FOGRA Forschungsgesellschaft Druck e.V. was set up to promote printing technology.

foil 1. Carrier for planned films 2. In book binding, short for stamping foil: a plastic film coated with clear or coloured lacquer and a thin layer of condensed aluminium that is used to block covers. The aluminium and coloured top lacquer detach from the plastic carrier under heat and pressure from a blocking brass during the blocking process to leave the design or lettering engraved on the block transferred into the surface of the case material with the thin coloured metallic layer on top. Popular colours are gold, silver and holographic designs.

foil papers Papers with metallic surface.

fold-out Folded sheet in text that opens out beyond the page size. Also, **gatefold**, **throw-out**.

folding boxboard High-quality carton maker's board that has good scoring and folding characteristics.

folding endurance Measure of deterioration of paper along a constantly repeated fold.

foliation The numbering of manuscript pages.

folio 1. Page number at the head or foot of a page of text. 2. Sheet of copy.

FolioViews A viewer, mainly for textual information, although links can be made to graphics. Requires **structured documents**, but not necessarily **SGML**. Can provide its own **database** structure.

follow style Instruction to compositor to set to the publisher's specified style.

Font (fount) A complete set of all of the characters making up a typeface.

font metrics The detailed design specifications of a font, that include the widths of individual characters, the **x-height**, how tall the capital letters are, the **kerning pairs** and many other items.

font size In the UK and US, font size is usually given in **points** (1 point = 0.351mm) and 12 points make up a **pica**, the basic unit of typographic measurement. Elsewhere in Europe, point sizes and measurements are given using the **Didot** system, based on a 12pt **cicero**, equal to 12.8 British points, so that 1 Didot point = 0.376mm.

foolscap Paper size measuring 13in×1in.

foot Bottom of a book or page.

footer In conventional books the running footline that sometimes appears at the bottom of each page. (See also **header**.)

footnotes Notes explanatory to the main text, set in smaller type at the bottom of the page.

footprint The surface area of a machine

force card Male die used in die-stamping.

fore-edge Outer edge of a book, opposite the binding edge.

foreword Introduction to a book, not written by the author. As distinct from a **preface**.

format Trimmed page size, or physical specification for a page or a book.

Format Output Specification Instance (FOSI) An **SGML-marked-up** document that uses the **CALS** output specification as its **Document Type Definition** (DTD). A FOSI contains formatting information structured according to SGML. FOSI styles define all features of composition: font, leading, quadding, spacing (about 125 characteristics in all). FOSIs map SGML documents to appearance-based mark-up ready for composition by a FOSI-capable system. FOSIs were originally intended for print but can equally be applied to composition on-screen. FOSIs use the same constructs as documents but apply them to format instead of to structure and content.

formation The fibre distribution of a sheet of paper. The two extremes are described as 'wild' or 'even'.

forme The printing surface as imposed and mounted ready for printing. By extension, a flat of pages imposed for printing one side of a sheet.

forme rollers Rollers in contact with the plate on a press.

former folder Type of web press folder which draws paper over a **kite** to make first fold. As distinct from a ribbon folder.

forwarding Binding stages after sewing till casing-in.

fountain Damping solution reservoir on a press. Fountain rollers measure out the damping solution to the damping rollers. Sometimes used to describe the flexo inking system.

fountain solution Solution of water and chemicals used in litho to prevent the non-printing areas from accepting ink. Also, damping solution.

four-colour process See **CMYK, colour separation**.

Fourdrinier Papermaking machine named after the brothers who invented it. Uses a wire belt to convey the wet paper.

fourth cover Outside back cover of a periodical.

FPO For position only. Using a low-resolution version of a graphic on a desktop computer for speed then replacing with the high-resolution version at final output.

fractal An irregular 'fragmented' geometric self similar shape. The term was invented by Benoit Mandelbrot in 1975. Fractal objects contain structures that are nested within each other, so that each smaller structure is a reduced version of the larger form, although not identical.

frame A sequence of contiguous **bits**, enclosed by opening and closing **flags**, transmitted over a **serial link**. A frame generally contains its own **addressing** and error-checking information and is sent between **datalink** layer entities. The size of the frame will depend upon the protocol used. Also a single image that forms part of a series that make up either a video or an animation.

frame grabber A device that allows a single **frame** of a video to be captured and subsequently used as a still image.

frames A browser facility that allows the screen to be broken into several different areas, some of which may remain static, acting as a menu, while new information is downloaded into the main screen area.

free sheet 1. Periodical or newspaper distributed free to its readers. 2. **Woodfree paper** (US).

free surface energy Measurement of the ink receptivity of plastic substrates, tested by **dyne** or **Sherman** fluids.

free-text search Searching text files for any combination of characters, often words. **Search engines** that are able to carry out free-text search often include **Boolean** facilities and **proximity searching** so that, for example, one can search for the occurrence of a group or string of characters within, say, 20 words of another group or groups. Such engines are usually based on **indexing** and the approach should be contrasted with **keyword search**.

freeness Measure of purity in woodfree pulp (i.e. the degree to which the pulp is free of **lignin** traces).

freeware Software made available by the author at no cost. The author still retains copyright and thus it is not quite the same as **public domain software** (PDS). (See also **shareware**).

freight forwarding The organisation of freight handling for customers. A freight forwarder can offer a variety of services, ranging from a comprehensive service including packing, full documentation, customs clearance, pick up and delivery of all his customer's freight, to a specialised service offering any part of the freight operation.

French fold The fold used on Christmas cards that folds a sheet into four pages, exposing only one side of the sheet and leaving the join at the edges.

French groove In binding, the groove or channel left by bringing the case board slightly away from the shoulder of the book. Also, **joint.**

French sewing Plain, conventional sewing. Also called **section sewing**.

frequency The number of repetitions per unit time of a periodic waveform. The number of cycles per second for an electromagnetic waveform is expressed in **hertz** (Hz, kHz, MHz or GHz).

friction glazing Form of glossy finish imparted to paper by a special calender.

frisket Device on a hand-press for holding down paper during printing.

front end General term for all the parts of a photosetting system before the output unit/imagesetter, e.g. input keyboards, screens or editing terminals.

front of book Part of a periodical before the bulk of the editorial pages, often dedicated to advertisements.

frontispiece Illustration on the page facing the title page of a book.

frontmatter Prelims of a book.

FTA Flexographic technical association. Founded in 1958 the FTA is the leading US technical society devoted exclusively to the flexo print sector.

ftp See **File Transfer Protocol**.

ftp archive See **archive site**.

fugitive inks Inks that fade or change colour in unstable atmospheric conditions or in bright light.

full capitals or **full caps** Full-sized, regular capitals as distinct from small capitals.

full colour Four-colour process.

full duplex Data transmission in both directions simultaneously. Contrast **simplex**, **half duplex**.

full measure Complete width of a column of text.

full point Full stop.

full run All the editions of a newspaper.

full-bound Binding style in which the case covering material is one piece of cloth or leather. As distinct from **quarter-bound**, **half-bound**, or **three-quarter bound**.

full-out Set flush with no indentations.

function codes Codes that control the function of a phototypesetter or output device rather than generating characters.

furnish The components in a paper.

fuzz Loosely bonded fibres projecting from the surface of paper.

fuzzy logic In the context of word searching, fuzzy logic programs encompass words that look or sound very similar to the word required, e.g. a search for the name Smith might also pull in Smithe, Smythe, Smyth, Smitt.

FWA Fluorescent Whitening Agent. A loading similar to an **OBA** added to paper to increase whiteness and brightness.

gamma A measure of contrast in photographic processing.

gamut See **colour gamut**.

gang printing Running more than one job on the same sheet.

gapless Refers to the elimination of any gap on the printing cylinder, so allowing smaller waste trim in the printed product and higher running speeds.

Garalde Generic term for the group of typefaces also known as **Old Face**.

gas plasma display An alternative to the cathode ray tube in a VDU, a gas plasma display consists of a sealed unit made from two sheets of flat glass filled with a neon/argon gas. Conductors are etched onto the glass plates (vertical on the front plate, horizontal on the rear plate) and images are formed when currents coincide at conductor junctions.

gate Part of a computer circuit that tests a precondition in a program, e.g. the statements 'and' and 'or'.

gatefold A page in a magazine or book which folds out to double its size.

gateway A communications device or program that passes data between networks that have similar functions but dissimilar implementations. Should not be confused with a **protocol converter**.

GATF Graphic Arts Technical Foundation, Pittsburg, US.

gather Collect sheets or signatures of a printed job into the correct sequence for binding. See also **collate**.

Gb Abbreviation for **gigabyte**.

GCR See **grey component replacement**.

gear streaks Marks on a printed sheet caused by the gears on a press cylinder.

GenCode A **generic coding** project set up by the US Graphics Communications Association. An important precursor of **SGML**.

Generalised Markup Language (GML) The **generic markup** language developed at IBM in 1969; the principal precursor of **SGML**. The acronym originally comprised the initials of the three inventors, Charles Goldfarb, Edward Mosher and Raymond Lorie.

generic coding Coding the structure of a document rather than its typographical constituents.

generic mark-up A method of adding information to text, indicating the logical components of a document, such as paragraphs, headers or footnotes. **SGML** is an example of such a system. Specific instructions for layout of the text on the page do not appear in the mark-up. Essentially the same as **generic coding**, the difference in emphasis between the two terms is more one of usage than of any real difference in meaning.

Ghent PDF Group A significant independent team working to establish and disseminate process specifications for best practices in graphic arts workflows.

ghosting An unintended faint printed image caused by problematic ink conditions, normally **ink starvation**.

GIF (Graphics Interchange Format); '.gif' is also the filename extension for files in Graphics Interchange Format.

gilt in the round Fore-edge of a book gilded after the book has been rounded. Achieves better cover than gilt in the square: gilded before rounding.

giveaway Free promotional leaflet or gift.

glair Substance that bonds gold leaf to leather.

glassine Tough but partially transparent paper used for protective purposes and for overlays on artwork.

glazed vellum Vellum paper with a glazed surface, used for decorative documents.

Global Network Service (GNS) The service that connects national PSS services. Formerly known as **International Packet SwitchStream** (IPSS).

global search and replace The facility of a computer program to find all examples of a word or group of words in a file and replace them with an alternative.

Global System for Mobile Communications (GSM) The standard for digital cellular communications.

gloss art Shiny art paper, as opposed to matt art or coated carriage which have a dull finish.

glossary Alphabetically arranged list of terms and their meanings.

glossy Photographic print with a glossy surface.

glueability Measure of speed of paper adhesive bonding and its strength.

glyph The actual shape of a character, as opposed to its identity within a **character set**. Whether two representations of the same character in two different **fonts** constitute one or two glyphs is not agreed, as long as they are basically similar, so the sans-serif 'g's in the typefaces Arial (g) and Helvetica (g) can be regarded as two glyphs or two representations of the same glyph. However, the letter 'g' in the Times typeface (sideways spectacles) is definitely a different glyph. It is possible for several characters to make up a single glyph (for example, a ligature), while equally a single character may be composed of more than one glyph.

Glyphic Typeface based on a chiselled rather than a calligraphic form.

glytch (glitch) Program error.

GML See **Generalised Markup Language.**

Goffering A process for shaping the surface of paper into a pattern, usually of fine grooves.

Google Leading internet search engine.

gold foil Paper with a foil coating. 'Gold leaf' comprises thin sheets of real gold.

gothic See **black letter.**

GPS Global positioning system, satellite location system to pinpoint a receiver to within a few metres anywhere on the earth's surface.

gradation of an image indicates the steps in which the gray values of the original are rendered. With a flat gradation, there are many steps between white and black, while a steep gradation has fewer steps or even just pure black-and-white. This is also referred to as a soft-to-hard rendition.

gradient fill Another term for a **graduated fill.**

graduated fill A gradual shift from one colour to another, from a dark tone to a light one in an object **fill**. An ideal graduated fill avoids **banding.**

grain direction Direction of fibres in a sheet of paper. **Long grain** describes fibres running parallel with the longest side of a sheet; **short grain** along the shortest side. See also **machine direction.**

graining 1. Mechanical roughening of a litho plate to retain water. 2. Treatment of paper, board, or laminated board to give a textured effect.

grainy Photographic film or print with coarse grain visible usually due to high speed of film.

grainy edge Surface roughness on edges of web caused in the drying process.

grammage Weight of paper expressed as grams per square metre.

graphic file format The format in which graphics are stored and transmitted. There are two main types: **raster** or **bitmap graphics** (in which the image is stored as a bitmap) and **vector** or **outline graphics** (in which the image is stored using geometric formulae). There are many different file formats, some of which are used by specific computers, **operating systems** or applications. Some formats use file compression, particularly those that handle colour.

graphic papers Papers for printing or writing.

graphical user interface (GUI) (Pronounced 'gooey'.) An interface that allows users to choose commands and other options by pointing to a graphical icon or by pulling down a menu and then activating the choice, either by using the keyboard or by **clicking** with a **mouse**. Provides what is often thought of as a more **user-friendly** approach than a **command line interface.**

graphics The creation, modification and manipulation of (usually static) graphic images. The two basic forms are **bitmap** or **raster graphics** and **vector graphics**. In general, bitmapped graphics are handled using **paint programs**, able to access individual **pixels** or groups of pixels, while vector graphics are handled using **draw programs**, which allow the manipulation of graphics as mathematical **objects**. A third way of representing images uses **fractals**. Graphics are stored in a wide variety of **graphic file formats.**

graphics adapter See **display adapter.**

graphics insertion Text and pictures photoset in one operation.

Graphics Interchange Format (GIF) (Pronounced with a hard 'G', as in 'gift'.) A **graphic file format** in which images are compressed with the LZW algorithm.

graphics primitive In a **vector** (**object-oriented**) **graphics** program, one of the basic graphic units, e.g. circle, rectangle, line.

graphics scanner An input device that allows **images** on paper to be input into computer systems as **bitmapped** graphics files.

gravure printing Process in which recesses on a cylinder are filled with ink and the surplus removed with a blade. The paper contacts the cylinder and 'lifts' the ink from the recesses.

gray scale See **grey scale**. 'Gray' is the US spelling and is widely used.

greaseproof Translucent paper with high resistance to grease penetration.

greeked text Simulated text used to display small type on a screen. Line breaks in greeked text correspond to the correct breaks in the text simulated.

grey balance The ability to print a neutral grey from four-colour printing plates with no coloured tinges showing through. Monitored by a grey balance patch on colour bars.

grey board or **Dutch grey board** Homogeneous case board made from newsprint furnish. Grey board or unlined **chipboard** are the normal boards used for case making. **Millboard** is used for specific heavy-duty bindings, e.g. stationery or archive bindings.

grey component replacement (GCR) Colour separations where the black printer carries more detail than conventional separations and the tertiary, or complementary, elements of any colour hue are removed. Also called **ICR (integrated colour removal)** or **achromatic separation**.

grey levels Separate tones of grey reflecting back from a continuous-tone original. Grey levels are frequently defined in 256 steps from pure white to pure black, each step identified by a different **8-bit** number. The grey-level value of each **pixel** of an **original** is sampled by an analyse **scanner** in scanning an original and allocated its grey level value as one of these 256 steps.

grey scale The use of (discrete) shades of grey, from black to white, to represent an image. If the **pixels** of a grey-scale image have N **bits**, then $2N-1$ levels can be represented. If $N = 1$ the image is **monochrome**, i.e. black and white. Grey-scale monitors represent pixels by using different intensities, often with up to 256 different levels. Grey scaling is used to represent **continuous tone** images. (Note the difference from **dithering**.) The US spelling of grey is 'gray'.

grid Systematic division of a page into areas and positions.

grip Margins needed at the feed edge of a sheet of paper for the grippers on the press. Also gripper edge and gripper margin.

gripper Device on a printing press for holding the sheet.

gripper edge See **pitch edge**.

grotesque Form of sans serif typeface.

ground An electrical connection or common conductor connected to the earth. Also known as the 'earth wire'.

groundwood American term for **mechanical pulp**.

groundwood sheet mechanical paper (US).

groupware General **applications software** intended to help groups of people working together over a **network** to coordinate and organise their activities (**workgroup computing**).

GSM See **Global System for Mobile Communications.**

gsm or **gm^{-2}** Grams per square metre: the measure of substance of paper or board.

guard Linen or paper put on the back of a book section to provide additional strength. The process of doing this is known as 'guarding' a section. The first and last sections of a heavy reference work may be guarded in this way.

GUI See **graphical user interface.**

guideline Line on artwork indicating the printing area. Also, **keyline**.

guilloche (from the French *guilloche* –graver) is the term used for fine, interwoven geometric patterns of lines or ornaments. They are printed on banknotes, securities, certificates, etc., in order to make forgery more difficult. Guilloches are also often used as screen lines for illustrations.

guillotine Machine that cuts paper into sheets. Programmatic guillotines can perform a whole series of measured cuts without re-setting for each measurement.

gum up To apply gum arabic to a litho plate. Gum arabic protects the image area and prevents oxidation.

gummed paper Paper coated on one side with adhesive.

gumming Applying adhesive to paper.

gun The component of a **cathode ray tube** that provides a continuous stream of electrons. A monochrome display will have a single gun while colour displays have three, one each for red, green and blue.

gusseting Waving occurring at the heads of untrimmed signatures.

Gutenberg Johannes Gutenberg, real name Johann Gensfleisch, (b. ~1397, d. 1468 in Mainz). During the period 1440 to 1450, Gutenberg invented 'printing with moving letters'. His invention was based on cast type, a corresponding manual casting instrument, a suitable metal alloy and a printing press. Gutenberg's invention spread throughout the whole of the then known world within a matter of years.

gutter Binding margin of a book.

H&J Abbreviation used for **hyphenation** and **justification**.

hair cut Curved cut in a web on a papermaking machine.

hair spaces Very thin letterpress spaces used between letters in a word.

hairline Very fine line or stroke in a letter. Hairline register is colour register within ± half a row of dots.

halation Blurred halo effect in the highlight areas of a photo, caused by reflection back from the emulsion substrate.

half duplex Asynchronous communication in which data can be relayed in only one direction at a time. Two-way transmission is possible but the transmissions must be alternate.

half page Advertisement occupying half a periodical page, horizontally or vertically.

half plate Photo measuring 6×4in.

half sheet work See **work and turn**.

half title Title of book, sometimes shortened, printed on the first right-hand page in the book – the half-title page. Sometimes called **bastard title**.

half-bound Book case binding style: covered in one material on the spine and corners, and another material – paper or cloth – on the remainder.

half-duplex Data transmission in both directions but not at the same time. Contrast **simplex**, **full duplex.**

halftone Illustration created by dots of varying size, resulting in the appearance of 'continuous tone'. Therefore, **halftone negative** and **halftone positive**.

halo effect Build-up of ink at edges of printed letters and halftone dots, creating a darker perimeter to the dot. An undesirable peripheral outline of the printed image that afflicts flexo; being overcome with thinner, harder plates.

handmade paper Paper made by hand in a mould. Decorative content can be introduced into the pulp. The edges are **deckled**.

handbill Publicity sheet, normally printed on one side only, for delivery by hand.

handling stiffness Rigidity of paper when held, e.g. stiffness of a newspaper held by the reader.

handout Publicity leaflet for handing out on the street, at exhibitions.

hanging indent Typesetting style in which the first line of a paragraph is set full out and the remainder are indented.

hanging punctuation Punctuation marks at the end of justified lines that are allowed to jut out very slightly in order to give a visually straight right-hand edge to a column or page. Effect achievable only on sophisticated hyphenation and justification programs.

hard carriage return A carriage return that is inserted by the user, i.e. at the end of paragraph, rather than the **soft carriage return** inserted by software.

hard copy Copy written, typed or printed as distinct from stored in electronic form.

hard disk A rigid magnetic storage disk capable of high data density and speed.

hard hyphen Hyphen essential to the spelling of a word. Contrast **soft hyphen** or **discretionary hyphen**.

hard-bound See **case-bound**.

hard-sized Paper with a high degree of **sizing**.

hard-wired Circuit or program, as constructed by the manufacturer of a piece of hardware, that cannot be changed.

hardcover See **case-bound**.

hardness Resistance of paper to indentation by printing plate, type or pen.

hardware Computer term for equipment as distinct from programs (software).

hardwood pulp Pulp made from hardwood (deciduous) trees, e.g. oak, beech, birch, eucalyptus. As distinct from **softwood pulp**.

harlequin Ornamented typographical character.

Harvard system System of bibliographical references that originated at Harvard University.

hash An index number, otherwise meaningless, that is generated from a list or series of 'pointers'.

hatch Draw closely-spaced lines in a drawing to give the effect of tone.

head 1. Top or top margin of a page. 2. **Heading**.

head margin The white space above first line on a page.

head-to-head, **head-to-tail** Alternative imposition schemes for a pair of books or printed covers/jackets, which are printed as one, and cut apart at the final stage.

headband Cotton or silk cord attached to the top of the back of a book. See also **tailband**.

headbox The part of a papermaking machine that dispenses the stock on the moving wire.

header The portion of a **packet**, preceding the actual data, containing source and destination addresses, error checking and other fields. Also used to describe the part of an **electronic mail** message or news article that precedes the body of a message and includes the sender's name and email address and the date and time when the message was sent. In conventional books it is sometimes used to describe the running headline appearing at the top of each page. (See also **footer**.)

heading 1. Title of a section or chapter in a work, set in displayed type. 2. See **headline**.

headline A displayed line or lines at the top of a page or a piece of text. See also **running head**.

heat seal paper Paper coated on one side with adhesive activated by heat.

heat sealing Closing plastic bags by semi-melting techniques.

heat transfer Transfer of ink from paper to another material (e.g. fabric) by heat and pressure. Special paper and ink are necessary.

heat-resistant splice Join in paper that will resist the heat of a heatset press.

heatset Drying of ink on paper using heat on a web offset machine. Hence heatset inks.

helio engraving or **photo engraving** A photochemical process for creating gravure cylinders.

help A method of providing information to the user.

hemp fibre Paper making fibre made from rope or the hemp plant.

hertz A frequency unit equivalent to one unit per second. In the case of computers, processing speed is reckoned in megahertz (MHz). Most micros are rated between 5MHz at the lower end, up to 20MHz at the top.

hertz (Hz) A measure of frequency. One hertz is one cycle per second; 1KHz = 1000Hz; 1MHz = 1,000,000Hz. (See also **bandwidth**.)

hexadecimal system A counting system based on 16, widely used in computing, essentially because it is based on powers of two (see binary system). In hex, decimals 0–15 become 00, 01, 02, 03, 04, 05, 06 07, 08, 09, 0A, 0B, 0C, 0D, 0E, 0F. Decimal 16 is then 10; decimal 17 is 11; decimal 27 is 1B; and so on. The hexadecimal digits are 0–9, followed by A–F so that, for example, the decimal number 12 is written as C, while hexadecimal 10 is equivalent to decimal 16.

hickey Spot on a printed sheet caused by dust, lint or ink imperfections. Particularly noticeable in solids, large type halftones or tints.

hierarchy An inverted tree structure. Examples in computing include: a directory hierarchy where each directory may contain files or other directories.

high key Tonal values lighter than mid-grey.

high resolution High density of detail. Is often used to describe the number of **pixels** or dots per unit area in an image. The higher the **resolution**, the more information there is in a given amount of visual space.

high-density plastic Thin, strong plastic film used for wrapping magazines where weight is critical.

high-level ASCII or **extended ASCII** The term often used to describe characters with code numbers from 128 to 255, as the true **ASCII** character set only includes the characters from 0 to 127.

high-level language A computer programming language that uses English-language instructions. Use of a high-level language then requires a translator program within the computer to convert these instructions from high-level language into machine-code. See also **low-level language**.

high-yield pulp Synonym for **CTMP**, or **chemithermomechanical pulp**.

highlights Lightest tonal values in a graphic.

hinting A method, to improve the rendering of fonts at small size or on low resolution output devices. It uses a series of priorities, either encoded as extra information in the font or applied using set mathematical formulae, to correct noticeable distortions, such as uneven stem weight. **PostScript Type 1** and **TrueType** fonts are hinted. Hinting is only required for small characters or for printers with a low **resolution** when the presence or absence of a single dot makes a visible difference to a character.

hold Retain matter for subsequent use.

holding fee Also called a **blocking fee**. The fee charged by a picture library when a picture is retained by a client beyond the agreed period.

holdout Resistance to ink absorption of a paper.

hollow 1. Space between the case and the back of the sewn sections in a hardbound book. 2. By extension, the material used for reinforcing the inside spine of a case. Examples include a **board hollow**, **presspahn hollow**, **oxford hollow**.

hologram or **holograph** A three-dimensional image created by lasers.

holography A method of recording and then reconstructing three-dimensional images (holograms) using coherent light beams from lasers. The laser beam is split into two and one part used to illuminate the object. The light waves scattered by the object are then recombined with the other, reference part of the original beam and the interference pattern thus created is stored as a hologram on a photographic plate. When the hologram is illuminated a three-dimensional image is created.

homogeneous board A homogeneous board is made on a Fourdinier machine of one furnish throughout. A **pasteboard** is made up of two or more plys of different papers or homogeneous boards which are pasted together.

hooked An illustration or plate can be hooked in a book by folding the paper along the edge and wrapping the edge round the outside of a section. The illustration/plate is then secured with that section in the binding.

hopper Station on a machine (especially in binding) where printed sections are stacked and dropped onto a conveyer belt.

host A computer system that provides services to users of a network. The **host** part of an **internet address**.

hotmelt Type of synthetic resin adhesive used in perfect binding. Can be used alone (one-shot binding) or in conjunction with PVA (two-shot binding).

house style See **style of the house**.

housekeeping File initialisation, creation, maintenance and back-up tasks.

HSWO Heatset web offset.

HTML See **HyperText Markup Language**.

http See **HyperText Transfer Protocol**.

hub A device or computer to which several other devices are connected (like spokes to the hub of a wheel). The central node of a network. Hubs provide flexibility in logical interconnection of networks and data equipment.

hue Essentially, a representation of how colour is perceived, based on the artist's colour wheel from violet to red (red and violet then being adjacent). The relationship between hues is thus represented in terms of the number of degrees separating them on the colour wheel.

Humanist Generic term for 'Venetian' style typefaces.

humidification Addition of water vapour to air.

humidity Quantity of water vapour in the atmosphere. See also **absolute humidity** and **relative humidity**.

Hunter Lab values American scales, used to measure colour.

hydrapulper Large circular metal tank in which dry pulp is mixed with water, and other ingredients added, in the first stages of paper making. The stock from the hydrapulper passes on for **refining** in a cone refiner system prior to release to the paper machine.

hygro-expansivity Growth or shrinkage of paper due to moisture content. Hence also 'hygro-instability'.

hygrometer Instrument used to measure relative humidity.

hygrometry Measurement of humidity.

hygroscopic Absorbing moisture.

hyperlink A **hypertext** link. A reference from some point in one hypertext document to (some point in) another document or another place in the same document. A hyperlink is usually displayed in some distinguishing way, such as a different colour, **font** or **style**, or even as a symbol or graphic.

Hypertag Electronic tag that transmits content to a mobile phone or PDA over a short range; used to make posters interactive.

HyperText Markup Language (HTML) The underlying **hypertext** language of the **World Wide Web**. HTML is based on an **SGML Document Type Definition (DTD)**. (See also **XML**.)

HyperText Transfer Protocol (http) The client-server **TCP/IP** protocol used on the **World Wide Web** for the exchange of **HTML** documents. (See also **uniform resource locator** (URL).)

hyphenation Literally, the use of a hyphen to connect two words or numbers. In typography, however, it is usually employed to mean the use of a hyphen at the end of a text line (often when **justification** is also used, whence **H&J** as an abbreviation for hyphenation and justification) to indicate that a word does not fit completely on that line and the remainder is at the beginning of the next line.

hyphenation exception dictionary A dictionary of words, held in computer memory, that if hyphenated by the normal rules of hyphenation logic may break at an unacceptable point. When the typesetting computer needs to break a word at the end of a sentence, it will first refer to its hyphenation exception dictionary to see if the word is there, and, if so, will break it at one of the discretionary hyphen points allotted to the word. If the word is not in the dictionary, it will break it according to the rules of logic programmed into it.

hyphenation logic Programming to break words according to logical rules.

hyphenation zone The area towards the end of a text line within which a program may break the line, hyphenating the final word if necessary.

hyphenless justification Justification without breaking words. On narrow measures this creates widely varying spacing characteristics.

hypo Abbreviation for sodium hyposulphite, a chemical used to fix photographic images after development.

Hz The standard abbreviation for the unit of frequency. (See **hertz**.)

IBC Inside back cover.

ICC The International Color Consortium brings together manufacturers of prepress products in order to promote colour management, device-independent processing of colour.

ICR 1. Integrated colour removal. See **achromatic separations**. 2. **Intelligent character recognition**.

idiot tape Unformatted tape with no line ending commands.

idle time Time on a machine when it is not in use for productive work.

Ifra An international association that has more than 2000 members from the newspaper publishing industry.

illustration board One-sided heavy drawing card.

image area The area of the printing plate that transfers ink to the substrate.

image area piling Build-up of lint and ink on litho press blanket in the image area.

image compression The reduction of the amount of information required to represent an **image**, so that the file size is smaller, which means that it will require less space in computer memory and storage and takes less time to transfer over networks and communications systems (See also **JPEG**, **compression**, **fractal**.)

image file formats There are many formats used to store images in files: **GIF**, **TIFF**, **pcx** and **JPEG** are common.

image processing The manipulation of **images**, usually using algorithms to, for example, enhance contrast, reduce noise (remove spots) or change colours.

imagesetter A high-resolution output device that provides output on film

imitation art Paper loaded with china clay in the pulp and highly finished to give an 'art paper' appearance. As distinct from true art paper, which has a china clay surface applied to a conventional base paper.

imitation cloth Reinforced and embossed paper commonly used for binding hardback books instead of cotton cloth. Also, fibrefelt. Contrast **woven material**.

imitation gold/silver foil Aluminium foil with lacquer on plastic carrier. Used for blocking the covers of books.

imitation parchment Tough greaseproof paper.

imperfection Printing or binding faults.

import To copy across from an external program into a current program, typically from a word processing application into a page make-up program.

import filter A program that accepts input from an external program and converts it into a format suitable for the user's current program.

imposed colour proofs Colour proofs produced from a large-format inkjet machine that are imposed to the final page sequence of the job. The effects of **tracking** can be properly considered.

imposition The arrangement of pages on a printing plate so that, when a publication is folded and bound, the pages are in the correct sequence.

impregnating Running book binding cloth through starches or chemicals to enhance its quality or appearance.

impression 1. Pressure of the plate in contact with paper or blanket at the moment of printing. 2. All the copies of a book from one printing.

impression cylinder Cylinder that holds the substrate against the printing surface.

imprint Publisher's and/or printer's identifying text printed in a book or other work.

in pro In proportion.

inclusive type area Type area inclusive of headline and folio. Contrast **exclusive type area**.

incunabula Early printing.

indent 1. Set type further in from the left-hand margin than the standard measure of surrounding text. 2. In paper trading, an indent paper is one that is available from the mill by special making order only, and is not held in common stock by the mill as a standard line.

index 1. Alphabetical list of subjects contained in the text of a work, together with their page numbers. 2. The contents of a file with references for locating the contents.

index board Board suitable for index cards and similar stationery.

india paper Very thin opaque rag paper often used for high-quality bibles.

Indian ink Intensely black drawing ink.

indicia Formal mailing information or permit printed on envelope or item to be mailed.

indirect printing Process where the printing surface is not in direct contact with the paper, e.g. offset litho.

inferior Small character set below the base line at the foot of another character.

information retrieval A term used in the context of obtaining information from online databases in response to a query formulated in an appropriate way.

infotainment The integration of **interactive** information and entertainment services or **software**.

infrared port Port that accepts data via a wireless infrared link.

ingrain paper Rough-surfaced paper for book covers.

initial First letter in text when set in such a way that it stands out, e.g. bigger than its normal cap text size. See **cocked-up initial**, **drop initial**.

initialise Run a program that sets all data values at nil and prepares a storage medium such as a floppy disk to be compatible with the system in use.

ink adhesion The bonding between ink and substrate, a key property when printing on plastics.

ink duct Part of printing machine that holds ink before it is released to the cylinders.

ink flotation sizing test Test that measures paper sizing by floating paper on ink and calculating penetration time.

ink fountain Device that supplies ink to the inking rollers.

ink hickey See **hickey**.

ink holdout See **holdout**.

inkjet A non-impact printing mechanism that forms the image at high speed by deflecting ink droplets electromagnetically.

ink mist Ink filaments thrown off the rollers during high-speed coldset web offset printing.

ink piling Build-up of ink on offset blanket.

ink receptivity Uniform acceptability of ink on paper surface.

ink rub Smears of ink caused when the surface of an abrasive paper, often matt art, rubs against the ink film before it is completely dry. Often occurs during binding.

ink set-off Unintentional transfer of wet ink from one printed sheet to another in the delivery stack.

ink starvation Ink starvation is caused by the image on one part of the plate cylinder requiring more ink to cover it than that particular track of the inking rollers can handle.

inkjet printer A printer that sprays very fine droplets of quick-drying ink onto the paper. The quality of printed text is not as good as that on a **laser printer** at the same resolution, but inkjet printers provide a relatively cheap way

of printing both monochrome and colour images of acceptable quality.

inkometer Instrument that measures the tack of ink.

inline 1. Typographic style in which the characters comprise white inner areas contrasting against the outlined shape. 2. Unit press configuration widely used in label manufacture.

inner forme The imposed forme that forms the inside of the sheet when folded and which therefore contains the second page of the section. Contrast **outer forme**.

input Data going into a computer system.

insert Plate section placed into the middle of a text section in a book. Contrast **wrap**.

inserting Placing loose material inside a section or book.

insertion Inclusion of an advertisement in a periodical.

insetting Placing and fixing one section inside another.

inspection copy Copy of a book sent to a potential customer (often a school) for inspection prior to buying.

instruction Order in a program telling a computer to carry out an operation.

intaglio Printing from a recessed image, e.g. gravure, die-stamping.

integrated circuit Silicon chip.

integrated colour removal 'ICR' See **achromatic separations**.

integrated services digital network (ISDN) A network that provides end-to-end digital connectivity to support a wide range of services, both voice and data. **Bandwidths** vary from 56kbps in the US and 64kbps in Europe upwards. ISDN has the advantage that lines can be combined to increase bandwidth.

Intel Company that designs and manufactures the microprocessors used in most PCs.

intellectual property rights The rights of an author or creator to the use and re-use of material created by him or her, including **copyright**.

intelligent agent An automated network information gathering tool that searches the **internet** either to locate documents on subjects specified by the user or to create indexes.

intelligent character recognition A form of **optical character recognition** (OCR) in which logic or fuzzy logic is used to aid recognition of letter forms and combinations of letter forms, making up words.

intelligent terminal A computer, with its own memory and processor, but not necessarily storage memory, which is used as a terminal to another system. (On a **dumb terminal** all the processing is carried out on the system accessed.) (See also **client server**.)

interactive Being able to accept and react to user input. This generally applies to a program or communications medium. Thus almost all computer applications are interactive, while normal television is not and Teletext is only interactive in that the user can choose the page to go to.

intercharacter spacing In word processing, the use of variable spaces between characters which, in conjunction with variable interword spacing, combine to give an impression of typeset quality. Also, **letter spacing**.

interface The physical boundary between two systems or devices (hardware interface). Also used to describe the specifications for the protocols, procedures, codes (software interface) that enable communication between two dissimilar systems or devices. (See also **user interface**: how the user is able to interact with the computer.)

interfacing codes Generic tags used for the electronic mark up of headings in text.

interlacing A technique for increasing resolution on graphic displays or screens. The electron beam traces alternate lines on each pass, providing twice the number of lines that would appear on a non-interlaced screen. However, screen refresh is slower and screen flicker may be increased over that seen on an equivalent non-interlaced screen because any given **pixel** is only refreshed half as often.

interleaves 1. Sheets of paper put between wet printed sheets to prevent set-off. 2. Different types of paper interleaved with the text paper in a book.

interline spacing Leading: space between lines in text.

internal sizing Rosin, alum or starch sizing added to the papermaking stock at the refining stage to prevent ink spread on paper. Also called **engine sizing** or 'beater sizing'. As distinct from surface sizing which is carried out at the size press on the papermaking machine.

International Organisation for Standardisation (ISO) A voluntary organisation, founded in 1946, responsible for creating international standards in many areas, including computers and communications. Some important standards are listed under their ISO number.

International Packet SwitchStream (IPSS) The service that connects national public data network PSSs to other national networks operated by **PTT**s. It is now known as **Global Network Service** (GNS).

International Phonetic Alphabet (IPA) A system that provides special characters (IPA characters) and **ASCII** equivalents for phonetics (how characters or combinations of characters are pronounced).

International Standard A standard that has been approved and published by the **International Organisation for Standardisation (ISO)**.

International Standard Book Number (ISBN) A 10-digit identification number, individual to each book (and edition) that is published. While there is no legal requirement for books to carry these numbers, they are used by both librarians and booksellers. The numbers are allocated on a national basis and part of the number is unique to the publisher of the book, while the last digit is a check digit.

International Standard Serial Number (ISSN) An eight-digit identification number that is allocated to each journal that is published. It remains the same for all issues and volumes of a journal. Unlike the **ISBN**, it does not contain any information that identifies the publisher, but is an arbitrary number made up of seven digits plus a check digit. The **PII** (see **Publisher Item Identifier**) has been developed partly to make it possible to identify individual articles within journals.

internegative Negative for a colour print.

Internet (With a capital 'I'.) The largest internet in the world, made up of a three-level hierarchy composed of backbone **networks**, such as ARPANET, NSFNet and MILNET, mid-level networks and stub networks. These are connected using the **Internet Protocol** (**IP**). Access to the Internet is from an Internet Service Provider **ISP**. Although the international links within the Internet operate at high **bandwidth**, the speed available to the individual user will usually depend on the speed of the local connection. Many utilities and services, such as **email**, **newsgroups**, **ftp**, are available on the Internet, but the **World Wide Web** is rapidly becoming the most important way of distributing and accessing information.

internet (Without a capital 'I'.) Any set of networks interconnected with routers.

Internet address (Or **IP address**, **TCP/IP** address.) The 32-bit host address defined by the **Internet** protocol and usually represented in dotted decimal notation, e.g. 158.152.28.130. The address can be split into a network number (or network address) and a host number unique to each host on the network, and sometimes also a **subnet address**. The way the address is split depends on its **class**. The term 'internet address' is sometimes incorrectly used to refer to a **fully qualified domain name**.

Internet Explorer Microsoft's browser for the **World Wide Web**.

Internet Protocol (IP) The **network layer** for the **TCP/IP protocol** suite widely used on **ethernet** networks. IP is a connectionless, best-effort **packet-switching** protocol, providing packet **routing** through the datalink layer.

Internet service provider (ISP) (Also called **access provider**.) A company providing a **point of presence**.

interpreter A program **translator**.

interword spacing The use of variable interword spacing to achieve justified text. See **intercharacter spacing**.

intranet A network providing similar services to those provided by the **internet**, but only within an organisation. (See also **extranet**.)

introduction Introduction to the subject matter of a book, as distinct from **preface**, **foreword**.

Inverform machine Type of papermaking machine used particularly in board making. A series of head boxes feed consecutive layers of wet stock over the main, first, layer at the wet end of the machine to build up a thick final layer of stock on the wire.

inverse video (Also called **reverse video**.) When the image on the screen appears as a 'negative', so that the parts which are conventionally black appear as white and vice versa. Inverse video is often used to indicate that something, for example a portion of text, has been selected for copying, moving, deletion.

invert halftone Gravure printing that uses halftone dot structures.

IP See **Internet Protocol**.

IP address See **Internet address**.

IPA 1. **International Phonetic Alphabet**. 2. An abbreviation for Institute of Practitioners in Advertising. 3 Abbreviation for iso-propyl alcohol (propan-2-ol), the alcohol used in fount solutions and for general cleaning.

IPC Integrated pollution control.

iph Impressions per hour. The normal measure of printing speed.

IR coating Coating varnish cured by infrared light.

ISBN See **International Standard Book Number**.

ISDN See **integrated services digital network**.

ISO See **International Organisation for Standardisation**. Also a prefix to the reference numbers of standards issued by that body. ISO is not actually an acronym for anything, rather a pun on the Greek prefix 'iso-' meaning 'the same'; nonetheless, it is an anagram of the initials of the organisation's name. Some relevant ISO standards are included as separate entries below.

ISO 646 The **ISO** standard for seven-bit characters. **ASCII** is the US equivalent, although it differs in a few bracket characters. (See **ISO 8859**.)

ISO 8859 (**ISO Latin**.) An **ISO** standard for eight-bit single-byte coded graphic **character sets** for the major European languages that can be represented using Latin characters. In addition, covers the Greek, Cyrillic, Hebrew and Arabic alphabets. Latin alphabet No. 1 is often used as an extension of and replacement for **ASCII**. **ISO 8879** includes some extra characters used in **SGML**.

ISO 8879 The **ISO** standard defining **SGML**.

ISO 9000 and **subsets**. Standards defining quality systems.

ISO 9735 or **EDIFACT** The **ISO** standard for **electronic data interchange** for administration, commerce and transport. Being superseded by e-commerce.

ISO 10179 The **ISO** standard for the **Document Style Semantics and Specification Language** (DSSSL).

ISO 10180 The **ISO** standard for the Standard Page Description Language (PDSL).

ISO 10646 The **ISO** standard for 32-bit and 16-bit character encoding, which includes **Unicode**. Originally ISO 10646 (32-bit) and Unicode (16-bit) codes were developed separately but, following the failure of the Draft ISO 10646 to be accepted, Unicode was taken within the scope of ISO.

ISO 10744 The **ISO** standard for **HyTime**.

ISO 12083 A revised version of the American Association of Publishers (AAP) **SGML DTD**, covering books and academic journals.

ISO 13818 The **ISO** standard for MPEG-2 compression.

ISO15930-1/2/3 standards that define how to produce PDF files for printing.

ISO Latin See **ISO 8859**.

ISO sizes Formerly **DIN** sizes. International range of paper and envelope sizes, comprising **A series**, **B series**, and **C series**.

ISP Internet Service Provider. Company providing individual and corporate access to internet services at a variety of speeds and costs.

ISSN See **International Standard Serial Number**.

issue All copies of a publication with the same content.

issue life Average reading life of a periodical before it is no longer topical.

italic Specially designed letters that slope forward. Contrast **sloped roman**.

ivory board Fine board manufactured by laminating two high-quality sheets together.

jacket Dust cover on book.

jacket paper High-quality one-sided coated paper used for book jackets.

jacketwrap US term for jacket paper.

jaggies The visual effect caused by **aliasing**, so that curves look like a series of steps. (See also **anti-aliasing**.)

JANET See **Joint Academic NETwork**.

Japanese vellum Paper made in Japan from the bark of the mulberry tree.

Java An **object-oriented** progamming language, designed for **programming** the internet. While it is possible to write complete **programs** in Java, one of its strengths is that **Java applets** can also be written, which can be run within **browsers** providing additional functionality.

Java applets A form of **Java** program, dedicated to performing a particular task, such as reading a particular type of file, e.g. an **MPEG** video.

Java beans A platform-independent application program interface that will enable **Java**-based **applets** and objects to interoperate with other **object** technologies such as OpenDoc.

JavaScript A version of the **Java** language that can be included directly within an **HTML** page in order, for example, to provide interaction between the user and the **host** system such as validating entries in a form. JavaScript lacks some of the functionality of Java, but is thus easier to learn. Using applications such as LiveWire, it is possible to produce the equivalent of **CGI-scripts**.

jaw folder A type of folder in which a partly-folded section is thrust into a jaw to complete its fold. Typically one of the units in a web offset folder system. Sometimes called a 'nip and tuck' folder.

JDF Job Description Format. A standard based on XML designed to allow easy comprehensive information interchange between customer and supplier. It may provide the basis for future administration systems, with the capability for real-time bi-directional links into specific manufacturing equipment.

JIS Japanese Institute for Standards. The Japanese equivalent to the **ANSI** in the US or the **British Standards Institution** in the UK.

JIT See **just-in-time**.

jitter Small changes in the timing or the phase of a signal transmitted over a **network**, possibly leading to errors or loss of synchronisation.

JMF Job messenger format, may be bi-directional transfer of JDF data.

jobbing General printing.

jog Align edges of a pile of papers by vibrating them.

joint Recessed part of a book case between the inside edge of the front and back boards and the shoulder, forming a hinge. Also, **French groove**.

Joint Photographic Experts Group (JPEG) A standard from the **ISO** and **ITU-T** for coding and **compression** of colour images. Named after the committee (sometimes also called the Joint Picture Encoding Group) that designed the image compression algorithm. JPEG works best on full colour or **grey-scale** digital images of real world scenes and not so well on non-realistic images, such as cartoons or line drawings, because the technique involves smoothing of the image and loss of detail. JPEG does not handle compression of black-and-white (1-bit-per-pixel) images or moving pictures.

jointing The process of forming the joint or groove in book binding. Also known as **backing**.

Jordan Type of paper machine refiner.

JPEG See **Joint Photographic Experts Group**.

jpg The usual file name extension for **JPEG** files.

jukebox A way of storing and accessing large numbers of **compact discs**. Used mainly in **document image processing** applications.

jumbo reel The large reel of paper formed and wound up at the end of a paper-machine.

just-in-time (**JIT**) Production technique based on the concept of acquiring materials and components at the very last moment that still allows production and selling to schedule.

justification The arrangement of text on a page or screen so that it is aligned with either the left or right margin, or with both. Fully justified text has lines of the same length that are perfectly aligned with both the left and the right margins. Both margins are even; full justification is produced by increasing (or sometimes decreasing) the space either between words (word spacing) or between letters (**letter spacing**) or both. **Hyphenation** is often used in conjunction with full justification, hence the use of the expression **H&J**. Full justification tends not to be used in electronic publications that are viewed on screen, particularly if the text **wraps** when the window size or the type size is changed.

justify In word processing and desktop publishing, the use of intercharacter and/or interword spacing to achieve even left and right margins.

jute Indian plant used to produce pulp for hard papers.

K Measure of computer storage. K = 1024 computer bytes but often used loosely as 1000.

K and N absorbency Test for comparing rate of ink absorbency of different papers.

Kalamazoo Proprietary system of scheduling and listing documents.

kaolin Fine clay used as a filler in paper making.

kamyr digester Digester used in production of chemical pulp.

Kb See kilobyte.

Kbps Kilobit(s) per second. Transfer rate of 1000 bits a second. (See **bps** and **Mbps**.)

keep standing Instruction to keep type made up for possible reprinting.

kenaf Type of plant fibre used in paper making.

Kermit A widely used **public domain asynchronous file-transfer protocol,** originally developed at Columbia University and made available without charge. Kermit is available as part of most communications packages and available on most operating systems. The UK centre for Kermit distribution is at the University of Lancaster. Kermit uses intensive encoding and error detection, and hence is fairly slow, but very robust.

kern Part of a typographic character projecting beyond the body.

kerning Adjusting the spacing between two letters to create a better visual fit, also called aesthetic kerning, which explains the rationale behind the procedure. Traditionally meant decreasing the amount of space, but has come to mean either increasing or decreasing the space between the letters. Note that this is not the same as **letter spacing**.

kerning pairs Pairs of letters that invariably need spacing adjustments made to them for visual neatness. **Autokerning** performs this function automatically.

kettle stitch Stitch joining one signature of a handsewn book to the next. See also **blind stitch**.

key A sequence of characters that is used in **encryption** and **decryption**.

key forme The forme or plate positioned first in colour work. Hence also 'key negative'.

key numbers Numbers on advertisements that identify the source in which they appeared.

key plate The printing plate that sets the register position for the other plates.

keyboard The array of keys used to input into a system.

keyword A word that is indexed to improve the speed of **searching**. (Contrast with **free-text searching**.) The term has a special meaning in **SGML** to indicate a property of an **element** or a **marked section**.

kicker Short line above a headline, set in smaller type.

kill Delete unwanted matter. Distribute type.

kinetic friction Resistance to sliding of one material over another.

kiss impression Very light printing impression.

kiss-fit Printing on an offset press different colours that touch each other, but using no **traps**. Kiss-fitting is not always suitable for all printing jobs but when it is, the result should be clearer than when traps are used.

kite 'V' shaped plate over which the web of paper is drawn to create first fold.

knife folder A type of folding machine that uses a knife between inwardly rotating rollers. Contrast **buckle folder**.

knocking up To line up the edges of a pile of paper.

kraft Strong brown paper used as a second lining, and in many forms of packing application.

kraft pulp See **sulphate pulp**.

Kromecote Proprietary name for a cast-coated paper with glossy finish.

L/C See **letter of credit**.

label 1. A record that identifies the items stored on a disk. 2. Caption on a technical line drawing.

label paper Paper gummed on one side and usually coated on the other, for labels.

laced-on-boards Signatures of a case-bound book 'laced on' to the case boards.

lacquer Coating applied to a printed piece for protection or gloss.

laid lines The narrow parallel lines in a laid paper, as opposed to the wider lines at right-angles to these called the **chain lines**.

laid paper Paper with watermark lines parallel to each other formed by a **dandy roll**.

lamination Thin plastic film applied by heat and pressure to a printed sheet for protection and/or appearance. See also **OPP lamination**.

lampblack Carbon pigment ink with dull, very black appearance.

LAMS Laser ablative masking system, where a laser-sensitive layer is coated over the plate material for flexo CTP exposure. The image is exposed on a platesetter, after which it requires normal exposure and processing.

LAN See local area network.

landfill site Area set aside to dump rubbish and waste into; concern over the space needed for many directories.

landscape The orientation of a picture, **screen** or page such that its width is greater than its height. Most screens are landscape, while most books, and certainly journals, are **portrait**.

language In computing, a structured communications vocabulary using codes and words that can be translated into the machine code that runs the computer. See **high-level language**, **low-level language**.

large post Standard size of paper 419×533mm.

laser An acronym of Light Amplification from the Stimulated Emission of Radiation (developed from Maser, where the initial 'M' stands for 'microwave'). Lasers create coherent light, i.e. with a single frequency and phase. This has two effects: the energy is concentrated, so that high powered lasers can be used for applications such as surgery and welding; and the coherence means that the beam can carry information. The second property is used in **laser printers**, **fibre optics** and **holography**.

laser printer A high-speed non-impact device that employs laser technology to sensitise selected areas of a photosensitive drum. As it revolves it picks up toner that is transferred to the paper via heated rollers.

last colour down The final colour to be printed in colour work.

lateral reversal Change of image from wrong to right-reading or vice versa.

latex-treated paper Paper impregnated with latex for toughness.

latin alphabet Western European alphabet

lay Guide on a printing machine that positions a sheet before printing. Hence, **lay edges**.

lay down Impose a job.

lay edge Edge of a sheet laid against the front or side lay of the machine.

layboy A stacking device on a paper sheeter.

layer, layering A technique used within **draw programs** for handling **vector** or **object-oriented graphics**. Each object is drawn on its own layer, so that objects can be placed 'in front of' or 'behind' any other object; this

arrangement can be changed with the draw program. In addition, most draw programs allow objects to be grouped on layers (each object still occupies its own layer within that group layer). This gives great flexibility to the expert user.

layer-on Machine-minder who feeds sheets to the machine.

layout Sketch of a book or other publication, showing the plan to work to.

lc See **lower case**. See also **U/L**, **ulc**; **caps**, **c&sc**.

LCD See **liquid crystal display**.

lead time The time it takes for a requirement to be satisfied.

leader 1. Row of dots used to lead the eye across a page. 2. See **editorial**.

leading The spacing between lines of type.

leading edge The edge of a sheet or plate at which printing begins. Also, **gripper edge**, **pitch edge**.

leaf Single sheet, comprising two pages.

leaflet Folded printed sheet comprising only a few pages.

leased line A private telephone circuit permanently connecting two points.

leather Leathers used in bookbinding include goat hides, pig skins, calf skins, vellum, sheep skins, forels.

leather pulp Pulp made from leather scraps and used for reconstituted leather coverings.

leathercloth Bookbinding grade of cloth: a plasticated cotton, dyed-through and calendered.

leave edge The edge of the sheet thatleaves the machine last as it goes through the printing rollers into the delivery.

LED See **light emitting diode**.

LED printer A printer, similar to a **laser printer,** that uses a bank of **LED**s as the image source, rather than a single **laser** beam.

ledger paper A strong paper for clerical use.

leg Short column of type.

legend Caption.

legibility The ease with which a page, design or typeface can be read.

length The 'flowability' of a printing ink. 'Short' ink does not flow as easily as 'long' ink.

LEP Light-emitting polymer.

letter of credit 'L/C' A letter addressed by a bank in an importing country to its agent bank in the exporting country, authorising the latter, providing an agreed set of conditions is met, to release a specified sum of money to the account of the exporter. A 'Confirmed Irrevocable Letter of Credit' carries the absolute guarantee of the issuing bank and cannot be revoked unless agreed by all parties.

letter-fit Spacing between characters in a typeface.

Letterflex plate Proprietary letterpress photopolymer plate, similar to an APR plate.

lettering Hand-drawn typography or a typeface designed to look hand-drawn.

letterpress Printing from images with a raised surface which impresses on the paper.

letterspace Space between letters.

letterspacing Adding or reducing the space between individual characters, as opposed to between words, in a formatted document. When used correctly, the effect should be pleasing. However, when done automatically in order to reduce the interword spacing in **justification**, the effect can often be the reverse.

levant Soft, pliable goatskin for bookbinding covers.

Lib Con number See **Library of Congress number**.

library binding Durable type of case binding used on books in libraries.

library material Text or pictures held on file for subsequent use.

Library of Congress number US system for bibliographical data. The number is printed on the title page verso.

lick-coated paper Paper with a very light coating. Also **pigmented paper**, **light-coated paper**, **size-press coated paper**.

ligature A **glyph** (or character) that is a combination of two or more single characters. For example, in many **fonts** when an 'i' follows an 'f', they are printed as a single character 'fi';

a ligature for 'fl' is also fairly common. In the past, particularly when hot metal or cold type were used for typesetting, a whole range of ligatures was used, but their use has become less common as computer typesetting has developed.

light box Box with glass top illuminated from within so that transparent artwork can be viewed on its surface.

light emitting diode (LED) A diode that glows red, green or amber when energised by low voltage.

light pen A device that looks like an ordinary pen, but which can be used to instruct the computer to modify part of a screen image. At its tip the pen has a photoreceptor that emits signals when it receives light from the screen.

light primaries See **additive primaries**.

light secondaries The complementary, or 'opposite' colours to the **additive primaries**.

light-coated paper See **size-press coated paper**.

lightface Lighter version of a roman typeface.

lightfast ink Ink that will fade less readily than normal ink on prolonged exposure to strong light. See **blue wool scale**.

lightweight coated paper (**lwc**) Coated paper (often part-mechanical) below 60gsm.

lightweight paper Normally taken to mean paper less than 60gsm in substance.

lignin The substance in wood that binds the fibres together. Removed during the pulping process.

limp binding Paperback binding.

limp-bound Referring to a book with a limp or paper binding. See also **case-bound**.

line 1. Rule. 2. Copy that consists of solid black lines or dots only, and has no intermediate grey tones. Contrast **tone**.

line block A relief plate produced from a line drawing.

line gauge Measuring ruler used for copy fitting and measuring type. Also called **type gauge** and **depth gauge**.

line length Column width.

line mechanical Paste-up of line copy ready for the camera.

Line work Vector graphics.

Lineale Typeface without serifs, otherwise known as **sans serif**.

linen finish Imitation linen texture on paper surface.

linen screen Halftone screen giving a linen effect.

liner Paper used to cover another paper or board for extra strength, thickness or finish.

line spacing Space between lines of type.

lining Part of the spine strengthening in a case-bound book. See **first and second linings**.

lining figures Arabic numerals the same height as capitals, also known as **aligning numerals**. As distinct from **non-lining** or **old-style figures**.

link (Also called **hotlink**.) In **hypertext** documents, a connection from one document to another (see also **anchor**). Linking is also used within **programs** and **applications** in order to save space by not duplicating data or to ensure that data is always up to date.

linked image A **graphic** image that is stored in a different file from the current **hypertext** page, so that it is displayed by selecting a **link**, although the image may also be included automatically, depending on the coding of the hypertext page.

Linotype Metal linecasting machine manufactured by Linotype.

lint Surface fibres released from paper during printing.

linting The build-up of lint on an offset blanket causing **hickies** in the printed result.

Linux Alternative operating system to Windows or MacOS for computers. It is open source and appeals to many as an alternative with a large community of developers and support available via the web. **Linux** is a free Unix-type operating system originally created by Linus Torvalds with the assistance of developers around the world.

liquid crystal display (**LCD**) Consisting of a sandwich of two glass plates and a fluid. The liquid darkens when a voltage is applied, thus creating an image.

list Often used for **mailing list**.

list broker Someone who sells lists of names and addresses in specific market-oriented categories.

listing Computer print-out of data or a file.

listing paper The paper used for computer listings, traditionally printed with light green horizontal stripes and punched with sprocket holes at the sides.

literal Mistake introduced in text input, often only affecting one or two characters.

litho, lithography Invented by Alois Senefelder in 1796, a planographic process in which ink is applied selectively to the plate by chemically treating the image areas to accept ink and the non-image areas to accept water.

live matter Copy that will go to press rather than be deleted.

loadings Minerals and fillers added to the furnish of paper.

loan A rag writing paper.

local area network (**LAN**) A geographically limited data communications network (typically to a 1km radius or within a building), that allows resource sharing. A **LAN** allows computers to have access to common data, **programs** and **peripherals**.

local loop That part of the telephone network that links individual premises to the local exchange of the network operator.

local papers Newspapers circulating in one town or area of the country.

loft-dried High-grade papers dried in a drying shed to allow natural evaporation.

log off An instruction issued by a user indicating the termination of a session.

log on An instruction, issued by a user, requesting access. A log-on sequence will usually include entry of a name and password.

logo Company name or product device used in a special design as a trademark. Shortened from **logotype**.

long grain Sheet of paper in which the grain direction (or machine direction) runs parallel with the longest side.

long ink An ink that flows easily.

long run A high printing number for a job.

look through Appearance of a sheet of paper when held up to the light. Also, **formation**.

loose leaf Binding that uses steel rings passing through drilled holes in the paper to hold the sheets together.

lossless compression A term describing a data **compression** algorithm in which all the information in a file is retained, allowing it to be recovered perfectly by decompression.

lossy compression A term describing a data **compression** algorithm in which the amount of information in the data, as well as the number of bits used to represent that information, is reduced. The lost information is usually assumed to be less important to the quality of the data (usually an **image** or **audio**) because it can be recovered reasonably by interpolation. **MPEG**, **JPEG** and **fractal compression** are examples of lossy compression techniques.

low resolution (Often shortened to low-res.) The opposite of **high resolution**. While some graphics are just low-resolution to begin with, other graphics are created or scanned as complex, high-resolution images (probably for offset printing). However, to save space, network traffic and to provide thumbnails for browsing low-res versions are produced for use in **page make-up** and placement of the image. Usually the high-resolution version is merged using the Open PrePress Interface. (See also **resolution**.)

lower case Small letters as distinct from capitals. Abbreviated as **lc**. The term is derived from the days of metal type, when the capitals were kept in the top typecase and the small letters in the bottom (or lower) case. Capitals are thus sometimes referred to as **uppercase letters**.

lumen The unit of luminous flux, the amount of light emitted by a light source with a luminous intensity of 1 candela.

lwc Lightweight coated (paper). Refers to coated papers, normally with a part-mechanical base, which are 60gsm or lighter in substance.

M 1 Used to indicate the machine direction (grain direction) of a sheet when placed against one dimension, e.g. 890(M)×1130 is a **short grain** sheet.

M2M Machine-to-machine communication, system whereby machines pass data across the internet and initiate actions accordingly.

M3D Maskless mesoscale materials deposition.

Mac Common abbreviation for the **Apple Macintosh** computer, widely used in publishing work.

machine clothing The various felts and wire materials on a paper machine.

machine coated Paper coated on the papermaking machine.

machine code Primary code used by the computer's processor. Few programs are written directly in machine code, but in a **high-level language** or **low-level language** which is then translated by a separate translator program into machine code.

machine deckle Width of the wet web on a papermaking machine.

machine direction The direction in which fibres lay on the wire of a paper machine, i.e. along the web. Also called grain direction. As distinct from the **cross direction**.

machine fill A making of paper which uses the full width of the **machine deckle**.

machine finished (MF) Smooth paper calendered on the paper machine.

machine glazed (MG) Glossy finish to one side of paper obtained by drying against the polished surface of a heated cylinder of a Yankee-type paper machine.

machine language See **machine code**.

machine minder Printer who supervises the running of a printing machine.

machine proof Proof made by printing from plates, as opposed to using plastic proofing techniques. Also known as a **wet proof**.

machine revise Printed sheet for checking against the press proof.

macro A combination of commands, used in various kinds of interactive programs. In an interactive program, a series of commands can be 'recorded' then 'played' to create the same effect by using either a function key, a menu command or a **button**. Alternatively, macros can be written essentially as small computer programs, including functions and conditional expressions. The more complex macros can take parameters such as a text string or a value for such items as page number, interline spacing or type size.

made ends See **joints**.

magazine supplement Magazine inserted in a newspaper.

magenta Process red. One of the colours used in four-colour process printing.

magnefite pulp A **sulphite pulp** made using magnesium bisulphite rather than calcium bisulphite in the cooking process. The magnesium waste liquor can be chemically recovered.

magnetic-ink character recognition (MICR) A character recognition system in which special characters printed in magnetic ink are read for rapid input to a specialist reader. Because magnetic-ink characters are difficult to forge, MICR is used extensively in banking for marking and identifying cheques.

mail merge Word processing utility enabling a name and address file to be merged with a text file containing a letter.

mailshot A single sending of promotional material to a list of names and addresses.

Mailsort method of obtaining discounts on postage By pre-sorting addresses into postcode order

mailing list List of names and addresses to which mailing pieces can be sent.

mailing piece Promotional material mailed out.

make-ready Setting up a printing machine ready to run a specific job.

makegood Periodical advertisement re-run because the original was faulty.

making order An order for paper to particular specifications needing to be made specially rather than withdrawn from stock.

making-up Assembly of printed sections prior to sewing.

management information system (MIS) Normally a computerised system to control all financial information to aid the management function.

mandrel A shaft onto which cylinders or sleeves are mounted.

manifold paper A lightweight paper used for copies or for airmail. See also **bank**.

manila A tough paper made from hemp and often used for envelopes.

manual Book giving instructions about a technique or details of operation of a device.

manuscript Abbreviated to MS. Typed or handwritten copy for setting. Also **typescript**, **copy**.

marbled paper Paper covered with a marbled design, used for endpapers of books. True marbled paper is made by hand: paper is dipped into a bath containing liquid pigment colours floating on a viscous gum solution, and then dried. Imitation marbled paper is normal paper printed with this pattern by litho: this is the sort normally used.

margin guides The non-printing dotted lines in programs that mark the basic **margins** of the page within which the text is fitted.

margins Areas of white space left around printed matter on a page.

mark-up Instructions on a layout or copy for the compositor to follow when typesetting or making up pages. See also **electronic mark-up**.

mark-up language A language (or **meta language**) designed to formalise the **mark-up** process for text. Mark-up languages also give facilities for including links to **multimedia** items, such as **graphics**, **audio** and **video**.

marked proof The proof on which the printer's reader has marked corrections.

marked section A section of an **SGML** document that is to be treated in a special, usually conditional, manner.

markings or **marks** Identifying description written onto a label, e.g. the title of a book on a consignment of paper sent to a printer to show the printer the use for which the paper has been sent.

mask Opaque overlay that masks out the unwanted portion of a photograph.

mass market Broadly-based market; in book publishing, general interest paperbacks.

master 1. A plate for a duplication machine. 2. Original file from which copies will be made.

master page grid The basic page layout, held in memory as a job **template** for the design and kept independently of the job itself.

master proof Printer's proof or reader's proof. See also **marked proof**.

masthead Graphic device that displays a newspaper's name on the front page.

matrix Also **matrice**. Mould from which typeface is cast or photographic master of type fount.

matt or matte Dull finish as distinct from glossy.

mature Acclimatise paper to pressroom humidity. Also called **conditioning**.

maximise button In Windows applications, resizes a window to fill the full screen rather than a small part of it.

Mb Abbreviation for **megabyte**.

Mbps Megabit(s) per second. Transfer rate of 1,000,000 bits a second. (See **bps**, **kbps**.)

McCain sewing See **side-sewing**.

MD In paper making, **machine direction**. As distinct from **CD**, **cross direction**.

mean line Imaginary line that runs along the top of the lowercase letters in a line of text. Also, **x line**. Compare **base line**.

measure Length of line of type.

mechanical binding Binding held together by metal or plastic coils. See also **spiral binding.**

mechanical composition See **machine composition**.

mechanical ghosting Ghosting caused by blanket irregularities.

mechanical paper Paper made from **mechanical pulp**.

mechanical pulp Pulp produced mechanically, by grinding, rather than chemically. There are several sorts. See

stone groundwood mechanical pulp (SGW), **refiner mechanical pulp (RMP)**, **thermomechanical pulp (TMP)**, **chemi-thermomechanical pulp (CTMP)**.

media The materials onto which data can be recorded, i.e. DVD, CD, DAT.

media converter Device that reads from one medium (normally a disk) and translates its content in order to output to another medium.

medium 1. The means of conveying something; an intermediate. 2. An extender – an ink constituent used to dilute coloured ink.

memory Internal storage of a computer. The memory of a computer is where it finds its instructions and the data it is to work with, as well as where it stores its results. It is organised as a series of locations or cells each of which can hold one computer word. The locations are given numbers which enable the computer to identify their positions. See **RAM**, **ROM**.

MEMS Microelectromechanical systems. Systems that can respond to a stimulus or create physical forces (sensors and actuators) and that have dimensions on the micrometre scale. They are almost exclusively made using the same lithographic techniques that produce silicon chips for computers.

menu A type of **user interface** in which the user is presented with a series of options, from which he or she can select, either with a **mouse** or by entering a text string, often just a number.

menu bar In a **graphical user interface** (GUI), the bar across the top of the **screen** or a **window** containing the names of **pull-down menus**.

menu-driven Software program laid out in the initial form of a number of questions to which the user replies in order to action the program.

merge Combine two or more files into one.

meta An **HTML** tag, defining **metadata**, which is used by many of the **World Wide Web's search engines**, either as part of the **indexing** or as part of a **keyword search**.

meta-information Information about information, e.g. how it is structured.

metadata Structured data that describes types of information. Often used for searching, although the data may not actually form part of the viewable document.

meta language A (computer) language in which the logic and statements of another language are discussed and specified. For example, **SGML** is a meta language in that it specifies how to do things, rather than what to do.

metallic inks Inks containing metallic powders to give a gold- or silver-printed effect. Often best printed in conjunction with a **primer**.

metamerism The phenomenon whereby certain colours shift in hue under different lighting conditions.

mezzotint Form of print used to simulate the effect of painting.

MF See **machine finished**.

MG See **machine glazed**.

MHz One million **hertz**. Most micros are ruled between 5–20MHz in microprocessor speed.

microchip See **chip**.

microfiche Sheet film, typically 105×150mm, containing a large number of pages of information photographically reduced to a very small size and readable only with a microfiche reader.

microfilm A roll of film, usually 35mm, onto which text and images are photographically reduced.

microform Generic name for media onto which text or images are photographically reduced. The main examples are **microfiche** and **microfilm**.

micrometre One-thousandth of a millimetre.

micron Alternative term for **micrometre**.

microprint Extremely small print that is only legible when magnified greatly. It is used as a security element on banknotes and other documents at risk of forgery. The image resolution of colour copiers is too low to reproduce the microprint.

microsecond One-millionth part of a second. Measurement used in computing. Compare **nanosecond**, **millisecond**.

mid tones or **middle tones** Tonal ranges between highlights and shadows.

mill conditioned Paper conditioned for normal atmospheric humidity.

mill finished See **machine finished**.

mill glazed See **machine glazed**.

mill waste Broke and other by-products of a paper mill's normal manufacturing processes which can be recycled within the mill. Paper made using mill waste as a majority furnish should not really be termed **recycled** even though it sometimes is.

millboard True millboard is a very dense hard board used in stationery binding and for archival use. The term millboard is sometimes used to describe normal case boards, which are more properly **grey board** or **unlined chipboard**.

millisecond One-thousandth part of a second. Measurement used in computing. Abbreviated to ms. Compare **nanosecond**, **microsecond**.

mini-web Small web offset machine typically producing 16pp A4 colour sections (8pp A4 to view). Also known as **narrow-web**, or **half-size press**.

miniscules Lower case.

mips Millions of instructions per second. Measurement of computer processing speed.

mirror duplication of storage on disk, for example in **RAID** systems.

MIS See **management information system**.

misprint Typographical error.

misregister One colour or more printed out of alignment with other colours.

mixed furnish Referring to papers that have mechanical and woodfree pulps in their furnish. Also see **part-mechanical paper**.

mixing Usually applied to typefaces of different founts in one line of text.

mnemonic codes Easily remembered codes: abbreviations or tags that suggest their meanings (e.g. bd1 = bold style 1).

mock-up A layout or rough of artwork. Also called a visual.

modem or **Modulator/Demodulator** Device that converts analogue communication (e.g. telephone transmission) into digital form and vice versa.

Modern Late 18th century typestyle, also called **Didone**.

modern figures See **lining figures**.

modular Hardware system capable of being expanded by adding on compatible devices.

moiré Undesirable pattern caused by incorrect angles of screens.

moisture content Amount of moisture in paper, expressed as a percentage of weight. A moisture content of around 7 to 8% is recommended for printing papers in optimum press room conditions (20°C, 55–65% RH).

moisture welts Wrinkles in a paper roll caused by moisture absorption after drying.

molleton Cotton material used on damping rollers.

monitor Screen that displays the operations of a machine in real time.

mono See **black and white**.

monochrome Literally means one colour, often black on white (although see **bi-level bitmap**), but used for **grey scales**.

monoline Typeface with all strokes appearing to have the same thickness, e.g. Univers.

monospaced Letters that have the same set widths, as in typewriter faces

monotone Illustrative material in one colour.

montage Several images assembled into one piece of artwork.

morgue Newspaper reference library.

morocco Goatskin with fine grain for bookbinding.

motherboard The printed circuit board containing the main components of a computer. See **add-on board**, **expansion board**.

mottle Uneven printing in solid areas caused by poor ink or uneven absorption characteristics in the paper.

mould-made paper Paper either made by hand, or made on a **cylinder mould machine**.

mounting The process of fixing plates onto a cylinder in position to register colour to colour as well as to the finishing of the product being printed.

mounting equipment Device to aid accurate positioning of plates onto the plate cylinder in flexo.

mouse Computer input device.

mouse mat A mat on which a **mouse** can be moved around. For a mechanical mouse, this is usually a plastic surface on a foam-rubber backing, while for an optical mouse, the surface is usually a firmer plastic carrying a grid ruled in two dimensions.

MP3 Format for storing digital audio files.

Moving Pictures Experts Group (MPEG) (Also called Motion Picture Encoding Group.) An **ISO** standard for coding full-motion **video** information in a compressed form. **Encoding** is done **offline** while **retrieval** is performed in **real time**. (See MPEG-1, MPEG-2, MPEG-3.) MPEG can also be used for **audio** files.

MPEG-7 Multimedia content description interface, a standard for describing the multimedia content data that supports some degree of interpretation of the information meaning, which can be passed onto, or accessed by, a device or a computer code.

MS-DOS The original **operating system** used on IBM PCs.

mull Muslin fabric fixed to the back of a case-bound book under the spine covering. See **first and second linings**.

multi-disk reader Machine that reads a variety of disks in different formats and translates their content to output disks. Also, **media converter**.

multi-layer headbox A **headbox** that distributes up to three different layers of stock onto the wire simultaneously.

multimedia An umbrella term used to describe media products and services that are saved, transmitted and depicted electronically as well as printed, allowing the recipient to use the content interactively.

multi-tasking The ability of a computer to work with more than one program at a time without any further action from the user. In fact, the computer uses **time-slicing** to switch between applications, but this happens so fast that users are unaware of it, although all the applications slow down to some extent.

multi-user Computer system allowing multiple users access to the same machine, software and data files.

Multilith Proprietary name of a small offset press in wide use.

multiplexor Switching device enabling communication between central storage and a number of peripherals.

Munsell system A colour gradation system which uses numbers for identification.

mux See **multiplexor**.

MWNT Multi-walled nanotube (see **nanotube**).

nanosecond One-thousand-millionth part of a second. Measurement of computer processing speed. Abbreviated to **ns**. Compare **microsecond**, **millisecond**.

nanotube Any tube with nanoscale dimensions. Carbon nanotubes are the most common but they can be made from other substances, e.g. boron nitride. The diameter can vary down to 0.4nm. Nanotubes can exist within nanotubes, creating multi-walled nanotubes, or MWNTs (q.v.). Besides remarkable tensile strength, nanotubes have electrical properties that depend on how the graphite structure spirals around the tube; they can be semiconducting or conducting (metallic).

nap roller Leather-covered ink roller.

narrow band Data transmission at speeds of less than 200 bits a second.

narrow-web See **mini-web**.

narrowcast (Also described as **personalcast**.) Transmission of information to a defined group of recipients. Contrast **broadcast**.

national characters An expression used for characters of the Roman alphabet with accents and other diacritical marks that are used in certain written languages, but not in English. They are listed in **ISO 8859**.

natural Case-covering material finish.

NC varnish Nitrocellulose varnish: a high-gloss finish.

NCR (no carbon required) A paper that, being impregnated with dye, transfers an image onto the sheet below when written or typed on.

nearside lay The sidelay on the operating side of the press. See also **offside lay**, **lay**.

neckline White space under a headline.

negative Reverse photographic image on film.

negative-working plates Litho plates that are exposed in the non-image area.

nest To place a program routine within a larger routine.

nested indent A left or right indent applied to a paragraph or more that insets the text affected inside the previous margin. Typically used to highlight a piece of **extract** setting within main body text.

net A rather loose term, sometimes applied to the **internet** itself, at others to specific networks.

network An arrangement of linked computers that typically draw on a common database of information resident on a file server while retaining considerable local processing capabilities.

network application A program, or combination of program and data, that performs a task over a **network**, usually involving more than one computer.

network computer A computer without any local storage, i.e. with no disks, that is designed to be used on a **local area network** (**LAN**) or connected to a **network** via an **intranet** or even the **internet**. Because of the lack of storage, network computers are cheaper than standard PCs.

network layer The third-lowest layer of the **ISO** seven-layer model, which determines the switching and routing of **packets** from the sender to the receiver using the **datalink layer**. It is in turn used by the transport layer. **IP** is a network layer protocol.

network operating system The system software used to integrate the computers on a **network**.

neutral sized paper That is sized with neutral pH7, acid-free size. This gives it considerable qualities of longevity, but less than those required for the standard of permanent paper that must be acid-free in furnish as well as surface.

newsprint Paper made from mechanical pulp for the printing of newspapers, usually between 45 and 58gsm.

next to editorial Instruction to position advertisement adjacent to editorial text.

nip Pressure point between two rollers.

nipping Pressing a book to flatten the signatures and remove air from between the sheets. This takes place after the book blocks are sewn and before they are rounded and backed, and sent on for further processing. Also known as **crushing** or **smashing**.

nm Nanometre (one billionth of a metre, the distance a fingernail grows in one second).

no break area In text setting, a defined sequence of words or characters within which hyphenation is not allowed for grammatical or contextual reasons.

noise Unwanted signals or information that interferes with the required information. This may be literal noise in telecommunications; it may be visual in computer **graphics**, where there are, say, spots on an image; or it may be metaphorical in the sense that a communication contains irrelevant information that obscures the real message.

nominal weight American system of specifying **basis weight** of paper.

non-consumable textbook Textbook that will be re-used constantly rather than written in.

non-impact printing Electronic methods of image transfer without striking paper. See **ink jet printer**, **laser printer**.

non-interlaced Not using **interlacing**.

non-reflective ink Light-absorbing ink used to print machine-readable characters.

non-reproducing blue See **drop-out blue**.

non-scratch inks Inks resistant to marking.

non-tarnish paper Paper free from chemicals that will tarnish metal surfaces in contact with it.

non-woven material See **imitation cloth**.

Nordsen binder Device that applies a line of glue beneath the shoulder of a book block to reinforce the casing-in process. Useful for heavy books.

notch binding A form of unsewn binding in which notches are punched in the backs of the sections as they are folded on the folding machine, and glue applied in through the notches to hold the leaves together. Also called **slotted binding**. See also **burst binding**.

ns A **nanosecond**.

NTSC National Television Standards Committee. Also used to describe the US television format defined by the committee.

numbering machine On or off-press device that numbers printed sheets consecutively, e.g. for tickets.

OBA Optical bleaching agent. Added to the furnish of bright white papers.

OBC Outside back cover.

object A combination of data that has a well-defined, distinct existence. This may be a graphic object, a group of database fields (see **object-oriented database**), a cell in a spreadsheet, a range of cells, or even an entire spreadsheet or a video clip. Such objects are handled in **object-oriented programming** and used by such systems and protocols as **Object Linking and Embedding** (OLE).

object code or **object language** Machine code, as translated from a **source program**.

Object Linking and Embedding (OLE) (Pronounced olé'.) A distributed **object system** and protocol from Microsoft.

object-oriented (OO) To do with **objects**, particularly the programming and manipulation of non-text items.

object-oriented programming (OOP) A type of programming that operates on **objects**, or data structures. Operations that can be performed on particular objects form part of those objects, and will be common to all objects in a particular **class**.

oblique Slanted, usually used of **type**, or sometimes **graphics**. Note that oblique type, that is, upright type slanted with the computer, is not the same as italic type, i.e.

a font that has been designed as italic. However, if a **sans serif type** is used, it may only be the expert who can tell the difference ; with serifed faces it should be clear to everyone.

oblong Bound at the shorter dimension. Also, **landscape**.

OCR Optical Character Recognition. The interpretation of type-written characters by a machine that scans the text and stores it in memory, often for subsequent typesetting.

OCR paper High-quality bond suitable for optical character recognition equipment.

OCR-A A typeface designed to aid machine readability. Compare **OCR-B**.

OCR-B A machine-readable typeface that is designed to be more legible to humans than OCR-A. In accordance with the specification laid out in this guide, so that it can be read by Royal Mail automated sorting machines.

OCR readable mail Mail whose address can be read by a postal service OCR machines that read the printed readable address on a letter, check the postcode and apply a phosphor code or barcode. This can then be read by other machines for sorting.

octavo Abbreviated as 8vo. The eighth part of the traditional broadside sheet. Used to describe book sizes, e.g. demy octavo.

ODBC Open database connectivity, a standard database access method developed by the SQL Access group.

oddment A book signature with fewer pages than the others and which has to be printed separately.

OEL Organic electroluminescence. The phenomenon of light emission as a result of electrical stimulation of an OLED.

OEM Original Equipment Manufacturer. An OEM product is one that is a rebadged and possibly enhanced version of an original manufactured product, and which sells under its rebadged name.

OFC Outside front cover.

off-machine coating Coating applied to a paper as a separate operation. Contrast **on-machine coating**.

offline The opposite of **online**, so that data cannot be transferred, for example, to a printer or a **network**.

offprint Part of a book or journal printed separately, e.g. an article from a journal.

offset Printing which uses an intermediate medium to transfer the image onto paper, e.g. a rubber blanket wrapped around a cylinder, as in **offset litho**.

offset letterpress See **letterset**.

offset paper Any paper suitable for offset litho printing.

offside lay The lay opposite the operating side of a press. As distinct from **nearside lay**.

Old Face Early 17th century typestyle. Also called 'Old Style' and **Garalde**.

old-style figures Also called **non-lining figures**. Numerals that do not align on the base line but have ascenders and descenders. As distinct from **modern** or **lining figures**.

OLE See **Object Linking and Embedding**.

OLED Organic light-emitting diode. Devices that use organic materials to produce light through electrical stimulation.

OLEP Organic light-emitting polymer.

on the fly Refers to any process that occurs as output is being performed, such as the screening of halftones simultaneously with output to an image recorder.

on-demand publishing The concept of printing books one at a time from a computer store 'on demand', rather than tying up capital by printing for stock.

on-machine coating Coating applied to the base paper on the paper machine itself. As distinct **from off-machine coating**, where the base paper is coated as a completely separate operation, giving a superior result.

1-bit, **8-bit** and **24-bit colour** The number of bits of information (**colour resolution**) that can be represented in the **pixels** (dots) on the screen. The higher the number of bits, the more colours or **grey scales** you can have. In turn, the higher the number of bits, the more memory is required to handle them, so the number of colours depends on the size of the computer memory, rather than on the monitor used. 8-bit and 24-bit are the most commonly used. 1-bit colour is **monochrome**.

one-shot binding Perfect binding with one application of hot-melt glue only. As distinct from **two shot binding**.

one-sided art Paper coated on one side only (such as jacket art).

onionskin Lightweight cockle finish blank paper often used for airmail stationery (30–39gsm).

online Connected, so that data can be transferred, say, to a printer or a **network**. The opposite of **offline**.

online Connected to the **internet**.

on-sert Apply a component onto a mailing piece, typically a plastic (credit) card or ticket.

opacity The quality of opaqueness in a paper. Opacity is measured in %, with around 90% being an average for 80gsm printing paper.

opaque printing An **MF** printing paper with high opacity.

OPC organic photo conductor, light reactive material forming the basis of electrophotographic imaging.

Open Source Software made freely available to users, suppliers gain revenue from implementation, training and updates.

open time In binding, the time between an adhesive being applied and when it sets. In printing, the time an ink stays fluid on the press.

opening Facing pages.

operating system The underlying computer software that controls the operation of a computer.

OPI (Open Prepress Interface) System of substituting high-resolution images with low-res and swapping back at output to save computer power when image processing was too intensive for desktop machines.

OPP lamination Oriented polypropylene lamination. The standard plastic lamination film.

optical brightener Dye that emits visible radiation. Used to 'brighten' paper.

optical centre The 'visual' centre of a page, about 10% higher than the mathematical centre.

optical character recognition See **OCR**.

optical density Light-absorbing capacity of an image area.

optical letter spacing Space between letters that accommodates their varying shapes and gives the appearance of even space.

orange peel 1. Multi-indentation effect on paper. 2. varnishing fault.

order form Form on which a buyer can fill in the detail of his intended purchase as an order to supply.

original Photograph or drawing to be reproduced.

origination All the processes involved in the reproduction of original material, including make-up, up to plate-making stages; and also including typesetting.

ornamented Typeface embellished with decorative flourishes.

ornaments Another term for **dingbats**.

orphan The first line of a new paragraph, or a subhead, that appears at the foot of a page. Considered undesirable. See also **widow**, **club line**.

OSI Open Source Initiative, a non-profit corporation dedicated to managing and promoting open source software on behalf of developers and users.

out of focus Blurred, not properly focused by a camera.

out of register One or more colours out of alignment with the others in a piece of printing.

out-of-round Distorted paper reel.

out-turn sheet Sheet of paper taken during manufacture or on delivery as a representative sample for checking specification.

outer forme The imposed forme that forms the outside of the sheet when folded and which contains the first page of the section. Contrast **inner forme**.

outline Typeface comprising only an outline with no 'solid' area. Contrast also inline, in which the characters have white inner areas against a bolder outline shape.

outline font (Also described as a **vector font** or **scalable font**.) A **font** that is stored in terms of its outline shape rather than as a **bitmap**. Because it is a type of object-oriented graphic, an outline font can be scaled to any size and transformed, e.g. by sloping or just using the outline.

outline graphics Another term for **vector** or object-oriented graphics.

output Data or any form of communication coming out of a computer after processing.

outsert Item of promotional material on the outside of, rather than inside, a pack or periodical.

outwork Operations put out to another company for reasons of specialism or capacity.

overexposure Too lengthy an exposure of film, causing a thin, 'chipped', image. **Underexposure** leads to a dense, dark, murky image.

overhang cover Cover larger than the text pages. Also **yapp cover**.

overmatter Text matter not used in the final printing.

overprinting Additional printing over a previously printed sheet.

overrun Copies in excess of the specified print number.

overs See **spoilage**.

oversewing Attaching single leaves to a sewn book with thread sewing.

Oxford hollow A **hollow** on the back of a book that consists of a tube of brown paper attached to the back of the folded sections and the inside of the case hollow. Used for heavy books where reinforcement is necessary.

oxidation Chemical action with the oxygen in the air: one of the principal ways in which sheetfed offset ink dries. Oxidation also affects litho plates, attacking the non-image area. Gumming up a plate helps prevent this.

ozalid Print made by a form of diazo copying process and often used for proofing film. See also **blueprints**.

P&L Profit and loss account.

package Set of software bought 'off-the-shelf' rather than specifically written for a purpose.

packager Organisation that provides complete publications ready to be marketed.

packet A block, or specified number of bytes, that contains both control information and data. Can be sent by connectionless (packet switching) or connection-oriented communications.

packet switch node (PSN) A computer used in a **packet-switched network** to accept, route and forward packets.

packet-switching network Computer-controlled communications network in which data is divided into 'packets' transmitted at high speed.

packing Paper placed under the plate or blanket in litho to adjust printing pressure.

PAF postcode address file Royal Mail's file of all correct postal addresses in the UK.

page One side of a leaf.

page count Synonym for extent (US).

page make-up Assembly of the elements in a page into their final design.

page pull test Test to determine the strength of binding of an adhesive-bound book.

pages per inch Number of pages per inch of thickness. US measurement of bulk. Abbreviated **ppi**.

pagination Page numbering.

paint program A software application that provides the ability to create and edit **bitmaps**. Also called **image-editing software**. (Contrast with a **draw program**, used for editing **vector graphics**.)

pair-kerning The automatic kerning of selected pairs of letters for better aesthetic effect.

palette An analogy to the paint palette used by artists, this is a **window** showing the colours available for use in a **paint** or **draw program**. The colours available in the palette will depend on the **screen** resolution (and thus the number of colours) chosen.

pallet Wooden base on which paper or books are stored. Also known as skid and stillage. The 'European standard' pallet size is 1000×1200mm, four-way entry. A maximum pallet weight of 1000kg and maximum height of 1219mm (4ft) are commonly specified. Typical pallet loads might come to 1000–1250 books of average octavo size; or around 12,500 sheets of quad demy (one tonne in 80gsm).

pamphlet Booklet comprising only a few pages.

pamphlet binding See **saddle stitching**.

panel Display board.

Pantone Proprietary name of a widely-used colour matching system.

Pantone Matching System (PMS) See **Pantone**.

paper basis weight See **basis weight**.

paper master Paper plate used on small offset machine.

paper surface efficiency (PSE) Printability of paper.

paperboard Lightweight board in the range 200–300gsm. See **board**.

papeterie Smooth, stiff paper used in greeting card manufacture.

papier maché Repulped paper with stiffening additives which can be used for moulding.

papyrus Egyptian reed from which the earliest form of paper was made (made from sedge).

paradigm Set of norms and values associated with an operation or environment which becomes the accepted way of doing things.

paragraph formatting The application of a format or style (including such factors as typeface, type style, indents, space before and after) to a whole paragraph. (Contrast with **character formatting**, where only the selected characters are affected.)

paragraph opener Typographic device marking the start of a paragraph that needs emphasising.

paragraph widow A short line (one or two words) appearing as the last line of a paragraph anywhere on a page. To be avoided if possible. (See **Widow**.)

parallel communication Data transfer in which each **bit** is transferred along its own line, in contrast to serial connection, in which bits are transferred one at a time. Parallel communication is generally used only over short distances, mainly because data integrity is lost over longer distances.

parallel folding Folding a sheet with all the folds parallel to each other. Contrast **right-angle folding**.

parallel interface An interface over which **parallel communication** is carried out. Also called a **Centronics interface**.

parallel port See **parallel communications**. Usually, parallel port describes the physical connection on a computer, most frequently used for connecting printers.

parallel transmission Data communications method where each bit in the computer byte travels in parallel with its fellows and bytes arrive intact. (Contrast **serial transmission**). Widely used for transmission to printers. See also **Centronics interface**.

parameter A variable set to a constant value for a specific operation.

PARC Xerox Palo Alto Research Centre, home of many key developments in communication technology.

parenthesis A round bracket.

parity In general, being either odd or even. In computing and communications, however, parity usually means the number of ones, as opposed to zeros, in a **byte** or **word**. A redundant parity bit is added to each byte and this is set to make the number of 1 bits in the byte even (for even parity) or odd (for odd parity). Parity bits are a basic form of **error detection**, but will detect only single bit errors because, if an even number of the bits are incorrect, then the parity bit will not show this. Also, unlike more complex **error detection and correction** systems, it is impossible to tell which bit is wrong. (See also **checksum**.)

parser An algorithm or program that is used to check the syntactic structure of a file or **structured document**. For example, an **SGML** parser checks that a **document instance** (i.e. a document coded in SGML) corresponds to the specified **Document Type Definition** and will report any errors. SGML parsers are often integrated with editing programs so that documents can be parsed as they are created or edited.

part-mechanical paper Paper containing up to 50% of mechanical pulp with the balance chemical pulp. Compare **mechanical paper**, **woodfree paper**.

partwork Publication issued in a number of parts which can be purchased separately and which then combine to make up the whole.

pass 1. One run through a machine. Also, working. 2. An operation that realises the completion of a job from input through processing to output.

pass for press Authorise the final form of a publication for printing.

pass4press Specification for the creation of PDF files for printing developed by the PPA.

passive matrix A design of **liquid crystal display**.

password A secret (or private) arbitrary string of characters that has to be typed into a computer in order to allow access to a system or a particular program. Normally it is not displayed on the screen, so that it remains private. There are many recommendations about choosing and changing passwords. The main problem is choosing something which is easy to remember and yet difficult for someone else to guess.

paste To insert text or graphics from the **clipboard** into an open document.

paste drier Type of drier used in inks.

paste-up Dummy or artwork comprising all the elements pasted into position.

pasteboard Board made from several laminations of thinner sheets. Also known as 'pasted board'. Contrast **homogeneous board**.

pasted unlined chipboard See **unlined chipboard**.
path The explicitly routed, node-by-node, **internet address** or the link between two machines. Path is also used in computer operating systems to specify the order in which directories should be accessed when a program (or executable file) is called.

PBX See **private (automatic) branch exchange**.

PC Personal computer.

PCB Printed circuit board.

PDF see **Portable Document Format**.

PDF/X A series of standards (**ISO15930-1/2/3**) that define how to produce PDF files for printing.

PE or **printer's error** Normally a literal in typesetting.

pebble finish Textured surface on paper, added after making or sometimes after printing.

pebbling Embossing paper after printing with a pebbled pattern.

peculiars Special characters outside a normal fount range.

peer-to-peer Network arrangement in which each computer has equal power: any can hold applications and data and control network traffic, as distinct from the more common **client-server** architecture.

pel See **pixel**.

penetration One of the ways in which inks dry. See **absorption**.

percentage dot area The percentage of a halftone that is black as opposed to white.

perfect binding Adhesive binding widely used on paperbacks. Glue is applied to the roughened back edges of sections to hold them to the cover and each other. Also called **adhesive binding**, **cut-back binding**, **thermoplastic binding**, **threadless binding**.

perfecting Printing both sides of a sheet at one pass. Such a press is called a 'perfector'.

perforating Punching a series of holes in paper, either as a coding process or to facilitate tearing off a part.

perforating rules Letterpress steel rules that indent the sheet.

peripheral Computer input or output device that is not part of the main CPU, e.g. a printer.

PERL Practical Extraction and Report Language. An interpreted computer language mainly used for processing and converting text and text strings.

permanence Paper's resistance to ageing.

permanent inks Inks that do not fade. Also, **lightfast inks**.

permanent paper Paper that is acid-free and made to stringent conditions for archival purposes. The accepted standard for manufacture is laid out in American standard

ANSI Z39 1984 and specifies neutral pH, alkaline reserve, chemical furnish, and specified tear resistance and fold endurance.

permissions Permission given to a publisher for him to reproduce material that is someone else's copyright. Normally the subject of a fee.

peroxide bleaching The bleaching of wood pulp using hydrogen peroxide. More environment friendly than **chlorine bleaching** that it is steadily supplanting.

Personal Digital Assistant (PDA) A small hand-held computer, often integrated into mobile phones.

personalcast See **narrowcast**.

PET Polyethylene terephthalate. The most common plastic used for bottles, replacing glass.

pH value Measure of acidity or alkalinity of a substance. 7 = neutral; less than 7 = progressive acidity; more than 7 = progressive alkalinity.

phase alternate/alternating line (**PAL**) The television standard used in most European countries. France, which uses **SECAM**, is the principal exception. (See also **NTSC**.)

phloroglucinol Chemical used on paper to test for woodfree or mechanical furnish. Phloroglucinol is applied to a paper: if the stain remains yellow it is woodfree; if the stain turns red it contains mechanical pulp. The depth of colour of the red stain indicates the percentage of mechanical fibre present.

photo retouching The modification of **bitmap** images, using **image-editing** or **paint programs**.

photocopy Duplicate of a photograph or a document produced on a copying machine.

photoengraving Letterpress printing plate.

photogram Print made by exposure of object directly on photographic paper.

photogravure Gravure printing in which the cylinder image is photographically produced.

photolettering Method of setting display-sized type from photographic founts.

photolithography Lithographic process with photographically produced plate image.

photomontage Print comprising several other photographs.

photopolymer Plate coating that polymerises (solidifies) on exposure to light. Used for long runs.

photopolymer plate Flexo or letterpress relief printing plate.

photoprint Photographic print.

PhotoShop An image manipulation (**paint**) program from **Adobe**. Probably the most widely used such program in the graphic arts industry.

phototypesetting Setting type onto photographic paper or film.

pi characters Special characters outside the normal alphabetic range and not normally contained in a standard fount, e.g. special maths symbols.

pic Abbreviation for picture. Plural: pix.

pica A typographical unit of measurement. Each pica is divided into 12 points. Although originally six picas equalled 0.996 of an inch, in the development of **PostScript** the point has been standardised, so that there are 72 points per inch (thus on a screen with 72 **pixels per inch**, one pixel equals one point). Type size is always specified in points.

pick-away See **pull-away**.

picking The lifting of areas of paper surface during printing which happens when ink tack is stronger than the surface strength.

picture element See **pixel**.

picture list List of illustrations intended for a book drawn up by a picture researcher.

picture research The process of locating illustrations for a book from picture libraries, museums, galleries.

pie Jumbled type. Sometimes spelt pi.

pie chart A graphic diagram representing a pie, the portions of which vary to indicate values or percentages.

piezo Mechanism of generating a droplet of ink in on-demand inkjet printing.

piggyback form A continuous stationery tractor-fed carrier designed to feed headed stationery and envelopes into a printer.

pigment The constituent of a printing ink that gives it its colour.

pigment foil Foil which is of coloured pigment rather than imitation gold or silver.

pigmented paper Size-press coated or **light coated paper**.

pin feed The method of feeding continuous stationery by lining up pins on the machines with a series of small holes in the paper, sprocket fed.

pinholes 1. mall holes in paper surface. 2. Small holes in the dense black image area of a film that let through the light, and need to be spotted out using an opaquing fluid.

pinholing Faults in gravure and flexo print, minute spots that remain unprinted in an image. It may be due to ink drying in the cells of the anilox or the surface being printed lacking receptivity.

pinless Refers to the elimination of the standard pin mechanisms that control paper webs going through folders and high-speed mono digital printers.

pitch edge The edge of the sheet which is fed into a printing or folding machine. Also known as the **gripper edge** or **leading edge**.

pixel An abbreviation for 'picture element' (or 'picture cell'). The smallest resolvable rectangular area that can be displayed on-screen or stored in memory. In a monochrome image the pixel may be just black or white but, if **grey scales** are used, then each pixel will have its own brightness, from 0 for black to the maximum value (255 for an eight-bit pixel) for white. On a colour monitor, each pixel is made up of a triple of red, green and blue phosphors (see **RGB**) and each is controlled by a number of bits (see **8-bit colour**, **24-bit colour**). This will affect the **palette** and will be related to the **screen** resolution.

pixel editing The ability to examine and delete individual pixels, typically around the outside of images, in order to tidy up outlines.

plain ASCII Means just the real **ASCII** characters including none of the **extended ASCII** characters. (See **flat ASCII**.)

plaintext A message before **encryption** or after **decryption**, in its readable form, rather than its encrypted form. (Compare with **ciphertext**).

pl Picolitre.

planning All the processes involved in imposition; laying pages down in imposition sequence ready for plate exposure.

planographic printing Printing from a flat (as distinct from indented or relief) image, e.g. litho.

plasma discharge Surface treatment technique to improve ink adhesion to a plastic substrate. The material is passed through a plasma, a gas containing electrons and ions that act to increase the free surface energy of the substrate.

plastic plate Printing plate made of polyester.

plastic wrapping Wrapping magazines in polythene.

plate 1. A one-piece printing surface. 2. Single leaf printed on separate paper and attached to a book.

plate cylinder The press cylinder that carries the plate.

plate finish High calendered finish given to paper.

plate folder See **buckle folder**.

plate hooked and guarded Printed plate fixed into a book by extending the back margin under a signature and sewing it in.

plate section Printed illustrations separated from the text matter and often on different paper.

plate size A size of negative or photographic print 8×6in.

platen Small letterpress printing machine on which the paper is pressed up against the vertically-held type bed.

plates joined on the guard Two printed plates joined by adhesive at the back margin to form a four-page section.

platesetter Imaging unit on a **ctp** device that exposes the plate either by laser or by **thermal imaging** techniques.

platform A combination of a particular computer and **operating system**.

PLED Polymer light-emitting diode. The most advanced display technology, based on the use of organic polymers that emit light when stimulated electrically. Also described as polymer light-emitting device or polymer light-emitting display. PLEDs are a form of OLED. PLEDs have the major advantage of being solution processable, and can therefore be applied to substrates using techniques such as inkjet printing.

plotter Device that draws graphics from computer instructions using either laser techniques or mechanical techniques.

plucking See **picking**.

plug-in A term describing add-on **applications** associated with software to extend specialist functionality.

ply Layer of paper or board joined to another for strength, thus: two-ply and three-ply.

PMS Pantone Matching System. See **Pantone**.

POD Print on demand. Using digital printing to produce the required order from a database

PODi Print on Demand Initiative. A group of the leading vendors of digital printer manufacturers and front-end suppliers working to promote variable data digital printing.

point (noun) A typographical unit of measure, one-twelfth of a pica. (See **pica** for more details.)

point (verb) To locate a **cursor**, controlled by a **mouse** on a screen item

point of presence (PoP) A site, run by an **internet service provider**, that users can access. Such a site will usually have banks of modems and other telecommunications, together with access to an internet backbone. PoPs may be geographically distributed to improve access and keep telephone costs down.

point system The main system of typographic measurement. 1pt = 0.351mm (0.013837). See also **didot**, **pica**.

point of sale (PoS) The place in a shop (or other business operation) where a sale is transacted, e.g. a supermarket check-out.

pointing device A device used to control the movement of a pointer or cursor on the screen, usually in a **graphical user interface** (**GUI**). The **mouse** is the most common pointing device.

polymerisation Drying of ink by ultraviolet curing.

polywrap Enclosing a magazine or brochure with plastic film for mailing.

POP Point of purchase, see **point of sale**.

pop-up menu A **menu** that is brought to the screen by clicking on a word or **icon**, which can be anywhere on the screen, or even in some applications just by **clicking** the right **mouse** button.

pop-ups Cardboard cut-outs that stand erect.

porosity The degree to which a paper is porous to air. Very open, porous papers give difficulties with feeding.

port An input and/or output connection to or from a computer.

portable document format (PDF) The format used by **Adobe Acrobat** files.

portrait The orientation of a picture, **screen** or page, such that its height is greater than its width. Most books, and certainly journals, are **portrait**. (See also **landscape**, **aspect ratio**.)

PoS See **point-of-sale**.

positive An image on film or paper in which the dark and light values are the same as the original, as distinct from **negative**.

positive-working plates Litho plates that are exposed using positives.

post To send an **email** message, usually to a **mailing list** or a newsgroup. (Contrast with **mail**, which is generally used to mean sending a message to specific recipients.)

post, telephone and telegraph administration (PTT) A provider of a public telecommunications service. May also be involved with setting national standards and policy on telecommunications issues.

postcode (zipcode, US) Alphanumeric code allocated by postal service to identify the location of an address or group of addresses.

post exposure UV light exposure of a dried and light finished flexo plate to complete polymerisation and attain maximum durability.

posting docket Four- or five-part document set describing the make-up of that mailing, that accompanies a Mailsort, Walksort or Presstream mailing for validation and invoicing purposes. Being replaced by electronic methods.

poster A single sheet in a large size printed on one side only for public display.

poster paper One-sided glazed paper with rough underside suitable for pasting.

posterisation A technique in which the number of colours or **grey levels** in a **bitmap image** is reduced – there is no longer a continuous variation in the shades.

PostScript Adobe System's page description language.

PostScript fonts See **outline fonts**,

PostScript interpreter Software that converts PostScript files to an imaging code command set supported by the output device.

powdering Build-up of paper dust on a blanket.

powderless etching Method of etching letterpress line plates in one step.

pp Pages.

PPA Periodical Publishers Association.

PPF Prepress Production Format. Early attempt by prepress vendors to develop a standard across their equipment, superseded into CIP3/4 and JDF

PPI Printed Postage Impression. Mark printed on an envelope or wrapper to indicate postage will be paid through a mail docket billed by the postal supplier.

ppi Pages per inch. American method of specifying the thickness of paper.

PPML An XML-based standard that facilitates the data handling of variable data jobs by any compliant press. It allows any front end to talk to any press, rather than having to use a turnkey solution from one supplier

preface Formal statement before the text of a book by the author. As distinct from **foreword**.

preferred position Advertisement location that an advertiser would prefer for his copy if it is available.

preflight checking software Method of systematically ensuring prepress files are complete and follow specification for printing

prekissing Paper and blanket making contact too early, resulting in a double impression.

prelims Abbreviation of preliminary matter. The matter in a book that precedes the text.

prepress costs All the costs associated with bringing a job ready for press, up to but not including printing the first copy. As distinct from **press costs**.

prepress proofs Proofs made by techniques other than printing.

preprinted Part of a job printed before the main run through the press.

presensitised plate Offset litho plate supplied by the manufacturer with a light-sensitive coating e.g. an offset litho plate. Often shortened to 'presen plate'.

press 1. Generic term for all periodicals. 2. Printing machine.

press costs The costs associated with printing and manufacturing a job from plates onwards. As distinct from **prepress costs**.

press proof Proof taken from the press after make-ready but before the full run.

press release News of an event sent to the press for publication.

press section In papermaking, the section of the paper machine where the web of paper is first pressed before it is passed onto the drying cylinders.

pressing Flattening folded sections before binding.

presspahn hollow Hollow made of a strip of brown reinforced card applied to the inside of the spine of a cased book. Less rigid than a board hollow, but more durable than paper.

Presstream A Mailsort service for the distribution of magazines, periodicals and newsletters meeting specific contractual requirements.

pressure-sensitive Adhesive when pressure is applied.

primary (subtractive) colours Yellow, magenta, and cyan which, with black, make up the four **process colours**.

primer Print working that acts as a base or undercoat for a colour which will otherwise lack covering power, e.g. a metallic silver or gold ink.

print 1. A photograph. 2. A common operating system command to print a specified file list.

printability Covers a range of paper properties that will impact the printed results: gloss, smoothness, whiteness, opacity, etc.

print engine In a digital printer, the mechanical part that performs the physical printing function. As distinct from the **RIP**.

print length See **repeat**.

print server A **server** (or computer) that handles the printer access and buffering for a **network**.

print to paper Instruction to the printer to use all available paper for a job rather than printing to a specific quantity of copies.

printed circuit board A plastic base with a copper coating onto which electronic components are attached. Unwanted areas of copper are removed by acid etching.

printer's error See **PE**.

printing cylinder See **plate cylinder**.

printing down Laying film over a light-sensitive plate or paper to produce an image.

printing sequence The order in which the four process colours are applied.

printings Papers suitable for printing.

printmaking Making fine art reproductions of originals.

printout The text printed out by a computer printer.

private (automatic) branch exchange (PABX/PBX) A switching telephone exchange located within an organisation to connect users both internally and to the public telephone network.

private line Another term for a **dedicated circuit** or line.

pro-forma invoice Invoice drawn up to show the value of goods, and needed either for documentation purposes or to obtain prepayment.

process blue, **red**, **yellow** Used to indicate the cyan, magenta and yellow colours of the **four colour process** inks.

process colour(s) The four colours **CMYK**, used in printing and the **colour separation** process.

process inks Cyan, magenta, yellow and black formulated as a set of four to print colour.

process set The four process inks.

program The complete set of instructions that control a computer in the performance of a task.

program paper A flabby, generally woodfree paper made from chemical pulp derived from the soft leaves of hardwood trees. Allows noiseless page-turning.

programmable Any device that can receive, store and act on a computer program.

programmer The person employed to write, develop or maintain computer programs.

programming A sequential list of instructions by which a computer performs its designated tasks.

progressive proofs or **progs** Proofs of each plate in a colour set showing each colour alone and in combination with the others as a guide to colour matching, at the printing stage.

projection platemaking equipment Equipment such as the Rachwal or DaiNippon SAPP systems, which make plates by exposing from 35mm or 70mm roll microfilms mounted in the head of computer-controlled step-and-repeat machines. The microfilm contains the pages of the job shot sequentially; the step-and-project machine is programmed to locate and expose each page in imposition order onto the plate.

prompt A message, usually displayed but sometimes audible, requesting an action from a computer user.

proof A trial printed sheet or copy made before the production run for the purpose of checking.

proofreader's marks Symbols used by a proofreader in marking corrections on proofs.

proofreading Checking typeset proofs for accuracy.

proportional fonts See **proportional spacing**.

proportional spacing Spacing letters in text so that each takes up its own width, rather than all taking the same width (see **monospaced fonts**). Thus 'm' and 'w' take up a comparatively wide space and 'i' a narrow one. Virtually all material is now set in proportionally spaced fonts, whether for printing or display on the screen. (See also **hyphenation**, **justification**.) In one sense, monospaced fonts can be seen as a transient development, forced on users by the limitations of the mechanical typewriter; handwriting is, after all, proportionally spaced.

protocol In general, an agreed set of rules on how something should be carried out. In communications and networks, these govern areas such as data format, timing, sequencing, access and error control and syntax of messages.

proximity search A **searching** technique in which, for example, one is able to search for the occurrence of a group of characters within, say, 20 words of another group or groups.

PS, ps Both an abbreviation for **PostScript** and the file extension which is often used for PostScript files.

PSDN See **public switched data network**.

PSN See **packet switch node**.

PSTN See **public switched telephone network**.

psychrometer Instrument used for determining **relative humidity 'RH'**.

PT Precision trimmed (paper).

PTT See **post**, **telephone and telegraph administration**. **public carrier** A provider of a public telecommunications service. (See **PTT**.)

public domain (PD) If **intellectual property** (books, computer programs, images) is in the public domain, it is available to anyone without charge. Most commonly, this applies to public domain software, which is usually software developed on behalf of the US government and which by law has to be available in this way. It is important to distinguish such software from **shareware**, which is not free, or at least free only for evaluation.

public switched data network (PSDN) Usually a digital network (and of a higher **bandwidth** than the **PSTN**), particularly suitable for data communications. Generally operated by a **PTT**.

public switched telephone network (PSTN) A public telephone network or the collection of them around the world, operated by **PTT**s. Sometimes called 'POTS' in contrast to **PSDN**.

publication window In **DTP**, the basic window which appears when a document is being worked on. It comprises one or two pages, the **pasteboard**, page **icons**, the **pointer**, **scroll bars**, **title bar**, **menu bar**.

Publisher Item Identifier (PII) An extension of the **ISBN** and **ISSN** system, introduced by a group of leading US academic (scientific) journal publishers to provide a way of identifying individual items, such as articles, within both books and journals. It also provides a unified identification system for books and journals.

publisher's statement Publisher's authorised notice of circulation and distribution statistics.

pull 1. A **proof**. 2. A single print for subsequent photolitho reproduction, often called a **repro pull**.

pull down menus Also referred to as pop-up menus. Options are revealed only when a menu type is accessed, usually by a pointing and dragging action with a **mouse**. Once the option has been selected the menu disappears off the screen free.

pull-away A section that contains several blank pages (typically 4pp) either in the middle or at front and back, which are to be removed before binding. Also, **pick-away**.

pull-down menu A **menu** that is brought to the screen by clicking on a word or **icon** in a **menu** bar.

pull-out Part of a publication that can be removed from the binding and used separately.

pulling Resistance between paper and printing surface.

pulp The raw suspension of wood fibre, which is treated either chemically, or mechanically, in water.

Chemical pulp Contains many fewer impurities than **mechanical pulp**.

pulp board A homogeneous board manufactured to its full thickness on the papermaking machine.

pulpwood Wood for the manufacture of wood pulp.

punch binding See **burst binding**.

punch register system Device that punches registered holes in sets of films or plates for positioning purposes.

PUR binding See **reactive hotmelt**

pure woodfree See **woodfree**.

PVA Polyvinyl alcohol, a water-based cold-melt emulsion adhesive which is flexible when dry and is used particularly in gluing the spines of cased books and in perfect binding. See also **two-shot binding**.

PVC Polyvinyl chloride. 1. Applied as a coating or impregnated into base paper for durability. 2. Substrate used in plastic card production.

QA Quality assurance.

QC Quality control.

QMP A quality mark awarded to qualifying mailing houses that supply enclosing and despatch services for direct mail. The award has been designed to help the buyers of direct mail services source proven, high-quality suppliers.

quad Paper terminology for a sheet four times the size of the traditional broadside sheet e.g. 'Quad Demy', 890×1130mm.

quad left, **right** or **centre** To set lines flush left, right or centre.

quad press Printing press designed for a maximum sheet approximately 1010×1400mm (40×56in) i.e. a 'quad' sheet.

quadrille Grid paper.

quadtone The use of four colours in combination to produce a particular effect in printing. May be used to produce a finer **grey-scale** effect. (See also **duotone**.)

quality The whole set of features of a product or service that relate to its being able to satisfy the needs of the end user.

quality assurance Abbreviated **QA**. Umbrella term for all activities associated with the creation and maintenance of a quality system within a company.

quality circles or **quality control circles** Small groups of company workers called to meet regularly to examine working practices, bring forward suggestions for improvement and discuss solutions to quality problems.

quality control System for checking quality of products during or after manufacture.

quality system Comprehensive, company-wide set of practices adopted in a firm to monitor the quality of its products and the effectiveness of its internal and external operations.

quantum computing Possible long-term successor to digital computing with far more power and capability.

QuarkXPress The leading **page layout** program.

quarter tone Illustration made by retouching a coarse-screen halftone print to emphasise the shadows by making them solid and the highlights by making them white, following which the illustration is reshot as fine line.

quarter-bound Binding with spine in one material (e.g. leather) and sides in another (e.g. cloth). Compare **full-bound**, **half-bound**, **three-quarter bound**.

quarto A page one-quarter of the traditional broadside sheet size, e.g. Crown Quarto.

Qubit Quantum bit, potential basic quantum computing information unit that can exist in several states and form complex interactions as pairs.

quire 1. One-twentieth of a ream (25 sheets). 2. Section or signature.

quirewise binding Saddle stitching.

quotes Inverted commas.

qwerty Standard typewriter keyboard layout, qwerty being the arrangement of keys on the top left-hand row of the board.

R type Colour print made from a transparency without any intermediate negative. Contrast **C type**.

r&b See **rounding and backing**.

R&D Research and development.

radiation drying Use of infrared, ultraviolet and electron beam to accelerate ink drying, and sometimes glue.

rag paper Paper made from stock containing a substantial percentage of rag.

ragged Text layout that is not justified. Most text on screen is ragged right, i.e. the left-hand margin is aligned while the right-hand margin is not. Ragged left and ragged centre (ragged on both margins) are also used in books, but only usually as a design feature.

ragged right Text with irregular line lengths, i.e. with an even left margin but an uneven right margin.

RAID Redundant arrays of inexpensive/independent disks.

rainbow printing Also known as iris printing – a form of multicolour printing from a single printing plate that is inked in different colours in different areas for this purpose. The ink duct is split into sectors with different inks.

raised printing See **thermographic printing**.

RAM Random access memory. RAM is the temporary, interactive area of memory in a computer in which programs work and manipulate the data. Data in RAM is lost when the computer is switched off unless it is first saved to disk. Compare **ROM**.

RAM disk A large area of RAM memory that holds some or all of the contents of a floppy or hard disk enabling far faster read-write operations. At the end of a session the contents of a RAM disk are rewritten back to floppy or hard disk.

ram stacker Machine that condenses stacks of printed sections ready for binding.

random access Method of directly accessing a specific address on a computer file without the need for a sequential process. Random access memory is often abbreviated to **RAM**.

range Align (type).

raster The horizontal pattern of lines on a video display or television that make up the picture. Each line is made up of a series of dots or **pixels**. Also used generally (as the equivalent of **bitmap**) to describe a similar pattern, as in **raster graphics** and **raster fonts**.

raster data Data held in raster form. Contrast **vector data**.

raster font See **bitmap font**.

raster graphics The same as **bitmap graphics**, in which an image is made up of an orthogonal array of **bits** (or **pixels**). Compare with **vector graphics**.

raster image processor (RIP) A program that converts a file in a **page description language**, possibly containing **vector graphics**, to a **raster** or **bitmap** image for output. The **RIP** will create a bitmap at the correct resolution for the output device, so that the page description file can be **resolution** independent.

raster scan The technique of plotting an image by the selective exposure of dots, line by line, in a series of horizontal sweeps following a raster pattern or grid.

rasterise Turn into a **raster** (bitmap) version by scanning or digitally processing.

rate card Leaflet or kit showing costs of advertisement space in a publication.

raw data Data before processing or preparation.

raw stock Base paper before coating.

reactive hotmelt Polyurethane (**PUR**)-based glue that reacts with moisture to form a strong flexible bond in perfect bound products.

red hat A company marketing **linux** OS and applications, providing development and support.

read-only memory See **ROM**.

read-write head The component that reads from and writes to a magnetic disk or tape.

real time Method of computing in which operations are performed on data simultaneously with input and output.

ream Five hundred sheets of paper.

ream-wrapped Sheets wrapped in lots of 500.

rebind Binding a set of stored sheets, set aside after the first binding.

reconstituted leather Leather made from pulp of different leather scraps.

record A discrete block of computer data, typically consisting of a number of **fields**.

recovered fibres Fibres from waste paper as opposed to virgin pulp.

recto A right-hand page.

recycled paper Paper for which the majority furnish is consumer waste paper of one sort or another, either printed or unprinted. Paper made mainly from **mill waste** does not fall under this definition although it is sometimes rather misleadingly termed recycled too.

redlining Facility available to use with some word processing packages which shows where alterations have been made to a document.

reducers Printing ink additives.

redundancy Inclusion of duplicate information. This is often used as a check, particularly in transferring information between systems, so that an additional check digit or bit is included. See also **validation**.

reel Roll of paper. Also, **web**.

reel-stand The unit housing a reel of paper at the feed end of a web offset press. Newspaper web offset machines may have up to 15 reel-stands feeding paper simultaneously. The printed webs are brought together in the folder.

reel-up The reeling section of a paper machine.

refiner mechanical pulp (RMP) Pulp made by passing wood chips through a refiner. Midway in quality between stone ground wood mechanical pulp (**SGW**) and **thermomechanical pulp** (**TMP**).

refining The second main stage of papermaking after dry pulp has been mixed in a **hydrapulper** at the first stage. The stock from the hydrapulper is further refined in a cone refiner and, after cleaning, is ready for pumping to the paper machine. Also known as **beating**.

reflection copy Copy viewed by its reflected light, e.g. a photograph, as distinct from **transmission copy**, which is viewed by transmitted light. Also known as 'reflective copy', and 'reflex copy'.

refusal When one ink film will not print on another.

register marks Marks in the same relative position on films or plates to enable correct positioning to be achieved.

register pins Pins that locate in holes made by a punch in a **punch register system**.

registration The alignment of the different colours in the printing of coloured material; see **CMYK**. Registration marks are printed for alignment purposes outside the area of the finished publication.

relational database A type of **database** in which entries are structured in defined **fields**, usually of a fixed length. By using tables that relate to one another by having a field in common, most information need only be stored once. Thus, for example, a database may include a table containing spare parts and another containing customer details. Ordering a part will entail referencing both these tables. Relational databases are increasing in their flexibility but are still not appropriate for **applications** including large amounts of unstructured text.

relative humidity (RH) Amount of water vapour in the atmosphere expressed as a percentage of saturation. Standard testing conditions for paper are 23°C and 50%RH. Optimum press conditions are 20°C and 55–65%RH.

relief Printing method using a raised image, e.g. flexo.

remainders Unsold books that are discounted for sale on preferential terms. Primarily used in relation to books.

remote Located away from main plant or, in the case of technical equipment, having no direct electronic link with the main processing plant.

remote log-in Connecting to and using a remote computer, via a **protocol** over a computer network, as though locally attached.

render, rendering The process of applying colour, shading and shadows to a computer-generated image on the basis of a mathematical model to make it appear realistic.

repeat The cut off (printing length or drop) of a plate cylinder, determined by one revolution of the plate cylinder gear. As the cylinders can be replaced flexo and gravure offers totally variable repeat lengths.

replacement fee Fee paid to a picture library to cover the cost of replacing a lost or spoiled picture.

repp Writing paper with a patterned surface.

reprint 1. Subsequent printing of the first edition of a publication. 2. Printing of part of a publication for promotional or editorial use.

repro Prepress process involving continuous tone reproduction.

reproduction fee Fee paid for the right to reproduce an illustration.

reproduction proof A proof taken from type for subsequent reproduction.

rescreen To take a subject that is already screened (e.g. a printed photograph) and rescanning it for reuse; it is important in doing this to avoid **moiré patterning**.

residual odour The odour of a printed material after drying, usually due to residual solvent not removed by the drying process but may be due to overheating the resin incorporated in the ink or releasing plasticisers from the substrate.

Residue selection Areas defined by a Postcode that accept mail unable to be sorted into **direct selections**. This may happen because there are not enough items to satisfy the minimum direct selection requirement, or because it has not been adequately postcoded. Attracts higher postal costs than **Mailsort** items.

resiliency Measure of paper surface condition after printing.

resin coated paper Abbreviated to 'RC paper'. Photographic paper with good longevity of image used in photosetting.

resist A protective chemical or coating.

resolution Measurement of image fineness stated in lines per inch (**lpi**), **dots per inch** (**dpi**), or **pixels** per inch as created by a platesetter or **imagesetter**.

retarders Printing ink solvents that reduce the drying rate of an ink, extending its **open time**.

reticulation A print fault where the ink runs into lines or beads, often due to over-thinning of an ink with diluent.

retouching Correcting a photographic print or transparency before reproduction.

retree Slightly damaged paper sold at a reduced price and often marked xx. See also **broke**.

reversal Creation of white text or images on a black background. Sometimes referred to as **WOB** (white on black). See **reverse out**.

reverse-reading See **wrong-reading**.

reversed out Type printing white out of another colour.

revise A revised proof for subsequent reading.

revision control system Programs that store and keep track of successive versions of a document or series of documents as they are amended.

RFID Radio frequency identification devices that will eventually replace barcodes. The tag can be printed, a simple chip with antenna that broadcasts its presence to a reader that sends data to a host computer. The chip stores information about the associated product and it updates the location status when the tag passes close to a reader. This enables great efficiencies and cost reductions in inventory management and control and enables innovative applications in locating and tracking people and assets.

RFQ Request for quotation.

RGB Red, green, blue. The (additive) colour system used in televisions and computer monitors. In a **computer** display, signals from three colour signals activate the appropriately coloured phosphor coating on the screen, creating a colour image. Compare this with the (subtractive) **CMYK** system. Note that the two systems do not always give the same colour for an equivalent image.

RH Relative humidity.

rheology The science and study of the deformation and flow of fluids, particularly inks and coatings.

ribbon folder Web press folder that cuts web into ribbons for folding. As distinct from a **former folder**.

Rich text format (RTF) It is a data format for texts that contain not only the text itself, but also information on the font, font size and formatting.

right side In papermaking, the top side or felt-side of the **web**.

right-angle folding Folding a sheet with one or more folds at right angles to each other.

right-angle folds Folds at 90° angles to each other.

right-reading Film that reads 'correctly', i.e. from left to right, when viewed from the emulsion side. As distinct from **wrong-reading**.

ring binding Binding by means of holes in paper which locate on metal rings.

RIP See **raster image processor**.

RISC Reduced instruction set computer. A type of computer processor architecture. The instructions are to the processor from the **operating system** and do not affect **applications**, except in that they are intended to increase processing speed.

river Undesirable formation of word spaces into a vertical 'river' of white in the text.

RMP Refiner mechanical pulp.

rocker sealer Heated element in film-wrapping machine that seals centre join.

roll Reel (US usage).

roll coating Coating applied to paper by rollers.

roll wrapping Rolling a magazine to wrap paper around it for mailing (as distinct from folding).

roll-out 1. Using a roller to spread ink on paper for sampling purposes. 2. In direct mail, the projection of orders that should come from a full mailing based on the response to a test mailing.

rolled Paper glazed by rolling.

rolling ball See **trackball**.

rollover A graphic or image that changes when the cursor is moved over it.

roman figures Roman numerals such as iii, xviii, xxv.

roman type 'Upright' letters as distinct from **italic**. Known as 'plain' or 'normal' in **DTP** systems.

root directory The top directory in an (inverted) tree-and-branch filing system. It contains all the other directories.

ROP Abbreviation for 'Run of Paper'. In magazines or newspapers, material printed as part of the main text.

rosette Pattern created from conventional process dots, visible at screen rulings of under 175dpi

rosin An important component in papermaking **size**.

rotary Printing from plates on cylinders.

rotogravure Gravure printing on rotary press.

rough A sketch or layout.

rough proof Proof for identification rather than reading.

rounding and backing Shaping a book so the back is convex. As distinct from **flat back** binding.

routine A computer program with a selective task.

routing Cutting away non-printing areas of a plate.

royal Standard size of paper 480×636mm (metric system)

RSS 1. Really simple syndication (rich site summary), a web feed of news and information to a browser 2. Reduced space symbology, an emerging barcode format that allows more information in a smaller space. The codes consist of a conventional linear barcode with an additional 2D (two dimensional) component that enables additional information about the product to be included.

rub-proof Ink with good abrasion resistance.

rule A line (of specified thickness).

ruler guides The electronic rulers used for the accurate alignment of text. See **guide**.

rules Printing lines, measured in points.

run 1. The activation of a computer **program**. 2. Number of printed copies of a publication.

run through Ruled lines stretching from one edge of the paper to the other with no breaks.

run-around The flow of text around a, usually irregularly shaped, graphic.

run-length encoding (RLE) A **compression** algorithm that replaces sequences of repeated characters (or groups of characters) with a single character and the length of the run. It is mainly used for storing **bitmaps**, since it encodes the points at which there is a change from black to white, on to off, 0 to 1, and the distance since the last switch (in the opposite direction).

run-of-book See **run-of-paper**.

run-of-paper Advertisement location allocated at the publisher's choice, anywhere in the publication.

runnability Ability of paper to be printed without problems.

running head A title repeated at the top of each page. Also known as 'running headline'.

running order 1. Set of notes indicating the order of events in a production. 2. List of the contents of a printed work to guide the printer in his imposition.

running text Columnar main text on a page (as distinct from displayed material).

runtime Cut-down version of a program that is bundled with another application in order to provide specific and limited functions.

RW Ream wrapped. RWOP is ream wrapped on pallets.

S paper See **stabilisation paper**.

s/s Abbreviation for 'same size' in reproduction specifications.

saddle stitching Binding inset books with **wire** staples through the middle fold of sheets.

saddle thread-sewing See **Singer sewing**.

safelight Darkroom lamp that does not affect photographic materials.

sans serif type (**Sanserif** is an alternative spelling.) A category of type in which there are no **serifs**, e.g. Avant Garde, Helvetica, Univers. Sans serif type tends to be used for display and for headings but less often for text. More formal documents use serif typefaces, while less formal documents are more likely to use sans serif faces.

sanserif type See **sans serif type**.

satellite press A printing press with multiple printing units, arranged around a central impression cylinder. In this way, all the colours are printed in a serial wet-on-wet process unless there is interdeck drying.

saturation In colour measurement, the measure of how much colour ('colourfulness' is the term used by experts) is present at a particular brightness.

Save The operation of storing data on disk or tape.

sawn-in-sewing Sewing with cuts in the backs of sections to take cords.

sc 1. **Small caps**. 2. **Supercalendered** (paper). 3. spray coating technology to allow reimageable DI plates announced by Creo.

scalable font A **font** that can be used at any size and any **resolution**.

scaling Calculating or marking the enlargement or reduction of an original for reproduction.

scamp Rough layout. Also, **rough**.

scan-a-web Method of scanning the image on a moving **web** by means of rotating mirror.

scanner Computer-controlled sampling device that reads the relative colour densities of a copy and produces digital image files.

schedule 1. Sequence of events and deadlines agreed for production. 2. Schedule of bookings for an advertising campaign.

score To impress paper with a rule to ease folding.

scratch resistance The ability of an ink to resist removal by scratching or rubbing

screen The display device on which computer input (and some output) is viewed. The term is also used in the traditional graphic arts industry to describe the **halftone** pattern overlaid on a continuous tone photograph so that it can be reproduced.

screen angles Varied angles of each screen used in colour halftones to avoid moiré patterns. The conventional screen angles are: black 45°; magenta 75°; yellow 90°; cyan 105° (15°).

screen capture, **screen dump** Copying the image on the computer screen (or part thereof) to a file or a printer. Often used in manuals and books about computer applications to illustrate what the screen looks like.

screen clash Moiré patterning caused by incorrect screen angles, or occurring when previously printed, screened halftones are rescreened.

screen finder A plastic viewer placed over a halftone to determine the screen ruling.

screen font A font that is designed specifically for viewing on screen.

screen process printing See **silk screen printing**.

screen resolution In the context of computer monitors, the number and layout of pixels that make up the image on the screen. It is expressed as the number of pixels across and down.

screen ruling The number of lines or dots per inch on a screen. The conventional screen rulings in common use for bookwork are 100, 120, 133, 150 lines per inch (40, 48, 54, 60 lines per centimetre).

screened print A print with a halftone screen, typically a **PMT**.

Script A series of commands that can be executed as a single unit.

script A typeface that simulates handwriting.

scroll, scrolling Upwards, downwards or sideways smooth motion of data across a screen, as if a window were being dragged across the data. In a **GUI** environment, it is usually activated with the **mouse**, although in other environments it may be activated by holding down the arrow keys on the keyboard.

SCSI Small computer system interface (pronounced scuzzy.) An 8-bit **parallel** interface used by the Apple **Macintosh** and the PC for connecting peripheral devices, such as disk and CD-rom drives, printers, and tape drives. SCSI can support high data transfer rates (up to 4 Mbytes a second). SCSI-2 and SCSI-3 are later versions with wider data buses, supporting even higher transfer rates.

SCSI device Any device, such as a scanner, CD-rom drive or external hard disk, that is connected to the computer by an **SCSI** port.

scuff test Testing a printed surface by placing it on a smooth hard plate and rubbing to see if any of the ink is removed.

scum or **scumming** Build-up of ink on the non-image area of an offset plate.

search and replace See **global search and replace**.

search engine Software that makes it possible to search files and/or **databases** for specific terms. The two principal approaches are **Boolean search** and **free-text search**, which usually involves using **indexing**. The more **structured** the queries, the more precisely a search can be defined, depending on the functionality of the search engine.

search fee Fee charged by a picture service to cover the cost of conducting research in its own files on a client's behalf.

search key An item to be compared with specified areas in a database search.

search routine Computer routine for finding specified words or groups of words in text.

searching Trying to locate required character strings or words. Examples are **keyword** searching and **free-text** searching. (See also **proximity searching**.)

SECAM (Sequential Colour and Memory or Système Electronique Couleur avec Mémoire.) A television coding standard used in Europe (mainly in France and some eastern European countries). (See also **PAL**, **NTSC**.)

second cover Inside front cover.

second-generation computers Early computers using transistors in place of vacuum tubes.

second-level heading Second in number (and importance) of a series of headings in a book.

secondary colour The colour made by a mixture of two primaries, e.g. yellow + red = orange.

secondary fibres See **recovered fibres**.

seconds See **retree**.

section A folded sheet forming part of a book.

section sewing Conventional sewing, as in most paperback or hardback books. The full specification is 'section-sewn continuous', or **French sewn** or **Smyth sewn** (US).

security firewall See **firewall**.

security paper Paper incorporating features that make counterfeiting difficult.

see-through See **show-through**.

selective binding Choosing only some of the sections to bind according to recipients profile **selectronic binding**.

self-assembly Spontaneous organisation of components into larger or more complex objects. It occurs widely in natural systems and is a central theme in much of nanotechnology, an example of bottom-up construction.

self copy paper Carbonless copy paper, see ncr.

self cover Cover of the same paper as text pages.

self-adhesive paper Gummed pressure-sensitive paper.

self-ends First and last pages of a **book block** used as **endpapers**.

self-mailer Printed piece mailed without envelope.

semantic Real meaning of words and expressions.

semantic web Internet development that will allow information to be stored as data rather than pages so improving the sharing and searching function between machines as well as people.

semi-chemical pulp Combination of chemical and mechanical pulp.

semi-display Advertisements displayed in boxes or laid out as a full or part-page within classified advertisement pages.

semiconductor Material used in the construction of transistors, diodes and photoelectric cells.

Senefelder, Alois (b. 1771 in Prague, d. 1834 in Munich) Invented lithography in 1796. By using a greasy substance to write on polished Solnhofen limestone which was then lightly etched with an acidic gum arabic solution, ink only adhering to the areas that have been written on.

sensitivity guide Piece of film with graded density used to monitor exposure.

separation See **colour separation, origination**.

separation negative See **colour separation negative**.

serial device Modems are probably the most commonly used serial devices, although a **mouse** and other devices can be connected in this way. Keyboards are also examples of serial devices.

serial interface An **interface** through which data is transmitted one **bit** at a time, unlike a **parallel interface**. Also described as an **RS-232** interface.

serial line Wires, or a telephone line, connecting two **serial ports**.

serial port Another term for a **serial interface**, although often used to refer to the physical connection on a computer. (See, in contrast, **parallel port**.)

serial printer One that prints a single character at a time. Compare **line printer**, **page printer**.

serial to parallel converter A device that converts the sequential input from a **serial transmission** device and passes it on via the required number of parallel lines.

serial transmission Data communications method in which each component bit of a character is transmitted in sequence down the wire, and is then reassembled with its fellows on arrival. Contrast **parallel transmission**. **series** A complete range of sizes in the same typeface.

serif The terminal stroke at the end of a line making up part of a character. Thus the characters in serif typefaces (such as the one used for this glossary) carry serifs, while characters in **sans serif** (or sanserif) typefaces do not (see example under **sans serif**).

serigraphy See **silk screen printing**.

server A computer that either holds information accessed by other computers over a **network**, e.g. a **file server** or **database server**, or provides a service, e.g. a **print server**, a dedicated computer that carries out the printing processes for all computers on a network, reducing the load on the other machines. The **internet** is based on a network of servers. Also a program providing a service to a 'client program'. (See **client-server**.)

service level agreement (SLA) Contracted levels of service provided by a supplier, usually guarantees of on-time deliveries

service provider See **internet service provider**.

set-off The transfer of wet ink to another sheet. Typically occurs at the delivery end of the printing press. Precautions can include the use of an **anti set-off spray**.

sew To fasten the sections of a book with thread.

SFL Sheetfed litho.

SGML Standard Generalised Mark-up Language. A complex generic coding scheme adopted as both an ISO International Standard and as a BSI British Standards Institution standard.

SGW See **stone groundwood mechanical pulp**.

shade The lightness or darkness of a colour, as distinct from its hue.

shaded watermark Watermark with opaque rather than transparent appearance.

shadows Dark parts in a photograph or halftone print represented by 70%–100% dot sizes. Contrast **highlights**, **mid-tones**.

shared file One that can be accessed by two systems and which may be used to provide a means of communication.

shareware Software that may be obtained and tested for free, usually for a limited time period. It is often distributed through **internet** file transfers or on floppy disk. After the trial period is complete, users are asked to pay a registration fee to the author or distributor of the package. Payment of the fee often brings additional facilities or documentation.

sheet The full-size piece of paper for printing, before folding or cutting.

sheet stock Publisher's printed sections held at the printer for binding up later.

sheetfed Printing by separate sheets as distinct from reels.

sheeter Machine that cuts reels into sheets.

sheetwork To print both sides of the sheet separately as two formes, cf **work and turn**, **work and tumble**.

sheetwise Printing one side of a sheet at a time. As distinct from **perfecting**.

sheetwork To print each side of the sheet from a separate forme. Each sheet yields one copy. As distinct from **work and turn**.

shelflife The usable storage life of a material (e.g. a plate).

Sherman tester range of mixed chemicals used to determine the free surface energy of a substrate.

shift A key which, when depressed, gives a different designation to all the other keys, e.g. turns a lowercase letter into uppercase.

shift codes Codes employed to increase a number of addressable characters. By reserving two characters to perform shift and unshift functions the number of available characters will be increased by adding shift to each character to effectively double those available.

shingle The allowance made in imposition for **creep**, i.e. the fractional space by which the back margins of the outer pages of a section need to be increased in order to make all the back margins appear to be equal when the section is folded.

shive Coarse fibre in paper or pulp.

shoot Photograph.

short grain Sheet of paper in which the grain is parallel to the short edge of the sheet.

short ink An ink that does not flow easily. The opposite is a long ink.

short sheet Sheet with too small a width dimension mixed in with sheets of the correct size.

short ton American ton (2000lbs) equal to .893 long (imperial) tons, or .9072 metric tonnes.

shoulder The raised shoulder of the book back which is formed in the **rounding and backing** process. The height of the shoulder should approximate to the thickness of the board to be used for the case.

shoulder head A form of **boxed head** that is ranged left on a line of its own. As distinct from a **side head**.

show-through Lack of opacity in a sheet of paper to the point where the printed image on one side of a page is excessively visible from the reverse side.

shrink wrap Plastic film wrapping.

side head A form of **boxed head** which is ranged left and from which the text runs on in the same line. As distinct from a **shoulder head**.

side lay The guide on a sheetfed press that positions the sheet sideways.

side notes Short lines of text set in the margins.

side run An addition to the 'making' on a paper machine that helps to fill up the maximum width.

side wire-stitching Binding by stapling through the back margin of the sections.

side-sewing Binding by sewing through the sides of the gathered sections. Also known as **McCain sewing**.

side-stabbing Used loosely to describe side **wire stitching**. But strictly, a form of stitching where the stitch on one side of the book penetrates only two-thirds distance, and a complementary stitch at the other side completes the securing.

signature 1. The letters of the alphabet or numerals printed at the bottom left-hand corner of sections to show the correct sequence of sections. 2. Synonym for section.

silk screen printing Method that employs a fine mesh to support a stencil through which ink is squeezed.

silurian Paper with a small percentage of long-fibre, dyed threads giving it a characteristic 'hairy' look. Used for covers or endpapers.

simplex Communication in one direction without any provision for transmission in the reverse direction. See also **duplex**, **half duplex.**.

simultaneous transmission The transmission of data in one direction simultaneously with messages transmitted in the other. See **full duplex**.

Singer sewing Saddle thread-sewing through the spine of an inset book.

size Rosin, starch and other chemicals used in papermaking to control the water and ink absorbency of the paper. Size can be added either at the refiner stage (engine-sizing) or on the papermaking machine at the size-press (surface sizing).

size-press coated paper Paper given a very light coating (around 4gsm per side) in the size press unit on the papermaking machine. Also known as **pigmented paper**, **light-coated paper** or **lickcoated paper**.

sizing 1. Treatment of paper with **size**. 2. See **scaling**.

skid A pallet.

skips Missing dots in gravure caused by lack of ink transfer.

skiver A book covering made of split sheep skins.

SLA See **service level agreement**

slabbing off Removing several outer layers from a reel of paper typically because they are unsatisfactory for printing through damage, dirt, marking.

slave or **slave unit** A device that uses logic from a separate CPU.

slice The outlet from a paper machine's headbox onto the wire.

slime spot Hole in paper resulting from a bacterial growth which developed during the making.

sling psychrometer Device for measuring relative humidity by whirling in the atmosphere.

slip case Cardboard case for book which displays the spine.

slip sheeting Placing sheets of paper between printed sheets to prevent set-off.

slit Divide a web of paper along its length using a disc or wheel. As distinct from 'cut', which is to divide a web across its width using a rotating knife or guillotine blade.

slitter marks Binder where a slit is to be made. Used in imposition schemes which require this.

sloped roman An imitation **italic** formed by electronically slanting the roman of a typeface.

slot punching Punching rectangular holes in paper.

slotted binding See **notch binding**.

slur Image distortion caused by drag on the printing machine. Monitored by a slur gauge in most colour bars. Often caused by an excess of ink on a non-absorbent coated paper, or machine-gearing wear.

slushing The disintegration of fibres in a liquid.

small capitals or **small caps** Abbreviated **sc**. Capitals the same size as the **x-height** of the normal lower case, i.e. about 70% of the size of the **full capitals** of the same fount.

smart materials Range of printed electronic devices that may be updated (e-ink) or broadcast to suitable receivers.

smartcard A plastic card containing a chip and memory used for identification or financial transactions.

smashed bulk The bulk of a book block under compression during casing-in a hard-bound book.

smashing See **nipping**.

smoothing press Rollers on a paper machine that smooth the web before drying.

smoothing roll coating Application of coating to paper surface by rollers revolving against the web direction.

smoothness Evenness of paper surface.

Smyth sewing Conventional **section sewing**.

snap to grids Function on graphics packages and electronic page composition systems which permits elements of a page to be positioned approximately and then automatically 'snapped' exactly into alignment to a grid by a command issued through the mouse by the operator.

snowflaking White dots on a printed piece caused by water droplets or debris.

soda pulp Pulp produced from hardwood chips cooked in caustic soda. See **sulphate pulp**.

soft cover Paper cover as distinct from case boards.

soft dot Halftone dot with soft (etchable) halation around it.

soft hyphen A hyphen introduced into a word by an **H&J** program, as opposed to a **hard hyphen** grammatically essential to the word.

soft proof A representation on screen of what will be printed rather than a proof on paper or in any **hard copy** form.

software package A set of programs written for a specific purpose, e.g. word processing.

software protection Technical and/or legal method adopted to prevent unauthorised usage.

softwood pulp Pulp made from softwood (coniferous) trees, e.g. fir, pine, spruce. As distinct from **hardwood pulp**.

solid 1. Typeset with no leading between the lines. 2. Printed area with 100% ink coverage.

solid density patches Patches of solid for each of the process inks in a colour bar testing strip. They reveal print density for each of the four colours across the sheet.

solid state Electronic components that use solid materials for current manipulation, e.g. transistors.

solvent The volatile liquid in which dyes and resins are dissolved and pigments are dispersed to produce printing ink.

sort 1. A single character of type. 2. To order data into a given sequence, e.g. alphabetical.

sort key Part of a data record used to determine the position into which the whole record will be sorted. See **sort**.

sound card A **plug-in** board usually for a PC, that provides **output** of high-quality stereo sound, controlled by **application software**.

source code or source language The programming language in which a user's program is written, usually a **high-level language**.

source program Program written in a language that requires subsequent translating into an **object** program which the computer can understand.

SP Spray polymer system from Creo to allow on-press re-imagable plates

SPC Statistical process control. Techniques of controlling and improving (manufacturing) efficiency and quality.

spec Specification.

special colour A printing ink colour mixed specially for a job rather than made up out of the process colour set. Means an extra printing working.

special furnish Papers made from a special mixture of pulps for a specific purpose.

special sort Unusual character necessary in a job.

specialty papers Papers for special industrial or commercial use, often with unusual properties.

specimen Sample page set to show the typography.

speckle See **skips**.

spectrophotometer Instrument that measures colour.

spectrum Complete range of colours from long wavelengths (red) to short wavelengths (blue).

speech recognition (Or voice recognition, **voice input**.) A technique in which spoken words are interpreted by a computer system. Most systems must be 'trained' by the user giving the interpretation of a series of representative words, and may need training for each individual using the system. Speech recognition is particularly useful in ideographic languages such as Chinese.

speech synthesis (Or voice output.) The generation from a textual or phonetic description of a waveform that sounds like human speech. The generation of numbers, e.g. associated with an on-screen calculator, is quite common. Speech synthesis is also used in **voicemail** systems.

Speedmaster Heidelberg tradename for sheetfed presses.

spelling check program or **spellchecker** or **spelling checker** A computer **program** that checks the accuracy of each word of input against the spellings of a dictionary held in **memory** and displays discrepancies on screen.

sph Sheets per hour, the standard measurement of **sheetfed** printing speed.

spiking Irregular surges in power on an electrical power line causing interference with sensitive electronic equipment.

spine The back edge of a book.

spine brass See **brass**.

spine lettering The words on a spine of a book, often blocked in gold or silver.

spiral binding Binding using a continuous spiral of wire or plastic threaded through punched holes in the back margin.

splice Crosswise joint in a web of paper, secured with adhesive. See also **flying paster**.

split boards Cover boards in two layers between which are glued the edges of the endpapers and section tapes in hand-bound books.

split fountain or **split duct working** Colour printing technique that divides the ink duct to achieve different colours across different parts of the same roller.

split run Print run of a publication divided in two (or more) stages to accommodate changes in text, changes of binding style.

splitting Tearing of paper suface areas on the press.

spoilage Waste incurred during the printing or binding processes.

spooling Refers to the simultaneous printing of a text while the user is engaged in some other activity, such as editing another text. The term comes from the acronym SPOOL, standing for Simultaneous Peripheral Output On Line.

spot colour Colour that is usually specified in a document as a particular, often **Pantone**, colour, say, for text or graphical features. This is in contrast to **process colour**.

spot varnish Varnish applied to selected parts of a printed sheet. Often used to enhance the sheen of photographs.

spraying Ejection of ink off the rollers, usually because it is too thin.

spread 1. Pair of facing pages. 2. See **trapping**.

spread coating Method of paper coating using a controlled flow of coating material onto the paper surface.

spreading Ink creep on printed areas.

spreadsheet A software package designed to perform financial calculations. Users are presented with a grid of alphabetically identified columns and numbered rows. Each intersection forms a cell that may contain text, numerics or algebraic formulae. As the contents of one numeric cell are altered, the contents of referenced formulae cells are updated automatically.

spring back A rounded springy back for stationery books made of strawboard or millboard.

sprinkled edges Edges of a book block sprinkled with blobs of ink.

sprocket holes Feed holes in paper tape.

SQL See **Structured Query Language**.

square back Flat back binding.

square serif Typeface with serifs heavier than the strokes.

squared-up halftone A photograph with right angle corners, rectangular or square.

squares The parts of a case that overlap the edges of the leaves on a case-bound book.

stabbing See **side-stabbing** and **side wire-stitching**.

stabilisation paper or **S paper** Photographic paper used for photosetting output. Has short image-retention span once processed and cannot be used when subsequent corrections will be stripped in at a later stage. Contrast **resin coated paper**.

stack 1. The calendering unit on a paper machine. 2. Pile of sheets, printed or unprinted.

stack press Printing press in which the printing units are stacked one above the other

stampers Hammers used to separate the fibres from rags in watermills.

stamping See **blocking**.

stamping die Steel or brass plate used for blocking. See **brass**.

stamping foil See **foil**.

stand-alone A self-contained hardware system that needs no other machine assistance to function.

standard document A file containing a document that can be merged with variable information to produce a letter. See **mail merge**.

standard testing conditions Officially specified conditions under which paper is tested: 50% relative humidity and 23°C.

standoff The distance between a graphic and its boundary. Text that is flowed around a graphic will not encroach into the standoff area. See also **graphic boundary**.

starred roll Paper roll with buckled inner layers caused by loose winding and forming a 'star' pattern when viewed from end-on.

start bit The **bit** that signals the start of a block of **data** in **asynchronous** communications. (See also **stop bit**.)

start-tag The tag that indicates the end of an **element** in **SGML** or **HTML**. For example, this entry could be represented as '<entry>starttag</entry>', where '<entry>' is the start-tag.

static IP address An **IP address** that is permanently allocated to a user.

static neutraliser An attachment on a litho press that removes static electricity from the paper.

station Unit of a binding or wrapping machine.

stationery binding Binding that allows books to remain flat when open (to facilitate writing in).

steel engraving Intaglio plate often used to reproduce fine designs on stationery (e.g. bank notes, share certificates).

stem Upright stroke of a letter or figure.

step index Index letters in the far edge margins of a book revealed by cutting the margins away progressively to expose the letters sequentially positioned from top to bottom throughout the text. Also known as **cut-through index**.

step-and-repeat machine A device that exposes the same image repeatedly according to pre-programmed instructions.

stet Proofreader's instruction meaning ignore marked correction, i.e. let it stand as it was.

stickyback US term for double-sided adhesive material, used for mounting printing plates to the plate cylinder; may be hard tape or cushioned tape and sheets.

stiffness Rigidity of a sheet of paper.

stillage Pallet.

stipple Dots used to give a background effect of colour tint.

stitch To stitch with thread or staple with wire as a binding function.

STM Scientific, technical and medical publishing.

Stochastic screening See **FM screening**.

stock 1. Liquid pulp prior to paper making. 2. (Loosely) the chosen paper to be printed.

stone groundwood mechanical pulp (SGW) Basic mechanical pulp, obtained by grinding debarked logs against a milling stone under heat and pressure. See also **refiner mechanical pulp (RMP), thermomechanical pulp (TMP), chemi-thermomechanical pulp (CTMP)**.

stop The ending of a rule where it crosses another line.

stop bit The bit (or bits) that signal the end of a block of data in **asynchronous** communications. See also **start bit**.

storyboard Illustrated board showing proposed camera shots or illustration sketches with script and technical annotation.

strawboard Originally, board made from straw fibres. Now used loosely to mean case boards of any description.

stream feeder Fast feeder on printing machine or folder that overlaps sheets as it arranges them for the grippers.

streaming Playing **audio** or **video** in real time as it is downloaded rather than storing the file and playing it when **download** is complete. For streaming to operate effectively, it is necessary to have a connection with a high **bandwidth**.

stress Angle of shading in typeface character design. May be oblique or vertical.

strike-through Too heavy a printing impression that leads to the printed image bleeding through to the underside of the sheet.

string A sequence of alphabetic or numeric codes in a computer program.

string variable Programming variables that may contain alphanumeric data.

strip and rebind Remove the case of a case-bound book and rebind as a paperback with a limp cover.

strip gumming Applying water-soluble adhesive to paper strips.

strip test Use of special paper to test the **pH** of an offset fountain solution.

structured document A document that is coded in such a way as to indicate its structure, rather than its formatting, so that, for example, there will usually be no concept of page, although sections and perhaps chapters may be coded since they are structural elements.

structured programming A method of program design and structure intended to aid the debugging process.

Structured Query Language (SQL) A language designed for searching for information within **relational databases**, usually within a **client-server** architecture, and retrieving the information in a structured form. SQL commands can also be used to add to or change the information in a database. SQL has a structure which is similar to natural language (English), which is intended to make it easy for non-specialists to use; however, the syntax must be adhered to, so it is not easy for a novice to use. Alternatively, it can be embedded in other languages.

stuffed Compressed with the compression utility **StuffIt** although the term is also used to describe a file compressed by other means. See also **zip**.

stuffer Publicity material sent out in the mail with other literature.

StuffIt A file **compression** utility for the **Macintosh**, developed by Aladdin Systems Inc. Also used for **archiving**. See **stuffed**.

stump The first half of a hyphenated word at the end of a line. Some typesetting systems permit the definition of a 'minimum stump' at the end of turned-over lines, i.e. the minimum number of letters that it is acceptable to leave before a hyphen.

stump line The last line of a page ending with a hyphen. Considered very undesirable.

style Typographically, whether text is bold, italic, reversed or underlined. The term is also used to describe a set of formatting characteristics, such as typeface, type size, interline spacing (**leading**), indents, **hyphenation** and **justification** parameters and even language, that can be applied to a paragraph and saved under a defined name.

style of the house Typographic and linguistic rules of a publishing house. Also **house style**.

style sheet A combination of **styles** or formatting (also called a **template**) which is appropriate for a particular type of document. Thus, there will be different style sheets for letters, invoices, reports.

sub 1. Sub editor, journalist who edits copy. 2. Subscription to a magazine or journal.

sub heading Secondary level of heading on a printed piece.

sub routine Set of instructions in a computer **program** that perform a constantly repeated operation such as a mathematical function.

subscript Inferior character. Small character printed below the base line as part of a mathematic equation.

subsidiary text Extracts, footnotes, and other secondary text in a book. Typically set smaller than the body text.

substance Paper weight measured in grams per square metre.

substrate 1. Base paper before coating. 2. Carrier for another material or coating, e.g. film. 3. Surface being printed on.

subtractive colour The colour seen when white light is reflected from a coloured object. Subtractive colour is used in printing (see **CMYK**). Screen displays use **additive colour**.

subtractive primaries Yellow, magenta and cyan, the process colours.

suction feeder Machine feeder that uses air blowers and suckers to separate and lift sheets.

sulphate pulp Also known as **kraft pulp**. Pulp made from wood fibres cooked in an alkaline mixture containing caustic soda (sodium hydroxide), sodium sulphide and sodium sulphate. Particularly suited to hardwoods, but increasingly used for softwoods.

sulphite pulp Pulp made from wood fibres cooked in an acidic mixture containing calcium bisulphite and sulphur dioxide in water. Particularly suited to softwoods.

supercalender A calendering stack with alternate hard steel rollers and soft rollers which imparts a high gloss finish to paper as it 'slips' between them. Usually off-machine.

supercalendered mechanical See **WSOP**.

superior Small character set above the line especially used in mathematical statements or to indicate footnotes.

supported sleeve Cylindrical, wire-mesh sleeve that can be fitted over the body of a **dandy roll** and removed when not required.

surface picking See **picking**.

surface sizing Sizing of paper carried out on the sizing press of the papermaking machine.

surface strength Resistance of paper surface to picking or lifting.

swash letter An ornamental character, usually an italic cap.

swatch Colour specimen printed on paper or a set of such specimens.

swelled rules Rules that are wider at the centre than at the ends.

sword hygroscope Probe used to determine the moisture content of a stack of paper.

synchronous In data transmission, signals coordinated by timing pulses. Blocks of data are transmitted at a measured rate dictated by timing devices at both ends of the interface. Compare **asynchronous**.

synchronous transmission A communications technique in which uninterrupted data blocks are transmitted at a fixed rate, the transmitting and receiving devices being synchronised. While each block is preceded by special synchronisation bits, no **start** and **stop bits** are used.

syntax The rules of grammar regulating the use of a language.

synthetic papers Synthetic materials, typically plastic, which have many of the properties of paper and can be printed. Usually expensive.

3-G Expensive development in mobile telephone technology based on Wide Code Division Multiple Access (W-CDMA); may provide more sophisticated and diverse range of services on telephones.

tab To determine the points where the text is to align vertically.

tab index Index letters printed on tabs which are stuck to the far edge margin of a book.

table Data stored in a form, often an array, that is suitable for reference.

table of contents generation The computer-aided compilation of a table of contents by taking specified headings from text, sorting and displaying them.

tabloid Newspaper size approximating to A3.

tabular material Typeset tables or columns of figures.

TAC Total area coverage. The maximum amount of ink that can be laid down as overprints to avoid trapping and drying problems will be determined in the output settings for a particular print technology at RIPping stage.

tack The viscosity and stickiness of ink.

tacketing Method of strengthening stationery binding using 'slips' or bands of leather.

tag A generic mark-up tag is one that identifies a particular attribute: an 'A' heading, for example, in the mark-up of text. Tags are converted to typesetting by allocating typographical specifications to them and translating them inside the front-end of the typesetting system.

TAGA The Technical Association of the Graphic Arts, founded in 1948 in the US, is an international technical association for professionals in graphic arts.

tagged image file format (TIFF) A **graphic file format** used for **bitmap** images. Tiff files can be black and white, **grey scale** or in colour.

tail-end hook See **back-edge curl**.

tail-piece Typographical device at the end of a chapter or book.

tailband Cotton or silk cord attached to the foot of the spine of a book. See also **headband**.

tails Bottom margins of pages.

tamper-evident The term used for labels and seals that indicate any manipulation.

taping Pasting strips of material to binding sections to add strength.

TAPPI See **Technical Association of the Pulp and Paper Industry**.

tare Weight of an empty container or unloaded vehicle.

taster Small sample of a book, typically a chapter, sent out by a publisher for promotion purposes.

TCF Totally chlorine free, relating to pulp and paper manufacture. See also **ECF**.

TCP/IP See **Transmission Control Protocol/Internet Protocol**.

tear test 1. Test that determines grain direction in paper by the ease of tearing. 2. Test to determine strength.

tearsheet Page from printed periodical used as proof or evidence of publication, especially of advertisement.

Technical Association of the Pulp and Paper Industry (TAPPI) American professional organisation.

technical press Periodicals concerned with technical subjects and circulating among specialists in those subjects.

telecommunications Communication via telephone systems. Telecommunications today range from simple voice communication over the telephone to complex systems involving computers, **fax** machines, **modems** and related equipment.

telecommuting The use of computers and telecommunications to enable a user to work away from the office.

teleconferencing Either audio-conferencing or videoconferencing.

telephony See **telecommunications**. Involving voice transmission, as opposed to **telegraphy**.

telescoped roll Reel of paper with progressively misaligned edge.

template A standard document that can be used as the basis of a class of documents. Templates are now widely used in many applications and in most cases any document can be saved as a template. A similar term is **style sheet**.

text The body type in a book as distinct from headings and display type.

text area Area occupied by text on a page, normally governed by a grid.

text block An area on a page into which the user has placed text.

text editing Any rearrangement or change performed upon textual material, such as correcting, adding and deleting.

text pages The principal matter in a book as distinct from the **frontmatter** and **endmatter**.

text paper 1. Fine quality paper for printed publicity work. 2. The body paper of a magazine or book as distinct from the cover stock.

texture A descriptor for the graphic properties of a surface in terms of smoothness/coarseness and regularity. Approaches used to define texture are statistical, structural and spectral.

textured inks Inks that create their colour impression not by means of pigments, but by their physical structure. They contain structures that selectively reflect light of a certain wavelength with the aid of interference effects. Textured inks create shimmering colour effects that can vary, depending on the viewing angle.

TFT LCD Thin film transistor liquid crystal display.

TFM Thin flexible microelectronics.

thermal imaging Exposure technique associated with **ctp** plates that uses heat to expose the image.

thermal printer A non-impact printer. Heat is applied to a ribbon carrying waxed ink which is transferred to the paper in the form of dots.

thermochromic inks Security inks that change colour with changes in temperature.

thermographic printing Relief effect created by heating special powder or ink on a sheet to give 'raised' typesetting.

thermomechanical pulp Abbreviated to **TMP**. Superior, stronger **mechanical pulp** produced from steam-heated wood chips.

thermoplastic binding See **adhesive binding**.

thesaurus A software feature of word processing. Synonyms for words can be accessed online by highlighting a word and activating the dictionary program behind it.

thin client A computer with a minimal 'thin' operating system held locally with access to resources from a remote server when needed. See **citrix**.

thinners Solvents added to ink to reduce tack.

thixotropic Viscous substances that become less viscous through mechanical action (stirring) and return to their original highly viscous form when left unagitated.

thread sealing Binding method using meltable threads as 'stitches' to secure individual sections before trimming and forwarding.

thread sewing Conventional sewing. Also known as **French sewing** or **section sewing**.

thread stitching Securing inset books by stitching through the spine with threads.

threaded Text is threaded when its several parts or **text blocks** are linked together by the user into a continuous **story**. Threaded text behaves as a single element of continuous text which the program identifies as such and keeps together in correct sequence no matter how much the page layout may be changed, or how many corrections are inserted or deleted.

threadless binding See **adhesive binding**.

three-colour process Process work using the yellow, magenta and cyan without black.

three-quarter bound Method in which the majority of the case of a book is covered in leather or cloth and the remainder in a different material.

throw-out A page that folds out of a book or magazine to a size larger than the book trim. Also **fold-out**, **gatefold**.

throwaway Free newspaper comprised largely of advertisements.

thumb index Index where the alphabetical divisions are cut into the edge of the book trim.

thumbnail sketch Small rough drawing.

tick marks 1. Alternative term for **crop marks** or **cut marks**. 2. Marks on rulers that define the increments being measured.

ticket board Pasteboard.

tied letters See **ligature**.

TIFF Tag Image File Format. A standard format for the storage of **bit-map graphics** and scanned images.

tight Laid out on a page so that there is little white space.

tight edges Referring to a stack of paper in which the edges of the sheets are stretched tight and the centre of the sheets are baggy. Caused by the stack having a higher moisture level than the surrounding atmosphere. Compare **wavy edges**.

tightback binding Binding in which the backs of the sections are stuck to the spine of the book, reinforcing its strength. Also known as **fastback binding**.

tile In the make-up of publications with a page size larger than A4, a portion of the page that is printed on a single sheet of paper. To make the complete page, the various tiles are assembled and pasted together.

tile, **tiling** The arrangement of **windows** in a **graphical user interface** (GUI) so that they but rather than overlap (or **cascade**).

time-out The use of a timer to limit the period of a program's operation. Often used in communications, so that if there is no transmission over a communications link during a specified time, then the link is broken.

time-sharing Concurrent processing of several jobs or **programs** on a computer.

time-slicing The technique used by computers to switch between concurrent **applications** and programs. Effectively a time slot is allocated to each process and the computer switches between them. On a powerful computer, the user appears to have access all the time. Time-division multiplexing uses a similar approach. (See also **multi-tasking**.)

tint 1. A solid colour reduced in shade by screening. Specified as a percentage of the solid colour, and in a particular **screen ruling**. 2. Transparent white ink.

tip in To fix a single leaf inside a section.

tip on To fix a single leaf, or endpaper, to the outside of a section.

tissue A fine, thin paper used for a variety of purposes where a delicate, lightweight paper is required.

titanium dioxide Mineral used in papermaking to add brightness and opacity.

title page Page of a book carrying the title, author's name and publisher's name. Always a recto.

titling Type font only available in full-faced caps.

TiVo US company supplying a digital video recording set-top device for personal television, allowing viewers to watch later, remove advertisements and access other content.

TMP See **thermomechanical pulp**.

to view Referring to the number of pages appearing on one side of a plate or sheet, e.g. 32-to-view = 32pp each side of the sheet = 64pp unit.

tombstone Basic advertisement for professional services which conforms to the limitations imposed by law or by professional associations.

tone Colour variation or **shade** of grey, as distinct from **line** which is solid black only.

toner Chemical used to create image in photocopying processes.

tonne Metric tonne, equivalent to .984 long (imperial) tons, or 1.102 short (US) tons.

toolbar An area of a **window**, usually at the top or bottom, carrying **buttons** for commonly used commands.

tooth Rough surface, as applied to a paper.

toothy Having a rough surface.

top of form A character printer feature that advances paper by one page.

top side The side of a web facing upwards during making, i.e. opposite to the wire side. Also called the felt-side and the right-side. Tends to be smoother than the wire-side.

touch screen An input mechanism in which a user can communicate with the computer by touching a particular location on the screen with his finger. Touch screens are most widely used in applications where the users are unfamiliar with computers, e.g. public information systems. The point at which the screen is touched is detected either using a sensitive membrane or as a result of light beams being interrupted.

touch-tone The method employed in telephony throughout the US to communicate the keys pressed when dialling.

tracing paper Transparent paper manufactured for tracing.

tracing programs See **autotracing**.

track In printing, the line or strip around the circumference of the printing plate governed by one inking key. All items positioned in this track will be subject to the same density of inking on the press run.

track kerning Global reduction in letter spacing to achieve a tighter visual effect. The same as **character compensation**.

tracking 1. When illustrations are in **track** on the press, they are subject to the same density of ink. The 'tracking' of subjects means their positions relative to each other along the same track. 2. See **track kerning**.

tractor feed A printer drive mechanism comprising a chain or belt equipped with teeth that engage with the sprocket holes of continuous stationery.

trade houses Companies in the printing industry whose main work is for other printers. Often specialists in a specific operation, e.g. laminating.

trade press Periodicals targeted to specific trades or businesses.

trade publishing The publishing of general interest books which are sold through the retail bookshop trade.

trade tolerance Allowances for under or over delivery quantities deemed acceptable commercially.

trademark Unique printing mark identifying a company.

traffic In general, transmissions over the **internet**, but usually used to indicate the number of transmissions at any one time.

Transitional Type style such as Baskerville which evolved between 'Old Style' and **Modern**.

transliterate Transcribe into characters of a different language.

transmission codes Standard code sets used in computers to represent alphanumeric characters and numbers. Examples include **ASCII** and **EBCDIC**.

Transmission Control Protocol/Internet Protocol (TCP/IP) (Transmission Control Protocol over Internet Protocol) Network protocols used on many systems and on the **internet**. It includes both **network layer** and **transport layer** protocols. The term is often used to include **telnet**, **ftp** and UDP.

transmission copy Copy that is viewed by transmitted light, e.g. a transparency. As distinct from **reflection copy** which is viewed by reflected light.

transparency Full-colour photographic positive on transparent film for viewing by transmitted light. Suitable as copy for separation.

transparency viewer Box arrangement with special light source to enable the viewing of transparencies under consistent conditions.

transparent In computing, a process is transparent to the user if he is unaware of it going on. Used particularly of computer processing that is taking place as an operator is doing something else.

transparent inks Inks such as process inks that permit other colours to show through when overprinted and so produce subsequent mixed colours.

transpose Abbreviated trs. Exchange the position of words, letters or lines, especially on a proof. Hence 'transposition'.

trap, trapping The overlap between two colours used in printing to ensure that there is no white appearing between them as a result of paper movement or poor registration. Gives a slightly less clear impression than **kiss-fit**, but allows for variation in printing conditions. When the border is around a character or an object lighter colours will be **spread** (made bigger) while darker colours will be **choked** (made slightly smaller) relative to each other.

trichromatic Using three process colours (**magenta**, yellow, **cyan**) to print in full colour.

trim Cut edges off sheets to square up or reduce size. Hence trimmed size is the size after trimming.

trim marks Alternative term for **crop marks** or **tick marks**.

trim to bleed Trim so that printed solids reach the edge of the trimmed sheet.

trimask Special photographic mask made of three-layer film and used in camera separation processes to colour correct separations as they are made.

trimetal plate Lithographic plate for very long-run work where three layers of metal are used in manufacturing the plate.

triplex board Board made up of three layers of thinner paper or of one central layer lined on both sides with paper.

tritone The use of three colours to produce a particular effect in printing. May be used (with cyan, yellow and magenta hues) to produce a finer **grey-scale** effect. See also **duotone**.

troubleshoot To find and rectify a fault.

true small caps Small caps designed as such, rather than created as a smaller size of main-text capitals (in which case the strokes frequently look too thin).

TrueType A **font** system.

trunk A high-capacity communications circuit that carries many channels.

trunk network The main part of the telephone network that passes through the country.

turned 1. A table or illustration turned sideways on a page so as to fit better. Such tables or illustrations should always be turned so that the foot of them is on the right-hand side of the page when the book is in normal, upright, position. 2. News setting carried over onto another page.

turned in Cover material turned over the edges of the board.

turner bar Bar on a web offset press that redirects the web through a right-angle degree.

turnkey system A system that is complete and designed for a specific use. With hardware this implies that the supplier has full responsibility for installation, with software the implication is that the user may initiate the package without necessarily understanding or even being aware of the operating system.

TVI Tone value increases. The increase in area of printing dots from computer to print; it is an effect of dot gain in making parts of an image heavy when uncontrolled.

twin-wire Smooth board or paper made from two separate webs which are brought together at the press section of the twin-wire paper machine. Contrast the **duoformer** principle with which it is sometimes confused.

twisted pair A cable in which pairs of conductors are twisted together in order that 'crosstalk' from nearby wiring and other noise is randomised.

two-colour press Two-unit machine that can print two colours on a sheet in a single pass.

two-sheet detector A device for stopping the press if more than one sheet is fed.

two-shot binding Adhesive binding in which the first application is of PVA adhesive, the second of hot-melt adhesive. Compare **one-shot binding**.

two-sidedness Undesirable differing finish between the **felt-side** and the **wire-side** of a sheet.

tying-up Using cord to secure type for storage.

Type 1 font A **PostScript outline font** having the highest typographic quality, mainly because Type 1 fonts incorporate **hinting**. As well as the outline specification, Type 1 fonts also include a screen, **bitmapped** font OpenType, has recently been developed with the aim of removing font-compatibility problems.

type area Area occupied by text on a page.

type family Roman, italic, bold and all other versions of one typeface.

type gauge A rule calibrated in picas for measuring type.

type height Distance from the foot of type to printing surface: 23.17mm in the UK and US.

type scale See **type gauge**.

type series All the sizes available in one typeface.

typeface A set of characters of a particular design. Text fonts will almost always include the **ASCII** character set, but symbol fonts may include a wide range of characters. Today the term 'face' tends to be used interchangeably with **font**, although historically they both had different meanings, there being several typefaces, e.g. bold or italic within a font.

typescript Typed copy.

typographer Designer of printed material.

typographic errors Abbreviated to typos. See **literals**.

u and **lc**, also **ulc**, **U/L** Abbreviation for upper and lowercase. Instruction to follow copy for caps and lowercase.

U/L or **ulc** Upper and lowercase.

UCR See **undercolour removal**.

UDF See **user-defined format**.

UGRA A Swiss association for the promotion of research in the graphics arts industry.

ultrawideband A fast wireless connection, from about 40Mbsec^{-1} to 600Mbsec^{-1}, that consumes about 10^{-4} the power of a cellphone.

un-shift Keyboard designation for lowercase.

unbacked Printed one side only.

unbundling Referring to the sale of software, training and services by a computer manufacturer independent of the sale of hardware.

uncoated paper Paper with no coating and not suitable for high-quality illustrated work.

undercolour removal Abbreviated to UCR. Technique that reduces unwanted colour in areas of overlaps. Results in better trapping and lower ink cost.

undercut The amount of space left for plate packing on press cylinders.

underexposure Inadequate exposure to light causing a mostly dense image. Contrast **overexposure**.

underline 1. Caption (US). 2. A facility to automatically underline text.

underrun Paper delivery or printing quantities that fall short of the order.

underside Bottom side of a web of paper. Also known as the wire-side or wrong-side. The other side is the **top side**, **felt-side**, or **right side**.

Unicode A 16-bit character-encoding system that is intended to include all characters in all languages (including Chinese and similar languages). It forms part of **ISO 10646** and is backwards-compatible with **ASCII** (7-bit encoding). Instead of the 128 characters that can be encoded with ASCII, 65,500 can be encoded with Unicode.

uniform resource identifier (**URI**) Formerly called universal resource identifier. A general way of addressing resources on the **web**, including **uniform resource locators** (URLs) and **uniform resource numbers** (URNs).

uniform resource locator (**URL**) A way of specifying an **internet** resource, such as a **file**, a **World Wide Web** site or a **newsgroup**. **URLs** are used in **HTML** documents to specify the target of a **hyperlink**. An example URL is http://www.piranet.com/. The part before the first colon specifies the **protocol** to be used, that may be **ftp**, **telnet**, **Gopher**, rather than **http** (http being perhaps the most common).

uniform resource number Former name for uniform resource name.

union paper Special wrapping paper comprising two webs joined by tar coating.

unit 1. Smallest sub-division into which the em character width measurement of a fount is divided. Used as the counting basis for all character widths in a fount. Actual size varies with the manufacturer's system. 2. One set of printing cylinders with associated machinery. A four-colour press will have four units, each printing one colour.

unit value The number of units in a character width. See **unit**.

universal resource identifier Former name for **uniform resource identifier**.

universal resource locator Former name for **uniform resource locator**.

UNIX A multi-user operating system allowing several operators to use the same computer simultaneously.

unjustified Typesetting with even spacing, therefore having a ragged right edge.

unlined chipboard Case board made from mixed waste furnish and consisting of a number of plies of thin board pasted together. See also **Dutch grey board**, **millboard**.

unsewn binding See **perfect binding**.

unsharp masking (USM) Feature that lowers the background resolution in pre-defined local areas increases the sharpness of detail in these areas.

unstuff To decompress a file that has been **stuffed**.

untrimmed size Dimensions of a sheet or printed piece before trimming.

unzip To decompress a file that has been **zipped**. See also **WINZIP**.

up 1. Running (in the case of equipment). 2. Several at once: two-up means two copies the same out of one sheet.

update Edit a file by adding current data.

upload To transfer files over a communications link or a **network**, usually from a smaller system to a larger **host**. The opposite of **download**.

uppercase Capital letters.

uppercase letters Capitalised letters, such as the first letter of this sentence. The term is derived from the days of cold type, when the capitals were kept in the top (upper) typecase and the small letters in the bottom (or lower) case.

upright Designation for binding along the longest dimension. Also, **portrait**.

upward compatibility The ability of one computer to run programs written for a later model, but not vice versa.

URI See **uniform resource identifier**.

URL See **uniform resource locator**.

USASCII USA Standard Code for Information Interchange. Synonymous with ASCII. Typically, the only difference lies with the character associated with code 123 (hash in USASCII, pound symbol in ASCII).

user area That part of computer memory allocated to user programs, the remainder being reserved for buffers and operating systems.

user interface The way in which a user interacts with a program or system. **Graphical user interfaces** (GUIs) are increasingly becoming the norm, although **command interfaces** are still used. Both of these may also include **menu**-driven interfaces.

user-defined format An instruction assigned to an input key to perform a particular command or string of commands over and above any normal function. Keys

programmable by the user in this way are known as 'UDKs', (user-defined keys), or 'user programmable keys' or **macros**.

user-friendly A term, perhaps obvious in meaning but difficult to define, used to describe systems, software and **user interfaces** that are easy to interact with, needing little or no prior training or documentation for the user.

USM See **unsharp masking**.

utilities Software programs designed as tools to assist in the development of systems, the recovery of data.

UV Ultraviolet, refers to inks dried by UV radiation.

UV fluorescent inks Security inks that fluoresce under UV light.

UV varnish Ultraviolet varnish. Sometimes installed inline with a printing machine, a UV varnish unit deposits a high-gloss varnish dried by exposure to UV light.

V series Series of recommendations for data transmission over telephone.

V.32 bis Modem protocol allowing data rates of up to 14.4kbps.

V.34 Protocol allowing data rates of up to 28.8kbps.

V.fast A 28.8kbps **modem protocol** proposed by some manufacturers before **V.34** had been approved.

vacuum frame Contact printing frame using vacuum pumps to hold copy in position.

validation Checking **data** to ensure that it is valid, which may mean that it is complete, accurate or reasonable. Validation may be carried out in a number of ways, including comparison with a mask, calculation of a **checksum** or **parity checking**.

value In **colour measurement** an alternative term for brightness.

Vancouver system Set system for laying out bibliographical references much used in **STM** publishing.

variable A name given to a memory location that is used to hold the current value of variable data.

variable space Space between words used to justify a line. Contrast **fixed space**.

varnish Thin, transparent coating applied to printed work for gloss or protection.

vat papers Handmade papers formed on a wire in a vat.

vector A line and its direction. Vector instructions given to a computer enable the computer to calculate and plot the outlines of graphics and type characters. A programmed instruction then fills in the outline. Contrast **bitmap**.

vector data Data held in vector (outline) form.

vector font Another name for an **outline font**.

vector graphics Another name for **object-oriented graphics**. The term arises because graphics are defined in terms of vectors, or geometric formulae, rather than **as bitmaps**.

vehicle Liquid component of ink that serves to carry the **pigment** and bonds it to the **substrate**.

vellum 1. Prepared inner side of calf-skin, used in **binding**. 2. Imitation of this type of surface on paper.

verification **Data validation** achieved by keying the information twice and then performing a character-by-character check.

version number Identification of a particular 'edition' of **software**.

verso Left-hand page with even number.

vertical justification Spacing a column or page of type to fit a predetermined depth. Automatic process on some typesetting systems. See also **feathering**.

vertical scrolling The ability to move text displayed on a screen up or down a line at a time to reveal other parts of the text.

video Moving images, conventionally considered in terms of television images and usually in a recorded form, but now extended to include moving-image files of all types and live images capable of being stored on computer systems and transmitted over **networks**.

video compression The **compression** of sequences of images. Algorithms for video compression take advantage of there usually being only small changes from one frame to the next, so that the first frame is recorded using similar techniques to those for still images (see **JPEG**, for example) and then only the differences between frames are recorded.

video display A text or graphics display device which may be a **cathode ray tube**, LED or gas plasma display.

video conferencing A meeting between two or more groups of people in different places, who can both see and hear one another using **video** and **audio** links. **Video compression** is often used but, because of **bandwidth** limitations, images are quite often disjointed and may sometimes break up. See also **virtual meeting**.

virus A **program**, usually written anonymously with malicious or mischievous intent, that attaches itself to executable program files when these are transferred from computer to computer. A virus is usually triggered by a particular stimulus, which may be running the program to which it is attached or just the system reaching a certain date, for example.

viscoelastic Flexible enough to return to original size after stretching.

viscosity Resistance to flow; tackiness.

visual A layout or rough of artwork. Also, **mockup**.

visual display unit (**VDU**) The unit of a computer system containing a **screen**; usually part of a **video display terminal**.

VLF Very large format platesetter capable of exposing large areas over 102×72cm.

VOC Volatile organic compounds that are frequently incorporated in solvent-based ink formulations and wash ups. Their use is potentially damaging to the environment and so is being reduced where practical.

voice action In speech recognition technology, an operation much the equivalent of a keystroke or mouse-click that can be invoked by a voice command.

voice activation (Or speech recognition, voice recognition, voice input.) Giving commands to a computer by speaking rather than by using the keyboard or **mouse**. Although frequently featured in science fiction, it is now a reality.

voice file In speech recognition technology, the file that contains the user's voice model.

voice input An alternative name for **speech recognition** or **voice activation**.

void hickey A **hickey** appearing as a white spot on the printed image.

volume 1. **Bound book**. 2. Thickness of paper expressed as a volume number (e.g. vol 18) equal to the thickness in millimetres of 100 sheets of paper in 100**gsm**.

volumetric A volumetric paper is one which is made to a guaranteed bulk. Typically an Antique wove.

vouchers Free copies of a periodical given to advertisers in that issue.

W3 An abbreviation (occasionally) used for the **worldwide web**.

W3, W3C Consortium See **World Wide Web Consortium**.

Walksort Discounted postal rates for high-density mailings where mail is sorted to individual post walks.

WAN Wide area network. A network of micros spread over a larger area than a **LAN**, and linked typically by telecommunication.

warm colours Red and yellow shades.

warp The long threads in a woven cloth that represent the machine direction. The cross threads are the **weft** or **woof**.

wash drawing Black and white illustration with **tones** created by grey or black ink or paint washes.

wash-up The cleaning of the printing units of a press prior to a change of ink or shut-down of the machine.

washing The unintended dissolving by water of pigment in ink during **litho** printing.

waste furnish Board or paper furnish consisting of waste paper – packaging, cardboard, newsprint, magazine papers.

water-based inks Used in **screen printing**, **flexo** and **gravure**.

water finish High finish to paper achieved by damping the **web** as it passes through the calender stack.

water immersion size test Test using water immersion to establish the effectiveness of **sizing** in a paper as a water repellent.

water miscible coatings A range of quick drying resistant sealer coatings to protect and enhance the finish of printed material.

water vapour transmission rate (WVTR) Test to determine the waterproof qualities of packaging paper.

waterleaf Moisture-absorbent paper such as blotting paper or filter paper.

waterless litho Offset litho process using special inks with plates that do not require damping.

watermark Design impressed into a paper web during manufacture by the **dandy roll**.

wavy edges Referring to a stack of paper in which the edges of the sheets are baggy and the centre of the sheets are stretched tight. Caused by the stack having a higher moisture level than the surrounding atmosphere. Compare **tight edges**.

wax test Test of **picking** of paper surface using graded wax sticks.

WCDMA (Wideband Code Division Multiple Access) Wireless data transfer standard offers data transfer rates of 2Mbsec^{-1} over a static indoor environment and 384Kbsec^{-1} outside.

web A continuous length of paper (i.e. a roll or reel) as distinct from sheets.

web browser See **browser**.

webDAV Web-based distributed authoring and versioning – a standard to extend HTTP to allow the content of documents to be accessed directly via the internet to allow a team to work on the content and structure of a document.

webMaster Administrator and contact of a website

web offset Reel-fed **offset litho**. May be heatset or coldset. A variety of configurations are possible ranging from one **mono** unit with a single **reel-stand** up to multi-unit colour presses with up to three reel-stands.

web page A **worldwide web** page, i.e. an **HTML** document.

web press See webfed.

web server A program that serves file and data to **web browsers**. (See **client-server**.)

website The related set of **web pages** operated by a single organisation or individual, usually identified by a single **IP** number (with the first part of the **URL** the same, e.g. 'http://www.'.

web sized mechanical sc paper See **WSOP**.

web sized offset printing paper See **WSOP**.

web tension Adjustable degree of lateral pull on a web of paper in a web press.

web to print System to generate content from remote web access as PDF or optimised file for digital printing.

webfed Presses printing on **webs** of paper rather than sheets.

webmaster The person responsible for maintaining and administering a **website**.

weft The cross threads in a woven material. Contrast **warp**.

weight 1. In typography, the degree of boldness of a **typeface** style (e.g. light, medium). 2. Loosely, in paper specification, the **substance**.

wet printing See **wet-on-wet**.

wet proof See **machine proof**.

wet stock Pump in its liquid form or during formation on the **wire**.

wet strength Tensile strength of saturated paper.

wet-end The **Fourdrinier** wire section and the pressing section of a paper machine.

wet-on-wet Superimposition of colours on a multi-unit press (i.e. before each colour has dried).

wettability The extent to which a substrate can be wetted evenly by a liquid ink. A material can be tested for wettability by dabbing ink on the surface and checking whether it spreads out (indicating good wettability) or runs into droplets (poor wettability). Good wettability is necessary for optimal reproduction and adhesion.

wetting agent An additive that decreases the surface tension of water.

wf Wrong font. Proofreader's mark indicating an incorrect typeface has been used.

whip stitching Sewing technique used to join sheets at the edges.

whiteback Cloth that is dyed on its surface only, with the reverse side remaining white. Contrast **dyed-through cloth**.

whitewater See **backwater**.

whiting A widely used **extender** for ink.

whole-bound **Full-bound** case of a **hard-bound** book covered in the same material all over.

wide area network (WAN) A **network** that covers areas larger than those serviced by a **local area network** (LAN). This usually means that **serial communications** are used, either via telephone lines (usually a **leased line**) or by satellite.

wideband A communications **bandwidth** higher than **voice band**, but how much higher is undefined. See also **broadband**. A wideband amplifier is one that will handle a wide range of frequencies.

widow The last line of a paragraph, printed at the top of a page, although sometimes this is described as an **orphan** and a widow is defined as the first line of a paragraph at the bottom of a page. In either case, good typographic design means avoiding them.

wild card A signifier used in searches to mean 'anything', and usually an asterisk or question mark.

WiMax Data transfer standard (802.16) that promises 70 megabits per second across a 30-mile range.

Window Portion of a VDU screen dedicated to a particular file/document. Several windows can be open on screen at one time, allowing the user to jump from one to another rapidly. Ideal operating conditions for on-screen cut and paste.

Windows (3.x, 95, 98, 2000, XP) Suite of operating systems provided by MicroSoft for the PC and server market, continually being upgraded to provide additional functionality and stability.

wing effect The result of out-of-square guillotining of a book: when the book is opened the edges look like a pair of butterfly wings rather than being parallel along the tops and bottoms.

Winzip Widely used data compression application to reduce the file transfer time in email across Windows applications.

wire The moving fine mesh belt on which liquid stock is formed into a **web** of paper by draining away the water. 'Wire-side' is the side of the web that rests on the wire (also known as the **underside** or **wrong side**). Wire mark is the impression left by the wire on the web.

wire stitching See **saddle stitching**.

wire-binding or **wire-O binding** Binding method comprising a continuous double loop of wire running through slots in the margin of a book.

with the grain In the direction of the length of the original web. Paper folds more easily with the grain. Contrast against the grain.

wizard Help feature which guides the user through the steps of a process.

WOB White on black (i.e. **reversed out**).

wood pulp Pulp made from wood.

wood-containing Referring to papers which are part-mechanical in furnish.

woodcut Hand engraving cut into a block of wood for print-making.

woodfree paper Full woodfree paper contains no mechanical pulp at all. This is sometimes known as pure woodfree. It is generally accepted, however, that woodfree paper may include up to 10% mechanical or other fibre and still fall within the definition of woodfree.

woodfree pulp Pulp that is processed chemically and which contains no mechanical groundwood.

woodtype Typographical characters (usually in sizes over 72pt) made from wood. Often called **poster type**.

woof The cross threads in a woven material. Also, **weft**. Compare **warp**.

word As a computer term, a set of **bits** recognised by the computer as the smallest logical unit of information for processing.

word break Division of a word at a line ending.

word search The process of finding a word within running text by computer matching. Word searches may be of several types: **free text**

searching, that is the simple identification of all occurrences of a word or phrase, **proximity searching**, that allows pairs of words or phrases to be found provided they are in a certain range of each other; and **Boolean searching** that allows word or phrase pairs to be found based on logical AND and OR statements.

word wrap The automatic wrapping of text onto the next line when a line end is encountered.

word processing composing, inputting and editing text through a dedicated word processor or specific word processing software.

Word processor An editing and formatting **program** with which documents, including graphics, can be input, edited, formatted and printed.

wordspace The variable space between words that may be increased or decreased to justify a line.

work and back See **sheetwork**.

work and tumble Printing the reverse side of a sheet by turning it over on its long axis from gripper to back and using the same plate. Each sheet, cut in half, yields two copies from a single set of plates.

work and turn Printing the first side of a sheet, turning the stack across its short axis, and then printing the reverse side of the sheet using the same plate and the same **gripper edge**. Each sheet, cut in half, yields two copies.

workflow The control of documents through their design and production.

work station A desk on which a computer is used.

worldwide web (**WWW, W3**) The internet.

wove Paper produced using a plain, woven dandy roll and therefore without laid lines, as distinct from **laid paper**.

woven material Genuine cloth, used for case covering. The two main qualities of woven cloth used for coverings are 'single-warp' and 'double-warp' buckram. In the case of single-warp buckram, the standard specification is '40/40', i.e. 40 strands of thread per linear inch in each direction.

wp See **word processor**.

wrap 1. See **word wrap**. 2. Plate section placed around the outside of a folded text section in a book and bound in. Contrast **insert**.

wraparound A **word processing** facility that moves a word to a preceding or following line to avoid word breaks or to allow for deletion or insertion.

wraparound plate Thin relief letterpress printing plate that is clamped around the plate cylinder.

wrapping Attaching a paper cover by gluing at the spine. See **drawn-on cover**.

wrinkles 1. Creases in printed paper caused by uneven moisture absorption. 2. Uneven surface of ink during drying.

write To record or output electronic data.

write enable A means of allowing data to be written to magnetic disk or tape. With floppy disks this is achieved by the removal of an adhesive tab from the disk's write-protect notch. Compare **write protect**.

write protect A means of preventing data being written to magnetic disk or tape. With floppy disks, this is typically achieved by placing an adhesive tab over the disk's write-protect notch, while with magnetic tape the same objective is achieved by repositioning a sliding tab on a cartridge or cassette enclosure or by the removal of a file protect ring from a reel of magnetic tape. Compare **write enable**.

writings Papers sized for writing without ink spread.

wrong font See **wf**.

wrong grain See **cross grain**.

wrong side See **underside**, **wireside**.

WSOP Web-sized offset printing paper. A calendered mechanical paper, mainly used for magazines, but appropriate for some grades of bookwork.

WWW See **worldwide web**.

WYSIWYG Acronym for 'What you see is what you get' and pronounced 'whizzy wig' what appears on the screen is a direct representation of what would be printed.

x-height The height of the **lowercase** letter 'x' in a particular **typeface** or **font**; 'x' is used because it the only letter that effectively has a clearly defined flat top. The x-height determines the appearing size of the font, while the relationship between the x-height and the **cap height** (the height of the capital letters) is a characteristic of a typeface and can affect its readability. Thus a typographic designer needs to take the differences into account when choosing a typeface.

x-line Alignment along the tops of lowercase letters. Also, **mean line**.

x-y coordinates Horizontal (x) and vertical (y) alignments used by computers for siting pixels in screen displays or output.

xerography Electrostatic copying process in which toner adheres to charged paper to produce an image.

XSLT The eXtensible Stylesheet Language Transformations. A language designed to transform one XML document into another or to transform the structure of an XML document.

XML See **eXtensible Markup Language**.

XP Version of MicroSoft Windows launched in 2002

xx Mark indicating **retree**.

Xxx Mark indicating **broke**.

YAG Yttrium aluminium garnet. A type of laser used offering very high power from a very small beam. Widely used to produce high-quality ceramic anilox rollers.

yankee dryer Steam-heated paper drying cylinder generating a glazed finish to the paper so treated.

yapp cover Binding material edges which overlap the case boards to provide a 'fringed' effect. Often used on bibles.

Zahn Cup A cup of known volume with a precisely sized hole in the base used to measure the viscosity of a liquid ink or varnish by determining the time it takes to empty.

Zapf Dingbats A **typeface**, designed by Hermann Zapf, which includes common **dingbats**. It is usually provided as one of the standard fonts with a **PostScript laser printer**.

zinc engraving Relief engraving made on zinc and often used for short-run blocking in preference to a chemac. Also called 'zinc'.

zip A **file** format widely used for **data compression**, for example in transferring **programs** and other large files on **floppy disk** or over the **internet**. The files used to compress and decompress are **PKZIP** and **PKUNZIP**. There is also now a **Windows** version, Winzip. Note that PKZIP is **shareware** and not **public domain** software, although the supplier, PKWare, provides runtime licences for Pkunzip.

zip drive A type of super-floppy drive with much higher capacity and operating at a much higher speed.

Zip-a-tone Proprietary name for patterned line or dot effects applied as rub-down film onto artwork. See also **transfer type**.

zoom In analogy with a photographic lens, to make what appears in a screen **window** (in a **graphical user interface**) larger (zoom in) so that a smaller area is seen, or smaller (zoom out), so that a larger area is seen. Depending on the **application**, either the magnification may be selected from a menu or, for zooming in, the **cursor** changes (usually to a magnifying glass) and the area to be zoomed in on is **marquee** selected. If zooming in is performed by the latter method, zooming out is usually achieved by **clicking** an **icon** which has the effect of undoing the last zoom in (marquee selection itself cannot be used because the desired area of viewing is larger than what can currently be seen on the screen).